Geoecology of the Colorado Front Range

Also of Interest

Precipitation History of the Rocky Mountain States, Raymond S. Bradley

Geomorphological Processes, E. Derbyshire, K. J. Gregory, and J. R. Hails

Man and Environmental Processes, edited by K. J. Gregory and D. E. Walling

Applied Climatology, John Hobbs

Submarine Permafrost on the Alaskan Continental Shelf, Michael E. Vigdorchik

Arctic Pleistocene History and the Development of Submarine Permafrost, Michael E. Vigdorchik

Institute of Arctic and Alpine Research
Studies in High Altitude Geoecology

Geoecology of the Colorado Front Range:
A Study of Alpine and Subalpine Environments
edited by Jack D. Ives

The Front Range of Colorado, especially Niwot Ridge, is one of the most intensively studied mountain areas of the world. The forty-four papers, critiques, and overviews collected here are the first concerted attempt to bring together a representative coverage of this research. Contributors from the earth, life, and atmospheric sciences examine the glacial geology, geomorphology, glaciology and hydrology, climatology, plant ecology, and animal ecology of the region. An overview and critique of the state-of-knowledge in each field are also included.

The book provides a model geoecology of a major mountain range, against which research in many other mountainous areas of the world can be assessed. Primarily scientific in scope, it lays as well the foundation for the use of environmental and geoecological data in the formulation of management policies for mountain wilderness land.

Jack D. Ives is professor of geography at the Institute of Arctic and Alpine Research, University of Colorado, Boulder, where he was director from 1967-1979. He has served as chairman of the International Geographical Union Commission on Mountain Geoecology and has been involved with the UNESCO Programme on Man and the Biosphere and the U.N. University Natural Resources Project on Highland-Lowland Interactive Systems.

Below the Continental Divide

Geoecology of the Colorado Front Range: A Study of Alpine and Subalpine Environments

edited by Jack D. Ives

Westview Press / Boulder, Colorado

This work was inspired by the UNESCO Programme on Man and the Biosphere (MAB) and the Commission on Mountain Geoecology of the International Geographical Union.

Institute of Arctic and Alpine Research
Studies in High Altitude Geoecology

Published in 1980 in the United States of America by
    Westview Press, Inc.
    5500 Central Avenue
    Boulder, Colorado 80301
    Frederick A. Praeger, Publisher

Library of Congress Cataloging in Publication Data
Main entry under title:
Geoecology of the Colorado Front Range
    (Institute of Arctic and Alpine Research Studies in high altitude geoecology)
    Bibliography: p.
    1. Earth sciences--Front Range, Colo. and Wyo. 2. Mountain ecology--Front Range, Colo. and Wyo. I. Ives, Jack D.
QE92.F7G46   551.4'32'097886   80-13955
ISBN 0-89158-993-7

Composition for this book was provided by the editor.
Printed and bound in the United States of America.

CONTENTS

PART 3: GLACIOLOGY AND HYDROLOGY

PART 5: PLANT ECOLOGY

PREFACE

THE DEVELOPMENT OF A FRONT RANGE MOUNTAIN RESEARCH STATION

In the early years of the Twentieth Century Professor Francis Ramaley, professor of biology at the University of Colorado, prophetically referred to that narrow north-south stretch of terrain, extending some 25 km westward from the Boulder campus to the Continental Divide, as an excellent natural scientific laboratory. He undoubtedly was prompted to this designation by the dramatic sequence of vegetation belts and their associated local climates, extending from the upper limit of the short-grass prairie of the High Plains across the lower treeline immediately west of a line joining Golden, Boulder, and Lyons through a series of altitudinally-arranged forest belts and their ecotones to the upper timberline and the alpine tundra close to the Divide. This spectacular transition across a distance of barely 25 km, the equivalent of a northward journey in the latitudinal sense of some 2,500 km, is further emphasized by the existence of small cirque glaciers and patches of permafrost at the higher levels.

Although Ramaley had no direct association with the facility which today is known as the Mountain Research Station of the Institute of Arctic and Alpine Research (INSTAAR), he should be credited with sowing seeds of interdisciplinary natural science teaching and research in the Colorado Front Range.

This teaching and research tradition has waxed and waned, but on the whole has slowly developed on the Boulder campus for three-quarters of a century. Ramaley's direct contribution to ecological teaching and early research had virtually ended when a group of energetic and recreationally-oriented University of Colorado (CU) faculty began to construct buildings at 2965 m, west of North Boulder Creek on the old Rainbow Lakes Road some 8 km north of Nederland, that originally were referred to as "University Camp." During the late 1900s the City of Boulder took over this property, and the camp was moved towards the southeast end of Niwot Ridge to the base of a moraine where a

spring provided a good supply of water. The present location
of the camp is designated "University of Colorado Camp" on the
Ward quadrangle (U.S.G.S. topographic map, 7.5 min. series).
During the 1920s other CU faculty, this time biologists and geologists, began to use the camp for summer school teaching aimed
at utilizing the natural laboratory around it, as previously
recognized by Ramaley, who himself had earlier used for a similar purpose a rustic hotel at Tolland, some 15 km further south.

With the summer school activity the name "Science Lodge"
became established and the purely recreational use was super-
seded. Doc Thompson, Hugo Rodeck and Ernie Wahlstrom, were some
of the leading figures who were long associated with this phase,
which extended with a short break during World War II until the
end of the 1940s. Teaching and summer season activities predominated although several faculty members undertook individual
research projects and undoubtedly, group experience in the
beautiful rustic mountain setting must have resulted in shared
ideas and the dissemination of results across disciplinary
boundaries.

Particularly noteworthy is the research on bedrock geology
and geomorphology by Wahlstrom, with his 1940 and 1947 papers
standing as fine examples of works that are still extensively
used as basic references. Another example is the prolific
publication record of Ronald L. Ives (not related to the editor
of this volume) in geology, geomorphology, climatology, and
archeology.

During the late 1940s a rather remarkable event occurred.
The "Science Lodge" organizing committee, considering the
facilities too primitive to support "modern" teaching, recommended that the University terminate the program. It is perhaps
permissible to claim that the vacuum so created, in the presence
of a large group of buildings and some thousand hectares of land
with no immediate or obvious use, prompted a positive and highly
constructive initiative by John W. Marr who at that time was a
young assistant professor of biology with field experience in
Greenland and northern Labrador-Ungava, as well as in the Front
Range. His initiative, along with the faith and foresight of
Robert L. Stearns, CU President, and the Board of Regents,
resulted in the establishment of an Institute of Alpine Ecology
in 1950. One of the institute's main functions was to admin-
ister "Science Lodge" and through this to develop a program on
long-range ecological research for the Front Range. The institute initially consisted of a single faculty member, Marr, as
its first director, and a modest support staff. Its activities
were guided by a governing Council consisting of a representative from each of the cognate academic departments, in those
days: biology, geography, and geology, the CU Museum, and the
Dean of the Graduate School. One of the earliest actions of
the Council under the chairmanship of Hugo Rodeck (which he
retained until his retirement from the University in 1970) was
to change the institute's name. Thus in 1951 the Institute of

of Arctic and Alpine Research came into formal existence, the name having been retained until the present day.

1950/1951, therefore, represents a major turning point in the history of the Mountain Research Station, as it is now named. First, it was institutionalized in that it became the Institute of Arctic and Alpine Research, and was given a permanent directorship and a regular, if modest, operating budget; and secondly, the task of the first director was the establishment of long-term scientific objectives. This took the form of a study of the Front Range ecosystems in a dynamic context, with the very important corollary of the operation of a series of permanent environment measurement stations (climatic recording stations), one in each of the major ecosystem belts: lower montane, upper montane, subalpine forest and alpine, through an altitudinal range from 2,195 m to 3,750 m. This massive effort culminated in the publication of Marr's classic monograph, "Ecosystems of the East Slope of the Front Range, Colorado Rocky Mountains" in 1961. Another feature of the early years of the Institute was the attention given to year-round ecological research and teaching, resulting in the development of a logistical system that provides access to alpine and subalpine research areas to a degree unparalleled in North America. This was also accompanied by the first year-round residents: Les and Teri Viereck, who later obtained their doctoral degrees at CU before "emigrating" to Alaska, were the first to overwinter (1955-1958). They were followed by establishment of a permanent, residential station manager post which has been continued to this day. Ralph (Skip) Greene, was the first manager who lived at the station with his family for 12 years. Skip's enthusiasm for the development of the mountain logistical system and his devotion to the concepts of the mountain research station were only surpassed in importance during the first seventeen years in the life of the Institute by the contribution of the first director himself. Also, during this period, John Clark adopted the maintenance and development of the climatological observing network as a personal commitment. Undoubtedly, without the assistance of Skip Greene and John Clark, often far beyond the call of duty, many doctoral and masters dissertations would never have been completed.

Marr introduced many graduate students to ecological research in the Front Range, many of whom have progressed to enter the leading ranks of ecological research and administration in the United States today. Amongst others, these include: Cliff Amundsen, Al Johnson, Phil Miller, Al Mooney, Bill Osborn, Les Viereck, and Beatrice Willard. A parallel development was that the institute attracted the interest and moral support of such well established members of the ecological community both nationally and internationally, as Dwight Billings, Larry Bliss, Eilif Dahl, Dave Gates, Martyn Caldwell, Hal Lutz, and Peter Wardle. The late Carl Troll, pursuing his world-wide studies in mountain geoecology, was one of many notable visitors. Sid

White and Gerry Richmond, geologists, and Pete Martinelli, snow
hydrologist, represent some of the non-biological interest that
have had both direct and indirect bearing on many of the more
recent developments. Particular mention must be made of Sid
White, who, from 1960 onwards, virtually established an Ohio
State University partnership by conducting research in the area
for 11 field seasons, and by introducing a succession of his
graduate students to Quaternary doctoral dissertation topics in
the Front Range. These included Richard Bonnett, Richard F.
Madole, Gary Wallace, Eileen McSaveney, and Gary McLaughlin,
who together have laid the foundation for the first systematic
mapping of the glacial and periglacial deposits of the Front
Range, a task still awaiting final collation from individual
sources. A few years later, a young graduate student from
Madison, Jim Benedict, working under the supervision of Bob
Black, took up residence at the Mountain Research Station for
completion of his doctoral dissertation, which later resulted
in award of the Kirk Bryan Medal of the Geological Society of
America in recognition of his 1970 paper, published in the
Journal of Arctic and Alpine Research. This study also established lichenometric techniques (Beschel, 1950; Webber and
Andrews,1973; Benedict, 1968) as an important geochronological
tool in the Front Range and was extended to a major study of
alpine game drive systems on and near the Continental Divide,
initially identified by Husted (1962, 1974). This flavoring of
glacial and geological research with archeology and biology
ensured a duality of research effort, a situation reflected in
Chapters 6 and 7. Finally, towards the end of his directorship
(1950-1967) Marr succeeded in attracting National Science
Foundation and University matching funds for the construction
of the Alpine Laboratory, a substantial, winterized laboratory
and office building completed in 1965.

The next step in the development of the Mountain Research
Station was the 1967 decision by the University to augment the
number of INSTAAR faculty positions from one to seven, to add
significantly to the staff, to establish a quarterly scientific
journal, Arctic and Alpine Research, and to provide a major
facility on the Boulder campus for office, laboratory, and
teaching activities. The administrative foresight and energy
of Jim Archer, then Dean of the Graduate School, was largely
responsible for this development and was sustained by Lawson
Crowe who succeeded him. It was provided at a time when there
was serious debate over whether to enlarge or terminate the
role of the Institute. As in 1950, the very presence of a significant physical plant at 3,000 m provided a bias in favor of
a positive outcome. But it was the creative mind of Archer,
intent on establishing a firmly-based "instant institute," to
quote his own words, with a truly interdisciplinary faculty and
mission and, for the first time, an Arctic program to rationalize
the Institute's name, that prevailed. From this point the
Mountain Research Station came to be only one part of the

Institute as a whole and the Arctic program, under the leader-
ship of John T. Andrews, and others subsequently, which gave
rise to more than 200 publications in the last twelve years and
which, through its very success, has possibly delayed realization
of the full potential for work in Mountain Geoecology in the
Front Range. Additional extensive research developments in the
San Juan Mountains (Steinhoff and Ives, 1976; Armstrong and Ives,
1976) and in Alaska and throughout the Canadian Northwest Territories and Labrador-Ungava, whilst of great value in enlarging
the role of INSTAAR, also served to reduce the available energy
for the firm establishment of a program of alpine research.
This volume, however, should serve to emphasize that the growth
in Front Range endeavor was still considerable and recent
efforts have been made to sustain and augment this momentum.
These include: creation of a resident field directorship;
location of a large program supported by the NASA Office of
University Affairs at the Alpine Laboratory (this has as its
objective the application of remote sensing to solution of land-
use problems in mountain Colorado); and a modest, but important,
schedule of winterizing "summer" buildings and constructing new
year-round living and utility buildings. Current activities
include a strengthening of the station's teaching program. The
field directorship, established as a two-to-three-year appointment to rotate amongst the cognate disciplines, was initially
filled by Mike Grant, biologist. The second appointment (Sept.
1976), was David Greenland, a climatologist, and the third
(Sept. 1978) was Misha Plam, whose special interest is snow and
avalanche research.

One of the important administrative and legal aspects of
developing and maintaining a viable mountain research station
relates to access to a major research area that encompasses a
wide variety of ecosystems. For the Mountain Research Station
this includes the subalpine and alpine ecosystems of the immediately adjacent sections of the Indian Peaks area and especially Niwot Ridge and the valleys of Green Lakes and Silver
Lakes, the latter two valleys comprising the City of Boulder
Watershed. The United States Forest Service, through Special
Use Permits, have provided INSTAAR and collaborating institutions and individuals with priority research access to some
5,000 acres. Recent developments in land-management decisions
for the Front Range promise to be of great significance for
research activities in general and the Mountain Research Station
in particular. In November 1978, President Carter established
the Indian Peaks Wilderness Area, thus protecting a wide area
of mountain land south of Rocky Mountain National Park. In May,
1979, following submissions by the U.S. Forest Service and the
Department of State, Unesco formally accepted designation of
INSTAAR's primary mountain research area as the Niwot Ridge
Biosphere Reserve. This should provide added protection and
support for alpine and subalpine research and facilitate application of research results into management decision-making for

the Indian Peaks Wilderness Area and for comparable mountain areas elsewhere. The formal link with the Unesco Man and the Biosphere (MAB) Programme provides an international setting of great potential. Similarly, the City of Boulder Watershed, a vital subalpine and alpine research area closed to the general public, has been made available for appropriately justified research activities. INSTAAR has greatly benefited over the 30 years of its existence from the collaboration of the U.S. Forest Service and the City of Boulder. As pressures for access to mountain lands continue to grow it is imperative that this collaboration continue and also be extended so that applied research can be undertaken as one means of ensuring development of appropriate management techniques for the wider area of the Front Range at large. It may be anticipated that the role of the Mountain Research Station will be greatly enlarged and that new and major challenges will fall upon INSTAAR.

The enlargement of INSTAAR to include seven faculty members in various disciplines, their graduate students, and the continued involvement of visiting scientists and their students, has resulted over the last ten years in a great increase in depth and breadth of research in the Front Range. Some highlights include the participation of INSTAAR in the International Biological Program (IBP) Tundra Biome research and designation of Niwot Ridge as an intensive alpine tundra study site; identification of INSTAAR as the United States headquarters of the Unesco Man and the Biosphere (MAB) Program -- Project 6A directorate: study of the impact of human activities on mountain ecosystems; and intimate association with the International Geographical Union (IGU) Commission of "High-Altitude Geoecology" (renamed following the Moscow 1976 Congress as "Mountain Geo-ecology"), founded in 1968 by the late Carl Troll. Most recently the University of Colorado, Boulder, became an Associate Institute of United Nations University, with a special relationship with the UNU Programme on the Use and Management of Natural Resources. Specifically this involves the UNU-NR project on Highland-lowland interactive systems and entails an important training component. This was initiated in 1979 with the incorporation of four Nepali and three Thai UNU fellows into its summer mountain training program.

All these relationships are doing much to augment the role of the Mountain Research Station in Mountain Geoecology. It seemed timely, therefore, to publish in book form an annotated collection of previously published papers, with some hitherto unpublished work, dealing primarily with the Colorado Front Range, many of them stemming either directly or indirectly from the Mountain Research Station and the activities of the scientists and teachers that its presence drew to the Front Range.

OBJECTIVES OF THE BOOK

1. To make available in a single volume research

publications that deal directly or indirectly with the mountain
environment of the Front Range of Colorado, with emphasis on
the alpine and subalpine ecosystems.

    2. To produce a basic research and teaching reference on
the geoecology of the Front Range through the addition of com-
mentaries on the various groups of papers, which have been arranged to form the specific chapters, together with additional
references.

    3. By the same means expressed in (2) to provide a state-
of-knowledge report on Front Range research, to identify strengths
and weaknesses and to indicate gaps in knowledge. It is hoped
that, on the one hand, this will assist individuals contemplating
research there and, on the other, that it will aid INSTAAR to a
more effective formulation of the next phase of its Front Range
research program. Hopefully, this will embrace a more rigorous
quantitative approach and a more effective interdisciplinary
balance.

    4. To provide background material for examination of many
of the applied, land-use management problems facing this and
comparable mountain environments.

    5. To illustrate the effectiveness of the Mountain Research
Station as a research and teaching facility set in the midst of
a superb mountain area and yet in close proximity to a major
university campus.

    6. To encourage scientists and students from other insti-
tutions to identify weaknesses, gaps in knowledge, and other
research opportunities, so that they consider using our facilities as a basis for future collaborative research and learning.

SELECTION OF PAPERS

    Papers selected for inclusion date primarily from 1965-1978,
with the majority having been published after 1968. The intent
is to give as good a cross-section as possible of the various
disciplines represented yet within reasonable constraints imposed
in terms of quality, quantity, and length of individual paper.
Also, to reduce costs, every attempt has been made to restrict
the amount of new text and illustrations. Again, the emphasis
on the alpine and subalpine ecosystems is underlined.

    While the majority of the papers represent the work of
INSTAAR faculty, present and former graduate students, and research associates, and visiting scientists to the Mountain Research
Station, there was no specific policy to restrict selection to this
group. Nor is there a wish to claim any exclusiveness on the part
of INSTAAR to Front Range research; rather the reverse. Papers
such as those by G.R. Richmond, M. Martinelli, Jr., P. Wardle, and
L.M. Hjermstad, provide added breadth and perspective and are also
intended to indicate the strong presence of the USGS, the U.S.
Forest Service, Rocky Mountain Forest and Range Experiment Station, and Colorado State University. In some areas, notably
animal ecology and soil microbiology, the groups of papers

are not cohesive, and many gaps are apparent. This in part
reflects gaps in the scope of past INSTAAR research and in part
a general lack of activity in certain fields of endeavor. One
paper, based on research in the San Juan Mountains (Caine, 1971),
is included in part to ensure coverage of some topics not treated
directly through Front Range research and in part because its
subject matter is applicable and highly relevant to the Front
Range. For the same reason several other papers have been included which do not deal directly with Front Range problems.
The individual papers selected have their own bibliographies,
but to supplement these additional references have been cited
in the overviews for each chapter.

The selection was made from over 300 titles. A determination to be representative and at the same time to keep the total
number of pages within reasonable limits has frequently resulted
in a difficult decision to exclude a particular paper, or in the
inclusion of only parts of a paper. Finally, there was a deliberate intent to include papers authored by students or produced
while their authors were students at the time of writing.

Research in several fields, especially glacial geology,
geomorphology, climatology, and tundra plant ecology, has been
particularly intensive and also active during the period of
compilation and printing of this collection. In particular,
there are many doctoral and master's dissertations recently
completed or in preparation. Thus, in several of these fields
time is almost ripe for preparation of major syntheses. Such
especially lies beyond the scope of this book. INSTAAR recognizes an obligation to produce a number of such syntheses.
Others, and original works, will undoubtedly appear, both with
INSTAAR collaboration and entirely independently (cf. Benedict
and Olson, 1978; Komárková, 1979). In addition, it must be
pointed out that several areas of research in the Front Range
have progressed well beyond the stage that might be inferred
from the arrangement of this book. These include archeology
and certain aspects of applied ecology and forestry. To ensure
that we keep within reasonable bounds of subject matter and
cost, it was decided to set such topics beyond the limits of
this project. To conclude this section of the preface, it
should suffice to state that we hope to have made an initial,
if humble, first step in the provision of a broad understanding
of the geoecology of a magnificent mountain range.

WHAT IS GEOECOLOGY?

The word may seem self-evident to many -- ecology with a
good basis of geology, or geoscience, thrown in! But this is
surely not enough, especially for the 1980s when words such as
"ecology" and "environment" have become overused and sometimes
even grossly distorted. Nevertheless, the initial sentence
provides a large part of the answer. Technically "ecology" has
been used by biologists to imply the study of the functioning

of plants and animals, their interrelationships and the interrelationships between them, the living elements of ecosystems,
and the abiotic elements. Frequently, in the practice of
ecology, the abiotic aspects have received only secondary
attention. The term geoecology, as used here, therefore, is to
underline the need to redress this imbalance; but it is intended
to do more than that by including man and his activities into
the system. This volume is virtually lacking the human element,
in large part because that aspect of an already complex research
effort has not yet been satisfactorily developed. The argument
is nevertheless stated here at the risk of inviting the criticism
that this collection does not represent a geoecology as defined.
Let me therefore claim that it is used as a statement of good
intentions for the future, because the very justification of
continued research in the Front Range must rest equally on contribution to the solution of human problems as well as on the
satisfaction of human curiosity. These aspirations are a reflection of the goals of Unesco's Man and the Biosphere (MAB) Programme and the reason why this collection is offered as a contribution both to MAB Project 6: study of the impact of human
activities on mountain and tundra ecosystems, and to the International Geographical Union Commission on Mountain Geoecology.
In conclusion, it must be emphasized that the very word "geoecology," as well as the founding of the IGU Commission, is a
reflection of the preeminent work and personality of the late
Professor Carl Troll.

ACKNOWLEDGMENTS

Even a modest collection of papers dealing with a single
region is not put together without effort. I have long debated
the wisdom of even making this first step, particularly in
worrying over whether or not overall Front Range research has
progressed far enough to allow a reasonable coverage of the
various disciplines. The step would not have been taken without
the assistance, advice and moral support of many people, some of
whom are no longer living, and a few of whom perhaps were not
even aware of the help and encouragement they rendered. Of
course, the primary acknowledgment goes to the authors of the
many papers selected, and perhaps of almost equal importance to
those of papers considered and read as background material
although not selected. I believe that many of the papers included are the results of outstanding research and many years
of difficult and even dangerous physical effort. Next in importance are the contributions of my colleagues who supervised
the final selection of papers for the specific chapters and who
undertook writing the accompanying overviews. Thanks are also
due to the publishers and editors of scientific journals who
have given permission to reprint. These are acknowledged
specifically below.
    Next, the encouragement of faculty colleagues, graduate

students, staff and visitors to the Mountain Research Station
has been invaluable. Five summers of residence at the station
with my family, and many winter days on Niwot Ridge, have provided valuable insights, many moments of excitement and com-
radeship and frozen fingers. Roger Barry allowed me to relin-
quish for a year the burdens of administration by taking on the
task of INSTAAR Acting Director. A University of Colorado
Research Fellowship and a John Simon Guggenheim Memorial Fellowship facilitated a year's research leave in Switzerland whilst,
between my main goals, much of this work was planned. Professor
Bruno Messerli and the Geographisches Institut, Universität Bern,
provided the encouragement and hospitality for the Swiss experience.

Finally, a number of far-sighted, tenacious, peculiarly
gifted, or stimulating individuals, each in his own way, was
responsible for the establishment and maintenance of an institute,
a mountain research station, and a research and teaching tradition, without which practically nothing produced or reproduced
between these covers would have materialized. So, to Francis
Ramaley for sowing the seeds of an idea; to Doc Thompson and
his colleagues, who I am sure shared many happy summers in the
Front Range, and who constructed the log cabins of the original
Science Lodge with their own hands, and established a summer
teaching tradition; to John W. Marr, who established an institute
and a year-round research and teaching tradition and who maintained them through seventeen difficult years of inadequate
financial support; to Jim Archer, who briefly passed through as
sometime Dean of the CU Graduate School, and in so doing, gave
us, with the blessings of the Colorado taxpayer an "instant
institute," with an opportunity to realize an Arctic and an
Alpine program; to Hugo Rodeck, who devoted time and affection
to both station and institute from 1929 to 1970; and to Carl
Troll, for developing the concepts of mountain geoecology;
finally to many others, far too numerous to mention; this collection is dedicated with the hope that it will indeed prove
only a first step.

REFERENCES

Armstrong, R.L. and J.D. Ives (eds.). 1976. *Avalanche Release
    and Snow Characteristics, San Juan Mountains, Colorado.*
    Institute of Arctic and Alpine Research Occasional Paper
    19. 256 pp.
Benedict, J.B. 1968. Recent glacial history of an alpine area
    in the Colorado Front Range, U.S.A. II. Dating the glacial
    deposits. *Journal of Glaciology*, 7(49): 77-87.
_____. 1970. Downslope soil movement in a Colorado alpine
    region: rates, processes, and climatic significance.
    Arctic and Alpine Research, 2(3): 165-226.
Benedict, J.B. and B.L. Olson. 1978. *The Mount Albion Complex:
    a Study of Prehistoric Man and the Altithermal.* Center for

Mountain Archeology, Ward, Colorado, Research Report No. 1. 213 pp.

Beschel, R.E. 1950. Flechten als Altersmasstab rezenter Moränen. *Z. Gletscherkd. Glacialgeol.*, 1: 152-161.

Caine, N. 1971. A conceptual model for alpine slope process study. *Arctic and Alpine Research*, 3(4): 319-329.

Husted, W.M. 1962. *A Proposed Archeological Chronology for Rocky Mountain National Park Based on Projectile Points and Pottery*. Unpubl. M.A. Thesis, University of Colorado, Boulder. 109 pp.

————. 1974. Prehistoric occupation of the alpine zone in the Rocky Mountains. *In* Ives, J.D. and R.G. Barry (eds.), *Arctic and Alpine Environments*. Methuen, London, pp. 857-872.

Komárková, V. 1979. *Alpine Vegetation of the Indian Peaks Area, Front Range, Colorado Rocky Mountains*. Flora et Vegetatio Mundi, VII. J. Cramer, Vaduz. 649 pp.

Marr, J.W. 1967. *Ecosystems of the East Slope of the Front Range in Colorado*. University of Colorado Studies, Series in Biology No. 8, Boulder, Colorado. 134 pp.

Steinhoff, H.W. and J.D. Ives (eds.). 1976. *Ecological Impacts of Snowpack Augmentation in the San Juan Mountains, Colorado*. San Juan Ecology Project Final Report to Bureau of Reclamation. 489 pp.

Wahlstrom, E.E. 1940. Audubon-Albion stock, Boulder County, Colorado. *Geol. Soc. Amer. Bull.*, 51: 1789-1820.

————. 1947. Cenozoic physiographic history of the Front Range, Colorado. *Geol. Soc. Amer. Bull.*, 58: 551-572.

Webber, P.J. and J.T. Andrews (eds.). 1973. Lichenometry: Dedicated to the memory of the Late Roland E. Beschel. *Arctic and Alpine Research*, 5(4): 293-432.

JACK D. IVES

CREDITS

The following journals and publishers gave permission to reproduce papers in part, or in their entirety, maps, and diagrams:
American Midland Naturalist; Arctic and Alpine Research - Regents of the University of Colorado; Bulletin of the Geological Society of America; Climatological Bulletin; Ecology; Geology; Journal of Glaciology, Journal of Research, U.S. Geological Survey; Journal of Wildlife Management; and Zeitschrift für Geomorphologie.

Thanks are due to all the authors of papers reproduced who granted permission to reproduce and who otherwise cooperated with the production of this book.

New photographic material, unless specifically credited, was contributed by the Editor.

The following persons contributed to various phases of manuscript production, preparation of camera-ready copy, correspondence, identification and collection of reprints, typing, cartography:
Betsy and Richard Armstrong, Cherie Baxley, Marilyn McVey, Jane Perry, Ann Stites; Laura Koch was responsible for the final typing, lay-out, and mounting of the reprints; without her contribution the book would never have been completed. Thanks are also due to Frederick S. Praeger, President, and Ms. Miriam Gilbert of Westview Press, for their advice and general support.

ABBREVIATIONS

Amer. Midl. Nat.: American Midland Naturalist.
AAR: Arctic and Alpine Research.
Bull. Geol. Soc. Amer.: Bulletin of the Geological Society
                    of America.
Climatol. Bull.: Climatological Bulletin.
J. Glaciology: Journal of Glaciology.
J. Res. U.S. Geol. Surv.: Journal of Research, U.S. Geo-
                    logical Survey.
J. Wildlife Management: Journal of Wildlife Management.
Univ. of Colo. Stud., Ser. in Earth Sci.: University of
   Colorado Studies, Series in Earth Sciences.
Univ. of Colo. Stud., Ser. in Geol.: University of Colo-
   rado Studies, Series in Geology.
Zeits. Geomorph.: Zeitschrift für Geomorphologie.

INTRODUCTION:
A DESCRIPTION OF THE FRONT RANGE

JACK D. IVES*

The Front Range of the Colorado Rocky Mountains is here somewhat arbitrarily defined as a north-south trending massif that extends southward some 150 km from the Wyoming state line to where it merges with the complex highland centered on Mount Evans and overlooking South Park (Figure 1). In the north the Mummy, Neversummer, and Medicine Bow ranges splay off in a north-northwesterly trend from the northern Front Range axis within Rocky Mountain National Park. In the south the Park Range of South Park creates a confused southwest trending transition to the Gore and Mosquito ranges, while the eastern edge, much lower south of Denver, continues the primary north-south axis down to Colorado Springs and to beyond the New Mexico state line. Some definitions of the Front Range include this lower southerly extension with the prominently offset summit of Pikes Peak. For the purposes of this collection Mount Evans is used as the southern limit and most emphasis is placed upon the middle, or Indian Peaks, section which is bisected by the 40 degree north parallel.

The eastern limit of the Front Range is the simplest to demarcate. It approximates the lower timberline at about 1,700 m (5,600 ft) where the first uplifted, tilted and contorted sedimentary rocks form the transition with the High Plains. The western limit is more diffuse, demarcated in part by North Park and Winter Park.

Figures 1 and 2 illustrate the areal and cross-sectional appearance in somewhat simplified form. Again, emphasis on the Indian Peaks section makes for ease of description and concentrates attention on the area where most of the research illustrated in this collection has been undertaken. However, many of the descriptions and conclusions drawn from work in this area

*Institute of Arctic and Alpine Research
University of Colorado
Boulder, Colorado 80309

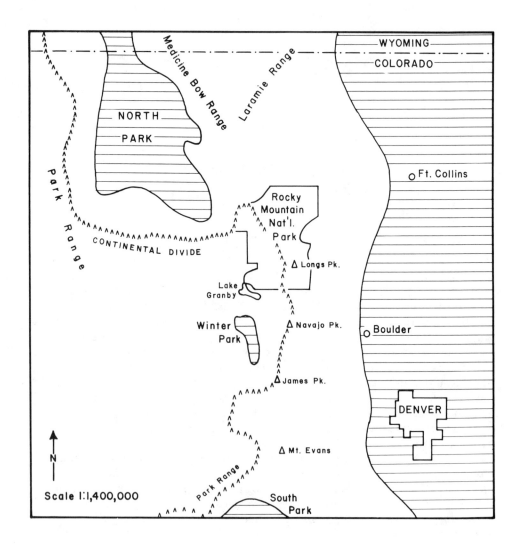

FIGURE 1. General sketch map of the Colorado Front Range
           vicinity.

are applicable, at least in a general sense, to the whole.

    Geologically the Front Range is framed by a series of nar-
row sedimentary formations forming cuestas and hogsbacks on the
east, and tectonic depressions, also underlain by sediments, on
the west and south. The main bulk of the range is composed of
a core of acidic Precambrian intrusives, themselves intruded by
acidic Tertiary plutons.

    The maximum relief from the High Plains to the crestline is
of the order of 2,500 m (8,200 ft). Viewed from the air one of
the most striking features is the north-south trending crestline, especially in the Indian Peaks section where maximum

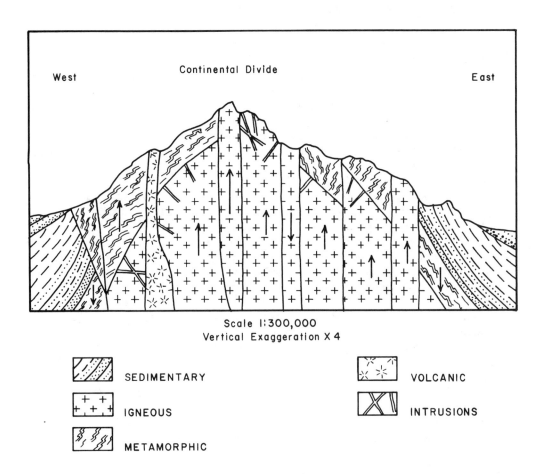

FIGURE 2. Generalized geological cross-section of the Colorado Front Range (derived from U.S. Geological Survey and other sources).

altitudes range between 3,800 and 4,200 m (12,600 and 13,500 ft). This crestline forms the Continental Divide. Viewed from a low angle it appears to slope off rather gently toward the east as a series of broad benches (belts of accordant summits) that have been described as remnants of former erosion surfaces. This relatively gentle east slope is dissected at right angles to the crestline by a succession of deep trenches formed initially as river valleys, with their upper courses subsequently modified by glacial erosion that occurred during Late Cenozoic times. The valley down-cutting has produced a fretwork of deep, U-shaped troughs and glacial cirques that have penetrated so far into the

heart of the main uplift in places as to leave a narrow and
precipitous rock wall as the actual crestline. The interfluves,
equally sharp near the crestline, become broad, gently contoured
ridges within a few kilometers before sinking below timberline
at about 3,400 m (11,200 ft). The lower sections of these east-
west trending valleys have cut spectacular V-shaped gorges before
debouching onto the High Plains.

Of the east-west trending ridges of the east slope, Niwot
Ridge, an objective of especially intensive research, is the
longest and most spectacular, extending a distance of 10 km from
the crestline at Navajo Peak (4,150 m; 13,404 ft) to Bald, or
Niwot, Mountain at 3,530 m (11,471 ft).

Westward from the Indian Peaks section of the crestline,
the land drops precipitously towards Winter Park and the water
bodies of Granby Reservoir, Grand Lake, and Monarch Lake.

The physique of the area has been heavily influenced, therefore, by the uplift of broad, flat, or gently rolling surfaces
that have been attacked by a combination of fluvial and glacial
erosion. Glacial erosion has not proceeded very far, so that
the higher parts of the Front Range (basically the area above
timberline) display a fairly even balance between steep, glaciated terrain and gently flowing upland surfaces. Thus the
area is characterized by two contrasting sets of landform
assemblages, one produced by glacial erosion and secondary mass
movement and frost-shattering, the other displaying the typical
smooth forms associated with periglacial processes (Figure 3).

Another important control on the overall physique of the
area is the prevailing westerly wind, present and presumeably
past. Thus drifting snow, snow accumulation, and topographic
control of glacier mass balance processes, have combined to
ensure that most of the tiny present-day cirque glaciers occur
on the east side of the crestline and most of the cirque forms
themselves are orientated predominantly toward the east. The
same wind-topographic-snowdrift relationship dominates the
disposition of the many perennial and late-lying snowbanks,
which, in turn, exerts a strong control on the patterns of
vegetation and animal populations.

After the broad physique of a mountain range, perhaps the
next most noticeable characteristic for the casual observer is
the vegetation cover. As seen from the air above the eastern
margins of Boulder, the westward rise of land displays a series
of semi-parallel vegetational belts, strongly influenced by the
progressive shift in climatic belts with increasing altitude.
The regional climate of the area can best be described as a mid-
latitude interior continental dry climate, that of the short-
grass prairie of the High Plains. The mountain climatic belts
are basically altitudinal variants of this regional climate,
the controlling factors being decreasing air temperatures and
increasing precipitation with increasing height above sea level;
thus the increasing precipitation with altitude provides sufficient moisture for vigorous forest growth until at extreme

altitudes temperature controls dominate a change to alpine herbs and shrubs. Thus the proportion of solid to liquid precipitation increases with altitude as does the total annual precipitation (from about 380 to 1,200 mm of water), and the mean temperatures of each of the four distinct seasons decrease. The length of the growing season, of especial importance to plant growth, also decreases with altitude. Thus four major ecosystems can be readily recognized above the short-grass prairie and the lower treeline: the colline belt, with ponderosa pine and Douglas fir predominating; the lower montane forest; the upper montane forest, with Englemann spruce, subalpine fir, and limber pine, and the alpine tundra. Lodgepole pine and aspen, also characteristic sub-dominants of the two uppermost forest belts are considered as successional after fire. Timberline, defined as the upper limit of tall, symmetrical trees, occurs at about 3,400 m (11,000 ft), with treeline, or species limit, at about 3,550 m (11,500 ft), with local variations due to a variety of factors. This transition from timberline to treeline, the so-called forest-tundra ecotone, or subalpine belt, is one of the most spectacular vegetation boundaries on earth. Ease of access from the Mountain Research Station ensured that it became an object of special scientific interest to the University of Colorado and other researchers.

Above timberline, major changes in the micro-topography and geomorphic processes become apparent. Patches of permafrost begin to occur at about 3,500 m (11,400 ft); in sheltered places snowbanks last throughout the summer, and periglacial terraces, needle ice patterns, and relict and subactual patterned ground, indicate a rapid increase in severity of climate. A myriad of tundra plant associations dominate the surface, showing rapid variation over short distances influenced by topography and snow accumulation patterns. Finally, at the higher levels, rock faces and small cirque glaciers predominate and the observer enters the true alpine landscape, or hochgebirge, as defined by Carl Troll.

It is upon this natural system that man has begun to leave an increasingly heavy stamp. Paleoindian game-drive walls are scattered across the area above timberline dating back at least to 7,000 years ago, but overall impact was slight prior to European penetration. Much more recently hunter and trapper left a minimum indication of their former presence. In the latter part of the last century the prospector and miner literally dug up much surface area, while the attendant need for lumber and firewood resulted in the first major impacts on the forests. This has left an impoverished forest, large areas being secondary growth after forest fire and logging, as indicated in part by the extensive stands of lodgepole pine and aspen and the young dense spruce-fir stands.

Finally, recreation is now making serious impacts. Summer and winter recreational use, principally from a booming Front Range population corridor stretching from Fort Collins to

6

FIGURE 3. The southern section of the Indian Peaks Wilderness Area with Niwot Ridge left center.

Colorado Springs, but heavily supplemented by out-of-state visitors, has been the basis for recently concluded and on-going land-management policy changes. These present-day uses, of course, are supplemented by hunting, water diversions, and the regrowth of many of the original mining towns. Land ownership patterns are quite complex and will themselves progressively differentiate a series of land-use regions as the level of human impact heightens.

The major land ownership patterns include: Rocky Mountain National Park, with its multi-million visitor impact on a small percentage of its total area; the newly created Indian Peaks Wilderness Area; the remaining National Forest land; the City of Boulder Watershed; the Niwot Ridge Biosphere Reserve; and amongst these larger areas, myriads of privately owned parcels.

Recreation, because of the many past and recent policy decisions, is destined to be the predominant land use of the Front Range. It can be shown, however, that even so-called protected areas, such as wilderness areas from which mechanized transport is excluded, can be extensively damaged, if not destroyed, by too many hiking boots and too many camp fires. The specialized papers of the subsequent chapters, while largely the result of intellectual curiosity, should form part of the data base and accumulated expertise from which wise land-use decision-making, or reasonably effective compromises, can be derived. These are already being supplemented, however, by more directly "applied" research, notable amongst which will be the Environmental Atlas of the Indian Peaks Wilderness Area.

FIGURE 4. The eastern margin of the Front Range; Mount Evans right skyline.

8

FIGURE 5. Upland surface dissected by cirque erosion.

FIGURE 6. The west slope; Monarch Lake drainage.

Part 1
Glacial Geology

Overview
*Michael J. Clarke**

It is now more than a century since the first tentative
suggestions for a Rocky Mountain chronology were made, yet
despite the massive proliferation of techniques, evidence, and
hypotheses, it is difficult to claim that the ensuing hundred
years have produced even a general concensus, let alone a definitive theory. To some extent, the current lack of accord is
simply a product of its scientific context: a generation of
young scientists dedicated to increasingly detailed study by
increasingly diverse means will be inherently less likely to
achieve easy unity than were their predecessors - fewer in
number, more generalist in outlook, and more closely bound to
a common tradition of investigative technique and explanatory
structure. Science is, of necessity, characterized by conflict.
Yet the feeling remains that part of this conflict may reflect
an unhealthy insistence on the verification of some cherished
hypothesis, rather than a progressive willingness to open all
ideas to the challenge of falsification. At times there is a
suspicion that the main conflict is between scientists rather
than between scientific ideas, yet even this may be forgivable.
Rocky Mountain glacial geology is open only to those with the
strength and perseverance to grapple with ambiguous evidence
scattered through a beautiful but extremely rugged fieldwork
environment - and ideas thus hard-won are unlikely to be easily
yielded. The story to be unfolded therefore has a double
fascination: part centered on the gradual illumination of the
Pleistocene history of a major mountain range; and part directed
to the equally significant task of elucidating the recent history
of research and creativity, in the hope that this understanding
might serve as a foundation for future progress.

Such a complex topic is trivialized by classification, but
as a compromise between brevity and clarity, it is convenient

*Department of Geography
 University of Southampton
 England

9

to divide the past century's activity into three developmental stages, to be followed by a discussion of the background to the debate of the present decade. The rest of the chapter is then devoted to a selection of papers which indicate the context of this debate. Attention will focus on the Colorado Front Range but not to the exclusion of other regions, for many vital stages in the growing awareness of the Rocky Mountain sequence were developed in other areas, and one of the primary motivating forces in a century of research has been the quest for regional, continental, and even global chronological synchroneity (an ideal the validity of which is discussed later). We will reach no conclusions, for the subject under discussion is characterized by flux rather than stability, but there is value and satisfaction to be gained from placing current research priorities into a regional and temporal perspective.

EMERGENCE OF THE HISTORICAL THREE-FOLD GLACIATION SEQUENCE

Although the period 1840-1860 saw the rapid spread of the concept of glaciation, and indeed of multiple glaciation, in both Europe and North America, there was little application of this idea to the Western Cordillera. The reasons for this time lag lay first in the great difficulty of access to the American West (which was not subject to substantial geological study of any kind until the middle of the Nineteenth Century), and second in the nature of valley glaciation. Whilst the great continental ice sheets of central, eastern, and northern North America might lay down extensive and chronologically complete depositional sequences, the evidence in the Rocky Mountains was fragmentary to start with, further reduced through part of the evidence of previous stages being removed during each subsequent valley-confined glacial period, and through disruption by the massive interglacial incision of the major rivers.

The Western glacial concept was born in the recognition by Whitney (1865) that a link must exist between the manifest fluctuation of lake levels and the equally manifest activity of valley glaciers at some point in the past. This idea was taken up by Gilbert (1875) and developed by him (1880) into the hypothesis that the joint history in the Lake Bonneville area was dominated by two periods of low lake level, with an intervening epoch of warmth and high water correlating with a major nonglacial episode between two glaciations in the surrounding mountains. This hypothesis received its fullest statement in 1890 when the evidence from moraines in the Wasatch Mountains and Sierra Nevada were combined by Gilbert with extensive use of argument by analogy to establish that "the relations of these moraines to the shores of the lakes and the associated deposits indicate that the maximum stage of the lakes coincided closely with the epoch of maximum glaciation. These phenomena sustain the theory that Pleistocene lakes of the western United States were coincident with the Pleistocene glaciers of the same district, and were produced by the same climatic changes. It follows as a corollary that the glacial history of this region was bipartite, two maxima of glaciation being separated, not by a mere variation in intensity, but by a cessation of glaciation" (p. 318). This wordy argument, coming as the conclusion of 53 pages of close discussion, indicates the degree to which Gilbert feared opposition to his ideas from the glacial "Establishment" of the East. In fact, the expected counterattack lacked real conviction, and the concept of multiple glaciation for the mountains of western U.S.A. has never since been seriously challenged.

Having once subdivided the Western Pleistocene, Gilbert paved the way toward a century of debate on the number of sub-divisions and their most appropriate classification. Given this system of multiple glaciation, together with the increasing momentum of settlement and economic exploitation in the West, Quaternary geologists moved into other parts of the region and brought the developing story of glacial chronology closer to the Front Range. In the early years of the Twentieth Century a number of published studies confirmed the two-glacial division; for example, Ball (1908), Atwood (1909), Capps (1909). However, the next really substantial advance came in the elaboration of this bipartite system to a three-fold division, which was applied to the San Juan Mountains by Atwood and Mather (1912). This careful and convincing study was followed shortly by Blackwelder's (1915) massive report on the Wind River Mountains, which both established that area of Wyoming as the classic center of dis-cussion for the glaciation of the Rocky Mountains and introduced the now-traditional stratigraphical trilogy of Pinedale, Bull Lake, and Buffalo. Although much refined in the subsequent 60 years, this tripartite system and its internal descriptions of characteristic tills both have very distinct reflections in the literature of today. Just why the Blackwelder terminology should have dominated the subject for so long is a matter of conjecture, especially in view of the great similarity of Atwood and Mather's concept. One might suggest that the explanation lies in the much more central geographical location of the Wind River Mountains with respect to the Rocky Mountain chain in the U.S.A., plus the fact that this area (and Blackwelder's study) caught the interest of G.M. Richmond, who was to be the dominant figure during the next two steps in the development of the chronology.

ELABORATION AND EXTENSION OF THE SEQUENCE

This phase as a whole occupies no less than half a century, a duration resulting in part from the fact that following Black-welder's study, geological interest in the Western Cordillera turned away from glacial history and the next significant local step was not taken until the publication of Bryan and Ray's 1940 work in the Cache la Poudre Canyon of the Colorado Front

Range. This study, plus Ray's extension (Ray, 1940), was important in the historical perspective mainly because it apparently deviated from the Blackwelder scheme. Bryan and Ray recognized evidence of pre-Wisconsin glaciation (their Prairie Divide stage, equivalent to Blackwelder's Buffalo glaciation) but divided Wisconsin time (as then conceived) into five substages of more or less equal status. Of these, perhaps the most significant was the fifth "Sprague" substage, which they suggested might well be post-Pleistocene -- one of the earliest recognitions of what was to become the Neoglacial of the Rocky Mountains. This suggestion may have been prompted by Matthes' (1939) introduction of the term "Little Ice Age" to the North American sequence as a whole, though the first identification of post-Pleistocene moraines in the West had been much earlier (Matthes, 1916). Hack's (1943) paper is worthy of mention mainly on the grounds that it apparently confirmed Bryan and Ray's views (except with respect to the Sprague substage) and was often quoted in the following years. As studies and substage-names proliferate, it becomes progressively more difficult to specify precise correlations between them. At this particular point in the development of a Rocky Mountain glacial chronology this task of precise correlation is conspicuously apparent. As will be seen in later sections of this review, the problem grows proportionally with the increase in number of workers and their publications. But at least we are about to embark on a long period of preponderance by a single scientist (G.M. Richmond). This should be of particular interest to the geological historian since it will probably mark the last such occasion in this specific area of study.

Paradoxically, the brief abstract published by Richmond in 1948 has had greater impact on subsequent thinking and research direction than the combined product of the previous quarter century, for it was this paper that returned the mainstream concept to an essentially tripartite scheme (plus a postglacial phase) and re-instituted Blackwelder's terminology and the pre-eminence of the Wind River Mountains. Using both morainal evidence and associated terraces, Richmond subdivided Blackwelder's three divisions, but gave great weight to the basic concept and terminology. He continued to extend these ideas to other parts of the Rockies for the next 25 years, culminating in the classic formulation of the glacial-stratigraphic sequence or model in 1965, which is further discussed below. Slowly but progressively, therefore, the Richmond view came to dominate the approach to Rocky Mountain glacial history.

In the 15 years following 1948, little happened to disrupt this underlying view, though certain internal modifications were made. An apparently transitory phase of digression is marked by Moss' 1949 and 1951 studies, which advanced the overall argument mainly in their recognition of the significance of the Temple Lake deposits. These had been erroneously classified as

"Wisconsin IV" (nearest current equivalent, Late Pinedale II) by Hack (1940), but Moss assigned them to an intermediate Pinedale/Neoglacial position which accords quite closely with the views expressed in several studies in the 1970s. As well as stipulating this pre-climatic optimum rank for the Temple Lake, Moss also introduced the term "Neoglacial" for the recent post-Pleistocene glacial activity. Whilst this term has survived relatively unscathed, the Temple Lake classification continued to evolve, and by 1955 Holmes and Moss allocated these deposits to the first stade of a two-stade Holocene. Although this change apparently adopted a Neoglacial age for the Temple Lake moraines, it may be significant that Holmes and Moss' second post-Pleistocene stade was termed "Little Ice Age," which some other authors have taken to be virtually the equivalent of the Neoglacial (and indeed, it had been so defined by Moss in 1949 and 1951). If this terminology is significant, then it follows that Holmes and Moss may be retaining a pre-Neoglacial age for the Temple Lake Stade, and that their Temple Lake/Little Ice Age interstade may actually equate with the climatic optimum.

The study by Madole (1963) introduced no major changes, but is significant in several ways. It apparently supported Holmes and Moss' two-fold subdivision of the Buffalo Glaciation, but more importantly, it followed Richmond in adopting a two-fold subdivision of the post-Pinedale in the format which was to become popular for a number of years, namely suggesting a simple two-fold Neoglacial separated from the Pinedale by a simple interglacial. This particular study is also of importance in that it represents a new medium for study-generation in the Front Range -- the Ph.D. thesis, destined to become a major source of detailed chronology. It also signified the influence S.E. White had on research in this area in the years following 1960, both personally and through the supervision of a series of graduate students. The institution of Ph.D. studies gave impetus to continued investigation, and by its nature and aims ensured that such study tended to be intensive, localized, and innovative -- both in terms of technique and interpretation. It is, therefore, possible to argue that there developed a conflict between the desire of young research workers not to offend established authority by seriously challenging accepted models, and the equally strong pressure to follow the new evidence and give vent to personal creativity by proposing new solutions to the problems at hand.

Madole's 1963 paper, therefore, is also of interest in that it firmly opts for the use of local type deposits and stade names, whilst equally clearly conforming to the macro-regional general model already stated by Richmond in a series of papers in the early 1960s. This conflict between local and regional terminology and concept strongly characterizes the development of the Front Range glacial sequence from this point onward (see, for example, Benedict, 1973, p. 585). Each has its advantages, and despite several attempts to assert the ascendancy of the

local material, there is no real sign of any breach in the
stability of the "Bull Lake" and "Pinedale" terminology, whether
or not the internal subdivisions are named locally. This represents the best and worst of the general sequence; the widespread
use of a general format certainly aids communication and easy
correlation, but at the same time it encourages researchers to
adopt frameworks that may be suboptimal for their region and to
use terminology for which there may be no agreed local type
deposit. Indeed, it gives implicit support to the notion of
macro-regional correlation, although the feasibility and reality
of such correlation are both unproven.

THE CLASSIC FORMULATION OF THE FIVE-GLACIAL PLEISTOCENE CHRONOLOGY

In the period 1957-1964, G.M. Richmond published a series
of ten important papers on aspects of the glaciation of the
Western Cordillera (including the 1960 paper reprinted in this
chapter), and then combined these with earlier work of his own
and of other researchers to produce his classic synthesis of the
Rocky Mountain glacial sequence of 1965. The Blackwelder (1915)
and Richmond (1948) parentage is clear, but there are modifications. Resting heavily on the Washakie Point till and interglacial soil sequence, a three-fold glaciation was proposed to
replace the Buffalo Glaciation, these early episodes being correlated with the Mid-continent Nebraskan, Kansan, and Illinoian.
The Bull Lake and Pinedale, each subdivided into two or three
stades, remained essentially as Wisconsin equivalents, and af-
firmation was given to a two-stade Neoglaciation. The Temple
Lake/Gannett Peak division placed the oft-studied Temple Lake
deposits firmly within the post-Altithermal (a term introduced
by Antevs, 1948). So entrenched has this aspect of the classification become, that more recent work has had great difficulty
in proposing ways of producing a modification in order to overcome what some felt to be a mis-classification (see section below). In Richmond's concept, Temple Lake is a part of the
Little Ice Age (Neoglacial), not its predecessor as suggested
by Holmes and Moss (1955). With the early availability of
radiocarbon dating, Richmond began the process of moving from
a relative sequence to an absolute chronology.
This study was a remarkably comprehensive and elegant
creation, apparently bringing the Western Cordillera at last
into line with the mid-continent and Europe in its broad five-
fold Pleistocene structure. The influence on later workers has
been remarkable, and once again we have a period during which
every effort is made to ensure that the data conforms to the
presumed sequence rather than vice versa. Whether this is to
the advantage of general progress in the field depends largely
on one's view of the validity of Richmond's 1965 glacial-
stratigraphic sequence, and whilst noting its powerful positive

influence on research it must also be said that the following
decade showed an increasing inability to accept the structure
in all its detail, but a widespread reluctance to break away
from it substantially. To an extent this must be regarded as
support for the validity of the model: even where subsequent
micro-studies have failed to verify it, they have at least
avoided falsifying it. However, a note of qualification may be
pertinent. Whilst elegance and general relationship within an
explanation are both highly regarded by scientists, these properties should not be assumed automatically to equate with Truth.
Furthermore, if regional synchroneity is found to be invalid,
it will be seen that different studies can quite appropriately
conclude with differing interpretations.

RECONSIDERATION AND DEVELOPMENT BASED ON NEW TECHNIQUES

The years since 1965 have seen an increasing tempo of
publication on Rocky Mountain glaciation in general and the
Colorado Front Range in particular. Alongside this increase
in the level of activity there has been a profound change in
the techniques available to the researcher. Improved mapping,
air photography, and remote sensing have eased the problem of
feature mapping. Relative age-dating has drawn upon a wider
range of parameters, and these have in turn been subject to
the application of much more rigorous and pseudo-objective
standard scales. Finally, absolute age-dating by radiocarbon,
obsidian hydration, amino acid, and, to an extent, lichenometric
techniques, has been developed to the point where it has become
a major basis for model building and for the controversy surrounding those models. At risk of over-simplification, four
components of particular importance can be identified in the
evolution of the Front Range glacial chronology during this
period:
    1. Whereas before 1965 most authors were concerned with
the full range of Pleistocene (or Pleistocene plus Holocene)
time, thereafter it is normal for papers to consider only a
part of the full sequence. The most common divisions for study
are the Neoglaciation on its own, Pinedale plus Bull Lake, or
Pinedale plus Bull Lake plus Pre-Bull Lake. This partial viewpoint is perhaps a reflection of the increased data yield of
modern publications and the technique-intensive nature of modern
academic research projects -- both of which militate against any
one study covering the whole of the Quaternary. A consequence
of this trend is that the high level of detail has in several
cases encouraged the additional subdivision which is considered
as trend (2) below. At the same time, progressive incorporation
of results from other areas (e.g., Iceland, the Arctic, and the
Antarctic) has thrown new light on assumptions about glacier
mechanics, relationship with climate, and the resulting chronological sequence. Attention has also returned to the possibility
of older (i.e., Tertiary) glaciations, perhaps reflected in the

tentative identification of high level diamictons as tills dating
from before the canyon-cutting phase. This critical question
of early glaciation in the Front Range, however, warrants great
caution. Madole's latest statement on the Front Range diamictons
is worth quoting:

> The overall pattern of glaciation documented thus far in
> the Front Range and in neighboring ranges suggests that
> the extent of early and late Pleistocene glaciation was
> not notably different. Therefore, a nonglacial origin
> should be considered for till-like diamictons that exist
> in localities where the presence of till would require
> early Pleistocene glaciers to have been much larger than
> those of Bull Lake and Pinedale time. (Madole, 1976,
> p. 303.)

2. Further subdivision of the major glacial periods has
continued, but this has mainly been applied to the Neoglacial,
where detailed evidence is at its freshest (though whether this
substantially decreases its ambiguity is questionable). Benedict (1968) initiated a popular move to recognize three Neoglacial stades, which he named Temple Lake, Arikaree, and
Gannett Peak (thus further entrenching Richmond's Neoglacial
attribution of the Temple Lake deposits). This broad framework
has been confirmed by several subsequent authors, including
Madole (1969, 1972), though often with some terminological
variation. For example, Mahaney (1972) renamed the Arikaree
stade the "Audubon" to avoid stratigraphic ambiguity; and Kiver
(1969) and Bonnett (1970) adopted the three-fold framework, but
used local stade names. Several further Neoglacial changes had
more profound effect. Kiver (1972) indirectly influenced Neoglacial interpretation by recognizing a probable Pinedale IV
stade, the result being the re-introduction of a stade between
the end of classic Pinedale and the onset of classic Altithermal
time. A similar line was taken by Graf (1971). Although he
postulated only two Neoglacial stades (a return to the Richmond
model), he did confirm the need to identify a Pinedale IV
following the end of the classic Late Pinedale.
    The full ambiguity of the situation is revealed in a series
of studies by Benedict (1973), Birkeland (1973, reproduced in
this chapter), Birkeland and Miller (1973), Miller and Birkeland
(1974), Currey (1974), and Carroll (1974, reproduced in this
chapter). Although complete agreement is lacking, these authors
all confirm the need for a pre-Altithermal stade intermediate
between Pinedale and Neoglacial time, though whether this stade
should be assigned formally to the Pleistocene or to the Holocene
appears to be a matter for conjecture. Birkeland and Miller,
and Currey, claim forcefully that this intermediate stade is
represented by the type Temple Lake moraine -- thus arguing in
favor of returning the Temple Lake to the pre-Altithermal position that it occupied in Moss' 1949 and 1951 chronologies. With

the Richmond-derived Neoglacial attribution of the Temple Lake firmly established in the literature, such a reevaluation clearly raises a situation of considerable potential ambiguity. Currey goes as far as to suggest that the original type Temple Lake deposit should be renamed "Miller Lake" and assigned a pre-Altithermal Pinedale IV position, whilst a new type deposit be found for the stade at the beginning of the Neoglacial, which could then retain the name "Temple Lake."

This complicated issue remains unresolved. Benedict (1973) currently holds the most advanced position. In a cautious and mature paper, he postulated a three-fold Neoglacial division (i.e., post-Altithermal) which he now terms Triple Lakes, Audubon, and Arapaho (thereby avoiding the overtones of the disputed Temple Lake/Gannett Peak terminology). In addition he postulated a major pre-Altithermal advance termed the Satanta Peak and possibly even a fifth post-classic Pinedale advance beginning about 8000 years BP, late in the interval between Satanta Peak and Altithermal maximum.* It is possible that there is a correlation (stratigraphical, if not terminological) between the Satanta Peak stade and the Pinedale V stade (Jim Creek Advance) proposed by Millington (1976) for the Upper Fraser Valley, Colorado (abstract of thesis reproduced here). Much of such ambiguity of classification and correlation stems from limitations of the relative age-dating techniques which have been extensively applied to Neoglacial deposits, and sometimes to the Pinedale also. The confusions that can result are admirably illustrated by Williams' (1973) substantial refutation of Mahaney's (1973a) lichenometrical, pedological, and geological study of the Neoglacial chronology of the Fourth of July Cirque, Colorado; and by Mahaney's (1973b) equally spirited defense of his interpretation. A further example of Mahaney's (1975) meticulous pedalogical approach is reproduced in this chapter. The problems and degree of success of various relative age-dating techniques also form the subject of Carroll's (1974) study (reprinted in this chapter), and White's (1974) invited comment on this paper. Clearly, the debate concerning the nature of Late Pinedale and Early Neoglacial time is one of the most important components of the contribution of the last decade, and is likely to remain a major priority.

3. Many authors, including Benedict (1973), have argued for a more extensive use of absolute age-dating techniques (particularly radiocarbon dating) rather than relying exclusively on relative techniques in the high valleys and cirques. This change is, in fact, being implemented, but first indications are that, far from clarifying the burning issues of the glacial chronology, these dates are at present deepening divisions of opinion -- though it is certainly too early to be able to view

---

*Editor's note: This important paper was amongst the original selections for inclusion in this book; it is not included because permission to reproduce could not be obtained.

the trend in perspective. An example of the approach by Madole (1976) is included in this chapter. Reference may also be made to Millington (1976), which is a pivotal contribution to Bull Lake-Pinedale chronology, being the first instance of absolute dating of a nonglacial episode about 30,000 BP. In addition to the question of being able to identify meaningful within-glaciation divisions, the absolute dates have raised the major issue of the correlation of the Rocky Mountain and mid-continent sequences, as is demonstrated on the chronology chart by the Richmond (1975) and Pierce, Obradovich, and Friedman (1976) studies. Further work on this topic appears to be widespread, and balanced judgement must await the publication of these studies. In general, though, it must be said that the root of the discussion will ultimately rest in the recognition of the subjective content of apparently objective techniques. It seems that whilst relative age-dating is subject to serious criticism of the objectivity and precision of the techniques themselves, the sampling is generally broad-based and clearly related to the overall stratigraphic and morphological significance of the feature or deposit concerned. With absolute age-dating, however, the techniques appear more reliable, but they are applied to such a small number of samples that the stratigraphical and morphological relevance of the results can be challenged by an author supporting an alternative chronological interpretation. "One clear illustration of this continuing challenge results from two sediment cores retrieved by P.T. Davis and S. Waterman from a lake within the type area Triple Lakes (early Neoglacial) moraines in Arapahoe cirque (Benedict, 1973, p. 589). Due to mechanical problems, both coring attempts failed to reach the lake bottom; however, ^{14}C dates on the organic fraction of the bottom sediments from the shorter of the two cores yielded ages of 4730 $\pm$ 200 yrs BP (W-4093, kindly provided by M. Rubin, U.S. Geological Survey; 430-450 cm depth) and 5400 $\pm$ 240 yrs BP (GX-5643, kindly provided by H. Krueger, Geochron Laboratories; 450-468 cm). The Geochron ^{14}C date was partially funded by a Grant-in-Aid of Research by Sigma Xi to P.T. Davis. Bottom sediments from the longer core, about 530 cm in length, have yet to be ^{14}C-dated. Palynological and sedimentological analyses are in progress and further lake sediment coring efforts in Arapahoe cirque are planned. It is already evident, however, that Benedict's Triple Lakes moraines may date to the Late Pinedale, as suggested by Birkeland and Shroba (1975, p. 253)." (Written communication, P.T. Davis, 1978).

4. Although less pronounced, a fourth trend of potentially equal importance is the emergence of a move to question the degree of subdivision of the major glacial periods. Whilst multiple moraines are common, these may not always be assumed to provide a reliable basis for the recognition of distinct stades, but rather may represent relatively minor within-stade fluctuation. This view is founded in part on the inability of absolute dating techniques to establish clear distinctions

between some of these moraines (e.g., Pierce, Obradovich, and Friedman, 1976), and in part on the feeling (e.g., Meierding; Ph.D. thesis, 1977; see note published in this chapter) that the process of subdivision is greatly affected by the method of combining different age-dating criteria, and that if multiple parameters are used it becomes increasingly difficult to recognize unambiguous divisions. Here again the issue is unresolved, and only time will tell whether the root of the problem lies in technique deficiencies, analytical weaknesses, or the simple fact that the major glaciations were not divided into fundamental and synchronous substages. Such qualifications are particularly significant in the Colorado Front Range, where glacier dynamics are thought to rely more heavily than usual on local topographic control of exposure and susceptibility to retention of wind-drifted snow (see Chapter 4).

PERSPECTIVES AND PRIORITIES

This background survey together with the chronological review and selection of reprinted papers which follow combine to demonstrate something of the range and vigor of debate which has characterized the last 25 years of study of Front Range glacial geology. The pace of publication precludes any final synthesis at this point, but it is clear that in common with many other branches of natural science, glacial geology is currently suffering some internal discomfort as it evolves from a small profession dominated by a few authorities and an established tradition, to a large technically varied investigative discipline in which no one scientist or center can hope to achieve long-term dominance.

In a recent study of the development of the Rocky Mountain chronology, Mears (1974) has suggested that a historical perspective of the varied models that have been proposed can be regarded as a macro-version of the method of multiple working hypotheses, whereby scientists advance their subject by the sequential testing of a series of ever more likely solutions to their problem. This is an imaginative and optimistic viewpoint, but if it is to be correct then the function of a historical review such as that provided here should be simply to present hypotheses for verification or falsification. Unfortunately, there are many indications both within the literature and behind it, that some authors prefer to regard the function of publication as being the defense of hypotheses rather than their testing. If this is the case, then this review may serve a valuable function in impressing upon the next generation of students that in an era of developing techniques and concepts, few hypotheses are worth defending in the face of conflicting evidence. Conflict is healthy, but the ultimate test of success is the ability to accept change when the reasons for that change become more pressing than the justification for resisting it.

This is not to say, however, that progress can be achieved only by rejecting presently established models out of hand, for these offer an invaluable framework within which future research can be formulated -- and it should be remembered that there are many precedents for the resurrection of classic hypotheses after an intervening phase of allegiance to alternative interpretations. Change does not necessarily mean progress, yet change is vital to ensure the continual investigative vigor and self-critical maintenance of standards of any subject. Thus, there remain just two questions to be asked, and for answers we may turn to the wisdom of authorities from other disciplines. First, is there scope for the implementation of a new research effort within the field of Rocky Mountain glacial geology? Despite the great advances made in the last two decades, the answer would clearly seem to be positive, if only in the sense of Einstein's dictum "As a circle of light increases, so does the circumference of darkness around it." Second, in what spirit might a new effort most effectively be formulated? The current debate within scientific methodology concerning the relative merits of hypothesis verification and falsification seems very relevant, and the latter approach might yield interesting results in the design of new studies. We can hardly do better than leave the last word to a comment by Francis Bacon, the many connotations of which offer us both a perceptive view of the past and a valuable guide for the future. "Facts will ultimately prevail; we must therefore take care that they be not against us."

REFERENCES AND RELATED SELECTIVE BIBLIOGRAPHY

Antevs, E.V. 1948. Climatic changes and pre-white man. *In:* A Symposium on the Great Basin, with emphasis on glacial and post-glacial times. *University of Utah Bulletin*, 38: 168-191.

Atwood, W.W. 1909. *Glaciation of the Uinta and Wasatch Mountains.* U.S. Geol. Surv. Prof. Paper 61. 96 pp.

Atwood, W.W. and K.F. Mather. 1912. The evidence of three distinct glacial epochs in the Pleistocene history of the San Juan Mountains, Colorado. *Journal of Geology*, 20: 385-409.

Ball, S.M. 1908. *Geology of the Georgetown Quadrangle, Colorado.* U.S. Geol. Surv. Prof. Paper 63, pp. 29-63.

Benedict, J.B. 1968. Recent glacial history of an alpine area in the Colorado Front Range, U.S.A.: Part II, Dating the glacial deposits. *Journal of Glaciology*, 7(49): 77-87.

_____. 1973. Chronology of cirque glaciation, Colorado Front Range. *Quaternary Research*, 3(4): 584-599.

Birkeland, P.W. 1973. Use of relative age-dating methods in a stratigraphic study of rock glacier deposits, Mt. Sopris, Colorado. *Arctic and Alpine Research*, 5(4): 401-416.

Birkeland, P.W., D.R. Crandell, and G.M. Richmond. 1971. Status of Quaternary stratigraphic units in the Western Coterminous United States. *Quaternary Research*, 1: 208-227.

Birkeland, P.W. and L.D. Miller. 1973. Re-interpretation of the type Temple Lake moraine and other Neoglacial deposits. Southern Wind River Mountains, Wyoming. *Geological Society of America, Abstracts with Programs*, Rocky Mountain Section, 5(6): 465-466.

Birkeland, P.W. and R.R. Shroba. 1974. The status of the concept of Quaternary soil-forming intervals in the western United States. *In* Mahaney, W.C. (ed.), *Quaternary Environments: Proceedings of a Symposium*. Geographical Monographs, 5, York University, Toronto, Canada.

Blackwelder, E. 1915. The post-Cretaceous history of the mountains of Central Western Wyoming. *Journal of Geology*, 23(4): 307-340.

Bonnett, R.B. 1970. Glacial sequence of the upper Boulder Creek drainage basin in the Colorado Front Range. Ph.D. thesis, Ohio State University.

Breckenridge, R.M. 1969. Neoglacial geology of upper Fall Creek basin, Colorado. M.A. thesis, University of Wyoming, Laramie.

Bryan, K. and L.L. Ray. 1940. Geologic antiquity of the Lindenmeier site in Colorado. *Smithsonian Misc. Coll.*, 99(2). 76 pp.

Capps, S.R. 1909. *Pleistocene Geology of the Leadville Quadrangle, Colorado*. U.S. Geol. Surv. Bulletin 386. 99 pp.

Carroll, T. 1974. Relative age dating techniques and a Late Quaternary chronology, Arikaree Cirque, Colorado. *Geology*, July, 1974, pp. 321-325.

Currey, D.R. 1974. Probable pre-Neoglacial age of the type Temple Lake moraine, Wyoming. *Arctic and Alpine Research*, 6(3): 293-300.

Fryxell, F.M. 1930. Glacial features of Jackson Hole, Wyoming. *Augustana Library Publication*, 13. 128 pp.

Gilbert, G.K. 1875. Explorations and surveys west of the 100th meridian. *Geology*, III: 97.

_____. 1880. *First Annual Report of the U.S. Geological Survey*, pp. 26.

_____. 1890. *Lake Bonneville*. Monographs of the U.S. Geological Survey, Vol. 1. 438 pp.

Graf, W.L. 1971. Quantitative analysis of Pinedale landforms, Beartooth Mountains, Montana and Wyoming. *Arctic and Alpine Research*, 3(3): 253-261.

Hack, J.T. 1943. Antiquity of the Finley site. *American Antiquity*, 8(3): 235-241.

Holmes, G.W. and J.H. Moss. 1955. Pleistocene geology of the southwestern Wind River Mountains, Wyoming. *Bulletin of the Geological Survey of America*, 66(6): 629-654.

Kiver, E.P. 1968. Geomorphology and glacial geology of the southern Medicine Bow Mountains, Colorado and Wyoming. Ph.D. thesis, University of Wyoming, Laramie.

_____. 1969. Neoglaciation of the Rawah Peaks, Colorado. *Geological Society of America, Abstracts with Programs,* Rocky Mountain Section, Part 5: 41.

_____. 1972. Two late Pinedale advances in the southern Medicine Bow Mountains, Colorado. *Contributions to Geology of the University of Wyoming,* 11(1): 1-8.

Madole, R.F. 1963. Quaternary geology of St. Vrain drainage basin, Boulder County, Colorado. Ph.D. thesis, Ohio State University. 288 pp.

_____. 1969. Pinedale and Bull Lake glaciation in upper St. Vrain drainage basin, Boulder County, Colorado. *Arctic and Alpine Research,* 1(4): 279-287.

_____. 1972. Neoglacial facies in the Colorado Front Range. *Arctic and Alpine Research,* 4(2): 119-130.

_____. 1976a. Bog stratigraphy, radio-carbon dates, and Pinedale to Holocene glacial history in the Front Range, Colorado. *Journal Research U.S. Geol. Survey,* 4(2): 163-169.

_____. 1976b. Glacial geology of the Front Range, Colorado. *In* Mahaney, W.C. (ed.), *Quaternary Stratigraphy of North America.* Dowden, Hutchinson and Ross, Inc., Stroudsburg, Pennsylvania, pp. 279-318.

Mahaney, W.C. 1972. Audubon, new name for Colorado Front Range Neoglacial deposits, formerly called 'Arikaree.' *Arctic and Alpine Research,* 4(4): 355-357.

_____. 1973a. Neoglacial chronology in the Fourth of July Cirque, central Colorado Front Range. *Bulletin of the Geological Society of America,* 84: 161-170.

_____. 1973b. Neoglacial chronology of the Fourth of July Cirque, central Colorado Front Range: reply. *Bulletin of the Geological Society of America,* 84: 3767-3772.

_____. 1975. Soils of post-Audubon age, Teton Glacier area, Wyoming. *Arctic and Alpine Research,* 7(2): 141-153.

Matthes, F.E. 1916. The post-Pleistocene moraines of the Sierra Nevada. *Annals of the Association of American Geographers,* 6: 128-129.

_____. 1939. Report of the Committee on Glaciers, April 1939. *Transactions of the American Geophysical Union,* 20: 518-523.

Mears, B. 1974. The evolution of the Rocky Mountain glacial model. *In* Coates, D.R. (ed.), *Glacial Geomorphology,* pp.11-40.

Meierding, T.C. 1977. Age differentiation of till and gravel deposits in the upper Colorado River basin. Ph.D. thesis, University of Colorado, Boulder.

Miller, C.D. and P.W. Birkeland. 1974. Probable pre-Neoglacial age of the type Temple Lake moraine, Wyoming: discussion and additional relative-age data. *Arctic and Alpine Research,* 6: 301-306.

Millington, H.C. 1976. Late Quaternary paleo-environmental
    history of the Mary Jane Creek valley, Grand County,
    Colorado. M.A. dissertation, University of Colorado,
    Boulder.
Moss, J.H. 1949. Possible new glacial stage in the middle
    Rocky Mountains. *Bulletin of the Geological Society of
    America*, 60: 1972.
_____. 1951. Late glacial advances in the southern Wind
    River Mountains, Wyoming. *American Journal of Science*,
    249(12): 865-883.
Pierce, K.L., J.D. Obradovich, and I. Friedman. 1976. Obsidian
    hydration dating and correlation of Bull Lake and Pinedale
    glaciations near west Yellowstone, Montana. *Bulletin of
    the Geological Society of America*, 87(5): 703-710.
Ray, L.L. 1940. Glacial chronology of the southern Rocky
    Mountains. *Bulletin of the Geological Society of America*,
    51: 1851-1918.
Richmond, G.M. 1948. Modification of Blackwelder's sequence
    of Pleistocene glaciation in the Wind River Mountains,
    Wyoming. *Bulletin of the Geological Society of America*,
    59(12): 1400-1401.
_____. 1960. Glaciation of the East Slope of Rocky Mountain
    National Park, Colorado. *Bulletin of the Geological
    Society of America*, 71: 1371-1381.
_____. 1965. Glaciation of the Rocky Mountains. *In*
    Wright, H.E. and D.G. Frey (eds.), *The Quaternary of the
    United States*, pp. 217-230.
_____. 1975. A partial Quaternary chronology from Yellow-
    stone National Park. International Geological Correlation
    Program, Project 73/1/24. *In* Sibrava, V. (ed.), *Quaternary
    Glaciations in the Northern Hemisphere*. Report No. 2.
Street, F.A. 1973. A study of tors in the Front Range of the
    Rocky Mountains in Colorado, with special reference to
    their value as an indicator of nonglaciation. M.A. dis-
    sertation, University of Colorado, Boulder.
White, S.E. 1974. Comment: relative age dating techniques...
    Geology, 2(7): 326.
Whitney, J.D. 1865. *Geology of California*, Vol. 1, pp. 452.
Williams, J. 1973. Neoglacial chronology of the Fourth of
    July Cirque, central Colorado Front Range: discussion.
    Bulletin of the Geological Society of America, 84: 3761-
    3766.

GLACIATION OF THE EAST SLOPE OF ROCKY MOUNTAIN NATIONAL PARK, COLORADO

By Gerald M. Richmond

Abstract

The eastern slope of Rocky Mountain National Park, Colorado, has been subjected to at least three separate Pleistocene glaciations, which from oldest to youngest are correlated with the Buffalo, Bull Lake, and Pinedale glaciations of Blackwelder in the Wind River Mountains of Wyoming.

In this area, deposits of the oldest glaciation are known from only one locality. Deposits of the Bull Lake glaciation comprise two sets of moraines indicative of two advances of ice separated by a significant recession; those of the Pinedale glaciation comprise three sets of moraines indicative of a maximum advance of the ice and two recessional halts or minor readvances.

Moraines of two minor advances of the ice, correlated with the Temple Lake and historic stades of Neoglaciation in the Wind River Mountains, occur in the cirque heads.

CONTENTS

Introduction

Among the reasons for establishing Rocky Mountain National Park in 1915 was the preservation of the scenic grandeur of its glacial setting—rugged snow-banked cirques, sparkling rock-bound tarns, steep-walled U-shaped canyons, and broad moraine-enclosed basins.

Lee (1917) was the first to describe and interpret the glacial history of this setting; he recognized two episodes—an older "pre-Wisconsin" glaciation[1] inferred primarily from the shape of some of the lower basins such as Estes Park or Tahosa Valley, and a younger "Wisconsin" glaciation, represented by large terminal moraines along the National

---

[1] The terms glaciation and stade are applied in lieu of the terms stage and substage throughout this report in the sense recommended by the American Stratigraphic Commission (1959), but informally and without capitalization.

Park boundary and by lesser recessional moraines upstream. Although Lee's interpretation of a glacial origin for the lower basins has received some support (Fuller, 1923), most subsequent workers have considered the lower basins to be erosional features of nonglacial origin (L. O. Quam, 1938, Ph.D. thesis, Clark Univ.; Ray, 1940; Jones and Quam, 1944).

The "Wisconsin" moraines have been interpreted in a variety of ways. Ray (1940) first recognized that they represented multiple glaciation and distinguished five "substages" of Wisconsin glaciation. Jones and Quam (1944) considered them to represent three "stages" of glaciation, believing that the three youngest substages of Ray were deposits of a single advance of the ice. Richmond (1953) suggested some further modifications which are here revised and elaborated upon. The present paper is based on studies made on weekends and other brief visits over a period of years beginning in 1952.

Bulletin of the Geological Society of America, Vol. 71, 1960, pp. 1371-1382.

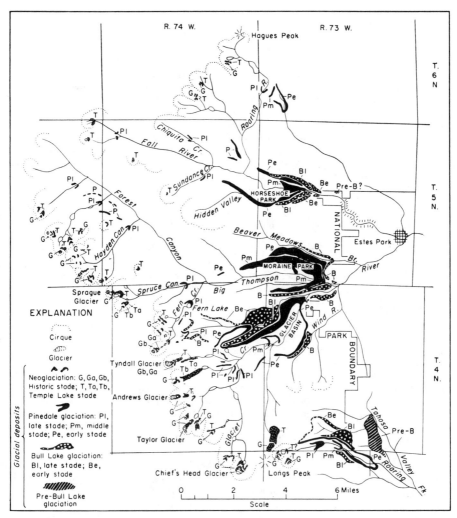

FIGURE 1.—GLACIAL GEOLOGY OF THE EAST SLOPE OF ROCKY MOUNTAIN NATIONAL PARK, COLORADO

NOMENCLATURE

The writer correlates the glaciations of this area with those of the Wind River Mountains of Wyoming where Blackwelder (1915) recognized and defined three glacial stages, from oldest to youngest, the Buffalo, Bull Lake, and Pinedale. The terms Bull Lake and Pinedale are used here to avoid introducing new names, but because deposits included in the Buffalo stage in the Wind River Mountains represent more than one glaciation (Richmond, 1957), correlative deposits in this area will be simply referred to as pre-Bull Lake.

Deposits of two Recent minor advances of

the ice, both restricted to the cirques, are referred to the Neoglaciation (term proposed by Moss, 1951a). The term Temple Lake (Hack, 1943; Moss, 1951a; 1951b) has been applied to deposits of the earlier stage in the Wind River Mountains; the term historic is here applied informally to those of the later stage.

CHARACTERISTICS OF THE GLACIAL DEPOSITS AND CRITERIA FOR CORRELATION

Distinction between deposits of the different glaciations in Rocky Mountain National Park is readily made on the basis of their physiographic, stratigraphic, and weathering characteristics, and their correlation with the glaciations of the Wind River Mountains is based on comparison of these characteristics. The deposits in both areas are derived primarily from Precambrian crystalline rocks.

PRE-BULL LAKE GLACIATION: Deposits of a pre-Bull Lake glaciation have been recognized with certainty in only one part of the area. W. S. Cooper (Personal communication, 1952; in Richmond, 1953) found numerous erratics and scattered areas of deeply weathered till in Tahosa Valley, east of Longs Peak (Fig. 1). The deposits lie beyond the outer limits of moraines of the Bull Lake glaciation and rest on a pre-canyon broad valley erosion surface underlain by deeply disintegrated and decomposed gneiss and schist.

The deposits of till are sheetlike and lack morainal topography. Their maximum observed thickness is about 6 feet. Boulders on the surface tend to be broken or deeply exfoliated, and no striations were found on them. At depth the deposits consist of a mixture of boulders, cobbles, sand, and silt. Exotic rock types are common. Many of the rock fragments and much of the matrix are derived from the underlying rotted rock. However, fresh cobbles and boulders from other sources are present. Most are angular to subangular, but a few are rounded. Some appear glacially soled and faceted, and striations were observed on a few of the dense fine-grained types.

The weathering of these deposits is unlike that on other tills in the area. The weathered zone, whose undulations suggest that it formed on a pre-existing topography, is clearly crosscut by the present land surface and surface soil. The maximum observed thickness of the weathered zone is about 4 feet, but its truncated character suggests that it may have been much thicker. The material is yellowish red (5YR 5/6) when dry, strong brown (7.5YR 5/6) when wet. When dry it is hard, compact, and has a coarse angular blocky structure. Although primarily sandy to silty, it contains sufficient clay to be plastic when wet. The pH is 4.5, which is considerably lower than the average 6.5 value for the surface soil.

These deposits are correlated with those of the Buffalo glaciations of Wyoming on the basis of their lack of morainal topography, the reddish color and clayey character of the weathered zone, abundance of deeply weathered boulders, and their location beyond the outer limits of moraines of the Bull Lake glaciation.

The degree of destruction of morainal topography and the very marked weathering of the till, together with the fact that the weathered zone is locally overlain by till of the Bull Lake glaciation, indicate that pre-Bull Lake glaciation was separated from Bull Lake glaciation by an interglacial interval.

BULL LAKE GLACIATION: Bull Lake glaciation is represented by remnants of low moraines representing two advances of the ice, along the valley walls and floors. Terminal moraines are broadly breached by axial streams; lateral moraines are segmented by tributaries. The morainal slopes are smooth and bear a scattering of boulders. Many of these are cracked, spheroidally spalled, or split apart, and most are sufficiently weathered so that striated surfaces are no longer identifiable.

The till at depth is gray brown, compact, sandy to silty and bouldery. The rock fragments although stained brown are for the most part fresh within. Some, however, are deeply disintegrated, especially those composed of mafic minerals. Both fresh and disintegrated rocks occur throughout the full thickness of the deposits. Striations are locally preserved on dense rock types, and soled and faceted stones are abundant.

A gray-brown podzolic soil about 5 feet thick is formed on the deposits. Its A horizon is 2 to 6 inches thick and consists of dark-grayish-brown, loose to friable sandy loam. An underlying A_2 horizon is 6 to 10 inches thick and consists of pale-brown (10YR 6/3), slightly hard, sandy material that has a fine angular blocky structure and a pH of 6.0. The B horizon is 36 to 48 inches thick and is composed of hard compact silty sand that has a coarse angular blocky structure when dry and contains sufficient clay to be slightly plastic when wet. The color is strong brown (7.5YR 5/6) to reddish brown (5YR 5/4), and the pH is 6.0. This material grades downward into fresh pale-brown (10YR 6/3) till that is compact but friable and has a pH of 7.0.

The terminal moraines of Bull Lake glaciation in Rocky Mountain National Park are unusually small as compared to those at the type locality in the Wind River Mountains. Other characteristics of the deposits, however, support their correlation. In both areas the deposits are the oldest and most extensive of those having well-preserved morainal topography. They have mature slopes that are relatively much less bouldery than those of the Pinedale glaciation and are breached by axial and tributary streams. The tills are compact, stained brownish, and contain the same general proportion of deeply weathered stones. The soils on the tills have similarly mature zonal profiles and are much less weathered than those on pre-Bull Lake tills but much more strongly developed than those on tills of the Pinedale glaciation.

The contrast in degree of development of the soils on deposits of the Bull Lake and Pinedale glaciations and the fact that till of the Pinedale glaciation locally overlies the soil developed on till of the Bull Lake glaciation suggest that these glaciations were separated by an interval of interglacial proportions. The fact that certain valleys, such as those northeast of Longs Peak, Hidden Valley, and the head of Forest Canyon were occupied by Bull Lake ice, but not by Pinedale ice, strengthens this hypothesis. The till in these valleys bears the post-Bull Lake soil, and the mouth of Hidden Valley is crossed by the outermost lateral moraine of Pinedale glaciation. The cirques at the heads of these valleys lack steep headwalls characteristic of Pinedale glaciation, and the slopes are thickly mantled with talus and solifluction debris which, although locally active in Pinedale time, bears a mature zonal soil like that on till of the Bull Lake glaciation in many places. The writer interprets these features as indicating that the ice probably withdrew entirely from the mountains between the Bull Lake and Pinedale glaciations.

PINEDALE GLACIATION: Pinedale glaciation in Rocky Mountain National Park includes moraines representing three pulsations of the ice. Moraines of the early stage are comparatively large and in places overlap those of Bull Lake glaciation. Their surface is irregular, hummocky, and littered with fresh boulders. Slopes are but little dissected, and kettles contain water at least seasonally. Terminal moraines are only partly breached by axial streams, and lateral moraines are but little dissected. The till is more sandy and much more bouldery than that of the Bull Lake glaciation. Many of the boulders are soled, faceted, or striated.

The deposits bear an immature brown podzolic soil about 12 to 18 inches thick. Its A horizon is 2 to 6 inches thick and consists of dark-grayish-brown to grayish-brown loose sandy loam. The B horizon is 8 to 14 inches thick and pale brown (10YR 6/3) to light yellowish brown (10YR 6/4). The material is friable, sandy, and lacks any distinct evidence of clay accumulation. Its pH is 6.5 to 7.0. The fresh till is light gray to light brownish gray (10YR 6/2-7/2), friable, and sandy; its pH is 7.0.

Moraines of the middle and late stades of Pinedale glaciation are relatively small, but their surface features, internal character, and soil are like those of moraines of the early stade. The deposits are distinguished as stades because their form and local relationships to outwash deposits indicate that they mark standstills or minor readvances of the ice. No soils or deposits suggestive of a major recession of the glaciers separate them.

Correlation of these deposits with those of the type locality of Pinedale glaciation in the Wind River Mountains is based on the comparable youthful aspect of the moraines, abundance of boulders at the surface, degree of dissection by axial and tributary streams, loose and sandy texture of the till, freshness and abundance of striations of the boulders, and comparable immature character of the soil. The deposits also represent the youngest major glaciation in both areas.

The interval between Pinedale glaciation and Neoglaciation is the so-called postglacial optimum or altithermal age. During this interval the glaciers are believed to have disappeared entirely from Rocky Mountain National Park. This is suggested by (1) the fact that many cirques occupied in Pinedale time were not reoccupied in Neoglacial time and only the more sheltered parts of others were reoccupied; (2) the contrast in character of the immature soil developed on till of Pinedale age in the cirques and the thin azonal soil developed on adjacent small moraines of Neoglacial age; (3) the presence, along cirque headwalls, of inactive talus, bearing the post-Pinedale soil, adjacent to and locally overlapped by fresh active talus; (4) the presence, on summit uplands cut by cirques, of extensive inactive block rubble, patterned ground and solifluction deposits, bearing a soil like that on till of the Pinedale glaciation, which are sharply truncated by smaller and younger areas of the same kind of periglacial deposits. Some of these are inactive and bear a thin azonal soil; others are active. Together these features lead the writer to the conclusion that the glaciers disappeared and that freezing and thawing, which had been active on slopes near the ice during Pinedale glaciation, essentially ceased.

NEOGLACIATION: Neoglaciation included two small advances of the ice in the cirques. End moraines and rock glaciers of the older or Temple Lake stade are at most a mile from the cirque headwall and commonly about half a mile. The deposits are small and very bouldery. Most of the boulders are blocky and angular, but a few display evidence of glacial abrasion.

The moraines tend to be covered by a scrub spruce or tundra vegetation, and boulders at the surface commonly bear lichens. The soil on the deposits is azonal. Its A horizon is 6 to 10 inches thick and consists of brown (10YR 4/3) humus and sandy mineral debris, which directly overlies the yellowish-brown (10YR 5/4) stony sandy till.

The moraines and rock glaciers of the younger or historic stade lie at the cirque heads above those of the Temple Lake stade. They appear very fresh, are blocky, and have no soil. The boulders are unweathered and in most places do not bear lichens, although a few annual plants grow on the deposits. Thirteen small glaciers, some of which are merely stagnant ice bodies, were observed back of these deposits in the area studied (Fig. 1).

Correlation of the deposits of the Temple Lake stade with those at the type locality in the Wind River Mountains (Moss, 1951a) is based on the position of the moraines at the mouths of the cirques, their freshness as compared to those of Pinedale age, and their relatively thin and weakly developed soil as compared to that on adjacent till of Pinedale age. Deposits of the historic stade are extremely fresh, lack vegetation, and lie in front of existing glaciers or in cirques from which glaciers have only recently disappeared in both areas.

Descriptions of Individual Canyons

Significantly different interpretations exist as to which groups of moraines in Rocky Mountain National Park represent major glaciations, which represent regionally widespread halts or readvances within glaciations, and which represent merely minor changes in ice regimen due, for example, to orographic differences from canyon to canyon. For this reason, the four major drainage systems on the east slope of the Park (Fig. 1) are discussed individually. The writer's correlation of the nomenclature assigned to specific moraines in three of the drainages by the several workers is shown in Table 1.

FALL RIVER: About 3 miles west of the town of Estes Park (Fig. 1) at an altitude of 7880 feet, the narrow V-shaped winding canyon of Fall River opens abruptly into a broad valley whose U-shaped profile suggests that it has been glaciated. Along the highway near the lower end of the valley are deposits that contain exotic rock fragments and may be pre-Bull Lake till (Fig. 1). They lack morainal form and lie downstream and upslope from moraines of Bull Lake glaciation. The soil on them, however, is like that on moraines of the Bull Lake glaciation. Although positive criteria are lacking, it seems likely that a glacier extended to the lower end of the U-shaped valley in pre-Bull Lake time.

Two distinct end moraines, differentiated as "Old Moraine remnants" by Jones and Quam (1944), characterize Bull Lake glaciation on Fall River (Fig. 1). They form low ridges which border the valley just outside the Park boundary and extend down to the valley floor at altitudes of 8040 and 8100 feet respectively. In places they extend across rock knobs which project through them. Both moraines possess the aspects of Bull Lake glaciation, and the characteristic soil profile is exceptionally well exposed in road cuts along the highway just outside the Park boundary. On the south side of the valley, the outer moraine grades into a bouldery outwash plain which, together with the moraine, is trenched about 30 feet by a lower outwash plain. This lower outwash heads against the inner moraine along an intermorainal outwash channel separating it from the outer moraine. Both the outwash plain and the inner moraine are in turn trenched by a still lower narrow outwash terrace that stems from moraines of Pinedale glaciation upstream.

These relationships indicate that the two moraines of Bull Lake glaciation represent separate stands of the ice, an early stage and a late stage. No evidence suggesting how far the ice may have receded between them was found. The dual character of Bull Lake glaciation is further indicated by the fact that the inner moraine cuts out the outer moraine headward along the south wall of the valley.

The oldest moraine of Pinedale glaciation is crossed by the highway just west of the Park boundary. It forms a narrow ridge about 200 feet high whose lowest point is at an altitude of about 8280 feet. Along both sides of the valley, this moraine successively overlaps and cuts out the lateral moraine of the late stage of Bull Lake glaciation. Just inside it is a second large moraine of Pinedale aspect which as a continuous ridge, not only cuts out the first

TABLE 1.—Correlation of Nomenclature of Moraines in Rocky Mountain National Park, Colorado

		Fall River			Big Thompson River-Spruce Canyon-Fern Creek			Glacier Creek		
		Richmond, This Paper	Jones and Quam, 1944	Ray, 1940	Richmond, This Paper	Jones and Quam, 1944	Ray, 1940	Richmond, This Paper	Jones and Quam, 1944	Ray, 1940
RECENT — Neoglaciation					Historic stade 11,850 Sprague; 11,600 Fern; 11,100 Spruce	Upper Valley moraine		Historic stade 10,750	Upper Valley moraine	
		Temple Lake stade 11,400*			Temple Lake stade 11,750 Sprague; 10,925 Fern; 10,800 Spruce	Upper Valley moraine	W V	Temple Lake stade 10,600		
LATE PLEISTOCENE — Pinedale glaciation		Late stade 10,600	Upper Valley moraine	W IV	Late stade 9100 Spruce; 9525 Fern	Upper Valley moraine	W IV	Late stade 9400, 9600	Upper Valley moraine	W IV
				W III	8050, 8100	Upper Valley moraine	W III		Upper Valley moraine	W III
		Middle stade 8250	Park Border moraine	W II	Middle stade 7850	Park Border moraine	W II	Middle stade 8760, 8800	Upper Valley moraines	
		Early stade 8280	Park Border moraine		Early stade 7850	Park Border moraine		Early stade 8200	Park Border moraines	W II

Table 1 *continued*

	Fall River			Big Thompson River-Spruce Canyon-Fern Creek			Glacier Creek		
	Richmond, This Paper	Jones and Quam, 1944	Ray, 1940	Richmond, This Paper	Jones and Quam, 1944	Ray, 1940	Richmond, This Paper	Jones and Quam, 1944	Ray, 1940
Bull Lake glaciation	Late stade 8100	Old Moraine remnants		Buried beneath later deposits?	Old Moraine remnants		Late stade 7800	Old Moraine remnants	W I
	Early stade 8040			Early stade 7850			Early stade 7800		

Empty box denotes that no moraine was differentiated by the author cited
W followed by a Roman numeral refers to Ray's substages of the Wisconsin glaciation

* Altitude in feet (from U. S. Geological Survey 7½′ topographic maps, 1957–1958) of the feature believed to be a significant moraine by one of the investigators

moraine headward along both walls of the valley but also breaches it on the valley floor to form a narrow terminal snout at an altitude of 8250 feet.

Both moraines are hummocky, little dissected, very bouldery, and bear only an immature brown podzolic soil. The till also contains many boulders, of which most are fresh and many are striated. The relationships and characteristics of these moraines suggest that they represent an early and a middle stade of Pinedale glaciation. They are the Park Border moraines of Jones and Quam (1944) and were mapped as Wisconsin II substage by Ray (1940).

Upvalley are a number of morainal deposits which together were called Upper Valley moraines by Jones and Quam (1944). Ray (1940, p. 1868) identified a "mass of jumbled morainal material" between altitudes of 8900 and 9300 feet on Fall River as his Wisconsin III substage. The writer would classify this deposit as bouldery ground moraine. A small but prominent end moraine with associated outwash plain at 10,600 feet on Fall River, called Wisconsin IV substage by Ray, is considered by the writer to mark the late stade of Pinedale glaciation. Similar moraines lie on Sundance Creek at 10,000 feet, on Chiquita Creek at 10,600 feet, and on Roaring River at 10,900 feet. All have an immature brown podzolic soil like that on moraines of the middle and lower stades downstream.

Many of the cirques at the head of Fall River and its major tributary, Roaring River, contain a moraine, protalus rampart, or talus lobe which, except where very blocky, is overgrown with tundra and scrub spruce, and bears a thin azonal soil. These deposits are referred to the Temple Lake stade of Neoglaciation. In cirques at the head of Roaring River and its tributaries, but not at the head of Fall River, are younger fresh moraines and protalus ramparts that lack vegetation and a soil profile, and are referred to the historic stade of Neoglaciation.

BIG THOMPSON RIVER: The oldest glacial deposits known along Big Thompson River are characteristic of Bull Lake glaciation and were mapped as Old Moraine remnants by Jones and Quam (1944). They form a single low boulder-strewn ridge which lies on the north slope of the valley at the Park boundary and terminates against bedrock a short distance to the east at an altitude of 7850 feet. From here, the deposits can be traced discontinuously to the lower end of Moraine Park, across the east end

of which they trend as a bouldery veneer between 8300 and 8400 feet in altitude. To the north, the deposits extend as a low northwest-trending ridge into the drainage of Beaver Meadows Brook, where a soil like that on moraines of Bull Lake glaciation along Fall River is exposed at roadcuts in them. To the south, the moraine forming the highest part of the south rim of Moraine Park is also a deposit of Bull Lake glaciation.

These several deposits outline only one advance of Bull Lake glaciation, probably the early stade, for no other glacial deposits occur downstream and the large size and close proximity of moraines of the Pinedale glaciation suggest that they may overlie a moraine of the late stade of Bull Lake glaciation.

Contrasting with the small mature moraine of Bull Lake glaciation is the broad high bouldery ridge of youthful appearance and shallow immature soil that encloses Moraine Park. This deposit, which attains a lower limit of 7850 feet, was mapped as Wisconsin II substage by Ray (1940) and as Park Border moraines by Jones and Quam (1944). It includes an outer and an inner ridge, separated in several places by an outwash channel. The writer considers these ridges to represent respectively the early and middle stades of Pinedale glaciation. Deposits on the floor of Moraine Park at about 8050 to 8100 feet, mapped as Upper Valley moraines by Jones and Quam, appear to be mainly areas of ground moraine, in part on bedrock knobs whose structural trend gives them a morainal aspect.

Moraines considered to represent the late stade of Pinedale glaciation occur on the three lower tributaries of Big Thompson River above the confluence of Spruce Canyon at altitudes ranging from 9800 to 10,700 feet. Ray inferred that the one in Hayden Canyon represented his Wisconsin IV substage. No trace of a moraine was found along Big Thompson River between Spruce Canyon and Hayden Canyon where Ray (1940, p. 1869, Fig. 5) suggested that a deposit of his Wisconsin III substage might exist.

In Spruce Canyon, a moraine which Ray believed might be between 9000 and 9500 feet altitude is at an altitude of 9100 feet and is believed to mark the upper stade of Pinedale glaciation. A high bedrock cliff occurs at the site (10,100, 1919 topography = 10,450, 1957 topography) of a moraine said by Ray (1940, p. 1969) to represent his Wisconsin IV substage.

In Fern Canyon, the moraine enclosing Fern Lake (Wisconsin III substage of Ray,

Upper Canyon moraine of Jones and Quam) at an altitude of 9525 feet represents the upper stade of Pinedale glaciation. The next lake upstream, Odessa Lake, considered to be enclosed by a moraine of the Wisconsin IV substage at 10,025 feet (Ray, 1940, p. 1869), is a rock-bound tarn.

All the prominent cirques in the upper drainage of Big Thompson River except the two at the head of Forest Canyon contain a succession of moraines, rock glaciers, or protalus ramparts whose character and relationships indicate two minor advances of Neoglaciation. The outer deposits are like those of the Temple Lake stade. The inner deposits have the fresh aspect characteristic of the historic stade and in a number of places lie immediately below a small glacier (Fig. 1).

Of particular interest is the sequence of moraines at the head of Spruce Canyon, one of which is the type locality of the Wisconsin V or Sprague substage of glaciation of Ray (1939; 1940) and Bryan and Ray (1940). The moraine (Ray, 1940, Pl. 2, fig. 1) lies at an altitude of 11,750 feet in a cirque on the north side of the head of Spruce Canyon below the lower of two lakes at the foot of Sprague Glacier. It is a broad, relatively smooth, bouldery deposit that supports a tundra vegetation and bears a thin azonal soil which contrasts markedly with the immature brown podzolic soil on nearby till of the Pinedale glaciation. The deposit thus has the aspect common to moraines of the Temple Lake stade of Neoglaciation, with which it is here correlated. The lake in which Sprague Glacier terminates (11,850 feet) is partly enclosed by fresh barren morainal debris on which no soil is developed. This deposit is distinctly younger than the type moraine of Ray's Wisconsin V substage and is similar to moraines formed during the historic stade.

Near Sprague Glacier on the floor of Spruce Canyon at an altitude of 10,800 feet are a pair of moraines, both characteristic of the Temple Lake stade and both derived from the same cirque on the south side of the canyon. The upper moraine transects the lower, and outwash from it cuts across the lower in such a way as to suggest that the Temple Lake stade locally included two minor pulsations of the ice. A small fresh moraine, characteristic of the historic stade, lies upstream at an altitude of 11,100 feet near the base of the cirque headwall.

GLACIER CREEK: The outermost glacial deposits in the valley of Glacier Creek attain a lower limit of 7800 feet altitude and represent the Bull Lake glaciation (Fig. 1). They were mapped as "Old Moraine remnants" by Jones and Quam (1944), who first observed the mature gray-brown podzolic soil, typical of these deposits, at a well-preserved exposure where the highway into Glacier Basin starts up the enclosing ridge. Just east of this exposure, the soil on till of Bull Lake glaciation is overlapped by the fresh, much more bouldery till of the Pinedale glaciation.

The large high lateral moraines that rim Glacier Basin join to form a narrow terminus at its lower end at an altitude of about 8200 feet. This moraine marks the early stage of Pinedale glaciation. It represents the Wisconsin II substage of Ray and the Park Border moraine of Jones and Quam. At the upper end of Glacier Basin, two low moraines, characteristic of Pinedale glaciation, branch across the valley at altitudes of 8760 and 8800 feet respectively from a single lateral moraine (Fig. 1). Both are considered to represent the middle stage of Pinedale glaciation. They are included in the Upper Valley moraines of Jones and Quam (1944, Fig. 3).

Upstream, where several tributaries branch from Glacier Creek, segments of small, irregular, but clearly delineated moraines outline the position of glaciers that formerly occupied each tributary. Their termini lie between 9400 and 9600 feet in altitude. The deposits are fresh and bouldery. Ray interpreted them as outlining a single large ice mass which he referred to the Wisconsin III substage. They were included as Upper Valley moraines by Jones and Quam and are considered herein to represent the late stage of Pinedale glaciation. The writer found no clearly distinguishable evidence of other halts or readvances of the ice between these deposits and the cirques.

Within each cirque are two sets of moraines, rock glaciers, or protalus ramparts whose character and contrasting habit clearly distinguish them as correlative with the Temple Lake and historic stades of Neoglaciation. Many of those of the historic stade lie at the foot of small headwall glaciers. Deposits of the Temple Lake stade in the canyon between Andrews and Tyndall glaciers constitute a large rock glacier whose morphology suggests that it formed during two episodes of movement. The relationships of two moraines of the historic stade at the foot of Tyndall Glacier also suggest two pulsations of the ice at that time. Such a twofold habit among deposits of the Temple Lake and historic stades is not uncommon in the Rocky Mountain region, but is not a consistent feature from one range to another, or from canyon to canyon with a single range.

ROARING FORK: The canyon of Roaring Fork, east of Longs Peak, is of interest because the moraine of the early stade of Pinedale glaciation breached and extended beyond those of Bull Lake glaciation (Fig. 1). The latter form a huge bulky lobate mass at 9000 feet altitude where the canyon issues from the mountain front. Both the outer and inner moraines can be distinguished on the north side of the canyon. Only the inner moraine was differentiated on the south side.

The moraine of the early stade of Pinedale glaciation, fresher and more bouldery than those of Bull Lake glaciation, extends as a narrow tongue through a gap, probably a former outwash channel in the older moraines, to a lower limit of about 8800 feet.

A similar morainal tongue farther up the canyon at an altitude of 9300 feet probably represents the middle stade of Pinedale glaciation. Still higher in the canyon, at an altitude of 10,400 feet, large angular blocks, chaotically jumbled, form a long narrow lobe which heads in lateral moraines on either side of the valley and probably represents the late stade of Pinedale glaciation. No other morainal deposits of Pinedale aspect were found upstream; the canyon is floored only by striated rock ledges over which numerous glacial boulders are scattered.

Chasm Lake, at the head of the canyon, is a rock-enclosed tarn, but morainal debris covered by grass and local patches of scrub spruce overlies the bedrock and may represent the Temple Lake stade of Neoglaciation. A more distinct moraine, characteristic of the Temple Lake stade, lies on the steep slopes of the cirque to the southeast. Fresh blocky moraines of the historic stade also spill from this cirque and from two sources in the east cirque of Longs Peak.

Two large boulder fields extend north from the north cirque of Longs Peak. The outer, which appears stagnant and is covered with vegetation, probably formed during the Temple Lake stade. The inner, which appears to consist of the reactivated headward portion of the outer and is intermittently active at present, is referred to the historic stade.

SUMMARY OF GLACIAL HISTORY

The east slope of Rocky Mountain National Park has been glaciated at least three times during the Pleistocene, and two small rejuvena-tions of the ice have occurred in Recent time. In Tahosa Valley, east of Longs Peak, the oldest or pre-Bull glaciation appears to be of pre-canyon origin, although the broad valley surface on which the deposits rest may have been entrenched by the canyon before the ice advanced over it. Deposits of a younger questionable pre-Bull Lake glaciation postdate canyon cutting along Fall River.

The interglaciation separating pre-Bull Lake from Bull Lake glaciation was of sufficient magnitude for deep weathering to have occurred, but little canyon erosion appears to have taken place at this time in the park.

Bull Lake glaciation was marked by two stades during which two distinct sets of moraines were formed. The major glaciers were 6 to 10 miles long and terminated just outside the Park boundary at altitudes of 7800 to 9000 feet. No positive evidence suggests the extent of interstadial recession, but the degree of development and widespread distribution of a soil buried between outwash deposits of the two advances elsewhere in the Rocky Mountains lead the writer to believe that the ice receded nearly to the cirques.

During the interglaciation separating the Bull Lake and Pinedale glaciations the ice probably disappeared entirely from the mountains. A mature zonal soil developed, and erosion of 20 to 30 feet took place locally along major streams below the terminal moraines.

During Pinedale time, glaciers failed to reoccupy some cirques that had been occupied in Bull Lake time. The Pinedale glaciation was characterized by three stades. During the early advance, glaciers in general attained a position immediately in back of moraines of Bull Lake glaciation but locally overlapped these moraines and in one place breached them. Moraines of the middle stade probably mark a readvance of the ice that on Fall River breached the terminal moraine of the early stade and in Moraine Park reached the same position attained during that stade. Elsewhere, the middle stade recorded a recession of the ice of at least 2 miles resulting in glaciers 3 to 8 miles long. During the late stade of Pinedale glaciation, the ice everywhere receded markedly and tended to subdivide into tongues that failed to coalesce in the major canyons. These glaciers ranged from 2 to 5 miles in length. A radiocarbon date from peat at the base of a bog on one of these deposits, the type locality of the Wisconsin IV or Long Draw substage of Ray, is 6170 ± 240 years (Rubin and Suess, 1955). The peat is gradational downward into glacial silt, outwash gravel, and till, suggesting that it began to form shortly after recession of the ice.

A variety of evidence suggests that the Pinedale glaciers disappeared entirely from the mountains during the succeeding postglacial optimum or altithermal age and that freeze and thaw processes ceased to be effective on cirque headwalls and adjacent upland slopes. An immature zonal soil formed and erosion of a few feet occurred along major streams below the terminal moraines of Pinedale glaciation. These moraines probably retained shallow lakes at this time.

Small glaciers, formed during Neoglaciation, failed to reoccupy many cirques occupied in Pinedale time and developed only in the more sheltered parts of others. Two advances of the ice, the Temple Lake and historic stades, are recorded. Both are included within the Little Ice Age of Matthes (1939; 1940), and both include local evidence of at least two secondary pulsations. Most of the ice bodies were less than half a mile long.

Deposits in the La Sal Mountains, Utah, which are correlated with the Temple Lake stade have been dated as 2800 ± 200 years old (Rubin and Suess, 1955) and are estimated to have formed from about 3800 to about 2000 years ago. The historic stade may have attained its last maximum in Rocky Mountain National Park about 1860. Thirteen small glaciers and stagnant ice bodies are relict from this advance in the area at present.

References Cited

American Commission on Stratigraphic Nomenclature, 1959, Report 6—Application of stratigraphic classification and nomenclature to the Quaternary: Am. Assoc. Petroleum Geologists Bull., v. 43, p. 663–673

Blackwelder, Eliot, 1915, Post-Cretaceous history of the mountains of central western Wyoming: Jour. Geology, v. 23, p. 97–117, 193–217, 307–340

Bryan, Kirk, and Ray, L. L., 1940, Geologic antiquity of the Lindenmeier site in Colorado: Smithsonian Misc. Coll., Pub. 3554, v. 99, no. 2, 76 p.

Fuller, M. B., 1923, The physiographic development of the Big Thompson River Valley in Colorado: Jour. Geology, v. 31, p. 126–137

Hack, J. T., 1943, Antiquity of the Finley site: Am. Antiquity, v. 8, p. 235–241

Jones, W. D., and Quam, L. O., 1944, Glacial landforms in Rocky Mountain National Park, Colorado: Jour. Geology, v. 52, p. 217–234

Lee, W. T., 1917, The geologic story of the Rocky Mountain National Park: U. S. National Park Service, 89 p.

Matthes, F. M., 1939, Report of the committee on glaciers: Am. Geophys. Union Trans., p. 518–523

—— 1940, Report of the committee on glaciers: Am. Geophys., Union Trans., p. 396–405

Moss, J. H., 1951a, Early man in the Eden Valley: Univ. Penna. Museum Monograph, 124 p.

—— 1951b, Late glacial advances in the southern Wind River Mountains, Wyoming: Am. Jour. Sci., v. 249, p. 865–883

Ray, L. L., 1939, Subdivision of the last glacial stage in the southern Rocky Mountains (Abstract): Geol. Soc. America Bull., v. 50, p. 2006–2007

—— 1940, Glacial chronology of the southern Rocky Mountains: Geol. Soc. America Bull., v. 51, p. 1851–1918

Richmond, G. M., 1953, Pleistocene field conference in Rocky Mountain National Park: Science, v. 117, p. 177–178

—— 1957, Three pre-Wisconsin glacial stages in the Rocky Mountain region: Geol. Soc. America Bull., v. 68, p. 239–262

Rubin, Meyer, and Suess, H. E., 1955, U. S. Geological Survey radiocarbon dates, II: Science, v. 121, no. 3145, p. 481–488

USE OF RELATIVE AGE-DATING METHODS IN A STRATIGRAPHIC STUDY OF ROCK GLACIER DEPOSITS, MT. SOPRIS, COLORADO

PETER W. BIRKELAND

Department of Geological Sciences
University of Colorado
Boulder, Colorado 80302

ABSTRACT

Data from several relative age-dating methods were collected on rock glacier debris mantles to test the usefulness of each in assigning a relative age to various parts of the mantles. Lichens, rock weathering, and soils provide the best information on age. No single method is adequate to differentiate all the deposits, most of which have been formed within the past 20,000 to 30,000 years. Each method has an ages to the Neoglacial deposits. The Neoglacial-of each method differs. Lichen data, specifically *Rhizocarpon geographicum* s.l. size, percentage of total lichen cover, and species composi-tion provide the best information for assigning ages to the Neoglacial deposits. The Neoglacial-Pinedale break is recognized from a much thicker surface deposit of loess, thicker and more common rock weathering rinds, and greater soil development on Pinedale deposits relative to early Neoglacial deposits. The Pinedale-Bull Lake break was not satisfactorily recognized in many places. Where exposures are present, however, the granitic rocks in the weathered zone in Pinedale deposits are fresh whereas a substantial number of those in Bull Lake deposits are grusified.

INTRODUCTION

Many Quaternary stratigraphic studies of alpine glacial deposits have relied strongly on the use of relative dating methods to assign ages to deposits and for correlation. The main reason for this is that material suitable for radiocarbon dating generally is lacking in the right stratigraphic position. Correlations based on relative dating vary in their accuracy, however, because of (1) inexperience in the use of the methods by certain workers, (2) failure to quantify the data, (3) various workers use different definitions of parameters to describe the state of rock weathering and soil formation in quantitative terms, (4) there are variations in weathering, soils, and lichens because of variations in lithology and environment, and (5) it is not uncommon for workers to use one or two age-dating criteria with which they have greatest familiarity to the exclusion of others.

My purpose here is to discuss the use of lichen, weathering, and soil data to assign relative ages to rock glacier debris mantles in western Colorado. Deposits formed in the last 20,000 to 30,000 years will be emphasized, but criteria useful in differentiating these deposits from still older ones will be discussed. It is concluded that no one or two criteria are suitable for differentiating all deposits within this time span. Instead, each relative age-dating method has a limited time span over which it is most effective and each method is effective over a different time span. Therefore, it will be shown that the most reliable indications of relative age come from the use of a combination of age-dating

Arctic and Alpine Research, Vol. 5, No. 4, 1973, pp. 401-416.

methods. Another reason for using several methods is that in correlation with one area perhaps one method will provide the best data, whereas perhaps some other method will provide data on the best correlation with another area.

LOCATION AND GENERAL GEOLOGY

The rock glacier deposits studied are located on Mt. Sopris, which is between Aspen and Glenwood Springs in western Colorado (Figure 1). The summit reaches 3,948 m altitude, and major valleys are cut into the mountain on all except the west-facing side. Active and inactive rock glaciers are present in all of the major valleys.

Mt. Sopris is a Tertiary stock that intruded the surrounding sedimentary rocks (Pilkington, 1954; Pillmore, 1954; Foland, 1967). The main rock type making up the rock glaciers is a fine- to medium-grained granodiorite which is porphyritic in places. Foland (1967) lists andesine plagioclase (46.6%), potassium feldspar (20.8%), quartz (21.3%), and biotite (5.3%) as the most common minerals. Hornblende usually makes up about 1% of the rock, and augite less than 0.5%.

THE ROCK GLACIERS

The main purpose of my work was to determine the ages of debris on the surfaces of rock glaciers (Figure 2). Few such data, based on semi-quantitative age-dating methods, are available for the Cordilleran Region (see Richmond, 1962; Birman, 1964; Benedict, 1968; Yount, 1970; Curry, 1971; C. D. Miller, 1973, this issue). The Mt. Sopris area is excellent for rock glacier stratigraphic studies in that the rock glaciers are quite long (some over 2 km long), their debris mantles increase in age downvalley and some contacts between mantles of different ages are quite sharp, and many of the rocks making up now-active rock glaciers were first incorporated in Pinedale time.

The rock glacier nomenclature used here should be explained. All of the data reported here pertain to the debris at the surface of the rock glacier, called the debris mantle. In many places there are no interstitial fines between the angular blocks at the surface. In other places, however, the interstices are filled either with a coarse-grained matrix derived from the valley headwalls or with fine-grained loess blown in from distant sources. Both active rock glaciers

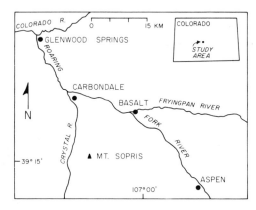

FIGURE 1. Location map of study area.

and inactive rock glacier deposits were studied. Active rock glaciers have downvalley fronts composed of extremely loose material that is on the verge of avalanching or has recently just avalanched. The slope of the front is 35 to 40° and forms an abrupt junction angle with the surface of the rock glacier (Wahrhaftig and Cox, 1959). In contrast, although inactive rock glaciers have steep downvalley fronts, the junction between the front and top of the rock glacier is rounded, the rocks on the fronts are lichen covered, and the fronts commonly have trees in growth position if they lie below tree-line.

Most of the rock glaciers described here seem to be similar in origin and in movement. Rockfalls at the valley heads are the main source of debris mantle. After rock debris is incorporated into the rock glacier at its upper end, the debris mantle moves downvalley in piggyback fashion. Although in some places the debris mantle moves downvalley relatively undisturbed, in other places the mantle has been churned, individual weathered rocks overturned, or buried, and fresh rocks brought to the surface. This replacement of weathered rocks by fresh rocks at the surface complicates stratigraphic studies directed toward determining when a particular part of the debris mantle first formed at the head of the rock glacier. Whereas these processes can cause underestimation of the age of the debris mantle, other processes can cause overestimation. For example, weathered talus can be shed onto a rock glacier at any time, be incorporated into the mantle, and thus give an apparent old age to that part of the rock glacier.

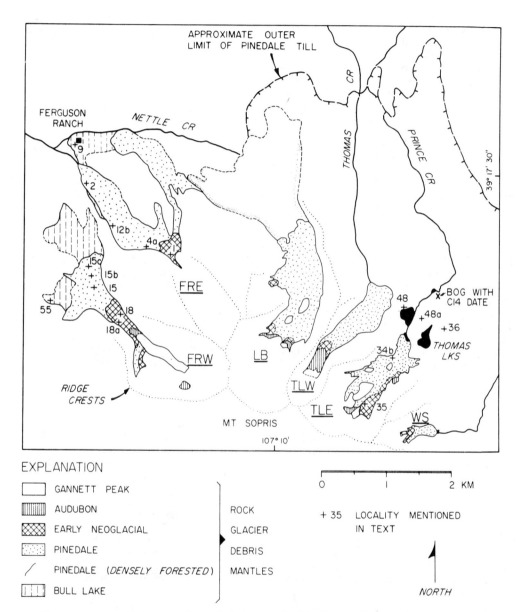

FIGURE 2. Generalized map of the rock glacier deposits, Mt. Sopris. The rock glacier names are as follows: FRW—Ferguson Ranch west; FRE—Ferguson Ranch east; LB—Lost Basin; TLW—Thomas Lakes west; TLE—Thomas Lakes east; and WS—West Sopris.

STRATIGRAPHIC NOMENCLATURE

The stratigraphic names assigned to the deposits discussed here have been used in various ways by most recent workers in the Rocky Mountains (Richmond, 1960, 1962, 1965; Benedict, 1967, 1968, 1970; Madole, 1969, 1972; Mahaney, 1971, 1973a; Williams, 1973; Birkeland and Miller, 1973). Because there is some controversy over the stratigraphic name assigned to deposits solely on the basis of relative age-dating methods (e.g., Mahaney, 1973a, 1973b; Williams, 1973), the nomenclature used here will be briefly discussed. Gannett Peak is used for deposits that probably are no more than several centuries old and these deposits are continuing to form at the present. Audubon is used for those deposits laid down between about 1850 to 950 years ago (Benedict, 1968, 1970; Mahaney, 1972). These deposits are readily distinguishable from those of early Neoglacial age, and therefore the Temple Lake "b" designation of Birkeland et al. (1971) for deposits in that age range should not be used. Although the Temple Lake moraine at the type locality (Hack, 1943; Moss, 1951) has not been radiometrically dated, recent work supports Moss's suggestion that it might be pre-Altithermal (Birkeland and Miller, 1973). A problem in nomenclature exists, therefore, because the name Temple Lake is entrenched in the literature as an early Neoglacial advance (Richmond, 1965; Porter and Denton, 1967). Because this problem is not resolved, the name Temple Lake will not be used here. Rather, the oldest post-Althithermal deposits will be called early Neoglacial. Although age limits are hard to determine for the early Neoglacial deposits they probably were formed between about 3,000 and 5,000 years ago (Benedict, 1970; in press; Andrews et al., 1973). Of special interest in this work is the minimum age for the Pinedale Glaciation because on Mt. Sopris a characteristic change in weathering features separates Neoglacial deposits from those considered to be of late Pinedale age. As used here, the Altithermal interval separates the early Neoglacial from the Pinedale. Benedict (1970) suggested an upper age limit of about 7,500 years ago for Pinedale deposits, and Curry (1973) put the upper limit at about 10,000 BP. In more recent work substantiated by radiocarbon dating, Benedict (in press) recognizes cirque moraines, informally designated Satanta Peak, that were formed just prior to about 10,000 years ago, and Andrews et al. (1973) and Carrara and Andrews (1973) have stratigraphic evidence for deglaciation of a high cirque in the San Juan Mountains at about this same time. I regard 10,000 years to be the approximate upper age limit for the Pinedale deposits at Mt. Sopris because this seems to allow sufficient time to develop the characteristic weathering features on them.

AGE-DATING METHODS

Several dating methods were used to assign relative ages to the deposits because no one method seems to differentiate satisfactorily all of the deposits in the area. Because there is no standardization of these methods, the methods I used will be described. All of the field localities and the data collected will be shown on maps and in tables in a subsequent paper.

LICHENS

Benedict (1967, 1968) has shown that the sizes of specific lichens, the percentage of cover of all lichens on rock surfaces, and the proportions of various lichen species change with time in the Colorado Front Range. It is commonly assumed that those lichens with the largest diameters are the oldest, so only the largest lichens were measured. Lichens measured were *Rhizocarpon geographicum, Lecanora thomsonii, Lecidea atrobrunnea,* and *Lecanora aspicilia.* Because I have not had formal training in lichen taxonomy, I cannot be sure that the lichens were properly and consistently identified. The greatest problem is the proper identification of *R. geographicum,* because it is easily confused with other *Rhizocarpon* species of similar appearance. Benedict (1967) makes the point, however, that *R. geographicum* grows as fast or faster than related species with which it might be confused, and that measuring the largest thalli tends to favor the selection of *R. geographicum.* On that basis, the measurements reported here would tend to favor *R. geographicum.* Because of this uncertainty in taxonomy, however, the name *R. geographicum, sensu lato,* will be used. Only lichens with circular or slightly elongate outlines were measured, and always in the direction of the smallest diameter. Lichen-measuring localities were not defined by a specific area, as in some previous works, but were places in which a lichen search of about 30 min duration was undertaken. The northwest to northeast sides of most boulders provided the maximum lichen sizes and percentage covers, and therefore the search was mainly restricted to those sides. At most localities the percentage of lichen cover on 50 boulders was estimated. Because there is a linear relationship between the mean cover

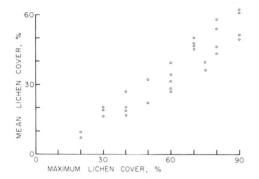

FIGURE 3. Comparison of mean lichen cover for 50 rocks at one locality with the maximum cover on one rock at the same locality.

for 50 boulders and the maximum cover on one boulder (Figure 3), it probably is sufficient to look only for maximum covers. In recent work (Birkeland and Miller, 1973), we have measured only the maximum lichen cover on a boulder at a locality; this tends to give higher percentage covers than does the procedure used on Mt. Sopris because the maximum cover might not be represented in the 50 boulders measured. Finally, at most localities a rough estimate on lichen species composition was made. It was noted that the green lichens predominate on young rock surfaces and that dark brown and black lichens are more dominant on older surfaces. Hence, it seemed sufficient to record whether the green species or brown-plus-black species predominated in the lichen population.

ROCK WEATHERING

Several different weathering parameters were measured on 100 or more rocks at many field localities. Counts were taken of the percent fresh, weathered, and pitted boulders. A weathered boulder is one in which part of the surface (an area greater than about 10 cm across) is so weathered that individual mineral grains stand in relief (Birman, 1964). A pitted boulder is weathered and contains small, usually closed, depressions on the surface. One major problem in the weathering study is that the lichen cover increases with age and some weathering features may be hidden.

A second weathering parameter is the change in angularity of boulder corners with age. Because most of the boulders fall onto the rock glacier surface, their corners are initially angular and impact scars are frequent. With time the corners become progressively rounded. About 100 boulders at each locality were classified as having angular, subangular, and subrounded corners (Powers, 1953). The radii of curvature for these three classes are modified from Caine (1968) and are approximately <0.5 cm for angular, 0.5 to 2.5 cm for subangular, and >2.5 cm for subrounded.

A third measure of rock weathering is the development of weathering rinds (Nelson, 1954). Rinds on 50 cobbles or boulders were generally measured at each locality. Over a period of time, the iron-bearing minerals weather and the weathering products discolor the outer parts of the rocks. The thickness of the rind probably is a rough measure of the duration of weathering. Rinds are as brightly colored as 2.5YR 5/4. Only the maximum rind thickness for each rock was recorded.

The weathering data reported on here are for rock surfaces that were probably never forested, and hence these data cannot be directly compared with those from forested areas. The reason for this is that periodic forest fires can cause spalling of rock surfaces (Blackwelder, 1927), and thus the weathering features may not accurately record the time interval since deposition. In one area, for example, nonforested blockfield deposits are more weathered than adjacent forested till of about the same age (Table 1). The major differences are that the surface rocks in forested till are not pitted, whereas the surface rocks in nonforested blockfield deposits have a significant amount of pitted rocks; in addition, although the maximum rind thicknesses in both environments are similar, the mean rind thickness is much higher in the nonforested deposit. One apparent discrepancy is that the forested till has a higher percentage of stones with subrounded corners; this rounding is mostly due to spalling during fire.

LOESS THICKNESS

A layer of fine-grained material, considered to be loess, overlies the coarse-grained rock glacier matrix in places. The differentiation between rock glacier matrix and loess is based on field and laboratory determinations of texture (Figure 4). Loesses have a smooth feel and generally are loams or silt loams. In contrast, rock glacier matrices have a gritty feel and they are sandy loams and loamy sands. Some samples have textures intermediate between loess and matrix, and both field and laboratory data suggest that they may be a mechanical mix-

TABLE 1

Comparison of weathering data between a forested till and a nonforested blockfield, both of Pinedale age, in the vicinity of Thomas Lakes, Mt. Sopris, Colorado

Locality[a]	Rock Weathering (%)			Corner Angularity (%)			Weathering Rind (mm)	
	Fresh	Weathered	Pitted	Angular	Subangular	Subrounded	Mean	Maximum
Forested till								
48a	76	24	0	10	48	42	9	24
Nonforested Blockfield								
36[b]	82	18	0					
	68	28	4	41	50	9	17.3	25
48	70	19	11	57	35	8	16.4	28

[a]These are located in Figure 2.
[b]Counts were made at two different times and both are given.

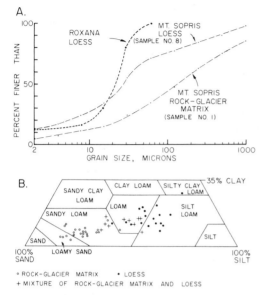

FIGURE 4. A: Representative cumulative curves for loess and rock-glacier matrix, Mt. Sopris. For comparison, Roxana loess from Illinois is shown. Sample no. 1 is from location 8 and sample no. 8 is from location 4a (Figure 2). B: Grain-size analyses of loess, rock-glacier matrix, and of deposits that may be a mixture of the two. Although many of these materials have weathered somewhat since deposition, the weathering probably has not been too extensive; hence, the distributions here probably closely approximate the unaltered material. Textural classes are from the U.S. Dept. of Agriculture.

ture of these two deposits. The extremely rough surfaces of the rock glaciers appear to be good

traps for loess, and thus the absence or presence of loess, as well as its thickness, provide data on relative age of the underlying deposits.

The interpretation that some silt-and-clay-rich material in the Rocky Mountains is loess is accepted by some workers (Williams, 1973), but not entirely by others (Mahaney, 1973b). A mineralogical test for derivation from distant sources has not yet been made. However, to call upon weathering on Mt. Sopris to produce the textural differences between the fine-grained surface material and the coarse-grained matrix underlying it in the time available would demand weathering rates out of line with those that students and I have observed in many parts of the Rocky Mountains.

SOIL PROPERTIES

Various soil properties change with time and can be used as indicators of relative age (Richmond, 1962). In most soil studies the aim is to identify the parent material at depth, determine if that material was the parent material for the soil horizons, and then ascribe departures (e.g., color or texture) from that original material to pedogenesis. At Mt. Sopris, however, loess of varying thickness locally overlies the rock glacier matrix and the soil has formed in both materials. This complicates the usefulness of soils in age dating. Another problem with using soils in this study has been that areally they are rather rare. In most places the rock glacier surfaces consist of open-work boulders. Where matrix material exists, trees are generally found, and these were the areas inspected for soils.

RELATIVE AGE ASSIGNMENT

The various data collected can be used to group the deposits on the basis of relative age. Although there are no useful radiometric ages with which to directly calibrate the relative age-dating methods on Mt. Sopris, comparisons with data from other areas are used to suggest correlations with the standard Rocky Mountain stratigraphic units. One radiocarbon date for Mt. Sopris is from the base of a bog lying on bouldery material considered to be Pinedale till (Figure 2); the sample gives an age of 9,100 ± 300 years (GaK-3161), and is just a limiting date for the till.

LICHEN DATA

Various lichen data can be used to group the rock glacier debris mantles into the three neoglacial ages recognized in the Front Range by Benedict (1968).[1] The most useful data are the combination of R. geographicum s.l. maximum thallus diameter with maximum percentage of lichen cover (Figure 5). Lichen cover on boulders of early Neoglacial age is 50% or

[1]With this exception: his Temple Lake is here termed early Neoglacial.

more, and diameters generally exceed 50 mm. In contrast, lichen cover on Audubon boulders is 50% or less and diameters are less than 42 mm, whereas the cover on Gannett Peak boulders is 5% or less and diameters are less than 22 mm. I probably have put more emphasis on percentage of lichen cover for relative age assignment than have previous workers; for example, in places where the percentage cover is high yet the *R. geographicum* s.l. diameter is low (Figure 5), I believe percentage cover to be more diagnostic of age.

The lack of closer correspondence in size of *R. geographicum* s.l. with age between Mt. Sopris and the Front Range (Figure 5) raises some question about the correlation of deposits between the two areas. One possible explanation for this size discrepancy is that perhaps rock glaciers do not provide a stable enough substrate for growth to maximum size whereas stabilized moraines, like those in the Front Range, do. Another explanation could be that some debris mantles assigned to the early Neoglacial may be younger, and instead have formed in the interval between the Audubon and the early Neoglacial.

Other lichen data suggest three Neoglacial ages for the Mt. Sopris debris mantles. One is the ratio of total green lichens to total dark-brown-plus-black lichens. Green species are predominant on rock surfaces of Gannett Peak and Audubon debris mantles, whereas the dark species seem either equal to or greater than the green on rock surfaces of early Neoglacial age. The maximum diameters of *Lecanora thomsonii* and *Lecidea atrobrunnea* also were measured at some localities. Size data on these two lichens also suggest three different ages (Table

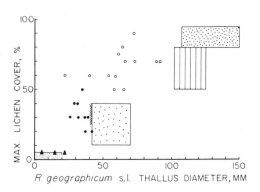

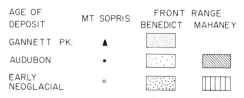

FIGURE 5. Plot of *R. geographicum* s.l. maximum lichen cover on one rock at the same locality, Mt. Sopris, compared with data for the Colorado Front Range (Benedict, 1968; Mahaney, 1973).

2), and the maximum values reported here are close to those reported by C. D. Miller (1973, this issue) for the Sawatch Range, about 55 km northeast of Mt. Sopris, and they agree with the Front Range data of Benedict (1968) for Audubon deposits. Mahaney's (1973) data, however, suggest that *L. thomsonii* are noticeably smaller in the Front Range than on Mt. Sopris.

WEATHERING DATA

Weathering rinds provide the best weathering index for relative age assignment; they were most useful in separating Pinedale from early Neoglacial deposits, a conclusion also reached by Williams (1973) for the Front Range. In general, many rocks from early Neoglacial debris mantles lack rinds whereas those from Pinedale mantles are characterized by well-developed rinds (Table 3). A frequency distribution of rinds for both Pinedale and early Neoglacial deposits was obtained from the Ferguson Ranch west rock glacier (Figure 6). The data there show that although some rocks from early Neoglacial mantles have rinds (24 to 42%), the rinds are generally thin. In contrast, over 78% of the rocks making up mantles of Pinedale age have rinds. This difference in

TABLE 2

Maximum diameters (mm) for Lecanora thomsonii *and* Lecidea atrobrunnea *on Neoglacial rock glacier debris mantles, Mt. Sopris*

Lichen Species	Age of Debris Mantle		
	Gannett Peak	Audubon	Early Neoglacial
Lecanora thomsonii	52	153	252
Lecidea atrobrunnea	not measured	179	202

rind development is obvious in the field because rocks with prominent rinds also are reddish due to fairly intense surface weathering, whereas those without rinds, or perhaps with only thin rinds, are gray.

Graphs of maximum rind thickness vs. age in several valleys give reasonable approximate ages for the deposits (Figure 7; Table 3). A basic assumption in this approach is that rinds on early Neoglacial rocks represent about 5,000 years of weathering. Although maximum rind thicknesses for the Ferguson Ranch west rock glacier are the greatest for the mountain, a linear plot of the data suggests an age of about 15,000 years for the Pinedale, an age that is not unreasonable (Birkeland *et al.*, 1971). A similar plot for the Thomas Lakes east rock glacier also suggests that the Pinedale mantle there may be 15,000 years old. In contrast, rind data for Pinedale mantle of the Lost Basin rock glacier would plot far beyond 20,000 years if a linear relationship is assumed. If 20,000 years is taken as the age of the Pinedale, an increasing rate of rind thickness development between the early Neoglacial and Pinedale is suggested. Obviously more field data are needed before we can be more certain of the uses and shapes of these curves.

Other data on rock weathering were not very useful in age differentiation. The data on percent fresh-weathered-pitted rocks do not fall into distinct groups on the basis of relative age (Figure 8). About the only meaningful trends are (a) most Neoglacial mantles contain over 65% fresh rocks, and (b) although generally only a small percentage of the rocks making up

TABLE 3

Range in thickness (mm) of maximum rinds on rock fragments in rock glacier debris mantles, Mt. Sopris

| | Age of Mantle | | |
Rock Glacier	Early Neoglacial	Pinedale	Older Pinedale?
Ferguson Ranch west	2-14	6-45	n.m.
Ferguson Ranch east	n.m.	14-22	—
Lost Basin	2	10-30	20-29[a]
Thomas Lakes west	n.m.	12-28	n.m.
Thomas Lakes east	2-7	12-28	—
West Sopris Creek	0	28	—

n.m. = not measured
[a]Shown as forested Pinedale in Figure 2.

Pinedale mantles are pitted, pitting is absent on rocks of Neoglacial mantles. Corner angularity data also do not fall into distinct age groups (Figure 9)—about the only discernible differences noted are that rocks with over about 5% subrounded corners probably are Pinedale, whereas those with less than 5% subrounded corners are most likely Neoglacial. Within the Neoglacial it was noted that the major differ-

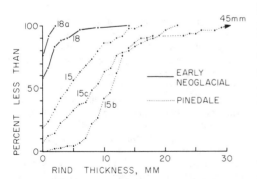

FIGURE 6. Cumulative frequency curves of weathering rind thicknesses for rocks in debris mantles of different age, Ferguson Ranch west rock glacier. Numbers refer to localities in Figure 2.

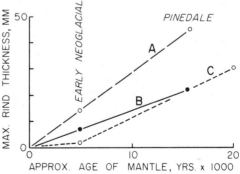

FIGURE 7. Plot of maximum rind thickness and approximate age of three rock-glacier debris mantles. A is for Ferguson Ranch west rock glacier, B for Lost Basin rock glacier, and C for Thomas Lakes east rock glacier.

44

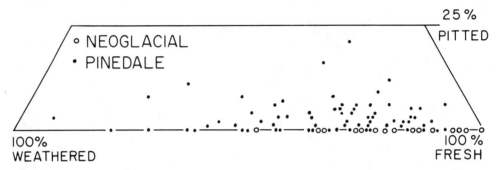

FIGURE 8. Partial triangular diagram of percentage of fresh-weathered-pitted rocks with age for rock glacier debris mantles, Mt. Sopris.

ence between Gannett Peak and Audubon deposits is the preservation of impact scars along the edges of the Gannett Peak rocks and their absence on Audubon and older rocks.

A determined effort was made to identify debris mantles of Bull Lake age on the basis of their surface and subsurface weathering. Rock glacier debris that is densely forested lies downvalley from some Pinedale rock glaciers. Although outcrops and unforested parts of the mantles are few, in some valleys Bull Lake deposits were tentatively identified (Figure 2). The extent of weathering on rock fragments at the surface of the Ferguson Ranch west rock glacier suggests that its downvalley, forested part is older than the unforested Pinedale part farther upvalley. In addition, 17% of the granitic stones are grusified at one outcrop (locality 55, figure 2). Several outcrops suggest that the downvalley part of the Ferguson Ranch east rock glacier also is of Bull Lake age (locality 9 and northwest of 12 b, Figure 2). About 67% of the granitic rocks in these cuts are weathered. The weathered stones have at least an outer grusified shell, or are so weathered that they lie flush against the face of the exposure. In addition, grusified rocks within the soil zone are oxidized. In contrast, granitic rocks in Pinedale till in soil pits and in shallow cuts along the road to Thomas Lakes are sound and not oxidized.

LOESS THICKNESS

The thickness of loess on a deposit is useful in differentiating Pinedale deposits from those of Neoglacial age. Loess thicknesses on Pinedale debris mantles range from 18 to 72 cm and loess mixed with some rock glacier matrix has been observed as thick as 83 cm. In contrast,

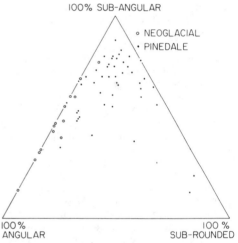

FIGURE 9. Triangular diagram of degree of corner angularity for rock fragments making up rock glacier debris mantles, Mt. Sopris.

most debris mantles on early Neoglacial rock glaciers lack loess, and it has been recognized only at the head of the Thomas Lakes east rock glacier. There, loess is 8 cm thick and loess mixed with rock glacier matrix is 4 cm thick. In other valleys, the meager evidence that I have does not suggest any differences in loess thickness between late(?) Pinedale mantles and forested deposits of older(?) Pinedale or Bull Lake age located farther downvalley. Loess also is thinner on till downvalley from the Thomas Lakes east rock glacier than on the rock glacier (Figure 10), perhaps because rock glaciers provide better surfaces for trapping and preserving loess. On smoother surfaces with interstitial fines, such as tills, loess can be removed by surficial processes.

45

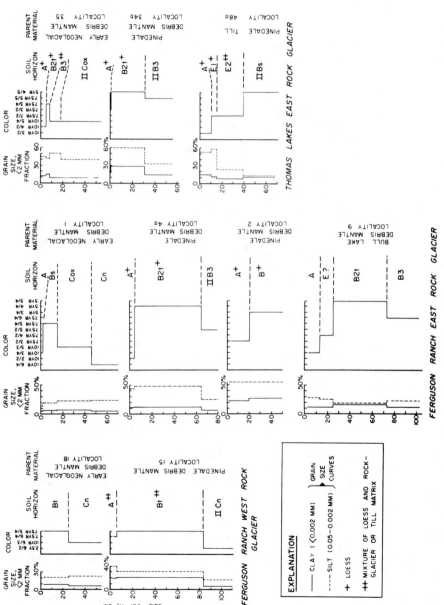

FIGURE 10. Grain-size and color data for selected soils formed from rock glacier debris mantle and loess of different ages. Some of the soil horizon nomenclature used is: E for light-colored eluvial horizon (also known as A2); Bs for color B horizon; Bt for textural B horizon; Cox for oxidized C horizon; and Cn for unweathered parent material.

The age and origin of the loess are problematical. Most of the loess is of pre-Neoglacial age, and thus it probably was deposited in late Pinedale and Altithermal time. Much of the loess could have been derived from nearby nonvegetated floodplains. Another possible source is the sparsely vegetated Colorado Plateau, to the west of Mt. Sopris.

Soil Data

Color of the B horizon and depth to the base of the B horizon appear to be the soil properties best associated with age of rock glacier debris mantles. Although it is difficult to make comparisons of soils formed on loess with soils formed on rock glacier matrix, some generalizations on developmental differences with age can be made (Figure 10). No soil has formed on Gannett Peak deposits. Audubon deposits with interstitial fines were not common enough to study soil development; if studies by Mahaney (1970, 1971, 1973) and those in progress elsewhere in the Rocky Mountains are representative (Birkeland and Miller, 1973), some subsurface oxidation but no B horizon development is expected. One of the most conspicuous differences in soils is that between those formed on early Neoglacial mantles and those formed on Pinedale mantles. Soils formed on early Neoglacial mantles have either color or textural B horizons with a color hue of 7.5YR, and the depth to the base of the B is 25 cm or less. The textural B horizons are recognized by a very slight increase in clay content relative to the C horizon, possibly due to the mixing of some loess particles with rock glacier matrix. In contrast, soils on Pinedale mantles are redder, with B horizon hues of 7.5YR to 5YR, and

the maximum depth to the base of the color or textural B horizon is 83 cm or more. The base of the B horizon coincides with the loess/till boundary in many places; in other places the textural B horizon extends downward into the coarse-grained matrix of the rock glacier deposit. In places where the base of the B horizon coincides with the base of the loess, and unaltered loess is not present, it is difficult to determine what pedologic changes have taken place in the loess since its deposition. The material surely has become redder, but it is difficult to determine if clay formation has taken place. Not uncommonly there is slightly more clay in the B horizon relative to the A horizon (Figure 10); however this relationship can be explained by the vertical translocation of original clay particles in the loess rather than by formation in place.

It is difficult to differentiate Pinedale from older Pinedale(?) or Bull Lake deposits solely on soils with the few data that are available. Color hue may help differentiate the deposits, because the older ones are all 5YR (Figure 10). Both Richmond (1962) and Madole (1969) report hue differences between soils formed on Bull Lake deposits and those formed on Pinedale deposits. In comparing soils formed from coarse-grained parent materials on Mt. Sopris, that formed from Bull Lake rock glaicer matrix of the Ferguson Ranch east rock glaicer has a slight textural B horizon, whereas that formed from Pinedale till just downvalley from the Thomas Lakes east rock glacier lacks a textural B horizon (Figure 10). The clay increase in this post-Bull Lake soil could be due to formation in place because a surface layer of loess from which clays could be translocated was not recognized at that site.

CONCLUSIONS AND RECOMMENDATIONS

This study demonstrates that no single relative age-dating method is sufficiently sensitive to date all the deposits at Mt. Sopris. Rather, a combination of several methods provides the best estimate of relative age. Each method has an approximate age span over which it is most useful in age determination, beyond which the usefulness of the method diminishes (Figure 11). Furthermore, the useful age spans of the methods used here partly overlap, so that in general when one method becomes less useful in age differentiation another becomes more useful.

Lichen data work best in differentiating Neoglacial deposits. One major problem in using lichens in this study is that there is no dated R. geographicum s.l. growth-rate curve for western Colorado. Lichenometric ages can not be assigned until we develop a local curve or demonstrate that the lichen growth-rate curve developed for the Colorado Front Range by Benedict (1967) can be used on Mt. Sopris. Because of this, I feel that lichen data are a good tool for relative age dating on Mt. Sopris, but I do not feel sure that lichenometric ages can be assigned to the rock glacier mantles.

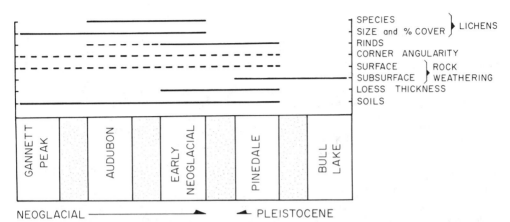

FIGURE 11. Plot of the relative age dating criteria vs. the approximate age span over which each appears to be most useful for age differentiation at Mt. Sopris. Extension of soil data to the Audubon and Gannett Peak deposits is based on work in the Front Range (Mahaney, 1970) and in the Wind River Mountains (Birkeland and Miller, 1973). Solid lines indicate strong correlation with age.

Succession of lichen species with time shows promise of being stratigraphically useful, and should be pursued by those more familiar with lichen taxonomy.

Rock weathering data vary in their usefulness for age dating. Weathering rinds provide the best information, because rocks from Gannett Peak and Audubon deposits have no rinds, a few from early Neoglacial deposits have thin rinds, and those from Pinedale deposits commonly have thick rinds. Corner angularity and surface rock weathering were of limited use on the mountain as a whole, and seemed to be most useful in local differentiation on a single rock glacier. Subsurface rock weathering, specifically the percentage of totally or partly grusified rocks, probably is the best criterion for differentiating Pinedale from Bull Lake deposits on Mt. Sopris and elsewhere in the Rocky Mountains (Richmond, 1965; Madole, 1969). Unfortunately, the lack of exposures limited the use of this method.

The lack of close correspondence between surface rock weathering and age came as a surprise because numerous studies in the Rockies and elsewhere have shown these data to be a primary source for age differentiation (Blackwelder, 1931; Nelson, 1954; Birman, 1964; Porter, 1969; Sharp, 1969). Detailed surface boulder weathering studies in the Rocky Mountains commonly show that Pinedale deposits have about twice as many fresh boulders as do Bull Lake deposits (Nelson, 1954; Miller, 1971; Weber, 1973; unpublished data of writer), but this was generally not the case at Mt. Sopris.

Two explanations for the lack of correspondence between surface weathering and age come to mind. One is that most previous studies have been on rocks that are coarser grained than the Mt. Sopris granodiorite. Initial weathering of a coarse-grained rock results in the development of a roughened surface (= weathered rock) more rapidly than is the case with a fine-grained rock, such as that making up Mt. Sopris. Another explanation could be related to the lichen cover. Because it is relatively fine grained, the mineral grains in the rock at Mt. Sopris do not stand out very prominently in relief when weathered. Hence, lichen cover can hide some evidence of weathring.

It therefore seems that rind development is a fairly good indicator of relative age with fine-grained rocks, but surface weathering features of these rocks are not very useful. In contrast, work by the writer and others in the Rocky Mountains indicates that coarse-grained rocks, because they weather fairly rapidly by granular disintegration, give a good sequence of surface weathering features with age, but they present a poor record of rind development because the surface is disintegrating more rapidly than most rinds can develop.

Loess thickness proved to be a good criterion for differentiating Pinedale from younger deposits, because it is relatively thick on Pinedale deposits and thin or absent on early Neoglacial deposits. Recent work in the Wind River Mountains also shows loess to be a good indicator of age (Birkeland and Miller, 1973).

Soils can be used to differentiate deposits

over the time span from the present to at least the Pinedale. In the past, however, few quantitative data have been used to support correlations based on soils, and correlations based mainly on soil descriptions are difficult to make. A major problem encountered in this study is that the pre-Neoglacial soils on rock glaciers commonly form from loess overlying rock glacier deposits, and, in places these have to be compared with soils formed entirely from rock or ice glacier deposits. Soil properties useful for age differentiation have to be found within the loesses, tills and rock glacier mantles; perhaps the progressive etching of weatherable heavy minerals could provide the necessary data. Another problem that needs more work is the origin of the textural B horizons. If the clay in these horizons can be ascribed to formation in place, the soil could be quite old. If, however, the clay is due only to the translocation of original clay, the soil may be much younger.

Much past stratigraphic work on young deposits has dealt with the construction of curves depicting the size of lichens vs. age of the substrate (work cited in this issue); however, similar curves could be derived for data on rock weathering. An example of these are the curves for lichen cover, rock weathering and pebble roundness vs. time of Carrara and Andrews (1972). These curves, and others (e.g., Figure 7), can be used to assign approximate ages to deposits. More curves for more areas and for other age-dating parameters need to be developed. Furthermore, we need to know more about the shapes of the curves, because some could be linear and others could be sigmoidal. We also need more data on the interaction of lichens and rock weathering, because Jackson and Keller (1970) have shown that rinds develop more rapidly in the presence of lichens than in their absence. It might be that increased rates of rind formation follow the attainment of a full lichen cover.

ACKNOWLEDGMENTS

This work was supported by funds from the University of Colorado Council on Research and Creative Work. All laboratory work was done by Rolf Kihl of INSTAAR. I thank John Empsall for assisting me during part of the field study, and J. T. Andrews, J. B. Benedict, W. C. Mahaney, S. E. White, Brian Whalley, and the graduate students in my Quaternary Stratigraphy course for their critical discussion in the field and office. In addition, Andrews, Benedict, and D. R. Crandell critically reviewed an earlier version of this manuscript and offered many helpful suggestions for its improvement. Finally, I am grateful to Mr. and Mrs. K. D. Ferguson of Carbondale, Colorado, for allowing me access to the north side of the mountain.

REFERENCES

Andrews, J. T., Carrara, P. E., Bartos, F., and Stuckenrath, R.
　1973 : Holocene stratigraphy and geochronology of four bogs (3,700 m), San Juan Mountains, SW Colorado, and implications to the Neoglacial record. *Geol. Soc. Amer. Abstracts with Programs*, 5(6): 460-461.

Benedict, J. B.
　1967 : Recent glacial history of an alpine area in the Colorado Front Range, U.S.A., I. Establishing a lichen-growth curve. *J. Glaciol.*, 6: 817-832.
　1968 : Recent glacial history of an alpine area in the Colorado Front Range, U.S.A., II. Dating the glacial deposits. *J. Glaciol.*, 7: 77-87.
　1970 : Downslope soil movement in a Colorado alpine region: rates, processes, and climatic significance. *Arct. Alp. Res.*, 2: 165-226.

　in press : Chronology of cirque glaciation in the Colorado Front Range. *Quat. Res.*

Birkeland, P. W., Crandell, D. R., and Richmond, G. M.
　1971 : Status of correlation of Quaternary stratigraphic units in the western conterminous United States. *Quat. Res.*, 1: 208-227.

Birkeland, P. W. and Miller, C. D.
　1973 : Re-interpretation of the type Temple Lake moraine, and other Neoglacial deposits, southern Wind River Mountains, Wyoming. *Geol. Soc. Amer. Abstracts with Programs*, 5(6): 465-466.

Birman, J. H.
　1964 : Glacial geology across the crest of the Sierra Nevada, California. *Geol. Soc. Amer. Spec. Pap.*, 75, 80 pp.

Blackwelder, E. B.
　1927 : Fire as an agent in rock weathering. *J. Geol.*, 35: 134-140.

1931 : Pleistocene glaciation in the Sierra Nevada and Basin Ranges. *Geol. Soc. Amer. Bull.*, 42: 865-922.

Caine, N.
1968 : The blockfields of northeastern Tasmania. *Australian Natl. Univ.* (*Canberra*), *Dept. Geogr. Publ.* G/6. 127 pp.

Carrara, P. E. and Andrews, J. T.
1972 : The Quaternary history of northern Cumberland Peninsula, Baffin Island, N.W.T., I: The late- and Neoglacial deposits of the Akudlermuit and Boas Glaciers. *Can. J. Earth Sci.*, 9: 403-414.

1973 : Holocene deposits in the alpine of the San Juan Mountains, SW Colorado. *Geol. Soc. Amer. Abstracts with Programs*, 5(6): 469-470.

Curry, R. R.
1971 : Glacial and Pleistocene history of the Mammoth Lakes Sierra, California, a geologic guidebook. *Univ. Montana Geol. Ser.*, Publ. no. 11. 49 pp.

1973 : Late glacial and Neoglacial chronology —a call for resolution. *Geol. Soc. Amer. Abstracts with Programs*, 5(6): 474-475.

Foland, K. A.
1967 : Structure and petrology of the Mount Sopris stock, Pitkin County, Colorado. Unpublished senior thesis, Bucknell Univ. 55 pp.

Hack, J. T.
1943 : Antiquity of the Finley site. *Amer. Antiquity*, 8: 235-241.

Jackson, T. A. and Keller, W. D.
1970 : A comparative study of the role of lichens and "inorganic" processes in the chemical weathering of recent Hawaiian lava flows. *Amer. J. Sci.*, 269: 446-466.

Madole, R. F.
1969 : Pinedale and Bull Lake glaciation in upper St. Vrain drainage basin, Boulder County, Colorado. *Arct. Alp. Res.*, 1: 279-287.

1972 : Neoglacial facies in the Colorado Front Range. *Arct. Alp. Res.*, 4: 119-130.

Mahaney, W. C.
1970 : Soil genesis during Neoglacial and late Pleistocene time in the Indian Peaks of the Colorado Front Range. Unpublished Ph.D. thesis, Univ. of Colorado. 246 pp.

1971 : Note on the "Arikaree Stade" of the Rocky Mountains Neoglacial. *J. Glaciol.*, 10: 143-144.

1972 : Audubon: New name for Colorado Front Range Neoglacial deposits formerly called "Arikaree." *Arct. Alp. Res.*, 4: 355-357.

1973a: Neoglacial chronology in the Fourth of July Cirque, central Colorado Front Range. *Geol. Soc. Amer. Bull.*, 84: 161-170.

1973b: Neoglacial chronology in the Fourth of July Cirque, central Colorado Front Range: Reply. *Geol. Soc. Amer. Bull.*, 84(11).

Miller, C. D.
1971 : Quaternary glacial events in the northern Sawatch Range, Colorado. Unpublished Ph.D. thesis, Univ. of Colorado. 86 pp.

1973 : Chronology of Neoglacial deposits in the Northern Sawatch Range, Colorado. *Arct. Alp. Res.*, 5(4): 385-400.

Moss, J. H.
1951 : Late glacial advances in the southern Wind River Mountains, Wyoming. *Amer. J. Sci.*, 249: 865-883.

Nelson, R. L.
1954 : Glacial geology of the Frying Pan River drainage, Colorado. *J. Geol.*, 62: 325-343.

Pilkington, H. D.
1954 : Petrography and petrology of a part of Mount Sorpris stock, Pitkin County, Colorado. Unpublished M.S. thesis, Univ. of Colorado. 27 pp.

Pillmore, C. L.
1954 : Petrography and petrology of a part of Mount Sopris stock, Pitkin County, Colorado. Unpublished M.S. thesis, Univ. of Colorado. 40 pp.

Porter, S. C. and Denton, G. H.
1967 : Chronology of neoglaciation in the North American Cordillera. *Amer. J. Sci.*, 265: 177-210.

Porter, S. C. and Denton, G. H.
1969 : *Pleistocene geology of the east-central Cascade Range, Washington.* Guidebook for third Pacific Coast Friends of the Pleistocene field conf. (Sept. 27-28, 1969). 54 pp.

Powers, M. C.
1953 : A new roundness scale for sedimentary particles. *J. Sed. Petrol.*, 23: 117-119.

Richmond, G. M.
1960 : Glaciation of the east slope of Rocky Mountain National Park, Colorado. *Geol. Soc. Amer. Bull.*, 71: 1371-1382.

1962 : Quaternary stratigraphy of the La Sal Mountains, Utah. *U.S. Geol. Surv. Prof. Pap.*, 324. 135 pp.

1965 : Glaciation of the Rocky Mountains. *In* Wright, H. E., Jr. and Frey, D. G. (eds.), *The Quaternary of the United States.* Princeton Univ. Press, Princeton, 217-230.

Sharp, R. P.
1969 : Semiquantitative differentiation of glacial moraines near Convict Lake, Sierra

Nevada, California. *J. Geol.,* 77: 68-91.

Wahrhaftig, C. and Cox, A.
    1959 : Rock glaciers in the Alaska Range. *Geol. Soc. Amer. Bull.,* 70: 383-436.

Weber, W. M.
    1972 : Correlation of Pleistocene glaciation in the Bitterroot Range, Montana, with fluctuations of Glacial Lake Missoula. *Mont. Bur. Mines and Geol. Mem.,* 42. 42 pp.

Williams, J.
    1973 : Neoglacial chronology of the Fourth of July Cirque, central Colorado Front Range: Discussion. *Geol. Soc. Amer., Bull.,* 84(11).

Yount, J. C.
    1970 : A Neoglacial chronology for the Independence Pass area, Colorado, using graph-theoretic classification methods. Unpublished M.S. thesis, Univ. of Colorado. 82 pp.

Relative Age Dating Techniques and a Late Quaternary Chronology, Arikaree Cirque, Colorado

ABSTRACT

Late Quaternary deposits in Arikaree Cirque are re-examined, using eight relative age dating methods including lichenometry. If snowkill of lichens is unrecognized, an erroneously young age may be assigned to Neoglacial deposits if only lichenometric methods are employed. The data were entered into two clustering programs, which were used to group sample sites according to age. The results of this study differ from those of Benedict (1968) in two ways: (1) no deposits of unequivocal Audubon age are believed to exist in Arikaree Cirque—those deposits previously thought to be Audubon age have an Audubon lichen cover because of snowkill of the original lichen cover sometime after deposition; and (2) deposits originally mapped as Temple Lake are thought to include both pre-altithermal (Pinedale) and post-altithermal (early Neoglacial) deposits.

Tom Carroll
Institute of Arctic and Alpine Research and
Department of Geography
University of Colorado
Boulder, Colorado 80302

INTRODUCTION

Recently, several workers have dated late Quaternary alpine glaciations in the Rocky Mountains by relative age dating methods. Mahaney (1973a, 1973b) and Williams (1973) used a variety of such methods to develop a chronology of the Fourth of July Cirque in the Colorado Front Range. Birkeland (1973) used these methods in a stratigraphic study of rock glacier deposits on Mt. Sopris, Colorado. In a re-examination of the type Temple Lake moraine and other deposits in the Wind River Mountains, Wyoming, Birkeland and Miller (1973) used a selection of relative age dating techniques.

This paper describes eight relative age dating methods and their application in mapping the late Quaternary deposits in Arikaree Cirque in the Colorado

Figure 1. Arikaree Cirque. Neoglacial deposits represented by arcuate moraine to left of Arikaree Glacier. Rock glacier of late Pinedale age shown at lower center.

Front Range. This particular cirque is important to Rocky Mountain studies because it was originally the type locality for the "Arikaree" of Benedict (1968), since renamed Audubon by Mahaney (1972). This study suggests that deposits originally mapped as Audubon (Benedict, 1968) are much older, and that deposits originally mapped as Temple Lake include both pre-altithermal and post-altithermal deposits. The study further suggests that several relative age dating methods give the best indication of the age of a deposit; the use of only one or two methods can give misleading age interpretations.

RELATIVE AGE DATING TECHNIQUES

A summary of relative age dating methods has been given by Birkeland (1973). Because each worker develops his own standards and definitions, however, a brief description of the criteria used in this study follows:

1. Fresh to weathered ratios: At each site a count of 100 coarse-grained granitic boulders was taken randomly. A boulder is considered weathered if more than 10 percent of its exposed area has individual grains standing in relief. A weathered boulder is rough to the touch, whereas a fresh boulder feels smoother (Birman, 1964; Blackwelder, 1931).

2. Pitted to nonpitted ratios: One hundred coarse-grained granitic boulders were randomly selected. A boulder is considered pitted if it has one or more closed depressions that appear to have formed as a result of grain-by-grain disintegration (in other words, there was no spalling).

3. Depth of pits: The depth of a pit was measured from the bottom to a reconstructed upper surface. This gives a minimum pit depth because the edge or crest of a pit probably also has

weathered; at each site the maximum pit depth found was recorded.

4. Thickness of oxidized weathering rinds: As the iron-bearing minerals weather with time, the weathering products discolor the outer parts of the rocks (Nelson, 1954). The maximum thickness of weathering rinds was recorded for coarse-grained granitic rocks at each site.

5. Maximum height of mafic inclusions: Mafic inclusions are the opposite of a pit; that is, grain-by-grain disintegration has taken place around an inclusion, leaving an upstanding rock knob. At each site the mafic inclusion in greatest relief was recorded.

6. Roundness analysis: Roundness analysis of glacial and fluvioglacial material has been used to help determine the age and origin of the deposit by Powers (1953). At the time of deposition, rocks and boulders were quite sharp and angular (for example, Gannett Peak deposits in the Colorado Front Range and the Wind River Mountains of Wyoming). As the deposit weathers, the sharp

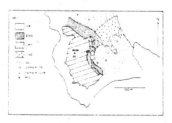

Figure 2. Arikaree Cirque. GP = Gannett Peak; ENG = early Neoglacial; LPD = late Pinedale; UND = undifferentiated ground moraine; SKL = lichen snowkill line; MS = meteorological station; P = point from where Figure 1 photograph was taken.

Geology, 2(7): 321-325.

TABLE 1. RESULTS OF RELATIVE AGE TECHNIQUES IN ARIKAREE CIRQUE

Site (Fig. 2)*	Weathered (%)†	Fresh (%)	Pitted (%)	Nonpitted (%)	Max. pit (mm)	Max. height of mafic (mm)	Max. depth of rinds (mm)	Lichen cover (%)	Max. R. geographicum lichen (mm)	Angular (%)	Subangular (%)	Rounded (%)	Well rounded (%)	Age§
4	0	100	0	100	0	0	0	0	0	100	0	0	0	GP
3	19	81	0	100	0	0	6	23	35	68	19	13	0	ENG
1	65	35	0	100	0	0	0	17	75	56	37	7	0	ENG
2	56	44	18	82	52	7	10	30	36	28	48	20	4	ENG
5	82	18	0	100	0	0	12	19	31	10	76	9	5	ENG
7	76	24	0	100	0	0	0	15	13	26	42	28	4	ENG
6	92	8	72	28	95	123	7			4	10	34	52	LPD
8	78	22	7	93	35	45	0			3	13	64	20	LPD
9	86	14	16	84	105	64	0			0	15	57	28	LPD
10	94	6	58	42	92	152	21			0	4	22	74	LPD
11	87	13	13	87	33	22	0			0	10	46	44	LPD
12	89	11	48	52	35	115	18			0	0	28	72	LPD
13	77	23	28	72	35	0	18			0	0	17	83	LPD
GL	83	19	39	61	41	37	16			0	7	24	69	LPD
ML	87	13	29	71	39	31	14			0	6	16	78	LPD
Relative age-dating technique	B 1	B 1	2	2	B 3	5	B 4	B 7	B 8	6	6	6	B 6	

* GL = Green Lakes site; ML = Mitchell Lake site.
† B = "best" variable.
§ GP = Gannett Peak; ENG = early Neoglacial; LPD = late Pinedale.

TABLE 2. RESULTS OF REVISIT BY ANDREWS AND BIRKELAND

Site (Fig. 2)	Pit (%)	No pit (%)	Weathered (%)	Fresh (%)	Max. rind thickness (mm) Coarse	Fine	Rind (%) Coarse	Fine	Age*	Worker†
1	0	100	44	56					ENG	JTA
1			4	96		5			ENG	PWB
2	16	84	40	44	2	9	4	20	ENG	JTA
2	12	88	16	84	5				ENG	PWB
3	8	92	32	60					ENG	JTA
5	32	68							LPD	JTA
5	24	76	64	12					LPD	JTA
10	65	35	55	45	15	5			LPD	PWB
10	44	56	44	16	15	4			LPD	JTA
10	46	54	40	16					LPD	JTA
10					12	3	32	48	LPD	JTA, PWB

Note: Boulder weathering criteria used by Andrews are described by Dugdale (1972) and are not the criteria described here.

* ENG = early Neoglacial; LPD = late Pinedale.
† JTA = J. T. Andrews; PWB = P. W. Birkeland.

edges become more rounded. Four roundness categories are used in this study: (a) angular, (b) subangular, (c) rounded, and (d) well rounded. At each site 100 coarse-grained granitic boulders were classified as belonging to one of the four categories.

7 and 8. Lichenometry: Beschel (1961) has shown that the diameter of *Rhizocarpon geographicum* s.1. (*sensu lato* because of uncertainty in taxonomy) and the percentage of cover of all lichens on rock surfaces increased with time. Consequently, the largest *R. geographicum* s.1. thalli was recorded for each of the sites. The percentage of cover of all lichens was also estimated at each site for all boulders in a circular area approximately 5 m in diameter (Dugdale, 1972).

STRATIGRAPHIC NOMENCLATURE

The stratigraphic nomenclature of late Quaternary glacial deposits in the Rocky Mountains has become increasingly confusing. Clarifications have been given by Birkeland (1973) and Benedict (1973). This paper refers to three Neoglacial advances (Benedict, 1968, 1973; Birkeland, 1973): Gannett Peak (ca. 100 to 300 yr B.P.), Audubon (ca. 950 to 1,850 yr B.P.), and early Neoglacial (ca. 3,000 to 5,000 yr B.P.). The altithermal, a period of possible warm, dry climate, occurred between 5,000 and 10,000 yr B.P., with a peak from 6,000 to 7,500 yr B.P. (Benedict, 1973). The late stade of the Pinedale glaciation closed at approximately 10,000 yr B.P. (Birkeland, 1973) and probably includes the type Temple Lake moraine (Birkeland and Miller, 1972).

STUDY AREA

The study area is located just down-valley from the Arikaree Glacier in the Indian Peaks area of the Colorado Front Range; the study concentrates on the glacial and rock glacier deposits located on the basin floor. Elevations of the area range from 3,780 to 3,800 m above sea level (Fig. 1).

Thirteen sample sites were examined within the cirque basin. Two additional sites of known late Pinedale age outside the cirque basin (R. F. Madole, oral commun., 1972) are included for comparison. The Green Lakes (GL on Table 1) sample site is in the alpine tundra 3.2 km downvalley from the Arikaree Cirque basin at an elevation of 3,410 m; the deposit appears to be ablation till. The Mitchell Lake (ML on Table 1) site, 5.8 km northeast of Arikaree Cirque at an elevation of 3,280 m, is a small moraine mapped as late Pinedale age (Madole, 1969). A C^{14} date from the base of the peat in a nearby bog gives a minimum date for local ice-free conditions of 7,690 ± 115 yr B.P. (St-3,898; Madole and Bachhuber, 1973; Madole, oral commun., 1973).

RESULTS

The data collected at each site are summarized in Table 1, and those from Arikaree Cirque are shown in Figure 2. Unquestionably, relative age dating techniques are subjective; no two workers are completely consistent in field definitions or in the classification of rock weathering and lichen parameters. It is desirable, however, that different workers get the same age differentiations in their data, which consequently will allow them to differentiate deposits of different ages even though their operational definitions may not be identical. To test this, Arikaree Cirque was revisited in September 1973 by P. W. Birkeland and J. T. Andrews, who collected data from selected sites (Table 2). A comparison of Table 1 (my data) with Table 2 (their

data) shows that different workers using subjective criteria can yield similar results.

COMPUTER ANALYSIS

One method of analysis of the data collected (Table 1) is the multivariate analysis of CHARANAL, a computer program using information- and graph-theory methods for nominal and ordinal scale data (Estabrook, 1966, 1967). This approach has been applied successfully to geologic problems and is discussed in detail by Andrews and Estabrook (1971) and Andrews and Dugdale (1971). A portion of the output from CHARANAL selects the "best" relative age dating methods used in the study (the methods that tell the most information about a deposit). The "best" methods

used in the study are denoted by "B" in Table 1. The data of the "best" methods used to describe the deposits can then be entered into GRAPH, a computer program that clusters similar field sites on the basis of the "best" weathering and lichen data (Andrews and Estabrook, 1971; Andrews and Dugdale, 1971; Estabrook, 1966, 1967; Hawksworth and others, 1968).

A portion of the output from GRAPH is a computer-drawn "skyline" grouping of sites of a similar age (Fig. 4). On the Y-axis of the cluster diagram is the similarity (C) value. If the ordinal representation of the weathering and lichen data of two sites were identical, those two sites would have a C-value of 1.0. For any given C-value, a corresponding number of clusters can be identified.

TABLE 3. SUMMARY OF RECENT RELATIVE AGE DATA FOR THE ROCKY MOUNTAINS

Age	Weathered (%)	Pitted (%)	Depth of pit (mm)	Maximum rind thickness (mm)	Max. R. geographi-cum diameter (mm)	Lichen cover (%)	Worker* Location†
Gannett Peak	0	0	0	0	7	0–5	PB, DM—WR
	0	0	0	0	<22	0–5	PB—MS
			1–3	0	15	0–5	WM—FR
			0	0	35	0–5	JW—FR
					20	0–5	JB—FR
Audubon	0	Few	25–30		46	30–50	PB, DM—WR
	27	0			<42	<50	PB—MS
			8–10	2–3	41	25–40	WM—FR
			3–7	0	60	50	JW—FR
					42–71	10–40	JB—FR
Early Neoglacial	30	53	70–80		107	85	PB, DM—WR
	48	0		14	>50	>50	PB—MS
			10–20	5–10	102–125	50–80	WM—FR
			6–14	3	85	60–80	JW—FR
					107–150	80–95	JB—FR
Late Pinedale	61	76	130–160		..	≥85	PB, DM—WR#
	90	21	60§	45			PB—MS
							WM—FR
			7–14	9			JW—FR
							JB—FR

* PB = P. W. Birkeland (1973); PB, DM = P. W. Birkeland and C. D. Miller (1973); JB = J. B. Benedict (1968); WM = W. C. Mahaney (1973); and JW = J. Williams (1973).
† MS = Mt. Sopris, Colorado; WR = Wind River Mountains, Wyoming; and FR = Front Range, Colorado.
§ From P. W. Birkeland (1973, oral commun.).
# Data collected at type Temple Lake.

54

Each cluster is composed of sites that are most similar to other sites in the same cluster. Because relative age dating criteria are used to characterize each site, each cluster represents sites of a similar age. When C = 0.64, two clusters are described. Cluster I is composed of sites 1 through 4; cluster II includes sites 5 and 6, 8 through 13, and ML (Fig. 2). Site GL (Table 1) was not entered into the cluster diagram (Fig. 4) because the ordinal representation of the weathering and lichen data of that site is identical to that of site 12. Consequently, because the two sites both have a C-value of 1.0, data from one of the two identical sites can be deleted from the analysis.

RELATIVE AGE ASSIGNMENTS

The above data can be used to assign relative ages to the study sites. Other workers in the Rocky Mountains have used relative age dating criteria for the assignment of ages to late Quaternary deposits. Table 3 is a summary of weathering and lichen data and age assignments by Birkeland (1973) for Mt. Sopris, Colorado; by Birkeland and Miller (1973) for the Wind River Mountains, Wyoming; and by Mahaney (1973a), Williams (1973), and Benedict (1968) for the Colorado Front Range. Based in part on the age assignments by these workers, ages were assigned to each of the 13 sites in the cirque (Table 1; Fig. 2).

Comparison with Previous Work in Arikaree Cirque. Benedict (1968) mapped the deposits in this cirque primarily on the basis of lichenometry (Fig. 3), whereas Mahaney (1970) worked on the soil genesis of the region. With the exception of one part of one moraine, Mahaney (1970) was in complete agreement with Benedict (1968) on the age of the deposits in the Arikaree Cirque. Based on my studies, I believe that Benedict (1968) was unable to differentiate between early Neoglacial and late Pinedale using lichenometric methods. The rock glacier (Fig. 2) was found, by using rock-weathering techniques, to be of late Pinedale age, whereas Benedict (1968), using lichenometric methods, assigned an early Neoglacial age (Fig. 3). It should be remembered that the maximum size of the growth curve for *R. geographicum* s.l. is reached by 3,000 yr (Benedict, 1967); consequently, *R. geographicum* s.l. on a 10,000-yr-old deposit may be no larger than on a 3,000-yr-old deposit.

The type locality of the "Arikaree" advance was established in the Arikaree Cirque (Benedict, 1968). However, it was subsequently moved to a lateral moraine on the north flank of Arapahoe

Cirque and was renamed Audubon (Mahaney, 1971, 1972). Benedict (1968, Fig. 3) identified a significant part of the deposits in the Arikaree basin as being Audubon in age on the basis of lichenometry. However, the results of the eight relative age dating methods described here indicate that all of the Audubon deposits mapped by Benedict (1968, Fig. 3) are no younger than early Neoglacial (Fig. 2).

What caused an Audubon lichen cover to develop on older deposits in the Arikaree Cirque? Probably the deposits were laid down during early Neoglacial time or earlier. During the Audubon stade, "as much as 90 percent of the floors of some alpine valleys were buried for a sufficient length of time to destroy the pre-existing lichen cover" (Benedict, 1973, p. 593). Although there is no conclusive evidence for an ice advance in the cirque during Audubon time, the extensive snow cover in the cirque during this time probably killed all pre-existing lichens in the snow-covered area. After the extensive snow cover deposited during Audubon time melted, an Audubon lichen cover developed on the rocks.

Relative Age Assignments of Sites. Figure 4 clearly shows that the 13 sites in the cirque cluster into two distinct age groups. Because the two clusters are derived from relative age criteria, each cluster includes sites of an inferred similar age. Both sites of known late Pinedale age are included in cluster II; this suggests that all the deposits in cluster II are probably of late Pinedale age. However, sites 5 and 7 are two of the last three sites to enter cluster II, indicating that *all* of their relative age characteristics do not necessarily reflect a late Pinedale age. This is expected because they both possess an Audubon-age lichen cover (Fig. 3; Benedict, 1968).

Cluster I includes three sites that have early Neoglacial weathering characteristics. Site 4 also clusters in the early Neoglacial grouping, even though it is clearly of Gannett Peak age (Table 1; Figs. 1 and 2; Benedict, 1968). This is expected because only one Gannett Peak site was examined; more than one Gannett Peak site would have to be entered into the GRAPH analysis before a "Gannett Peak cluster" could result.

"BEST" ROCK-WEATHERING TECHNIQUES

As previously mentioned, part of the output from the CHARANAL analysis tells which dating technique contains the most information about all the sites (Andrews and Dugdale, 1971; Andrews and Estabrook, 1971). In this study, oxidized weathering rind thickness was the

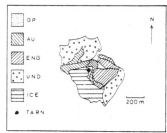

Figure 3. Arikaree Cirque (after Benedict, 1968). GP = Gannett Peak; Au = Audubon; ENG = early Neoglacial; UND = undifferentiated talus.

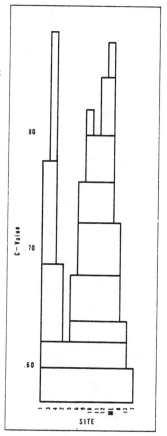

Figure 4. "Skyline" age cluster. ML = Mitchell Lake site.

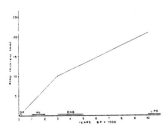

Figure 5. Plot of maximum rind thickness found at sites of different ages. GP = Gannett Peak; Au = Audubon; ENG = early Neoglacial; LPD = late Pinedale.

"best" rock weathering method used (that is, the technique that gave the most information about each site). On Mt. Sopris, "weathering rinds provide the best weathering index for relative age assignment" (Birkeland, 1973, p. 408); in the Fourth of July Cirque, weathering "rinds were particularly useful for distinguishing Neoglacial from older deposits" (Williams, 1973, p. 3761). Figure 5 is a plot of the *single* thickest weathering rind from coarse-grained granitic boulders found on deposits of each age. The 12-mm rind at site 5 (Table 1), an Audubon locality of Benedict (1968), falls far off

the curve. If the debris at site 5 were deposited during Audubon time, Figure 5 would suggest that the maximum rind thickness should be about 3 mm. In support of this, Mahaney (1973) reported rind thicknesses of 2 to 3 mm on deposits of Audubon age. Also, I found rinds of 2 mm on coarse-grained granitic rocks of Audubon age at the new type locality of Mahaney (1971). This seems to strongly suggest that the material of site 5 (Fig. 2) was deposited during early Neoglacial time at the latest.

CONCLUSIONS

Radiometric techniques are the most desirable method of dating late Quaternary deposits, but reliable C^{14} dates of western United States alpine glaciations are few and too often give only minimum or maximum dates. In the absence of C^{14} dates, relative age dating techniques may be used to assign relative ages to glacial deposits. However, some techniques may be subject to processes unrelated to time (Benedict, 1973). It seems that lichenometry is quite susceptible to influences unrelated to time because various environmental factors can affect the growth of *R. geographicum* s.l.

(Beschel, 1961; Benedict, 1967). Of particular importance is the loss of a lichen cover caused by a period of prolonged snow cover. This seems to have happened in Arikaree Cirque. Deposits previously mapped as Audubon have an Audubon lichen cover because the lichen cover that initially grew on these deposits was killed during Audubon time. These deposits are now thought to be pre-Audubon in age, as shown by the eight relative age dating methods. No deposits of unequivocal Audubon age were found in Arikaree Cirque.

Rock-weathering techniques can be used to identify deposits older than 3,000 yr B.P., the limit of the *R. geographicum* s.l. growth curve in the Colorado Front Range. By employing these techniques in the Arikaree Cirque, deposits of both late Pinedale and early Neoglacial age can be differentiated; all these particular deposits were previously mapped as early Neoglacial on the basis of lichenometry alone.

Deposits similar in age to the Audubon stade were recognized by Denton and Karlén (1973) as resulting from a relatively minor glacial expansion limited to western North America. Thus it is important to re-examine many areas for possible Audubon-equivalent deposits.

REFERENCES CITED

Andrews, J. T., and Dugdale, R. E., 1971, Quaternary history of northern Cumberland Peninsula, Baffin Island, N.W.T. Pt. V. Factors affecting corrie glacierization on Okoa Bay: Quaternary Research, v. 1, no. 4, p. 532–551.

Andrews, J. T., and Estabrook, G., 1971, Application of information and graph theory to multivariate geomorphological analysis: Jour. Geology, v. 79, p. 207–221.

Benedict, J. B., 1967, Recent glacial history of an alpine area in the Colorado Front Range, U.S.A., I. Establishing a lichen-growth curve: Jour. Glaciology, v. 6, no. 48, p. 817–832.

—— 1968, Recent glacial history of an alpine area in the Colorado Front Range, U.S.A., II. Dating the glacial deposits: Jour. Glaciology, v. 7, no. 49, p. 77–87.

—— 1973, Chronology of cirque glaciation, Colorado Front Range: Quaternary Research, v. 3, no. 4, p. 584–599.

Beschel, R. E., 1961, Dating rock surfaces by lichen growth and its application to glaciology and physiography (lichenometry), in Raasch, G. O., ed., Geology of the Arctic. Vol. 2: Toronto, Univ. Toronto Press, p. 1044–1062.

Birkeland, P. W., 1973, Use of relative age dating methods in a stratigraphic study of rock glacier deposits, Mt. Sopris, Colorado: Arctic and Alpine Research, v. 5, 401–416.

Birkeland, P. W., and Miller, C. D., 1973, Re-interpretation of the type Temple Lake moraine, and other Neoglacial deposits, southern Wind River Mountains, Wyoming: Geol. Soc. America, Abs. with Programs, v. 5, no. 6, p. 465–466.

Birman, J. H., 1964, Glacial geology across the crest of the Sierra Nevada, California: Geol. Soc. America Spec. Paper 75, 80. p.

Blackwelder, E. B., 1931, Pleistocene glaciation in the Sierra Nevada and Basin Ranges: Geol. Soc. America Bull., v. 42, p. 865–922.

Denton, G. H., and Karlén, W., 1973, Holocene climatic variations—Their pattern and possible cause: Quaternary Research, v. 3, no. 4, p. 155–205.

Dugdale, R. E., 1972, Quaternary history of the northern Cumberland Peninsula, Baffin Island, N.W.T. Pt. III. The late glacial deposits of Sulung and Itidlirn Valleys and adjacent parts of the Maktak-Narpaing Trough: Canadian Jour. Earth Sci., v. 9, p. 366–374.

Estabrook, G. F., 1966, A mathematical model in GRAPH theory for biological classification: Theoretical Biology, v. 12, p. 297–310.

—— 1967, An information theory model for character and analysis: Taxon, v. 16, p. 86–97.

Hawksworth, F. G., Estabrook, G. F., and Rogers, D. J., 1968, Application of an information theory model for character analysis in the genus *Arceuthobium viscaceal*: Taxon, v. 17, no. 6, p. 605–619.

Madole, R. F., 1969, Pinedale and Bull Lake glaciation in upper St. Vrain drainage basin, Boulder County, Colorado: Arctic and Alpine Research, v. 1, p. 279–287.

Madole, R. F., and Bachhuber, F. W., 1973, Geomorphology, palynology, and paleomagnetic record of glacial Lake Devlin, Front Range: Geol. Soc. America, Rocky Mtn. Sec., 26th Ann. Mtg., Boulder, Univ. Colorado, 25 p.

Mahaney, W. C., 1970, Soil genesis during

Neoglacial and late Pleistocene time in the Indian Peaks of the Colorado Front Range [Ph.D. thesis] : Boulder, Univ. Colorado, 246 p.

—— 1971, Note on the "Arikaree Stade" of the Rocky Mountains Neoglacial: Jour. Glaciology, v. 10, p. 143–144.

—— 1972, Audubon: New name for Colorado Front Range Neoglacial deposits formerly called "Arikaree": Arctic and Alpine Research, v. 4, p. 355–357.

—— 1973a, Neoglacial chronology in the Fourth of July Cirque, central Colorado Front Range: Geol. Soc. America Bull., v. 84, p. 161–170.

—— 1973b, Neoglacial chronology in the Fourth of July Cirque, central Colorado Front Range: Reply: Geol. Soc. America Bull., v. 84, p. 3767–3772.

Nelson, R. L., 1954, Glacial geology of the Frying Pan River drainage, Colorado: Jour. Geology, v. 62, p. 325–343.

Powers, M. C., 1953, A new roundness scale for sedimentary particles: Jour. Sed. Petrology, v. 23, p. 117–119.

Williams, J., 1973, Neoglacial chronology of the Fourth of July Cirque, central Colorado Front Range: Discussion: Geol. Soc. America Bull., v. 84, p. 3761–3765.

ACKNOWLEDGMENTS

Reviewed by P. W. Birkeland, R. F. Madole, and J. T. Andrews.

Comment : Relative Age Dating Techniques . . .

Sidney E. White

Department of Geology and Mineralogy

Ohio State University, Columbus, Ohio 43210

The combination of several relative age dating techniques by Carroll (1974, accompanying paper), and thereby the consequent establishment of a Neoglacial chronology for Arikaree Cirque in the Colorado Front Range, is an example of the professional effort expected of one currently working in late Quaternary stratigraphy. Carroll's eight age-dating methods increase the number of elements a specialist should examine to meet the approval of the scientific community in this proliferating field. Based upon studies in the southern and middle Rocky Mountains, the western United States, Alaska, northeastern Arctic Canada, Greenland, Scandinavia, New Zealand, and Antarctica, more than 25 papers on Neoglaciation using most, but not all, of these parameters were published in 1972 and 1973 alone.

Earlier workers in Colorado mapped Neoglacial deposits, some quite meticulously, on the basis of Carroll's methods 3, 4, 7, and 8, as well as on the degree of soil-horizon development and on loess thickness. Methods 1 and 2 seemed to be automatically included during any consideration of methods 3 and 4 and were commonly used in any determination of multiple glaciation of regions at lower altitudes. Angularity of rock fragments from cirque headwall or valley-side cliff, whether produced by freeze-thaw or by glacier abrasion in moraine, rock glacier, or talus, seemed expected and hence precluded the need for roundness measurements. Roundness (or sphericity) may be more likely a measure of distance traveled. Carroll's method 5—maximum height of mafic inclusions—is a welcome and viable new reinforcement of age assignment in the alpine region. It is encouraging to note that the parameters previously used in mapping are among the CHARANAL "best" relative age dating techniques, as are Carroll's method 1 and his "well-rounded" category of method 6.

In Arikaree Cirque, Carroll's thesis, that on the basis of a post-early Neoglacial snow cover Audubon stade deposits as mapped by Benedict are not younger than early Neoglacial, is certainly a valid idea. Benedict's Temple Lake—now his Triple Lakes, 1973—deposit (1968, Fig. 2) probably is originally as old as late Pinedale but reactivated in early Neoglacial time and then covered with snow on its lower (less high) parts in Audubon time. Even today, after heavy spring snowfall, a late-lying snowbank covers the end moraine part of this deposit (between Carroll's sample sites 10 and 13) for most of each summer. This has resulted in subdivision by Benedict of one deposit because of differences in the percentage of lichen cover and in sizes of *Rhizocarpon* spp. thalli on it. On the basis of separate mapping, average maximum *Rhizocarpon* thalli diameters of 67 mm occur on the lower part (Benedict's end moraine), 35 mm on the middle part ordinarily beneath snow almost every summer (Carroll's undifferentiated ground moraine), and 88 mm on the windswept upper part exposed each summer (Benedict's rock glacier; Carroll's sites 10 and 9; compare Carroll's "Max Pit" on Table 1).

In addition, the explanation for such a large area of undifferentiated ground moraine on the cirque floor also is a cover of snow that lies there most summers until early August; this ground moraine likewise is of late Pinedale age, because active sorted nets and sorted polygons are well established on it.

Except for the arcuate moraine shown on Carroll's Figure 1, snow covers the moraine around the east and north periphery of Arikaree Glacier long into any summer. The rarely exposed unweathered boulders of this moraine (Benedict's [1968] Arikaree Stade end moraine–ground moraine, Fig. 2) east, north, and northwest of the tarn have a lichen cover of less than 5 percent. The moraine might have been mapped as Gannett Peak (now named Arapahoe Peak; Benedict, 1973) stade, but Benedict recognized the snow-cover situation here and mapped it as the Arikaree (now Audubon) stade. Benedict cautioned against indiscriminate use of lichen measurements, and he carefully indicated seven environmental factors known to affect lichen growth (1967, p. 818–821); it is clear that he used great care in his mapping here in Arikaree Cirque.

Alternatively, the north wall of Arikaree Cirque is a steep slope of loose rocks that moved downslope since Pinedale glaciers swept clean that north wall. The rock debris was produced after late Pinedale time and later was reactivated during the several Neoglacial Stades. This has produced complex blockfields (frost rubble sheets of Richmond) on the uppermost slopes, midslope rubble lobes and festoons, and small protalus lobes on the lower slopes (one is Benedict's type locality of his Arikaree stade). Windblown snow, caught between lobes and remaining in hollows in summer on this slope ever since late Pinedale time, produced marked differences in lichen cover and sizes. Any attempt at mapping Neoglacial deposits on such a slope is fraught with problems and has wisely been avoided: Benedict mapped it as being undifferentiated talus, Carroll, as being late Pinedale.

The mapping of Neoglacial deposits in the cirques and eastward along valley walls and ridge tops to the north and south of Arikaree Cirque has revealed many similar places where various lengths of snow-free growing seasons provide anomalous lichen covers and sizes. Carroll has successfully confronted one of the most bothersome problems in mapping Neoglacial deposits.

REFERENCES CITED

Benedict, J. B., 1967, Recent glacial history of an alpine area in the Colorado Front Range, U.S.A., I. Establishing a lichen-growth curve: Jour. Glaciology, v. 6, no. 48, p. 817–832.

—— 1968, Recent glacial history of an alpine area in the Colorado Front Range, U.S.A., II. Dating the glacial deposits: Jour. Glaciology, v. 7, no. 49, p. 77–87.

—— 1973, Chronology of cirque glaciation, Colorado Front Range: Quaternary Research, v. 3, no. 4, p. 584–599.

SOILS OF POST-AUDUBON AGE, TETON GLACIER AREA, WYOMING

W. C. Mahaney

Geography Department
York University
Toronto, Ontario, Canada

ABSTRACT

Glacial deposits of late Neoglacial age in the Teton Range are dated by use of relative age-dating criteria. Soils of post-Audubon (1,850 to 950 BP) and post-Gannett Peak (300 to 100 BP) age are recognized on moraine surfaces. Morphological, physical, and chemical characteristics of the post-Audubon soils are discussed and correlated with soils of the Colorado Front Range. Recent geomorphological and pedological investigations suggest that glacier fluctuations in the Teton Range during the late Neoglacial may be broadly synchronous with those defined elsewhere in the Rocky Mountains.

INTRODUCTION

Neoglaciation refers to the renewal of glaciers in western North America following a maximum shrinkage and/or disappearance during the Altithermal Interval (7,500 to 5,000 BP) (Benedict, 1973). Three Neoglacial advances are recognized in the Colorado Rocky Mountains: Triple Lakes, 5,000 to 3,000 BP (Benedict, 1973); Audubon, 1,850 to 950 BP (Benedict, 1968; Mahaney, 1972); and Gannett Peak, 300 to 100 BP (Richmond, 1960; Benedict, 1973). In the Wind River Mountains of Wyoming three stades of Neoglaciation are recognized: an early stade[1] correlating to the Triple Lakes in Colorado; an Audubon equivalent stade defined in the Temple Lake area (Birke-

land and Shroba, 1974); and the Gannett Peak (Richmond, 1965). Deposits of each stade are recognized largely on the basis of topographic position, landform morphology, weathered state of surface boulders, vegetation cover, and soil development. Attempts to produce absolute age-controls are generally restricted by the location of moraines well above existing timberline, absence of volcanic ash, and lack of organic materials suitable for radiocarbon dating (Mahaney, 1973a, 1973b). Recent pedological work on a large end moraine system at 3,000 to 3,160 m, in proximity to the Teton Glacier, suggests that the late Neoglacial in the Teton Range consists of two glacier fluctuations.

FIELD AREA

The Teton Glacier, one of a number of small cirque glaciers in Grand Teton National Park, lies in a northeast-facing position 1,000 m beneath the summit of the Grand Teton (4,198 m; Figure 1). Late 19th century positions of the

glacier have been sketched from photographs taken in 1898 by W. O. Owen indicating that the ice margin had receded 10 to 50 m from the crest of the terminal moraine (Fryxell, 1935). Later studies by Reed (1964, 1965,

---

[1]Temple Lake moraines at the type locality in the Wind River Mountains are referred to in the literature as both post- and pre-Altithermal (Birkeland, 1973; Birkeland and Miller, 1973; Currey, 1974; and Miller and Birkeland, 1974). Since

there is considerable controversy over the age of Temple Lake units, the name Temple Lake will not be used here. The earliest Neoglacial units are referred to as "early."

58

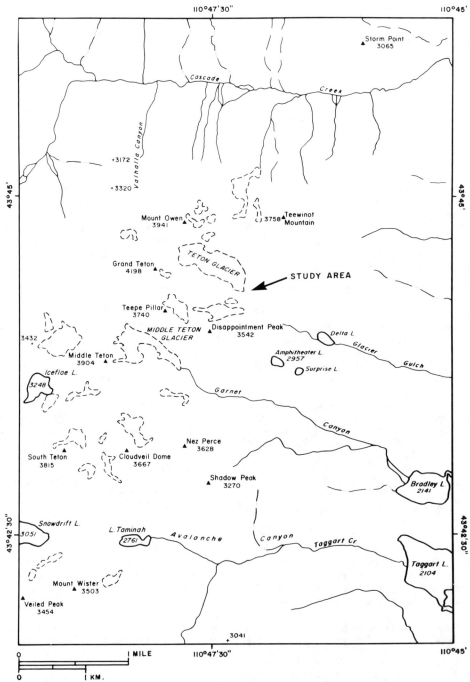

FIGURE 1. Map of the Teton Range showing major drainage features and location of the Teton Glacier. Adapted from the Grand Teton and Mount Moran quadrangles, U.S. Geol. Surv., 1:24,000 scale.

1967) show that the glacier had receded sharply since the early 20th century, with a decreasing rate of ice loss in the lower glacier, and an increase in the upper glacier from 1954 to 1963.

The moraine system in Glacier Gulch, near the terminus of the Teton Glacier, consists of fine-grained white and light gray granite, granite with large flakes of white mica, garnet-rich pegmatite, and gneiss.

Climatic data for the alpine zone in the Teton Range are lacking. A summary of 15 years (1955 to 1970) of nearly continuous meteorological data is available for Moran, Wyoming (elevation 2,071 m). The average air temperature for the 15-year period is 2.11°C, with mean maximum and minimum extremes of 9.83 and −5.67°C, respectively. Mean annual precipitation for the 30-year period 1941 to 1970 is 57.2 cm, with 480 cm of snow (U.S. Dept. Commerce, 1970). Employing the average lapse rate of 0.6°C · 100 m^{-1} (Cole, 1970), the average temperature at the terminus of the Teton Glacier is −4.7°C, with extreme mean maximum and minimum temperature of 3.0 and −12.5°C, respectively.

METHODS

The methods currently employed by the Soil Conservation Service (Soil Survey Staff, 1951, 1960) are used in the study, with the exception of the particle-size analysis which follows the Wentworth scale (Folk, 1968). Coarse grades (64 mm to 63μ) were calculated from dry sieving, and fine grades (less than 63μ) by sedimentation (Bouyoucos, 1962; Day, 1965). Clay samples were air-dried and X-rayed, following procedures outlined by Whittig (1965) and Birkeland (1969), on a Toshiba ADG-301H diffractometer with CuK α radiation.

Reactions were obtained from a 1:1 soil paste by glass electrode; total nitrogen by the Kjeldahl method (Bremner, 1965); organic matter by the Walkley-Black method (Walkley and Black, 1934); exchangeable basic cations and cation exchange capacity by ammonium acetate methods (Schollenberger and Simon, 1945; Peech et al., 1947); total soluble salts by electrical conductivity (Bower and Wilcox, 1965); exchangeable hydrogen by the Triethanolamine method (Olsen and Dean, 1965); and free iron oxide by the sodium dithionite-citrate method (Mehra and Jackson, 1960).

DATA AND RESULTS

A large, steep-sided (25 to 30°) and sharp-crested end moraine system at the terminus of the Teton Glacier has been dated by means of topographic position, lichen growth, and soil development (Figure 2). The younger proximal slopes of the moraine (Figure 3) generally have lichen-free boulders with occasional maximum diameters of *Lecanora thomsonii* and *Lecidea atrobrunnea* reaching 8 mm. *Rhizocarpon geographicum* is absent from these slopes. In most instances weathering profiles are not found on the proximal slopes as surface materials are fresh and occur as an open network of boulders. Where present, weathering profiles of 5 cm depth have Cn horizons bearing a light gray color (2.5Y 7 to 2.5Y 8), cobbly coarse sandy loam texture, massive structure, loose moist consistence, nonsticky and nonplastic when moist, with a surface pH of 7.0 to 8.0. This younger weathering profile correlates with the Gannett Peak stade defined elsewhere in the Rocky Mountains (Benedict, 1967, 1968, 1973; Mahaney, 1970, 1973a, 1973b, 1974).

Older distal slopes of the end moraine (Figure 4) display a lichen cover of 20 to 25% and maximum diameters of crustose lichens as follows: *Lecanora aspicilia*, 132 mm; *L. thomsonii*, 126 mm; *L. atrobrunnea*, 143 mm; and *R. geographicum*, 52 mm. Weathering pits are generally small, but where rocks are encrusted with lichen cover, pits may reach 6 to 10 mm in depth.

Representative soil profiles are described in Table 1. The post-Audubon soil consists of an A/Cox/Cn horizon sequence (Figure 5) with a total depth of weathering of 48 to 58 cm, which is somewhat deeper than those described by Birkeland and Shroba (1974) in the Wind River Range. A horizons vary from 8 to 10 cm thickness, while C horizons range from 40 to 48 cm. Soil colors for the A horizons are darker than colors in the subsurface horizons owing to slightly greater accumulation of organic matter. Sandy loam textures dominate in the horizons. Structure is granular in surface horizons where sufficient organic matter is available, and massive in the subsurface horizons. Unconfined shear strengths average 0.75 kg cm^{-2} for A horizons, and 1.10 kg cm^{-2} in C horizons.

The particle-size data suggest that coarse

60

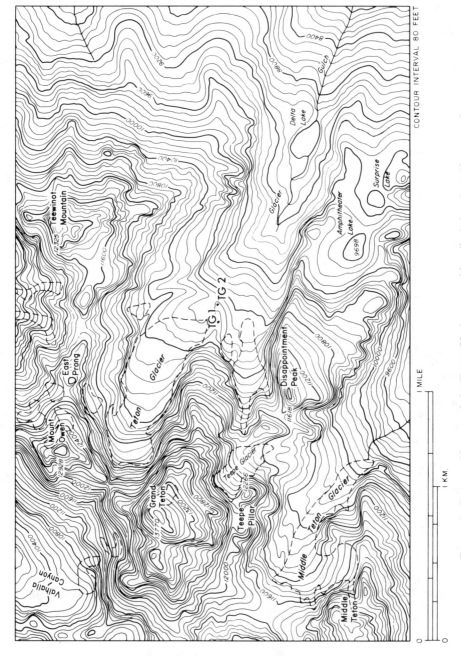

FIGURE 2. Topographic map of the Teton Glacier area with soil pit locations (for example, TG1). Adapted from the Grand Teton quadrangle, U.S. Geol. Surv., 1:24,000 scale.

FIGURE 3. Proximal slopes of Gannett Peak age and debris-laden ice of the Teton Glacier. The east flank of Mt. Owen is shown at left, and the east ridge of Teewinot at right.

FIGURE 4. Massive distal slopes of Audubon age.

grades (64 to 2 mm) are dominated by large and very large pebbles (Table 2). Insofar as the finer material (less than 2 mm) is concerned, sand dominates over silt and clay with values ranging between 72.9 and 56.4% in the A horizon. Data in Table 3 and Figures 6 and 7 indicate that sand is fairly evenly distributed between grades; silt tends to group in the coarse grades; and clay is dominated by the fine grade (less than 1.95μ). If the sand-plus-silt grades are considered the reactants and the clay grades the products (Barshad, 1967), the particle-size composition indicates only slight differences be-

tween the horizons (e.g. TG1). The TG2 profile, on the moraine crest, shows appreciable accumulation of silt and clay when compared with the parent material. In general, the distributions correlate closely with grain size curves for post-Audubon soils in the Colorado Front Range (Mahaney, 1974).

The clay mineralogy of the post-Audubon profiles was studied by X-ray diffraction and the dominant clay minerals detected are given in Table 4. Clay minerals vary among the different soil horizons as shown by differences in the quantity of 1:1, 2:1, and 2:1:1 clays. In gen-

TABLE 1

Neoglacial soil profiles[a]

Profile: TG1

Age: Post-Audubon

Location: Distal moraine slope, 3,120 m

Parent Material: Till, predominantly of granitic and gneissic materials

Soil Horizons	Depth below surface (cm)	Description
A	0-8	Dull yellowish-brown color (10YR 5/3), sandy loam texture, granular structure, friable moist consistence, nonsticky and nonplastic when moist.
Cox	8-48	Dull yellow orange color (10YR 7/3), sandy loam texture, massive structure, friable moist consistence, slightly sticky and plastic when moist.
Cn	48+	Grayish yellow color (2.5Y 7/2), sandy loam texture, massive structure, very friable moist consistence, slightly sticky and plastic when moist.

Profile: TG2

Age: Post-Audubon

Location: Moraine crest, 3,100 m

Parent Material: Till, predominantly of granitic and gneissic materials

Soil Horizons	Depth below surface (cm)	Description
A	0-10	Brownish-gray color (10YR 5/1), sandy loam texture, weak-granular structure, friable moist consistence, plastic and sticky when moist.
Cox	10-58	Dull yellowish-brown (10YR 5/3), sandy loam texture, massive structure, very friable moist consistence, slightly sticky and plastic when moist.
Cn	58+	Dull yellow color (2.5Y 6/3), sandy loam texture, massive structure, loose moist consistence, slightly sticky and plastic when moist.

[a]Terms and horizon nomenclature employed are in standard use with the U.S.D.A. (Soil Survey Staff, 1951, 1960). Soil pits (e.g., TG1) can be located on Figure 2.

TABLE 2

Grain size distribution for material > 2 mm in weight-percentage of dry mineral matter
and bulk weight percentages of sand, silt, and clay (< 2 mm)[a]

| Sample[b] (Site-Horizon) | Depth (cm) | Pebble | | | | Granule | % Pebble 64-4 mm | % Granule 4-2 mm | % Sand-Silt and Clay < 2 mm | % Granule 4-2 mm | % Sand 2 mm - 63μ | % Silt 63-4μ | % Clay < 4μ |
		Very Large 64-32 mm −6 to −5φ	Large 32-16 mm −5 to −4φ	Medium 16-8 mm −4 to −3φ	Small 8-4 mm −3 to −2φ	4-2 mm −2 to −1φ							
TG1-A	0-8	20.3	9.0	7.5	7.2	6.5	44.0	6.5	49.5	72.9	22.1	5.0
TG1-Cox	8-48	13.3	16.8	11.7	7.8	6.9	49.6	6.9	43.5	67.7	26.3	6.0
TG1-Cn	48+	31.5	18.3	11.6	6.4	5.1	67.8	5.1	27.1	69.3	24.2	6.5
TG2-A	0-10	3.8	9.4	8.2	7.3	6.3	28.7	6.3	65.0	56.4	27.1	16.5
TG2-Cox	10-58	13.9	9.7	9.9	7.0	7.1	40.5	7.1	52.4	59.2	25.8	15.0
TG2-Cn	58+	10.7	12.2	10.9	9.1	8.1	42.9	8.1	49.0	68.5	24.5	7.0

[a]Coarse grain sizes (64 mm-63μ) determined by sieving, fine grain sizes (63-1.95μ) determined by hydrometer.
[b]Soil pits (e.g., TG1) can be located on Figure 2.

FIGURE 5. Post-Audubon soil at site TG2. The mattock is 68 cm long.

of the original mineral, suggesting a moderate weathering environment. The presence of both kaolinite and montmorillonite in the same soil profile is difficult to interpret as they are generally considered representative of different environments (Barshad, 1966; Keller, 1968; Mahaney, 1974), e.g., leaching or nonleaching environments. The data suggest that the origin of each clay mineral is due to weathering from different parent minerals and recrystallization within the soil microenvironment and/or aeolian deposition.

Examination of the chemical data (Table 5) shows a soil reaction ranging from strongly acid in TG1 to slightly alkaline in TG2. The data for TG1 indicate a decrease in H^+ ion activity with depth in the profile, while TG2 is uniform throughout with little change between the surface horizon and the parent material. The pH data correlate closely with the organic matter and indicate the intersite variability in acidity. Cation exchange capacity is highest in the surface horizons, and parallels the low quantities of clay minerals. The presence of the mobile cations Na^+ and Ca^{+2} indicates poor leaching. As indicated by the distribution of basic cations and pH, base saturation tends to increase slightly with depth in the profiles. The leaching process appears sufficient to move basic constituents from the surface horizons downward, but is not sufficient to leach them from the profiles. The poor leaching power in the soil systems is further substantiated by the distribution of salts, which tend to concentrate in the surface horizons.

Water retention in the surface horizons is low in both cases reflecting the low amount of organic matter. Free iron oxide reaches 0.55% in the A horizon of TG1, and decreases with depth. Profile TG2 shows lower overall "free" iron of 0.32% in the A horizon, decreasing with depth. This degree of oxidation is similar to that measured in soils forming in other continental alpine climates of the Rocky Mountains (Mahaney, 1970, 1971, 1974). Organic matter, organic carbon, and nitrogen decrease from the surface downward as a function of distance from the zone of maximum organic matter input.

eral, chlorite, kaolinite, and illite appear to be inherited from the original parent material, which consists largely of granite and gneiss. Montmorillonite and mixed-layer illite-montmorillonite may form from the weathering of illite, or from aeolian deposition. The upward fining sequence of silt and clay in the TG2 profile and the overall high concentration of silt in both profiles tend to support the latter argument of aeolian deposition. In the Colorado Front Range, montmorillonite has been identified in the subsurface of late-Quaternary soils (Mahaney, 1970, 1974), owing its origin to the recrystallization of illite. The data in profile TG1 indicate that montmorillonite may develop from illite. This process requires a complete change in the chemical composition

CONCLUSION

Morphological properties consisting of horizon sequences, depth of weathering, texture, color, water retention, pH, as well as clay mineral development and certain aspects of the organic and chemical profiles correlate closely with post-Audubon soils in other areas of the Rocky Mountains. Alpine soil genesis appears to be a response to the incorporation of organic

TABLE 3

Grain size distribution[a] for material < 2 mm in weight-percentage and cumulative weight-percent of dry mineral matter

Sample[b] (Site-Horizon)	Depth (cm)	Sand					Silt				Clay	
		Very Coarse 2 mm-1,000μ (-1-0φ)	Coarse 1,000-500μ (0-1φ)	Medium 500-250μ (1-2φ)	Fine 250-125μ (2-3φ)	Very Fine 125-63μ (3-4φ)	Coarse 63-31.2μ (4-5φ)	Medium 31.2-15.6μ (5-6φ)	Fine 15.6-7.8μ (6-7φ)	Very Fine 7.8-3.9μ (7-8φ)	Coarse 3.9-1.95μ (8-9φ)	Fine <1.95μ (>9φ)
TG1-A	0-8	14.10 / 14.10	14.68 / 28.78	16.74 / 45.52	15.06 / 60.58	12.34 / 72.92	9.08 / 82.00	6.50 / 88.50	4.70 / 93.20	1.80 / 95.00	1.00 / 96.00	4.00 / 100
TG1-Cox	8-48	16.62 / 16.62	14.32 / 30.94	15.50 / 46.44	11.80 / 58.24	9.44 / 67.68	10.52 / 78.20	7.30 / 85.50	5.50 / 91.00	3.00 / 94.00	1.50 / 95.50	4.50 / 100
TG1-Cn	48+	17.48 / 17.48	14.56 / 32.04	15.50 / 47.54	12.32 / 59.86	9.48 / 69.34	11.16 / 80.50	6.50 / 87.00	4.00 / 91.00	2.50 / 93.50	1.00 / 94.50	5.50 / 100
TG2-A	0-10	10.28 / 10.28	10.84 / 21.12	13.80 / 34.92	11.84 / 46.76	9.60 / 56.36	5.64 / 62.0	6.0 / 68.0	11.0 / 76.0	4.5 / 83.5	5.5 / 89.0	11.0 / 100
TG2-Cox	10-58	10.70 / 10.70	11.90 / 22.6	14.42 / 37.02	12.50 / 49.52	9.72 / 59.24	6.76 / 66.0	6.0 / 72.0	6.0 / 78.0	7.0 / 85.0	3.5 / 88.5	11.5 / 100
TG2-Cn	58+	10.48 / 10.48	14.30 / 24.78	17.90 / 42.68	15.08 / 57.76	10.76 / 68.52	6.48 / 75.0	5.0 / 80.0	7.0 / 87.0	6.0 / 93.0	3.5 / 96.5	3.5 / 100

[a] Coarse grain sizes (2,000-63μ) determined by sieving, fine grain sizes (63-1.95μ) determined by hydrometer.
[b] Soil pits (e.g., TG1, TG2) can be located on Figure 2.

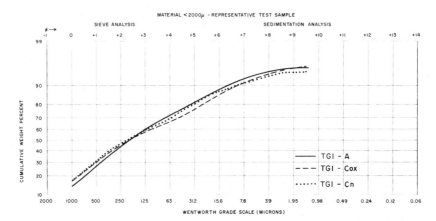

FIGURE 6. Particle-size analysis of the TG1 soil profile.

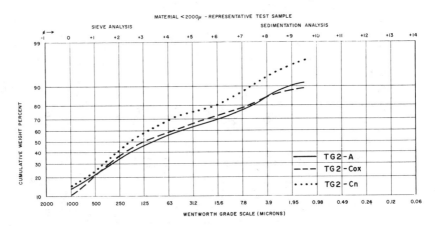

FIGURE 7. Particle-size analysis of the TG2 soil profile.

TABLE 4

Clay mineral analyses of the horizons in Table 1[a]

Sample[b] (Site-Horizon)	Depth (cm)	Chlorite	Illite	Kaolinite	Montmorillonite	Mixed Layer Illite-Montmorillonite
TG1-A	0-8	tr	x	tr	tr	tr
TG1-Cox	8-48	tr	xxx	x	—	tr
TG1-Cn	48+	tr	xxx	x	—	—
TG2-A	0-10	—	x	tr	—	—
TG2-Cox	10-58	tr	xxx	x	—	—
TG2-Cn	58+	—	xx	tr	—	—

[a]Mineral abundance is based on peak height: minor amount (tr); small quantity (x); medium (xx); and abundant (xxx). Dash (—) indicates not present.
[b]Soil pits (e.g., TG1) can be located on Figure 2.

TABLE 5

Chemical properties of the < 2 mm fraction of the post-Audubon soils

Sample[a] (Site-Horizon)	Depth (cm)	pH	H+	Exchangeable bases (meq 100 g^{-1})				CEC (meq 100 g^{-1})	Salts (mmhos/ cm)	O.M. (%)	O.C. (%)	N (%)	Fe$_2$O$_3$ (%)	C:N	(%) Oven-Dried Moisture
				K+	Ca++	Mg++	Na++								
TG1-A	0-8	5.35	3.62	.16	2.3	.35	.14	2.41	.55	1.78	1.03	.07	.55	15:1	.44
TG1-Cox	8-48	6.45	1.51	.10	2.2	.41	.20	.60	.30	.16	.09	trace	.48	nil	.34
TG1-Cn	48+	6.60	2.01	.11	2.3	.35	.16	1.21	.37	.22	.13	trace	.41	nil	.32
TG2-A	0-10	7.5	.3	.21	1.3	.36	.09	1.76	.23	.49	.29	.004	.32	nil	0.26
TG2-Cox	10-58	7.7	.5	.30	1.5	.43	.07	1.72	.22	.29	.17	.001	.37	nil	0.30
TG2-Cn	58+	7.6	.3	.15	.7	.20	.07	.98	.20	.34	.20	.003	.20	nil	0.18

[a]Soil pits (e.g., TG1) can be located on Figure 2.

matter in the surface soil accompanied by a slow build-up of nitrogen, slight illuviation of clay, and accumulation of Fe_2O_3.

The data indicate that the distal slope of the large terminal moraine complex was built-up during the Audubon advance when the terminus of the Teton Glacier occupied a position 175 to 225 m east of the present terminus. Lichen cover and soil development indicate that the dis-

tal moraine slope was free of ice approximately 1,000 years ago. The proximal moraine slope, varying from 75 to 150 m from the present terminus, was free of ice during the late 19th and early 20th centuries. Geomorphologic and pedologic data suggest that glacier fluctuations during the late Neoglacial may be broadly synchronous with those defined elsewhere in the Rocky Mountains.

ACKNOWLEDGMENTS

I thank B. D. Fahey, Guelph University, for reading and criticizing the manuscript; the National Park Service and R. P. Wood for permission to work in Grand Teton National Park; M. D. Kauffman, Oregon State University, for providing the chemical analyses; C. Grounds, York University, for drafting the illustrations; and the students in my Rocky Mountain geomorphology courses for assistance in the field. This research was partially supported by a grant from York University.

REFERENCES

Barshad, I.
1966 : The effect of variation in precipitation on the nature of clay mineral formation in soils from acid and basic igneous rocks. *In* Heller, L. and Weiss, A. (eds.), *Internat. Clay Conf. Proc.,* Jerusalem, Israel, 1: 157-173.
1967 : Chemistry of soil development. *In* Bear, F. E. (ed.), *Chemistry of the Soil.* Reinhold, New York, 1-70.

Benedict, J. B.
1967 : Recent glacial history of an alpine area in the Colorado Front Range, U.S.A. I. Establishing a lichen-growth curve. *J. Glaciol.,* 6: 817-832.
1968 : Recent glacial history of an alpine area in the Colorado Front Range, U.S.A. II. Dating the glacial deposits. *J. Glaciol.,* 7: 77-87.
1973 : Chronology of cirque glaciation, Colorado Front Range. *Quat. Res.,* 3: 584-599.

Birkeland, P. W.
1969 : Quaternary paleoclimatic implications of soil-clay mineral distribution in a Sierra Nevada-Great Basin transect. *J. Geol.,* 77: 289-302.
1973 : Use of relative age-dating methods in a stratigraphic study of rock glacier deposits, Mt. Sopris, Colorado. *Arct. Alp. Res.,* 5: 401-416.

Birkeland, P. W. and Miller, C. D.
1973 : Re-interpretation of the type Temple Lake moraine, and other Neoglacial deposits, southern Wind River Mountains, Wyoming. *Geol. Soc. Amer. Abstr. with Programs,* 5(6): 465-466.

Birkeland, P. W. and Shroba, R. R.
1974 : The status of the concept of Quater-

nary soil-forming intervals in the western United States. *In* Mahaney, W. C. (ed.), *Quaternary Environments: Proc. of a Symposium,* Geogr. Monogr., 5, York Univ. Ser. in Geogr., 241-276.

Bouyoucos, G. J.
1962 : Hydrometer method improved for making particle size analyses of soils. *Agron. J.,* 54: 464-465.

Bower, C. A. and Wilcox, L. V.
1965 : Soluble salts. *In* Black, C. A. (ed.), *Methods of Soil Analysis,* Part 2. Amer. Soc. Agron., Madison, Wisc., 933-951.

Bremner, J. R.
1965 : Total nitrogen. *In* Black, C. A. (ed.), *Methods of Soil Analysis,* Part 2. Amer. Soc. Agron., Madison, Wisc., 1149-1176.

Cole, F. W.
1970 : *Introduction to Meteorology.* Wiley, Toronto. 388 pp.

Currey, D. R.
1974 : Probable pre-Neoglacial age of the type Temple Lake Moraine, Wyoming. *Arct. Alp. Res.,* 6: 293-300.

Day, P.
1965 : Particle fractionation and particle-size analysis. *In* Black, C. A. (ed.), *Methods of Soil Analysis,* Part 1. Amer. Soc. Agron., Madison, Wisc., 545-567.

Folk, R. L.
1968 : *Petrology of Sedimentary Rocks.* Hamphill Press, Austin, Texas. 170 pp.

Fryxell, F.
1935 : Glaciers of the Grand Teton National Park of Wyoming. *J. Geol.,* 43: 381-397.

Keller, W. D.
  1968 : *Principles of Chemical Weathering.* Lucas Publishers, Columbia, Mo. 111 pp.
Mahaney, W. C.
  1970 : Soil genesis on deposits of Neoglacial and late Pleistocene age in the Indian Peaks of the Colorado Front Range. Unpublished Ph.D. Thesis, University of Colorado. 246 pp.
  1971 : Note on the "Arikaree Stade" of the Rocky Mountains Neoglacial. *J. Glaciol.,* 10: 143-144.
  1972 : Audubon: New name for Colorado Front Range Neoglacial deposits formerly called "Arikaree." *Arct. Alp. Res.,* 4: 355-357.
  1973a: Neoglacial chronology in the Fourth of July Cirque, central Colorado Front Range. *Geol. Soc. Amer. Bull.,* 84: 161-170.
  1973b: Neoglacial chronology in the Fourth of July Cirque, central Colorado Front Range, reply. *Geol. Soc. Amer. Bull.,* 84: 3767-3772.
  1974 : Soil stratigraphy and genesis of Neoglacial deposits in the Arapaho and Henderson Cirques, central Colorado Front Range. *In* Mahaney, W. C. (ed.), *Quaternary Environments: Proc. of a Symposium,* Geogr. Monogr., 5, York Univ. Ser. in Geogr., 197-240.
Mehra, O. P. and Jackson, M. L.
  1960 : Iron oxide removal from soils and clays by a dithionite-citrate system buffered with sodium bicarbonate. *In* Swineford, A. (ed.), *Nat. Conf. on Clays and Clay Minerals 1958.* Pergamon Press, London, 317-327.
Miller, C. D. and Birkeland, P. W.
  1974 : Probable pre-Neoglacial age of the type Temple Lake Moraine, Wyoming: discussion and additional relative-age data. *Arct. Alp. Res.,* 6: 301-306.
Olsen, S. R. and Dean, L. A.
  1965 : Phosphorus. *In* Black, C. A. (ed.), *Methods of Soil Analysis,* Part 2. Amer. Soc. Agron., Madison, Wisc., 1035-1048.
Peech, M. L., Alexander, T., Dean, L. A., and Reed, J. F.
  1947 : Methods of soil analyses for soil fertility investigations, *U.S. Dep. Agric. Circ.* 757, p. 25.
Reed, J. C.
  1964 : Recent retreat of the Teton Glacier, Grand Teton National Park, Wyoming. *U.S. Geol. Surv. Prof. Pap,* 501-C: C147-C151.

  1965 : Rate of ice movement and estimated ice thickness in part of the Teton Glacier, Grand Teton Natl. Park, Wyoming. *U.S. Geol. Surv. Prof. Pap.,* 525-B: B137-B141.
  1967 : Observations on the Teton Glacier, Grand Teton Natl. Park, Wyoming, 1965-1966. *U.S. Geol. Surv. Prof. Pap.,* 575-C: C154-C159.
Richmond, G. M.
  1960 : Glaciation of the east slope of Rocky Mountain National Park, Colorado. *Geol. Soc. Amer. Bull.,* 71: 1371-1381.
  1965 : Glaciation of the Rocky Mountains. *In* Wright, H. E. and Frey, D. G. (eds.), *The Quaternary of the U.S.* Princeton Univ. Press, Princeton, 217-230.
Schollenberger, C. J. and Simon, R. H.
  1945 : Determination of exchange capacity and exchangeable bases in soils-ammonium acetate method. *Soil Sci.,* 59: 13-24.
Soil Survey Staff
  1951 : Soil Survey Manual. U.S. Gov. Printing Off., Washington, D.C. 503 pp.
  1960 : *Soil Classification; 7th Approximation.* U.S. Gov. Printing Off., Washington, D.C. 265 pp.
U.S. Dep. Commerce.
  1970 : *Climatography of the U.S., No. 20-48,* N.O.A.A., Climatological Summary, Moran, Wyoming.
Walkley, A. and Black, I. A.
  1934 : An examination of the Degtjareff method for determining soil organic matter and a proposed modification of the chromic acid titration method. *Soil Sci.,* 37: 29-38.
Whittig, L. D.
  1965 : X-ray diffraction techniques for mineral identification and mineralogical composition. *In* Black, C. A. (ed.), *Methods of Soil Analysis,* Part 1. Amer. Soc. Agron., Madison, Wisc., 671-696.

BOG STRATIGRAPHY, RADIOCARBON DATES, AND PINEDALE TO HOLOCENE GLACIAL HISTORY IN THE FRONT RANGE, COLORADO

By RICHARD F. MADOLE, Denver, Colo.

Abstract.—Radiocarbon dates and stratigraphic cores from bogs, kettle ponds, and former ice-marginal lakes on the east and west sides of the Front Range, Colo., between lat 40°00′ and 40°24′ N. suggest that (1) valley glaciers of Pinedale age began to recede from their terminal positions between about 14,600 and 13,000 yr ago, (2) revegetation of glaciated areas at altitudes of 2,600–2,900 m (8,600–9,500 ft) was complete by 11,000–10,000 yr ago, (3) at one site, 3,500±1,000 yr elapsed before peat began to form after deglaciation, (4) the formation of bogs within the glaciated areas kept pace with glacier recession in a general way, beginning at progressively later times as deglaciation proceeded upward, (5) Pinedale glaciers had disappeared or were reduced to small remnants by about 8,000 yr ago, (6) moraines that have been mapped as belonging to the early stage of Pinedale Glaciation are no younger than 13,000 yr B.P. and may be older than 14,600 yr, and those delimiting what has been mapped as late stage are no younger than about 7,600 yr B.P. and are probably older than 7,800 yr, and (7) most of the till mapped as Pinedale was deposited between about 14,600 and 8,000 yr ago.

This paper describes the stratigraphy and radiocarbon dates of four localities in the Front Range and gives interpretations that bear on the beginning and end of Pinedale deglaciation, on the ages of moraines mapped as delimiting the early and late stages of Pinedale Glaciation, and on postglacial revegetation. Although the dates and stratigraphic data are too few to be interpreted rigidly, they offer insights not provided by morphology and weathering, criteria which of necessity have been relied on heavily by Quaternary stratigraphers in the Front Range and southern Rocky Mountains in general.

My work on a radiocarbon correlation of stades of Pinedale Glaciation began in 1969. Sediment for dating was collected from the base of bogs, kettle ponds, and former ice-marginal lakes. Samples from bogs and kettles were recognized as providing only minimum dates, and their interpretation was known to be subject to the kinds of errors discussed by Florin and Wright (1969) and Porter and Carson (1971). However, no radiometrically datable materials have yet been found in till in the Front Range or any other part of the southern Rocky Mountains.

Bogs were found to vary in degree of utility for radiocarbon dating, not only because of their location relative to a stratigraphic boundary or moraine system, but also because of conditions which influenced how soon after deglaciation they formed. Closed depressions, preferably those unassociated with landforms produced by stagnant ice, are the best sites for sampling because the imperfect drainage needed to form bogs was present as soon as they became free of ice. Where closure is not complete, bogs can take hundreds or even thousands of years to get started.

Acknowledgments.—Most of the work described was made possible by National Science Foundation Grant GA–29137. Geological Society of America Grant 16644 supported mapping at the Winding River site. Mark Anders, Jim Clark, Jeff Davis, Bonnie Gray, Barbara Madole, Mark Madole, Thomas Madole, Tom Meierding, Joe Noffsinger, and Katie Thorsheim helped with coring. Rolf Kihl made grain-size analyses and prepared samples for radiocarbon dating. Estella Leopold, Harold Malde, G. M. Richmond, and Van Williams provided several valuable suggestions for improving the organization and presentation of the results of this study.

SETTING AND STRATIGRAPHY OF SAMPLE SITES

The location, stratigraphy, and radiocarbon dates of four key sites are described in the following sections. Figure 1 shows the locations of the four sites plus others mentioned later in the paper. (See table 1.)

Winding River kettle pond

Winding River kettle pond is on the Pinedale terminal moraine, 250 m west of the Colorado River in the southwest corner of the Grand Lake quadrangle. This is the lowest of the four key sites (alt 2,640 m or 8,660 ft), and Madole, Fahnestock, and Meierding (1972) correlated the moraine on which it is located with the early stage of Pinedale Glaciation of Richmond (1960) and Madole (1969). Four metres of sediment overlie the till of the kettle floor. This sediment is divisible

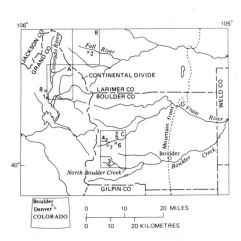

FIGURE 1.—Location of key sample sites: (1) Winding River kettle pond, (2) Hidden Valley, (3) Devlins park, (4) Mitchell bog. Others referred to: (5) Stapp Lakes, (6) Red Rock, (7) Long Lake, (8) Supply Creek bog. Quadrangles (7½-minute): (A) Grand Lake, (B) Trail Ridge, (C) Ward. Sites 4 and 7 are near the upper limit of continuous till at altitudes of 3,250 and 3,200 m (10,660 and 10,500 ft); the others are nearer the lower limit of glaciation at altitudes between 2,640 m (8,660 ft) and 2,953 m (9,690 ft).

into three principal parts (fig. 2): (1) an upper unit of peat 2.1 m thick, (2) a middle unit of black organic mud about 0.3 m thick, and (3) a lower unit of grayish-olive silt and clay 1.5 m thick, of which at least the lower half is finely laminated. Compared to other localities in the region, this is a large amount of sediment for so small a basin. Several kettle ponds of similar size at comparable altitudes in the Ward quadrangle contain only 25 to 100 cm of sediment.

The lower unit (3a and 3b) contains very little coarse sediment. Sand makes up only 2–12 percent of six samples that were analyzed (fig. 3), whereas silt ranges from 40 to 59 percent. The dominance of silt suggests a windblown origin. Laminations in this sediment indicate that the kettle hole contained water when the sediment was deposited. A lack of deformed laminae shows that subsequent collapse or slumping due to the melting of buried ice was insignificant. An absence of laminations in the upper part may reflect a decrease in water depth and a corresponding change to more turbulent conditions.

The lower unit also has only a few percent organic matter, whereas the middle unit (unit 2) is nearly half

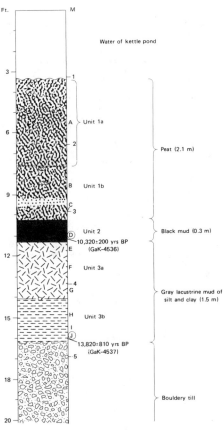

FIGURE 2.—Winding River kettle pond core.

Description of units shown in figure 2

Unit 1a: Olive-brown to dark-olive-brown (2.5Y 4/3 to 2.5Y 3/3 rootlet mud (fresh). Darker in lower 20 cm. Approximately 80 percent organic matter, dominated by a dense network of rootlets as much as 1 cm across. Remainder is mud consisting of 12 percent sand, 42 percent silt, and 46 percent clay. pH 4.8. When squeezed, the organic matter yields relatively clear water that has suspended dark material.

Unit 1b: Brownish-black to olive-black (2.5Y 3/2 to 5Y 3/1) rootlet mud (decomposed); 49 to 57 percent organic matter, much more decomposed than above. Few rootlets, but sedgelike remains occur throughout. Sand-silt-clay content of mud component ranges from 22–48–34 percent at top to 12–40–48 percent at bottom. Amount of sand is two to six times greater than in other units. pH 5.0. Waterlily seeds abundant in upper 55 cm. Horizontally bedded fragments of wood and laminae of sand and granules occur throughout. Flakes of muscovite are particularly prominent in middle 23 cm. Lower boundary is recognized by an abrupt decrease in plant remains.

Unit 2: Black (5Y 2/1) silty clay mud; 46 percent organic matter, almost all fine grained (microscopic). Remaining sediment is 6 percent sand, 41 percent silt, 53 percent clay. pH 5.1. Sand grains, flakes of muscovite, lily seeds, and decomposed rootlets are sparse.

Unit 3a: Grayish-olive (7.5Y 6/2) mud of silt and clay (nonlaminated). Samples E, F, and G have 6.7, 6.0, and 9.5 percent organic matter, respectively, all colloidal sized; amounts of sand-silt-clay in these samples are, respectively, 6.5–54.1–39.4, 3.4–53.4–43.2, and 1.7–41.9–56.4 percent. pH 4.6, 4.5, and 4.6. Not visibly laminated but has perceptible differences in shades of gray from layer to layer. Microscopic laminations may be present in lower 38 cm. Micaceous throughout. Generally devoid of visible sand grains. Basal part particularly low in sand.

Unit 3b: Light-olive-gray (5Y 6/2) mud of silt and clay (laminated). Samples H, I, and J have 5.2, 3.3, and 3.7 percent organic matter, all colloidal sized; amounts of sand-silt-clay in these samples are 3.3–48.1–48.6, 9.1–57.9–33, and 10.3–47.6–42.1 percent. pH 4.4 in all. Micaceous, especially near the bottom.

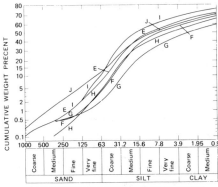

FIGURE 3.—Grain-size distribution for samples E–J from Winding River kettle pond core (fig. 2). The grain size (40–59 percent silt, 2–12 percent sand, and no grains larger than 1 mm) suggests that this interval consists of windblown material.

organic. This abrupt increase in organic content is interpreted as marking the return of an abundant growth of plants near the site following deglaciation.

The upper unit (1b and 1a) consists predominantly of organic matter, which, unlike that in unit 2, is chiefly in the form of visible plant remains. Unit 1b is about half organic matter, while 1a is four-fifths organic. Unit 1b contains scattered grains of coarse sand and granules and fragments of wood—materials derived from adjacent slopes. These constituents suggest that the setting had changed from what it was during deposition of unit 2 to something similar to that of today—a small pond surrounded by forest and filling with peat.

A small quantity of colloidal-sized organic matter, presumably consisting of pollen, humus, and other windblown organic debris of the kind described by Bonde (1969), which was concentrated from the bottom 12 cm of the lower unit, yielded a radiocarbon date of 13,820±810 yr B.P. (Gakushuin Univ. sample GaK–4537). Black mud of the middle unit gave a radiocarbon date of 10,320±200 yr B.P. (Gakushuin Univ. sample GaK–4536).

Hidden Valley bog

Hidden Valley, in the southeast corner of the Trail Ridge quadrangle, Rocky Mountain National Park, was once tributary to Fall River, but it has been blocked by a large lateral moraine of the early stade of Pinedale Glaciation (Richmond, 1960). Drainage from Hidden Valley is diverted eastward along the flank of the moraine, and sediment deposited behind the moraine has formed a broad relatively flat marsh. The marsh is at an altitude of about 2,802 m (9,180 ft), approximately 4.8 km west of the Pinedale terminal moraine that closes off Horseshoe Park, a broad meadow, 180 m below Hidden Valley, on the valley floor of Fall River.

A boring at the marsh penetrated 2.4 m of peat and the upper 1.5 m of coarse sand and granules that underlie it. Two or three thin layers of sand (a few centimetres or less thick) were found in the peat, of which the most conspicuous is at a depth of 2 m. The bottom 5 cm of the peat, which is a mixture of organic mud and highly decomposed plants, provided a radiocarbon date of 10,630±250 yr B.P. (Gakushuin Univ. sample GaK–3977). As at other localities discussed here, dates from basal peat or organic mud are interpreted as marking the time when plants reoccupied the area of the sample site after glaciers of Pinedale age retreated.

Devlins park

Devlins park (a name for a mining claim not shown on most maps) is the site of a former ice-marginal lake at the south edge of the Ward quadrangle, western Boulder County (fig. 1). Drainage from Devlins park was blocked by a moraine in a manner similar to Hidden Valley. The site is at an altitude of 2,953 m (9,690 ft), approximately 2.3 km upvalley from the glacial terminus. During Pinedale Glaciation, Devlins park was covered by water 30–50 m deep, which was backed up 1.5 km behind the impounding moraine. The lake persisted long enough to form a large delta, wave-cut terraces, and a spillway across crystalline rocks (fig. 4).

While sand and fine gravel were being deposited in the delta and along the shoreline, clay and silt were accumulating over most of the lake basin. Water depth and temperature probably inhibited organisms from disturbing most of this sediment, and the lake's orientation and configuration limited disturbance by waves. Hence, thin horizontal laminations thought to represent seasonal layers are perfectly preserved.

Approximately 7 m of core from Devlins park was obtained during the summer of 1971 using a hand-operated modified Livingston piston-sampler. During the following summer a power-driven rig using a split-barrel sampler recovered nearly 12 m of section. Unfortunately, the split-barrel sampler seriously deformed the sediments. Most of the section cored is sticky, unoxidized, gray, rhythmically layered silty clay consisting of dark-gray laminae generally <2 mm thick that alternate with light-gray laminae of variable thickness, ranging from 0.5 to 20 mm, but being typically from 2 to 4 mm. Most such rhythmites, the pairs of dark- and light-gray laminae, are from 1 to 6

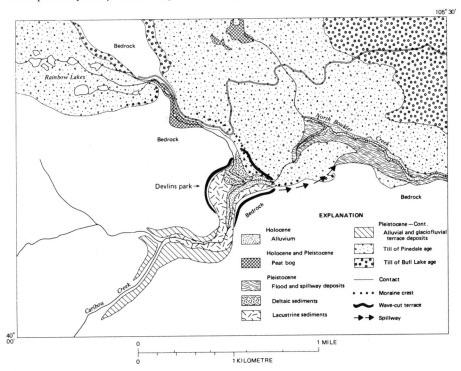

FIGURE 4.—Surficial geology of the Devlins park area. From Madole, Bachhuber, and Larson (1973) and Gable and Madole (1975).

mm thick. These are interrupted intermittently, as for example every 20–25 rhythmites, by layers of fine sand or silt, most of which are from 12 to 20 mm thick. The thicker the interrupting layers, the coarser is the sediment composing them. Those 25–30 mm thick tend to be coarse sand.

The dark layer of the rhythmites contains organic and inorganic colloids. The organic fraction consists of pollen and probably also of humus and other organic debris. Much of this organic material is believed to have been transported by wind. Organic material concentrated from the uppermost lakebeds exposed in the south bank of the creek that drains from Rainbow Lakes (fig. 4) yielded a date of 12,180±240 yr B.P. (Gakushuin Univ. sample GaK–4834). This is believed to date the end of glacial Lake Devlin, which drained catastrophically when the glacial dam was breached and left a swath of flood deposits in the valley of North Boulder Creek (fig. 4).

Mitchell bog

Mitchell bog fills an oval depression in a moraine 0.5 km east of Mitchell Lake in the northwestern part of the Ward quadrangle (fig. 1). The bog is at an altitude of 3,255 m (10,680 ft), approximately 3.6 km from cirques at the valley head and about 0.9 km downvalley from the upper limit of nearly continuous till. Mitchell bog is the highest of the four key sites. The moraine on which it is located was mapped as delimiting the late stade of Pinedale Glaciation (Madole, 1969). The bog is 80–115 m across and slightly more than 2 m deep on the west side, becoming progressively more shallow toward the east and southeast. It is saturated with melt water most of the summer and drains by seepage through a swale on the southeast that is filled with about 30 cm of peat.

Seven cores removed from Mitchell bog were from 0.3 m to 2.2 m long and composed entirely of peat. The absence of a basal unit of silt and clay such as that found at the Winding River kettle is tentatively attributed to a sparse supply of sediment upvalley from the site. Cores near the west edge of Mitchell bog contain more black inorganic sediment, especially in their upper parts, than those on the east. Thin streaks of scattered sand occur within the peat on the west, whereas wood is relatively abundant in the cores from the center and the east. The wood is of interest because woody plants do not grow in this bog. The wood may mark episodes of milder climate when the timberline rose and forests encroached on the bog. The site is essentially at timberline now. A spruce-fir krummholz (stunted, wind-battered trees) flanks it on the west, and a normal subalpine forest lies only a fraction of a

kilometre to the east and south. The bottom 10 cm of the longest core, taken about halfway between the center of the bog and the west edge, yielded a radiocarbon date of 7,690±115 yr B.P. (Stockholm Univ. sample St 3898).

DISCUSSION

Radiocarbon dates and stratigraphic evidence from Winding River kettle and Devlins park provide an indication of when Pinedale deglaciation began in the Front Range. Judging from the date of 13,820±810 yr B.P. for lake sediment at the base of Winding River kettle, Pinedale ice in this area began to recede from its maximum reach between about 14,600 and 13,000 yr ago. Undisturbed laminae in the lowermost sediment in this kettle indicate a lack of disturbance by collapse over melting ice and imply that all ice had disappeared from this locality by the time the sediment was deposited. Furthermore, the absence of megascopic plant remains and the paucity of organic matter in the sediment seem to refute the notion that it could have accumulated over stagnant ice long after deglaciation, as described by Florin and Wright (1969) in Minnesota. The location of Glacial Lake Devlin and the radiocarbon date for the uppermost rhythmites indicate that the Pinedale glacier in the valley of North Boulder Creek had receded at least 2.3 km from its terminal moraine by 12,180±240 yr B.P.

Data from the Winding River core indicate that a large time lag may occur between glacier recession and revegetation. From 2,500 to possibly as many as 4,500 yr elapsed between the disappearance of ice at Winding River kettle and the deposition of the fine, black, organic mud of unit 2 (fig. 2). Whether or not the lag recorded between these two events at this site is typical of the region as a whole is unknown.

The accord between the 10,320±200 yr B.P. date for unit 2 of the Winding River core and three other dates from similar settings (two of which were not discussed in the previous section) suggests that the dates from the bottom of organic-rich sediment in bogs and ponds probably mark the time of revegetation and bog formation rather than glacier recession. The other three dates include one of 10,630±250 yr B.P. from the base of Hidden Valley bog (alt. 2,802 m or 9,180 ft), a second of 10,340±285 yr (Stockholm Univ. sample St 3894) from a streak of organic matter in gravel just below peat near Stapp Lakes (site 5, table 1; alt 2,890 m or 9,480 ft), and a third of 10,530±230 yr (Gakushuin Univ. sample GaK–4165) from charcoal-like fragments in mud beneath peat in a kettle on the outermost (early stade) Pinedale lateral moraine, 2 km upvalley from the Winding River site (site 8, fig. 1; alt 2,750 m or

9,025 ft). These dates are interpreted as indicating that revegetation of deglaciated areas had extended to altitudes of at least 2,900 m (9,500 ft) by 11,000–10,000 yr ago.

Radiocarbon dates from peat obtained from a variety of settings (see also table 1) suggest that bogs did not all form at the same time, but kept pace with glacier recession. Those from similar settings, but at successively higher altitudes, tend to be progressively younger. However, as shown in table 1, there are exceptions. Local peculiarities of topography and drainage also influence how soon after deglaciation bogs begin to form. Apparently, the poorer the drainage, the sooner peat began to form. The age difference between the bogs at site 4 (7,690±115 yr B.P.) and site 7 (5,250± 120 yr B.P.) (table 1), which have comparable settings, is attributed to incomplete topographic closure—and, hence, continuing drainage—at site 7. The same explanation is offered for the anomalously youthful date (7,085±100 yr B.P.) at site 6, which lies only about 300 m from another site known to have been free of glacier ice by 9,490±150 yr B.P. (I-4581) (Maher, 1972).

A single radiocarbon date provides an estimate of when Pinedale deglaciation ended. The date, 7,690± 115 yr B.P., for peat from Mitchell bog, a site within 3.6 km of the cirque headwalls, shows that Pinedale ice was nearly, if not entirely, gone from the east slope of the Front Range by 8,000 yr B.P. The time at which peat began to accumulate in Mitchell bog probably postdates the end of Pinedale deglaciation in this area.

The moraines at the key sites have been correlated with either the early or late stage of Pinedale Glaciation of Richmond (1960), Madole (1969), and Madole,

Fahnestock, and Meierding (1972). The radiocarbon date from the base of the Winding River core shows that the early stade moraine there is no younger than 13,000 yr B.P. and may be older than 14,600 yr. Likewise, the date from Mitchell bog suggests that the moraine system originally mapped as late Pinedale is no younger than about 7,600 yr B.P. and may be older than 7,800 yr—a distinct probability inasmuch as some lag probably occurred between glacier recession and peat formation. Again, it should be noted that all dates reported here are minimal.

Finally, all the radiocarbon dates reported, but especially those from Winding River kettle and Mitchell bog, which are sites near the lower and upper limits of Pinedale Till, indicate that most of the till mapped as Pinedale was deposited between about 14,600 and 8,000 yr ago. This would help explain the lack of success in using soil studies and weathering to subdivide and correlate stades of Pinedale Glaciation. The times at which soil formation began near the lower and upper limits of till would not be notably different, at least not different enough to override the influence of differences in climate and vegetation.

REFERENCES CITED

Bonde, E. K., 1969, Plant disseminules in wind-blown debris from a glacier in Colorado: Arctic and Alpine Research, v. 1, no. 2, p. 135–139.

Florin, Maj-Britt, and Wright, H. E., Jr., 1969, Diatom evidence for the persistence of stagnant glacial ice in Minnesota: Geol. Soc. America Bull., v. 80, p. 695–704.

Gable, D. J., and Madole, R. F., 1975, Geologic map of the Ward quadrangle, Boulder County, Colorado: U.S. Geol. Survey Geol. Quad. Map GQ-1277. (In press.).

TABLE 1.—*Time of beginning of peat formation with respect to altitude and physiographic setting as determined at bogs in Ward quadrangle, Colorado, listed in order of ascending altitude*

Site No. (fig. 1) and location	Lat N.	Long W.	Approximate altitude		Physiographic setting	Age of basal peat (yr B.P.)
			Metres	Feet		
5. 700 m southeast of the lodge at Stapp Lakes.	40°07′	105°32′	2,883	9,460	Kettle hole 650 m behind outermost Pinedale moraine and about 4–6 km from lower limit of glaciation. Seasonal stream drains through saddle on the encircling moraines.	[1] 8,930±245
5. 775 m west-southwest of the lodge at Stapp Lakes.	40°06′ 52″	105°33′ 34″	2,890	9,480	Peat over fluvial and glaciofluvial gravel in poorly drained, but not closed, area just beyond Pinedale terminal moraines.	[2] 10,340±285
6. 300 m west of Red Rock Lake__	40°04′ 54″	105°32′ 41″	3,104	10,185	Imperfectly drained area on till of Pinedale age near valley wall a little below the midpoint between upper and lower limits of glaciation. Bog is thought to have formed gradually and progressively outward from the base of the valley wall.	[3] 7.085±100
7. 150 m east of Long Lake _____	40°04′ 30″	105°31′ 10″	3,200	10,500	Poorly drained, but not closed, area on till of Pinedale age 4.6 km from the cirque area at the head of South St. Vrain Creek.	[4] 5,250±120
4. Mitchell bog, 500 m east of Mitchell Lake.	40°05′ 13″	105°35′ 18″	3,255	10,680	Closed depression on crest of a Pinedale moraine 3.6 km from cirque area.	[5] 7,690±115

[1] Stockholm Univ. St 3896   [2] Stockholm Univ. St 3894   [3] Stockholm Univ. St 3897   [4] Gakushuin Univ. GaK–3976   [5] Stockholm Univ. St 3898

Madole, R. F., 1969, Pinedale and Bull Lake Glaciation in upper St. Vrain drainage basin, Boulder County, Colorado: Arctic and Alpine Research, v. 1, no. 4, p. 279–287.

Madole, R. F., Bachhuber, F. W., and Larson, E. E., 1973, Geomorphology, palynology, and paleomagnetic record of glacial Lake Devlin, Front Range: Geol. Soc. America Rocky Mtn. Section Ann. Mtg., 26th, Guidebook (Trip 1), 25 p.

Madole, R. F., Fahnestock, R. K., and Meierding, T. C., 1972, Glaciation of the west slope of the Colorado Front Range: Geol. Soc. America Abs. with Programs, v. 4, no. 7, p. 583–584.

Maher, L. J., 1972, Absolute pollen diagram of Redrock Lake, Boulder County, Colorado: Quaternary Research, v. 2, no. 4, p. 531–553.

Porter, S. C., and Carson, R. J., III, 1971, Problems of interpreting radiocarbon dates from dead-ice terrain, with an example from the Puget lowland of Washington: Quaternary Research, v. 1, no. 3, p. 410–414.

Richmond, G. M., 1960, Glaciation of the east slope of Rocky Mountain National Park, Colorado: Geol. Soc. America Bull., v. 71, p. 1371–1382.

LATE-QUATERNARY PALEOENVIRONMENTAL HISTORY OF THE MARY JANE CREEK VALLEY, GRAND COUNTY, COLORADO

(Abstract)

ANDREW CLAVERLEY MILLINGTON*
(M.A., Geography)

This study was undertaken to investigate the environmental history of the upper Fraser valley. The bulk of the work concerns the paleoecology of the pollen-bearing strata of an excavation at the Mary Jane Ski Area. Complementing this aspect, the sedimentology of the excavation and the surficial geology of the valley are synthesized.

A thirteen meter excavation contains five series of cyclothems (till-lake sediment, and occasionally peat) above the basal outwash. Sedimentological analyses were undertaken to distinguish the outwash, tills, and lake sediments: these were texture, pH, and percent of organic matter. The outwash was a distinct sandy horizon with little organic matter. The tills corresponded to those in the valley, being mainly silty-sands with little organic matter. The upper lake sediments are clays with much organic matter, but the lower sediments are coarser ice- or moraine-dammed lake sediments. The lower horizons in the excavation are contaminated with groundwater.

Palynological analyses were completed on the upper two peats and the lowest, organic-rich, lake sediment: radiocarbon dates provided chronological control for these sediments. The lowest lake sediments accumulated about 30,500 B.P. (30,480+2,800/ -4,300 B.P. DIC-482); the lowest peat accumulated between 13,740+ 160 B.P. and 12,380+180 B.P. (DIC-516) and the upper peat and lake sediments between 4,260+130 B.P. (DIC-130) and the present. The analyses were done at five centimeter intervals using modified, acetolysis procedures; 'absolute' counts were obtained by a combined dry weight/exotic tracer method. To aid the interpretation of the fossil pollen spectra, the modern pollen rain was sampled in a series of moss polsters. This series was devised to sample the pollen rain in all the local

*Institute of Arctic and Alpine Research
University of Colorado
Boulder, CO, 80309, U.S.A.

vegetation zones, and within the different stands in each zone. Except for the more diverse valley floor and meadow stands, few intra-zonal differences were found. However, there are quite broad distinctions between vegetation zones, and between the spectra on the east and west slopes of the Front Range. To clarify these distinctions the 'absolute' pollen values were summed into lifeforms and diversity indices and the Picea/Pinus ratios were calculated. Also, two multivariate analyses were applied to the data, Q-mode factor analysis and canonical discriminant analysis. When the fossil pollen spectra were examined it became relatively simple to assign a vegetation zone on the basis of the lifeforms and Picea/Pinus ratio. The more detailed environmental components of each spectra were elucidated by detailed examination of the pollen taxa present.

The sedimentological and palynological analyses enabled a partially time-controlled paleoenvironmental history to be established for the excavation. This was then compared to the surficial mapping of the upper Fraser valley. Before 30,500 B.P. the Fraser glacier retreated upvalley and the basal outwash was deposited (late Bull Lake time), this outwash was weathered during the Bull Lake/Pinedale Interglacial. In early Pinedale time the Fraser glacier retreated-advanced three times, at each retreat phase an ice- or moraine-dammed lake was formed in the Mary Jane Creek valley. The first of these interstadials is dated at 30,480+2,800/-4,300 B.P. (DIC-482), during which the temperatures were similar to the present but the climate was slightly moister. After the first mid-Pinedale advance the interstadial culminated in peat growth from 13,740+160 B.P. to 12,380+180 B.P. (DIC-516). During this time the climate became warmer than present and upper Montane Parkland covered the site; at the end of the interstadial the climate cooled. Ice advanced over the site at 12,380+180 B.P. (DIC-516) - this is the ice of the Winter Park Advance. Evidence of a late Pinedale advance is seen upvalley of the site. The late Pinedale and early Holocene sediments are missing from the section, they appear to have been eroded by a flood episode. After 4,260 B.P. subalpine forest reestablished around the site, but was being constantly burnt by forest fires until about 4,000 B.P. After this time the forest began to regenerate itself but productivity fell off at about 1,400 B.P.

GLACIATION OF THE UPPER COLORADO RIVER BASIN

(Summary of Doctoral Dissertation)

T. C. Meierding*

During the Pleistocene glacial periods, much of the Upper Colorado River Basin on the west side of the Front Range was covered by ice. Large glaciers fed by numerous tributaries descended the Kawuneeche, Inlet, and Monarch Valleys, attaining maximum lengths of 32 km, 24 km, and 24 km respectively. Several smaller glaciers were also active in the area during the same periods. Glaciers with multiple outlets and transection-type glaciers were common. Quaternary till and outwash deposits mantle much of the region today. Outwash deposits from the many glaciers now form extensive terraces along the Colorado River. Near the town of Granby these terraces merge with those from the Fraser River Basin.

Previous works on the glacial chronology of the Front Range west side have been few. Lee (1917), Boos (1929), and Richmond (1974) presented maps of the reconstructed Pleistocene glaciers of the area in connection with work on the geology of Rocky Mountain Park. Ives (1936, 1938) found evidence for five glaciations in the Monarch Valley, whereas Ray (1940) believed that only four glaciations were represented there. Madole et al. (1973) correlated tills in the region with Pinedale, Bull Lake, and pre-Bull Lake deposits of other areas. Benedict (1973) and Madole (1976) collected radiocarbon dates from Holocene and Pinedale deposits, respectively.

Detailed stratigraphic work and the use of multiple relative age dating criteria establish a complex glacial and glaciofluvial chronology for a portion of the Upper Colorado River Basin. Weathering criteria differentiate terrace gravels into as many as eight age groups--one Holocene, three Pinedale, two Bull Lake, and one pre-Bull Lake (?) till. Many terraces can be traced to moraines: thus, terraces help to correlate tills from valley to valley within the study area. Except for pre-Bull Lake deposits, till and outwash deposits of any glacial period

*Department of Geography
University of Delaware

are similar to one another in degree of weathering. Glacial
readvances are indicated in some localities where outwash is
buried by till or where till texture is similar to outwash
terrace.

The most useful relative age dating criteria for differentiating deposit age groups include subsurface granitic cobble
weathering, soil B horizon clay percentage and thickness,
strength of soil color, thickness and B horizon development of
loess mantles. Moraine form and presence of kettles also aided
in till differentiation. On terraces, carbonate accumulation
and degree of terrace dissection were helpful. The criteria
often differ one from another in deposit age assignment, so the
number of glacial stages depends partly on the method used to
combine the relative dating criteria.

PRE-BULL LAKE EVENTS

The oldest Pleistocene pre-Bull Lake deposit in the field
area is a 25 m-thick terrace gravel on Granby Mesa. The terrace
tread is presently about 80 m above the Fraser River. Though
the gravel cannot be traced to till, it is thought to represent
outwash, because the gravels are the same size and the terraces
have the same gradient as lower level terrace gravels which can
be traced to moraines. Outwash of the high terrace is tentatively correlated to the 600,000 year-old Verdos alluvium of
the Colorado Piedmont (Scott, 1965; Machette, 1975) and is
labeled middle pre-Bull Lake here. The gravel is not as weathered as Rocky Flats alluvium of the Piedmont, but it appears to
be significantly older than lower terrace gravels of probable
pre-Bull Lake age in terms of degree of terrace dissection, subsurface stone weathering (100% grusified granitic cobbles), clay
accumulation in loess (43% clay), and loess thickness (200 cm).
The greater loess thickness on the high terrace than on the next
lower terrace suggests that eolian deposits occurred between
formation of the two terraces.

Two terraces on Granby Mesa at 70 m and 47 m above the main
rivers may correlate to the Slocum alluviums (late pre-Bull Lake)
of the Colorado Piedmont. The gravels are more weathered (78%
grusified), contain much more carbonate (68% $CaCO_3$ in K horizons),
and have thicker loess mantles (122 cm) than gravels in lower
terraces. The 70 m terrace tread can be traced upstream to the
outermost moraine in the Monarch Valley. Following deposition
of that pre-Bull Lake (?) moraine in the Monarch Valley, the
glacier retreated and then readvanced. Late pre-Bull Lake (?)
till buries outwash on the 47 m terrace at an island in Lake
Granby. Further upstream, the 47 m terrace may correlate with
a moraine on Green Ridge in the Inlet Valley.

Pre-Bull Lake (?) moraines all have a low rounded form and
occupy ridge-top positions well above the Colorado River, but
they are no more weathered than stratigraphically younger
moraines of probable Bull Lake age. Either these moraines are

of Bull Lake age and have overridden older terraces, or they have lost much weathered surface material by local erosion of the crests subsequent to moraine deposition.

BULL LAKE EVENTS

The glaciers readvanced in early Bull Lake time to a position close to the outermost moraines of each valley. In the Kawuneeche Valley, moraines of early Bull Lake age cross-cut and bury pre-Bull Lake (?) moraines. Well preserved outwash terraces (20 m above the Colorado River near Granby) are connected to recessional moraines of early Bull Lake till. The early Bull Lake terrace gravels and moraines have moderately to strongly developed soils, contain up to 63% grusified granitic cobbles and 3% carbonate, and have up to 80 cm-thick loess mantles. The moraine crests range from moderately sharp to rounded.

After recession of early Bull Lake ice, the glaciers readvanced in late Bull Lake time to a point less than two kilometers upvalley from the outer Bull Lake moraines. At several valley-center locations, late Bull Lake tills are excessively sandy and contain many round cobbles, as if the glaciers had advanced over outwash. The moraines are small, possibly indicating a short time at the maximum glacial position. Late Bull Lake moraines appear only slightly less weathered and eroded than earlier tills, and the mapped boundary between Bull Lake tills is not certain. Few terrace remnants can be specifically connected to late Bull Lake tills. A terrace 15 m above the Fraser River at Granby may relate to the late Bull Lake advance, and is significantly less weathered than the early Bull Lake terrace. It contains only 28% grusified cobbles and 1% carbonate. Up to 36 cm of loess were deposited on the late Bull Lake and earlier deposits before deposition of Pinedale till and outwash. Most of this eolian material has since moved downslope away from moraine crests.

PINEDALE EVENTS

The earliest event of possible Pinedale age recorded in the field area is the deposition of a terrace gravel which now forms a small terrace remnant 6 m above the Fraser River. The gravel is intermediate in elevation, weathering (11% grusified cobbles), and carbonate content (0.2%) between Pinedale and Bull Lake terrace gravels. The terrace may relate to an early Pinedale glaciation in the Fraser River Basin dated at approximately 30,000 years B.P. by Millington (this chapter), but it cannot be specifically correlated with that till.

According to the relative age-dating criteria, a substantial amount of time elapsed between the late Bull Lake glaciation and deposition of most Pinedale till and terrace gravels now exposed in the Upper Colorado River Basin. Pinedale moraines and terrace

gravels (less than 5 m above the main streams) are much less
eroded and weathered than Bull Lake deposits, and are seldom
covered with loess. They contain neither carbonate nor grusified granitic cobbles. The moraines are commonly sharp or
pitted, and original channel patterns are readily identified on
the terrace treads.

The oldest Pinedale till exposed in the study area has a
minimum radiocarbon age of 13,820+810 yr B.P. (Gak-4537), and
is thought to be not more than a few thousand years older than
that date (Madole, 1976). The date and the youthful appearance
of the deposits suggests that the outermost Pinedale moraines
were laid down at some time in the middle of the Pinedale period
rather than in early Pinedale time.

The numerous kettles in the outermost Pinedale moraine of
the Kawuneeche Valley indicate that at least the upper layers
of till were deposited by stagnant ice. The Kawuneeche Pinedale
glacier had a lower gradient than that of most Front Range
Pleistocene glaciers, and faced southward, receiving more direct
solar radiation than other glaciers. It is suspected that the
Kawuneeche glacier was more sensitive to climatic changes than
other glaciers in the area. It would respond to a slight rise
of the equilibrium line elevation either by rapid recession or
stagnation of the ice front. Kettles are also common in the
outermost Pinedale moraines of the North Inlet Valley. Ice
stagnation in that case is due to the fact that thin ice was
stranded on a lateral bench well above the main glacial valley
now occupied by Shadow Mountain Lake. Many recessional moraines
were deposited by the retreating middle Pinedale glaciers. The
outermost tills of the North Inlet Valley could not have been
deposited until the Kawuneeche glacier had receded several km.
Moraines of the North Inlet Valley cross-cut Kawuneeche and
Tonahutu Valley Pinedale tills.

After recession of more than 8 km, late Pinedale ice readvanced in the East Inlet and Monarch valleys, and perhaps also
in North Supply and Tonahutu valleys. Late Pinedale till buries
an outwash terrace in the Monarch Valley and a bog in the Inlet
Valley (Richmond, 1974). The later Pinedale tills seem only
slightly less weathered than earlier Pinedale tills, indicating
a short time span before readvance.

Following deposition of the later Pinedale moraines, the
ice fronts then retreated rapidly to the cirques, depositing
little till on the exposed bedrock of the valley floors. Only
in the Kawuneeche Valley are there substantial till deposits
along the valley walls. Ice in the Monarch Valley had retreated
to the cirque near Satanta Peak by at least by 9,915+165 yr B.P.
(I-6335) (Benedict, 1973). Holocene tills, rock glaciers, and
protalus ramparts were mapped from air photographs, but not differentiated by relative age data. They are particularly abundant
in cirques of the Neversummer Range. Outwash gravels near stream
level may be either late Pinedale or Holocene in age and are
slightly less weathered than middle Pinedale gravels.

REFERENCES

Benedict, J.B. 1973. Chronology of cirque glaciation, Colorado Front Range. *Quaternary Research*, 3(4): 401-416.

Boos, M.F. 1929 (revised 1963). *Guide to the Geology of Rocky Mountain National Park, Colorado*. Unpublished manuscript, National Park Service.

Ives, R.L. 1936. *Glaciology of the Monarch Valley, Grand County, Colorado*. Unpublished M.A. thesis, University of Colorado, Boulder.

_____. 1938. Glacial geology of the Monarch Valley, Grand County, Colorado. *Bulletin of the Geological Society of America*, 49: 1045-1066.

Lee, W.T. 1917. *The Geologic Story of the Rocky Mountain National Park*. National Park Service, U.S. Dept. of the Interior. 89 pp.

Machette, M.N. 1975. *The Quaternary Geology of the Lafayette Quadrangle, Colorado*. Unpublished M.A. thesis, University of Colorado, Boulder.

Madole, R.F. 1976. Bog stratigraphy, radio-carbon dates, and Pinedale to Holocene glacial history in the Front Range, Colorado. *Journal of Research U.S. Geological Survey*, 4(2): 163-169.

Madole, R.F., P.K. Fahnestock, and T.C. Meierding. 1973. Glaciation of the west slope of the Colorado Front Range. *Abstracts with Programs, Geological Survey of America*, 4(7): 583.

Meierding, T.C. 1977. *Age Differentiation of Till and Gravel Deposits in the Upper Colorado River Basin*. Unpublished Ph.D. thesis, University of Colorado, Boulder.

Ray, L.L. 1940. Glacial chronology of the Southern Rocky Mountains. *Bulletin of the Geological Society of America*, 51: 1851-1918.

Richmond, G.M. 1974. *Raising the Roof of the Rockies*. Rocky Mountain Nature Association. 80 pp.

Scott, G.R. 1965. Nonglacial geology of the Southern and middle Rocky Mountains. *In* Wright, H.E. and D.G. Frey (eds.), *The Quaternary of the United States*, pp. 243-254.

Part 2
Geomorphology

Overview
Jack D. Ives*

Of the seven papers selected for this chapter, six involve process studies that necessitated long periods of data acquisition in high mountain terrain and in various seasons. When it is considered that, during three months of the year (December through February), the alpine environment of the Front Range is so severe that, on average, exposed flesh will freeze within two minutes, the large year-round component of this work must serve as a tribute to the dedication of a few masochistic individuals. It also demonstrates one of the vital roles of the Mountain Research Station and associated logistical system, for without it much of this work would have been too dangerous to have been justified, or at least too exacting to have permitted collection of adequately reliable data. It illustrates the basis of one of the components of the underlying philosophy of an institute of arctic-alpine research, whereby year-round access from a field station and major university campus to cold-climate alpine environments can facilitate an understanding of processes operating during the winter half-year in the much less accessible arctic.

Any definition of geomorphology must encompass the application of scientific method to achieve an understanding of the shape of the relief elements that together comprise the landscape of a particular area. Since the pioneering work of Anders Rapp (1960) in Swedish Lapland, arctic and alpine geomorphic research has been more and more preoccupied with process studies aimed at understanding the development of landforms of cold-climate environments. It is not intended here to minimize the value of understanding those processes per se, either as components of present-day cold-stressed ecosystem dynamics, or in relation to types and rates of processes operating in other ecosystems. Nevertheless, it follows that process studies must be related to an absolute chronology of landscape events, including

*Institute of Arctic and Alpine Research
University of Colorado
Boulder, Colorado 80309

an understanding of the foregoing glacial sequence. Thus a
primary benchmark for effective process study is frequently the
date that a particular landscape element became free of its ice
cover during the waning phase of the Last Glaciation, or else a
determination of the maximum extent of different past glacial
stades. It is only upon this kind of base that quantitative
determinations of the rates at which various geomorphic processes
operate (calculated rarely from more than six to ten years of
observation) can be extrapolated back in time to facilitate reconstruction of landscape development. A comparable foundation
is also necessary if we are to apply our knowledge to a prediction of the impacts of a possible range of land-management alternatives into the future. But herein lies a formidable ob-
stacle, since a single catastrophic event with a long recurrence
interval may account for more "work" than the operation of a
continuous slope process for more than a decade. Whether the
catastrophic event falls within or outside the period of field
study, the uncertainty of any estimate of its recurrence interval creates a research design problem of considerable magnitude.
This realization has been at least partially responsible for
the recognition that geomorphic studies in the Front Range must
go hand-in-hand with studies in glacial geology. Thus, as with
the papers authored by White and Benedict, the geomorphologist
is frequently glacial geologist and vice versa, or else, as in
the case of the remaining papers, the geomorphologist relates
closely to the glacial geologist. Papers reproduced in chapters
2, 3, 4, and 5, therefore, repeatedly demonstrate a high degree
of interdependency.

The arctic relationship is also demonstrated in this selection. Thus Benedict's paper shows a heavy dependency on the
arctic work of Washburn (1967) and it demonstrates the application and development of relative and absolute lichenometric
dating techniques initiated by Beschel (1950, 1961) and Andrews
and Webber (1964), frequently in an arctic setting. Fahey's
attempts to analyze freeze-thaw and frost-heave cycles through
a range of altitudes follows the conceptual advances in the
arctic made by Fraser (1959), Cook and Raiche (1962), and Cook
(1960, 1967), amongst others, and employs a ground-heave measuring device developed at the McGill Sub-Arctic Research Laboratory in central Labrador-Ungava by Haywood (Andrews, 1963).
Thorn's important contribution to bringing the study of nivation
into the late-20th Century quantitative rigor and out of the
myths of the Century's beginning demonstrates a linkage with
the Cambridge University tradition of Lewis (1939, 1949, 1950),
Clark and Lewis (1951), McCall (1960), and Battle (1952 unpubl.,
1960).

With the exception of Caine's paper, which develops a conceptual model for alpine slope process study and is basically
theoretical in nature, all the papers selected involve long-term
field observations on a variety of actual geomorphic processes.
Caine's paper relates more specifically to the San Juan Mountains

and derives from a major Colorado State University-University of Colorado study of the ecological impacts of winter cloud-seeding (Steinhoff and Ives, 1976). It is included, nevertheless, because of its thought-provoking nature, its demands for systematic rigor in mountain geomorphology, and its applicability to the Front Range and elsewhere.

White's paper provides a valuable description of three rock glaciers in the Front Range and an analysis of five years of detailed measurements. It shows that the Arapaho rock glacier was initiated about 1,000 radiocarbon years ago and that its uppermost two-thirds conceals a core of glacier ice. The three individual rock glaciers show a range of annual movement from 5.0 to 9.7 cm and of volume transfer from 215 to 770 m^3. It provides the best available information on this important land-form component of the Front Range.

Benedict's[*] paper deals with the classification of stone-banked and turf-banked lobes and terraces, the processes influencing their development, and their changing rates through the last several thousand years. It is one of the most significant papers on mountain geomorphology of the last decade, recognized by the Kirk Bryan Award of the Geological Society of America.

Benedict shows that where field conditions favor solifluction, turf-banked lobes and terraces occur, whereas stone-banked lobes and terraces occur preferentially in frost-creep environments. Modern rates of downslope movement on Niwot Ridge vary between 0.4 and 4.3 cm/yr and this movement is confined to the upper 50 cm of soil. Much higher rates of movement occurred in the past at times believed to coincide with the melting of a more extensive snow cover than exists today, such as during the close of three Neoglacial stades. This current and past dependency on moisture is well demonstrated and the author concludes that autumnal availability of moisture, not characteristic of Front Range climate today, is the critical factor. Radiocarbon dating and lichenometry indicate that turf-banked terrace sites were used as paleoindian camping and butchering areas at least 7,650 ± 190 years ago. One intriguing conclusion is that current patterns of snow distribution have a negligible effect upon depth of winter freezing (p. 212-213 and Figure 53). Comparable observations by Fahey and Thorn (see below), Ives and Fahey (1971), Ives (1961, 1973), and Nicholson (1976, 1978), either on Niwot Ridge or in Labrador-Ungava, would seem to challenge this conclusion. That it was based upon a limited number of observations during a single autumn and winter would indicate that it be viewed with caution. However, the subsequent argument, that depth of freezing relates to timing of snow accumulation and snowmelt, would seem eminently supportable.

---

[*]It was not possible to obtain author's permission to reproduce this paper; the decision to do so is based on copyright held by the journal *Arctic and Alpine Research*.

Benedict's study set the stage for a major excursion into Front Range alpine archeology (Benedict and Olson, 1978) beyond the scope of the present volume. However, it has left in abeyance additional work: rates of slope retreat could be calculated for different micro environments; replication of the dating of variation through time in rates of stone-banked terrace movement is needed to obtain confidence limits that should be placed, for instance, on Figure 56; systematic palynological investigations are needed to test the proposed scheme of inferred climatic change and synoptic climatologic and climatic simulation studies may more nearly approach the problem of resolving when and how the critical autumnal moisture increases occurred.

Fahey's 1973 paper discusses variations in diurnal freeze-thaw and frost-heave cycles with altitude. He concludes that air temperature data obtained from standard climatological instrumentation cannot be used to predict either the number or geomorphic significance of surface and sub-surface events. Cycles of all three kinds decrease with increasing altitude, and frost-heave cycles and freeze-thaw events are confined to the upper 10 cm of soil, thus supporting Benedict's conclusion concerning the limited effectiveness of present-day down-slope processes. The major inference from this aspect of Fahey's work is that the widespread occurrence of mechanically weathered material, so characteristic of many arctic and alpine environments, cannot be explained by assuming that freeze-thaw cycles are more numerous in these areas even if it could be proved that they were geomorphically effective in the first place. This conclusion, of course, was anticipated in an arctic setting by the work of Fraser (1959), Cook and Raiche (1962), and Cook (1960). Fahey is responsible for making the first systematic attempt to tackle these issues in a mid-latitude, high-altitude setting. It is also important to realize that the unfortunate, yet time-honored, freeze-thaw cycle hypothesis is still widely disseminated through the standard literature (Ives, 1973, p. 3-4).

Fahey's 1974 paper (not reproduced here) presents the results of studies of seasonal frost-heave and frost penetration. Based upon a massive array of hard-won data he shows, for instance, that maximum vertical displacements in excess of 30 cm are to be anticipated on frost boil surfaces just above timberline in the Front Range, while intervening vegetated areas also heaved, but to a much lesser degree. The maximum surface heave is associated with the absence of prolonged snow cover and with scant vegetation cover, and directly related to the proximity of the water table to the ground surface.

Thorn's paper shows that the case for intensified mechanical weathering as a component of nivation must be made exclusive from the assumption of increased freeze-thaw cycle efficiency. He thus supports Fahey's findings and extends them to the permanent and semi-permanent snowbank environments. He demonstrates that two widely accepted hypotheses must be dismissed: (1) that freeze-thaw cycles are generally common in alpine environments, and (2) that such cycles specifically increase in frequency in and around snowbanks. He further shows that removal of sand-, silt-, and clay-sized particles is increased between 20 and 30 times by nivation as compared with surrounding control slopes, but that the specific processes are sheetwash and rivulet flow. Chemical weathering is also accelerated two to four times in a snow bank environment. He finds that, at contemporary rates of removal 500,000 years would be required to excavate a modest-size nivation hollow and, even allowing for the postulated climatic changes of Benedict, erosion and transport required to produce a small cirque would be several orders of magnitude greater. Also, once the nivation hollow becomes sufficiently large to accumulate snow to a thickness such that some survives through the subsequent ablation season, the role of the snow becomes protective. Thus the hypothesis that nivation hollow excavation leads directly into the development of cirques, and snowbanks into cirque glaciers, breaks down.

Reheis examines the sources of debris and methods of transport and deposition of the Arapaho Glacier. This is a very small cirque glacier little more than 500,000 m^2. Debris was divided into two classes on the basis of stone roundness and the presence or absence of glacial striations and polish; that produced by subglacial erosion, and that resulting from rockfall and snow avalanching. Of the current glacial load 70% derives from subglacial erosion, compared to 88% during the Gannett Peak Neoglacial stade[*]. Rockfall rates are 35 to 50 m^3/yr at present compared with 290 to 485 m^3/yr during Gannett Peak time. Total cirque area denudation, based upon present rates, is 95 to 165 mm/1000 yr compared with 5,000 to 8,000 mm/yr during the Gannett Peak stade. Even when full allowances are made for possible miscalculation, incorporation of possible buried older till, and so on, it would appear that the erosive power of Arapaho Glacier was greater by a factor of 5 during Neoglacial stades than today. An equally important conclusion, derived from a comparison with available rates of erosion on valley glaciers and ice sheets, is that the rate of glacial denudation is relatively constant regardless of glacier size.

The final section for this chapter is a paper by M.J. Bovis. This work also involves extensive geomorphic process data collection but concentrates on a large number of slope sites chosen deliberately to maximize environmental variation below the upper timberline. The most important findings include: demonstration of a summer seasonal maximum in surficial movement, the apparent heterogeneity of soil loss rates over relatively small areas within the forest ecosystems, and the existence of a possible soil loss maximum within the montane forest ecosystem. The paper provides a vital counterweight to the preponderance of

---

[*]See overview by M. Clark, chapter 2, for recent changes in Neoglacial terminology.

studies in the alpine belt, and gives a strong indication that both montane and alpine environments in temperate mountain areas are relatively very stable at the present time.

From the studies included, together with many others, both from the Front Range and other areas of the Colorado Rocky Mountains, it would appear that progress in mountain geomorphology has been substantial over the last ten to fifteen years. Replication would be valuable in the same and comparable environments and the challenge of accommodating the catastrophic event with a large recurrence interval remains to be tackled. Finally, the application of the great growth in our understanding of geomorphic processes on mountain slopes to policy development and decision-making in the management of mountain land has barely begun. The continued presence of the Mountain Research Station should be of fundamental importance in all of these areas, and its facilitation of graduate student dissertation work, which lies at the base of all the papers reproduced here except those by Caine and White, is especially significant.

REFERENCES

Andrews, J.T. 1963. The analysis of frost-heave data collected by B.H.J. Haywood from Schefferville, Labrador-Ungava. *Canadian Geographer*, 7(4): 163-173.

Battle, W.B.R. 1952. *Corrie Formation with Particular Reference to the Importance of Frost Shatter at Depth*. Unpublished Ph.D. dissertation, University of Cambridge. 181 pp.

_____. 1960. Temperature observations in bergschrunds and their relationship to frost shattering. *In* Lewis, W.V. (ed.), *Norwegian Cirque Glaciers*. R. Geogr. Soc. Res. Ser. 4, pp. 83-95.

Benedict, J.B. and B.L. Olson. 1978. *The Mount Albion Complex: a Study of Prehistoric Man and the Altithermal*. Res. Rept. No. 1, Center for Mountain Archeology, Ward, Colorado. 213 pp.

Beschel, R. 1950. Flechten als Altersmasstab rezenter Moränen. *Z. Gletscherkd. Glazialgeol.*, 1: 152-161.

_____. 1961. Dating rock surfaces by lichen growth and its application to glaciology and physiography (lichenometry). *In* Raasch, G.O. (ed.), *Geology of the Arctic*. Vol. 2, Univ. Toronto Press, Toronto, pp. 1044-1062.

Clark, J.M. and W.V. Lewis. 1951. Rotational movement in cirque and valley glaciers. *Journal of Geology*, 59: 546-566.

Cook, F.A. 1960. Periglacial-geomorphological investigations at Resolute, 1959. *Arctic*, 13: 132-135.

_____. 1967. Fluvial processes in the High Arctic. *Geogr. Bull.*, 9(3): 262-268.

Cook, F.A. and V.G. Raiche. 1962. Freeze-thaw cycles at Resolute, N.W.T. *Geogr. Bull.*, 18: 64-78.

Fahey, B.D. 1974. Seasonal frost heave and frost penetration measurements in the Indian Peaks region of the Colorado Front Range. *Arctic and Alpine Research*, 6(1): 63-70.

Fraser, J.K. 1959. Freeze-thaw frequencies and mechanical weathering in Canada. *Arctic*, 12: 40-53.

Ives, J.D. 1961. *A Pilot Project for Permafrost Investigations in Central Labrador-Ungava*. Geographical Papers (Ottawa, Canada), No. 28. 28 pp.

_____. 1973. Permafrost and its relationship to other environmental parameters in a midlatitude, high-altitude setting, Front Range, Colorado Rocky Mountains. *Permafrost: North American Contribution (to the) Second International Conference*. International Conference on Permafrost, Yakutsk, Siberia, 1973. National Academy of Sciences, Washington, D.C., pp. 121-125.

_____. 1973. Arctic and alpine geomorphology - a review of current outlook and notable gaps in knowledge. *In* Fahey, B.D. and R.D. Thompson (eds.), *Research in Polar and Alpine Geomorphology*. 3rd Guelph Symposium on Geomorphology, 1973, Proceedings. Geo Abstracts, Ltd., University of East Anglia, Norwich, England, pp. 1-10.

Ives, J.D. and B.D. Fahey. 1973. Permafrost occurrence in the Front Range, Colorado Rocky Mountains, USA. *Journal of Glaciology*, 10(58): 105-112.

Lewis, W.V. 1939. Snow patch erosion in Iceland. *Geogr. J.*, 94: 153-161.

_____. 1949. Glacial movement by rotational slipping. *Geog. Annaler*, 31: 146-158.

_____. 1960. *Norwegian Cirque Glaciers*. R. Geogr. Soc. Res. Ser. 4. 104 pp.

McCall, J. 1960. The flow characteristics of a cirque glacier and their effect on glacial structure and cirque formation. *In* Lewis, W.V. (ed.), *Norwegian Cirque Glaciers*. R. Geogr. Soc. Res. Ser. 4: 39-62.

Nicholson, F.H. 1976. Permafrost thermal amelioration tests near Schefferville, Quebec. *Canadian Journal of Earth Science*, 13: 1694-1705.

_____. 1979. Permafrost spatial and temporal variations near Schefferville. *Geogr. Phys. et Quater.*

Rapp, A. 1960. Recent development of mountain slopes in Kärke-vagge and surroundings, Northern Scandinavia. *Geogr. Annaler*, 17: 73-200.

Steinhoff, H.W. and J.D. Ives (eds.). 1976. *Ecological Impacts of Snowpack Augmentation in the San Juan Mountains, Colorado*. Occasional Paper No. 19 (INSTAAR), Boulder, Colorado. 256 pp.

Washburn, A.L. 1967. Instrumental observations of mass-wasting in the Mesters Vig district, northeast Greenland. *Medd. om Grønland*, 166. 296 pp.

Webber, P.J. and J.T. Andrews (eds.). 1973. Lichenometry: Dedicated to the Memory of the Late Roland E. Beschel. *Arctic and Alpine Research*, 5(4): 293-425.

A CONCEPTUAL MODEL FOR ALPINE SLOPE PROCESS STUDY

Nel Caine

*Institute of Arctic and Alpine Research
and Department of Geography
University of Colorado
Boulder, Colorado 80302*

ABSTRACT

This paper presents the model around which a geomorphic study of the impact of artificially augmented snowfall on alpine terrain has been designed. It consists of a two-order hierarchy which can be fitted into a single drainage basin to give three stages. On the smaller scale is a "plot model" which indicates the possible links between geomorphic controls, processes, and responses of plots of 10 m² or less. On a larger scale (about 1,000 m²) a more extensive system, defined by directions of waste transfer and enclosing a number of plot-size units, is modeled. This system is simplified to a single slope profile, the most adequate estimator of transfer directions. The drainage basin concept, into which the present model fits, has already been examined by Chorley (1969) and so is not considered in detail. Further work is intended to yield data from which the relative significance of the control-response links, and the importance of snow in these links, can be estimated.

INTRODUCTION

The study of the geomorphic "processes" involved in the movement of surficial waste is normally concerned with two sets of measurements which are considered as dependent and independent variables. The dependent variables are generally responses to physical or chemical processes, that is, they involve strains in the mechanical sense, such as waste movement or sediment yield rates. Strahler (1952) provides the classical review of such responses and his work has been the basis for recent advances in this area. The independent variables usually comprise descriptive elements of the system within which this adjustment occurs. These are frequently morphometric variables like relative relief, surface slope, and drainage density but also include geologic, climatic, and biotic factors.

By common consent we refer to studies of this kind, which involve an attempt to link system responses to controlling characteristics, as process studies. It should be noted, however, that in many of these studies the precise link between characteristic and response is not clearly defined; my own work on surficial creep rates is an example of this (Caine, 1963; 1968). Such a link should be capable of definition in terms of the physical-mechanical or chemical process by which it is made (Strahler, 1952), but often this is not possible. An alternative approach, though not always a satisfactory one, is to define empirical connections, usually by some form of correlation analysis; this would, in the ideal case, lead to a hypothesis about mechanisms which can then be tested. In a geomorphic investigation a crucial point is the fact that the mechanical process link is frequently either inaccessible or is not amenable to such accurate estimation as other system parameters. In part, this problem arises from a lack of adequate definition of the process involved. This paper is intended to alleviate that lack.

The model discussed here is intended to focus attention on the interaction of geomorphic processes with themselves and with their environment in a particular situation. It is not a model of the alpine ecosystem but represents only a subsystem of that larger one. Because we have little quantitative knowledge of the working of the system it represents, it does not allow dynamic simulation. Its application to specific field studies may, however, lead to development along both these lines. In its present form, the model is essentially a "Black Box" (Weiner, 1961, p. xi) and is presented for discussion in the hope that it contains the potential for improvement and its own replacement.

THE MODEL

The model consists of two parts, distinguished here by scale considerations. On the local scale is a "plot model" intended for application to areas of 10 m^2 or less. This is based upon the classical conceptual beach model of Krumbein (1964) which has been quoted on many occasions since its first presentation (e.g., Krumbein and Graybill, 1965, p. 22; Chorley, 1967; Harbaugh and Bonham-Carter, 1970, p. 26). It consists of a simple division of system components into boundary conditions (i.e., controlling characteristics), process mechanisms, and response elements between which the mechanisms of change operate. The second step is on a larger scale (about 1,000 m^2 area): a "site model" is intended to involve responses through a wider system comprised of a number of plots from the first stage. This is then capable of yet further expansion to include larger systems such as individual small drainage basins which make up logical units for geomorphic study (Chorley, 1969).

THE PLOT MODEL

Components

If one considers this model (Table 1) to represent a simple chain of effects, from controls to responses, the logical order of treatment is from left to right across the table. This procedure will be followed here but it should not prejudice the consideration of interaction between different members of the same component group or of feedback effects. Both of these are likely to be as important as direct, causal chains of effects.

Boundary conditions, comprising the first component, tend to define the condition of the system. They derive basically from the lithosphere, the atmosphere/hydrosphere, and the biosphere and have been classified in that sense here (Table 1). Within this grouping one can distinguish a basic dichotomy (or dialectic [Tricart, 1965]) between the conditions which influence the stress to which geomorphic materials are subject and those affecting their resistance to stress. The first of these lie mainly in the categories of climatic and biological controls but also include characteristics, like slope angle and direction, which have been included in Table 1 as geologic controls. The set of resistances is basically geologically derived but does include biologic factors like the protective influence of ground cover and litter cover and the binding effect of plant roots on the soil. This indicates that the sets of boundary conditions indicated in Table 1 are not closed: there is obviously much interaction between sets and between members of the same set. Frequently set members will tend in different directions and, occasionally, the same variable may do this, either sequentially through time or even contemporaneously.

The stresses defined by boundary conditions find their expression in material transfer within the system (or between the system and its environment). This occurs through the second component (processes) in so far as it is permitted by the resistance of the material being stressed. Both the stress and the resistance to it are subject to notoriously wide variances in most geomorphic situations and the low level of statistical explanation afforded by multiple regression models of responses on boundary conditions probably reflects this (e.g., Slaymaker, 1969). The processes that are involved in mass wasting in this component are essentially mechanical in nature although, on a long time scale, such as that required for the movement of a "waste package" across an entire slope profile, chemical processes and changes will also be significant. The mechanical processes involved are classifield into four groups in Table 1 and these encompass the

TABLE 1

The plot model

Boundary conditions	Processes	Responses
I. Geologic-pedologic controls	I. Bulk mechanical stresses	I. Soil surface set
(a) Mantle thickness	(a) Tangential stress	(a) Sheet erosion
(b) Surface shear strength	(b) Particle expansion-contraction	(b) Gully erosion
(c) Bulk shear strength	(c) Ice crystal growth	(c) Surface compaction
(d) Infiltration capacity		(d) Talus settling
(e) Permeability	II. Surface water stresses	(e) Avalanche erosion deposition
(f) Slope angle	(a) Overland flow drag	(f) Needle ice transport
(g) Aspect	(b) Rill discharge drag	
(h) Slope position	(c) Ground freezing	II. Bulk soil set
		(a) Soil creep
II. Climatic controls	III. Soil and groundwater stresses	(b) Solifluction
(a) Temperature variations	(a) Soil moisture fluctuations	(c) Landsliding
(b) Rainstorm periodicity	(b) Soil moisture gradients	(d) Groundwater solution transport
(c) Rainfall intensity	(c) Interflow discharge	(e) Frost creep
(d) Snow cover duration	(d) Pore water pressure	
(e) Snow depth-density	(e) Water table fluctuations	III. Rock weathering set
(f) Snowdrift factors		(a) Mechanical shattering
(g) Snowmelt conditions	IV. Meteorological stresses	(b) Solution effects
	(a) Raindrop kinetic energy	(c) Mechanical corrosion
III. Biologic controls	(b) Snowpack pressure	
(a) Ground cover	(c) Avalanche shear stress	
(b) Litter cover	(d) Stem flow discharge	
(c) Phenologic characteristics		
(d) Root density		
(e) Root strength		
(f) Burrowing organisms		
(g) Surface animal movement		

TABLE 2

Linkage matrices[a]

a. Boundary conditions versus processes

			Boundary Conditions																					
			I								II							III							Sum
			a	b	c	d	e	f	g	h	a	b	c	d	e	f	g	a	b	c	d	e	f	g	
I	a		1	1	1			1		1														1	1	7
	b		1	1	1	1		1	1		1	1	1	1	1			1	1	1	1					15
	c		1		1		1	1	1	1	1	1	1	1	1			1	1	1	1		1	1		17
II	a		1		1	1	1		1		1	1	1	1	1	1	1	1	1			1				15
	b		1		1	1	1		1		1	1	1	1	1	1	1	1	1							14
	c		1	1	1	1		1	1		1	1	1	1	1	1	1	1	1	1						16
III	a		1		1	1	1	1	1	1	1	1	1	1	1			1	1		1	1		1		17
	b		1			1	1		1		1	1	1			1	1	1	1		1			1		13
	c		1		1	1	1	1																		5
	d		1			1	1	1		1			1	1				1	1		1					10
	e		1			1	1	1			1	1	1	1		1								1		10
IV	a		1			1		1			1	1	1					1	1	1						9
	b		1			1	1	1			1	1	1	1	1											9
	c		1			1	1	1			1	1	1	1	1											9
	d		1								1	1						1	1				1			6
Sum			7	12	7	9	8	15	6	11	5	13	12	6	11	8	13	14	7	10	4	1	5	2		192

(Left axis label: Processes)

processes of waste movement on alpine slopes. They are classified according to whether they derive from physical forces in the waste mantle itself (Group I) or are associated with water on the surface (Group II) and in the ground (Group III), or are extraneous to the slope (Group IV). Again there is likely to be a considerable amount of interaction between these sets; surface water stresses are associated, at least at their inception, with the same controls of infiltration as are groundwater processes and are closely bound, in terms of their effects, with the turbulence induced in overland flow by raindrop impact.

The geomorphic responses of Table 1 fall into three basic sets involving either a large part of the waste mantle or only the immediate surface layer. Again, interaction between these sets is very likely and so the distinction should not be construed as anything more than an aid in implementing the model. The fact of interaction is made even more important when one considers the possiblity of feedback influences from any one variable in the response component to other components eventually being reflected in different responses elsewhere in the final product. The case of surface soil compaction by raindrop impact as an immediate response which might then influence soil creep rates through its effect on infiltration and soil moisture fluctuations exemplifies this kind of mechanism.

Links

The components of the model are linked in many ways; it is these links which effect geomorphic work and the transfer of waste and sediment. If Table 1 is considered as a three dimensional matrix with axes defined by the three components, it contains 5,175 cells each representing a possible link between three variables, without any statement about the direction of that link. Since not all of these links are physically possible, we can assign a value to each cell in binary or nominal fashion as: 1 = a conceivable link; and 0 = a physically impossible one. Obviously only the cells containing unit values will be of interest but, with over 5,000 cells initially, even the number of these will be high ($\simeq 2,500$?). For this reason, analysis in this form has not been attempted here. Instead the links between variables in contiguous components have been examined (Table 2). This represents a basic

b. Processes versus responses

Processes

Responses		I a	I b	I c	II a	II b	II c	III a	III b	III c	III d	III e	IV a	IV b	IV c	IV d	Sum
I	a			1	1	1	1						1			1	6
	b				1	1	1						1	1			5
	c		1		1			1					1	1			5
	d	1	1	1			1	1				1	1	1	1		9
	e		1				1								1	1	4
	f		1	1			1	1	1			1					6
II	a	1	1				1	1	1	1	1	1		1			9
	b	1					1	1	1		1	1					6
	c	1	1				1	1	1		1	1		1			8
	d						1	1	1	1	1	1					6
	e	1		1			1	1	1								5
III	a			1			1	1				1					4
	b							1	1	1		1		1			5
	c		1											1	1		3
Sum		5	7	5	3	2	11	10	7	3	4	8	4	7	3	2	81

c. Boundary conditions versus responses

Boundary Conditions

Responses		I a	I b	I c	I d	I e	I f	I g	I h	II a	II b	II c	II d	II e	II f	II g	III a	III b	III c	III d	III e	III f	III g	Sum
I	a		1	1	1	1	1	1	1	1	1	1	1	1	1	1	1	1	1				1	18
	b		1	1	1	1	1	1	1	1	1	1	1	1	1	1	1	1	1				1	18
	c	1	1	1	1	1	1	1	1	1	1	1	1	1	1	1	1	1	1	1		1	1	21
	d	1	1	1	1	1	1	1	1	1	1	1	1	1	1	1	1	1	1	1		1	1	21
	e	1	1	1	1	1	1	1	1	1	1	1	1	1	1	1	1	1	1					18
	f	1	1	1	1	1	1	1	1	1	1	1	1	1	1	1	1	1	1	1		1		20
II	a	1	1	1	1	1	1	1	1	1	1	1	1	1	1	1	1	1	1	1		1	1	21
	b	1	1	1	1	1	1	1	1	1	1	1	1	1	1	1	1	1	1	1		1	1	21
	c	1	1	1	1	1	1	1	1	1	1	1	1	1	1	1	1	1	1	1		1	1	21
	d	1		1	1	1	1	1	1	1	1	1	1	1	1	1	1	1	1	1		1		19
	e	1	1	1	1	1	1	1	1	1	1	1	1	1	1	1	1	1	1	1		1	1	21
III	a	1	1	1	1	1	1	1	1	1	1	1	1	1	1	1	1	1	1	1	1	1		21
	b	1	1	1	1	1	1	1	1	1	1	1	1	1	1	1	1	1	1	1				19
	c	1	1	1	1		1	1	1	1	1	1	1	1	1	1	1		1			1		17
Sum		12	13	14	14	13	14	14	14	14	14	14	14	14	14	14	14	13	14	10	1	10	8	276

[a]1 = reason to believe a link between the two variables is likely. Zero values have been omitted for clarity.

simplification in that it ignores interaction between variables in the same component and between more than one pair of variables at a time. The result is still somewhat surprising: 192 links are defined between boundary conditions and processes and 81 links between processes and responses. The range of possibilities in the operation of a geomorphic system is obviously very wide. This conclusion is reinforced by considering similarly defined links between boundary conditions and responses made through an intermediate process.

In this case 276 links are defined and this does not include multiple links between the same boundary control and response, i.e., the linkage between rainfall intensity and sheet erosion is only counted once even though it may go through overland flow mechanisms, frozen ground factors, raindrop impact, or stem flow discharge.

For a single point in the landscape it may be possible to assume that many of these links have negligible importance and to ignore them. (This is likely to be an important next-step if the matrices of Table 2 are to be collapsed to manageable size.) Nevertheless, an analysis such as this indicates the complexity of process work in alpine geomorphology, especially when the entire landscape of the stream basin is considered. The row totals in Table 2c, which indicate the number of boundary conditions capable of affecting each response, show this very clearly. Any of the listed responses are likely to be the result of a highly complex, multivariate interaction: all of those named in Table 1 may be influenced by more that 17 boundary conditions. Even this situation may be an over simplification since many of the defined boundaries and responses of Table 1 include what would be measured as more than one variable in a field study. Furthermore, there will be great variation in the strength of different links, just as there is variability in the directness and direction in which they are made. At present, we have little information on which to base even an ordinal scaling of the large number of links involved (for this reason the binary analysis was used here). The accumulation of such information is a basic requirement of any study of a single geomorphic system and is also required for the deletion of any links from consideration.

Groups

Simplification is possible if the system components of Table 1 are clustered into like-groups, although this will mean further loss of information as individual variables are omitted. This has been done in Table 3 which shows only 10 groups and 18 links between adjacent components. Now the level of interaction between groups in the system can be seen more clearly. Because it involves the lumping of disparate variables, however (as in the climatic boundary conditions or the soil surface responses) this model is probably too simple to be of use in a field enquiry. A compromise is needed between this and the full plot model which may be found by defining subsystems, i.e., sets of links rather than the whole model. This is one approach that is being taken in a study of the geomorphic effects of increased snowfall in the alpine of the San Juan Mountains. In this approach, the variables associated with snowfall, snowpack, or snowmelt have been isolated from the rest of the general model to make up two mutually exclusive process sets—one associated with snow and the other associated with all other boundary conditions. The relative importance of these two sets in the work of waste movement is considered as a test of the net effectiveness of snow on geomorphic processes.

The Site Model

A model such as that developed above may be considered dimensionless in a spatial sense but the local variablity of many geomorphic boundary conditions makes it inapplicable in practice to large areas. While boundary conditions and the processes and responses developed from them are continuously variable in space, and therefore theoretically open to analysis by infinitesimal calculus, the complexity of their gradients necessitates much simplification. It is likely that the partial differential equations needed in the study of more than two variables in a two dimensional space would be impossible to solve, anyway (Harbaugh and Bonham-Carter, 1970, p. 170).

Two stages of approximation offer means of making this simplification; both are probably required in geomorphic process work at the present time. First, there is the possibility of a reduction from the two dimensions of an area to the single dimension of a slope profile or transect. Given the basic contraint on most geomorphic processes imposed by gravity which leads to movement approximately along the profile, this is a useful simplification. It allows process measurments to be used in testing deductive models developed from the denudation balance concept, like those of Ahnert (1967). Second, there is the reduction of continuous trends along the profile to finite steps. This may be done by sampling rather than by considering the entire continuum as a unit. It means that the plot model would be fitted to a slope profile at a sequence of points along the profile, rather than as a continuously changing set of factors applied to the whole profile. At a later stage, smoothing of points to a trend line, or even a surface, is possible by standard statistical techniques.

TABLE 3

Summary plot model

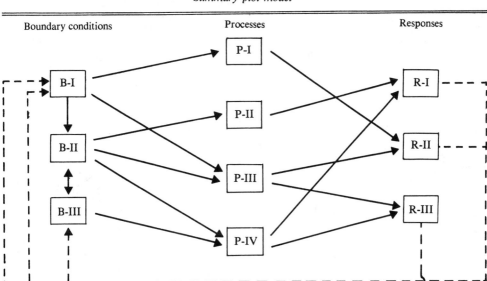

Boundary conditions   Processes   Responses

⟶ Direct important links, showing direction of influence

– – ➤ Feedback effects

The Plot Budget

For each of these points, the resultant of all responses in the plot model can be expressed as a simple budget:

$$A + W - R = dS \qquad (1)$$

in which A is the waste moved onto the plot area from upslope, W is the waste accumulated on the plot by the weathering of bedrock below it, R is the waste removed from the plot and moved downslope; and dS is any change in the volume of waste stored on the plot. The nature of slope systems that have been simplified in this way, and the results of inequalities in their budgets have been examined by Ahnert (1967) who used these considerations to develop deductive slope models. Here, we need only note that equation (1) represents something close to a *reductio ad absurdum* of the response component in Table 1. Any member of response sets I and II is capable of con-

tributing to A and R while W is comprised of every member of response set III. Therefore, the measurement of all the responses in the model may be required to adequately explain the denudation budget of a single plot. Even though the budget is conceptually simple, the estimation of its terms in practice is not simple and the further step to the explanation of their magnitude is even more problematic. These problems are parallel to those met in work on glacier mass budgets (Paterson, 1969, Chapt. 3).

Nevertheless, one may now consider a slope profile as a sequence of contiguous plots that are linked by the fact that R from one plot constitutes A at the next plot downslope or, to express this more succinctly:

$$R_n = A_{n+1} \qquad (2)$$

In a slope profile, the form of the linkage of R strongly suggests a hydrologic cascading system and may be capable of analysis as a first order, single dependence Markov chain to which W and storage change (dS) provide independent or random effects. To my knowledge, modelling of slope responses in this manner has not been attempted but, although it would be an interesting potential extension of any study of geomorphic processes, the subject need not be considered further here.

An Alpine Slope Model

Alpine slopes may be considered axiomatically steep. Given the characteristic of high relief which this implies, they seem to conform quite closely to the classical slope model defined by Wood (1942) and King (1953). (This has yet to be convincingly demonstrated, however, by generalizing or averaging alpine slope profiles.) This model breaks a typical slope into four

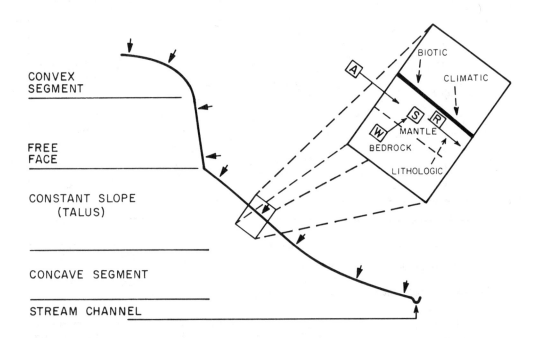

FIGURE 1. The site model.

components—a convex segment at the inter-fluve, a cliff or freeface below this, a constant slope below the cliff, and a concave segment extending across the valley floor to the stream channel. This set of four segments, not necessarily in this sequence, accounts for every slope profile form if partial or multiple sequences are allowed as well. Such a profile (Figure 1) is easily adapted to the alpine situation, especially where the problem of contemporary glacial activity does not arise. Although multiple sequences are likely to be the rule rather than the exception, the simplification afforded by the model profile is a real gain and does not appear to distort the natural system too badly.

In a field situation one cannot usually consider the entire population of 1-m² plots along a slope profile and so a sampling problem arises. An intermittent chain of plots along the profile has a serious disadvantage in that the equality of equation (2) will be lost. This is serious because change in storage between two neighboring, but separated, plots may disqualify the extension of budgets from the plots across the intervening area. This problem is probably best overcome by stratified random sampling (within slope segments), with replication, to allow estimation of segment mean values. It might also be approached by testing the representativeness of plots on the same segment by a comparison of boundary conditions. A weakness of the latter approach is that many significant boundary conditions are not apparent on superficial examination since they are "buried" below the ground sur-face. Nevertheless, they only need to be measured once in the life of most research projects, since they are unlikely to undergo drastic changes in a period of, say, 5 years.

The base of a slope profile like Figure 1 is likely to be defined by a stream channel, the activity of which represents an important boundary condition to the slope. The influence of this boundary will be fed back up the slope through budget links like those defined in equations (1) and (2). The significance of the stream channel end point in the development of the slope has been examined on many occasions (e.g., Scheidegger, 1961, p. 109, Ahnert, 1967; Carson, 1969). Often the stream is assumed to be neither aggrading, degrading, nor migrating laterally and thus to be simply removing waste supplied to the slope foot by processes acting on the slope. This assumption is implicit in the preceding discussion. Channel behavior has been ignored here for the sake of simplicity but it would not be difficult to extend the model to include active stream influences. A further extension into three dimensions to represent a natural system such as a drainage basin, in which the stream channel has basic importance, would be possible but, for the present, the complexity of the plot model, expanded by replication on a multiplicity of profile segments, represents a meaningful limit to which both field and analytical techniques can be pressed. The introduction of the stream channel to this creates new sets of boundary conditions, processes, and responses controlled by open channel hydraulic forces.

CONCLUSION

This basis for the study of alpine slope processes has been developed as the framework for a study of the direct effects of artificially increased snowfall on the stability of slopes above timberline in the San Juan Mountains of southwestern Colorado. In such an inquiry the model becomes somewhat simpler than its presentation here suggests since only the boundary conditions and processes related to snow, or capable of being affected by snow, need be considered. Table 4, a modification of Table 3, shows the results of this simplification. It suggests that the most probable direct geomorphic results of an increase in average snowfall should be found at the soil surface, rather than at greater depths in the waste material.

This is a basic justification for concentrating the field effort on the study of surface movement rates and surface sediment loss.

Two other factors, however, tend to complicate implementation of the model in a field situation. First is the problem of the timing of the geomorphic process controls that are subject to temporal variability. For the sake of simplicity this has been ignored here although it has already been examined in a more general context (Wolman and Miller, 1960). It introduces a second dimension (time) to the sampling problem that has been discussed (the spatial one) and is, therefore, capable of seriously complicating the field study. The second factor concerns only the immediate

TABLE 4

Cross-component sets

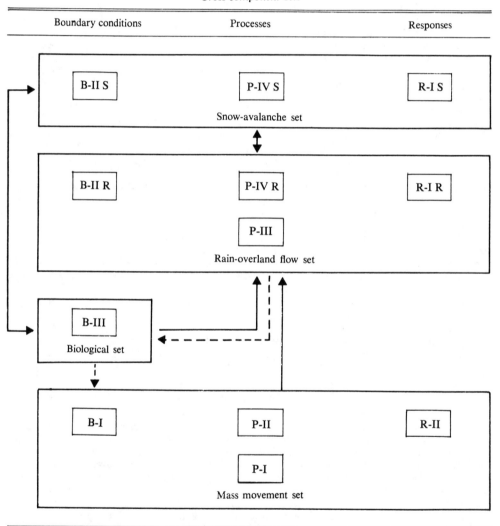

| Boundary conditions | Processes | Responses |

Strong between-set interaction, with direction

Weak between-set interaction, with direction

The groups B-II, P-IV, and R-I of the original model have been split here. The split is as follows:
S = variable associated with precipitation as snow
R = variables associated with precipitation as rain

application of the model to the San Juan situation. It derives from the fact that an increase in snowfall may have indirect effects on geomorphic processes, as well as the direct ones defined by Table 4. These could, for example, work through a chain of ecological exchanges from an initial impact on the vegetation and so may be felt anywhere in the whole set of geomorphic responses. Hence, it is important that the model be implemented as a single whole, even though such indirect effects may be lagged relative to any direct ones.

ACKNOWLEDGMENTS

This work has been financed by the U.S. Department of the Interior, Bureau of Reclamation (Contract No. 14-06-D-7052) as part of a study of the ecological effects of augmented snowfall in the San Juan Mountains. I am particularly indebted to J. T. Andrews, M. A. Carson, J. D. Ives, P J. Webber, and S. E. White for discussion, comments, and advice on earlier versions of this paper.

REFERENCES

Ahnert, F.
    1967 : The role of the equilibrium concept in the interpretation of landforms of fluvial erosion and deposition. In Macar, P. (ed.), *L'Evolution des Versants.* Univ. de Liège, 23-41.
Caine, N.
    1963 : Movement of low angle scree slopes in the Lake District, northern England. *Rev. Geomorph. Dyn.,* 14: 171-177.
    1968 : The log-normal distribution and rates of soil movement: an example. *Rev. Geomorph. Dyn.,* 18:1-7.
Carson, M. A.
    1969 : Models of hillslope development under mass failure. *Geogr. Analysis,* 1: 76-100.
Chorley, R. J.
    1967 : Models in geomorphology. *In* Chorley, R. J. and Haggett, P. (eds.), *Models in Geography.* Methuen, London, 59-96.
    1969 : The drainage basin as the fundamental morphic unit. *In* Chorley, R. J. (ed.), *Water, Earth and Man.* Methuen, London, 77-99.
Harbaugh, J. W. and Bonham-Carter, G.
    1970 : *Computer Simulation in Geology.* Wiley-Interscience, New York. 575 pp.
King, L. C.
    1953 : Canons of landscape evolution. *Bull. Geol. Soc. Amer.,* 64: 721-751.
Krumbein, W. C.
    1964 : A geological process-response model for analysis of beach phenomena. Northwestern Univ. Geology Dep. Tech. Rep., 8: 1-15.

Krumbein, W. C. and Graybill, F. A.
    1965 : *An Introduction to Statistical Models in Geology.* McGraw-Hill, New York. 475 pp.
Paterson, W. S. B.
    1969 : *The Physics of Glaciers.* The Commonwealth and International Library, Pergamon Press, Oxford. 250 pp.
Scheidegger, A. E.
    1961 : *Theoretical Geomorphology.* Springer Verlag, Berlin. 333 pp.
Slaymaker, H. O.
    1969 : A reinterpretation of some fluvial landforms of mid-Wales. Unpublished paper, mimeographed. 19 pp.
Strahler, A. N.
    1952 : Dynamic basis of geomorphology. *Bull. Geol. Soc. Amer.,* 63: 923-938.
Tricart, J.
    1965 : *Principes et Méthodes de la Géomorphologie.* Masson, Paris. 496 pp.
Weiner, N.
    1961 : *Cybernetics; or Control and Communication in the Animal and the Machine.* 2nd Edition. M. I. T. Press, Cambridge. 212 pp.
Wolman, M. G. and Miller, J. P.
    1960 : Magnitude and frequency of forces in geomorphic processes. *J. Geol.,* 68: 54-74.
Wood, A.
    1942 : The development of hillside slopes. *Proc. Geol. Assoc.,* 53: 128-140.

ROCK GLACIER STUDIES IN THE COLORADO FRONT RANGE, 1961 TO 1968

SIDNEY E. WHITE

Department of Geology
The Ohio State University
Columbus, Ohio 43210

INTRODUCTION

Three of nine tongue-shaped rock glaciers in Colorado Front Range were selected for study in 1961 (Figure 1). Two are east of the Continental west of the Divide at the head of Cascade Creek, tributary to the Colorado River. Arapaho and Taylor rock glaciers are easily accessible, but the need to study one west of the Divide for comparison made it necessary to choose the relatively inaccessible Fair rock glacier.

This study became part of a larger research program in 1964 concerned with identification and mapping, including motion studies, of many forms of alpine mass movement due to past and present periglacial action in the upper glaciated valleys and cirques of this part of the Front Range.

Divide—Arapaho rock glacier, 31 km west of Boulder, and Taylor rock glacier in Rocky Mountain National Park. The third, Fair rock glacier, is This paper reports on the rock glaciers and the first 5 years (1961 to 1966) of movement data.

Other tongue-shaped rock glaciers are between latitudes 40°00′ and 40°19′N (Figure 1). Lobate rock glaciers, so named by Wahrhaftig and Cox (1959), and also called valley-wall rock glaciers by Outcalt and Benedict (1965), occur at various altitudes and exposures in all upper valleys nearby. Rock glaciers of this paper are accumulations of unsorted till-like, coarse to fine rock debris, with an ice core and/or interstitial ice, having a glacier shape and spreading downvalley.

(*Editor's Note:* Material has been omitted at this point.)

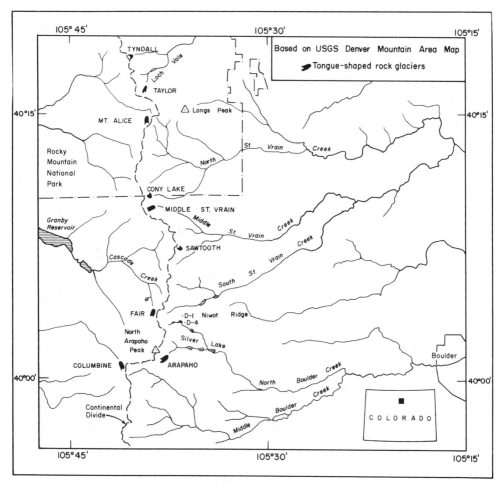

FIGURE 1. Location map of tongue-shaped rock glaciers.

(*Editor's Note:* Material has been omitted at this point.)

104

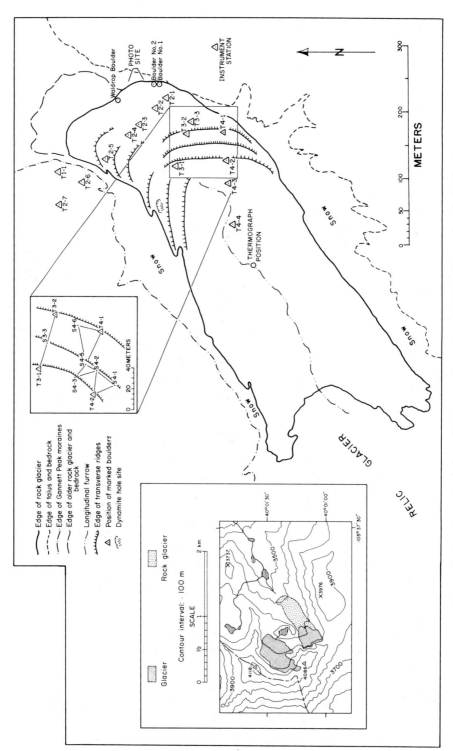

FIGURE 2. Arapaho rock glacier, with traverse lines of marked boulders, enlarged sketch of movement net between transverse ridges, thermograph position, photo site, and other places of specific study. Inset map of rock glacier and Arapaho Glacier adapted from U.S.G.S. Monarch Lake quadrangle, 7.5 min. ser., 1958. Relic glacier at west edge of Arapaho rock glacier is un-named. Peak at 4,086 m is South Arapaho Peak. Continental Divide is dashed line.

DESCRIPTION OF ARAPAHO, TAYLOR, AND FAIR ROCK GLACIERS

Arapaho, Taylor, and Fair rock glaciers are shown by topographic maps (insets in Figures 2, 6, and 9); character of boundaries, means of supply, surface microrelief, and composition are given for each. Altitude, length, width, area, surface slope, crest height, thickness, and data on the front are in Table 1. Terminology and techniques of Wahrhaftig and Cox (1959) on rock glaciers in the Alaska Range are followed.

ARAPAHO ROCK GLACIER

Arapaho rock glacier lies along the southeast side of a double cirque (Figure 2); Arapaho Glacier, a small drift glacier, is in the northwest corner of the same cirque. The rock glacier is separated from Arapaho Glacier by ice-cored terminal moraines of Gannett Peak stade and by a lateral trough along its north side, and separated from talus on the south wall of the cirque also by

a lateral trough (Figures 2, 3, and 4). The north side of the rock glacier stands 4 to 10 m above the snow surface, and the south side, 7 to 12 m. This height depends in part upon amount of winter snow and extent of summer melting in the lateral troughs. Boulders only reach the troughs on rare occasions, as in the summer of 1965 when unusually severe cloudbursts triggered mudflows from the south valley wall.

The rock glacier head is separated from the cirque wall by a small saucer-shaped relic glacier (Figure 2) of unknown thickness, with an area of about 43,720 m². Blocks from avalanche rockfalls rarely leave the headwall cliffs except during extreme summer deluges or rapid spring melting. Both tabular and cubical blocks pried loose from the cirque wall failed to slide or roll across the surface of the relic glacier to the rock glacier. Photographs that I took in 1939 and since show

TABLE 1

Data on Arapaho, Taylor, and Fair rock glaciers

	Arapaho rock glacier (40°01'15"N, 105°38'20"W)	Taylor rock glacier (40°16'30"N, 105°40'15"W)	Fair rock glacier (40°03'50"N, 105°39'20"W)
Altitude of head	3,710 m	ca. 3,540 m	ca. 3,520 m
Altitude of toe	3,570 m	3,330 m	<3,320 m
Mean length	640 m	625 m	405 m
Mean width	205 m	ca. 170 m	215 m
Surface area	126,480 m²	113,700 m²	93,325 m²
Slope of head	13-16°	9°	10°
Slope near toe	21°	13°	14°
Estimated thickness	21 m	24 m	>37 m
Frontal[a] crest height Range (mean)	13-27 m (23 m)	18-30 m (25 m)	20-40 m (36 m)
Slope of front Range (mean)	37-55° (44°)	36-44° (40°)	42-50° (46°)
Frontal talus slope Range (mean)	36-39° (38°)	35-38° (37°)	38-40° (39°)
Frontal talus height Range (mean)	8-11 m (9.5 m)	8-11 m (10 m)	5-30 m (14 m)
% talus on front Range (mean)	40-62% (52%)	36-54% (46%)	41-80% (55%)

[a]"Frontal" includes data near the corners as well as along the actual front.

FIGURE 3. Upper ice-cored end of Arapaho rock glacier. Unnamed relic glacier is at upper left edge of photograph. August 8, 1959.

FIGURE 4. Center and terminus of Arapaho rock glacier, showing transverse ridges and furrows. Gannett Peak moraines and older debris along top of photograph. Matches right edge of Figure 3. August 8, 1959.

that the appearance of the south valley wall, the relic glacier surface, and the head of the rock glacier have not changed appreciably in the past 30 years.

Thickness may be determined only at the front and southeast corner where the rock glacier rests on thin till on bedrock. Height to crest varies, but is as much as 27 m. Average crest height is 23 m (incorrectly stated as 6 m by White, *in* Waldrop and White, 1965); this gives a thickness of 21 m using $T = H \cos S$, where T is thickness, H height of front, and S slope of upper surface (Wahrhaftig and Cox, 1959). Wherever height

was acquired, slope angle also was obtained. Steepest slopes are where many blocks protrude, gentlest where mostly finer material occurs. Talus along the base of the front or sides rests at still lower angles.

Microrelief features on the surface of rock glaciers often reveal their internal character. A central longitudinal furrow extends for 360 m down the rock glacier surface. The downvalley two-fifths of the surface has transverse ridges and furrows convex in plan downvalley (Figures 2 and 4). Here the V-shaped furrows provide relief of 8 to 10 m. The gentler upvalley slope of

(*Editor's Note:* Material has been omitted at this point.)

each transverse ridge is made of angular rock rubble, but much finer debris is exposed on the 42° front slopes of a ridge, such as the ridge along traverse positions T4-2 to T3-1 (*see* Figures 2 and 5). Fine debris is rarely exposed on front slopes of the transverse ridges downvalley from here, except along the rock glacier front.

As with rock glaciers studied by Wahrhaftig and Cox (1959) and Foster and Holmes (1965) in the Alaska Range; by Vernon and Hughes (1966) in the Ogilvie Mountains, Yukon Territory; by Roots (1954) in the Swannell Ranges, British Columbia; by Potter (1967) in northern Absaroka Mountains, Wyoming; and with those I have studied in the Uncompahgre and the Elk Mountains, Colorado, the upper one-fourth to one-fifth thickness of the rock glacier is coarse blocky rubble, whereas the inside is mainly finer material. Blocks along the south side are by far the largest; more than 50% of those on the surface there are 25 m³ or larger. This reflects homogeneity of the granitic source rocks, easily traced to their cliff positions, as well as scarcity of jointing. Mean particle size on the rock glacier surface is about 1 m. Roots (1954, pp. 27-28) measured the coarser sizes on rock glaciers in the Swannell Ranges of northern interior British Columbia and learned from a mean diameters study that more than 75% are between 0.5 and 1 m. In Graubünden Canton, Switzerland, Domaradzki (1951) obtained a mean particle size of 0.7 m on rock glacier surfaces of sedimentary rocks and 1.5 m on those of crystalline rocks.

Voids between large blocks are open to depths of 4 to 6 m and permit passage of air, rainwater, drifting snow, and meltwater. Water drains away wherever possible, or freezes upon contact with the frozen material inside. Water that reaches the front emerges about two-thirds of the height above the base. The zone of emergence is marked by moist, darkly colored fine debris.

Here and there on the surface pockets of fine debris support immature soil and a growth of grasses, sedges, and many alpine herbaceous plants. Lichens grow on all but freshly exposed or overturned rock surfaces on all the rock glaciers; frontal areas are conspicuously barren. Lichen cover is about 10% on rock surfaces on the transverse ridge along traverse positions T4-2 to T3-1 and all upvalley, but is more than this downvalley, possibly as much as 40%. Benedict's study (1967, 1968) of lichen growth and percentage cover is much more extensive.

The lower fine material is similar to till, consisting of unsorted, angular to subangular blocks embedded in a matrix of gray sand, silt, and clay; except where seasonally thawed, it is cemented with interstitial ice. Mechanical analysis of particles less than 4 mm in diameter, at 6 exposures around the sides and front, show a matrix of 68% sand and 9% silt and clay. During an attempt with James B. Benedict on August 22, 1966, to learn if the rock glacier has an ice core, a hole was dynamited 2.5 m deep into only the fine debris, 170 m behind the front and 25 m in from the north side (Figure 2). All material encountered below a depth of 0.5 m to the base of the hole was tightly frozen, and was aggregates of muddy sand embedded in clusters of ice granules 1 to 2 cm long. Creep of this interstitial ice may be responsible in part for the rock glacier movement.

Temperatures and Ice Core Within Arapaho Rock Glacier

In 1961, I followed the sound of running water and entered the rock glacier via the voids in the blocky rubble, and was surprised to discover, at a depth of 4 m, water flowing across solid ice. Although I assumed the ice was derived from drifted snow of the previous winter, and that it would disappear at the end of the melt season, it did not. In a 15-day period (August 7 to 21), this ice surface lowered 35 cm. A thermograph in a wooden frame was suspended 25 cm above the ice, 4.5 m below the rock glacier surface (see Figure 2 for location). Daytime air temperatures for the 15-day period rarely reached 4.4°C (40°F) at noon, fluctuated about 1.6°C (35°F), and dropped to −0.5°C (31°F) the first 8 nights and to −1.1°C (30°F) the last 7 nights. Minimum temperature for 1961 to 1964 here was −10°C (14°F), and for the winter 1964-65 −21°C (−6°F). In ·1966, in a new position 6 m below the rock glacier surface, night temperatures dropped to 0.6°C (33°F) in late July and to −1.1°C (30°F) in late August. Minimum 1966-67 winter temperature at this new place was −11°C (12°F).

At the 1961 thermograph position on July 28, 1966, water flowing 5 m below the rock glacier surface was −4.4°C (24°F), an unexpected temperature that remained this low during an hour of repeated testing. On August 16, 1966, using a new thermometer for verification, −2.2°C (28°F) was recorded for the flowing water at the same place. Domaradzki (1951) obtained temperatures at the point of emergence of water from nine rock glaciers in Switzerland; these ranged from 0.5°C to 2.5°C, and averaged 1.5°C.

It is now known that a relic glacier (ice core) exists under the blocky rubble of the upvalley part of the rock glacier. The surface stream flowing on the relic glacier in the depression of the central longitudinal furrow becomes entrenched first through 2 to 3 m of blocky debris and then into underlying clean glacier ice to depths of 9 to 12 m. Annual repetition of this process is responsible for the longitudinal furrow. Water flowing through the relic glacier inside is so cooled it is momentarily below freezing while in motion. The existence of this ice core was first noted by J. B. Benedict in late August 1963, and first recorded by him on August 21, 1964, in an exceptional photograph (see Outcalt and Benedict, 1965, Figure 6). In late August 1966, water had melted a channel 3 to 5 m wide and at least 12 m deep into the ice of the relic glacier, proving minimum ice thickness of at least this amount.

The relic glacier does not extend inside any farther downvalley than about 330 m from the rock glacier head because this point is (1) shortly before the transverse furrows and ridges begin (suggesting pressure by the downvalley end of the buried relic glacier); (2) about 70 m downvalley from the 1961 thermograph site where ice was seen at depth; and (3) where water audibly flowing on ice inside drops out of hearing, presumably over the front of the ice core.

The area underlain by ice is estimated to be 55,700 m². Along the south and north sides, blocky rubble on the ice is about 10 and 6 m thick, respectively. In the center, it has the observed thickness of 2 to 3 m. Using 0.4 for porosity, a figure employed by Wahrhaftig and Cox (1959, p. 430), so that volume of debris is 60% of total volume, this part of the rock glacier is about 143,080 m³. The part not underlain by ice forms about 56% of surface area. Volume here also may be calculated, provided it truly does not contain an ice core. Again using porosity of 0.4, surface area of 70,780 m², and thickness of 21 m, volume of the non-ice-cored part is 891,830 m³. Volume of the whole rock glacier is about 1,034,910 m³, giving an estimate of the amount of debris moving downvalley.

Taylor Rock Glacier

Taylor rock glacier fills almost all of a narrow cirque inset into the west-sloping surface that forms the Divide (Figure 6). It has a concave surface where it merges into Taylor Glacier (Figure 7), but flattens near the terminus where many irregular pits and depressions abound (Figure 8).

Debris from the north wall rarely reaches the north edge of the rock glacier. Above the northwest corner, however, several couloirs allow a continuous stream of rockfall- and avalanche-produced talus to reach the rock glacier there. Taylor Glacier is supplied by snow blown across the smooth periglacial slopes (Figure 6) to the west. Heads of the couloirs above receive the drifting snow first; it then avalanches across the concave glacier below onto the rock glacier. Rock debris, transported by this avalanching snow added to that from the northwest couloirs, is the supply of material today. The area of avalanched snow and nonsorted rock debris, transitional between ice of Taylor Glacier and blocky rubble of the rock glacier (Figure 7), is 38% (43,400 m²) of the rock glacier surface. Evidence of this avalanching is a higher zone where mainly erosion occurs,

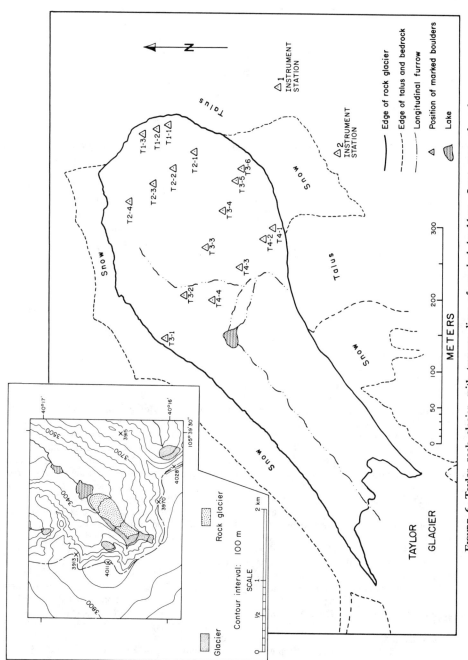

FIGURE 6. Taylor rock glacier, with traverse lines of marked boulders. Inset map of rock glacier and Taylor Glacier adapted from U.S.G.S. McHenrys Peak quadrangle, 7.5 min. ser., 1957. Continental Divide is dashed line. Broad periglacial surface is west of Divide.

(*Editor's Note:* Material has been omitted at this point.)

with typical boulder-protected debris tails (Rapp, 1959, pp. 39-40), and a lower zone where mainly deposition occurs, with rocks of all sizes perched precariously everywhere.

Near the southeast front corner, the crest is 30 m high, but thickness along the front is about 24 m. The younger upvalley part of the rock glacier is relatively smooth with one microrelief feature, a longitudinal furrow separating debris from the northwest couloirs from debris that avalanches across Taylor Glacier (Figure 6). Annual layers of avalanched snow and firn alter- of seasonal thaw must contain interstitial ice. Again using porosity of 0.4 and surface area and thickness (Table 1), volume of the rock glacier is about 1,091,500 m³, providing a measure of amount of debris moving out of the cirque today.

FAIR ROCK GLACIER

Fair Glacier and Fair rock glacier, deeply set into the head of a narrow cirque, are confined by

nating with layers of nonsorted rock rubble concentrated by summer ablation are exposed in the walls of the furrow. This avalanched part stands 5 to 10 m above the lower irregularly pitted down-valley part (Figure 8). There are no transverse ridges or furrows across the rock glacier anywhere.

The rock glacier is made of rock rubble of fine sizes as well as of angular blocks. No obvious upper layer of coarser blocks rides on finer material inside. The avalanched debris when concentrated after summer ablation is homogeneous and appears similar to till. Voids below the limit arêtes on the east, west, and south sides (Figure 9). Crest height along the rock glacier front is 38 to 40 m. Both east and west sides are high enough to prevent inundation by talus from valley walls, but at one place active rockfall and alluvial talus from the west wall may supply blocks to the rock glacier. Steep-sided, ice-cored Gannett Peak moraines in front of Fair Glacier shed debris onto the rock glacier head. A gap 80 m wide in these

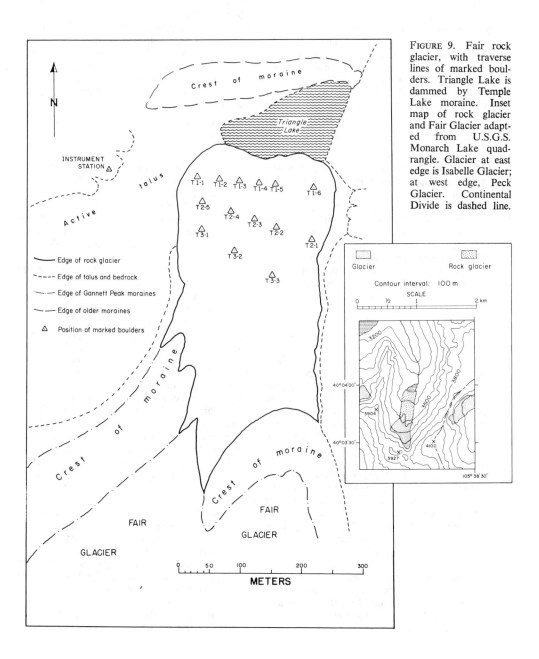

FIGURE 9. Fair rock glacier, with traverse lines of marked boulders. Triangle Lake is dammed by Temple Lake moraine. Inset map of rock glacier and Fair Glacier adapted from U.S.G.S. Monarch Lake quadrangle. Glacier at east edge is Isabelle Glacier; at west edge, Peck Glacier. Continental Divide is dashed line.

moraines allows additional rocks from cirque cliffs to the south to slide through onto the rock glacier. Scores of freshly broken rock chips, and one granite block weighing 58×10^3 kg, moved within 60 m of the front between 1961 and 1966, presumably skidding across drifted snow during a winter.

Most of the rock glacier surface is compressed into transverse ridges and furrows. These ridges extend not more than half rock glacier width in from each side, alternating from one side and then from the other (see Ives, 1940, Plate 1). Ridges are steepest (39°) on downvalley sides and stand 6 m above the bottom of adjacent furrows. No central longitudinal furrow is present. Blocky rubble overlies finer material over most of the rock glacier; many large blocks are granite, 12 to 15 m³, and could have come from any valley wall. Random pockets of fine debris sustain an immature soil and alpine plants between blocks. Fine debris is visible along the rock glacier front and also on the forward edges of the transverse ridges. Mechanical analyses of particles less than 4 mm in diameter indicate a matrix of 71% sand and 8% silt and clay. Flowing water at 0°C emerges at the front, 3.3 m above Triangle Lake. Interstitial ice probably occurs within the fine material. Assuming no ice core within, and using porosity of 0.4 and surface area and thickness (Table 1), volume of the rock glacier is about 1,381,200 m³.

MOVEMENT OF THE ROCK GLACIERS

Movement studies carried out on Arapaho rock glacier include measurements of (1) surface movement of marked boulders, (2) differential movement between transverse ridge crests, (3) movement of individual blocks in the base at the front, and (4) movement shown indirectly by identifiable rock debris falling down the front. Only surface motion measurements were made on Taylor and Fair rock glaciers. A study of frontal talus heights pertinent to velocity gradient is included.

SURFACE MOVEMENT OF MARKED BOULDERS

To obtain the movement of boulders on the rock glacier surfaces, the method of Wahrhaftig and Cox (1959, p. 394) was followed. Three traverse lines were run on both Arapaho and Fair rock glaciers, but four on Taylor rock glacier using two instrument stations. Lengths of traverse lines ranged from 110 to 272 m on Arapaho rock glacier, 167 to 386 m on Taylor rock glacier, and 142 to 316 m on Fair rock glacier. Bedrock for an instrument station in Arapaho cirque was not within workable distance, and a granite block of about 48 m³ (124×10^3 kg) was chosen; location by resection before each survey verified its stability. Boulders along each traverse were marked by drilling holes 1 cm deep in exact line with cliff targets and alidade axis. The center of each hole was indicated with a deeper cut and encircled with paint. In resurveying, movement was measured directly on the boulder at right angles to the traverse line using a millimeter rule extended between the center of the drilled hole and the center of the base of the rod, repositioned again in line with the cliff target. Accuracy of this measurement is within 2 mm.

Results of the measurements of surface movement of 12 marked boulders on Arapaho rock glacier are in Table 2, of 17 boulders on Taylor rock glacier in Table 3, and of 14 boulders on Fair rock glacier in Table 4. Annual movement and average downvalley movement (excluding apparent upvalley movement) are included in the tables.

Downvalley movement is erratic across the surfaces of the rock glaciers. This is especially noticeable across Arapaho rock glacier where forward movement of some marked boulders is 5 to 10 times more than adjacent ones. Of the 12 marked boulders on Arapaho rock glacier, only 5 moved continuously downvalley. For Taylor rock glacier, motion differences between adjacent marked boulders are less variable, with 9 of the 17 moving continuously forward. Arapaho rock glacier moved downvalley 50% faster in 1964 to 1966 than it did in the three previous years, whereas Taylor rock glacier slowed by 27% in the same period. Average annual movement of Arapaho rock glacier was the least of all three (5 cm). Taylor rock glacier moved only slightly farther each year (6.6 cm), but Fair rock glacier moved almost twice as far (9.7 cm) as Arapaho rock glacier.

Assuming the annual surface movement of marked boulders on Arapaho rock glacier represents motion or velocity for the whole body, and using thickness and mean width (Table 1), then discharge from Arapaho cirque of rock glacier debris is calculated to be 215 m³ year⁻¹; for Taylor rock glacier, 269 m³ year⁻¹; and for Fair rock glacier, 771 m³ year⁻¹.

In addition to the erratic downvalley movement is the apparent upvalley movement of certain

TABLE 2

Movement of marked boulders on Arapaho rock glacier[a]

Marker no.	1961-64 3 yr	1964-66 2 yr	1961-66 5 yr	1961-64	1964-66 Annual movement	1961-66
T2-1	n.c.[b]	34	34	n.c.	17	6.9
T2-2	7.5	12	19.5	2.5	6	3.9
T2-3	n.c.	45	45	n.c.	22.5	9
T2-4	14	4	18	4.6	2	3.6
T2-5	*26*[c]	35.5	*9.5*[d]	*8.6*	17.7	*1.9*[d]
T3-1	16.5	12.5	29	5.5	6.2	5.8
T3-2	n.c.	17.5	17.5	n.c.	8.7	3.5
T3-3	*4.5*	11	*6.5*[d]	*1.5*	5.5	*1.3*[d]
T4-1	*16*	*27.5*	*43.5*	*5.3*	*13.7*	*8.7*
T4-2	*8*	*1*	*9*	*2.6*	*0.5*	*1.8*
T4-3	9	4	13	3	2	2.6
T4-4	48	12.5	60.5	16	6.2	12.1
Avg. total downvalley movement	19.0 (5)[e]	18.8 (10)	25.2 (10)	6.3 (5)	9.4 (10)	5.0 (10)

[a]Data given in centimeters. Initial survey, August 9, 1961; resurvey, August 5, 1964; resurvey, July 11, 1966.
[b]n.c. = no measurable change.
[c]Numbers in italics = apparent upvalley movement.
[d]Downvalley only, past original position.
[e]Numbers in parentheses = number of markers averaged.

marked boulders. Four were on Arapaho rock glacier, three on the south side (Figure 2, Table 2), surveyed in line with the direction of rock glacier motion toward the instrument station, and one on the northwest corner (Figure 2, Table 2), again surveyed in line with rock glacier motion but away from the instrument station. Five were on Taylor rock glacier, three of them on the south side (Figure 6, Table 3), surveyed along the line of rock glacier motion. (This movement of four boulders on Arapaho rock glacier and three on Taylor rock glacier is explained by the combination of forward motion simultaneous with slight spreading toward the sides and hence toward the instrument station (or away from it), giving the apparent upvalley displacement.) The other two boulders at the center of Taylor rock glacier were in an area of melting and collapse (*see* near right edge of Figure 8).

Taylor rock glacier shows two gross patterns of movement. Over the 5-year period, the front of the rock glacier (traverses T1 and T2) moved at twice the speed of the rest of the rock glacier. No increase in surface slope reveals the location of this velocity change; an increase in bedrock slope may be responsible. If this trend continues and the rock glacier behaves as glacier ice, transverse furrows may develop similar to transverse crevasses, or that part of the rock glacier may thin.

The second gross pattern of movement of Taylor rock glacier is the mean greater movement in the center and less on the sides (traverses T3 and T4), a movement characteristic of slow flow of such features. Chaix (1923, p. 12; 1943, p. 125) measured two rock glaciers in the Swiss National Park over a 24-year period which had greater movement at their centers. Wahrhaftig and Cox (1959, Figure 6), over an 8-year period along two traverses on rock glacier 51 in Clear Creek, Alaska Range, demonstrated greater movement in the center. Outcalt and Benedict (1965, Figure 3), for 1 year on one traverse, showed greater movement in the center of Arapaho rock glacier. Potter (1967) measured Galena Creek rock glacier in northern Absaroka Mountains along two traverses over periods of 3 years and of 23 days. Movement of the upvalley two-thirds for the most part is greater in the center (1967, pp. 21-22; Figures 25, 26). Barsch (1969) measured Macun 1 rock glacier in the lower Engadine,

Switzerland, at 125 places for 2 years and disclosed greater movement within the central area.

All three Colorado rock glaciers have lower velocities than do those few that have been measured elsewhere. The rock glaciers listed in the previous paragraph have, respectively, annual velocities of 136 and 158 cm (Chaix, 1943, p. 122), 64 cm (Wahrhaftig and Cox, 1959), none by Outcalt and Benedict, 64 cm (Potter, 1967), and 25 to 30 cm (Barsch, 1969). Foster and Holmes (1965) figured annual velocity of 58 cm for one in the Johnson River area, Alaska Range,

TABLE 3

Movement of marked boulders on Taylor rock glacier[a]

Marker no.	1961-64 3 yr	1964-66 2 yr	1961-66 5 yr	1961-64	1964-66 Annual movement	1961-66
T1-1	67	*7*[c]	60[d]	22.3	*3.5*	12[d]
T1-2	51	10	61	17	5	12
T1-3	41	9	50	13.7	4.5	10
T2-1	25	15.5	40.5	8.3	7.7	8
T2-2	22.5	14.5	37	7.5	7.2	7.4
T2-3	33.5	15	48.5	11.	7.5	10
T2-4	27	8	35	9	4	7
T3-1	n.c.[b]	19.5	19.5	n.c.	9.7	4
T3-2	30.5	*16*	14.5[d]	10	*8*	3[d]
T3-3	38	*10*	28[d]	12.6	*5*	5.6[d]
T3-4	18	7	25	6	3.5	5
T3-5	n.c.	13	13	n.c.	6.5	2.6
T3-6	*9*	*5*	*14*	*3*	*2.5*	*2.8*
T4-1	*18*	20	2[d]	*6*	10	0.4[d]
T4-2	n.c.	13	13	n.c.	6.5	2.6
T4-3	16.5	26	42.5	5.5	13	8.5
T4-4	9	31	40	3	15.5	8
Average total downvalley movement	31.6 (12)[e]	15.5 (13)	33.1 (16)	10.5 (12)	7.7 (13)	6.6 (16)

[a]Data given in centimeters. Initial survey, August 17-18, 1961; resurvey, August 18-19, 1964; resurvey, August 3, 1966.

[b]n.c. = no measurable change.

[c]Numbers in italics = apparent upvalley movement.

[d]Downvalley only, past original position.

[e]Numbers in parentheses = number of markers averaged.

and Hughes (1966) estimated velocity at the terminus of one in the Logan Mountains, Yukon Territory, at 250 cm year^{-1}. The Colorado rock glaciers with 5 to 10 cm year^{-1} velocities are conspicuously slow.

MOVEMENT BETWEEN TRANSVERSE RIDGE CRESTS

In an attempt to establish existence of differential movement or expanding and contracting near the terminus of Arapaho rock glacier, a simple network (*see* Figure 2) between boulders on transverse ridge crests, suggested by Noel Potter, Jr., was set up in mid-summer 1966. Distance between centers of steel spikes 1 cm in diameter driven into cracks in boulders to centers of drilled holes or driven spikes in other boulders was measured with a steel tape. Three transverse ridge crests were spanned with a range of distances of 11.93 to 34.87 m. Accuracy of these measurements is estimated to be within 0.5 cm. The network was remeasured in July 1967 and August 1968; results are in Table 5. Movement is of a magnitude of a few cm year^{-1}, varying from 27 cm to none at all.

Four positions in the network are on previously marked boulders in traverses T3 and T4 of the surface motion study. Where opening or closing was greatest at the north end of the network in 1966 to 1968, marked surface boulders there had moved most in 1961 to 1966. Where opening or closing was least at the south end, marked boulders had moved least in 1961 to 1966. When distances between ridge crests were lengthening at the north end, they shortened at the south end, displaying torsional extension and compression. Compression between certain ridges in one year and extension in another is interpreted as possibly due to overthrusting or shear along one or another plane within the rock glacier. Greater shear in the same period of time at one place than at another results in compression and extension at the surface. Presence of transverse ridges and furrows implies downstream velocity decrease with possible thickening. This is accomplished by internal distortion and is expressed externally by ridges and furrows (Wahrhaftig and Cox, 1959, p. 434). Pressure from upvalley due to residual creep of the relic glacier inside Arapaho rock glacier may be responsible also in part for the overthrusting or shear, and therefore for the transverse ridges. Analysis of the compressive-extensive relations and construction of strain-rate fields and of orientation and magnitude of principal strain rates is not warranted at this time due to inadequacy of data.

MOVEMENT OF BOULDERS AT BASE OF FRONT

Two boulders, 4 and 6 m above the base of Arapaho rock glacier near its southeast corner, were selected for motion measured directly to bedrock. A steel spike 1 cm in diameter was driven into a rock ledge. Distance from center of spike to center of hole drilled into each boulder was measured with steel tape every year of observation. A boulder painted (in 1959?) by H. A. Waldrop was discovered at the base of the front (Figure 2). Its distance to painted crosses on two reference boulders in a line 19 and 30 m beyond the front was measured. Movement of these boulders is in Table 6.

Boulder No. 1, 4 m above the base, moved 41.5 cm in 7 years or almost 6 cm year^{-1}. Boulder No. 2, originally 6 m above the base, rotated 4 m out of position one winter, and 3 years later rolled to the bottom; although it gave a less reliable

TABLE 4
Movement of marked boulders on Fair rock glacier[a]

Marker no.	1961-66 5 yr	Annual movement
T1-1	20	4
T1-2	58	11.6
T1-3	56	11.2
T1-4	50	10
T1-5	39	7.8
T1-6	75	15
T2-1	67	13.4
T2-2	73	14.6
T2-3	52	10.4
T2-4	44	8.8
T2-5	29	5.8
T3-1	22	4.4
T3-2	29	5.8
T3-3	66	13.2
Avg. total downvalley movement	48.5	9.7

[a]Data given in centimeters. Initial survey, August 27, 1961; resurvey, August 8, 1966.

long-term record, it had greater absolute movement when in position 2 m above Boulder No. 1. The Waldrop boulder, although inaccessible during some summers due to drifted snow, and almost covered with talus by 1968, moved 27 cm in 7 years, or almost 4 cm year^{-1}. On the surface of the rock glacier above, the four nearest marked boulders moved a mean annual downvalley distance of 5.8 cm. Least movement at the base and greater movement higher in the front support Wahrhaftig and Cox's inference that "velocity of material within the rock glacier probably decreases gradually downward from the surface" (1959, p. 395). By assuming the more reliable figure of 6 cm year^{-1} provided by Boulder No. 1 as velocity for the whole front, and using average height (thickness) and width at the front, discharge of material through the frontal cross section is calculated to be about 239 m^3 year^{-1}.

FRONTAL TALUS HEIGHTS

Along the front of Arapaho rock glacier, talus rises 8 to 12 m above the base. This is 40 to 45% of frontal height. At the southeast corner, talus rises 8 to 10 m above the base, 60 to 62% of height there. These talus heights vary but average 52% (Table 1). This is significant because it indicates, indirectly, vertical distribution of velocity within the rock glacier. According to Wahrhaftig and Cox's Figure 8, case b (1959, p. 398, 400), a talus height equal to half the total height of rock glacier front (52% here) indicates velocity gradient evenly distributed throughout. Average talus height at the front of Taylor rock glacier is 46%. This corresponds more closely to Wahrhaftig and Cox's case c of their Figure 8, where velocity gradient is greater nearer the base than nearer the rock glacier surface. Talus heights are more variable along the front of Fair rock glacier but average 55%. This fits case a more closely where velocity gradient is greater closer to the rock glacier surface.

DEBRIS FALLS AT THE FRONT

Most of the boulders exposed on the 43° front of Arapaho rock glacier in an area between the top of the talus and about 3 m below the crest were painted red in 1961. A photograph site (Figure 2) on bedrock was monumented and the painted sector photographed on August 9, 1961, August 10, 1964, August 11, 1965, July 22, 1966, July 10, 1967, and August 24, 1968. The photograph site and nearby front was revisited as early each summer as possible to observe and obtain dimensions of the maximum number of fallen boulders still resting on the previous winter snow

TABLE 5

Measurements across transverse ridges of Arapaho rock glacier[a]

Boulder to boulder	Initial distance	1966-67	Movement	1967-68	Movement
S3-3 to T3-1	2555	27	Opened	12	Closed
S3-3 to T3-2	2876.5	0.5	Opened	2	Closed
S4-5 to S4-6	2529	0	None	0	None
S4-5 to T4-1	3485	2	Opened	1	Closed
S4-6 to T4-1	2929	5	Opened	9	Opened
S4-2 to S4-5	1186	7	Opened	4	Closed
S4-2 to S4-3	2198	2.5	Closed	0.5	Closed
S4-5 to S4-3	1540	2	Opened	1.5	Closed
S4-2 to S4-1	2744	0	None	1.5	Opened
S4-2 to T4-2	2226.5	2	Closed	2	Closed
S4-1 to T4-2	2270	2.5	Closed	3	Closed

[a]Data given in centimeters. Initial survey, July 27 and August 13, 1966; resurvey, July 10, 1967 and August 24, 1968.

TABLE 6

Movement of boulders at front of Arapaho rock glacier[a]

	1961-64 3 yr	Annual 1961-64	1964-65 1 yr	1965-66 1 yr	1966-67 1 yr	1967-68 1 yr	Avg. annual 1961-68
Boulder No. 1	18	6	4	4.5	9	6	5.9
Boulder No. 2	31.5	10.5	—[b]	1	17	—[c]	12[d]
			(1964-66, 2 yr)		(1966-68, 2 yr)		
Waldrop Boulder	6	2	—[e]	7	—[e]	14	3.8

[a]Data given in centimeters.
[b]Boulder rotated out of position during 1964-65 winter, continued to move.
[c]Boulder rolled to bottom during 1967-68 winter.
[d]Average of best record: 1961-64 and 1966-67.
[e]Inaccessible under snow.

surface. By personal observation both early and late each summer, and by comparison of photomosaics and of superimposed transparent sketches of boulders made from photographs taken over the 7-year period, it was possible not only to obtain a record of annual debris fall and talus accumulation with volume and weight of rock transferred downslope, but also to ascertain the mechanism of transfer. For future reference, white bars were painted on boulders exposed 3 to 5 m below the crest and photographed from the photo site on July 26, 1966.

Not only were painted boulders that had fallen recognizable, but they helped in identifying concurrent falls of other unpainted debris. Recognition of the winter snow surface was necessary for identification of an early spring debris fall. Autumn or early winter debris falls were not identifiable by the following spring. Table 7 shows volumes and weights of debris fallen at and near the photograph site for the 7 years. Unpainted rocks that fell onto older debris undoubtedly were missed in the field. These were identified, however, on the photomosaics and estimates of their dimensions made. Boulders were turned over, but those buried by later falls or too large to turn, with painted surfaces downward, certainly were missed. A relatively small amount of debris fell in 1961 to 1964 compared to later years. Personal observations were not possible and photomosaics for years 1962 and 1963 cannot be constructed. Significance of the meager debris falls for 1967 and 1968 is not known.

Information in Table 7 represents a minimum estimate of material transferred at the photograph site. This sector, however, is about one-eighth of the distance along the front. If it is typical of the whole front, and assuming that 20 m^3 weighing

45×10^3 kg (minus that from the southeast corner and above the Waldrop boulder) actually is the total amount of talus that fell at the photograph site, then 164 m^3 (366×10^3 kg), released at the annual rate of 23 m^3 (52×10^3 kg), may be the total transfer of debris along the front for

TABLE 7

Volumes and weights of fallen debris at and near photgraph site at front of Arapaho rock glacier

	Only boulders painted in 1961 (m^3)	Only boulders painted in 1961 ($\times 10^3$ kg)	All debris, including painted boulders (m^3)	All debris, including painted boulders ($\times 10^3$ kg)
3-yr total, 1961-64	0.9	2.3	1.6	2.5
Spring 1964	3.5	9.5	6.2	16.3
1 yr, 1964-65	1.8[a]	4.6[a]	6.4[a]	10.0[a]
SE corner, spring 1965	—	—	2.5	6.2
Spring 1966	0.5	1.3	5.6	14.6
Spring 1967	0.1	0.4	0.2	0.6
Above Waldrop Bldr., 1967-68	—	—	2.0	5.2
Spring 1968	—	—	0.6[a]	1.8[a]
Totals	6.8	18.1	25.1	57.2

[a]Estimate for that year based upon debris in photomosaics.

the 7-year period. If the average volume of debris that fell for one year (23 m^3) is divided by the photograph site area (crest height, 18.5 m; length about 20 m), this becomes the average distance, 0.063 m, the upper half of the front moved above the top of the talus. Because this distance is annual, it is the same as a velocity of 6.3 cm year^{-1}, giving a discharge of about 251 m^3 year^{-1}. This is very close to that obtained using the movement of a single boulder near the base.

Between 1961 and 1964 a comparatively small amount of debris fell annually at the photo site. During the same period, the nearest marked boulders on the rock glacier surface moved very little or not at all. And in 1964 to 1966, when a great amount of debris fell down the front, the same marked boulders had moved greater distances. There is a definite relation here between surface movement and talus activity along the front. Furthermore, because (1) debris falls originate high on the front and not in the middle, (2) talus accumulating at the base eventually is buried by the advancing front, and (3) velocity gradient probably is evenly distributed throughout the frontal height, the rock glacier then must lay down a rough boulder pavement over which it rides. This behavior is similar to that of lava blocks at the front of an aa lava flow.

CONCLUSION

The main purpose of the motion study was not to analyze in depth mechanisms of rock glacier movement, but to obtain in part some measure of the existing volume and discharge of rock glacier material leaving the cirques. This has been accomplished and with reasonable assurance of accuracy. The total volumes of the three rock glaciers as a form of alpine mass movement represent a respectable amount of rock debris. The results obtained using different measurement data for discharge of Arapaho rock glacier are strikingly similar. All these data will be used in reinforcing current studies of alpine mass movement and periglacial activity in adjacent valleys.

SHEAR STRESS AND VISCOSITY OF THE ROCK GLACIERS

SHEAR STRESS

Maximum shear stress may be obtained for each rock glacier by using formula (2a) derived by Wahrhaftig and Cox (1959, pp. 401-403): $\tau_{max} = \rho\, g\, H / \cosec A$ where τ is shear stress, ρ density of flow (1.8 g cm^{-3} is used for rock glacier flow), g acceleration of gravity, H thickness of rock glacier, and A slope of rock glacier surface. Wahrhaftig and Cox estimated τ_{max} for 28 Alaskan and 2 Swiss rock glaciers. Shear stresses conformed to two groups, those between 1 and 2 bars for active rock glaciers and those less than 1 bar for inactive rock glaciers. Rock glaciers with shear stresses greater than 2 bars were on steep slopes with unusually high fronts. Several active rock glaciers had shear stresses slightly less than 1 bar. Using data from Table 1, τ_{max} near the front of Arapaho rock glacier is 1.35 bar, but is 0.97 bar in mid-section. Taylor rock glacier with its flatter, long profile has τ_{max} of 0.97 bar near the front, and 0.66 bar near its head. Fair rock glacier on steeper slopes has τ_{max} of 1.34 bar near its front and 1.13 bar near the middle.

VISCOSITY

Apparent viscosity of the rock glaciers may be obtained by adapting formula (6), derived by Wahrhaftig and Cox (1959, pp. 405-406) for calculating velocity at the surface of a flow, to obtain viscosity: $\eta = \rho\, g\, H^2 \sin A / 2V_s$ where η is viscosity, ρ density of flow, g acceleration of gravity, H thickness, A slope of rock glacier surface, and V_s velocity at the surface. Gross flow viscosities for rock glacier 51 in Clear Creek, Alaska Range, and the two studied by Chaix in Switzerland for which data were available, range from 1.6×10^{14} to 9×10^{14} poises (Wahrhaftig and Cox, 1959, Table 5). Using data previously reported here, apparent viscosity near the front of Arapaho rock glacier is 90×10^{14} poises, and at mid-section 65×10^{14} poises (where $A = 15°$). Viscosity near the front of Taylor rock glacier is 54×10^{14} poises, and near the front of Fair rock glacier, 92×10^{14} poises.

NEOGLACIATION

A small glacier still remains in the southwest corner of Arapaho cirque. It now is a thin relic, protected at times of the year from solar radiation by high valley walls. Its foot is buried under debris called here Arapaho rock glacier and its head is a saucer-shaped firn field. During the past 100 years nearby Arapaho Glacier receded 90 to 275 m; during the past 60 years it thinned an estimated 32 m (Waldrop, 1964). The glacier in the southwest corner presumably kept pace with this recession although not at the same rate. It is not known for certain how long ago this glacier was big enough to have added debris to its terminal moraine. One associated study, however, permits an estimate of the age of the relic glacier inside Arapaho rock glacier and allows an inference of glacial history in the cirque.

Benedict has documented (1966, 1967, 1968) growing evidence for three stades of Neoglaciation in this part of the Colorado Front Range. "The earliest advance (Temple Lake Stade) is dated at 2500-700 B.C. A later advance (Arikaree Stade) began in about A.D. 100 and ended in A.D. 1000. The most recent advance (Gannett Peak Stade) is dated at A.D. 1650-1850." (Benedict, 1968, p. 77) Deposits of all three stades are in the upper Arapaho Valley (Silver Lake Valley). Arapaho rock glacier is on Benedict's map (1968, p. 80) as an Arikaree stade rock glacier. To confirm this in part, Benedict collected debris from dirt bands, probably marking annual ablation surfaces, from the buried relic glacier overlain by blocky rubble of Arapaho rock glacier with a late Arikaree lichen cover (Benedict, written comm., September 30, 1966, and March 10, 1969). Radiocarbon age of organic matter in the dirt bands is 1,000 ± 90 BP (I-2562) or A.D. 950 (Benedict, written comm., March 15, 1967). This corresponds closely to the end of Arikaree advance and lends convincing support to his stade of glaciation intermediate between Temple Lake and Gannett Peak stades.

Porter and Denton (1967) assembled data on Neoglacial ice advances throughout the world, and noted other mid-Neoglaciation radiocarbon-dated advances in south-central Sierra Nevada, Trinity Alps of northern California, Brooks Range of Alaska, central Norway, and southern Patagonia, but caution that some of these may be glacier surges. Likewise, Curry (1969) finds in central Sierra Nevada, mainly on the basis of ages of lichen on several types of periglacial deposits and on moraines but based also upon historical and tree-ring data, "three major periods of Sierran neoglacial activity during the last 5,000 to 6,000 years" (1969, p. 22). Curry's oldest Neoglaciation is about 700 to 600 B.C. to O.B.C./ A.D., the mid-glaciation is A.D. 850 to 1050, and the latest is between A.D. 1250 and 1898 (1969, pp. 22-23).

Inasmuch as Benedict's date of A.D. 950 fits with Curry's intermediate Neoglaciation, the relic ice inside Arapaho rock glacier indeed seems to belong to a middle stade. A Gannett Peak glacier then should have filled the basin between the head of the glacier of Arikaree stade and the cirque wall sometime after A.D. 1650. This younger glacier should have pushed the ice of Arikaree stade with its thick ablation moraine downvalley, shortening and thickening the ice sufficiently to set it in motion. Gannett Peak moraines should have been formed, and their debris added to the up-valley end of Arapaho rock glacier. Based on lichen studies, however, Benedict dates the blocky rubble at the rock glacier head as no younger than late Arikaree (written comm., March 10, 1969). This is sustained by the late Arikaree age of the relic ice inside. If this be true, there is no Gannett Peak debris between the upper end of Arapaho rock glacier and the head-wall. Not only has there not been a Gannett Peak glacier of size enough to produce moraines against the rock glacier head, but also the rock glacier was not supplied rock debris to any extent within at least the last 1,000 years. This would explain the slow velocity of the rock glacier. And yet Arapaho Glacier, not more than 200 m distant, created voluminous Gannett Peak stade moraines.

Wind-drifted snow and avalanching ice and snow maintain Arapaho Glacier and prevent its complete stagnation (Waldrop, 1964). Glacier regime was and is now dependent to a degree upon configuration of the windward slopes and of the arête to the west that allows snow to pass over the Continental Divide. Arapaho Glacier is fed by snow blown out of a large cirque due west of the Divide. The southwest part of Arapaho cirque, with only the rock glacier in it, has South Arapaho Peak and the east-west-oriented Divide west of it (Figure 2) effectively preventing most of the drifting snow today from entering. This configuration of windward slopes and the arête hindered glacier growth and rock glacier expansion in that part of the cirque since late Arikaree time. This means the large cirque west of the Divide during Arikaree stade and even Temple Lake stade was filled with ice of these stades and/or eroded less deeply to allow concurrent growth of glaciers in the southwest corner of Arapaho cirque.

As long as morainal cover is thicker than depth of summer thaw, buried ice may be preserved for great lengths of time (Østrem, 1965, pp. 20, 22-23). For many centuries rock rubble and fine debris protected the buried glacier of Arikaree stade. As an active glacier, it developed about A.D. 100 or some time later. In the past 960 to 1,860 years, morainal debris that started in front of the now buried glacier either moved or was pushed downvalley about 300 m. At its present slow velocity, a distance of only 50 to 100 m would have been covered. Whatever motion Arapaho rock glacier now has, it most likely is due to residual creep of the enclosed relic Arikaree stade glacier.

In the north part of Arapaho cirque and downvalley beyond the Gannett Peak moraines, Benedict's map (1968, p. 80) shows a rock glacier of Arikaree stade in front of these moraines and a Temple Lake stade rock glacier a few meters beyond (all being 10 to 20 m north of Arapaho rock glacier). I am not as confident that these steepsided deposits of till-like debris should be labelled rock glaciers, but this may be a matter only of terminology. Two earlier Temple Lake stade morainal complexes are 0.7 to 1 km farther downvalley, so that this Temple Lake rock glacier, if truly of this stade, denotes a third episode of Temple Lake refrigeration. Certainly the debris of these deposits is older than the Gannett Peak moraines they are in front of, but they appear like ice-cored moraines. Two traverse lines across Arapaho rock glacier in 1961 included three marked boulders on them (Figure 2). By 1966 all three boulders had rotated upvalley, although earlier two had moved downvalley; this suggests a melting ice core.

Details of glaciation at the head of the valley containing Taylor rock glacier are not known, but a history somewhat comparable to that of Arapaho cirque might be expected. The downvalley two-thirds of the rock glacier with flatter profile, irregular pits and depressions, and rotating boulders may be of Arikaree stade, whereas the upvalley higher, smoother, concave part may be of Gannett Peak stade and recent. This upvalley sector has the uniform appearance and internal layering of a rock glacier supplied without interruption for years by avalanched snow and rock debris.

In front of Fair rock glacier and damming Triangle Lake (Figure 9) is a Temple Lake stade moraine. After retreat of Temple Lake ice, a stade of glaciation resulted in a moraine-covered ice body older than the present Gannett Peak moraines. This older glacier of Arikaree stade, now become Fair rock glacier, may have had a history rather similar to that of Arapaho rock glacier. Later, a Gannett Peak glacier built moraines between Fair rock glacier and the cirque wall. Activity of Fair rock glacier today may be due in part to residual creep of a buried Arikaree stade glacier.

Some cirques are favorably situated for development of healthy glaciers with terminal moraines and rock glaciers representing each stade of Neoglaciation. Arapaho cirque is such a cirque with two and possibly three Temple Lake stade moraines, one and possibly two Arikaree stade rock glaciers (one being Arapaho rock glacier), and three Gannett Peak stade moraines. Other less favorably oriented cirques have only rock glaciers built during each Neoglacial stade. Still others with least favorable exposure contain extensive talus and lobate rock glaciers or protalus lobes along cirque walls for each Neoglacial stade. All the reasons for the differences are not yet identified, but cirque orientation and the nature of windward slopes have a strong influence.

ACKNOWLEDGMENTS

The initial program of reconnaissance and survey in 1961 was assisted by INSTAAR and by The Ohio State University Institute of Polar Studies. The University of Colorado Department of Geological Sciences loaned all surveying equipment in 1961. Field work and graduate assistants for the years 1964 through 1968 were supported by National Science Foundation Grant GP-2822. Field participants were made available 1964 to 1966 through NSF Research Participant Programs operated by INSTAAR. All facilities of INSTAAR'S Mountain Research Station were at my disposal.

I am indebted to John W. Marr, director of INSTAAR through 1967, for his kind assistance, encouragement and advice; to M. Martinelli, Jr., of the U.S. Forest Service for help with alpine snow studies photography in 1961; to Thomas Platt of the City of Boulder for permission to work in the Boulder Watershed area; to Ralph Greene, manager of the Mountain Research Station, for help in so many ways; to the several superintendents and naturalists of Rocky Mountain National Park for permission to conduct research within the Park; to Anders Rapp of Geografiska Institutionen, University of Uppsala, for consultation in the field in 1965; and to Jack D. Ives, present director of INSTAAR, for so much support in 1968.

Many individuals gave generously of their time as participants in the field work, or as surveyors, recorders, packers, or wranglers: they are J. B. Benedict, N. C. Berry, J. W. Blagbrough, J. W. Davis, G. A. Dolezal, R. E. Foreman, R. C. Johnson, S. Johonnott, R. L. Laughlin, P. J. Lehr, R. Lynn, C. Opperman, K. L. Petersen, J. H. Richards, J. M. Roelofs, C. C. Rust, R. G. Wallace, R. Weaver, K. Westerling, and M. L. White. I am obligated to my colleagues J. B. Benedict, Charles E. Corbató, J. W. Marr, Noel Potter, Jr., and Clyde Wahrhaftig who have kindly read and criticized this paper, helped with the calculations, or made valuable suggestions for its improvement. Responsibility for its content, of course, still rests with me.

REFERENCES

Barsch, D.
  1969 : Studien und Messungen an Blockglet-
         schern in Macun, Unterengadin. *Z.
         Geomorph.*, Suppl. 8: 11-30.
Benedict, J. B.
  1966 : Radiocarbon dates from a stone-banked
         terrace in the Colorado Rocky Moun-
         tains, U.S.A. *Geog. Annaler*, 48A(1):
         24-31.
  1967 : Recent glacial history of an alpine area
         in the Colorado Front Range, U.S.A.
         I. Establishing a lichen-growth curve.
         J. Glaciol., 6(48): 817-832.
  1968 : Recent glacial history of an alpine area
         in the Colorado Front Range, U.S.A.
         II. Dating the glacial deposits. *J.
         Glaciol.*, 7(49): 77-87.
Bonnett, R. B.
  1970 : The glacial sequence of upper Boulder
         Creek drainage basin in the Colorado
         Front Range. Unpublished Ph.D. dis-
         sertation, The Ohio State University.
         318 pp.
Chaix, A.
  1923 : Les coulées de blocs du Parc National
         Suisse d'Engadine (Note préliminaire).
         Le Globe (J. Géog.; Organe Soc.
         Géog. Genève), 62 (Mém.): 1-34.
  1943 : Les coulées de blocs du Parc National
         Suisse: nouvelle mesures et comparison
         avec les "rock streams" de la Sierra
         Nevada de Californie. *Le Globe* (J.
         Géog.; Organe Soc. Géog. Genève),
         82 (Mém.): 121-128.
Curry, R. R.
  1969 : Holocene climatic and glacial history of
         the central Sierra Nevada, California.
         Geol. Soc. Amer. Spec. Paper 123,
         1-47.
Domaradzki, J.
  1951 : Blockströme in Kanton Graubünden.
         Ergebnisse d. Wissenschaft. Untersu-
         chungen d. Schweiz. Nationalparks, 3
         (N.F.)(24): 173-235.
Foster, H. L. and Holmes, G. W.
  1965 : A large transitional rock glacier in the
         Johnson River area, Alaska Range.
         U.S. Geol. Surv. Prof. Paper 525-B,
         B112-B116.
Hughes, O. L.
  1966 : Logan Mountains, Y.T.: Measurements
         on a rock glacier. *Ice*, (20): 5.
Ives, R. L.
  1940 : Rock glaciers in the Colorado Front
         Range, *Geol. Soc. Amer. Bull.*, 51:
         1271-1294.
Madole, R. F.
  1963 : Quaternary geology of St. Vrain drain-
         age basin, Boulder County, Colorado.
         Unpublished Ph.D. dissertation, The
         Ohio State University. 288 pp.

  1969 : Pinedale and Bull Lake glaciation in
         upper St. Vrain drainage basin, Boulder
         County, Colorado. *Arctic and Alpine
         Res.*, 1(4): 279-287.
Marr, J. W.
  1961 : Ecosystems of the east slope of the
         Front Range in Colorado, *Univ. Colo-
         rado Stud.*, Ser. Biol. No. 8. 134 pp.
  1967 : Data on mountain environments. I.
         Front Range Colorado, sixteen sites,
         1952-1953, *Univ. Colorado Stud.*, Ser.
         Biol. No. 27. 110 pp.
Marr, J. W., Johnson, A. W., Osburn, W. S.,
  and Knorr, O. A.
  1968a: Data on mountain environments. II.
         Front Range Colorado, four climax
         regions, 1953-1958, *Univ. Colorado
         Stud.*, Ser. Biol. No. 28. 169 pp.
Marr, J. W., Clark, J. M., Osburn, W. S., and
  Paddock, M. W.
  1968b: Data on mountain environments. III.
         Front Range Colorado, four climax
         regions, 1959-1964, *Univ. Colorado
         Stud.*, Ser. Biol. No. 29. 181 pp.
Østrem, G.
  1965 : Problems of dating ice-cored moraines.
         Geog. Annaler, 47A(1): 1-38.
Outcalt, S. I. and Benedict, J. B.
  1965 : Photo-interpretation of two types of
         rock glaciers in the Colorado Front
         Range, U.S.A. *J. Glaciol.*, 5(42):
         849-856.
Outcalt, S. I. and MacPhail, D. D.
  1965 : A survey of Neoglaciation in the Front
         Range of Colorado, *Univ. Colorado
         Stud.*, Ser. Earth Sci. No. 4. 124 pp.
Paddock, M. W.
  1964 : The climate and topography of the
         Boulder region. *In* Rodeck, H. G.
         (ed.), *Natural history of the Boulder
         area*. Univ. Colorado Museum, Leaflet
         No. 13: 25-33.
Porter, S. C. and Denton, G. H.
  1967 : Chronology of Neoglaciation in the
         North American Cordillera. *Amer. J.
         Sci.*, 265: 177-210.
Potter, N., Jr.
  1967 : Rock glaciers and mass-wastage in the
         Galena Creek area, northern Absaroka
         Mountains, Wyoming. U.S. Army
         Natick Laboratories, Natick, Massa-
         chusetts, Tech. Rept. (Mimeographed).
         75 pp.
Rapp, A.
  1959 : Avalanche boulder tongues in Lappland.
         Geog. Annaler, 41(1): 34-48.
Richmond, G. M.
  1960 : Glaciation of the east slope of Rocky
         Mountain National Park, Colorado.
         Geol. Soc. Amer. Bull., 71: 1371-1382.

1962 : Quaternary stratigraphy of the La Sal Mountains, Utah. U.S. Geol. Surv. Prof. Paper 324, 1-135.

Roots, E. P.
1954 : Geology and mineral deposits of the Aiken Lake map-area, British Columbia. Geol. Surv. Can. Mem. 274, 1-246.

Vernon, P. and Hughes, O. L.
1966 : Surficial geology, Dawson, Larsen Creek, and Nash Creek map-areas, Yukon Territory. *Geol. Surv. Can. Bull.*, 136: 1-25.

Wahrhaftig, C. and Cox, A.
1959 : Rock glaciers in the Alaska Range. *Geol. Soc. Amer. Bull.*, 70: 383-436.

Waldrop, H. A.
1964 : Arapaho Glacier: a sixty-year record, *Univ. Colorado Stud.*, Ser. Geol. No. 3. 37 pp.

Waldrop, H. A. and White, S. E.
1965 : Trip 1: Arapaho Glacier and Arapaho rock glacier. *In*: *Guidebook for one-day field conferences, Boulder area, Colorado*. Int. Assoc. Quaternary Res., VIII Congr., 5-10.

DOWNSLOPE SOIL MOVEMENT IN A COLORADO ALPINE REGION: RATES, PROCESSES, AND CLIMATIC SIGNIFICANCE

James B. Benedict

Institute of Arctic and Alpine Research
University of Colorado
Boulder, Colorado 80302

ABSTRACT

Soil-movement rates, processes, and landforms were studied above timberline on the east slope of the Colorado Front Range. Maximum rates of downslope movement measured in sorted stripes, turf-banked lobes and terraces, and stone-banked lobes and terraces at fined to the upper 50 cm of soil; columns of small cement rods placed in vertical drillholes showed no downslope displacement below this depth after four years of burial.

Periodic measurements of downslope movement and frost heaving during the 1965-66 annual freeze-thaw cycle suggest that solifluction is a more effective process than frost creep in the saturated axial areas of turf-banked lobes in wet sites, but is less effective than frost creep at their edges. Potential frost creep at one experimental site exceeded theoretical values calculated from heave and slope measurements. Retrograde movement was larger than anticipated. At a site where frost creep is the dominant movement process, stone-banked lobes moved three times as rapidly as the finer-textured soil between them; at a site where shallow solifluction is important, stripes of coarse debris moved only half as rapidly as stripes of fine material.

Turf-banked lobes and terraces are the result of intense solifluction beneath a cover of vegetation; they form where downslope movement is impeded, and are normally associated with a decrease in gradient such as occurs on concave lower slopes. The shape of the front (linear or lobate) is determined by the uniformity of moisture distribution parallel to the contour of the slope. At least two generations of turf-banked lobes and terraces occur in the Niwot Ridge area. Terraces with gentle, subdued fronts and patterned treads date from the late Pleistocene, and were used as camping and butchering areas by prehistoric man as long ago as $7,650 \pm 190$ radiocarbon years. Most bear an Altithermal soil: five dates for the soil

nine experimental sites on Niwot Range ranged from 0.4 to 4.3 cm/yr. Rates of displacement were strongly influenced by differences in moisture availability and gradient, but were relatively unaffected by differences in soil texture and temperature. Movement is currently con- at an average rate of 0.19 cm/yr during the past $2,340 \pm 130$ radiocarbon years.

Stone-banked lobes and terraces are caused by frost creep and are favored by an absence of vegetation; they commonly develop where moving sorted stripes or blockfields encounter a decrease in gradient. Sorting is partially inherited, but is accentuated as the lobe or terrace moves downslope. Stone-banked lobes and terraces in the Niwot Ridge area developed late in the Temple Lake Stade of Neoglaciation. A series of radiocarbon dates from the buried A horizon in one stone-banked terrace suggests that its front has advanced at an average rate of 0.34 cm/yr during the past $2,470 \pm 110$ radiocarbon years. Movement was slow during the Temple Lake-Arikaree* interstade (2,650 to 1,850 BP), a time of soil formation and intense cavernous weathering, and during the Arikaree glacial maximum, when lichen measurements show that the slope was covered with an insulating blanket of perennial snow. Disappearance of the snowbank led to an eight-fold increase in the rate of terrace advance between about 1,150 and 1,050 BP.

The widespread occurrence of stone-banked lobes and terraces, sorted polygons, and sorted stripes on the treads of turf-banked lobes and terraces suggests a general decline in the availability of moisture and the effectiveness of solifluction since the end of the Middle Stade of Pinedale (Late Wisconsin) Glaciation. During the latest Pinedale and earliest Neoglacial ice advances frost creep replaced solifluction as the dominant movement process on many slopes. Neither process is particularly effective today, except in specialized microenvironments

Arctic and Alpine Research, Vol. 2, No. 3, 1970, pp. 165-226.

range from 5,800 ± 125 to 5,300 ± 130 BP. Lobes and terraces with overhanging fronts and unpatterned treads postdate the Altithermal interval: radiocarbon and stratigraphic evidence suggest that they formed late in the Temple Lake Stade of Neoglaciation. The front of one small Neoglacial turf-banked lobe has advanced that are saturated with meltwater in the autumn.

---

*The term Arikaree, as used in this context, has been preempted. No alternative name has been established (Editor).

INTRODUCTION

An eight-year study of soil-movement processes above timberline in the Colorado Front Range has recently been completed. The objectives of the study were threefold:

(1) To describe, classify, and determine the origins of landforms produced by moving soil on slopes in the Front Range alpine region.

(2) To measure modern rates of downslope soil movement, evaluate the processes involved, and relate modern rates of movement to present environmental conditions.

(3) To determine former rates of movement, date previous intervals of intense frost action, and infer past changes in the Front Range environment.

(*Editor's Note:* Material has been omitted at this point.)

PERIGLACIAL GEOMORPHOLOGY OF NIWOT RIDGE,
BOULDER COUNTY, COLORADO

Contour Interval 50 m

FIGURE 2.

MOVEMENT PROCESSES

Frost creep and solifluction are the two main processes responsible for downslope soil movement in the Colorado Front Range. Because of a lack of consistency in the definition of these terms by different authors, their use in this paper is explained below.

Frost Creep

Frost creep is defined as *the net downslope displacement that occurs when the soil, during a freeze-thaw cycle, expands normal to its surface and settles in a more nearly vertical direction.* Expansion, or heaving, is proportional to the total thickness of segregated ice layers that form in the freezing soil, and is generally directed at right angles to the ground surface. Heaving is favored by saturated conditions and by slow, deep freezing, and is important only in soils that contain sufficient fine-textured material to permit water to move upward to the base of the frozen layer.

In analyzing movement data from Niwot Ridge, frost creep was broken down into two components: (1) *potential frost creep,* the downslope displacement caused by frost heaving during the fall and winter freeze, and (2) *retrograde movement,* the apparent upslope displacement caused by non-vertical settling during the spring and summer thaw (*see* Washburn, 1967, Figure 5). Potential frost creep can be calculated from slope angles and heave measurements.

Solifluction

Following Andersson (1906), solifluction is defined as *"the slow flowing from higher to lower ground of masses of waste, saturated by water...."* This definition does not restrict the process to a periglacial environment (Butrym *et al.,* 1964), and special terms such as "gelisolifluxion" (Baulig, 1956), "gelifluction" (Washburn, 1967), and "congelifluxion" (Dylik, 1967) are sometimes used for solifluction operating over a frozen subsoil.

Solifluction is favored by an impermeable substratum, such as frozen ground, which limits the downward movement of water through the soil. The process is most effective where melting ice layers weaken the soil and provide a source of excess water that reduces *internal friction and cohesion* (Williams, 1957, 1959). The importance of ice-lensing is illustrated by the restricted occurrence of solifluction on Niwot Ridge. Although much of the alpine region is saturated during the spring thaw, significant solifluction occurs only in areas where the water table remains high enough during the fall freeze to permit thick ice-lens development. A. L. Washburn (pers. comm., 1969) has cautioned that autumn moisture may *not* be required for solifluction in other periglacial regions.

In the analysis of movement data from Niwot Ridge, all downslope displacement occurring during the spring thaw has been attributed to solifluction. Frost creep also occurs during this interval, but is too shallow to affect the movement of wooden stakes used in measuring displacement.

CLASSIFICATION AND DESCRIPTION OF LANDFORMS

Introduction

Frost creep and solifluction commonly operate together. The importance of each process varies from site to site and from year to year, and has varied, on a much larger scale, during the climatic oscillations of late Pleistocene and Recent time. As a result, most landforms produced by downslope soil movement are polygenetic. In classifying landforms, we should avoid the use of genetic names that stress the importance of one process at the expense of another (solifluction terrace, gelifluction lobe, etc.), unless the processes involved are clearly separable. This is rarely possible. In the present paper I have adopted a descriptive terminology based on the parameters used by Washburn (1956) in his classification of patterned ground. These are surface expression and the presence or absence of sorting (Table 2). Moving soils that lack distinct topographic expression are included in the classification, but are not discussed in the paper.

Turf-Banked Terraces

Turf-banked terraces (Lundqvist, 1949; Galloway, 1961; Embleton and King, 1968) are defined as *bench-like accumulations of moving soil that lack conspicuous sorting.* Synonymous terms include "soil terraces" (Sigafoos and Hopkins, 1952), "solifluction terraces" (Billings and Mark, 1961; Rapp and Rudberg, 1960), and "nonsorted terraces" (Osburn *et al.,* 1965). Representative turf-banked terraces are illustrated in Figure 3.

FIGURE 3. Turf-banked terraces at tree limit on Niwot Ridge. A lush cover of sedges gives the moist treads of the terraces a dark appearance. Winter snow accumulation is moderately heavy on this 9 to 11°, northeast-facing slope. The mountains on the skyline are (left to right) unnamed, Pawnee Peak, Mount Toll, Paiute Peak, and Mount Audubon. July 27, 1967.

FIGURE 4. Miniature *Dryas*-banked terraces on Albion Ridge. The fronts of the terraces are covered by *Dryas octopetala,* but their treads are relatively free of vegetation. *Dryas* terraces are aligned either parallel, or at right angles, to the local prevailing winter wind direction, whichever orientation comes closest to paralleling the contour of the slope. The terraces form as a result of surficial frost creep, modified by wind and by the restraining influence of the vegetation cover. August 1, 1967.

TABLE 2

Classification of landforms produced by downslope soil movement in the Colorado Front Range

	No surface expression	Lobate	Terrace-like
Nonsorted	Nonsorted sheet	Turf-banked lobe	Turf-banked terrace
Sorted	Blockfield	Stone-banked lobe	Stone-banked terrace

"*Dryas*-banked terraces," such as those shown in Figure 4, are miniature turf-banked forms produced by the interaction of vegetation, wind, and surficial frost creep.

Turf-banked terraces in the Niwot Ridge area occupy slopes of 2 to 19°, with an average gradient of 10°. The terraces are largely restricted to south- and east-facing snow-accumulation slopes (Figures 5 and 6), where moisture is abundant and evenly distributed along the contour, and where the deposition of windblown soil eroded from exposed west-facing slopes replenishes the

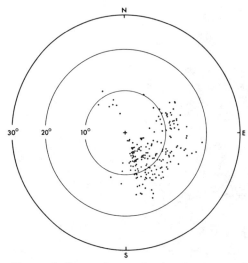

FIGURE 5. Scatter diagram showing the slopes and exposures of 195 turf-banked terraces on Niwot Ridge. The terraces show a preference for gentle southeast-facing snow-accumulation slopes.

supply of fine-textured material. Concave lower slopes are favored, but terraces also occur in convex slope positions.

For about 1.5 km east of the D-1 weather station, turf-banked terraces form giant stairsteps, whose arcuate fronts trend parallel to the contour of the ridgecrest (Figure 2). The largest terrace is 580 m long, 95 m wide, and 4 m high. Farther to the east, on steeper slopes, the terraces are almost as long and high, but are considerably narrower; Wilson (1952) has noted a similar relationship between gradient and terrace width on Jan Mayen Island. The fronts of the Niwot Ridge terraces slope at angles of 10 to 50° and rarely bulge or overhang; in plan they may be either straight or irregularly lobate, and commonly trend obliquely across the contour of the slope.

Where winter snow accumulation is deep, sorting processes are ineffective, and turf-banked terraces are covered with dense vegetation. Where winter snow is shallow, the moist treads of the terraces show the effects of intense frost activity. Inactive sorted polygons, 3 to 10 m in diameter, occur near the fronts of terraces at the western end of Niwot Ridge. Elsewhere in the study area, small active polygons, 1 to 4 m in diameter, occupy the floors of shallow ponds on terrace treads. Most of the terrace ponds are irregularly shaped, but some are elongated parallel to the prevailing wind direction. Earth hummocks occur where winter snow is deep enough to provide protection from

wind erosion, but shallow enough (generally 10 to 50 cm) to permit deep frost penetration; in less protected sites the hummocks are replaced by frost boils, which form in narrow, relatively snow-free zones atop the risers of the terraces. Paralleling the fronts of the terraces, and associated with the frost boils, are tension cracks caused by differential heaving. Many of the cracks are filled with stones; rock-filled depressions mark the junctions of branching cracks.

Representative transects across terraces in areas of moderate and light snow accumulation (Figure 7) illustrate the effects of topography upon snow cover, vegetation, and patterned ground.

TURF-BANKED LOBES

Turf-banked lobes (Galloway, 1961; Embleton and King, 1968) are defined as *lobate accumulations of moving soil that lack conspicuous sorting*. Other terms commonly used for these features include "soil lobes" (Sigafoos and Hopkins, 1952), "soil tongues" (Williams, 1959), "solifluction lobes" (Washburn, 1947; Dahl, 1956; Holmes and Colton, 1960; Rapp, 1960; Jahn, 1961; Rudberg, 1964), "nonsorted lobes" (Osburn et al., 1965), "nonsorted congelifluction lobes" (Dutkiewicz, 1961), and "gelifluction lobes" (Washburn, 1967). A representative turf-banked lobe is illustrated in Figure 8.

Turf-banked lobes on Niwot Ridge occur on slopes of 4 to 23° (Figure 9). Like turf-banked terraces, their average slope angle is 10°. The lobes are best developed in winter snow-free areas, where moisture, instead of being uniformly distributed across the slope, is confined to linear drainageways. Lobes form one below the other wherever moisture is channeled along definite drainage routes (Figure 6). North- and south-facing slopes that receive runoff from nearby snow-accumulation areas provide the ideal combination of snow-free winter conditions and abundant moisture.

On Niwot Ridge turf-banked lobes are 3 to 50 m wide and extend downslope for distances of 3 to 100 m. Spoon-shaped recesses lie at the rear of most lobes. Frontal banks are 0.5 to 3.5 m high, and generally slope at angles of 10 to 35°; the fronts of a few particularly active lobes bulge outward over the soil that they are overriding. Treads are gently inclined downslope at angles of 2 to 14°.

Because of their restriction to winter snow-free areas, turf-banked lobes are particularly susceptible to erosion by wind. Wind-erosion

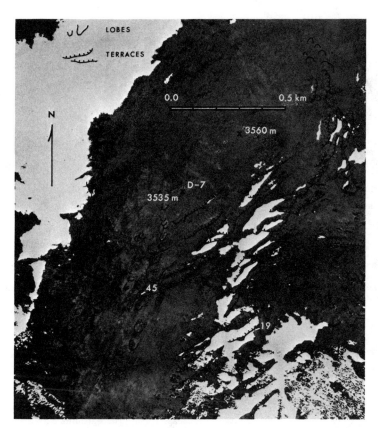

FIGURE 6. Vertical air photograph showing the distribution of turf-banked lobes and terraces on the flanks of the D-7 knoll, Niwot Ridge. The winter snow cover was still in the process of melting off turf-banked terraces when this photograph was taken on June 19, 1962. Other terraces remain buried beneath the large snowbank (upper left). Lobe 45 and terrace 19 are movement-study sites. U.S. Air Force photograph courtesy of Ronald Foreman and William S. Osburn.

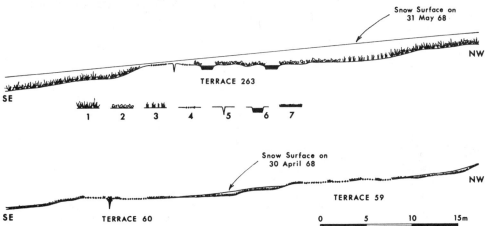

FIGURE 7. Topographic profiles across the fronts of turf-banked terraces in areas of moderate (top) and light (bottom) winter snow accumulation. Frost boils and frost cracks occur only where winter snow is shallow or absent. Plant distribution is controlled by differences in snow depth and growing-season moisture; these factors are related to terrace topography and orientation. 1—*Deschampsia caespitosa-Sibbaldia procumbens* snowbank community. 2—Wet *Carex scopulorum-Caltha leptosepala-Salix anglorum* meadow. 3—*Juncus drummondii-Carex nigricans* meadow. 4—Frost boil area, sparsely vegetated. 5—Frost crack. 6—Pond. 7—Dry *Kobresia myosuroides-Carex rupestris* meadow.

FIGURE 8. View looking downvalley onto the surface of a turf-banked lobe. This is lobe 26, a movement-study site on Niwot Ridge. September 23, 1967.

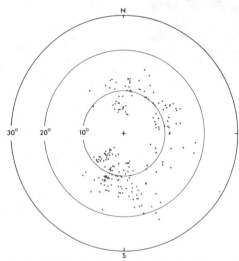

FIGURE 9. Scatter diagram showing the slopes and exposures of 208 turf-banked lobes on Niwot Ridge. Winter snow-free north- and south-facing slopes with gradients of 5 to 15° are favored.

scarps occur on steep, west-facing frontal banks; oriented ponds, aligned in the direction of the prevailing winter winds, occupy the gently sloping treads. Patterned ground is active at the surfaces of all but the driest and most steeply sloping lobes. Frost boils occur in exposed sites with abundant moisture, and earth hummocks are prominent in sheltered locations. Frost cracks are also common; unlike

the cracks on turf-banked terraces, they tend to be aligned in the direction of slope. The cracks are caused by tensional forces resulting from differential frost heaving (Benedict, 1970). Stones move into the frost cracks during periods of daily freezing and thawing, producing sorted stripes or crude polygonal patterns. Except for areas of patterned-ground activity, turf-banked lobes on Niwot Ridge are completely covered with vegetation.

STONE-BANKED TERRACES

Stone-banked terraces (Lundqvist, 1949; Galloway, 1956; Benedict, 1966; Embleton and King, 1968) are defined as *terrace- or garland-like accumulations of stones and boulders overlying a relatively stone-free moving subsoil* (Figure 10). Synonymous terms include "stone garlands" (Antevs, 1932), "block-banked terraces" (Thompson, 1961), "boulder steps" (Lundqvist, 1962), and "sorted terraces" (Osburn *et al.,* 1965).

Stone-banked terraces on Niwot Ridge occupy south- and east-facing snow-accumulation slopes with an average gradient of 16° and a range of 9 to 23° (Figure 11). There is partial overlap between the slope and exposure requirements of turf-banked and stone-banked terraces; where both occur on the same slope, the latter commonly override the former, suggesting a difference in age or in rate of movement. In Figure 12, profiles b and c show the positions of stone-banked terraces on representative snow-accumulation slopes, and

FIGURE 10. Stone-banked terrame on Niwot Ridge. The terrace is composed of coalescing lobes of blocky debris, and occupies a 14°, southeast-facing snow - accumulation slope. This is terrace 328, a movement - study site. September 13, 1968.

illustrate a common slope catena in the Front Range alpine region. The catena begins with sorted polygons at the crests of windswept knolls. With increasing slope, the polygons become elongated and their borders spread to form a blockfield with scattered debris islands. Irregularly branching sorted stripes extend from the lower edge of the blockfield; where movement is retarded, normally by a decrease in gradient, the stripes spread and merge to form stone-banked lobes and terraces. Gentle lower slopes tend to be smoothed by sheetwash, and are broad and featureless except where turf-banked terraces are present.

The fronts of stone-banked terraces are lobate, steep, and rocky. On Niwot Ridge, they slope at angles of 20 to 50°, and have a maximum height of 2.7 m. The terrace treads may be as wide as 60 m, and extend along the contour of the slope for distances of 200 to 400 m. Material at the rear of the tread is a mixture of soil and rock, covered with vegetation except where sorted stripes are present or where crudely sorted polygons are currently active. Closer to the front, stones and boulders form an arcuate strip of openwork rubble, 3 to 20 m wide, in which fines are lacking. Most boulders near the front range from 20 to 50 cm in maximum dimension, but some are as large as 180 cm. Tabular gneisses and blocky granites, syenites, and monzonites are rock types that occur in stone-banked terraces on Niwot Ridge. As noted by Lundqvist (1949), the long axes of stones tend to be oriented at right angles to

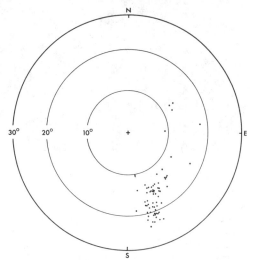

FIGURE 11. Scatter diagram showing the slopes and exposures of 66 stone-banked lobes and terraces on Niwot Ridge. Relatively steep, south-southeast-facing slopes are favored.

the terrace front except immediately behind the riser, where they are rotated to an orientation paralleling the front. Rocks on the surfaces of the terraces commonly are cavernously weathered, with pitted surfaces and grotesquely irregular shapes. Maximum-diameter measurements suggest that lichens became established on most stone-banked terraces at the close of the Arikaree Stade of Neoglaciation, 900 to 1,000 years ago.

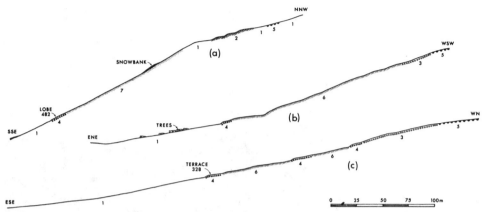

FIGURE 12. Topographic profiles of snow-accumulation slopes in the Indian Peaks region. Profiles a and c are from Niwot Ridge. Profile b is from the crest of a ridge east of the summit of Pawnee Peak. 1— Nonsorted sheet. 2—Turf-banked terraces. 3—Block-field with debris islands. 4—Stone-banked lobe or terrace. 5—Sorted polygons. 6—Sorted stripes. 7—Unstable scree in late snowbank area.

FIGURE 13. Lobes of debris with steeply-sloping fronts and pavement-like surfaces occur in stream channels at high elevations in the Indian Peaks region. These lobes were photographed in the valley north of Niwot Ridge. The terminus of the Navajo Glacier is visible beneath low clouds in the background. September 26, 1966.

STONE-BANKED LOBES

Stone-banked lobes (Galloway, 1961; Embleton and King, 1968) are defined as *lobate masses of rocky debris underlain by relatively stone-free, fine-textured, moving soil.* Other names for these features include "stone-banked flow earth cones" (Lundqvist, 1949), and "stone-banked solifluction lobes" (Rudberg, 1964).

Stone-banked lobes occur on south- and east-facing snow-accumulation slopes with gradients of 12 to 24° (Figure 11). The average slope angle is 17°. Stone-banked lobes and terraces frequently occur together in the same areas, and many of the terraces have developed from the merger of closely spaced stone-banked lobes (Figure 10). Stone-banked lobes also occur at the fronts of isolated "stone streams," and along the lower margins of scree slopes below persistent snowbanks (Figure 12a). Lobate accumulations of boulders found in stream channels near and above timberline (Figure 13) may be related in origin, although they have formed under conditions of total saturation.

The treads of stone-banked lobes are composed of stones and boulders without visible fine material. Cavernous weathering is conspicuous where the lobes are composed of medium-textured crystalline rocks. Maximum-diameter lichen measurements suggest that the lobes became available for lichen colonization at the close of the Arikaree Stade of Neoglaciation.

The fronts of stone-banked lobes are rarely more than 1 m high. In other respects, the lobes are comparable in size to the individual lobate components of stone-banked terraces.

(*Editor's Note:* Material has been omitted at this point.)

FIGURE 14. Lobe 499. The bulging, overhanging front of this small turf-banked l o b e contrasts sharply with the subdued terrace riser on which it has developed. Flowing water is present at the surface of the lobe throughout the ice-free season. July 10, 1962.

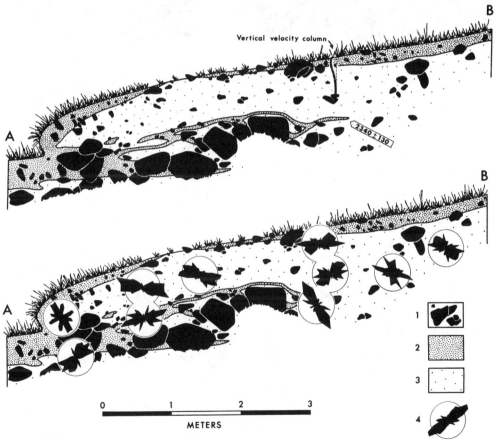

FIGURE 21. Soil profile, lobe 499. 1—Stones, drawn to scale. 2—Very dark grayish brown to very dark brown gravelly sandy loam. Mucky and less gravelly where buried. 3—Dark grayish brown to dark yellowish brown sandy loam, becoming finer textured near the front of the lobe. Locally mottled. Cohesive, with weakly platy structure. 4—Rose diagrams showing the long-axis orientations of elongate sand grains, measured in thin section. Each diagram is a summary of 200 individual measurements, with circles representing frequencies of 10%.

FIGURE 41. Oblique aerial view of the stone-banked terrace slope west of D-7. Sorted stripes near the top of the knoll merge to form stone-banked terraces where they encounter a decrease in gradient. On lower slopes the stripes become buried by rapidly moving fine-textured soil. Rates of downslope movement were measured annually near the front of ter-race 328 (A) and at two sorted-stripe localities (B and C). A profile trench was dug at D. Maximum *Rhizocarpon geographicum* diameters were measured at 9 stations along the line transect. In the background, large turf-banked terraces dominate the western crest of Niwot Ridge. September 1, 1964.

(*Editor's Note:* Material has been omitted at this point.)

COMPARISON WITH RATES OF MOVEMENT IN OTHER AREAS

INTRODUCTION

Maximum rates of downslope movement measured at experimental sites on Niwot Ridge ranged from about 0.4 to 4.3 cm/yr. Measure-able displacement was confined to the upper 50 cm of soil. This section of the paper compares the results of studies in the Front Range with measurements from other regions and environments.

ARCTIC, SUBARCTIC, AND ALPINE REGIONS

Reported maximum rates of downslope soil movement at 71 experimental sites in periglacial environments range from 0 to 71 cm/yr, with a median value of 2.7 cm/yr. Comparisons between individual areas are complicated by the variety of measurement techniques that have been used. Movement rates have been estimated from the displacement of plant stems (Sandberg, 1938) and of ancient strandlines of known age (T. Lindell, cited in Rapp, 1963). More-standard techniques involve the resurvey of painted stones (Dege, 1943; Rudberg, 1958, 1962, 1964; Rapp, 1960; Smith, 1960; Macar and Pissart, 1964; Pissart, 1964; Caine, 1968), nails (Budel, 1961), or wooden stakes (Washburn, 1947, 1967; Dahl, 1956; Jahn, 1960, 1961; Rapp, 1960; Smith, 1960) inserted to varying depths in the soil. The effect of differences in the depth of insertion of movement markers is illustrated by a study on the island of South Georgia (Smith, 1960). Twenty stones on the ground surface moved at an average rate of 47 cm/yr, whereas stakes inserted to depths of 10 and 25 cm moved at average rates of only 5 cm/yr and 3 cm/yr respectively. Stakes inserted to a depth of 50 cm experienced no movement at all. Smith's study clearly illustrates the need for standardizing measurement techniques.

Rates of subsurface movement in periglacial environments have been measured using spring-steel strain gauge probes (Williams, 1959), polyethylene tubing (Williams, 1966), vertical columns of plastic or wooden cylinders (Rudberg, 1958, 1962, 1964; Dutkiewicz, 1967), and linear motion transducers (Zhigarev, 1960; Everett, 1966). Maximum depths of movement are highly variable, ranging from about 10 cm at a site in Spitsbergen (Dutkiewicz, 1967) to 130 cm at the Anadyr Permafrost Station in the Soviet Union (Zhigarev, 1960). The median depth of movement measured at 19 arctic, subarctic, and alpine sites is 50 cm, which corresponds closely to the thickness of the layer of soil in which the long axes of elongate stones are oriented downslope (Rudberg, 1958; Rapp, 1967).

TEMPERATE AND SEMIARID REGIONS

Rates of downslope movement have been reported from 45 experimental sites in temperate and semiarid regions. Measured rates of displacement depend upon the nature of the vegetation cover and the technique of measurement.

On grassy and wooded slopes, downslope movement is minor, regardless of the measurement technique employed. Maximum rates of movement range from 0 to 1.4 cm/yr, with a median value of 0.1 cm/yr at 23 sites (Young, 1960, 1963; Everett, 1963; Hamilton, 1963; Iveronova, 1964; Emmett, 1965; Kirkby, 1967). Displace-ment is confined to depths of less than 30 cm, and is caused by expansion and contraction of the soil due to wetting and drying or to shallow freezing and thawing.

Comparably low rates of movement have been reported from studies in which wooden stakes or pipes were used in measuring soil movement on sparsely vegetated hillslopes in the western United States (Emmett, 1965; Leopold *et al.*, 1966). Because the markers used in these studies penetrated the soil to depths greater than 20 cm, they were relatively unaffected by rapid displacement in the upper few centimeters of soil.

Where rates of movement on bare and sparsely vegetated slopes have been measured using lines of small stones or other markers capable of responding to movement within a thin surface layer, maximum rates of displacement have proven to be exceptionally high (Gradwell, 1957; Caine, 1963; Schumm, 1964, 1967; Owens, 1967, 1969). Movement is confined to the upper 20 cm of soil. It is rapid (5 to 334 cm/yr) and usually random because of the tendency for small stones to roll and slide downslope after they are dislodged by surficial frost creep, needle ice, and raindrop impact.

CONCLUSIONS

Downslope soil movement in the Niwot Ridge area is comparable, both in rate and in the thickness of the layer of moving soil, to downslope movement in other alpine, arctic, and subarctic locations. Movement is generally more rapid, and extends to greater depth, in the Colorado mountains than on vegetated slopes in semiarid and temperate regions. Regardless of the environment, pebbles and small stones embedded in steep, bare slopes move rapidly under the influence of surface processes. Differences in measurement technique result in large differences in measured rates of movement, making it difficult to compare the results of studies in different environments.

ENVIRONMENTAL FACTORS

INTRODUCTION

Annual movement surveys on Niwot Ridge provide a basis for evaluating the effects of different environmental factors on rates of downslope movement. Despite their obvious interrelationship, soil texture, soil temperature, soil moisture, and gradient are treated as separate factors.

SOIL TEXTURE

A minimum of five textural samples were collected from the moving subsoil at each of eight experimental sites. In Figure 52, the combined silt and clay contents of samples from each site are plotted as a function of average maximum rates of movement. No correlation exists between

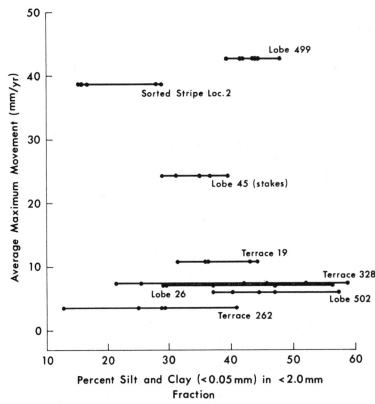

FIGURE 52. Silt and clay content of the moving subsoil at 8 experimental sites on Niwot Ridge, shown as a function of maximum rate of downslope movement.

the silt and clay content of the soil and the rate at which it moves downslope: some of the coarsest-textured soils have moved most rapidly. The effects of grain-size variation in moving soils on Niwot Ridge are apparently obscured by the effects of other, more important, environmental factors.

As shown in Figure 52, textural variations are greatest at experimental sites where present-day movement is due almost entirely to frost creep, and are smallest where solifluction is also an important process. Solifluction obliterates many of the textural differences produced by frost sorting within the finer fractions of the soil.

SOIL TEMPERATURE

Soil temperatures were measured at two movement sites selected because they represented opposite extremes of winter snow accumulation and downslope movement. Thermistor readings were taken at weekly intervals during the winter of 1964-65.

Soil Temperatures in a Winter Snow-Free Area

Because its surface is blown free of snow in winter, lobe 45 was expected to undergo particu-

larly deep freezing. Thermistor probes were inserted to depths of 1.2 m in bare and vegetation-covered soil on the lobe. Temperature fluctuations were largest, and freezing occurred most rapidly, where the soil was bare. By late January, however, the ground at both locations had frozen to a depth greater than 1.2 m. Both probes recorded a minimum temperature of $-3.6°C$ at this depth in late March. Temperatures rose in April and May. As ice lenses thawed, the soil surrounding the thermistor probes collapsed around them; with their bases still firmly frozen in the subsoil, the probes could not be reinserted, and temperature measurements were discontinued. Heaving of the probes relative to the ground surface continued until late June, when the depth of thawing exceeded 1 m. Total heave within the upper 1.2 m of soil amounted to 18 cm where vegetation was absent, and 11 cm where the ground surface was covered with *Carex* turf.

Soil Temperatures in a Winter Snow-Accumulation Area

Because of heavy winter snow accumulation, terrace 328 was expected to undergo relatively shallow freezing. Data from thermistors installed

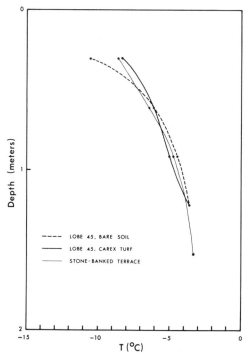

FIGURE 53. Minimum soil temperatures recorded during the winter of 1964-65 at experimental sites on Niwot Ridge.

to a maximum depth of 1.5 m in the terrace, however, show that freezing was deep during the winter of 1964-65. Interstices in the rubble layer were filled with snow continuously after mid-November, but heavy snow accumulation above the thermistor installation did not begin until mid-January. On January 16, 1966, the temperature of the soil at 1.5 m depth had dropped to $-2.9°C$. A minimum temperature of $-3.3°C$ was recorded at this depth in early April, when snow above the thermistors had reached a thickness of 2.6 m. Thawing did not begin until mid-July, when the site became free of snow. The highest temperature recorded at a depth of 1.5 m was $1.9°C$, in mid-September.

Conclusions

Comparison of minimum soil temperatures measured during the fall and winter of 1964-65 (Figure 53) indicates that current patterns of snow accumulation have a negligible effect upon the depth of freezing at experimental sites on Niwot Ridge. Except in very sheltered depressions or unusual years, snow does not accumulate early enough in the winter to be an effective insulator against deep frost penetration. Similar temperature regimes in lobe 45 and terrace 328 suggest

that factors other than depth of freeze are responsible for differences in movement rates at the two sites.

The time of the year when thawing occurs is probably more critical. Winter snow-free areas such as lobe 45 begin to thaw in April or May, when air temperatures are still relatively low; slow, intermittent melting prolongs the period of active solifluction. Areas of heavy winter snow accumulation, such as sorted stripe locality 2, begin to thaw later in the summer, when air temperatures are high; thawing is rapid, and solifluction is brief but intense. Differences in net downslope movement resulting from differences in rate of thaw may be minor, as suggested by comparable rates of displacement measured in lobe 45 and sorted stripe locality 2. But where thawing begins very late in the year, the persistence of frozen ground at shallow depth increases the amount of moisture available for autumn freezing, and thus encourages rapid movement.

SOIL MOISTURE

A close relationship between rates of downslope movement and soil-moisture availability is suggested by the restriction of lobes and terraces to meltwater-drainage areas and snow-accumulation slopes, and by the correlation of movement rates with depths to groundwater in individual turfbanked lobes and terraces (Figures 30, 31, and 32).

In Table 5, experimental sites are grouped according to the availability of moisture at critical times during the year. Three of the sites are saturated throughout the ice-free season. Part of a fourth is saturated during the spring thaw and, in very wet years, at the beginning of the fall freeze. The remaining five sites are wet in the spring, but relatively dry in the fall. Differences in maximum movement rates at the sites suggest that moisture is a critical environmental factor, and that, at least in the Front Range, abundant moisture *at the beginning of the fall freeze* is required in order for solifluction to occur.

Depths to groundwater were measured in early November alongside movement stakes on lobe 45 (1964 to 1966) and lobe 499 (1965). In Figure 54, displacement is plotted as a function of depth to the water table at the beginning of freeze. Slope angles are not comparable at the two sites, stakes varied in length, and measurements could not be made at exactly the same stage in the freeze-thaw cycle each year. The data indicate, nevertheless, that maximum rates of downslope movement are limited by the depth to the water table at the beginning of the fall freeze.

TABLE 5
Summary of movement data from experimental sites on Niwot Ridge

Feature	Eleva-tion	Slope	Ex-posure	Markers	Period of measurement	Avg. annual displacement (mm/year)		
						Minimum	Maximum	Mean
Saturated in spring and fall								
Turf-banked lobe 499	3,640	13°	NE	10 stakes	1962-1967	1.1	42.7	17.0
Sorted stripes (locality 2)	3,490	12.5°	NE	35 stones	1964-1967	12.8	38.8	22.1
Turf-banked lobe 45	3,480	6-7°	SW	14 stakes (line A)	1963-1967	0.0	22.8	9.8
Turf-banked lobe 45	3,480	6-7°	SW	10 stakes (line B)	1965-1967	0.2	24.2	9.4
Turf-banked lobe 45	3,480	6-7°	SW	7 cement blocks	1966-1967	8.3	42.9	21.8
Saturated in spring, locally in fall								
Turf-banked terrace 19	3,440	11-12°	SE	14 stakes	1964-1967	—1.9	10.9	2.0
Saturated in spring, but never in fall								
Stone-banked lobes 502-3	3,420	16-18°	S	20 stones	1965-1967	0.4	6.0	3.1
Stone-banked terrace 328	3,560	14°	SE	7 stones	1961-1967	1.5	7.3	4.2
Turf-banked lobe 26	3,480	13.5°	SW	8 stakes	1961-1967	—0.5	7.2	3.4
Sorted stripes (locality 1)	3,570	12°	SE	30 stones	1964-1967	—1.0	6.0	0.3
Turf-banked terrace 262	3,510	5-7°	SSE	7 stakes	1961-1967	0.8	3.6	2.0

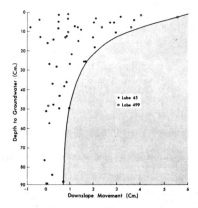

FIGURE 54. Rates of downslope movement plotted as a function of depth to groundwater at the beginning of the autumn freeze. Movement rates greater than 2 cm/yr occurred only where the water table lay within 20 cm of the ground surface.

GRADIENT

On shale hillslopes in semi-arid western Colorado, Schumm (1967) found a direct relationship between rates of surficial frost creep and the sine of the slope angle. On wet slopes in northeast Greenland, Washburn (1967) noted a similar relationship between rate of movement and sine of gradient. Gradient is important in the Front Range, but here, as in Greenland, its influence is partially obscured by the overwhelming effect of differences in moisture availability. In comparable moisture environments, movement rates tend to increase as the angle of slope becomes steeper (Table 5).

CONCLUSIONS

Local differences in rates of downslope movement in the Front Range result almost entirely from differences in soil-moisture conditions and gradient. Autumn moisture is the single most important factor. As a rule of thumb, rates of downslope movement on moderate slopes exceed 1 cm/yr only where the water table lies within 0.5 m of the ground surface at the beginning of the fall freeze. Rates of movement exceed 2 cm/yr only where the water table is shallower than 0.2 m (Figure 54).

The effect of gradient is secondary, but can be seen by comparing sites that are located in comparable moisture environments. Soil texture and temperature are not generally limiting, and affect rates of downslope movement only because of their influence on moisture availability.

Because slope angles remain virtually constant, changes in movement rates with time are a reflection of changing moisture conditions, and particularly of differences in the availability of autumn moisture. By reconstructing former rates of movement, it should be possible to infer past moisture fluctuations. A later section of the paper will deal with the ages of lobes and terraces in the Niwot Ridge area, and with former rates of downslope movement.

ORIGIN

TURF-BANKED LOBES AND TERRACES

Turf-banked lobes and terraces develop where the velocity of rapidly moving soil decreases downslope. Reduced rates of movement cause the soil to thicken; it acquires a bench-like, lobate, or transitional form depending upon the uniformity of moisture distribution along the contour of the slope. A vegetation cover is probably required to prevent destruction by slope-wash processes. The absence of pronounced sorting in the deposits suggests that solifluction is the major downslope movement process involved in their formation.

Terraces develop in snow-accumulation areas, where moisture is distributed more-or-less uniformly along the contour of the slope. Somewhere in the concave lower section of the slope, a zone exists in which the combination of moisture and gradient is optimum for rapid movement. Above this zone, movement rates increase downslope, and the soil becomes thinner; below it, movement rates decrease, and the soil thickens. Turf-banked terraces develop in the zone of compressive flow, where rapidly moving soil overtakes and overrides the more slowly moving material in its path. Because the terraces develop parallel to lines of equal velocity, their fronts are seldom strictly parallel to the contour of the slope, but cross it at low angles. Flow along the terrace axis prevents "cross-contour dips" from becoming larger than a few degrees.

Lobate forms develop in snow-free areas and on slopes where winter snow accumulation is patchy and irregular. Moisture conditions alternate between wet and dry in short distances across these slopes. Where changes in gradient or soil-moisture content along meltwater drainage routes cause the soil to move more slowly, lobate deposits of earth and rock accumulate. The widths of individual lobes are proportional to the widths of the drainage channels in which they form.

Many turf-banked lobes, including lobe 45 and others illustrated in Figure 6, are located where there are no obvious downslope changes in gradient or soil-moisture conditions. As Rapp (1960) has suggested for similar features in the Karkevagge Valley, these lobes may have developed from the tongues of small earth slides; their physical resemblance to earth slides is strong. Although earth slides do not occur under present conditions on Niwot Ridge, wet intervals during the Pleistocene would have favored their occurrence along drainage routes and their subsequent modification by frost creep and solifluction.

STONE-BANKED LOBES AND TERRACES

Stone-banked lobes and terraces develop where moving sorted stripes, blockfields, or other accumulations of bouldery debris on slopes undergo a decrease in velocity. They are commonly associated with a reduction in gradient, and occur on concave slopes, valley floors, and the gently sloping treads of older, turf-banked terraces. Where a decrease in gradient causes the debris to move more slowly, it thickens and spreads laterally. Lobes develop at the fronts of isolated sorted stripes and stone streams. Terraces develop at the leading edges of sloping blockfields, or where stripes are spaced so closely that the lobes at their fronts merge to form a single unit. The formation of stone-banked lobes and terraces does not require a vegetation cover, and is probably favored by its absence.

Sorting is largely inherited. Stone-banked terraces at the edges of blockfields retain their characteristic blockfield sorting, with a surface layer of rocks and an underlying layer of stone-free soil. Lobes and terraces at the fronts of stripes become sorted when rocks in the stripes spread laterally over the stone-poor surface soil between them. As the terrace moves downslope, continued frost ac-

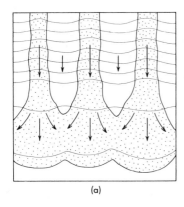 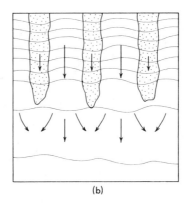

FIGURE 55. D i a g r a m showing the effect of a decrease in gradient upon moving sorted stripes. Arrows give the directions and relative magnitudes of movement. (a) Stones are moving more rapidly than fines. (b) Fines are moving more rapidly than stones.

tivity accentuates the separation of fine- and coarse-textured material, and stones that fall from the surface of the terrace at its front are recycled upward to the base of the rubble layer.

Stone-banked lobes and terraces can develop from sorted stripes only if the rocky stripes are moving more rapidly than intervening fine-textured material (Figure 55a). Where the opposite is true, a decrease in gradient causes fine material to override and bury the slowly moving blocky debris (Figure 55b). Both situations are illustrated in Figure 41. Near the top of the slope, terraces are well developed at the lower ends of sorted stripes; near the bottom of the slope, terraces are poorly developed or absent, and stripes that encounter a decrease in gradient tend to disappear beneath the surface.

Measurements on stone-banked lobes 502 and 503 have shown that rapid movement of blocky debris is characteristic of a *frost-creep* environment; measurements at sorted stripe locality 2 suggest that rapid movement of fine material relative to coarse debris is characteristic of a *solifluction* environment. If this relationship is generally true, stone-banked lobes and terraces will be able to form only where frost creep is the dominant movement process. This hypothesis is supported by the strong vertical sorting of the features and by the fact that they are best developed on steep upper slopes. On gentler, moister, lower slopes, solifluction becomes increasingly important; the relative velocity of fine-textured soil increases, and stone-banked lobes and terraces are unable to develop from sorted stripes.

AGE, PAST MOVEMENT RATES, AND CLIMATIC SIGNIFICANCE

TURF-BANKED LOBES AND TERRACES

Several periods of turf-banked lobe and terrace formation have occurred in the Front Range alpine region. "Older" and "younger" lobes and terraces can be distinguished from each other by differences in morphology. The "older" features are topographically subdued, covered with patterned ground, and dissected by meltwater streams; the "younger" features are topographically fresh, with bulging, overhanging fronts, unpatterned treads, and surface drainage.

Stratigraphic and archaeological evidence suggests that many of the "older" turf-banked lobes and terraces developed during the interval separating the Middle Pinedale glacial maximum and the beginning of the Altithermal.

(1) Topographically-subdued lobes and terraces occur on moraines of Early and Middle Pinedale age, suggesting that conditions favorable

for widespread solifluction have occurred since the Middle Pinedale maximum. The absence of lobes and terraces on Late Pinedale and Neoglacial moraines may indicate a minimum age for the features, or may result solely from the small size and limited extent of the younger moraines.

(2) A turf-banked terrace at archaeological site 5 BL 67, east of the summit of Mount Albion (Figure 1), is older than a prehistoric game drive system and occupation area dated at 5,800 to 5,300 BP (Benedict, in preparation). The terrace is located on a southeast-facing slope with a gradient of 10 to 12°. Detailed stratigraphic studies at the site suggest the following sequence of events:

(a) Formation of the terrace.

(b) Development of sorted polygons and frost cracks on the terrace surface.

(c) Human occupation of the terrace during a

period of patterned-ground inactivity and soil formation.

(d) Intermittent reactivation of polygon centers, alternating with periods of renewed soil formation, during Neoglaciation.

Radiocarbon dates of 5,800 ± 125 BP (I-3267), 5,730 ± 130 BP (I-3817), and 5,300 ± 130 BP (I-4418) have been obtained for charcoal associated with Archaic projectile points, grinding tools, and hide-working implements in the occupation level. The dates provide a minimum age for both the terrace and the sorted polygons.

(3) A turf-banked terrace at archaeological site 5 BL 70, also on Albion Ridge, is older than 7,650 radiocarbon years. The terrace is located on a relatively dry southeast-facing slope with a gradient of 11 to 12°. Excavations have shown that the terrace tread was used by Archaic hunters and gatherers for butchering, seed or root preparation, and tool manufacture (Olson, 1969). The following sequence of events occurred at the site:

(a) Formation of the terrace.

(b) Development of sorted stripes on the terrace tread.

(c) Occupation of the terrace surface by an unidentified cultural group.

(d) Deposition of a culturally sterile sandy unit.

(e) Occupation of the terrace surface by Archaic hunters and gatherers during a period of soil formation.

(f) Deposition of colluvium, followed by development of the modern A horizon.

Terrace formation and the development of patterned ground both preceded initial occupation of the site, which is dated at 7,650 ± 190 BP (I-3266). The sterile unit overlying the lower occupation level was deposited early in the Altithermal. Soil formation and reoccupation of the site occurred during a moist phase of the Altithermal, and are dated at 5,650 ± 145 BP (I-3023) and 5,350 ± 130 BP (I-4419). Colluvium was deposited during Neoglaciation.

After a long period in which no new lobes or terraces developed in the Indian Peaks region, "younger" turf-banked lobes formed during Neoglacial ice advances. Only one of these, lobe 499, has been studied in detail. Because of its fresh appearance and its location on the riser of an older and more subdued turf-banked terrace, the lobe is clearly younger than the Pinedale Glaciation. A radiocarbon date from the upslope end of the buried A horizon (Figures 20, 21) indicates that the lobe began to form during the

Temple Lake Stade of Neoglaciation, and has advanced a distance of 4.45 m during the past 2,340 ± 130 years (I-4045).[2] Despite heavy precipitation during the Arikaree and Gannett Peak Stades, the average rate of frontal advance during this interval (1.9 mm/yr) is comparable to, or lower than, the probable modern rate. Slow average movement is a result of the absence of important snow-accumulation areas higher on the slope. Snowbanks form only in the lee of terrace risers, and are limited in size by the height of the terrace front; even if winter snowfall were drastically increased, the amount of moisture available for downslope movement in lobe 499 would remain relatively constant.

Because they are indicators of widespread and effective solifluction, turf-banked lobes and terraces provide information about former moisture conditions. We can infer that they originated at times when the soil was weakened and saturated by melting ground ice, and when at least a rudimentary plant cover was present. Such conditions apparently existed on a broad scale at the close of one or more Pinedale ice advances, and on a much smaller scale during the Temple Lake Stade of Neoglaciation. The occurrence of patterned ground on terrace treads indicates that significant frost sorting occurred after formation of the older terraces; a likely time, suggested by the limiting date of 7,650 years BP from site 5 BL 70, would have been the most recent stade of Pinedale Glaciation.

Snowdrift patterns in the Indian Peaks region are controlled by the interaction of wind and topography. Significant snow accumulation occurs only in lee situations, and these are the slopes most likely to be saturated during the spring and fall. Because turf-banked terraces are restricted almost entirely to south- and east-facing exposures, prevailing winter wind directions during the latter part of the Pinedale Glaciation are inferred to have been northwesterly, as they are today.

STONE-BANKED LOBES AND TERRACES

Stratigraphic, lichenometric, and radiocarbon evidence suggest that stone-banked lobes and terraces in the Niwot Ridge area formed at the close of the Temple Lake Stade of Neoglaciation:

---

[2]Rootlets were removed by repeated flotation. The radiocarbon date was obtained from soil humates extracted by boiling in 2% NaOH and acidifying with 6N̄ HCl, as recommended by C. Vance Haynes, Jr.

142

(1) Stone-banked lobes and terraces commonly override and bury the treads of turf-banked
terraces that formed in middle or late Pinedale
time. A post-Pleistocene age is implied.

(2) Stone-banked lobes and terraces lack the
buried Altithermal soil that occurs elsewhere in
the region, suggesting that they began their downslope advance after this soil had been destroyed
by Temple Lake nivation processes.

(3) Lichen measurements show that stone-
banked lobes and terraces are older than the beginning of the Arikaree-Gannett Peak interstadial,
when their treads reappeared from beneath perennial snowbanks. Strong cavernous weathering
suggests formation prior to the Temple Lake-
Arikaree interstadial.

(4) A radiocarbon date from the upslope end
of the buried A horizon in terrace 328 (Figure
46) indicates an age in excess of 2,470 ± 110
years (I-1792).

Stone-banked lobes and terraces are the products of intense frost creep, which requires autumn
saturation and a temperature regime that encourages deep freezing and thawing. Frost creep
is most effective where vegetation is absent. In
the coarse-textured and permeable soils that
blanket slopes above timberline in the Front
Range, autumn saturation is limited to areas that
are irrigated with water from melting snowbanks.
The close of the Temple Lake Stade of Neoglaci-

ation must have been a time in which perennial
snowbanks were shrinking, so that upper slopes—
formerly snow-covered throughout the year—became free of snow and saturated with meltwater
in early fall.

Past rates of downslope movement, determined
by dating samples collected at regular intervals
along the buried humus layer overrun by terrace
328 (Figure 46), provide information about subsequent Neoglacial climatic fluctuations. Dates
were corrected for the approximate radiocarbon
age of the soil at time of burial, assuming a linear
increase from 0 to 355 years during the period
of A-horizon development on this slope. Details
are given in Benedict (1966). Corrected dates
(Table 6) were used in reconstructing past rates
of downslope soil movement, which are shown in
Figure 56. Trenches in three additional stone-
banked terraces and a stone-banked lobe failed to
produced datable organic material to supplement
the results of this initial study.

An inferred period of rapid movement at the
end of the Temple Lake Stade of Neoglaciation
came to a close about 2,500 years ago, when
plants recolonized the slope and an A horizon
began to develop. During the Temple Lake-
Arikaree interstadial, movement rates were roughly comparable to modern rates. Near the close of
the Arikaree Stade, rates of downslope movement
increased dramatically, and the front of the terrace
advanced at an average velocity of 23 mm/yr.
After several hundred years of rapid movement,
the terrace slowed to a velocity comparable to
that occurring under modern climatic conditions.

Accelerated movement at the close of the
Arikaree Stade reflects emergence of terrace 328
from beneath a cover of perennial snow. Lichen
measurements have shown that a major snowbank
covered the slope during the Arikaree glacial
maximum. Between about 1,150 and 1,050 years
BP the terrace became free of snow in late fall;

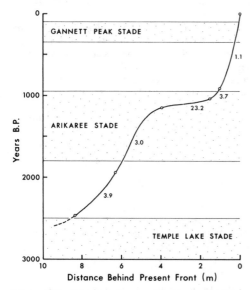

FIGURE 56. Diagram showing changes in the position of the front of terrace 328 during the past
2,500 years. Average rates of movement (mm/yr)
have been calculated for 5 intervals.

TABLE 6

Radiocarbon dates from terrace 328, Niwot Ridge

Sample number	Distance behind present front (m)	Uncorrected age (years BP)	Corrected age (years BP)
I-1510	0.00	355 ± 115	0
I-4044	1.04	1,140 ± 90	915
I-1697	1.52	1,250 ± 120	1,045
I-1698	3.96	1,340 ± 110	1,150
I-1371	6.31	2,020 ± 110	1,945
I-1792	8.35	2,470 ± 110	2,470

average movement rates greater than 20 mm/yr during this interval suggest that groundwater lay at a depth of less than 0.2 m at the beginning of the annual freeze.

Although evidence for accelerated movement during the Gannett Peak Stade of Neoglaciation is lacking, the expanded snowbank that occupied the rear of the terrace during the Gannett Peak maximum should have favored rapid movement.

The virtual restriction of stone-banked lobes and terraces to south-southeast-facing exposures suggests that prevailing winter wind directions late in the Temple Lake Stade were from the north-northwest.

CONCLUSIONS

CLASSIFICATION AND DISTRIBUTION

(1) Moving soils in the Colorado Front Range are classified on the basis of their surface expression and sorting. The deposits may be sorted or nonsorted; they may be uniform and sheetlike, lobate, or terrace-like. Intergradations in surface expression are common, but intergradations in sorting do not occur.

(2) Turf-banked lobes and terraces in the Niwot Ridge study area occupy gentle slopes with an average gradient of 10°. Terraces are confined almost entirely to snow-accumulation slopes, whereas lobes are best developed along meltwater drainage routes that pass through winter snow-free areas.

(3) Stone-banked lobes and terraces occur on snow-accumulation slopes with average gradients of 16 to 17°; they commonly form at the lower edges of blockfields, sorted stripes, stone streams, and unstable scree slopes.

INTERNAL STRUCTURE

(1) Beneath their surface humus layers, turf-banked lobes and terraces in the Front Range consist of stones and soil, mixed together without conspicuous sorting. The soil is commonly mottled or gleyed and has a pronounced platy structure. Its texture becomes gradually finer toward the front of the lobe or terrace. One or several buried organic layers are commonly present. The long axes of elongated sand grains, cobbles, and boulders tend to lie parallel to the ground surface or to be slightly imbricated.

(2) In profile, stone-banked lobes and terraces in the Front Range consist of (a) a surface layer of cobbles and boulders, thickening toward the front of the lobe or terrace; (b) an underlying unit with distinct platy structure and very few stones, becoming thinner and finer-textured toward the front; (c) a buried A horizon, locally disrupted or absent because of deep freezing and thawing; and (d) the buried subsoil. Rocks in the rubble layer tend to be orientated with their long axes pointing in the direction of slope and their flat faces parallel to the lobe or terrace surface. Near the fronts of individual lobes, the long axes of stones are rotated into orientations paralleling the fronts, and tabular stones are moderately to strongly imbricated.

MODERN RATES OF MOVEMENT

(1) Average maximum rates of downslope soil movement at nine experimental sites on Niwot Ridge ranged from 0.4 to 4.3 cm/yr. Comparison with other areas is difficult because of the inconsistency with which results are often reported and the variety of measurement techniques that have been used. Rates of movement are generally comparable to rates measured in other alpine and arctic regions, are higher than rates measured on grassy and forested slopes in temperate and semiarid regions, and are lower than rates of surface displacement on stony, unvegetated slopes in temperate and semiarid climates.

(2) Movement rates vary erratically along the treads of stone-banked and turf-banked terraces; movement is most rapid where moisture is most abundant.

(3) Movement rates vary systematically in turf-banked and stone-banked lobes. Movement is greatest along the axis of the lobe, with maximum values occurring just below its midpoint. Variations in movement rates are related to groundwater levels, which are typically highest along the axis and near the midpoint of the lobe. Directions of movement tend to preserve an equilibrium surface profile: flow is directed toward the lobe axis where movement is accelerating, and away from the axis where movement is retarded.

(4) Differential movement within the surface rubble layer of stone-banked lobes and terraces on Niwot Ridge is minor under present conditions, and occurs mainly in parts of the lobe or terrace that adjoin areas of finer-textured soil.

(5) Important frost heaving is currently restricted to microenvironments that are saturated at the beginning of the fall and winter freeze. Heaving at the axis of a turf-banked lobe on Niwot Ridge exceeded 36 cm during the winter of 1965-

66. Although small stones on the ground surface are affected by short-term freeze-thaw cycles during the spring and fall, only the annual cycle influences the movement of larger stones and wooden stakes.

(6) Differential heaving and downslope movement at experimental sites on Niwot Ridge are currently confined to a layer of soil 50 to 75 cm thick. The shape of the vertical velocity profile reflects differences in the relative importance of frost creep and solifluction, as well as the presence or absence of a restraining turf layer.

EVALUATION OF PROCESSES

(1) Downslope soil movement is the resultant of potential frost creep, solifluction, and retrograde displacement. Retrograde movement and solifluction both occur during the spring thaw. Each minimizes the effect of the other, making it impossible to accurately determine their individual contributions to net downslope movement.

(2) Under present conditions, frost creep is the dominant movement process on Front Range slopes. Only in specialized microenvironments, such as the saturated axial areas of turf-banked lobes in wet sites, do the effects of solifluction exceed the effects of frost creep. Along the axes of turf-banked lobes on slopes of 6 and 13°, displacement due to solifluction exceeded 2.5 and 2.2 cm/yr respectively. Potential frost creep amounted to 3.0 and 2.2 cm/yr, but much of this displacement was only temporary, and was cancelled by retrograde movement during the spring thaw. At the edges of both lobes, movement was entirely the result of frost creep.

(3) Saturation during the spring thaw is not, in the Front Range, sufficient to cause solifluction. In order for solifluction to occur, the soil must have previously been "conditioned" by ice-lens formation, which requires saturation at the beginning of freeze.

(4) Measured rates of potential frost creep in a turf-banked lobe on Niwot Ridge were as much as seven times greater than values calculated from slope and frost-heave measurements. Soil movement during the fall freeze is a more complicated process than previously suspected.

(5) In wet sites, retrograde movement may significantly exceed potential frost creep. It is uncertain whether this is a result of annual differences in the depth of summer thaw, of desiccation, or of other factors.

(6) Fine-textured soil sometimes moves faster and sometimes moves more slowly than nearby coarse material, depending upon the relative importance of different movement processes. On a

saturated 12 to 13° slope subject to intense solifluction, fine-textured soil moved twice as rapidly as stripes of coarse debris (Figure 43). On a relatively dry 16 to 18° slope subject only to frost creep, and perhaps to wetting and drying, stone-banked lobes moved three times as rapidly as adjacent nonsorted soil (Figure 49).

RELATIONSHIP OF MOVEMENT TO ENVIRONMENT

(1) Rates of downslope soil movement in the Front Range are largely determined by the depth to groundwater at the beginning of the autumn freeze. At experimental sites on Niwot Ridge, the displacement of 25-cm-long wooden stakes exceeded 2 cm/yr only where the water table lay within 0.2 m of the ground surface at the beginning of freezing, and exceeded 1 cm/yr only where it lay within 0.5 m of the ground surface.

(2) Gradient exerts a secondary influence upon rates of downslope movement. Under comparable moisture conditions, movement increases as a direct function of slope angle.

(3) Differences in soil texture and temperature affect soil movement indirectly, by influencing the availability of moisture, but otherwise have little control upon rates of downslope movement in the Front Range alpine region.

ORIGIN

(1) Turf-banked lobes and terraces develop where rapid downslope movement is impeded, normally by a decrease in gradient. Terraces with linear fronts develop in snow-accumulation areas, where moisture is more-or-less uniformly distributed along the contour of the slope. Where snow accumulation is patchy, the fronts of terraces are irregularly lobate. On winter snow-free slopes, where moisture is confined to narrow drainageways, lobate forms dominate the landscape.

(2) The absence of sorting in turf-banked lobes and terraces together with their restriction to relatively moist lower slopes reflect the importance of solifluction in their formation. Solifluction largely obliterates the results of vertical frost sorting and produces deposits in which stones and fines are mixed together without obvious layering. Because solifluction is no longer an important process in most lobes and terraces in the Front Range, sorted polygons have developed and are preserved at their surfaces. The formation of turf-banked lobes and terraces requires a coherent plant cover, and is favored by perennially frozen ground at shallow depth.

(3) Stone-banked lobes and terraces develop

where a decrease in gradient causes rocky debris to accumulate and spread laterally. Topographic form is less an expression of moisture distribution than of the source of the stones that supply the lobe or terrace. Lobes develop where isolated stone streams and widely-spaced sorted stripes encounter a decrease in gradient. Terraces form at the lower edges of sloping blockfields and scree slopes, and where sorted stripes are so closely spaced that the lobes at their fronts coalesce and merge. Stone-banked lobes and terraces can develop only where coarse debris is moving more rapidly than adjacent finer-textured soil; thus they are characteristic of a frost-creep, rather than a solifluction, environment.

(4) The pronounced vertical sorting of stone-banked lobes and terraces, and their occurrence on steep, upper slopes, reflect the importance of frost creep in their formation. Most of the sorting currently observed in stone-banked lobes and terraces is inherited from the blockfields or sorted stripes that formerly supplied debris to their surfaces. Sorting is accentuated as stones that fall from the terrace fronts are recycled upward to the base of the rubble layer by frost heaving.

Ages of the Deposits

(1) Stratigraphic and archaeological evidence from Niwot Ridge and the surrounding area suggest that many turf-banked lobes and terraces with gentle fronts and patterned surfaces formed during the interval between the Middle Pinedale glacial maximum and the beginning of the Altithermal. The closing phases of the Middle Stade of Pinedale Glaciation were a likely time. Lobes and terraces undoubtedly also formed during earlier periods of favorable climate. Sorted polygons and stripes developed on terrace treads during the final stade of Pinedale Glaciation, prior to 7,650 radiocarbon years ago.

(2) Turf-banked lobes with overhanging fronts and fresh topography developed in the Front Range during Neoglaciation. A radiocarbon date of 2,340 years on organic material from the upslope end of the buried A horizon in a small turf-banked lobe on Niwot Ridge suggests formation during the Temple Lake Stade. Costin et al. (1967) have shown that comparable features were forming in the Australian mountains at approximately the same time.

(3) Stratigraphic, lichenometric, and radiocarbon evidence indicate that stone-banked lobes and terraces in the Front Range originated in late Temple Lake time. A minimum age for their development is provided by a date of 2,470 years for organic material overrun by a large stone-banked terrace on Niwot Ridge. Conditions would have been favorable for frost creep and intense sorting when lee slopes were emerging from beneath perennial snowbanks and when vegetation was absent.

Past Movement Rates

(1) A radiocarbon date from the upslope end of the buried humus layer in a turf-banked lobe on Niwot Ridge shows that the front of the lobe has advanced at an average rate of 1.9 mm/yr during the past 2,340 years. This value is comparable to the estimated modern rate of frontal advance.

(2) Radiocarbon dates for samples of buried humus collected from beneath a stone-banked terrace on Niwot Ridge suggest an average rate of terrace advance of 3.4 mm/yr during the past 2,470 years. Rates of movement have varied with changing climatic conditions. An inferred initial period of rapid movement came to a close at the beginning of the Temple Lake-Arikaree interstadial, a time of general slope stability, vegetation growth, and soil formation. Movement was slow during the Arikaree glacial maximum, when all but the upper sections of the slope were covered with perennial snow. Movement rates increased by a factor of almost eight at the close of the Arikaree Stade, when the slope again became free of snow in the fall. During the past 1,050 radiocarbon years, average rates of movement have been relatively low. Wide spacing of dated samples has made it impossible to determine whether expanded snowbanks during the Gannett Peak Stade caused increased rates of downslope soil movement.

Climatic Significance

(1) Modern rates of downslope movement in the Colorado Front Range reflect differences in gradient and the availability of autumn moisture. Because gradient has remained virtually constant through time, former periods of rapid downslope movement are inferred to have been times when moisture was plentiful at the beginning of freeze. Such intervals occurred at the close of the Middle Stade of Pinedale Glaciation, and during the waning phases of the Temple Lake and Arikaree Stades of Neoglaciation (Figure 57).

(2) Soil-moisture distribution in the Front Range is intimately related to winter snowdrift patterns. The locations of terraces on Niwot Ridge suggest that prevailing winter winds were from the northwest during Middle Pinedale time,

146

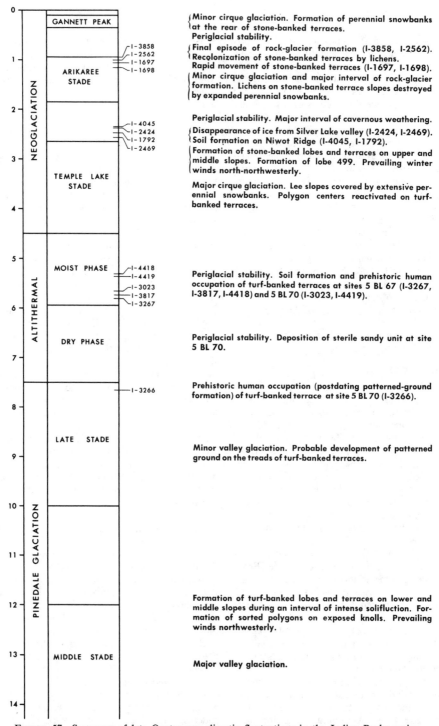

FIGURE 57. Summary of late Quaternary climatic fluctuations in the Indian Peaks region. Dates for the close of the Middle Stage and beginning of the Late Stage of Pinedale glaciation are from Richmond (1965, Table 2). The time scale is in thousands of years BP.

and from the north-northwest at the close of the Temple Lake Stade of Neoglaciation.

(3) The relative importance of frost creep and solifluction varies with the moisture content of the soil. Frost creep is generally associated with upper slope positions, and solifluction with lower slope positions. The line separating the zones dominated by each of these two processes has shifted upward and downward with changes in climate. During the late Pleistocene, solifluction was the dominant movement process on all but the driest ridgecrests and the upper flanks of knolls. Neither process seems to have been particularly important during the Altithermal. During Neoglacial intervals of rapid downslope movement, solifluction was restricted to lower slopes, and frost creep became the most important movement process in middle slope positions formerly dominated by solifluction. Under present climatic conditions, solifluction occurs only in specialized, saturated microenvironments; frost creep is the dominant movement process on upper, middle, *and* lower slopes.

(4) Sorted landforms characteristic of frost creep are often superimposed upon landforms characteristic of solifluction. The occurrence of sorted polygons and stripes, stone-banked lobes, and stone-banked terraces on the treads of turf-banked lobes and terraces reflects a general decline in the availability of moisture and the effectiveness of solifluction since the close of the Middle Stade of Pinedale Glaciation.

(5) A tentative reconstruction of climatic fluctuations in the Front Range alpine region is given in Figure 57.

ACKNOWLEDGMENTS

Many people have contributed to this project. My special thanks go to William C. Rense, Kenneth L. Petersen, Dennis Rasmussen, and Bryon Olson, whose help in the field was made possible by INSTAAR summer research participation programs sponsored by the National Science Foundation. Charles Schweger, Ronald Foreman, Mrs. Katharine T. Benedict, Mrs. Diane G. Benedict, and Mrs. Barbara Madole provided voluntary assistance on a number of occasions. The map of periglacial landforms on Niwot Ridge (Figure 2) is the result of fieldwork by Mrs. Jody Fitzgerald during the summer of 1965. David F. Murray and Donald L. Pattie identified plants collected at several of the movement sites. Transportation problems, particularly in winter, were minimized thanks to the talents of Skip Greene. Surveying equipment was made available by the University of Wisconsin Geology Department and by the Geological Sciences and Geography Departments at the University of Colorado. Discussions with Robert F. Black and William C. Bradley led to the adoption of several techniques that were used in the study. Much of the fieldwork was accomplished while I received financial aid in the form of National Science Foundation Graduate Fellowships and a University of Colorado INSTAAR Postdoctoral Fellowship; the Society of the Sigma Xi and the Geological Society of America contributed additional support. INSTAAR provided living accommodations at its Mountain Research Station, as well as other forms of assistance during the period of study. Robert F. Black, Nel Caine, Jack D. Ives, Cuchlaine A. M. King, A. Lincoln Washburn, and Peter J. Williams made helpful comments on the manuscript. My thanks go to these individuals and institutions, and others not mentioned.

REFERENCES

Andersson, J. G.
    1906 : Solifluction, a component of subaërial denudation. *J. Geol.,* 14: 91-112.
Antevs, Ernst
    1932 : *Alpine zone of Mt. Washington Range.* Merrill & Webber, Auburn, Maine, 118 pp.
Baulig, Henri
    1956 : Pénéplaines et pédiplaines. *Bull. Soc. Belge d'Études Géog.,* 25(1): 25-58.
Benedict, J. B.
    1966 : Radiocarbon dates from a stone-banked terrace in the Colorado Rocky Mountains, U.S.A. *Georg. Annaler,* 48A (1): 24-31.
    1967 : Recent glacial history of an alpine area in the Colorado Front Range, U.S.A., I. Establishing a lichen-growth curve. *J. Glaciol.,* 6(48): 817-832.
    1968 : Recent glacial history of an alpine area in the Colorado Front Range, U.S.A., II. Dating the glacial deposits. *J. Glaciol.,* 7(49): 77-87.
    1969 : Microfabric of patterned ground. *Arctic and Alpine Res.,* 1(1): 45-48.
    1970 : Frost cracking in the Colorado Rocky

148

Mountains. *Geog. Annaler* (in press).
In preparation: Prehistoric man and environment in the Colorado Rocky Mountains.

Beschel, R. E.
1961 : Botany: and some remarks on the history of vegetation and glacierization. *In* Müller, B.S.(ed.), *Jacobsen-McGill Arctic Research Expedition to Axel Heiberg Island. Preliminary Report 1959-1960,* 179-199.

Billings, W. D., and Mark, A. F.
1961 : Interactions between alpine tundra vegetation and patterned ground in the mountains of southern New Zealand. *Ecology,* 42: 18-31.

Büdel, Julius
1961 : Die Abtragungsvorgänge auf Spitzbergen im Umkreis der Barentsinsel. *In: Deutscher Geographentag Köln: Tagungsbericht und wissenschaftliche Abhandlungen.* Franz Steiner Verlag, Weisbaden, 337-375.

Butrym, J., Cegła, J., Dzułynski, S.,
and Nakonieczny, S.
1964 : New interpretation of "periglacial structures." *Folia Quaternaria,* 17: 1-34.

Caine, T. N.
1963 : Movement of low angle scree slopes in the Lake District, northern England. *Rev. Géomorph. Dyn.,* 4: 171-177.
1968 : The log-normal distribution and rates of soil movement: an example. *Rev. Géomorph. Dyn.,* 18(1): 1-7.

Costin, A. B., Thom, B. G., Wimbush, D. J., and Stuiver, Minze
1967 : Nonsorted steps in the Mt. Kosciusko area, Australia. *Geol. Soc. Amer. Bull.,* 78: 979-992.

Curry, R. R.
1969 : Holocene climatic and glacial history of the central Sierra Nevada, California. *In* Schumm, S. A. and Bradley, W. C. (eds.), *United States Contributions to Quaternary Research,* Geol. Soc. Amer. Spec. Paper, 123: 1-47.

Czeppe, Zdzisław
1960 : Thermic differentiation of the active layer and its influence upon the frost heave in periglacial regions (Spitsbergen). *Bull. Acad. Polonaise Sci.,* Série des sci., géol., et géog., 8(2): 149-152.
1966 : Przebieg głownych procesow morfogenetycznych w południowo-zachodnim Spitsbergenie. *Zeszyty Naukowe Uniwersytetu Jagiellonskiego,* 127: 1-129 (Polish with English summary).

Dahl, Eilif
1956 : Rondane: Mountain vegetation in south Norway and its relation to the environment. *Skrifter utgitt Det Norske Vid.-Akad. i Oslo, Mat.-Nat. Klasse.* No. 3: 273-282.

Dege, Wilhelm
1943 : Über Aussmass und Art der Bewegung arktischer Fliesserde: Z. *Geomorph.,* 11: 318-329.

Dutkiewicz, Leopold
1961 : Congelifluction lobes on the southern Hornsund coast in Spitsbergen. *Biul. Peryglac.,* 10: 285-289.
1967 : The distribution of periglacial phenomena in NW-Sörkapp, Spitsbergen. *Biul. Peryglac.,* 16: 37-83.

Dylik, Jan
1967 : Solifluxion, congelifluxion and related slope processes. *Geog. Annaler,* 49A (2-4): 167-177.

Embleton, C. and King, C. A. M.
1968 : *Glacial and periglacial geomorphology.* St. Martin's Press, New York, 608 pp.

Emmett, W. W.
1965 : The Vigil Network: Methods of measurement and a sampling of data collected. *In:* Symposium of Budapest, *Representative and experimental areas,* 1. Int. Assoc. Sci. Hydrol., Publ. No. 66: 89-106.

Everett, K. R.
1963 : Slope movement, Neotoma Valley, southern Ohio. Ohio State University, Inst. Polar Studies, Rep. No. 6: 1-62.
1966 : Slope movement and related phenomena. *In* Wilimovsky, N. J. and Wolfe, J. N. (eds.), *Environment of the Cape Thompson region, Alaska,* U.S. Atomic Energy Comm., Div. Tech. Info., 175-220.

Galloway, R. W.
1961 : Solifluction in Scotland. *Scot. Geog. Mag.,* 77(2): 75-87.

Goldthwait, R. P.
1960 : Development of an ice cliff in northwest Greenland. U.S. Army CRREL, Tech. Rep. 39. 106 pp.

Gradwell, M. W.
1957 : Patterned ground at a high-country station. *N.Z. J. Sci. and Tech.,* 38(sec. B, no. 8): 793-806.

Hamilton, T. D.
1963 : Quantitative study of mass movements, southeastern Wisconsin. Unpublished M.S. thesis, University of Wisconsin, Madison. 103 pp.

Holmes, C. D. and Colton, R. B.
1960 : Patterned ground near Dundas (Thule Air Force Base), Greenland. *Medd. om Grønland,* 158(6): 1-15.

Iveronova, M. I.
1964 : Stationary studies of the recent denudation processes on the slopes of the R. Tchon-Kizilsu Basin, Tersky Alatau

ridge, Tien-Shan. Z. *Geomorph.*, N.F. Suppl. Bd. 5: 206-212.

Jahn, Alfred
1960 : Some remarks on evolution of slopes on Spitsbergen. Z. *Geomorph.*, N.F. Suppl. Bd. 1: 49-58.
1961 : Quantitative analysis of some periglacial processes in Spitsbergen. *Uniwersytet Wrocławski im Bolesława Bieruta Zeszyty Naukowe Nauki Przyrodnicze,* Ser. B, Nr. 5: 1-54.

Kirkby, M. J.
1967 : Measurement and theory of soil creep. *J. Geol.,* 75(4): 359-378.

Leopold, L. B., Emmett, W. W., and Myrick, R. M.
1966 : Channel and hillslope processes in a semiarid area, New Mexico. U.S. Geol. Sur. Prof. Paper, 352-G: 193-253.

Lundqvist, G.
1949 : The orientation of the block material in certain species of flow earth. *Geog. Annaler,* 31(1-4): 335-347.

Lundqvist, Jan
1962 : Patterned ground and related frost phenomena in Sweden. *Sveriges Geologiska Undersökning,* 55(7): 1-101.

Macar, P. and Pissart, A.
1964 : Études récentes sur l'évolution des versants effectuées à l'Université de Liège. Z. *Geomorph.,* N.F. Suppl. Bd. 5: 74-81.

Madole, R. F.
1969 : Pinedale and Bull Lake Glaciation in Upper St. Vrain drainage basin, Boulder County, Colorado. *Arctic and Alpine Res.,* 1(4): 279-287.

Marr, J. W.
1961 : Ecosystems of the east slope of the Front Range in Colorado. *Univ. Colorado Stud.,* Ser. Biol., No. 8: 1-134.

Marr, J. W., Clark, J. M., Osburn, W. S., and Paddock, M. W.
1968 : Data on mountain environments III. Front Range, Colorado, four climax regions, 1959-1964. *Univ. Colorado Stud.,* Ser. Biol., No. 29: 1-181.

Munsell Color Company, Inc.
1954 : *Munsell soil color charts.* Baltimore.

Olson, B. L.
1969 : An Archaic site in the Colorado Front Range (abstract). *J. Colorado-Wyoming Acad. Sci.,* 6(2): 43.

Osburn, W. S., Benedict, J. B., and Corte, A. E.
1965 : Frost phenomena, patterned ground, and ecology on Niwot Ridge. *In* Schultz, C. B. and Smith, H. T. U. (eds.), *Guidebook for one-day field conferences, Boulder area, Colorado,* VIIth INQUA Congress, 21-26.

Østrem, Gunnar
1965 : Problems of dating ice-cored moraines. *Geog. Annaler,* 47A(1): 1-38.

Owens, I. F.
1967 : Mass movement in the Chilton Valley. Unpublished M.A. thesis, University of Canterbury, N.Z. 92 pp.
1969 : Causes and rates of soil creep in the Chilton Valley, Cass, New Zealand. *Arctic and Alpine Res.,* 1(3): 213-220.

Pissart, A.
1964 : Vitesses des mouvements du sol au Chambeyron (Basses Alpes). *Biul. Peryglac.,* 14: 303-309.

Rapp, Anders
1960 : Recent development of mountain slopes in Karkevagge and surroundings, northern Scandinavia. *Geog. Annaler,* 42: 71-200.
1963 : Solifluction and avalanches in the Scandinavian mountains. Proc. Permafrost Int. Conf., 11-15 November 1963, Lafayette, Indiana, 150-154.
1967 : Pleistocene activity and Holocene stability of hillslopes, with examples from Scandinavia and Pennsylvania. *In: L'Evolution des versants,* Les Congrès et Colloques de l'Université de Liège, 40: 229-244.

Rapp, Anders and Rudberg, Sten
1960 : Recent periglacial phenomena in Sweden. *Biul. Peryglac.,* 8: 143-154.

Richmond, G. M.
1965 : Glaciation of the Rocky Mountains. *In* Wright, H. E., Jr. and Frey, D. G. (eds.), *The Quaternary of the United States,* Princeton University Press, Princeton, 217-230.

Rudberg, Sten
1958 : Some observations concerning mass movements on slopes in Sweden. *Geologiska Föreningens i Stockholm Förhandlingar,* 80(1): 114-125.
1962 : A report on some field observations concerning periglacial geomorphology and mass movement on slopes in Sweden. *Biul. Peryglac.,* 11: 311-323.
1964 : Slow mass movement processes and slope development in the Norra Storfjäll area, southern Swedish Lappland. Z. *Geomorph.,* N.F. Suppl. Bd. 5: 192-203.

Sandberg, Gustaf
1938 : Redogörelser för undersökningar utförda med understöd av sällskapets stipendier. *Ymer,* 58: 333-337.

Schumm, S. A.
1964 : Seasonal variations of erosion rates and processes on hillslopes in western Colorado. Z. *Geomorph.,* N.F. Suppl. Bd. 5: 214-238.
1967 : Rates of surficial rock creep on hillslopes in western Colorado. *Science,* 155(3762): 560-562.

150

Sigafoos, R. S. and Hopkins, D. M.
    1952 : Soil instability on slopes in regions of perennially-frozen ground. *In: Frost action in soils,* Highway Research Board, Spec. Rep. No. 2: 176-192.

Smith, Jeremy
    1960 : Cryoturbation data from South Georgia. *Biul. Peryglac.,* 8: 73-79.

Soil Survey Staff
    1951 : *Soil Survey Manual.* U.S. Department of Agriculture Handbook No. 18, U.S. Government Printing Office, Washington, 503 pp.

Thompson, W. F.
    1961 : The shape of New England mountains, Part II. *Appalachia,* June: 316-335.

Washburn, A. L.
    1947 : Reconnaissance geology of portions of Victoria Island and adjacent regions, Arctic Canada. *Geol. Soc. Amer. Memoir,* 22: 1-142.
    1956 : Classification of patterned ground and review of suggested origins. *Geol. Soc. Amer. Bull.,* 67: 823-866.
    1967 : Instrumental observations of mass-wasting in the Mesters Vig District, Northeast Greenland. *Medd. om Grønland,* 166(4): 1-297.

Williams, P. J.
    1957 : The direct recording of solifluction movements. *Amer. J. Sci.,* 255: 705-715.

    1959 : An investigation into processes occurring in solifluction. *Amer. J. Sci.,* 257: 481-490.
    1966 : Downslope soil movement at a subarctic location with regard to variations with depth. *Can. Geotech. J.,* 3(4): 191-203.

Wilson, J. W.
    1952 : Vegetation patterns associated with soil movement on Jan Mayen Island. *J. Ecol.,* 40: 249-264.

Young, Anthony
    1960 : Soil movement by denudational processes on slopes. *Nature,* 188(4745): 120-122.
    1963 : Soil movement on slopes. *Nature,* 200: 129-130.

Zhigarev, L. A.
    1960 : Eksperimental'nye isseldovaniia skorostei dvizheniia gruntovykh mass na solifliuktsionnykh sklonakh. *Trudy Inst. Merzlotovedeniia im V.A. Obrucheva,* 16: 183-190.

AN ANALYSIS OF DIURNAL FREEZE-THAW AND FROST HEAVE CYCLES IN THE INDIAN PEAKS REGION OF THE COLORADO FRONT RANGE

B. D. Fahey

Department of Geography
University of Guelph
Guelph, Ontario, Canada

ABSTRACT

Measurements were made along an altitudinal transect at five sites in the Colorado Front Range in order to determine the inter- and intrasite variability of diurnal freeze-thaw and frost heave cycles in an alpine region. Meteorological screen data showed the number of diurnal freeze-thaw cyles to decrease from 238 at 2,600 m to 89 at 3,750 m over a 22-month period. The same trend was established for diurnal freeze-thaw and frost heave cycles at the surface of snowfree sites. However, daily cycles based on air temperature could not be relied upon to accurately predict the number of frost heave events at the soil surface. The number of frost heave cycles also diminished sharply with depth; none was recorded at a depth of 20 cm, suggesting that their geomorphic effectiveness is limited to the upper 10 cm.

INTRODUCTION

It is customary to regard freeze-thaw action and frost heaving as two of the prevailing geomorphic agents operating in periglacial environments. However, recent investigators, e.g. Dahl (1955), Andrews (1961), Cook and Raiche (1962), have questioned the emphasis often given to the frequency of short-term freeze-thaw and frost heave cycles in the formation of landforms characteristic of these environments. Moreover, hypotheses elevating the importance of cycle frequency often rest on the assumption that the number of freeze-thaw cycles recorded in meteorological screens represent the number occurring at the ground surface. Such an assumption may be misleading (Cook and Raiche, 1962; Chambers, 1966). Russell (1943) and Fraser (1959) assigned arbitrary limits for available air temperature data in an attempt to make screen temperatures more representative of surface temperatures. However, this ignores the effect of other environmental factors such as soil moisture and snow distribution.

In order to evaluate the geomorphic effectiveness of diurnal events in a periglacial environment, measurements should be made within the active zone of frost heaving and freeze-thaw. Direct measurements of short-term cycles have been conducted at Resolute in the Canadian Arctic (Cook and Raiche, 1962), in northeast Greenland (Washburn, 1967), in northern Quebec (Matthews, 1962; Gray, 1966), on Signy Island off the coast of Antarctica (Chambers, 1966, 1967), and in Yorkshire in Great Britain (Matthews, 1967). With few exceptions, e.g. Brockie (1967), comparable measurements in mountain regions have not been forthcoming; yet, it is in these environments that the importance of short-term cycle frequency has been the subject of some debate (Dahl, 1966a, 1966b; Ives, 1966).

The primary objective of this paper is to examine the inter- and intrasite variability of diurnal frost heave and freeze-thaw events in the air and in the ground over a range of elevations in an alpine region. It is hoped that the results may help resolve some of the questions recently raised concerning variations with altitude in short-term cycle frequency, the geomorphic significance of diurnal cycles, and the practice of employing meteorological screen data to estimate the number of geomorphically effective cycles.

THE STUDY AREA

The investigation was conducted in the Indian Peaks region of the Colorado Front Range west of Boulder, Colorado. Since 1952 a transect of climatic stations down the eastern flank of the Front Range has been maintained as part of an environmental measurement program (Marr, 1961). Four of these stations are still operating: Ponderosa (A-1) at 2,200 m, Sugarloaf (B-1) at 2,600 m, Como (C-1) at 3,050 m, and Niwot Ridge (D-1) at 3,750 m. Significant elements of the air temperature data are furnished in Table 1. Temperature and precipitation regimes at Ponderosa and Sugarloaf are representative of many continental locations, while Como, located some 400 m below treeline, is more characteristic of a subalpine location. Niwot Ridge station is situated in the alpine tundra at the western end of Niwot Ridge, a major east-west ridge extending approximately 9 km from Navajo Peak at its junction with the Continental Divide. The mean annual air temperature at Niwot Ridge is −3.2°C and no month has an average above 10°C. (See also Barry, 1973.) Periglacial landforms are numerous and widespread above timberline in the study area (Benedict, 1970) and permafrost occurs in favorable locations (Ives and Fahey, 1971; Ives, 1973).

Measurements of frost heave and freeze-thaw cycles, and related environmental parameters were made at the five sites shown in Figure 1. The program began at Como and Niwot Ridge in the winter of 1968 and was extended to Ponderosa and Sugarloaf in mid-1969. The fifth site (designated the Saddle site) was added in order to incorporate into the study an area of active patterned ground. It was situated on the tread of a turf-banked lobe whose surface was characterized by nonsorted circles known locally as frost boils. Owing to its exposed location the Saddle site is normally snowfree during the winter.

INSTRUMENTATION AND TERMINOLOGY

Frost heave recording devices similar to those described by Matthews (1962) were installed at each site to monitor on a continuous basis frost heave at the soil surface and at depths of 10 and 20 cm (Figure 2). The two rods at depth were sleeved in the manner suggested by Chambers (1967) to guard against premature heaving. At Como, the Saddle site, and Niwot Ridge the heavographs were attached to a 3 × 3 m frame of angle iron designed to measure areal variations in seasonal heave (Fahey, in preparation). Freeze-thaw cycles in the air were recorded on thermographs housed in meteorological screens. Soil thermographs were

TABLE 1

Mean daily temperatures (1), and the range between the mean daily maxima and minima (2) for January and July, and the mean annual temperature for climatic stations in the Indian Peaks region[a]

Location	Elevation	January		July		Annual
		1	2	1	2	
A-1[b]	2,200 m	−1.6	13.2	20.7	18.9	8.3
B-1[b]	2,600 m	−5.4	11.7	17.8	13.4	5.6
C-1[b]	3,050 m	−7.2	9.6	12.2	15.0	1.7
Saddle[c]	3,500 m	−10.4	4.5	9.7	7.3	−2.8
D-1[b]	3,750 m	−12.6	6.0	8.3	7.8	−3.2

[a]Data are given in °C.
[b]Based on the data summary compiled by Marr et al. (1968) for the period 1953-1964.
[c]Based on data collected for 1969 only.

153

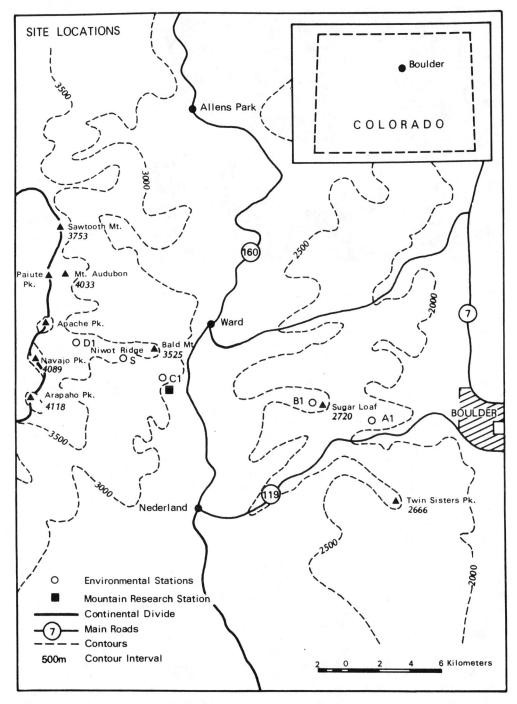

FIGURE 1. Location map of the study area.

154

FIGURE 2. The heavo-graph at Ponderosa show-ing two of the diurnal frost heave cycles experi-enced at the surface in April 1970. Note the lack of corresponding cycles at 10 and 20 cm.

used to record ground temperatures at depths of 1, 10, and 20 cm. The 1-cm depth was chosen as the best compromise in trying to approximate temperature fluctuations at the soil-air interface. Only those cycles which fell below 0°C were tallied in order to allow for the depression of the freezing point. Soil moistures were determined with Colman units. Observations at the four environmental stations were made on a standard soil. This should have eliminated any variance in frost heaving which otherwise might have been attributed to differences in intrinsic soil properties. At the Saddle, the *in situ* soil of the frost boil was used; its textural and mineralogical properties closely resembled those of the standard soil.

The current study is confined to diurnal cycles; seasonal events will be the subject of a later paper. A diurnal freeze-thaw cycle is here defined as a fall in temperature below 0°C, fol-

lowed by a rise above 0°C within 24 hr. Russell (1943) proposed that a potentially effective freeze-thaw would constitute a fall in air temperature to 28°F (−2.2°C) after a rise to 32°F (0°C). Cycles based on these limits were computed in this study, but the order was reversed to make them comparable with the definition used above. A diurnal frost heave cycle constitutes a rise of the soil surface in response to ice formation, followed by a collapse within 24 hr. It is counted as a cycle only if the movement is at least 1.0 mm. This takes account of any error arising from thermal expansion and contraction of the heavograph rods. Differential melting of snow around the rods was occasionally observed but its effect could not be estimated. Figure 3 illustrates the manner in which frost heave and freeze-thaw events are related.

RESULTS

FROST HEAVE/FREEZE-THAW RELATIONSHIPS

Table 2 demonstrates that no frost heave cycles were recorded at the ground surface at Niwot Ridge from October 1968, through September 1969. A persistent snowcover accounts for the absence of cycles during the spring of 1969. In contrast, 13 freeze-thaw cycles were recorded in the meteorological screen in June although only four could be classed as "effective" according to Russell's (1943) terminology. In the fall of 1969, 9 frost heave cycles

were recorded at the surface, while the earlier ablation of the protective snowpack led to 24 cycles being recorded in the following spring. At the snowfree Saddle site 17 frost heave events were recorded at the surface in the fall of 1968. After November, no cycles were recorded through to April 1969, on account of the below-freezing winter temperature regime, whereas the opposite condition of above-freezing temperatures explains the lack of cycles during July and August. By September diurnal

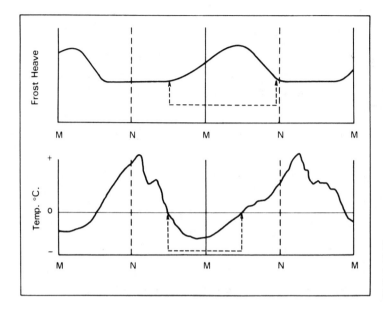

FIGURE 3. Idealized profiles designed to demonstrate the relationship between diurnal frost heave and freeze-thaw cycles.

heaving began again; eight cycles were recorded at the surface in October. The spring thaw produced 16 cycles in May and nine in June. No data are available on diurnal frost heave events in the fall of 1968 at Como. There were 16 cycles the following spring and 19 in the fall of 1969. The shorter freeze season at this elevation resulted in cycles beginning again by February and continuing intermittently through to June.

Due to the extended winter snowcover at Niwot Ridge, monthly totals of diurnal frost heave cycles at no time approached the number of freeze-thaw alternations in the air. A similar lack of agreement is apparent at Como where once again persistent snow frequently prevented diurnal frost heave and freeze-thaw activity at ground level. On the other hand, the virtual absence of a snowcover at the Saddle site provided an opportunity to compare the number of frost heave cycles with potentially effective freeze-thaw cycles. In the 3-month period April to June 1969, "effective" cycles numbered seven, five, and seven compared to eight, nine, and four, respectively, for frost heave cycles. However, only two "effective" cycles occurred in the following October, whereas there were eight daily movements at the surface and 11 freeze-thaw cycles. In November there were 15 freeze-thaw cycles just below the surface, but no corresponding frost heave cycles. Additional information on the degree

of correlation between monthly totals of air and surface events at the Saddle site is given in Table 3.

Table 4 summarizes the frost heave and freeze-thaw data from Ponderosa and Sugarloaf. The most notable feature is the large number of freeze-thaw cycles recorded in the air at both sites. At Sugarloaf, the presence of a snowcover throughout the winter prevented the occurrence of surface events except on a few occasions early in the fall. Of all the sites, Ponderosa exhibited the best agreement between the different events (Table 3). Frost heave cycles showed the highest correlation ($r = 0.911$) with freeze-thaw cycles at a depth of 1 cm. This is reinforced by the chi-square data. Using the distribution of frost heave cycles through eight time intervals as the observed and the distribution of freeze-thaw cycles at 1 cm as the expected, the calculated chi-square value was 8.62. The critical chi-square value for seven degrees of freedom at the 0.05 level of significance is 14.06. Thus the two distributions are not significantly different. However, in all other cases, the probability levels show convincingly that the observed distributions do not approach the expected distributions.

DATA ANALYSIS ON A DAILY BASIS

Figure 4 shows the daily relationships between the various sets of data for representative

TABLE 2

Monthly totals at the three upper sites of freeze-thaw cycles in the air (1), Russell's "effective" freeze-thaw cycles (2), freeze-thaw cycles at a depth of 1 cm with minima less than 0°C (3), frost heave cycles at the surface (4), freeze-thaw cycles at a depth of 10 cm with minima less than 0°C (5), and frost heave cycles at a depth of 10 cm (6)

Month	Niwot Ridge (1)	(2)	(3)	(4)	(5)	(6)	Saddle (1)	(2)	(3)	(4)	(5)	(6)	Como (1)	(2)	(3)	(4)	(5)	(6)
Sept. 1968	9	5	*	*	*	*	7	5	*	*	3	*	13	6	*	*	*	*
Oct.	8	3	*	*	0	0	12	2	*	14	2	1	18	9	*	*	*	*
Nov.	0	0	*	0	0	0	0	0	*	3	0	0	6	4	*	0	0	0
Dec.	0	0	*	0	0	0	0	0	*	0	0	0	5	5	*	0	0	0
Jan. 1969	0	0	*	0	0	0	0	0	*	0	0	0	5	3	*	0	0	0
Feb.	0	0	*	0	0	0	0	0	*	0	0	0	3	3	*	1	0	0
Mar.	0	5	*	0	0	0	0	7	*	0	0	0	5	5	*	8	0	0
Apr.	7	9	*	0	0	0	9	5	*	8	0	0	19	15	*	5	6	0
May	18	9	*	0	0	0	12	7	*	9	0	0	20	9	*	2	0	0
June	13	4	*	0	0	0	17	0	*	4	0	0	12	3	*	0	0	0
July	0	0	*	0	0	0	0	0	*	0	0	0	0	0	*	0	0	0
Aug.	0	0	*	0	0	0	0	2	0	0	1	1	0	0	*	1	0	0
Sept.	11	0	0	6	0	0	9	2	0	4	0	0	6	0	0	15	0	0
Oct.	2	1	0	3	0	0	2	2	11	8	0	0	12	12	13	3	0	0
Nov.	2	0	0	0	0	0	1	1	15	0	0	0	8	8	15	0	0	0
Dec.	0	0	0	0	0	0	3	3	10	0	0	0	10	10	8	0	1	0
Jan. 1970	0	0	0	0	0	0	0	0	0	0	0	0	1	1	0	2	0	0
Feb.	0	0	0	0	0	0	0	0	0	0	0	0	8	7	0	2	0	0
Mar.	0	0	0	0	0	0	0	0	0	0	0	0	4	4	*	5	0	0
Apr.	1	1	0	0	0	0	2	2	12	16	1	2	12	9	14	5	0	0
May	12	4	9	15	2	4	15	9	12	9	0	0	20	9	*	5	0	0
June	6	4	0	9	1	3	12	5	7	0	0	0	9	2	5	0	0	5
Total	89	36	9	33	3	7	101	50	67	75	7	4	196	124	50	54	7	5

*No data available.

TABLE 3

Linear regression and chi-square data relating monthly totals of frost heave cycles to freeze-thaw cycles in the air (1), Russell's "effective" free-thaw cycles (2), and freeze-thaw cycles recorded at a depth of 1 cm (3), at the Saddle site and Ponderosa

Site	Factor	Correlation Coefficient	Number of Observations	Standard Error of the Estimate	Significance Level (%)	Chi-square	Degrees of Freedom	Probability Level
Saddle								
	(1)	0.652	12	4.42	5	19.85	7	0.01
	(2)	0.539	12	4.69	NS	35.94	6	0.001
	(3)	0.063	7	5.62	NS	68.19	2	0.001
Ponderosa								
	(1)	0.800	8	6.67	5	19.02	7	0.01
	(2)	0.815	8	6.56	5	36.26	7	0.001
	(3)	0.911	8	5.58	1	8.62	7	0.20

TABLE 4

Monthly totals at Ponderosa and Sugarloaf of freeze-thaw cycles in the air (1), Russell's "effective" freeze-thaw cycles (2), freeze-thaw cycles at a depth of 1 cm with minima less than 0°C (3), frost heave cycles at the surface (4), and frost heave cycles at a depth of 10 cm (5)

Month	Sugarloaf (1)	(2)	(3)	(4)	(5)	Ponderosa (1)	(2)	(3)	(4)	(5)
Sept. 1969	0	0	1	0	0	0	0	0	0	0
Oct.	15	12	2	8	0	8	6	3	3	0
Nov.	16	7	4	10	1	14	9	12	19	3
Dec.	6	2	2	0	0	14	5	13	12	0
Jan. 1970	15	14	0	0	0	14	8	6	8	0
Feb.	18	14	0	0	0	20	16	26	28	0
Mar.	18	15	0	0	0	14	14	16	22	0
Apr.	23	20	0	1	0	18	15	18	13	0
May	3	2	*	0	0	2	1	1	1	0
June	0	0	*	0	0	0	0	0	0	0
Total	114	96	9	19	1	104	74	95	106	3

*No data available.

158

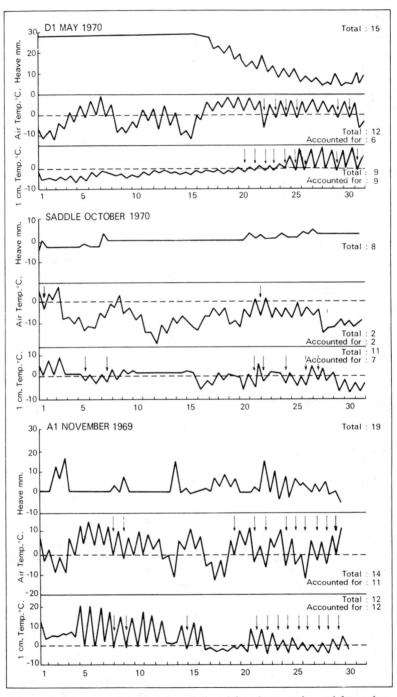

FIGURE 4. Diagrammatic presentation of diurnal frost heave cycles, and freeze-thaw cycles in the air and at a depth of 1 cm for selected months at three sites. Arrows indicate those freeze-thaw events corresponding with frost heave.

months at three sites. Thus, while neither freeze-thaw cycles in the air nor those at the ground surface can fully account for frost heave cycles on a daily basis, the latter do come closer to the ideal situation. At Ponderosa, for example, 19 frost heave events took place in November with 11 corresponding meteorological screen alternations and 12 surface temperature fluctuations. At the Saddle in October 1970, it was eight, two and, seven, respectively. Nevertheless, there are many exceptions. For example, 15 and 10 freeze-thaw cycles were recorded just below the surface at the Saddle site in November and December 1969, respectively, yet no frost heave cycles were noted in either month even though the near-surface soil moisture regime was sufficient to support ice formation at the time. Some of the anomalous freeze-thaw events occurred when the temperature fell to, or fractionally below, 0°C. This suggests that the temperature sensor at 1 cm may at times respond to fluctuations in heat inputs at the surface insufficient to melt surface ice. However, there are just as many cases when the monthly totals of frost heave cycles exceed the number of freeze-thaw cycles at 1 cm.

VARIATIONS IN FROST HEAVE AND FREEZE-THAW CYCLES WITH ELEVATION

The data has been rearranged in Table 5 to depict more clearly variations in the different events with elevation. At Niwot Ridge and the Saddle freeze-thaw cycles in the air are normally confined to the spring and fall. Station Como also exhibits a pronounced double maximum, although the spread is wider. This station has almost twice the number of cycles recorded at the higher sites. The distribution shifts to a winter maximum at the two lower sites. The lower overall total at Ponderosa can be explained by the slightly warmer temperatures in the early fall and late spring compared with Sugarloaf.

Due to the snowcover at Niwot Ridge only 9 freeze-thaw cycles occurred at a depth of 1 cm between September 1969 and June 1970, whereas 67 were recorded in the same period at the Saddle site. Despite the incomplete record at Como, available data suggests a further increase in frequency with decreasing elevation. At Sugarloaf, the very marked decrease is again a reflection of an insulating snowpack; in its absence the total would most likely have approached the maximum of 95 cycles observed at Ponderosa. Disregarding the fewer

cycles at Sugarloaf, the monthly frost heave totals for the period August 1969 through June 1970 increase with decreasing elevation. Diurnal frost heave cycles were three times more numerous at Ponderosa compared with the Saddle site.

GEOMORPHIC SIGNIFICANCE OF DIURNAL FROST HEAVING

The data in Tables 2 and 4 clearly demonstrate that, at least in this region, diurnal frost heaving is essentially a surface phenomena. No cycles were recorded at a depth of 20 cm during the entire investigation, and very few reached 10 cm. If the number of cycles at 10 cm is expressed as a percentage of the number at the surface, there is a general decrease with elevation from 21% at Niwot Ridge to 3% at Ponderosa. The same trend is evident in the case of freeze-thaw cycles at 10 cm. The average vertical displacement due to diurnal frost heaving and subsidence at the surface ranged from 2 to 7 mm depending upon site and season. Values tended to be higher at the lower stations, particularly when soil moisture readings were near 25% which is close to saturation for the standard soil. A maximum displacement of 21 mm was recorded at Ponderosa at the end of October 1969. Needle ice, which was observed at every site on a number of occasions, is believed responsible for many of the pronounced diurnal events such as those illustrated in Figure 2. When soil moisture values were high, needle-ice action often heaped the soil into small mounds. These features comprised a thin layer of relatively dry material supported from below by a layer of needle ice up to 1 cm thick. The lateral extension of individual layers seldom exceeded 10 cm. Occasionally two layers were observed, separated by a dry section of mineral soil. The needle ice layers were often attached to a thin plate-like base of frozen mineral soil.

During the early fall and late spring, small earth mounds, similar in morphology and size to the hummocky relief of the standard soil surface, appeared on the frost boil surfaces at the Saddle site. Pockets of coarse sand, gravel, and small cobbles frequently separated individual mounds which, by sunrise, comprised a mixture of needle ice and fines. By mid-morning, melting of the needle ice had reduced these forms to low hummocks of saturated soil. It is believed that their sorted nature is a product of small scale differential frost heaving. If one or two cobbles are present in an area of saturated fines, they could be subjected to diurnal heaving. During the early stages of the subsidence (melting) phase the cobbles may lose the support of the underlying ice needles, fall, and collect in adjacent depressions.

DISCUSSION

Diurnal freeze-thaw cycles are often used in hypotheses attempting to account for periglacial landforms. During an investigation of weathering forms near a fiord coastline in northern Norway, R. Dahl (1966a) observed that Narvik close to sea level experienced an average of 64 freeze-thaw days per year, while 81 were recorded at Bjornfjell at an elevation of 500 m. He assumed that this trend continued into a blockfield zone above 1,100 m, implying that the restriction of blockfields to upland areas reflects the increased likelihood of freeze-thaw oscillations at high elevations. Ives (1966) stressed that Dahl's hypothesis was questionable on the grounds that the incidence of freeze-thaw events in valley bottoms and at sites partially surrounded by open water would not be comparable to sites at higher elevations and farther removed from open water. Also, E. Dahl (1955) had already noted that freeze-thaw cycles actually decreased with increasing elevation in topographically comparable areas further inland. Irrespective of the questionable importance of short-term cycles in the production of mountain-top detritus, the results of the present study support E. Dahl's contention that the occurrence of blockfields in mountain areas cannot be explained by inferring a direct relationship between cycle frequency and elevation.

Since it is seldom possible to obtain a reliable and meaningful record of frost heave and freeze-thaw cycles at ground level in periglacial environments, researchers have often resorted to more readily available air temperature data. However, this study has shown a significant disparity between the number of freeze-thaw cycles in the air (even when rendered potentially effective according to Russell's reasoning) and the number of diurnal frost heave events at the surface. Air temperatures cannot be used to predict accurately either the number or geomorphic effectiveness of surface events. Never-theless, providing these limitations are recognized. air temperature data can still furnish worthwhile information on the broad variations in freeze-thaw frequency with respect to altitude and latitude. Fraser (1959) for example, who used 34°F (1.1°C) as the upper limit for an effective thaw, computed and mapped the distribution of the annual freeze-thaw frequencies for 42 stations in Canada. The observed decrease in both the mean annual freeze-thaw frequency, and the diurnal range of temperature with increasing latitude corresponds with the altitudinal pattern depicted in Tables 1 and 5.

It is generally recognized that diurnal frost heaving is of little consequence in the development of large scale patterned ground but opinions are divided over the role played by these events in the formation of miniature varieties. In the present study needle ice development seemed responsible for the more pronounced diurnal heave events, but its geomorphic significance is the subject of a continuing debate. Troll (1944), for instance, emphasized the importance of needle ice in the formation of small-scale "tropical mountain" varieties of patterned ground. On the other hand, Brockie (1967) advocated that needle ice activity is essentially confined to the surface. The latter view is supported by the observation that, at the time when maximum surface displacements were occurring at Ponderosa, no movement was recorded at 10 cm. In fact the restriction of diurnal cycles to the upper 10 cm suggests that these events are incapable of producing features beyond the dimensions of the micro-hummocks observed on the surfaces of the frost boil and standard soils. However, diurnal frost movements generated by needle ice may assist in the migration of small cobbles to the slightly depressed margins of miniature sorted nets and polygons found on some of the frost boils at the Saddle site.

SUMMARY AND CONCLUSIONS

(1) Apart from at Ponderosa, there is little correspondence between monthly totals of freeze-thaw cycles in the air, and freeze-thaw and frost heave cycles in the upper layers of the soil at any site. The same applies in the case of Russell's "effective" freeze-thaw cycles.

TABLE 5

Altitudinal variations in (1) freeze-thaw cycles recorded in the air, (2) freeze-thaw cycles recorded at 1 cm depth in the soil, (3) frost heave cycles recorded at the surface (September 1968 through June 1970)

Sta.	Elev. (m)	S	O	N	D	J	F	M	A	M	J	J	A	S	O	N	D	J	F	M	A	M	J	Total[a]	Total[b]
(1) Freeze-thaw cycles recorded in the air																									
D-1	3,750	9	8	0	0	0	0	0	7	18	13	0	0	11	2	0	0	0	0	0	1	12	6	89	34
S	3,500	7	12	0	0	0	0	0	9	12	17	0	0	9	2	1	0	0	0	0	2	15	12	101	44
C-1	3,050	13	18	6	5	3	5	19	20	12	0	0	0	6	12	8	10	1	8	4	12	20	9	196	100
B-1	2,600	5	6	16	18	21	14	17	6	5	0	0	0	15	15	16	14	15	18	18	23	3	0	238	114
A-1	2,200	1	8	14	10	15	20	14	14	2	2	0	0	8	14	14	14	20	14	18	2	0	0	194	104
(2) Freeze-thaw cycles recorded at 1 cm depth with minima less the 0°C																									
D-1	3,750	*	*	*	*	*	*	*	*	*	*	*	*	0	0	0	0	0	0	0	0	9	0	*	9
S	3,500	*	*	*	*	*	*	*	*	*	*	*	*	11	15	10	0	0	0	0	12	12	7	*	67
C-1	3,050	*	*	*	*	*	*	*	*	*	*	*	*	13	15	8	0	0	*	*	14	*	*	*	50
B-1	2,600	*	*	*	*	*	*	*	*	*	*	*	*	1	2	4	2	0	0	0	0	*	*	*	9
A-1	2,200	*	*	*	*	*	*	*	*	*	*	*	*	0	3	12	13	6	26	16	18	1	0	*	95
(3) Frost heave cycles recorded at the surface																									
D-1	3,750	*	0	0	0	0	0	0	0	0	0	0	0	6	3	0	0	0	0	0	0	15	9	33	33
S	3,500	*	14	3	0	0	0	0	8	9	4	0	0	4	8	0	0	0	0	0	0	16	9	75	37
C-1	3,050	*	*	*	0	1	8	5	2	0	0	0	0	15	3	0	3	2	5	5	5	0	0	54	38
B-1	2,600	*	*	*	*	*	*	*	*	*	0	0	0	8	10	0	0	0	0	0	1	0	0	19	19
A-1	2,200	*	*	*	*	*	*	*	*	*	0	0	0	3	19	12	8	28	22	13	1	0	0	106	106

*No data available.

[a]Period September 1968 through June 1970.

[b]Period September 1969 through June 1970.

Occasionally, the number of freeze-thaw cycles just below ground level agree with the number of surface frost heave movements.

(2) Diurnal frost heave and freeze-thaw events are normally confined to the upper 10 cm of soil. None was recorded at a depth of 20 cm during the entire investigation.

(3) Freeze-thaw cycles in the air decrease with increasing elevation from Sugarloaf (2,-600 m) to Niwot Ridge (3.750 m). There is a slight reduction from Sugarloaf to Ponderosa (2,200 m). Measurements of frost heave cycles at the surface follow the same trend but only at snow-free sites.

(4) There is an absence of freeze-thaw cycles in the air above treeline from late fall to early spring. Cycles occur throughout the winter in the forested zone below 3.050 m. Freeze-thaw activity ceases in July and August at all locations.

(5) Needle-ice activity gives rise to the development of microhummocks and may assist in the sorting process through small scale differential heaving on the surface of miniature polygons.

The findings of this paper strongly support the contention held by a growing number of investigators that the widespread occurrence of mechanically weathered material in arctic and alpine regions cannot be explained by assuming that freeze-thaw cycles are more numerous in these areas. Furthermore, the observed restriction of most diurnal frost heave and freeze-thaw cycles to the upper few centimeters of the soil suggests that the role played by these events in the formation of periglacial landforms other than small scale varieties, is insignificant. Many workers (e.g., Rapp. 1960; Washburn, 1969) now feel that prolonged winter freezing coupled with low temperatures may be a more effective geomorphic agent in periglacial environments than diurnal oscillations with a high annual frequency insofar as temperature conditions alone are considered. However, the significance of the annual cycle as a formative mechanism in the development of periglacial features, other than certain varieties of patterned ground, has yet to be adequately confirmed by measurements in the field.

ACKNOWLEDGMENTS

Field facilities and logistical support for year-round research toward a doctoral degree in the Front Range were made available through the Institute of Arctic and Alpine Research (INSTAAR). I wish to acknowledge Dr. J. T. Andrews, Dr. T. N. Caine, and Dr. J. D. Ives of INSTAAR, and Dr. W. C. Mahaney of York University, Toronto, for their helpful suggestions both in discussions and in the field, and for their critical examination of early drafts of this paper. Special thanks are due to Mr. J. Clark, Mr. R. Greene, and Mr. R. H. Kihl for their support and encouragement in the field. Mrs. Laurel Matthews, Summer Research Participant supported by the National Science Foundation Grant No. GY 4550 to Dr. J. D. Ives (Secondary Science Training Program), assisted in the field in the summer of 1968. Assistance in the preparation of maps and diagrams was received from Mr. Fred Adams. Department of Geography, University of Guelph. Living and transportation costs during the latter part of the investigation were defrayed by a Penrose Bequest Research Grant from the Geological Society of America.

REFERENCES

Andrews, J. T.
    1961 : "Vallons de gelivation" in Central Labrador-Ungava: a reappraisal, *Can. Geogr.*, 5: 1-9.
Barry, R. G.
    1973 : A climatological transect on the east slope of the Front Range, Colorado. *Arct. Alp. Res.*, 5(1): 89-110.
Benedict, J. B.
    1970 : Downslope movement in a Colorado Alpine region: rates, processes, and climatic significance. *Arct. Alp. Res.*, 2: 165-266.
Brockie, W. J.
    1967 : A contribution to the study of frozen ground phenomena—preliminary investigations into a form of miniature stone stripes in east Otago. *Proc. Fifth N. Z. Geogr. Conf*: 191-201.
Chambers, M. J. G.
    1966 : Investigations of patterned ground at Signy Island, South Orkney Islands: II. Temperature regimes in the active layer. *Brit. Antarct. Surv. Bull.*, 10: 71-83.
    1967 : Investigations of patterned ground at Signy Island, South Orkney Islands: III. Miniature patterns, frost heaving and general conclusions. *Brit. Antarct. Surv. Bull.*, 12: 1-22.

Cook, F. A. and Raiche, V. G.
1962 : Freeze-thaw cycles at Resolute, Northwest Territories. *Geogr. Bull.,* 18: 67-78.

Dahl, E.
1955 : Biogeographic and geologic indications of unglaciated areas in Scandinavia during the Ice Ages. *Geol. Soc. Amer. Bull.,* 66: 1499-1517.

Dahl, R.
1966a: Block fields, weathering pits, and tor-like forms in the Narvik mountains, Nordland, Norway. *Geogr. Ann.,* 48: 55-85.

1966b: Block fields and other weathering forms in the Narvik Mountains. *Geogr. Ann.,* 48: 224-227.

Fraser, J. K.
1959 : Freeze-thaw frequencies and mechanical weathering in Canada. *Arctic,* 12: 40-53.

Gray, J. T.
1966 : Frost heave studies at Knob Lake 1964-1965. *In:* *Field Research in Labrador-Ungava,* McGill Sub-Arctic Res. Pap., 21: 108-125.

Ives, J. D.
1966 : Block fields, associated weathering forms on mountain tops and the nunatak hypothesis. *Geogr. Ann.,* 48: 220-223.

1973 : Permafrost and its relationship to other environmental parameters in a mid-latitude, high-altitude setting, Front Range, Colorado Rocky Mountains, U.S.A. *Second International Conference on Permafrost, Yakutsk, U.S.S.R., July 1973.* Nat. Acad. Sci., Wash., D.C. (in press).

Ives, J. D. and Fahey, B. D.
1971 : Permafrost occurrence in the Front Range, Colorado Rocky Mountains, U.S.A. *J. Glaciol.,* 10: 105-111.

Marr, J. W.
1961 : Ecosystems of the east slope of the Front Range in Colorado. *Univ. Colorado Stud., Ser. Biol.,* 8. 134 pp.

Marr, J. W., Clark, J. M., Osburn, W. S., and Paddock, M. W.
1968 : Data on mountain environments III Front Range, Colorado, Four Climax Regions, 1959-1964. *Univ. Colorado Stud., Ser. Biol.,* 29. 181 pp.

Matthews, B.
1962 : Frost-heave cycles at Schefferville October 1960-June 1961 with a critical examination of methods used to determine them. *McGill Sub-Arctic Res. Pap.,* 12: 112-125.

1967 : Automatic measurement of frost heave: results from Malham and Rodley (Yorkshire). *Geoderma,* 1: 107-115.

Rapp, A.
1960 : Talus slopes and mountain walls at Templefjordan Spitzbergen. A geomorphological study of denudation slopes in an Arctic locality. *Norsk Polar Skr.,* 119. 96 pp.

Russell, R. J.
1943 : Freeze-thaw frequencies in the United States. *Trans. Amer. Geophys. Union,* 24: 125-133.

Troll, C.
1944 : Strukturböden, Solifluktion, und Frostklimate der Erde. *Geol. Rundschau* 34: 545-694 (Engl. Transl. by H. E. Wright Jr., 1958, *U.S. Army SIPRE Transl.* 43. 121 pp).

Washburn, A. L.
1967 : Instrumental observations of mass-wasting in the Mesters Vig district, northeast Greenland. *Medd. om Grønland* 166. 318 pp.

1969 : Weathering, frost action, and patterned ground in the Mesters Vig district, northeast Greenland. *Medd. om Grønland* 176. 303 pp.

Quantitative evaluation of nivation in the Colorado Front Range

COLIN E. THORN *Department of Geography, University of Maryland, College Park, Maryland 20742*

ABSTRACT

A quantitative evaluation of nivation in a mid-latitude alpine environment has been derived from an intensive study of two snow patches on Niwot Ridge, in the Colorado Front Range. Four research hypotheses were tested: nivation intensifies (1) mechanical weathering, (2) mechanical transport, (3) chemical weathering, and (4) chemical transport.

Nivation does not increase the number of freeze-thaw cycles (mechanical weathering); rather, snow patches redistribute the pattern of occurrence of freeze-thaw cycles by preventing wintertime cycles and increasing springtime cycle totals. Intensification of mechanical weathering can only result from increased cycle effectiveness. In contrast to a snowfree site, nivation increases the mechanical transport of sand, silt, and clay by an order of magnitude. Sheetwash and rill flow dominate mechanical transport. The snowpack itself is protective, sediment removal being focused downslope of the retreating snow margin. Chemical weathering is increased by a factor of two to four by a snow patch. Variations in weathering rinds indicate that chemical weathering is produced by concentration of meltwater and (or) snowpack free water.

Within a nivation hollow, chemical and mechanical degradation are approximately equal. On Niwot Ridge, degradation increased from 0.0001 mm/yr on a snowfree site to 0.0074 mm/yr within a nivation hollow. Slope profile through a nivation hollow corresponds to slope forms derived theoretically from the continuity equation. Snow-patch enlargement leads to downslope lengthening of the nivation hollow, whereas regular, complete meltout promotes incision of the hollow headwall into the hillside.

INTRODUCTION

Nivation is the term introduced by Matthes (1900) to designate the geomorphic impact of late-lying snow patches. The term embraces the idea that such snow patches intensify both weathering and mass wasting processes. Despite the cursory nature of Matthes's study, the elegance of his paper led to rapid, universal acceptance of the nivation concept. A few subsequent papers focused on the processes involved in nivation (Lewis, 1936, 1939; Boch, 1946, 1948; Lyubimov, 1967; Hall, 1975), but the great majority of investigators described landforms derived from nivation processes and gave little or no consideration to the mechanisms involved. The variety of forms assigned a nivation genesis is large, ranging from miniature hollows (Nichols, 1963) through fully formed nivation hollows (St. Onge, 1969) to multistaged cirques (Watson, 1966). Overall, the contemporary literature assigns a major role to nivation in the development of periglacial and glacial landscapes (for example, Flint, 1971, p. 134). Quantitative verification of nivation, however, is all but absent, a fact highlighted by the brief treatment of nivation in such specialized texts as Bird (1967), Embleton and King (1968, 1975), and Washburn (1973). In this paper, I examine the mechanisms of nivation as observed in the Colorado Front Range.

RESEARCH DESIGN

Table 1 lists the four established models of nivation; extensive studies have characterized all four, and several major conflicts are apparent. The research reported here was intensive and designed to determine which processes are involved in nivation, the magnitude of intensification produced by nivation, and the areal and temporal distribution of the intensification. The concept of nivation is founded on process intensification; therefore, the collection of comparative data is critical. In this study, data were collected within snow patches and compared with identical measurements made on nearby snowfree (control) sites. Wherever possible, instrumentation was deployed so that the data generated were suitable for analysis of variance or more specific alternatives, such as Duncan's multiple range test.

The hypothesis that nivation produces measurable intensification or acceleration of periglacial weathering and (or) transport processes was tested by examination of four component hypotheses — namely, nivation produces measurable intensification of (1) mechanical weathering, (2) mechanical transport, (3) chemical weathering, and (4) chemical transport. In the strict sense, these subdivisions are arbitrary; in the field, however, they provide manageable focal points.

RESEARCH AREA AND SITES

The general research area, the Indian Peaks area of the Colorado Front Range, and the individual research sites are shown in Figure 1. Selection of a single site with comprehensive characteristics was impossible; therefore, three sites on the southern flank of Niwot Ridge were chosen on the assumption that the well-documented higher insolation receipts of southerly aspects (for example, Barry and Chorley, 1970, p. 27–28) would be reflected by a local maximum in geomorphic activity. The principal sites, Martinelli and Longitudinal, were used to study the characteristics of a snow patch on unconsolidated debris and bed rock, respectively. A subsidiary debris site, Saddle, was also studied.

The Martinelli site (Fig. 2) has a single snow patch in winter with a maximum extent of approximately 450 m in length downslope and maximum width across slope of 175 m. Snow accumulation takes place in the lee of a pre-Pleistocene or early Pleistocene diamicton of glacial or possibly fluvial origin (Madole, unpub. results). Early in the ablation season the snow patch subdivides: a circular snow patch [Lewis's (1939) classification terminology] occupies an upper basin approximately 245 m wide and 165 m long downslope; a longitudinal snow patch (Lewis, 1939) occupies the lower basin, which is approximately 83 m wide and 183 m long. The two basins are floored by syenite colluvium with little to no vegetation cover. The subsidiary site (Saddle) is 500 m to the east, where a heavily vegetated turf-banked terrace (Benedict, 1970, terrace 19) is occupied by a transverse snow patch (Lewis, 1939) with a maximum winter size of approximately 90 m across slope and 40 m downslope. The second principal site, the Longitudinal site (Fig. 3), lies 1.4 km west of the other two sites. This small snow patch collects against a 4- to 5-m-high wall of gneiss and extends 30 to 40 m along the west wall of a narrow gully.

Only a small core area of the upper basin at the Martinelli site fails to melt out; this permitted instrumentation throughout the snow-patch area. The Martinelli site was the focus for evaluating the intensification of mechanical transport, chemical weathering, and chemical transport; supporting evidence came from the Saddle site. The Longitudinal site was the focus for testing the hypothesis

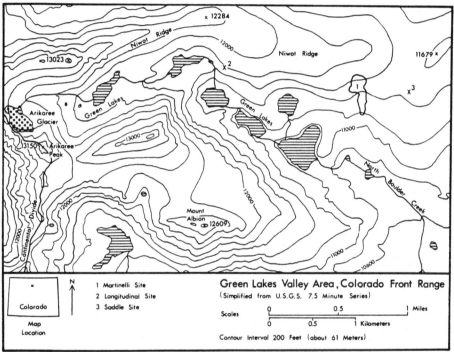

Figure 1. Map of the research area showing the three research sites.

of intensified mechanical weathering, with supplementary data coming from the Martinelli site.

MECHANICAL WEATHERING

The important role assigned to mechanical weathering within nivation stems from the belief that a snow patch intensifies freeze-

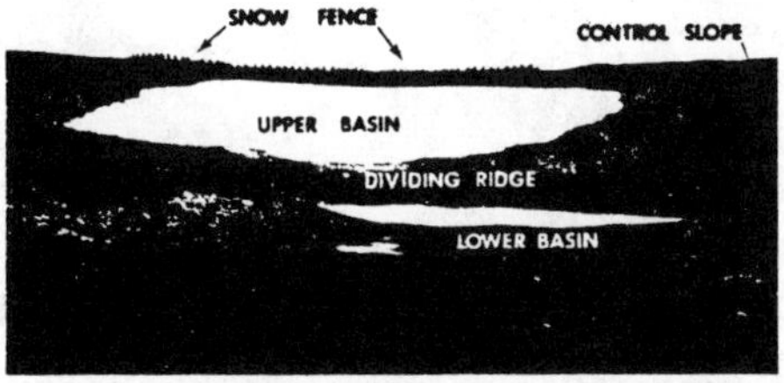

Figure 2. View toward north at Martinelli site (early August 1972); snow remains in the upper and lower basins, which are separated by the snowfree dividing ridge. The snowfree control slope is immediately to the east (right) of the upper basin. Snow fence is approximately 2 m high.

thaw cycle activity (Table 1). However, many unresolved problems concerning freeze-thaw cycles remain, both in the general context of all periglacial environments and in the specific case of nivation. Older viewpoints (Matthes, 1900, p. 180–181, 189; Lewis, 1936, p. 432; Boch, 1948, p. 1) were that freeze-thaw cycles were frequent in the vicinity of snow patches; more recently, the low frequency of freeze-thaw cycles in the Arctic (Cook and Raiche, 1962) and in alpine areas (Fahey, 1973) has been established.

Laboratory research has highlighted the complexity of the freezing and thawing processes (for example, Williams, 1964). A distinction has been made between a freeze-thaw cycle as a purely thermal event (the oscillation through 0°C) and a geomorphologically significant freeze-thaw cycle that disrupts bed rock. It is not precisely clear what determines the intensity of freeze-thaw weathering. All laboratory experiments indicate that the presence of moisture is critical. However, some experiments (for example, Coutard and others, 1970; Potts, 1970) suggest that the frequency of oscillations through the freezing mark is the dominant factor, although others (for example, Tricart, 1956; Wiman, 1963) suggest that freezing intensity is at least an important secondary factor.

The particular problems of freeze-thaw activity relative to nivation are the mechanism and location of intensification. Most workers have believed that increased freeze-thaw cycle intensity results from the copious water supply provided by the melting snow patch (for example, Matthes, 1900; St. Onge, 1969). A secondary

TABLE 1. SUMMARY OF NIVATION ACCORDING TO PRINCIPAL AUTHORS

Topic	Matthes (1900)	Lewis (1936, 1939)	Boch (1946, 1948)	Lyubimov (1967)
Data base				
Extensive observations*	Yes (Wyoming)	Yes (Iceland)	Yes (Ural Mountains)	No (Literature)
Intensive observations*	None	Minimal	Minimal	None
Quantified contrast†	None	None	None	None
Snow-patch classification	No	Yes	Yes	No
Snow-patch profile	Text (generalized)	Diagram (example)	Diagram (generalized)	Diagram (generalized)
Specifics				
Freeze-thaw cycles, intensified	Yes (snow margin)	Yes (throughout)	Yes (snow margin)	Yes (headwall base)
Snow-patch core	Protective	Intensified activity	Protective	Protective
Bedrock disruption	Not mentioned	Intensified	Intensified	Intensified
Sediment transport	Intensified	Intensified	Intensified	Intensified
Principal transport process	Not specified	Solifluction	Solifluction	Solifluction
Snowpack	Static	Static	Partially mobile	Static
Absence of vegetation	Brief comment	Comment	Comment	Extended comment
Chemical activity	Not mentioned	Not mentioned	Intensified	Intensified (in karst areas)

Note: All authors listed defined nivation as intensification of known processes by a snow patch.
* Extensive observations involved reconnaissance study of numerous snow patches. Intensive observations are detailed, continuous observations and measurements of one or more snow patches.
† Quantified contrast requires that a process be measured within the area of snow-patch influence and contrasted directly with the same process elsewhere.

hypothesis is that intensification also results from increased cycle frequency (for example, Matthes, 1900, p. 189; Lyubimov, 1967, p. 2; Gardner, 1969, p. 114). Lewis (1936, 1939) suggested that meltwater movement would extend freeze-thaw activity beneath the entire snow patch; however, Lewis's idea has been replaced by acceptance of Matthes's original idea that freeze-thaw cycle activity is confined to the snow-patch margins.

Ground temperature data in this study came from two 30-channel recorders located at the Martinelli and Longitudinal sites. Once every 2 hr the recorders automatically swept all channels, producing 30 spot readings. A freeze-thaw cycle was defined as each period in which the temperature dropped below+0.5°C and warmed again or, alternatively, each interval than a negative temperature rose above −0.5°C and subsequently cooled below this value. The definition is an attempt to accommodate the temperature range over which freezing and thawing are known to occur (Williams, 1964) with the discontinuous temperature recording system.

Because field data on moisture conditions could not be recorded automatically, a thermal freeze-thaw cycle had to be accepted as a surrogate measure for a geomorphologically significant freeze-thaw cycle. Therefore, the data represent a maximum frequency and must be accepted with caution. All seasons are represented, and the fall freeze up and spring meltout were monitored comprehensively. Thermistors were arranged in vertical profiles (surface to 5 cm deep in bed rock; surface to 40 cm deep in debris) and arrayed to include environments ranging from a snow-patch core to snowfree conditions. Regular photography, snow-depth probing, and tape measurements provided precise location of freeze-thaw activity.

The best illustration of freeze-thaw cycle frequency is provided by data from the Longitudinal site (Table 2). Results from only

thermistors that experienced no breakdowns are shown, but partial records from other thermistors support the interpretation below. A chi-square test of the data shown in Table 2 for the 1-cm-deep level indicates that there is no difference in annual freeze-thaw cycle frequency between snow-patch and snowfree sites. Similar chi-square tests on seasonal periods [including data not shown (Thorn, 1974)] indicate the following statistically significant differences: (1) the

Figure 3. View toward northeast at the Longitudinal snow patch. Photograph (early June 1973) shows the snow patch near its maximum extent. Large snowfree buttress (top right) served as the control site. Person seated in top center gives scale.

TABLE 2. LONGITUDINAL SITE, FREEZE-THAW CYCLE TOTALS FROM SELECTED THERMISTORS

Date	Thermistors* (buried depth)							
	11 (1 cm)	12 (5 cm)	19 (1 cm)	20 (5 cm)	23 (1 cm)	24 (in crack)	25 (1 cm)	26 (in crack)
09/14/71–10/27/71	31	30	34	30	20	25	19	21
12/13/71–12/22/71	0	0	3	6	5	5	0	0
02/19/72–02/26/72	0	0	0	0	4	4	3	2
03/12/72–03/31/72	0	0	0	0	18	14	13	12
04/15/72–04/26/72	0	0	0	0	7	7	6	6
05/13/72–07/06/72	35	35	32	30	13	11	10	10
Total (144 days)	66	65	69	66	67	66	51	51

* Thermistors 11 and 12 located at base of rock wall, snow-patch core; 19 and 20 located at base of rock wall, snow-patch core; 23 and 24 located at south face of buttress, snowfree control site; 25 and 26 located at west face of buttress, snowfree control site.

sites of snow patches that melt out in summer undergo more cycles than nearby snowfree sites during some falls, (2) snowfree sites undergo frequent cycles in winter when snow-patch sites record no cycles, and (3) during meltout, but prior to exposure, sites within snow patches have more cycles than snowfree sites. The same general picture emerged from the record at the debris site. Although impossible to compare directly, these thermal patterns are in overall agreement with those measured by Fahey (1973, 1974) at nearby but substantially different sites.

Increased freeze-thaw cycle frequency occurs when the thickness of the snowpack is reduced to approximately 1 m or less. This conclusion from the debris-site data agrees well with theoretical calculations of the depths to which solar radiation is able to penetrate (for example, Geiger, 1950, p. 165–166). Measurement of snow depths at the margins of the Martinelli snow patch shows snow depths of 0.83 ± 0.28 m at a distance of 5 m into the snow patch.

The important influence of a nearby snowpack on newly exposed ground is implied in several of the models in Table 1, but this implication appears to be false. Strong diurnal fluctuations occurred at a depth of 1 cm in bed rock forming one side of a narrow randkluft at the Longitudinal site. (A randkluft is a small crevasse that forms between a bedrock wall and a snow patch. It is caused by the snow patch undergoing accelerated melting due to heat from the bed rock.) However, no freeze-thaw cycles were recorded. Surface temperatures (Fig. 4) were measured at the debris site using an infrared thermometer (PRT 10). As Figure 4 shows, temperatures from 2 m beyond the snow margin are comparable to those 10 m or more away. Maximum snow-margin retreat rates were 1.8 m/day (4-day period) along the lateral margins and 6.8 m/day (3-day period) at the toe of the snow patch. In temporal terms, the impact of a retreating snow margin lasts little more than a day at the ground surface. Even when meltwaters extend the period of snow-margin influence, very few freeze-thaw cycles were recorded

subsequent to meltout (Table 3); in many instances, no cycles were recorded.

Accelerated mechanical weathering as a component of nivation is by no means firmly established. The claim for such intensification rests not with an increased number of cycles, but with more effective cycles. Such an argument can only be based on analogies with laboratory experiments (for example, Potts, 1970; Martini, 1967), where frequent crossings of the freezing point in the presence of abundant moisture, as beneath a shallow melting snowpack, produce effective disruption. The area of maximum freeze-thaw activity within a snow-patch hollow such as the one at the Martinelli site is a narrow zone beneath the snowpack but adjacent to the margin.

MECHANICAL TRANSPORT

Mechanical transport as a component of nivation may occur as the result of (1) inclusion in snow creep, (2) acceleration of one or more of the mass movement processes, or (3) fluvial processes associated directly with the melting snow. Traditionally, assumptions were that the snowpack is static, that solifluction is the principal process accelerated by snow meltwaters, and that where fluvial processes occur they are not dominant (Table 1). More recently, snowpack creep (first described by Matthes, 1909, and Dyson, 1938) has been supported as the major transport process by Costin and others (1964, 1973) for bedrock surfaces, although it does not seem to be major for debris surfaces (Mackay and Mathews, 1974).

TABLE 3. NUMBERS OF DIURNAL
FREEZE-THAW CYCLES SUBSEQUENT TO MELTOUT
AT MARTINELLI (DEBRIS) SITE, 1972

Thermistor no.	Buried depth (cm)	Meltout date	Total no. of cycles
1	5	June 1	1
3	20	June 1	1
6	10	June 19	3
7	5	June 19	0
11	10	July 24	0
12	5	July 31	0
13	10	July 31	0
14	20	July 31	0
15	5	July 20	10
16	10	July 20	10
17	20	July 20	10
18	5	July 19	6
20	5	July 27	3
21	10	July 27	2
22	5	July 31	4
24	5	July 31	2
25	10	July 31	2

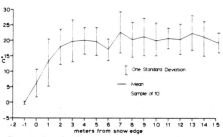

Figure 4. Ground-surface temperature profile away from edge of the melting snow patch, Martinelli site, June 28, 1972.

Three experiments were conducted at the Martinelli site, each designed to compare activity between the upper basin, the dividing ridge, the lower basin, and the control slope (Fig. 2). Figure 5 shows the detailed locations of experimental plots. Experiments were as follows: (1) tethered spheres designed to provide comparative data on snow creep (a simplified version of the instrument reported by Mathews and Mackay, 1963); (2) lines of painted pebbles (-2 to -6ϕ) to measure movement of intermediate material through the winter period; and (3) groups of sediment traps designed to measure both winter and summer transport of material. Data from these experiments were subjected to analysis of variance, the Scheffé statistic test (Scheffé, 1959, p. 68–72), or Duncan's multiple range test (Malik and Mullen, 1973, p. 272–273) to test the null hypothesis that there is no difference between the transport of material between snow-patch and snowfree sites.

Analysis of variance of the four profiles from the four tethered spheres led to the acceptance of the null hypothesis, possibly because of the small number of spheres used and their extremely erratic movements. However, inspection of surface characteristics revealed that the core of most snow patches is composed of relatively stable coarse fragments. Meltwaters appear to wash out fines, thereby undercutting coarse fragments. The coarse material creeps downslope until it interlocks with other fragments to form a partially imbricated layer. Excavations in winter revealed coarse fragments cemented in a snow-ice matrix. Evidence for this surface stability may be drawn from the fact that several spheres moved only 1 or 2 cm, whereas the hollow steel pipes (1.27-cm internal diameter, projected approximately 30 cm above the surface) to which they were anchored were bent until they were lying along the ground surface. These data in no way conflict with rapid movement of loose rock fragments across snow-covered bedrock surfaces (Costin and others, 1964, 1973), but they do indicate that a debris surface is a different case.

The movement recorded by marked pebbles is summarized in Table 4. Data were subjected to a logarithmic transformation prior to analysis, a necessary step (Caine, 1968) given the log normal distribution of such markers. Application of the Scheffé statistic indicated significant differences (1 percent confidence level) between all groups except those from the dividing range and the sheetwash area of the lower basin (Fig. 5, P4). Regular examination of the research plots permits explanation of the processes at work. Winter movement on a snowfree slope can only be the product of ground heave, needle-ice growth, and wind — in essence, a creep-dominated context. All of those processes are precluded within a snow patch once freeze up is completed. Snow-covered sites reveal less movement as well as greater homogeneity of movement. Within the snow-patch area substantial movement was recorded only by markers located in meltwater channels and in sections where lateral undercutting of an alpine sod was active in the spring.

Design of a suitable sediment trap (Fig. 6) was extremely difficult. The need for comparability dictated that all traps be identical. Each trap had to handle large amounts of water and be stable on a completely mobile debris surface. Traps were used in groups of five; the large amount of meltwater made it necessary to use traps that permitted the throughflow of water. Sediment data from the traps are summarized in Table 5, and the results of the statistical analyses appear in Table 6. It is apparent that the mechanical transport component of nivation produced a statistically significant increase in the transport of fines, although there are statistically significant differences between the various areas subjected to nivation. At the 10 percent confidence level, the upper basin is completely isolated from its surrounds, which serves to emphasize that the transport of fines is localized redistribution within the nivation hollow. The failure to distinguish statistically between the sediment yields in groups T3 and T4, despite a 5-week difference in meltout dates, indicates that rates of sediment yield increase toward the core of a snow patch.

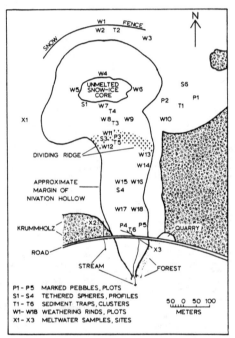

Figure 5. Sketch map of Martinelli site, showing the salient features and location of the principal experimental plots.

TABLE 4. COMPARISON OF INTERPLOT MOVEMENT OF PAINTED PEBBLES, MARTINELLI SITE, WINTER, 1972–1973

	Plot P1	Plot P2	Plot P3	Plot P4	Plot P5
n	720	446	217	594	817
x	9.71	6.76	1.93	31.39	5.67
s	10.23	9.01	4.19	36.69	14.32
*Logarithmic transformation**					
n	720	446	217	594	817
x	1.63392	1.37803	0.66797	0.76543	1.12946
s	0.73705	0.77677	0.76394	1.10463	0.85610
Geometric mean and standard deviation					
n	720	446	217	594	817
x	4.30	2.39	0.47	0.58	1.35
s	0.55	0.60	0.58	0.58	0.72

Note: n = number in sample, x = group mean (cm), s = standard deviation. Plot P1 = control slope; plot P2 = control slope, snow margin; plot P3 = dividing ridge; plot P4 = lower basin, sheetwash area; plot P5 = lower basin, east margin (see Fig. 5, P1 to P5).
* Data transformed as the logarithm of the movement in millimetres. Zero values assigned a value of 1 mm; no uphill (negative) movement accepted.

TABLE 5. SEDIMENT TOTALS FOR INDIVIDUAL TRAPS IN TRAP GROUPS
AT MARTINELLI SITE, MELTOUT, SEPTEMBER 25, 1972

	T1 (June 26)	T2 (July 6)	T3 (July 7)	T4 (August 14)	T5 (July 7)	T6 (July 20)
Trap no.						
1	5.1	6.8	1.2	187.2	0.6	20.7
2	10.4	3.9	77.0	300.9	2.4	237.3
3	1.7	7.9	73.7	47.7	0.2	51.6
4	2.9	207.3	685.2	444.6	3.1	48.7
5	1.7	140.8	546.1	379.0	1.5	120.0
x^*	4.4	73.3	276.6	271.9	1.6	95.7
s^*	3.7	94.9	314.8	157.8	1.2	87.2
n^*	5	5	5	5	5	5

Note: Analysis of variance $F = 3.32$, with 5 and 24 degrees of freedom; null hypothesis rejected at 5 (and 2.5) percent level. Trap groups as follows: T1 = control slope; T2 = upper basin (top); T3 = upper basin (bottom, A); T4 = upper basin (bottom, B); T5 = dividing ridge; T6 = lower basin (see Fig. 5, T1 to T6). Dates in parentheses under trap group numbers are the meltout dates.
$^*x$ = Group mean (g); s = standard deviation; n = number in sample.

The initial emptying of the trap after meltout provided an estimate of undersnow movement, although it is an overestimate, because some postmeltout sheetwash occurred prior to emptying. Trap group T3 recorded only 9 percent of the sediment total at the first emptying and trap group T6, 25 percent. Excluding the first emptying, trap group T3 caught 83 percent of the sediment total, and trap group T6 caught 67 percent when water was observed flowing through the traps. Sheetwash and rivulet flow, subsequent to meltout, are the dominant processes in the mechanical transport of material by nivation.

Surficial grab samples taken immediately upslope of each trap were compared with the larger sediment trap totals from individual emptyings. Both surface samples and trap samples were dominated by the sand fraction, which averaged more than 80 percent of the sand-silt-clay fraction; however, all trap samples were finer than the surficial samples. Attempts to locate the zone of maximum removal by regressing sediment totals against distance downslope of the retreating snow-patch margin were not successful. Similar sediment trap data were collected at the Saddle site, where a thick alpine turf mat is exposed to abundant meltwater. The extremely low sediment totals (Table 7) demonstrated the protective properties of such a vegetative mat.

Major studies (Table 1) have emphasized solifluction as the principal transport mechanism of nivation. This is the result of observing solifluction lobes in the toe area of nivation hollows (as is the case at Martinelli) and assuming that the same process dominates

throughout the basin. In fact, solifluction dominates only in peripheral areas where increased channelization of meltwaters and briefer periods of sheetwash reduce the importance of sheetwash and rivulet flow. Corroboration of this conclusion is available from theoretical relationships between slope form and process (Carson and Kirkby, 1972); this relationship indicates that solifluction-dominated slopes develop convex profiles, although nivation hollows exhibit concave profiles in the core areas and convex profiles only at the foot of the hollows.

CHEMICAL WEATHERING

In accordance with the general trend in periglacial geomorphology, chemical weathering has been largely ignored in nivation studies (Table 1). The study reported here included some preliminary investigations of chemical weathering, using principles derived from Quaternary studies (Thorn, 1974). Quaternary stratigraphers have found the weathering-rind thickness of rocks to be a good relative age indicator (for example, Birkeland, 1973). If a surface is time-synchronous, weathering-rind thickness should indicate process intensity, not process duration. The evidence for minimal downslope movement of coarse material suggests that across-slope comparisons through a snow-patch hollow are essentially a time-synchronous profile.

Data were obtained from stones selected at random from the 10-m by 10-m plots at the Martinelli site shown in Figure 5. A matrix of results from use of Duncan's multiple range test is presented

TABLE 6. RESULTS OF APPLYING THE DUNCAN MULTIPLE
RANGE TEST TO THE SEDIMENT TRAP DATA,
MARTINELLI SITE, SUMMER 1972

	T1	T2	T3	T4	T5	T6
T1	x					
T2		x				
T3	S	T	x			
T4	S	T		x		
T5			S	S	x	
T6			T	T		x

Note: Results have been laid out in a matrix. Numerical values on the x and y axes refer to the sediment trap groups shown in Figure 5. S indicates that there is a statistically significant difference (5 percent confidence level) between the two trap groups; T indicates that the statistically significant difference was established only at the 10 percent confidence level. Trap groups are numbered as follows: T1 = control slope; T2 = upper basin (top); T3 = upper basin (bottom, A); T4 = upper basin (bottom, B); T5 = dividing ridge; T6 = lower basin (see Fig. 5, T1 to T6).

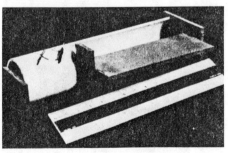

Figure 6. Individual sediment trap. Note fixed 10-cm-wide trap lip and partial blockage of one end to permit flow through trap.

TABLE 7. TOTAL YIELD OF SADDLE SEDIMENT TRAPS,
JUNE 8 TO SEPTEMBER 19, 1972

Trap no.	Yield (g)	Trap no.	Yield (g)
S1	0.0	S6	0.0
S2	0.0	S7	0.0
S3	0.0	S8	19.1
S4	0.0	S9	0.5
S5	1.5	S10	3.7

Note: Snow patch melted out on July 24, 1972. Trap S8 located in frost crack followed by meltwaters.

in Table 8. It is apparent from Table 8 that weathering-rind thickness is an extremely sensitive measure of localized environment. Only the salient aspects of the distribution are discussed below.

All available evidence points to the fact that the upper basin at Martinelli is younger than the lower basin, a relationship confirmed by the general distribution of rind thicknesses. Comparisons across slope through the nivation hollows (for example, plots W1, W2, W3, W4, W5, W6, and W7) indicate as much as a twofold increase in chemical activity; comparisons between absolute maxima and minima within either basin or around them indicate as much as fourfold increases. Similar studies at the Saddle site showed increases in rind thickness of a factor of 2.5 in a horizontal distance of less than 50 m. Increasing rind thickness appears to be accompanied by increased homogeneity within the sample. Examination of the research plots shows that rind maxima are directly related to zones of meltwater concentration. Such zones are undoubtedly also focal areas for free water moving through an isothermal snowpack. The dominant mechanism has not been identified, but residence time appears to favor free water in the snowpack.

CHEMICAL TRANSPORT

Although the objective of this project was to compare water chemistry within a snow-patch environment to that of snowfree slopes, a comparison of contemporary chemical weathering and transport on snow-patch and snowfree sites was prohibited by the absence of prolonged surface flow on the snowfree areas. On the

assumption that the Martinelli site exhibits typical relationships for the research area, its snow and meltwater chemistry were investigated.

A summary of snowpack aluminum and silica contents, total hardness (indicative of calcium and magnesium content), and total dissolved solid content is given in Table 9. Subdivision into clean and dirty snow reflects an attempt to contrast the surface snow that becomes littered with wind-borne material (dirty snow) with the "clean" snow that occurs at depth. No statistically significant differences were found between the two snow types. Analyses of snowpack pH were undertaken but are not reported, because pH values are extremely unstable and require determination in the field, which was not possible (Clement, 1966).

Meltwater values for the same parameters appear in Table 9. Statistically significant differences (analysis of variance, 1 percent confidence level) were found for all measures between snowpack and meltwater values. Despite probably brief residence periods in such a small basin, rapid but not intense chemical solution occurs. The solution load is comparable with that recorded for snow and meltwater elsewhere in the western United States (Feth and others, 1964) but is low by worldwide standards (Livingstone, 1963).

In addition to meltwater solutes, meltwater temperatures were recorded. Temperature is widely regarded as a control of chemical activity, although Tamm (1924) presented data demonstrating that very little change occurs in the intensity of chemical weathering in the range +2° to +15°C. Figure 7 illustrates meltwater heating upon emergence from beneath the snowpack. Both regressions are statistically significant (according to the t test) at the 1 percent level. Meltwater temperatures at the point of emergence varied from 0° to +1°C, and, despite the small range, statistically significant differences (analysis of variance, 5 percent confidence level) were detected between localities. Clearly, residence time and subsnowpack pathways influence meltwater temperatures only through a very narrow range.

DISCUSSION

The importance of these data rests not only in identification of the elements of nivation but also with the opportunity to place nivation and nivation forms in larger developmental, spatial, and temporal contexts. An important limitation of this study is that it pertains to a mid-latitude alpine environment with no permafrost;

TABLE 8. RESULTS OF THE DUNCAN MULTIPLE RANGE TEST APPLIED TO WEATHERING RIND DATA
BY PLOTS, MARTINELLI SITE

	W1	W2	W3	W4	W5	W6	W7	W8	W9	W10	W11	W12	W13	W14	W15	W16	W17	W18
W1																		
W2	5																	
W3	5	x																
W4	5	5	5															
W5	x	5	5	5														
W6	x	5	5	5	x													
W7	5	5	5	5	5	5												
W8	5	5	5	5	5	5	5											
W9	5	5	x	5	5	5	5	x										
W10	5	5	5	5	5	5	5	x	x									
W11	5	5	5	5	5	5	5	x	x	x								
W12	5	x	x	5	5	5	5	x	x	x	x							
W13	5	x	x	5	5	5	5	x	x	x	x	x						
W14	5	5	5	5	5	5	5	x	x	x	x	x	x					
W15	5	x	x	5	5	5	x	5	5	5	5	5	5	5				
W16	5	x	x	5	5	5	x	5	x	5	x	x	x	x	x			
W17	5	x	x	5	5	5	x	5	5	5	5	5	5	5	x	x		
W18	5	x	x	5	5	5	x	5	5	5	5	5	x	5	x	x	x	

Note: 5 = statistical difference established (5 percent confidence level); x = no statistical difference established (5 percent confidence level); see Fig. 5, W1 to W18, for plot locations.

TABLE 9. CONCENTRATIONS OF SOLUTES IN MELTED SNOW AND MELTWATERS, MARTINELLI SITE

Snow type	Aluminum			Silica			Total hardness			Total dissolved solids		
	n	x (ppm)	s	n	x (ppm)	s	n	x (ppm)	s	n	x (ppm)	s
Dirty snow	18	0.11	0.14	18	0.10	0.31	17	2.00	3.39	18	5.27	4.03
Zero readings*	9			16			11			0		
Clean snow	16	0.08	0.00	16	0.12	0.33	15	1.20	2.36	16	3.52	2.60
Zero readings*	8			14			11			0		
Meltwater sites†												
X1	23	0.20	0.10	23	6.69	1.25	23	20.86	8.28	23	26.54	1.42
X2	19	0.18	0.10	19	4.36	0.75	19	12.94	3.96	19	15.43	1.47
X3	26	0.19	0.10	26	2.03	0.76	26	7.53	5.63	26	6.48	2.34

Note: n = number in sample, x = sample mean, s = sample standard deviation.
* Zero readings indicate the number of occasions when the specified material was absent.
† See Figure 5 for the location of the meltwater test sites.

the model and comments likewise pertain only to this environment.

The principal elements of nivation may be summarized briefly. Mechanical weathering may be accelerated by nivation, but this is not established definitively. The case for intensified mechanical weathering must be derived exclusively from increased freeze-thaw cycle efficiency. Both the ideas that freeze-thaw cycles are generally common in the alpine environment and that the cycles are specifically of increased frequency in and around snow patches must be dismissed. The removal of sand, silt, and clay is increased 20 to 30 times by nivation, with sheetwash and rivulet flow dominant over solifluction in the core area of the nivation hollow. Mobility of coarse material may be very limited on debris surfaces where imbrication and winter cementation enhance stability. Chemical weathering is increased two to four times by a snow patch. Soil development is retarded within a nivation hollow owing to the absence of vegetation and the removal of fines.

Table 10 provides a comparative guide to denudation rates recorded in the Colorado Front Range. Whereas denudation rates within a debris-mantled nivation hollow represent an order of magnitude increase over the nearby control site, these rates are two to three orders of magnitude less than those calculated for nearby cirques, which probably represent bedrock denudation rates. A calculation of the volume of the Martinelli nivation hollow shows it to be three orders of magnitude less than that of the cirque occupied by the Arikaree Glacier (Fig. 1). Furthermore, at contemporary rates of removal, excavation of the Martinelli nivation hollow would have required 500,000 yr. The possibility that climatic de-

terioration during glaciation accelerated nivation must not be overlooked, nor must the alternative possibility — that nivation decelerates owing to a greatly shortened ablation season — be ignored.

There has been a widespread assumption that nivation hollows are precursors to cirques (for example, Flint, 1971, p. 134). This continuum concept is based exclusively on the ergodic hypothesis "that, under certain circumstances, space and time can be considered as interchangeable" (Chorley and Kennedy, 1971, p. 349). However, in the example at hand, the continuum hypothesis is confused, and it appears that either (1) there is a continuum of process, (2) there is a continuum of form, or (3) there is a composite continuum of both process and form. Given the disparity in denudation rates and volume recorded herein, none of the options appears feasible. The study reported here is by no means definitive, but in the total absence of previous data it provides a basis for reevaluating an "article of faith."

Comparison of known relationships between process and slope form (Carson and Kirkby, 1972; Fig. 8) and the evidence from this study are compatible; combined, they refute the claim that solifluction is the dominant process within the core area of a nivation hollow. The upper convexity associated with a nivation hollow is produced by the dominance of creep processes outside the realm of nivation dominance; on Niwot Ridge, evidence from this study and from Benedict (1970) supports this contention. The nivation hollow is slightly to distinctly concave as a product of soilwash (sheetwash), with concavity varying with the intensity of gullying. The lower convexity is the result of temporary storage and

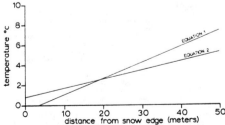

Figure 7. Regression analysis of two meltwater stream temperature profiles. Equation 1, $T = 0.16D - 0.52$, $r = 0.99$, sample size = 22, 2σ = 0.60. Equation 2, $T = 0.09D + 0.84$, $r = 0.91$, sample size = 14, 2σ = 0.71. In both equations, T = meltwater temperature, and D = distance from snow edge; r = product moment correlation coefficient.

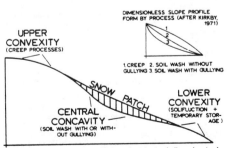

Figure 8. Idealized slope profile through a nivation hollow, showing location of dominant processes derived from this study and the process-slope form relationships derived from the continuity equation (Kirkby, 1971).

TABLE 10. SELECTED DENUDATION RATES, COLORADO FRONT RANGE

Area	Dominant erosion process	Erosion rate (mm/1,000 yr)	Method of estimation	Author
Rocky Mountain National Park	Cirque Glaciation	2,000 – 8,000 100 – 2,000	Moraine volume Cirque volume	Andrews (1971)
Arapaho Cirque Present Past	Cirque Glaciation	140 – 235 } 1,260 – 2,040 }	Suspended load and moraine volume	Reheis (1974)
Niwot Ridge Martinelli site	Nivation*	7.5	Sediment trap and solute analysis	Thorn (1974)
Control slope	Creep*	0.1	Sediment trap	Thorn (1974)

* Data from this study are based on one year's values. Bedrock density was used in the calculation to make results compatible with the other studies.

the transition to solifluction dominance, resulting from a drop in the amount of surface flow, an increase in vegetation, and an abundance of fines.

Lewis's (1939) classification of snow patches into longitudinal, transverse, and circular is accepted in the literature with the implication that form has genetic significance. The evaluation of processes in this study indicates that nivation is always focused downslope of the available snow. A corollary is that lateral modification of a nivation hollow is minimal. Combining this evaluation of nivation with the idea that nivation can only modify a hollow, not initiate one (Matthes, 1900; Carson and Kirkby, 1972), it would appear that a morphologic classification of snow patches and nivation hollows provides no genetic insight for a mid-latitude alpine environment.

Finally, the temporal role of nivation must be considered. Evidence indicates that snowpack is essentially protective. Headward incision of a nivation hollow is dependent on regular, complete meltout of the resident snow patch (Boch, 1948; this study); spatially, this implies subarctic or high-energy alpine environments; temporally, the onset or decline of glacial phases appears significant. The concept of "paraglaciation" (Ryder, 1971; Church and Ryder, 1972) appears to be pertinent, because logically, abundant meltwaters crossing an unconsolidated debris surface, deprived of its vegetative mat by prolonged burial, should make a deglacial phase the optimal context for nivation.

The study reported here represents a preliminary step toward a quantitative model of nivation processes in a mid-latitude alpine environment. Further research must be directed toward testing both the temporal and spatial representativity of the model. We also need to know the impact of a shallow permafrost table, as is common in most arctic nivation hollows, and the point at which climate deterioration ceases to accelerate nivation processes and begins to produce perennial snow patches that cause the cessation of nivation processes.

ACKNOWLEDGMENTS

The Institute of Arctic and Alpine Research, University of Colorado, provided the logistical support for this project; in particular, I thank J. T. Andrews, Associate Director, and J. D. Ives, Director, for their support. Many tedious chores in the field were undertaken cheerfully by John Craig, Janet Herman, and Eric Orr while they were National Science Foundation Summer Research Participants. Partial financial support came from two Penrose Bequest Research Grants from the Geological Society of America, University of Colorado Graduate School, and an award from the University of Colorado Council on Research and Creative Writing to J. D. Ives. I also thank D. Alt, J. T. Andrews, and M. Webber for reading the manuscript.

REFERENCES CITED

Andrews, J. T., 1971, Estimates of variations in glacial erosion from the volume of corries and moraines: Geol. Soc. America Abs. with Programs, v. 3, p. 493.

Barry, R. G., and Chorley, R. J., 1970, Atmosphere, weather and climate: New York, Holt. Rinehart and Winston, Inc., 320 p.

Benedict, J. B., 1970, Downslope soil movement in a Colorado alpine region: Rates, processes and climatic significance: Arctic and Alpine Research, v. 2, p. 165–226.

Bird, J. B., 1967, The physiography of Arctic Canada: Baltimore, Md., Johns Hopkins Univ. Press, 336 p.

Birkeland, P. W., 1973, Use of relative age dating methods in a stratigraphic study of rock glacier deposits, Mt. Sopris, Colorado: Arctic and Alpine Research, v. 5, p. 401–416.

Boch, S. G., 1946, Snow patches and snow erosion in the northern part of the Urals: Vses. Geog. Obshch. Izv., v. 78, p. 207–222.

———1948, Some remarks on the nature of snow erosion: Vses. Geog. Obshch. Izv., v. 80, p. 609–611.

Caine, T. N., 1968, The log-normal distribution and rates of soil movement: An example: Rev. Géomorphologie Dynam., v. 18, p. 1–7.

Carson, M. A., and Kirkby, M. J., 1972, Hillslope form and process: London, Cambridge Univ. Press, 475 p.

Chorley, R. J., and Kennédy, B. A., 1971, Physical geography: A systems approach: London, Prentice-Hall Internat., Inc., 370 p.

Church, M., and Ryder, J. M., 1972, Paraglacial sedimentation: Consideration of fluvial processes conditioned by glaciation: Geol. Soc. America Bull., v. 83, p. 3059–3072.

Clement, P., 1966, Snow water acidity in Wyoming: Water Resources Research Inst., Water Resources Ser., no. 3, 11 p.

Cook, F. A., and Raiche, V. G., 1962, Freeze-thaw cycles at Resolute Bay, N.W.T.: Geog. Bull., 18, p. 79–85.

Costin, A. B., Jennings, J. N., Black, H. P., and Thom, B. G., 1964, Snow action on Mount Twynam, Snowy Mountains, Australia: Jour. Glaciology, v. 5, p. 219–228.

Costin, A. B., Jennings, J. N., Bautovich, B. C., and Wimbush, D. J., 1973, Forces developed by snowpatch action, Mt. Twynam, Snowy Mountains, Australia: Arctic and Alpine Research, v. 5, p. 121–126.

Coutard, J. P., Gabert, P., Helluin, M., Lantridou, J. P., and Pellerin, J., 1970, Recherches de gélifraction expérimentale au centre de géomorphologie. II, Calcaires de Normandie et de Provence: Caen Univ. Centre Géomorphologie, Centre Natl. Recherche Scientifique, 72 p.

Dyson, J. L., 1938, Snowslide erosion: Science, v. 87, p. 365–366.

Embleton, C., and King, C.A.M., 1968, Glacial and periglacial geomorphology: New York, St. Martin's Press, 608 p.

———1975, Glacial and periglacial geomorphology, Vol. 2 (2nd ed.): New York, John Wiley & Sons, 203 p.

Fahey, B. D., 1973, An analysis of diurnal freeze-thaw and frost heave cycles in the Indian Peaks region of the Colorado Front Range: Arctic and Alpine Research, v. 5, p. 269–281.

———1974, Seasonal frost heave and frost penetration measurements in the Indian Peaks region of the Colorado Front Range: Arctic and Alpine Research, v. 6, p. 79–84.

Feth, J. H., Rogers, S. M., and Robertson, C. E., 1964, Chemical composition of snow in the northern Sierra Nevada and other areas: U.S. Geol. Survey Water-Supply Paper 1535-J, 39 p.

Flint, R. F., 1971, Glacial and Quaternary geology: New York, John Wiley & Sons, 892 p.

Gardner, J., 1969, Snowpatches: Their influence on mountain wall temperatures and the geomorphic implications: Geog. Annaler, v. 51A, p. 114–120.

Geiger, R., 1950, The climate near the ground: Cambridge, Mass., Harvard Univ. Press, 482 p. (English trans. of 2nd ed. by M. Stewart and others).

Hall, K. J., 1975, Nivation process at a late-lying, north-facing snowpatch site in Austre Okstindbredalen, Okstindan, northern Norway [M.S. thesis]: Reading, England, Univ. Reading, 307 p.

Kirkby, M. J., 1971, Hillslope process-response models based on the continuity equation, in Brunsden, D., compiler, Slopes, form and process: Inst. British Geographers Spec. Pub. 3, p. 15–30.

Lewis, W. V., 1936, Nivation, river grading and shoreline development in southeast Iceland: Geog. Jour., v. 88, p. 431–437.

——1939, Snow-patch erosion in Iceland: Geog. Jour., v. 94, p. 153–161.

Livingstone, D. A., 1963, Chemical composition of rivers and lakes, in Fleischer, M., ed., Data of geochemistry (6th ed.): U.S. Geol. Survey Prof. Paper 440-G, 64 p.

Lyubimov, B. P., 1967, On the mechanism of nival processes: Podzemnyy Led, Pt. III, no. 3, p. 158–175.

Mackay, J. R., and Mathews, W. H., 1974, Needle ice striped ground: Arctic and Alpine Research, v. 6, p. 79–84.

Malik, H. J., and Mullen, K., 1973, A first course in probability and statistics: Reading, Mass., Addison-Wesley Pub. Co., 361 p.

Martini, A., 1967, Preliminary experimental studies on frost weathering of certain types from the West Sudetes: Biul. Peryglacjalny, v. 16, p. 147–194.

Mathews, W. H., and Mackay, J. R., 1963, Snowcreep studies, Mount Seymour, B.C.: Preliminary field investigations: Geog. Bull., v. 20, p. 58–75.

Matthes, F. E., 1900, Glacial sculpture of the Bighorn Mountains, Wyoming: U.S. Geol. Survey, 21st Ann. Rept., 1899–1900, p. 167–190.

——1909, Debris tracks on the domes of the Yosemite region: Science, v. 30, p. 61–62.

Nichols, R. L., 1963, Miniature nivation cirques near Marble Point, McMurdo Sound, Antarctica: Jour. Glaciology, v. 4, p. 477–479.

Potts, A. S., 1970, Frost action in rocks, some experimental data: Inst. British Geographers Trans., v. 49, p. 109–124.

Reheis, M. J., 1974, Source, transportation, and deposition of debris on Arapaho Glacier, Front Range, Colorado [M.S. thesis]: Boulder, Univ. Colorado, 71 p.

Ryder, J. M., 1971, Some aspects of the morphometry of paraglacial alluvial fans in south-central British Columbia: Canadian Jour. Earth Sci., v. 8, p. 1252–1264.

Scheffé, H., 1959, The analysis of variance: New York, John Wiley & Sons, Inc., 477 p.

St. Onge, D. A., 1969, Nivation landforms: Canada Geol. Survey Paper 69-30, 12 p.

Tamm, O., 1924, Experimental studies on chemical processes in the formation of glacial clay: Sveriges Geol. Undersökning Årsb., v. 18, no. 5, 20 p.

Thorn, C. E., 1974, An analysis of nivation processes and their geomorphic significance, Niwot Ridge, Colorado Front Range [Ph.D. dissert.]: Boulder, Univ. Colorado, 351 p.

Tricart, J., 1956, Étude expérimentale du problèm de gélivation: Biul. Peryglacjalny, v. 4, p. 285–318.

Washburn, A. L., 1973, Periglacial processes and environments: New York, St. Martin's Press, 320 p.

Watson, E., 1966, Two nivation cirques near Aberystwyth, Wales: Biul. Peryglacjalny, v. 15, p. 79–101.

Williams, P. J., 1964, Unfrozen water content of frozen soils and soil moisture suction: Géotechnique, v. 4, p. 231–246.

Wiman, S., 1963, A preliminary study of experimental frost weathering: Geog. Annaler, v. 45, p. 113–121.

SOURCE, TRANSPORTATION AND DEPOSITION OF DEBRIS ON ARAPAHO GLACIER, FRONT RANGE, COLORADO, U.S.A.

By MARITH JEAN REHEIS

(Department of Geological Sciences and Institute of Arctic and Alpine Research, University of Colorado, Boulder, Colorado 80302, U.S.A.)

INTRODUCTION

Detailed studies of existing glaciers have been performed in many areas of the world for well over a century. The majority of these studies have concentrated on ice movement and glacial mass and energy balance, but there has been a general absence of research on modern glacier processes relevant to glacial geology. As a result, theories of transportation mechanisms and glacial deposition rest largely on information from studies of till rather than on information derived from active glaciers. In addition, studies on existing glaciers have been mainly concerned with ice bodies of at least valley-glacier size up to those of ice-cap dimensions. There is at present an obvious gap between glacial geology and glaciology.

This study attempts partially to fill that gap by considering the sources of debris and the methods of transportation and deposition of debris of a small cirque glacier at present and during the recent past, and to evaluate methods and rates of bedrock erosion. An attempt was also made to determine if there had been any changes in source of debris, and in the transport and deposition of debris, by an analysis and comparison of both the material currently in transport by the glacier and the material previously deposited in the neoglacial moraine.

(*Editor's Note:* Material has been omitted at this point.)

Journal of Glaciology, Vol. 14, No. 72, 1975, pp. 407–420.

Arapaho Glacier

Arapaho Glacier is a small cirque glacier, but the largest in Colorado. It lies in the Colorado Front Range and ranges from 4 054 to 3 680 m in elevation (Figs. 1 and 2). Crevasses in mid-glacier penetrate 17 m of ice.

The climate in the cirque may be approximated with data from the Niwot Ridge weather station, 5 km to the north-east. There, the mean annual air temperature is $-3.8°$ C, the ablation season average temperature (June, July, August) is 6.8° C, the average annual precipitation is 102 cm, and the average wind velocity is 10.3 m/s (Barry, 1972). Snow accumulation is much higher in the cirque due to wind-drift accretion in the lee of the continental divide.

Rotational slip probably accounts for most of the glacier motion, as indicated by the changing dip angles of the accumulation layers in the ice and firn. Some internal deformation is indicated by the decrease in ice velocity from 5.2 m/year at the firn line to 1.7 m/year at the terminus of the southern lobe of the glacier (Waldrop, 1964; 1960–61 data). Alford (unpublished) measured a mean specific winter balance of $+330$ cm H_2O, and a mean specific summer balance of -305 cm H_2O, for the 1969–70 balance year. The high value of mass exchange, or the sum of the absolute values of the mean specific winter and summer balances,

Fig. 2. *Oblique air photograph of Arapaho Glacier cirque, showing Arapaho Glacier, its moraines and Arapaho rock glacier.* (*Photograph by J. D. Ives.*)

would appear to indicate that Arapaho Glacier should have a high potential for glacial erosion.

The glacier has undergone extensive retreat in the past 100 years, having lost over 30% of its area and having thinned considerably (Waldrop, 1964). Since about 1960, however, it has remained fairly stable, as shown by evidence which indicates that the mass balance of the glacier has been zero to slightly positive (Alford, unpublished; personal communication from J. B. Johnson, 1973).

Methods

The parameters sampled characterized the debris; they included lithology, roundness, striations, polish, and surface and sub-surface till fabrics. Debris sampling was donei at 26 sites on the moraines and the glacier for every stone touched by a 20 m long tape lad out, on the surface; in addition, small pebbles 2–10 mm in diameter were taken from each site and examined under a binocular microscope.

The relative age of the debris is based on diameters of *Rhizocarpon geographicum* (?), a slow-growing species with a known growth rate (Benedict, 1967), and *Lecanora thompsonii*, a fast-growing species. Lichens were sampled at 63 sites of 25 m² on the terminal moraine. Up to five large individuals of each species were recorded; only the maximum diameters of the two species at each location are presented here. The assumptions upon which lichenometry is based and its biological prerequisites and limitations have been discussed by many workers (cf. Beschel, 1961; Benedict, 1967; Webber and Andrews, 1973).

Suspended sediment in the moraine lake outlet was measured using a Norwegian sediment sampler.

Sand-sized quartz grains were separated from samples collected from several sites on the moraine and on the glacier ice. In order to try to differentiate grains that had been transported in different ways, the surfaces of the quartz grains were examined using a scanning electron microscope (Cambridge Stereoscan Model S-4).

The raw data and detailed descriptions of sampling and laboratory techniques may be found in my thesis (Reheis, unpublished).

Model for derivation and transportation of debris

The debris Arapaho Glacier carries derives from three sources: rockfall off the cirque walls, rock debris contained in avalanches, and glacial quarrying and abrasion of the bedrock. It is next to impossible to differentiate debris derived by rockfall from that contributed by

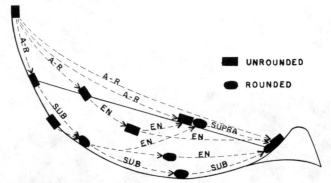

Fig. 3. Schematic diagram showing sources of debris and possible paths of travel through a small cirque glacier. Solid blocks represent unrounded material; solid ovals represent rounded material. Avalanche and rockfall debris is indicated by A–R; SUPRA means supraglacial transport; EN means englacial transport; SUB means subglacial transport.

avalanches, particularly once the debris has been covered by the next year's snow accumulation. Hence, avalanche and rockfall material will be considered together as rockfall debris.

Transport of debris occurs in several ways on Arapaho Glacier. These include subglacial, englacial and supraglacial transport, movement along shear planes (probably negligible), and rockfalls or avalanches which carry material across the glacier directly to the moraine. Interplay among the various sources of debris and the modes of transportation is complex (Fig. 3).

RELATIVE AGE OF MORAINE AREAS

The moraine fronting Arapaho Glacier (Fig. 2) has generally been considered as Gannett Peak, or no more than about 300 years old (Benedict, 1968). Benedict has mapped the north-eastern part of the moraine as an Audubon (1850–950 years B.P.) rock glacier, and has mapped the extreme northern edge as an Audubon lateral moraine. Lichenometry was used to test these age assignments and to see if Gannett Peak debris represents one or more different age groups and hence depositional episodes.

Six age groups are recognized on a basis of similarity of lichen diameters (Fig. 4). Application of the non-parametric Kolmogorov–Smirnov test (Campbell, 1967) for significant differences in the populations from which the lichen diameters were drawn indicated that the groupings are valid for *L. thompsonii*, but were generally invalid for *R. geographicum* (?). This result merely indicates that slow-growing *R. geographicum* (?) lichens are not useful for making fine age distinctions on very young deposits.

Tills of different ages form the moraine south of survey point A (Fig. 4). The lichen data support at least three (groups 1, 2 and 3 and/or 4) and not more than five intervals of deposition during the Gannett Peak stade. Three is probably the more accurate figure in consideration of the effects of snowkill and the instability of the substrate on the steep morainal slopes.

The lichen diameters in group 6 are decidedly larger than those in any of the other groups. *R. geographicum* (?) diameters range up to 30 mm and the *L. thompsonii* diameters up to 113 mm. The north-eastern area of the moraine falls within group 6 and is classed as Audubon by Benedict (1968). Two additional areas of group 6 lie on the southern boundary of the till on the distal slope. The lichens in those two areas were measured on large angular boulders with a relatively high percentage lichen cover as compared to the surrounding debris. If these lichen-covered boulders are not of rockfall origin off the cirque walls, they could be Audubon till partially masked by Gannett Peak till. If so, the accumulation of till in the moraine fronting the glacier could have occurred over 1 200 years rather than only 300 years; this may help to explain how a small glacier like Arapaho Glacier could produce the tremendous volume of debris in its moraine.

CHARACTERISTICS OF THE TILL

A major problem was to find some means of determining the various sources and transportation mechanisms which affected rock fragments in the till. During glacial transport, rock fragments may be rounded, striated, polished or not affected at all; the effect produced is dependent on the mode of transportation and the lithology of the stones. In a cirque glacier which rotates as a rigid body, stones must be moved relative to bedrock to become polished, striated or rounded. In addition, till fabric may provide clues on the transporting mechanism.

In recent years, many workers (Krinsley and Donahue, 1968; Margolis and Kennett, 1971; Brown, 1973) have attempted to use electron microscopy to determine the depositional histories of quartz sand grains based on surface textures characteristic of various transportational processes. This technique was attempted here on quartz grains collected from moraines and glacier ice, including subglacial, englacial, supraglacial and rockfall sites. However,

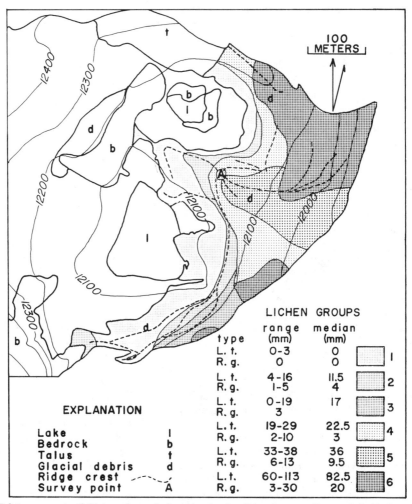

Fig. 4. *Relative age groups of debris on the terminal moraine, based on lichen diameters. L.t. stands for L. thompsonii, R.g. for R. geographicum (?).*

features diagnostic of glacial textures and of chemically weathered textures were found on grains from all sites. It was concluded that electron microscopy on grains in the till could give no conclusive evidence concerning the amounts of material contributed to a glacier by various sources.

Preliminary observations on debris in different parts of the moraine and glacier indicated varying degrees of rounding and occurrences of striations and polish. These three characters are closely associated; it is worthwhile to note that polish and striations were never found on stones with a roundness of only 0.1. To examine these characteristics in greater detail, two maps were constructed: one showing the average roundness of stones and the percentage of stones rounded >0.1 at each sampling site, and one showing the percentages of striated and polished stones at each site (Fig. 5). The sampling sites were divided into four groups on the basis of these characteristics. These four groups were tested for differences in populations using the Kolmogorov–Smirnov test (Campbell, 1967) and were found to be significantly different for all characteristics at a 5% confidence level.

Group A shows the least amounts of polish, striations and degree of rounding, and includes sites on the Audubon rock glacier, on the northern limb of the moraine, and on the ablation moraine and the glacier. The site on the northern limb receives talus from the cirque wall

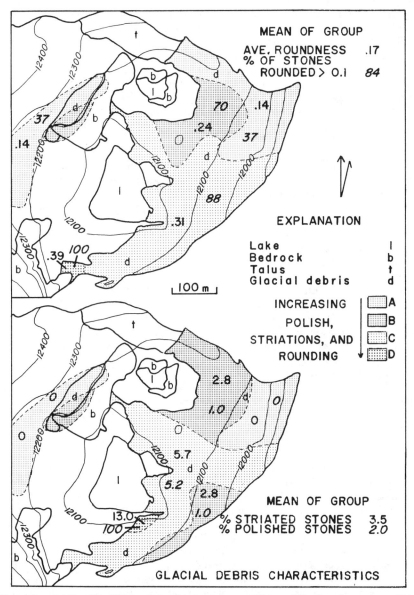

Fig. 5. *Glacial characteristics of the debris are compared in two maps, one with two aspects of roundness and one with percentages of striated and polished stones. These characters were used to divide the moraine into four areas representing debris which exhibits varying amounts of the effects of subglacial transportation.*

above. That area and the rock glacier down-valley were deposited by the northern lobe of the glacier, suggesting that that lobe had less effect on the material it carried than did the southern lobe of the glacier. Sites on the ablation moraine and the glacier probably consist largely of englacial material (Fig. 3).

One site on the ablation moraine and, in general, the northern half of the bilobate moraine comprise group B. Debris in the ablation moraine lies partly on the bedrock knob which might induce rounding, striations and polish. Data from the other sites support the notion above that the northern lobe of the glacier was generally less active than the southern one.

The highest degree of rounding and the most polish and striations are exhibited by sites in the southern half of the moraine (groups C and D). This suggests that the southern ice lobe contributed more subglacial material to the terminal moraine.

The amount of roundness, and occurrences of striations and polish, might significantly be controlled by lithology (Holmes, 1960). In order to test this hypothesis, a study was made of the relative proportions of rounding, striations and polish among pegmatites, schists, coarse-grained gneisses, fine-grained gneisses and hornblendites in the moraines. Contingency tables were constructed for comparison of the occurrence of polish and striations, and the amount of rounding (range 0.1–0.6 on the Powers scale), with these lithologic types. At a 5% level of confidence, the results showed that the fine-grained hornblende-gneisses and the hornblendites proportionally exhibit significantly greater amounts of striations, polish and rounding than do the coarser-grained gneisses, pegmatites and schists. However, the fine-grained rocks should have little effect on the data because they constitute only 6% of the sampled debris.

The characters of till, discussed above, are also a function of the distance of glacial transport. Goldthwait (1971) stated that rounding of stones will increase from 0.1 to 0.5 in the first mile of transport; till of Arapaho Glacier has been carried slightly over 0.5 mile (0.8 km), and the maximum roundness of stones was found to be 0.6. Drake (1971) reported that basally deposited continental till, similar in lithology to Arapaho Glacier till, has roundness (0.48) and per cent of stones striated (2.9) that are comparable to the till in this study. A maximum average roundness of 0.39 and 13% of stones striated was found on the Arapaho Glacier moraine. An average of 0.1% striations was reported for a continental ablation till (Drake, 1971) and this is comparable to striation frequency on englacial debris from the glacier and the ablation moraine (Fig. 5).

Rounding, striations and polish are, in summary, three associated characters which can be used to differentiate subglacially derived and transported stones from those derived from other sources and carried in other ways. Striations and polish, however, occur on a very small proportion of the debris (Fig. 5) and this is probably a function of the predominantly coarse-grained lithologies present.

PRESENT SOURCES AND TRANSPORTATION OF DEBRIS

Estimates of the contributions of the various sources and transportation mechanisms can be made based on the percentage of rounded stones. A stone is considered rounded if its roundness is greater than 0.1. It is assumed that debris which shows even a slight degree of rounding has been subglacially transported at some time during its history, while completely angular debris was derived from rockfall and has undergone only englacial, supraglacial, rockfall or avalanche transport (Fig. 3). The complex interplay of rockfall and avalanche accretion with englacial and supraglacial transport precludes the possibility of identifying material moved by an individual mechanism, so these types of transportation will be considered together. Hence, discussions that follow will attempt to differentiate between material that has been carried subglacially at some time and material that has undergone only englacial transport.

Estimates of the present contributions of various sources of debris, and on the modes of transport, were derived from five sampling sites located on the ablation moraine and on the ice immediately to the south in the central part of the glacier (Fig. 5). Two complicating factors are present. (1) The bedrock knob below the ablation moraine may be forcing the ice behind it to behave as if it were in a small sub-cirque, while the presence of this bedrock high would induce more rounding. (2) The fact that the samples used for the estimates are from the central part of the glacier means that they cannot be wholly representative of the total glacial product.

Taking Waldrop's (1964) figure of 0.9 m for the average thickness of the ablation moraine, and assuming that this deposit has been produced in a time span of 30–50 years during the rapid retreat of the glacier, I obtain a volume of 470 m³ and an average rate of production of 9.4–15.7 m³/year (these and all subsequent volumes and rates have been adjusted to allow for 40% pore space in the moraine). Of that amount, rounded debris (subglacially eroded and transported) comprises 35% or 3.3–5.5 m³/year, and unrounded debris (rockfall or avalanche material carried englacially or supraglacially) comprises 65% or 6.1–10.2 m³/year. The area of ice which contributes debris to the ablation moraine is approximately 20% of the entire glacier. Assuming that the debris production of this portion of ice is representative of the entire glacier, I obtain rates of 15–30 m³/year (30–60 mm/1 000 year) for rounded material and 35–50 m³/year (70–95 mm/1 000 year) for unrounded material. The latter figure is equivalent to a rockfall rate for the cirque.

The ablation moraine lies at a position a little more than half the distance from the headwall to the main part of the terminal moraine. Stones in the ablation moraine have therefore been carried only about half as far as stones in the terminal moraine. A reasonable assumption might be that transporting material from the headwall to the moraine could result in twice the number of rounded stones that occur in the ablation moraine. This assumption yields a present approximate production of 70% subglacially transported debris and 30% rockfall debris carried englacially or supraglacially.

To obtain the present rate of debris transport by Arapaho Glacier, an estimate of the volume of debris in the ablation moraine was combined with suspended sediment measurements made in mid-July and late August of 1972 at the moraine lake outlet on the east shore. The bedload of the stream may safely be ignored because all drainage occurs through the moraine. Error in the amount of suspended sediment load may be quite high, owing to the short time span covered by measurements, and the probable existence of other subterranean drainages. In addition, discharge records for the summer of 1972 were irregular owing to repeated malfunctions of the stream-level recorder. Accordingly, the following figures for rates and volumes from suspended sediment data must be taken as minimum estimates.

Assuming that discharge through the moraine occurs only in the summer for an average of 100 d/year, the yearly load of suspended sediment carried by the outlet stream ranges from 1.0 to 4.7 m³. Because the area of the cirque is 514 740 m², a denudation rate of 2–9 mm/1 000 year is obtained. A rate of 9.4–15.7 m³/year for the production of the debris in the ablation moraine was given previously. If the area of ice contributing material to the ablation moraine constitutes 20% of the total glacier area and is representative of the whole glacier, present deposition occurs at 48–82 m³/year or a denudation rate of 93–155 mm/1 000 year. Combining the figures obtained from the ablation moraine with those on suspended sediment, a total denudation rate of between 95 and 165 mm/1 000 year is obtained.

PAST SOURCES, TRANSPORTATION AND DEPOSITION OF DEBRIS

Data on stone roundness for the Gannett Peak moraine (Figs. 4 and 5) can be used to calculate past relative contributions of the various sources and of the various transportation mechanisms. If an estimate of 15–25 m is used for the average thickness of the moraine, and its area is 80 945 m², a total of 728 000–1 214 000 m³ is obtained for the volume of Gannett Peak debris in the terminal moraine. Assuming the Gannett Peak stade lasted approximately 300 years, the rate of production of debris was 2 430–4 050 m³/year. Data from 16 sampling sites on the moraine indicate that 88% of the debris is rounded, and thus derived and/or carried subglacially; the remainder is unrounded and thus derived by rockfall, and carried englacially or supraglacially. These data yield a production rate for rounded debris of 2 140–3 560 m³/year and for unrounded debris of 290–485 m³/year.

Calculation of the total volume of Gannett Peak material deposited by Arapaho Glacier should give an estimate of the rate of debris transport and deposition over the last 300 years. The volume of the Gannett Peak part of the end moraine was given as 728 000–1 214 000 m³. If the average thickness of the ground moraine beneath the lake is 3–5 m, its volume is 32 000–53 000 m³. The volume of the ablation moraine is approximately 785 m³. Over the whole of Gannett Peak time, transport of debris occurred at 2 500–4 200 m³/year for a denudation rate of 4 920–8 160 mm/1 000 year.

Deposition of glacial debris is the process which forms the link between debris sources and transportation methods on the one hand, and till deposits, which frequently constitute the only remaining evidence of former glaciation, on the other. Data on deposition are derived from a study of till fabric. It is recognized that the stones in an undisturbed till usually possess a fabric best shown as preferred orientations and dips of the stones. Boulton (1970, 1971) pointed out that either transverse or parallel preferred stone orientations may be exhibited by ablation, melt-out or lodgement till, depending on a number of factors. Without collecting exhaustive data, it seems impossible to differentiate between the three types of till in Arapaho Glacier cirque except in a very general way.

Data on surface and sub-surface till fabrics allow some division of sampling sites. The till-fabric strength at each of 26 sites was calculated by applying the χ^2 test, assuming that if the stones were not orientated, the numbers of stones should be equally distributed in all directions (Reheis, unpublished). Surface sites with relatively strong till fabrics are, in general, those in the southern half of the moraine, plus one site on the ablation moraine. Areas on the moraine with relatively weak till fabrics are generally those in which subsequent movement of material by surficial processes is expected, such as the steep down-valley side of the moraine, and in the northern talus-fed area.

Till fabrics combined with information on plunge, taken from below the moraine surface, provide the best information about the deposition of debris (site locations are shown on Figure 6). At site 3 the preferred orientation is down-slope, which could indicate a strong component of mass movement. However, all the stones plunged down at an angle 10° less than the dip of the moraine slope; therefore, this orientation may represent the original one parallel to the direction of glacial movement and later modified by mass movement. If so, site 3 consists either of melt-out till or lodgement till, probably the latter. At site 5, the stones have a plunge equal to the slope angle, suggesting a combination of melt-out and ablation till. Stones at site 7 nearly all plunge down into the moraine slope, representing either melt-out or lodgement till. There is a predominance of stones at sites 10 and 13 pointing down-slope with a plunge equal to the slope dip; ablation till seems to have been deposited here, along with talus material. Site 16 shows no preferred orientation as expected from its location on the rock glacier.

RELATIONSHIP OF TILL FABRIC TO GLACIAL-DEBRIS CHARACTERISTICS

An investigation was made to determine if those till fabrics with the strongest preferred orientations might be associated with debris which exhibited the most effects of glacial transportation: that is, rounding, striations and polish. The range of values for each para-meter—vector strength, percentage of striated stones, percentage of polished stones, average

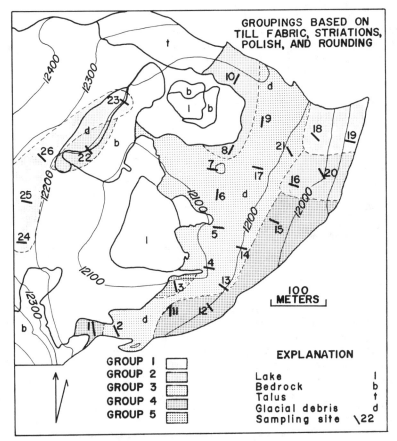

Fig. 6. *Map showing groups of sampling sites based on glacial characteristics of stones (including till fabric, polish, striations and rounding) using the GRAPH computer program. Note the similarity to the maps in Figure 5. Ranking of the groups is subjective and is based on the known values of glacial characteristics found at the sampling sites.*

roundness and percentage of stones rounded >0.1—was arbitrarily divided into six groups. The 26 moraine sites were each assigned a set of five characters according to these groups. A computer analysis resulted in the division of the moraine sites into five clusters (Estabrook, 1966) (Fig. 6). Since the characters are believed to represent effects of glacial transportation, each cluster of sites reflects an amount of such glacial characteristics, the amount increasing with the group number (Fig. 6).

Membership in the clusters was then considered to be a sixth character. A computer program called CHARANAL, developed by Estabrook (1967), showed that all characters were significantly associated with each other, with one exception. The percentage of stones rounded >0.1 is not significantly associated with till-fabric strength, or with percentages of striated and polished stones. The association between percentages of polished stones and average roundness is borderline. In general, the glacial characteristics do associate significantly with the clusters of characters for each sampling site in Figure 6. Strong till fabrics are present at sites with high rounding of stones, polish and striations.

Comparisons of past and present processes

There is a large difference between the percentages of rounded material produced over the last 50–100 years (70%) compared with that produced during the whole of the Gannett Peak stade (88%) (Table I). Accordingly, a tentative estimate of a 10–20% increase in erosive power of Arapaho Glacier during the Gannett Peak stade is proposed.

TABLE I. Data on areas, volumes and rates pertaining to the Arapaho Glacier area

Parameter	Past		Present
Cirque area			514 740 m²
Glacier area	368 250 m²		250 900 m²
Maximum velocity	8.4 m/year		5.2 m/year
Moraine volume: minimum		728 000 m³	
maximum		1 214 000 m³	
Gannett Peak debris volume: minimum		761 000 m³	
maximum		1 268 000 m³	
Estimated subglacial contribution	88%		70%
Rockfall rate	290–485 m³/year		35–50 m³/year
Denudation rate from suspended sediment load			2–9 mm/1 000 year
Denudation rate from ablation moraine			93–155 mm/1 000 year
Glacial denudation rates	4 920–8 160 mm/1 000 year		95–165 mm/1 000 year
Denudation rates corrected for ice area, minimum debris thickness, possible Audubon age of part of terminal moraine	1 260–2 040 mm/1 000 year		140–235 mm/1 000 year

This estimated increase in erosive power is seconded by the figures for rate of rockfall. Rockfall rate was observed to have diminished from 290–485 m³/year during the Gannett Peak stade to 30–50 m³/year at present (Table I).

It is apparent that well over an order of magnitude difference exists between present (95–165 mm/1 000 year) and past (4 920–8 160 mm/1 000 year) denudation rates by Arapaho Glacier (Table I). Several factors that may account for this difference can be introduced into the calculations in an effort to see if present and past rates could have been comparable. The present denudation rate was calculated using the present ice area; if this rate is adjusted for the area at the Gannett Peak maximum, I obtain a rate of approximately 140–235 mm/1 000 year for the present. In addition, the estimates of average thickness of morainal debris may be too large. If the terminal moraine is only an average of 10 m thick, and the ground moraine under the lake only 1 m thick, the denudation rate in the past would be 3 560 mm/1 000 year. Even with these adjustments, there is still more than an order of magnitude difference in the denudation rates.

Two factors remain which could resolve the discrepancy in present and past denudation rates. One is that rockfall rates and glacial erosion were greatly accelerated during the times of maximum extent of Arapaho Glacier. The second factor involves the presence of Audubon-aged debris on the south-eastern boundary of the till. If these areas truly represent Audubon till and are not relict rockfall boulders, it is probable that a substantial proportion of the terminal moraine actually consists of Audubon till covered by Gannett Peak till. Since Audubon time lasted approximately 900 years, the terminal moraine could have been produced in 1 200 years rather than in only 300 years. This results in a denudation rate of 1 260–2 040 mm/1 000 year and reduces the discrepancy between past and present denudation rates to an order of magnitude. Carrying this analysis one step further, suppose that between the Audubon and Gannett Peak stades, Arapaho Glacier shrank considerably but did not disappear, and in fact maintained its present denudation rate. Allowing the present rate of transport to extend over 2 000 years results in a theoretical volume of debris of 142 000–242 000 m³ as compared to the actual amount of 761 000–1 268 000 m³. The calculated volume is smaller than the actual volume by a factor of 5.

Having made all imaginable allowances for variables affecting the estimates of debris-production rates, it seems justifiable to state that during the periods of maximum extent of Arapaho Glacier the combined contributions of rockfall and glacial erosion of the bedrock to the glacial load increased by at least a factor of 5. Similar conclusions were given by Broecker and others (1958) for late Wisconsin deep-sea clay sedimentation rates, and by Church and Ryder (1962) in a review on denudation rates world-wide.

The amount of time required to erode Arapaho Glacier cirque below the height of its surrounding arête may be calculated from the data in Table I, assuming the cirque floor extends out to the terminal moraine. Using the adjusted Gannett Peak denudation rate, 200 000–300 000 years are required. Only 40 000–70 000 years, however, are required if the unadjusted Gannett Peak rate is employed. This may have important implications concerning the duration of cirque and valley glaciation in the Colorado Front Range, and suggests the possibility that some of the older Pleistocene glaciations may have been represented by ice-cap glaciers.

Past and present denudation rates in Arapaho Glacier cirque have been calculated as 1 260–2 040 mm/1 000 year and 140–235 mm/1 000 year, respectively. The denudation rate for Arapaho Glacier in Audubon and Gannett Peak times is quite comparable to rates quoted for other glaciers (Table II), even though all the data presented are derived from valley glaciers except for that of Andrews (1971) and Andrews and LeMasurier (1973). Even the lower rate of present erosion for Arapaho Glacier is within the range of figures quoted. Perhaps glacial denudation rate is relatively constant without regard to the size of the glacier.

TABLE II. A SUMMARY OF SOME DENUDATION RATES FROM BOTH GLACIAL AND NON-GLACIAL AREAS

Area	Erosion rate mm/1 000 year	Method	Reference
World	50–100	River loads lowering on granite	Ritter (1967)
Norway	1.05–1.28	River loads lowering on granite	Dahl (1967)
Glacial–periglacial	615		Corbel (1959)
Alps, Norway, Iceland	700	Stream load	Flint (1971, p. 120)
Iceland	640, 5 500	Suspended load	Okko (1955, p. 32)
Baffin Island	280–300	River load	Church and Ryder (1972)
British Columbia 10 000–6 000 years B.P.	25–7 300		Church and Ryder (1972)
Baffin Island	25–90	Moraine volume	Andrews (1971)
Rocky Mountains National Park (RMNP)	2 000–8 000	Moraine volume	Andrews (1971)
Baffin Island and RMNP	100–2 000	Cirque volume	Andrews (1971)
Marie Byrd Land	360–460	Cirque volume	Andrews and LeMasurier (1973)
St. Sorlin Glacier (France)	7 700	Suspended load and moraine volume	Corbel (1962)
Arapaho Glacier: past	140–235	Suspended load and moraine volume	Reheis (unpublished)
present	1 260–2 040		

ACKNOWLEDGEMENTS

I should like to express my thanks to the Institute of Arctic and Alpine Research (INSTAAR), University of Colorado, for their field support over the summers of 1972 and 1973. The Warren O. Thompson Fund, administered by the Department of Geological Sciences, University of Colorado, supported work on the electron microscope. Alisa Swartz, Keith Echelmeyer, Doug Duncan and Ted Cassman, high-school participants in INSTAAR's summer research program, assisted in the field work. Mr James B. Johnson, of Mesa College, Colorado, was an invaluable source of suggestions and patience. Drs John T. Andrews and Peter Birkeland, University of Colorado, supervised the research, read the manuscript, and offered much help and constructive criticism.

REFERENCES

Alford, D. L. Unpublished. Cirque glaciers of the Colorado Front Range: mesoscale aspects of a glacier environment. [Ph.D. thesis, University of Colorado, 1973.]

Andrews, J. T. 1971. Estimates of variations in glacial erosion from the volume of corries and moraines. *Abstracts with Programs, Geological Society of America*, Vol. 3, No. 7, p. 493.

Andrews, J. T., *and* LeMasurier, W. E. 1973. Rates of Quaternary glacial erosion and corrie formation, Marie Byrd Land, Antarctica. *Geology*, Vol. 1, No. 2, p. 75–80.

Barry, R. G. 1972. Climatic environment of the east slope of the Colorado Front Range. *University of Colorado. Institute of Arctic and Alpine Research. Occasional Paper* No. 3.

Benedict, J. B. 1967. Recent glacial history of an alpine area in the Colorado Front Range, U.S.A. I. Establishing a lichen-growth curve. *Journal of Glaciology*, Vol. 6, No. 48, p. 817–32.

Benedict, J. B. 1968. Recent glacial history of an alpine area in the Colorado Front Range, U.S.A. II. Dating the glacial deposits. *Journal of Glaciology*, Vol. 7, No. 49, p. 77–87.

Beschel, R. E. 1961. Dating rock surfaces by lichen growth and its application to glaciology and physiography (lichenometry). (*In* Raasch, G. O., *ed. Geology of the Arctic: proceedings of the first international symposium on Arctic geology held in Calgary, Alberta, January 11–13, 1960*. Toronto, University of Toronto Press, Vol. 2, p. 1044–62.)

Boulton, G. S. 1967. The development of a complex supraglacial moraine at the margin of Sørbreen, Ny Friesland, Vestspitsbergen. *Journal of Glaciology*, Vol. 6, No. 47, p. 717–35.

Boulton, G. S. 1970. On the deposition of subglacial and melt-out tills at the margins of certain Svalbard glaciers. *Journal of Glaciology*, Vol. 9, No. 56, p. 231–45.

Boulton, G. S. 1971. Till genesis and fabric in Svalbard, Spitzbergen. (*In* Goldthwait, R. P., *ed. Till: a symposium*. [Columbus], Ohio, Ohio State University Press, p. 41–72.)

Broecker, W. S., *and others*. 1958. The relation of deep sea sedimentation rates to variations in climate, by W. S. Broecker, K. K. Turekian and S. C. Heezen. *American Journal of Science*, Vol. 256, No. 7, p. 503–17.

Brown, J. E. 1973. Depositional histories of sand grains from surface textures. *Nature*, Vol. 242, No. 5397, p. 396–98.

Campbell, R. C. 1967. *Statistics for biologists*. Cambridge, University Press.

Church, M., *and* Ryder, J. M. 1972. Paraglacial sedimentation: a consideration of fluvial processes conditioned by glaciation. *Geological Society of America. Bulletin*, Vol. 83, No. 10, p. 3059–71.

Corbel, J. 1959. Vitesse de l'érosion. *Zeitschrift für Geomorphologie*, Bd. 3, Ht. 1, p. 1–28.

Corbel, J. 1962. *Neiges et glaciers*. Paris, Armand Colin.

Dahl, R. 1967. Post-glacial micro-weathering of bedrock surfaces in the Narvik district of Norway. *Geografiska Annaler*, Vol. 49A, Nos. 2–4, p. 155–66.

Drake, L. D. 1971. Evidence for ablation and basal till in east central New Hampshire. (*In* Goldthwait, R. P., *ed. Till: a symposium*. [Columbus], Ohio, Ohio State University Press, p. 73–91.)

Estabrook, G. F. 1966. A mathematical model in graph theory for biological classification. *Journal of Theoretical Biology*, Vol. 12, No. 3, p. 297–310.

Estabrook, G. F. 1967. An information theory model for character analysis. *Taxon*, Vol. 16, No. 2, p. 86–97.

Flint, R. F. 1971. *Glacial and Quaternary geology*. New York, John Wiley and Sons, Inc.

Goldthwait, R. P. 1971. Introduction to till, today. (*In* Goldthwait, R. P., *ed. Till: a symposium*. [Columbus], Ohio, Ohio State University Press, p. 3–26.)

Harris, S. A. 1968. Till fabrics and speed of movement of the Arapahoe Glacier, Colorado. *Professional Geographer*, Vol. 20, No. 3, p. 195–98.

Holmes, C. D. 1960. Evolution of till-stone shapes, central New York. *Bulletin of the Geological Society of America*, Vol. 71, No. 11, p. 1645–60.

Krinsley, D. H., *and* Donahue, J. 1968. Environmental interpretation of sand grain surface textures by electron microscopy. *Geological Society of America. Bulletin*, Vol. 79, No. 6, p. 743–48.

Margolis, S. V., *and* Kennett, J. P. 1971. Cenozoic paleoglacial history of Antarctica recorded in subantarctic deep-sea cores. *American Journal of Science*, Vol. 271, No. 1, p. 1–36.

Okko, V. 1955. Glacial drift in Iceland, its origin and morphology. *Bulletin de la Commission Géologique de Finlande*, No. 170.

Reheis, M. J. Unpublished. Source, transportation, and deposition of debris on Arapaho Glacier, Front Range, Colorado. [M.S. thesis, University of Colorado, 1974.]

Ritter, D. F. 1967. Rates of denudation. *Journal of Geological Education*, Vol. 15, No. 4, p. 154–59.

Sharp, R. P. 1949. Studies of the supraglacial debris on valley glaciers. *American Journal of Science*, Vol. 247, No. 5, p. 289–315.

Waldrop, H. A. 1964. Arapaho Glacier, a sixty-year record. *University of Colorado Studies. Series in Geology*, No. 3 p. 1–37.

Webber, P. J., *and* Andrews, J. T. 1973. Lichenometry: a commentary. *Arctic and Alpine Research*, Vol. 5, No. 4, p. 295–302.

Soil loss in the Colorado Front Range: Sampling design and areal variation

by

Michael J. Bovis, Vancouver, Canada

with 3 figures and 7 tables

Zusammenfassung. Raten der oberflächlichen Bodenabtragung werden zunächst für die montane, subalpine und alpine Vegetationszone der Front Ranges, basierend auf 30 Meßstellen verglichen. Ein zufällig angeordnetes Meßnetz mit flächenhaften Wiederholungsmessungen wurde benutzt, um zonale, intrazonale und lokale Veränderungen durch Varianzanalyse voneinander zu trennen. Die ursprüngliche Aufteilung in die Vegetationszonen erwies sich als unbrauchbar in bezug auf die statistischen Vergleiche der durchschnittlichen Raten. Eine Neugruppierung der Meßstellen bezüglich ihrer Resultate stimmt gut überein mit der Verteilung von Standortstypen und Pflanzengesellschaften. Signifikante Unterschiede in den durchschnittlichen Abtragungsraten wurden gefunden zwischen a) Tundra-Wiesen, b) subalpinen Wäldern und dicht bewachsenen montanen Standorten und c) trockenen montanen und alpinen Lagen. Innerhalb von c) liegt der montane Mittelwert höher, was darauf hindeutet, daß die größten Bewegungen beträchtlich unterhalb der Waldgrenze stattfinden. Der dominante Prozeß ist Erosion durch Regenaufschlag.

Summary. Rates of surficial soil movement are compared between montane, subalpine and alpine zones of the Front Range. The comparison is based on 30 sites. A randomized, stratified design, with replication, is employed to separate zonal, intra-zonal and local variations by analysis of variance. The initial sub-division of sites by major cover types proved unworkable in statistical comparisons of mean rates. Re-stratification according to soil movement controls, measured in the field, corresponded closely with stand types and species associations. Mean rates are significantly different between: a) tundra meadows, b) subalpine forest and dense montane stands, c) dry alpine and montane sites. Within c), the montane mean is higher, suggesting a regional maximum of movement well below timberline. The dominant process is rainsplash erosion.

Résumé. Les vitesses des mouvements surficiels du sol sont d'abord comparées entre les zones principales de vegetation montane, subalpine et alpine du Front Range. Cette comparaison est bassée sur 30 emplacements. Une selection au hasard des points de meusure avec des répétitions spatiales est utilisée pour séparer des variations zonales, intrazonales et locales avec l'analyse de variance. La stratification initiale par types de couverture a donnée des résultats non-significants lors d'une comparaison des vitesses moyennes d'érosion. Une nouvelle stratification des emplacements, basée sur les variables qui controlent les déplacements du sol, correspond bien avec la distribution des associations des espèces. Les moyennes des vitesses montrent une différence significative entre: a) les prés du toundra, b) des forêts subalpines et des parties denses

188

de la forêt montane, c) les emplacements montane et alpine sèches. Dans dernier cas c), la moyenne de montane est plus haut, indiquant une maximum du mouvement bien sous la ligne de la forêt. Le processus dominant est l'érosion par la pluie.

Introduction

This study is a comparison of surficial soil movement between forested and alpine tundra zones, conducted along a topographic transect down the east slope of the Front Range (fig. 1). The study is based on a 22-month record of observations. The impetus for the study derives from the fact that previous work on soil movement rates in the Boulder area had been confined to the alpine zone: for example, WALLACE (1968); BENEDICT (1970); WHITE (1971); FAHEY (1973); THORN (1976). These studies, in keeping with many others conducted in arctic and alpine environments over the past 25 years, have reported rates of movement from specific landforms, including rock glaciers, stone stripes, solifluction lobes, talus slopes and nivation hollows. While it may be argued that these forms reflect the dominant processes of cold environments, both at present and in the recent past, they may not be representative of tundra conditions from an *areal* standpoint. Also, it is possible that the rates of movement reported from some of these features are well above the average rate for the tract in which they occur. This implies bias toward the selection of relatively active sites, for which three causes are suggested. First, some studies have been concerned primarily with process mechanisms, with no intention of providing areally weighted estimates of movement. Selection of active features is therefore logical, in that the components of movement attributable to various mechanisms may be more easily separated than at less active sites. Secondly, techniques to monitor rates of soil movement are usually relatively crude. Selection of active sites therefore ensures that measured displacements exceed measurement error by an appreciable factor. Finally, many

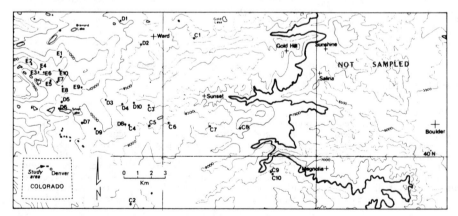

Fig. 1. Locations of study sites. Thickened contour line is approximate demarcation between sampled and non-sampled areas.

studies involve a time constraint, which favours selection of sites that will yield measurable changes over the period of study. These points may be overlooked when measured rates are compared between different environments (for example, BENEDICT 1970; CARSON & KIRKBY 1972), although it is difficult to assess the degree to which comparisons are invalidated by bias in site selection.

In this study, an attempt is made to overcome some of the problems of sampling bias. Although beset by practical constraints, the design adopted allows apparent differences in rates of movement between montane, subalpine and alpine environments to be qualified in terms of intrazonal and local variations.

The study area

The relief of the area ranges from 1,650 m at the western edge of the Great Plains to about 4,000 m along the Continental Divide, just beyond the western margin of the study area (fig. 1). Virtually all of the area is underlain by granites, gneisses and schists (LOVERING & GODDARD 1950) that weather to non-cohesive soils. Much of the area above 2,700 m has been glaciated.

Relatively short climatic records (BARRY 1973) point to a precipitation increase from about 55 cm per annum (areas below about 2,600 m) to over 100 cm at 3,750 m. Over this same range, the proportion falling as snow increases from about 50 percent to 80 percent.

MARR (1967) recognized four major vegetation zones related to the topographic and precipitation gradients: Lower Montane forest (2,00—2,600 m); Upper Montane forest (2,600—3,000 m); Subalpine forest (3,000—3,600 m); Alpine tundra (above 3,600 m). Below about 2,700 m, aspect is an important cover type control. Above about 2,700 m aspect contrasts gradually diminish as the montane forest is replaced by dense subalpine stands of aspen, Lodgepole pine and, at higher elevations, Engelmann spruce and Subalpine fir. Litter cover is virtually unbroken through this zone and mosses provide further protection to the soil surface.

Areal sampling design

Three principles of experimental design: randomization, stratification and replication, were followed as closely as the practical constraints of the study would allow. The first step involved the generation of 210 random pairs of co-ordinates over the study area to provide locations for potential study sites and a framework for stratifying the study area according to soil movement controls. At each of the 210 points (each one actually an area 50 m × 50 m at a map scale of 1:24,000), five variables were measured from existing source material: (1) rock type (from LOVERING & GODDARD 1950); (2) cover type (from MARR 1967); (3) slope angle; (4) slope aspect; (5) elevation (all from U.S. Geological Survey topographic maps).

Stratification of sites into major clusters, using the five control variables, was performed by a similarity-clustering routine described by ANDREWS & ESTABROOK (1971). A nominal coding of variables (1) and (2) ruled out the use of conventional Q-mode techniques. A coefficient of similarity is computed for any pair of objects (sites), based on nominally coded information, although subjective decisions must be made as to the number of levels, or 'states' of each variable, and the degree of similarity between adjacent states. This is a major weakness of the method. For any two objects A and B, the similarity index over all variables measured on those objects is defined to be:

$$S = \frac{1}{N} \sum_{i=1}^{N} f(K_{im}, K_{in}) \qquad 0 < S < 1$$

N is the number of variables and $f(K_{im}, K_{in})$ is an empirical function describing the similarity between states m and n of variable K_i, assigned to objects A and B respectively. If m = n over N variables, then both objects are identical and S = 1. Clustering begins with pairs or trios that are identical or have S values close to 1.0. Relaxation of S allows additional objects to be drawn into existing clusters until all clusters are joined. Five primary clusters are identified, that correspond roughly with the geographic limits of major vegetation zones identified by MARR (1967) (see table 1).

Table 1.   Stratification of sites

Stratum	Description of Cover Type	Number of sites
A	Piedmont grasses and ecotome area	19
B	Lower montane forest	12
C	Upper montane forest	98
D	Subalpine forest	59
E	Alpine tundra	22

Sites were established in strata C, D and E only. Ten sites were selected from each stratum, providing a balanced statistical design, by drawing three-digit random numbers. To allow regular servicing of sites (most of the work was conducted single-handed), points located more than 1 km. from a vehicular access point could not be included as field study sites. This practical constraint means that the sites selected are no longer random but are considered to be representative of the study area. This assertion is examined under 'Discussion'.

To provide a measure of local variation, two sites were picked at random from the ten in each of the three groups by drawing random single digits. At each of these six sites, two replicate sites were installed within a sample space 50 m × 50 m. Each replicate was located by drawing random two-digit co-ordinates. This brought the total number of installations to 42.

Design of installations

A Gerlach trough, virtually identical to that described by LEOPOLD & EMMETT (1967), was installed at each of the 42 sites to measure surficial soil movement (hereafter referred to as *soil loss*) (see fig. 2). The concrete base was cast in situ and moulded to the micro-relief features at each site. This minimized site disturbance,

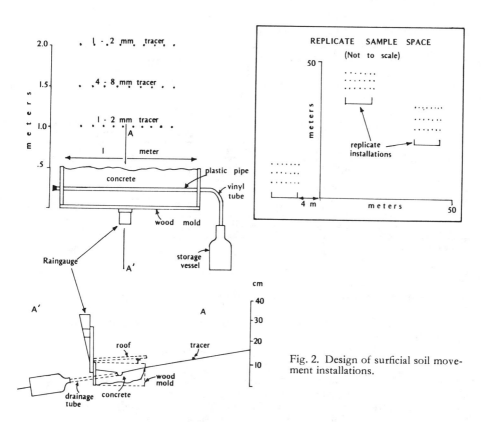

Fig. 2. Design of surficial soil movement installations.

especially in areas of coarse-textured soils. The mass of each trough was about 20 kg and none suffered perceptible displacement over the study period. To further reduce disturbance, a decision was made not to install enclosed plot boundaries above each trough. Previous work has indicated some serious drawbacks of using fractional-acre plots in steep mountain terrain (HAYWARD 1967). To provide an estimate of the area contributing material, painted tracers, diameters 1—2 mm and 4—8 mm, were placed at distances 1 m, 1.5 m and 2 m upslope of each trough, the latter providing a reference frame for monitoring particle displacements.

Areal variation in soil loss

Sites with replicates are examined first to evaluate the relative importance of zonal, intra-zonal and local variations in soil loss. Since replicates were not installed until May 1972, this first phase of the analysis is restricted to the period June 1972—June 1973. In this context, the term *site* refers to the sample space containing the three Gerlach troughs (fig. 2); the term *plot* is reserved for an individual Gerlach trough. Zonal variation between the montane, subalpine and alpine zones occurs as a column effect in table 2; intrazonal variation as a row effect; and local

Table 2   Soil loss (grams), replicated sites June 1972 —June 1973*

	Zones		
Sites (2 per zone)	Montane forest (Zone C)	Subalpine forest (Zone D)	Alpine tundra (Zone E)
1	C2: 68.6 (4.2) C2A: 91.3 (4.5) C2B: 330.1 (5.8)	D7: 2.8 (1.0) D7A: 47.4 (3.9) D7B: 20.1 (3.0)	E6: 85.2 (4.4) E6A: 156.8 (5.1) E6B: 62.8 (4.1)
Geometric means	127.4	13.9	94.3
2	C8: 517.4 (6.3) C8A: 149.0 (5.0) C8B: 41.5 (3.7)	D10: 0.9 (—.1) D10A: 7.1 (2.0) D10B: 2.4 (.9)	E9: 118.1 (4.8) E9A: 70.9 (4.3) E9B: 102.2 (4.6)
Geometric means	147.4	2.5	94.9
Zone means	137.0	5.9	94.6

Grand mean 42.4

* $\mathrm{Log}_e X$ transformed values in parentheses.

variation as 'within cell' differences. The following analysis of variance model is used:

$$(1) \qquad x_{ijk} = \mu + a_i + \beta_{ij} + e_{ijk}$$

in which μ is the grand mean; a_i the departure of the ith zone mean from μ; β_{ij} the departure of the ijth site mean from its zone mean, μ_i. The e_{ijk} are 'error' terms that measure the statistical fluctuation of the soil loss random variable, X, at each site (i.e., plot values). Two null hypotheses are tested:

H_0: $a_i = 0$ for equality of the three zone means, or: $\mu_C = \mu_D = \mu_E$

H_0: $\beta_{ij} = 0$, an assertion of no intra-zonal variation with respect to site means. An important requirement is that the error terms by independent of one another. Since plots are never closer than about 15 m apart, plot interactions may be disregarded. The requirements of a normal distribution and common variance for the e_{ijk}, which amounts to the x_{ijk} having these properties also, appear to have been violated (table 2). This is problematical in view of the small sample sizes and the question of transforming the data to meet these two requirements arises. SCHEFFÉ (1967, Chapter 10) suggests that the transformation used should reflect theoretical or empirical knowledge of the particular variable. Empirical evidence (CAINE 1968) points to a strong lognormal tendency in the sample distribution of tracer displacements, measured at the 'plot scale', and in the study reported here, the distribution of both annual soil loss and tracer displacement show this same tendency (fig. 3). This was also detected by the writer in data presented by COSTIN et al. (1960) and HAYWARD (1967). A logarithmic transformation of the data in table 2 therefore seems appropriate.

The first null hypothesis is rejected for zone means (table 3) and inspection of table 2 suggests $\mu_D < \mu_E < \mu_C$, (C = montane, D = subalpine, E = alpine). The second null hypothesis is retained, suggesting that between-site differences, within zones, are small. Between-plot variation at sites accounts for about 22 percent of the total variance. Table 2 indicates that most of this occurs at forested sites, probably a reflection of the interaction between canopy closure and litter protection to the soil surface.

Table 3   Analysis of variance, soil loss: June 1972–June 1973

Source of variation	Degrees of freedom	Sum of squares	Mean square	F-ratio
Between zones	2	35.58	17.79	18.53 $F_{.05}(2,12) = 3.89$
Between sites, within zones	3	4.47	1.49	1.55
Between plots	12	11.50	.96	$F_{.05}(3,12) = 3.49$
Total	17	51.54		

Table 4   Soil loss (grams) 29 sites: September 1971–June 1973*

Sites	Montane forest (Zone C)	Subalpine forest (Zone D)	Alpine tundra (Zone E)
1	1,300.6 (7.2)	1.0 (0.0)	2.2 (.8)
2	97.7 (4.6)	73.8 (4.3)	49.6 (3.9)
3	0.9 (—.1)	26.2 (3.3)	2.8 (1.0)
4	6.9 (1.9)	10.3 (2.3)	15.0 (2.7)
5	42.3 (3.7)	0.2 (—1.6)	82.1 (4.4)
6	1.8 (.6)	0.5 (—.7)	132.4 (4.9)
7	18.9 (2.9)	4.0 (1.4)	17.3 (2.9)
8	864.2 (6.8)	9.2 (2.2)	3.6 (1.3)
9	14.5 (2.7)	9.2 (2.2)	136.8 (4.9)
10	51.2 (3.9)	2.6 (1.0)	No data
Geometric means:	30.6	4.2	19.6

* Log $_e$ X transformed values in parentheses

The foregoing remarks are based on a limited number of replicated sites; therefore zonal means are tested using all sites over the full 22 month period of study (table 4). In this context, *site* refers to an original trough installation (i.e., prior to the replication phase of May 1972). No data are presented for E—10 since this was not established until May 1972. The null hypothesis H_0: $\mu_C = \mu_D = \mu_E$ is tested using log-transformed data in the one-way model:

(2) $x_{ij} = \mu + a_i + e_{ij}$

in which μ and a_i are as defined previously, and e_{ij} now refers to sites rather than plots. The null hypotheses is retained at the 5 percent level (table 5) and although the zonal geometric means in table 4 again suggest $\mu_D < \mu_E < \mu_C$, this is not statistically significant on account of considerable intrazonal variation. There are two

Table 5   Analysis of variance, soil loss: Sept. 1971—June 1973

Source of variation	Degrees of freedom	Sum of squares	Mean square	F-ratio
Between zones	2	21.49	10.74	2.74
Within zones	26	101.98	3.92	$F_{.05}(2,26) = 3.37$
Total	28	123.47		

interpretations of this result. First, there are in fact no real differences between the mean rates for the three zones. Alternatively, differences exist, but for a variety of reasons, the design has not detected them. This amounts to lack of sensitivity, probably resulting from the method used to stratify sites: notably, the use of map data and the use of subjective criteria in the cluster analysis.

In view of the large intrazonal component, the homogeneity of clusters C, D and E was examined using site characteristics, measured adjacent to each trough subsequent to their installation. This yielded a total of 19 variables composed as follows: slope angle; elevation; arboreal canopy closure (subjective estimate); ground cover (4 variables); grain-size parameters and organic content of surface soil (4 variables); soil 'strength' (4 variables); infiltration characteristics (4 variables). Site clusters were generated from these data by a method developed by CLARK (1974). Since the original score axes are not orthogonal, a principal components analysis is conducted first. Component scores then define the co-ordinates of each plot, from which the Euclidean distances between plots are known and held in an M X M matrix (assuming M plots). Initially, M single-member clusters exist; then proximate points form clusters and the distance matrix is collapsed. Three distinct clusters emerge (table 6) that transgress the boundaries of clusters C, D and E. This is not surprising in view of the three-orders-of-magnitude scale change from map 'points' (areas about 50 m × 50 m) to 'plots' (about 1 m²). Sites C4, C5, C7, D5 and E6B (second plot of E6 series) do not belong to any of the primary clusters, but do not form a separate sub-cluster.

The stratification of sites based on controls measured at the plot scale provides a more sensitive framework for detecting overall zonal differences. The hypothesis $H_0: \mu_1 = \mu_2 = \mu_3$ is tested (table 7) using the one-way model (equation 2). Subscripts refer to clusters in table 6. Since the error component in table 7 refers to intrazonal variation, replicate plots are excluded. The sample sizes in clusters 1, 2 and 3 are therefore 13, 7 and 7 respectively. Exclusion of replicates allows the test to be based on the full 22 month period of study.

H_0 is clearly rejected in table 7. The geometric means for clusters 1, 2 and 3 are 6 g, 155 g and 7 g over the 22 month period. Rates within dense forest stands and stable tundra meadow areas are therefore roughly equal and about 20 times lower than the mean rate from sparsely covered montane forest and alpine tundra areas in Cluster 2. Comparison of alpine and montane means within Cluster 2 is instructive, albeit based on very small samples (table 6). The geometric mean of C1, C8 and D2 = 436 g; the mean of E5, E6, E7 and E9 = 71 g. This suggests that the regional maximum of soil loss may be located within sparsely vegetated montane forest areas.

Table 6   Site clusters based on component scores and areal assessment by cover types.

Cluster number	Sites included in cluster	Geometric mean soil loss (grams)	Cover types	Percent* of study area
1	C2 C3 C6 C9 C10 D1 D3 D4 D6 D7 D7A D7B D8 D9 D10 D10A D10B	6	(a) Ponderosa pine/Douglasfir (b) Douglasfir/Engelmann spr. (c) Lodgepole pine/aspen (d) Lodgepole pine/Ponderosa pine/Douglasfir/aspen (e) Engelmann spruce/subalpine fir (f) Lodgepole pine/Ponderosa pine Sub-total:	11.2 2.0 5.2 16.3 9.1 9.3 53.1
2	C1 C2A C2B C8 C8A C8B D2 E5 E6 E6A E7 E9 E9A E9B	155	(a) Ponderosa pine with shrub (b) Dry alpine tundra and dry sites within forest-tundra ecotone region Sub-total:	3.4 5.7 9.1
3	E1 E2 E3 E4 E8 E10	7	(a) Alpine meadow	11.5
			Total:	73.7

* Study area as defined by sampled area in fig. 1.

Table 7   Analysis of variance, soil loss: Sept. 1971—June 1973 (Component-score clusters)

Source of variation	Degrees of freedom	Sum of squares	Mean square	F-ratio
Between zones	2	97.46	48.73	178.68
Within zones	22	6.00	.27	$F_{.05}(2,22) = 3.37$
Total	24	103.46		

Discussion

The analysis of areal variation assumes a representative sample of sites. This can be tested with respect to vegetal units, since table 6 indicates the broad correspondence between cover types and clusters derived from soil movement controls. The cover type areas (table 6) were generated from the maps in KREBS (1973) and KOMARKOVA & WEBBER (1976), both published after the completion of this study. Sites were located in eight of the 20 units recognized by KREBS, representing 60 percent of the sampled area. Although cover types (e) and (f) of Cluster 1 (table 6) were not sampled, it is likely that their soil movement characteristics would be very close to those of units (b) and (d) respectively. The 30 sites are therefore considered to represent about 74 percent of the sampled area (see fig. 1).

196

Cluster 3 in table 6 has a very low mean rate of soil loss and yet occupies about two-thirds of the alpine tundra zone. This fact, in combination with the very low figure for the subalpine forest suggests that the overall soil loss from the alpine and subalpine zones is quite low. This provides an important counter-weight to previous studies which leave the impression of high rates of surficial and mass movement within the alpine zone. The suggestion of a montane zone maximum of soil loss also accords with the observations of HEEDE (1970) in a similar Front Range environment near Colorado Springs. He noted that gullying was most pronounced between the foothills and the *lower* boundary of the sub-alpine forest. Both the soil loss maximum and the incidence of gullying appear to be the product of summer convectional rainstorms. Also, in this study, there is a pronounced summer maximum of soil loss at all elevations, including the alpine tundra. This points to rainsplash as the dominant agent of surficial erosion in the Front Range. This is supported by the recent findings of CAINE (1976) in the San Juan Mountains of southwest Colorado.

The cover type associated with maximum soil loss occupies about three per-cent of the study area (table 6). Taken in conjunction with the low mean rate in cluster 1, this implies that a representative sample of sites should possess a positi-vely skew distribution such as the lognormal (fig. 3). The detection of this effect in other studies indicates that it is not simply local to the study area. In the present context, the representative sample is drawn from a range of environments, each of

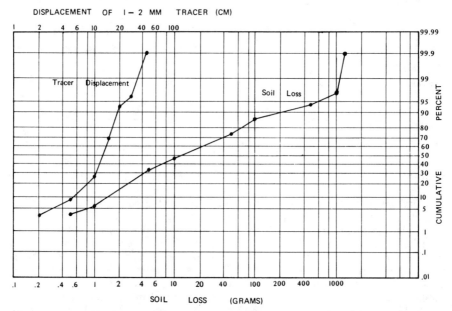

Fig. 3. Log X probability plots of: (1) Total soil loss, September 1971—June 1973 (29 sites), (2) Mean displacement of 1—2 mm tracer, October 1971—June 1973 (26 sites).

which possesses a theoretical soil loss mean and variance. Although the form of the soil loss distributions in each of the three primary site clusters cannot be known with certainty from such small samples (table 6), the coefficient of variation (c) in each case provides a clue. The values are: $c_1 = 1.6$; $c_2 = 1.4$; $c_3 = 1.4$, where subscripts refer to clusters, and c is the ratio of the sample standard deviation to the sample mean, based on the original untransformed data. Non-normality is indicated in each case, since all c-values are much greater than 0.5 (AGTERBERG 1974: 211). The roughly equal values of c from the three environments suggest a tendency toward constant proportionality between the standard deviation and the mean, in each cluster.

Conclusion

The physical constraint of accessibility in this study means that the sample of sites is not strictly random, though it represents approximately three-quarters of the sampled area. This demonstrates the advantage of starting with a set of randomly generated co-ordinates when areally weighted estimates of soil movement are required. Unless randomization and replication are included explicitly in studies of rates of slope erosion, there is little or no basis for making comparisons between different environments.

Areal stratification by stand types or species associations provides a surrogate for 'ground level' measurement of erosion controls at the plot scale. Also, vegetal information is less 'point specific' since relatively homogeneous areas up to 1 km² in size or larger often emerge, and provide a natural framework for replication. A strong tendency to lognormal distribution is shown for soil loss data when sites are drawn from a mixed population composed of strata which differ considerably in mean rate yet only slightly in terms of coefficient of variation. Correlation between the mean and variance will require the allocation of a disproportionate number of replicate sites to areas where slope erosion processes appear to be operating most intensively. These should occupy a very small proportion of the total area.

Acknowledgements

This study was supported by equipment grants from the Geological Society of America (Penrose Award). Logistical support was provided by the Institute of Arctic and Alpine Research, University of Colorado, Boulder. Thanks are due to NEL CAINE, R. F. HADLEY and J. D. IVES for support and guidance. Field assistance was provided during two summers under the INSTAAR Summer Program, funded by the National Science Foundation.

References

AGTERBERG, F. P. (1974): Geomathematics: mathematical background and geo-science applications. — Elsevier Scientific, Amsterdam.

ANDREWS, J. T. & G. F. ESTABROOK (1971): Applications of information and graph theory to multivariate geomorphological analyses. — J. Geology, **79**: 207—221.

BARRY, R. G. (1973): A climatological transect along the east slope of the Front Range, Colorado. — Arctic and Alpine Research, **5**: 89—110.

BENEDICT, J. B. (1970): Downslope soil movement in a Colorado Alpine Region: Rates, processes and climatic significance. — Arctic and Alpine Research, **2**: 165—226.

CAINE, T. N. (1968): The log-normal distribution and rates of soil movement: an example. — Révue Géom. Dynamique, **18**: 1—7.

— (1976): Summer rainstorms in an alpine environment and their influences on soil erosion, San Juan Mountains, Colorado. — Arctic and Alpine Research, **8**: 183—196.

CARSON, M. A. & M. J. KIRKBY (1972): Hillslope Form and Process. — Cambridge, 475 pp.

CLARK, J. (1974): Mud flows in the San Juan Mountains, Colorado: Controls and Work. — Unpubl. M. A. Thesis, Univ. of Colorado.

COSTIN, A. G., WIMBUSH, D. J. & C. Kerr (1960): Studies in catchment hydrology in the Australian Alps. II — Surface runoff and soil loss. — CSIRO Div. of Plant Industry.

FAHEY, B. D. (1973): An analysis of diurnal freeze-thaw and frost heave cycles in the Indian Peaks region of the Colorado Front Range. — Arctic and Alpine Research, **5**: 269—281.

HAYWARD, J. A. (1969): The use of fractional-acre plots to predict soil loss from a mountain catchment. — Lincoln Papers in Water Resources, **7**, Canterbury, New Zealand, 93 p.

HEEDE, B. H. (1970): Morphology of gullies in the Colorado Rocky Mountains. — Bull. of the Internat. Assoc. of Sci. Hydrol., **15**: 79—89.

KOMARKOVA, V. & P. J. WEBBER (1976): Vegetation map, Niwot Ridge, Colorado. — (U.S. 1BP Tundra Biome program). Inst. Arctic & Alpine Research, Boulder, Colorado.

KREBS, P. V. (1973): Vegetation. — In: MADOLE, R. F. (Ed.): Environmental inventory and land-use recommendations, for Boulder County, Colorado, pp. 63—79. — Inst. Arctic & Alpine Research Occasional Paper, No. 8.

LEOPOLD, L. B. & W. W. EMMETT (1967): On the design of a Gerlach trough. — Révue Géom. Dynamique, **17**: 172.

LOVERING, T. S. and E. N. GODDARD (1950): Geology and ore deposits of the Front Range, Colorado. — USGS Prof. Paper, **223**: 219 p.

MARR, J. W. (1967): Ecosystems of the east slope of the Front Range in Colorado. — Univ. of Colorado, Stud. in Biol., **8**: 134 p.

SCHEFFE, H. (1959): The analysis of variance. — Wiley, New York.

THORN, C. E. (1976): Quantitative evaluation of nivation in the Colorado Front Range. — Geol. Soc. Amer. Bull., **87**: 1169—1178.

WALLACE, R. G. (1968): Types and rates of alpine mass movement, west edge of Boulder County, Colorado Front Range. — Unpubl. Ph. D thesis, Ohio State Univ., Columbus, Ohio.

WHITE, S. E. (1971): Rock glacier studies in the Colorado Front Range, 1961—68. — Arctic and Alpine Research, **3**: 43—64.

Address of the author:
M. J. BOVIS, Department of Geography, University of British Columbia, Vancouver, B.C. V6T 1W5, Canada.

Part 3
Glaciology and Hydrology

Overview
*T. Nel Caine**

The snow and ice of the alpine zone in Colorado constitute
its most important economic resource - at least 20% of the state's
streamflow comes from the 5% of its area that lies above timberline. This snow and ice has, however, received relatively little
study, in contrast to the annual snow cover of the more extensive zone below timberline. This imbalance has been somewhat
redressed by work done in the last 20 years, but knowledge of
alpine hydrologic processes remains empirical in nature and includes few general theories and models.

It is evident from the sample of results reproduced here
that studies of alpine snow and ice in the Colorado Front Range
have followed two lines. Glaciological research with an academic
bias so far has been conducted almost entirely through the University of Colorado. In contrast, applied research aimed at man-
aging the snow cover for water resources and hazard mitigation
has developed through the U.S. Forest Service (Rocky Mountain
Forest and Range Experiment Station). The latter work has been
comprehensively summarized by Martinelli (1975) while Leaf (1975)
provides a companion summary of work in the forests just below
timberline.

Although only relatively recent work is included in the
first five papers of this collection, the small glaciers of the
Front Range have been studied scientifically since the beginning
of the century (e.g., Lee, 1900). The start of modern glaciological research in the area is represented here by Waldrop (1964)
who provides a 60-year history of the Arapaho Glacier, based upon
the early written records and his own observations (these include
some of the few measurements of glacier movement made in the
Front Range). This work is complemented by selections from the
survey of the Front Range glaciers by Outcalt and MacPhail (1965).

*Institute of Arctic and Alpine Research
 University of Colorado
 Boulder, Colorado 80309

The latter clearly states the hypothesis, first enunciated early in the century (e.g., Lee, 1922), that the continued existence of these cirque glaciers depends upon the contribution of wind-blown snow to their mass balance.

Since the mid-1960s, mass balance studies on the Front Range glaciers have continued almost constantly, if not entirely consistently. Research interest has shifted from glacier to glacier in such a way that few observational records have been maintained on the same glacier for more than one or two years. At the University of Colorado, J.T. Andrews has been the main inspiration for this work and a number of reports included here derive from theses completed under his direction. Johnson's work (1978) is of this kind and includes the longest continuous study of a single glacier in the Front Range. It clearly illustrates the wide year-to-year variability of the mass balance components of Arikaree Glacier, a variability that seems characteristic of all the glaciers in the Front Range. A similar level of variability is also evident in the spatial dimension and is apparent from Alford's study (1977) of 13 glaciers during the 1969-1970 budget year. This work explains the spatial variability by the orientation of the cirques as a control of both accumulation and ablation. This modification of the snow drifting hypothesis emphasizes the importance of winter storm tracks and the wind conditions following the few major storms that account for most of the snowfall in any Colorado winter. The differences in ablation rates between glaciers which are explained by Alford's model are further analyzed in the work of Cofer (1972). This study was conducted during the same balance year as that of Alford.

The hydrologic processes of the alpine zone and their management provides the common theme for the last three papers reproduced here. In general, these are empirical studies although the work of Berg (1977) is important for introducing a theoretical basis to the study of snow redistribution by the wind.

Carroll (1976) offers the only available quantitative study of the water budget of a single alpine catchment in the Front Range. This paper is important for its recognition that the alpine belt is one of unusually high hydrologic efficiency (it does, however, ignore the water lost through sublimation in winter), and for its empirical record of the early season discharge. The latter shows wide and rapid fluctuations that have not yet been adequately explained in physical terms but which seem to reflect the complexity of the hydrologic system as the snow pack ripens unevenly. A more specific study of the parts of the system which contribute large amounts to the summer stream-flow appears in the early paper of Martinelli (1959; not reproduced here). This describes conditions during the ablation of large snowdrifts and, in its last paragraphs, records the potential for additional water storage in such accumulation areas. In a longer paper published 14 years later (1973), the same author evaluates this potential more rigorously and shows it to be

realizable through structural modification of the up-wind side
of snowdrifts. Finally, the summary of Berg's work illustrates
some of the physical processes whereby snow redistribution into
drifts is performed by the wind. Berg describes a model which
is based upon the physics of fluid transport and sediment deposition and which realistically simulates snow deposition during
drifting. This work, therefore, is relevant to many glaciologic
and hydrologic problems in the alpine belt of the Front Range,
a belt in which the influence of the wind is ever-present.

REFERENCES

Alford, D.L. 1973. *Cirque Glaciers of the Colorado Front
     Range: Mesoscale Aspects of a Glacier Environment.* Ph.D.
     thesis, Department of Geography, University of Colorado,
     Boulder, Colorado.
Leaf, C.F. 1975. *Watershed Management in the Rocky Mountain
     Subalpine Zone: the Status of our Knowledge.* U.S.D.A.
     Forest Service Res. Paper RM-137. 31 pp.
Lee, W.T. 1900. The glacier of Mt. Arapahoe, Colorado. *Jour.
     Geol.*, 8: 647-654.
_____. 1922. Peneplains of the Front Range and Rocky Moun-
     tain National Park, Colorado. *U.S. Geol. Surv. Bull.*, 730A:
     1-19.
Martinelli, M., Jr. 1959. Some hydrologic aspects of alpine
     snowfields under summer conditions. *Jour. Geophys. Res.*,
     64: 451-455.
_____. 1975. *Water-yield Improvement from Alpine Areas:
     the Status of our Knowledge.* U.S.D.A. Forest Service Res.
     Paper RM-138. 16 pp.

THE ARAPAHO GLACIER:
A SIXTY-YEAR RECORD

(Abstract)

H. A. WALDROP

Arapaho Glacier occupies a cirque just east of the Continental Divide and twenty miles west of Boulder, Colorado. It is the largest glacier in Colorado, and is probably the southernmost active glacier in the Rocky Mountains. Its accumulation basin rises to 13,300 feet, and its front terminates at 12,075 feet in a moraine-dammed lake. In 1960 the glacier covered 62 acres. Average altitude of the firn limit was 12,400 feet.

Annual accumulation layers, which originally dipped downslope parallel to the glacier surface, have been rotated by glacier movement until they dip steeply back into the cirque. In places ablation surfaces separating these accumulation layers contain rubble of ancient rockfalls that was incorporated into the glacier beneath firn layers of succeeding years. Ice wastage slowly releases this rubble to the glacier surface, where it forms apron-like patches below outcrops of ablation surfaces.

Recent investigations have thrown doubt on the occurrence of overthrusting along ablation surfaces in cirque glaciers. On Arapaho Glacier a small vertical fault that offsets several ablation surfaces is in turn offset along an ablation surface, indicating that overthrust has occurred along that surface.

Maximum annual movement has decreased from about 28 feet measured in 1904-05 to about 12 feet measured in 1960-61.

The glacier has receded 300 to 900 feet across its front since its Historic stade maximum around 1860, losing 29 acres or 32 percent of its area. Since 1900, when it was first studied, it has receded 250 to 750 feet across its front, losing 22 acres, and has thinned an estimated average of 106 feet, losing 315,-412,200 cubic feet or 7,218 acre-feet of water.

Published in full as:
Univ. Colorado Studies
Ser. in Geology, No. 3
Univ. Colorado Press
Boulder, Colorado (1964); 37 pp.

A SURVEY OF NEOGLACIATION
IN THE FRONT RANGE OF COLORADO

(Summary)

S. I. OUTCALT AND D. D. MACPHAIL

THE REGION AND ITS DRIFT GLACIERS

The rugged beauty of the Front Range is due to the effects of cordilleran ice caps and valley glaciers which occupied the region during Pleistocene time. Above timberline, along the Continental Divide, the serrated ridges and awesome amphitheater walls exist in a state of imbalance with the forces of water, gravity, and frost which now replace glacial ice as the major sculpturing agents.

From the Canadian border to northern New Mexico, the mountains of the nation's backbone still hold small glaciers and perpetual snowfields within the chaotic topography of the highest ridges and peaks. In the Front Range of Colorado, between 40° 00'N. and $40^{\circ}20$'N, the general area of this study, there are about 30 small glaciers or stagnant ice bodies. Most of these show ice, annual bands, and the crevasses of movement.

These are drift or Ural-type glaciers. For a variety of reasons, they are unique and interesting. They occur below the theoretical snowline of the region which Flint (1957) calculates to be at 14,000 feet (4,267 m) above sea level. The average size is about one-fifth of a square mile (0.518 km^2) and they have vertical limits of less than 1,000 feet (304.8 m). These dimensions seem too small to develop any strong responses to climatic gradients as on larger alpine glaciers. Indeed, the towering valley walls, which enclose the Front Range glaciers, produce shadows which strongly condition the behavior patterns of these ice bodies (Figure 3). In other ways, too, the drift glaciers relate more dramatically to the surrounding environment

Published in full as:
Univ. Colorado Studies
Ser. in Earth Sci., No. 4
Univ. Colorado Press
Boulder, Colorado (124 pp.)

FIGURE 3. The Tyndall cirque heading in the Flattop erosion
surface which lies in the middle distance behind
Flattop Mountain, foreground.

than valley glaciers emanating from a cordilleran ice field.
The entire drift glacier responds to physical effects which are
simply peripheral to the regime of the typical alpine glacier.
It appears that the microenvironment becomes increasingly more
significant as the area and vertical corporal range of the glacier decreases. The strength of this hypothesis is constantly
tested in the subsequent parts of this study.

Remnants of the Pleistocene glaciers probably disappeared
from the Front Range during the warm "altithermal" of 5,000 to
2,500 B.C. (Thomas, 1962). Since that time, that is during Neoglaciation, there were two stades (substages) of glacial activity
which are defined as "Temple Lake" (2,800 ± 200 years ago) and
the "Historic" which may, Richmond believes, have reached its
maximum during the middle of the last century (Blackwelder, 1915;
Richmond, 1960). The zone of maximum Neoglaciation occurs
between timberline (approximately 11,500 feet or 3,500 m) and the
mountain crests. However, this region contains features produced

by several successive glaciations, some of them Pleistocene such as "Bull Lake" (early Wisconsin) and "Pinedale" (late Wisconsin) (Richmond, 1960). Within the valleys, on both sides of the Continental Divide, are representative erosional and depositional features associated with the pre-existing glaciers--cirque basins, moraines, rock glaciers, and talus cones. The resulting landscape is a fascinating mosaic of features which reflect the effects of several distinct superimposed stages of glacial and periglacial activity acting upon the exposed Pre-Cambrian igneous and metamorphic bedrock and detrital materials. During the Pleistocene, glaciers extended down the valleys as far as points such as Estes Park and Nederland on the eastern slope and Grand Lake west of the Continental Divide with average distances outward 8 to 10 miles (13 to 16 km).

Not all of the landscape above timberline appears to have been glaciated, however. There are significant remnants of flat or gently rolling erosion surfaces on both flanks of the Continental Divide which now form broad interfluves between deeply incised glaciated valleys. Relic headwalls, terminal moraine positions, and progressively higher cirque floors of more recent glaciations suggest evacuation of the valleys during interglacial stages and reoccupation at higher levels in response to fluctuating climatic conditions and snowline positions. Richmond presents several arguments in support of this idea--failure of glaciers to reoccupy Pinedale cirques, contrasting soil characteristics on Pinedale and Neoglacial tills, the presence of dormant talus with a veneer of Pinedale soil covered by fresh and active talus, and the fact that a variety of periglacial deposits on the gentle surfaces above the cirque headwalls bear strong similarity to Pinedale till; these have been truncated by youthful and active deposits (Richmond, 1960). Carrying Richmond's criteria into Neoglacial time, there appears to be similar evidence for distinguishing the Historic stade from the Temple Lake. All along the Continental Divide, there are extremely fresh surfaces in juxtaposition with those showing slight weathering and lichen formation. The tandem rock glaciers below Tyndall Glacier in Rocky Mountain National Park are a case in point. There, the upper rock glacier appears active and is a functional part of the glacier, while the lower one appears to be stagnant, weathered, and lichen covered (see Figure 3; Outcalt and Benedict, 1965).

Topographic orientation plays a critical role in the formation and activity of glaciers of the region. A glance at the large-scale relief maps of the U.S. Geological Survey, which cover a 30-mile stretch between Big Horn Flats in Rocky Mountain National Park and the Indian Peak Section of the Roosevelt National Forest, reveals that the Continental Divide follows a northwest-southeast trend for a quarter of this distance before it zig-zags southward to the Arapaho Peak (U.S. Geological Survey, 1957-58). The northern part of the Continental Divide in the study area and four major western subsidiary, unnamed ridges

jut northwestward en echelon. These stand at the same relative
elevation of the Divide itself which is consistently between
12,000 feet (3,658 m) and 12,500 feet (3,810 m) except for soli-
tary peaks which may be another 1,000 feet to 1,700 feet (304.8
m to 518.2 m) higher. The northeast facing slopes of the five
ridges are deeply and continuously scalloped by cirque basins
while the southwest slopes opposite are smooth and relatively
free of glacial erosion. The topographic effect is similar to
that produced along the crest of the Uinta Range in northeast
Utah and the Wind Rivers of central Wyoming (Thornbury, 1965).
It is precisely on the southwesterly slopes that the remnants
of the Flattop erosion surface are best preserved. Functionally,
these are important to the Ural-type glacier of today, since
they serve as catchment areas for snow which high-velocity,
westerly winds then drive into the cirque basins on the opposing
slopes (Figure 3).

East of the Divide, there are five major spurs extending
almost due east. Among these are Niwot and Baldy Ridges, and
Mount Albion and Mount Audubon. Superficial inspection of the
surface morphology of these ridges suggests that they have not
been subject to strong glaciation since the early Pleistocene.
The exception is the Long's Peak Massif where small slab glaciers
cling to the north-facing slopes. The relative scarcity of
recent glaciation on the flanks of the eastern spurs may be attributed partially to leeward position, to the axial orientation
of the ridges, and to the varying interaction of insolation on
topography.

The predominant northeast exposure of the existent drift
glaciers underscores the importance of topographic control and
climate. Of 28 cirques occupied by these between Notchtop
Mountain and South Arapaho Peak, all but two are oriented in the
90° quadrant between north and east. The mean, downslope axial
orientation of the glacial cirques is 51.26° E and the median
orientation is 54.50° E (Figure 5). The two cirques containing
Ural-type glaciers which are exceptions, deviate only 6° from
the limits of the northeast quadrant, 5.5° W and 96.5° E,
respectively.

The relatively close correlation between the attitude of
the axes of the cirque basins and the orientation of the axes
of the main ridges and spurs along the Divide suggests an underlying topographic control. Over 20 percent of the 28 cirque
basins previously mentioned are oriented within 10° of normalcy
to their own ridge or spur, and over half are situated within
20° of perpendicularity. While the explanation is not clearcut,
it seems reasonable to assume a relationship between preglacial
valleys developed below the Divide and those valleys now occupied
by drift glaciers. This aspect of topographic control, however,
appears secondary to the role played by climate in influencing
the affinity of the glaciers to a northeast exposure.

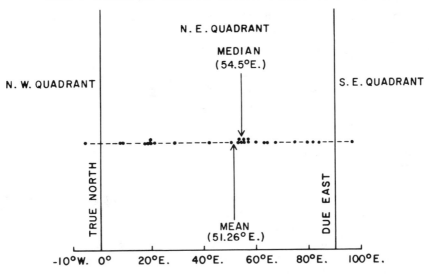

FIGURE 5. Azimuthal orientation of axes of drift glacier cirque basins from true north (28 glaciers).

THE GLACIERS UNDER STUDY

One-third of the glaciers between Notchtop Mountain in Rocky Mountain National Park and South Arapaho Peak have been under study for the past two years under a grant from the National Science Foundation. The criteria for selecting the glaciers for study included: (1) location, (2) type, and (3) accessibility. Those investigated are distributed in several localities along the Divide. One, the Fair, is situated on the slope immediately west of the Indian Peaks. The rest of the glaciers studied occur on the eastern and leeward flanks of the Divide. The Andrews and Tyndall Glaciers occur in the high, central part of Rocky Mountain National Park; further south, one of the St. Vrain group was selected. The Moomaw Glacier, one of the few located between the latter and the cluster of the Indian Peak Section, was chosen; and finally, several among the Indian Peaks, the Navajo, the Isabelle, the Arapaho, the Arikaree, and the Fair, previously mentioned.

Among these particular drift glaciers and others throughout the Front Range, there are distinct morphologic subtypes. Considering surface form and topographic environment, there seem to be three such classes in the study area: (1) the col-fed glacier, (2) the cornice-fed glacier, and (3) the gully glacier (U.S. Geological Survey, 1957). Their distinct appearance and variance in mode of accumulation are helpful in recognizing them.

The col-fed glacier occurs on the lee side of a col leading to one of the high-level erosion surfaces. The surface contours maintain a convex pattern in opposition to the typical concave morphology of the cirque headwall. Such a subtype may develop where snow drifts from large source areas on the windward side of the col. Example: Andrews Glacier, 40°17'15" N, 105°41'00" W.

The cornice-fed glacier occurs at the cirque headwall where there is no pronounced col leading to an erosion surface. The surface contours of this subtype are concave, conforming to the morphology of the headwall. The cornice-fed subtype seems to persist on feeding by avalanches which are frequent during the accumulation season and by the collapse of cornices which form early in the ablation season. Example: Tyndall Glacier, 40° 18'18" N, 105°41'20" W.

The gully-glacier is an extremely narrow glacier heading in one or more steep gullies. It requires only a minimal ac-cumulation to maintain movement because of extreme surface gradients. Cornice collapse seems to be the prime accumulation process. During the summer months, shadowing along the sides of the steep gully greatly retards ablation. Example: Taylor Glacier, 40°16'15" N, 105°40'40" W.

These three subtypes appear to be the "classic" glacial forms for the research area. Yet, even so, several other drift glaciers in the Front Range, especially in the Indian Peak Sec-tion, appear to possess complex combinations of the three rela-tively simple morphologic alternatives.

REFERENCES

Blackwelder, E. 1915. Post-cretaceous history of the mountains of central western Wyoming. *J. Geology*, 23: 97-117, 193-217, 307-340.

Flint, R.F. 1957. *Glacial and Pleistocene Geology*. John Wiley & Sons, New York, p. 304.

Outcalt, S.I. and J.B. Benedict. 1965. Photointerpretation of two types of rock glaciers in the Colorado Front Range, U.S.A. *J. Glaciology*, 5(42).

Richmond, G.M. 1960. Glaciation of the east slope of Rocky Mountain National Park, Colorado. *G.S.A. Bulletin*, 71: 1371-1381.

Thomas, H.E. 1962. *The Meteorologic Phenomenon of Drought in the Southwest*. Geological Survey Professional Paper 372-A, U.S. Government Printing Office, Washington, D.C., pp. A-33-A-34.

Thornbury, W.D. 1965. *The Regional Geomorphology of the United States*. John Wiley & Sons, New York, pp. 363, 368.

U.S. Geological Survey. 1957-58. McHenry's Peak, Isolation Peak, and Monarch Lake Quadrangles. 7.5 Minute Series (Topographic).

MASS BALANCE STUDIES ON THE ARIKAREE GLACIER

(Summary of Doctoral Dissertation)

JAMES B. JOHNSON*

Arikaree Glacier, at the head of the Green Lakes valley, is one of the most accessible of the Front Range glaciers and for that reason was chosen for continuous study during five mass balance years in the early 1970s. This ice body lies immediately east of the Continental Divide on the north flank of Arikaree Peak where it faces the northeastern quadrant. It has an elongate, along-the-contour shape and a relatively steep surface slope (up to 45° gradient). Its foot rests against the proximal face of a neoglacial moraine on the almost flat cirque floor (the deposits in the cirque have been described by Benedict (1968). With an area of about 5.6 ha. and a known depth of at least 5.5 m (from excavation and drilling), it contains at least 300,000 m^3 of water.

MASS BUDGET

Probe surveys, snowpits, and ablation stake observations were used for evaluating mass balance components on Arikaree Glacier during the ablation season of the five water years 1968 to 1973. During this time, the glacier showed a generally positive budget (Table 1) which amounted to an annual mean net accumulation (b_n) of about 0.22 m water equivalent. In three of the five years, the net balance was approximately zero; one of the remaining two years showed a clear net deficit and the other a net gain of over 1 m w.e. (Alford's analysis of one of these years shows that Arikaree Glacier responds in concert with the other glaciers of the Front Range (Alford, 1973). The volume of summer ablation (Table 1) and the best available estimate of the volume of water stored as ice in the glacier suggest a high instability index (I_i) (LaChapelle, 1965) for Arikaree Glacier. I_i exceeds 0.1 which suggest that Arikaree Glacier is in a marginally glacial environment and so should respond rapidly to

Mesa College
Grand Junction, Colorado

TABLE 1
Arikaree Glacier: Mass Budget, 1968-1973

Budget Year	Net Budget	Accumulation	Ablation
1968 - 1969	0.1	2.08	1.98
1969 - 1970	0.4	3.15	2.75
1970 - 1971	1.14	3.36	2.12
1971 - 1972	-0.7	2.62	3.32
1972 - 1973	0.2	2.27	2.07
Mean	0.23	2.70	2.45

All values in meters, water equivalent.

climatic variations.

In common with all of the Front Range glaciers, it is usually not possible to define accumulation and ablation zones on
Arikaree Glacier. When the glacier balance is negative, the
local balance is negative over most of its surface and up to six
years of accumulation layers may be exposed (e.g., Figure 1).
Conversely, a strongly positive balance, like that of 1971, shows
as net accumulation over the entire glacier surface. This characteristic is common among glaciers with a high instability index.

ACCUMULATION

Since wind-blown snow is thought to contribute significantly
to accumulation on the Front Range glaciers, the measurement of
wind speeds and directions was attempted in the Arikaree cirque
during this study. Unfortunately, the winter records are intermittent and of uncertain quality, but they do tend to support
the observations made by Lloyd (1970) on the moraine below Isabelle Glacier. Wind speeds tend to be lower than those recorded
at similar elevations on Niwot Ridge (Sept. to March mean of
5.26 m sec^{-1} in Arikaree cirque) and wind directions during
storms consistently show an easterly or northeasterly component.
The suggestion of a 'rotor-type' circulation within the cirque
indicates that drift accumulation on this topographic scale is
not as simple as that on the smaller scale examined by Berg
(this chapter).

A further complication to the pattern of accumulation on
Arikaree Glacier is due to avalanching from two gullies on Arikaree Peak. This process is known to contribute snow to the
glacier surface, but its magnitude has not been estimated.

Snowpits dug in late-June have shown the presence of multiple ice lenses and layers similar to those found in the seasonal snow cover at lower elevations in the Front Range (e.g.,
Carroll, 1976). More than 30% of the thickness of accumulation

FIGURE 1.   Arikaree Glacier from Navajo Peak.

consisted of ice layers in all years, except 1972. By the end
of the ablation season in September, the ice lenses have been
replaced by a layer of superimposed ice. This is usually of
high density ice with only large isolated air bubbles.

MASS TRANSFER

A number of attempts have been made to monitor movement of
Arikaree Glacier, none with a high level of success. Creep
within the winter accumulation is evident each spring, and predictably so given the depth of snow accumulation and the steep
slope on which it lies (e.g., Perla and Martinelli, 1976, p. 57).
This movement is not, however, considered here.

Between 1969 and 1972, there was no observed movement of 15 rocks arranged in line 10 m apart across the ice surface. This suggestion of little or no motion was corroborated in the 1971 to 1974 period when two strain nets of 4 and 5 points each were established on the glacier. Later recovery of the nets was only partially successful and not sufficient to allow strain analysis. It was, however, sufficient to allow estimates of horizontal movement and showed less than 0.1 m yr^{-1} in both of the two years of record. A survey of the ice surface in 1972, when much of the glacier was exposed during a strongly negative budget year, also showed little evidence of ice movement. The only features indicative of motion were a 12 m long bergschrund with a width of 0.1 m and a thin (less than 0.02 m wide) crevasse aligned parallel to, and near, the toe of the glacier. Inactivity is also in accord with the sedimentary evidence from the shallow ponds through which the drainage from the glacier passes. These ponds contain little rock flour like that in the drainage from Arapaho Glacier (Reheis, 1975), and their sediment content appears to be largely derived from wind-blown dust.

In light of the lack of clear evidence to the contrary, it seems best to conclude that Arikaree Glacier is stagnant at the present time.

ABLATION

The rates of snowmelt and meltwater production on Arikaree Glacier are similar to those reported by Carroll (this chapter) for the entire Green Lakes valley, to which the glacier contributes runoff. Once the winter snow cover becomes isothermal, changes in the ablation rate during the summer can be explained by atmospheric conditions and variations in the snow surface albedo. The latter varies with the 'age' of the surface: snowfalls in June producing an increase from about 0.6 to more than 0.8. Later in the ablation season as dust accumulates on the snow surface, its albedo falls gradually to reach 0.5 by July and 0.4 in August. In 1972, when large areas of ice were exposed in late July and August, the albedo in the latter month was below 0.2 over the ice and averaged .32 over the glacier as a whole. Similarly low albedo values have been found in other years with high winds and a correspondingly high influx of dust.

CONCLUSION

The net mass balance of Arikaree Glacier during the early 1970s has been approximately stable and balanced, and this state seems to have continued unchanged to the present (1979). The glacier is clearly in a critical situation as indicated by its present stagnation, its high instability index and the magnitude of its mass balance deficit in the occasional negative years it experiences. It can, therefore, be expected to respond rapidly, and perhaps obviously, to climatic variations capable of influencing its budget on the scale of 5 to 10 years. In this it appears to be reasonably typical of the other glaciers in the Front Range (cf. Cofer and Alford, this chapter). Allied with its accessability, this makes Arikaree Glacier a candidate for further work on glacier mass balances and their controls.

REFERENCES

Alford, D.L. 1973. *Cirque Glaciers of the Colorado Front Range: Meso-scale Aspects of a Glacier Environment.* Ph.D. thesis, Department of Geography, University of Colorado, Boulder, Colorado.

Benedict, J.B. 1968. Recent glacial history of an area in the Colorado Front Range, U.S.A. II. Dating the glacial deposits. *Journal of Glaciology*, 7(49): 77-87.

Berg, N.H. 1976. *Prediction of Natural Snowdrift Accumulation in Alpine Areas.* Ph.D. thesis, Department of Geography, University of Colorado, Boulder, Colorado.

Carroll, T. 1976. Hydrology of an alpine basin in the Colorado Front Range. *Proceedings 44th Annual Western Snow Conference*, Calgary, Alberta, Canada, April 20-23, 1976 (reprinted in this volume).

Johnson, J.B. 1979. *Mass Balance Studies on the Arikaree Glacier.* Ph.D. thesis, Dept. of Geology, University of Colorado, Boulder, Colorado.

LaChapelle, E.R. 1965. The mass budget of Blue Glacier, Washington. *Journal of Glaciology*, 5(41): 609-623.

Lloyd, D.T. 1970. *The Isabelle Glacier, Front Range, Colorado During the 1968-1969 Budget Year.* M.A. thesis, Department of Geography, University of Colorado, Boulder, Colorado.

Perla, R.I. and M. Martinelli, Jr. 1976. *Avalanche Handbook.* U.S. Department of Agriculture, Agriculture Handbook No. 489. 238 pp.

Reheis, M.J. 1975. Source, transportation and deposition of debris on Arapaho Glacier, Front Range, Colorado, U.S.A. *Journal of Glaciology*, 14(72): 407-420.

THE ORIENTATION GRADIENT:
REGIONAL VARIATIONS OF ACCUMULATION
AND ABLATION IN ALPINE BASINS

Donald Alford*

INTRODUCTION

The alpine region of the mountains of western North America represents an extension of an arctic-maritime climate deep into what is generally otherwise a continental, semi-arid environment. If it were not for the humid mountain "islands" which character- ize the western deserts of North America, it is doubtful that any significant human habitation would be possible.

Generally speaking, in the past, man has centered his ac- tivities and dwellings along the major river courses which flow from these mountain ranges. The demands on the water output of the mountains were normally less than the output until recently when two trends have worked to upset that balance. These are: (1) the increasing population pressure, developed within the traditional centers of habitation of the west, and (2) the ac- celerating development of other resources of the west, primarily coal.

It is apparent that a more detailed knowledge of the loca- tion, volume and timing of the water resources of western North America is needed. The real question is how best to obtain this knowledge.

The basin approach to the hydrologic evaluation of an area of interest is not new and yet relatively little effort has been expended in determining the extent to which a given basin is, in fact, "representative" of the area in which it lies. The question

*Water Resources Research Institute
University of Wyoming
Laramie, Wyoming

Text of a paper presented at the Symposium-Workshop on Northern Research Basins, U.S. National Committee on Scientific Hydrol- ogy; Fairbanks, Alaska; August 15-17, 1977, and derived from the author's doctoral dissertation.

of how to relate objectively to the data obtained from a particular research basin to other basins in its vicinity should be
a fundamental concern of anyone concerned with "basin" studies
in general.

The alpine basins in the western part of North America,
which are probably the most hydrologically productive portion
of the entire continent on a unit runoff/area basis, have received remarkably little attention from the scientific community.
Any consideration given to studies of "northern basins" must
surely include them and yet the vast numbers of them make it
difficult to rationalize any particular research scheme without
some concept which will set empirical studies into a regional
framework.

It is the purpose of this paper to present a preliminary
approach to the evaluation of regional variations of accumulation and ablation in alpine basins. This is a problem which is
relevant to the concept of basin studies and which will require
far more extensive studies than those on which the model presented here is based. At the same time, it is felt that,
without a systematic basis for the selection of research basins
and a technique for evaluating the regional significance of the
data obtained from them, the entire concept of "research basins"
lies open to serious questions.

ACCUMULATION: THE WINTER BALANCE

The ultimate depositional pattern of snow in the alpine
zone bears only limited resemblance to the original trend of
precipitation resulting from storms crossing a mountain range.
Snow falling on the forests of the mountain zone or the adjacent valley floors is, in some measure, protected from the
winds which are a common feature of major storm systems. The
alpine zone is fully exposed to them. These winds sweep the
falling and freshly deposited snow across the low vegetation
and boulder fields, first filling up minor depressions in the
lee of these features, then building drifts behind larger
boulders and in gullies and finally, major deposits of snow
begin to form in the cirque basins, which may or may not already contain a semi-permanent ice deposit. These cirques
constitute the primary accumulation area for alpine snow.

Morphologically, the cirque basin has been defined as
"...a deep, steep-sided recess, roughly semi-circular in plan,
cut into a slope..." (Flint, 1971, p. 133). The individual
cirque basin may be described in three-dimensions, such that x
represents its width; y, the direction toward which it opens,
and z, the elevation between the cirque floor and surrounding
ridge crests (Figure 1). A given cirque may be described by
one or more sets of axes, depending upon its morphologic complexity and the use to which the measurements are to be put.

Assume that windblown snow is the only source of accumulation in the alpine zone. Total net accumulation, B_w, in a

216

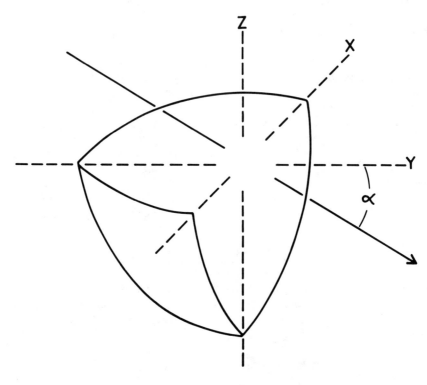

FIGURE 1

cirque basin, could then simply be expressed as:

$$B_w = \cos \alpha \, m \qquad (1)$$

where: α = angle between mean storm path trajectory and principal axis of cirque, measured toward open end (Figure 1),

m = a proportionality constant, related to the amount of snow transported by the wind.

As a first approximation, α is constrained to $\pm\frac{1}{2}\pi$ so that accumulation only occurs in the leeward hemisphere. The primary problem with Equation (1) is that as m approaches 0, so does B. To make the expression more reasonable in terms of real conditions, Equation (1) may be rewritten as:

$$B_w = \cos \alpha \, m + B_z \qquad (2)$$

where: B_z = normal nondirectional accumulation at the elevation (z) of cirque floor.

Equation (2) is sufficiently general to apply to a wide

range of conditions of mean wind transport of snow.

B_w is the total volume of net accumulation in the cirque so the specific volume ($\bar{b}_w$) is obtained through division by the cirque floor area (A):

$$\bar{b}_w = \frac{\cos \alpha \; m + B_z}{A} \qquad (3)$$

Some justification for the relationships expressed in Equations (2) and (3) is provided by the mass-balance studies conducted on cirque glaciers and snowfields in the Colorado Front Range during the period June-September, 1970 (Alford, 1973). Using standard mass balance techniques (snow pits and probe lines and ablation stakes) the balance quantities were determined for 13 cirque basins. It was found that specific accumulation, $\bar{b}_w$, varied by more than a factor of two among the basins. An attempt to relate these variations to elevation was made, in keeping with conventional analyses of mass-balance data, but no obvious correlation was found. This confirms the results obtained by Dugdale (1972) from an analysis of data from nine Norwegian glaciers. When the values of $\bar{b}_w$ were plotted as a function of cirque orientation, however, a curvilinear relationship was found (Figure 2). The equation which best fits the line in the 180° range centered on east was:

$$\bar{b}_w = \cos \alpha \; 2.05 + 2.23 \qquad (4)$$

$$S.E._y = 0.328$$

$$r = 0.879 \; (p > 0.99)$$

This "orientation gradient" was interpreted as the result of differential redeposition of snow by wind with the most favored location for accumulation being a cirque basin with a y-axis parallel to the mean storm trajectory.

ABLATION: THE SUMMER BALANCE

Ablation is a complicated process and has received more attention in the literature than the processes which influence accumulation. At the same time, this attention does not seem to have led to a generally acceptable understanding of (1) the importance of the various energy transfer mechanisms, or (2) the relative importance of melt and evaporation as elements of ablation. In all probability, there is no fixed relationship from region to region; either among the energy transfer processes or the elements of ablation. At low elevations, in the vicinity of bare ground or vegetation, and in those areas where a cloud cover predominates over clear skies, one would expect that long wave radiation and advected sensible heat would be the primary energy sources and that snowmelt would be the primary

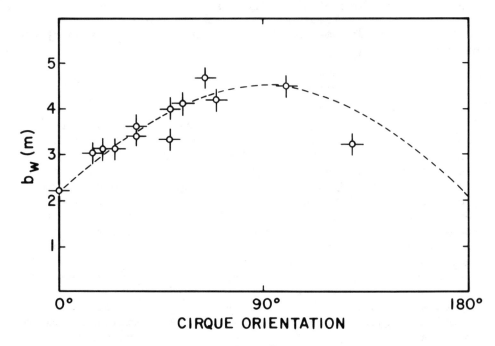

FIGURE 2

type of ablation. At higher elevations, or on more continental sites, where the absolute humidity of the air is low and the ground surface has a more-or-less uniform albedo during much of the year, one would expect short-wave radiation and the advective processes leading to evaporation to increase in importance.

Whatever the relationship existing among the energy budget components in the alpine environment, it is suggested here that direct solar radiation serves as a useful index of the total energy exchange, and that the relative significance of melt and evaporation in ablation deserves additional study.

Based upon the assumption that direct short-wave radiation is either the primary process or at least an index of it, an expression similar to that used to describe the alpine accumulation pattern may be written for the summer balance of alpine snowfields, B_s:

$$B_s = \cos \beta' \, m + B'_z \quad \text{(see Figure 3)} \quad (5)$$

where: β' = angle of incidence of short-wave solar radiation,
m = (1) ablation losses, expressed in units of length or volume, or
(2) effective incident energy in $cal\text{-}cm^{-2}$,
B' = ablation resulting from nondirectional components of energy transfer.

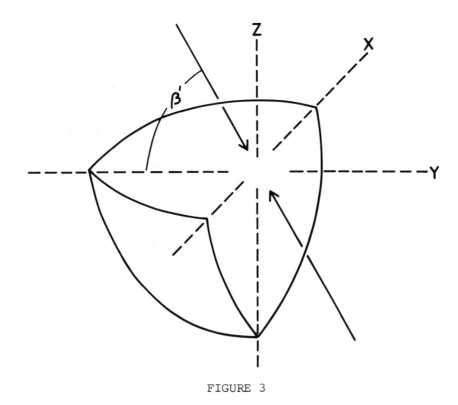

FIGURE 3

Equation (5) can also be written in terms of cirque orientation (β):

$$B_S = \sin \beta \, m + B'_z \tag{6}$$

and for specific values of ablation, b_S:

$$\bar{b}_S = \frac{\sin \beta \, m + B'_z}{A'} \tag{7}$$

where A' is equal to the surface area of the snowfield.

It is apparent that, using a general radiation theory, m could be replaced by a longer expression for the total energy receipt based on elevation, latitude, longitude, degree of cloudiness, albedo, time of year and time period of interest. This has been omitted here in the interest of brevity.

The study of the glaciers and snowfields of the Colorado Front Range also provided empirical evidence of an "orientation gradient" in the summer balance, $\bar{b}_S$. As with values for $\bar{b}_w$, $\bar{b}_S$ was first plotted against elevation and, again, no correlation

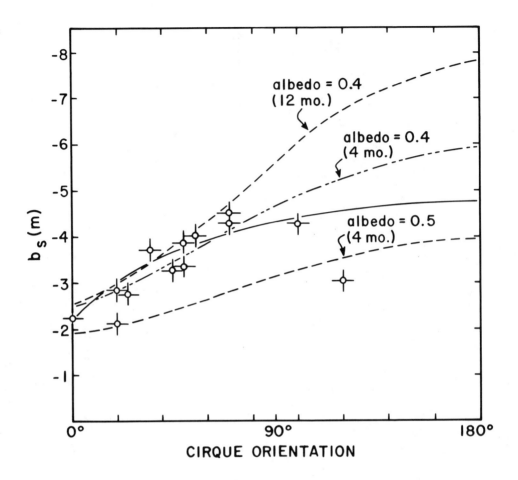

FIGURE 4

was found. When $\bar{b}_S$ was plotted as a function of cirque orientation, however, the relationship shown in Figure 4 resulted.
This is described in terms of basin orientation by:

$$\bar{b}_S = \sin \beta \ 2.37 + 1.82 \qquad (8)$$

$$S.E._y = 0.405$$

$$r = 0.866 \ (p > 0.99)$$

This "orientation gradient" of the summer balance was interpreted as the result of differing receipts of short-wave
radiation during the study period (late June to mid-September,
1970). Using standard equations for radiation intensity and
albedo estimates of 0.4 and 0.5, curves of relative radiation
melt balance for the period of study and for a 20° slope at

different orientations were also plotted in Figure 4.

A curve for the maximum possible melt on a 20° slope, constructed in the same manner, is also shown in Figure 4. This illustrates the "time-transgressive" nature of the ablation-orientation gradient and suggests that potential ablation may approach eight meters of water-quivalent annually at an orientation of 180° (south). This implies that the beginning and ending dates for mass-balance studies are important in determining the results obtained and their physical meaning, depending upon the orientation of the basin under study.

THE ANNUAL BUDGET OF AN ALPINE BASIN

In glacier mass-balance studies, the "net balance," $\bar{b}_n$, or state of health of the glacier is expressed:

$$\bar{b}_n = \bar{b}_w + \bar{b}_s \tag{9}$$

or,

$$B_n = B_w + B_s \tag{10}$$

From the standpoint of the majority of alpine cirque basins, however, it is probable that:

$$B_n = B_w = B_s = 0 \tag{11}$$

For these basins, it could be useful to calculate a "pseudo net balance." For example, in the case where a management scheme involved increasing the amount of accumulation in a basin, this could suggest the approximate amount which could be added before a permanent ice deposit formed and how the additional accumulation might affect the shape of the annual hydrograph. Using the model presented in this paper, this may be done with the expression:

$$B_n = (\cos \alpha \, m + B_z) + (\cos \beta \, m + B'_z) \tag{12}$$

Specific net values, $\bar{b}_n$, can be similarly calculated:

$$\bar{b}_n = \frac{(\cos \alpha \, m + \bar{b}_z) + (\cos \beta \, m + \bar{b}_z)}{A} \tag{13}$$

if it is assumed that A and A' are the same areas. This relationship is shown in Figure 5, along with the empirical data from the Colorado Front Range.

DISCUSSION

The model presented here requires extensive testing before it can be accepted with any confidence, but such testing is

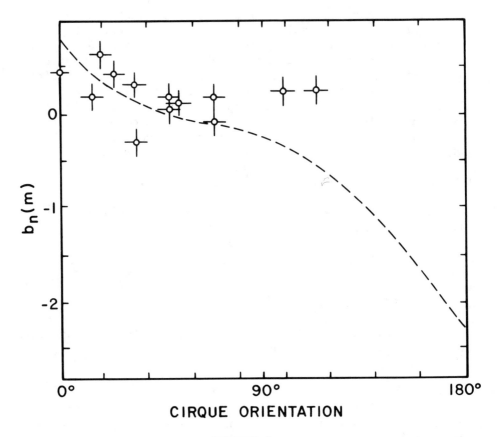

FIGURE 5

relatively straightforward. It involves a small number of variables and a fraction of the effort currently being expended in
hit-or-miss studies of unrelated basins.

Several important implications for water management and
runoff forecasting schemes are apparent in Equation (12). Perhaps the most important of these is the fact that the hydrologic year in any given mountain range is not composed of two
seasons, accumulation and ablation, of the same length at all
orientations. The duration of either season is, instead, a
time-transgressive function of the basin orientation and is
determined by the energy available for ablation at that orientation. In all cases, ablation will begin earliest and end
latest in the southern hemisphere. In predominantly N-S trending
ranges, such as the Rocky Mountain and Coast Ranges in North
America, the most probable orientation for the buildup of a
permanent ice deposit will be in the northeast quadrant. Conversely, the longest snow-free period should occur in the
southwest quadrant.

The model also points to the need for more study of wind

transport and redeposition of snow on natural terrain in the
alpine zone, particularly in major terrain features. Some consideration should be given to modeling this process under natural conditions. A second need defined by the model is for the
study of systematic relationships between melt and evaporation
in ablation, either as responses to the general environment or
to the time of year.

Perhaps the principle benefit of a conceptual model like
that here is a firmer foundation on which to base the selection
of a "representative" basin for glacial hydrology, or other
problems related to the alpine snow pack. It is the impression
of this writer that this type of selection is usually based on
subjective criteria. Whether or not the model presented here
will lead to the development of more objective criteria can
only be determined by tests in a variety of areas.

REFERENCES

Alford, D.L. 1973. *Cirque Glaciers of the Colorado Front
Range: Meso-scale Aspects of a Glacier Environment*. Ph.D.
thesis, Department of Geography, University of Colorado,
Boulder, Colorado.

Dugdale, R.E. 1972. A statistical analysis of some measures
of the state of a glacier's "health." *Journal of Glaciology*, 11: 73-79.

Flint, R.F. 1971. *Glacial and Quaternary Geology*. John Wiley
& Sons, New York. 892 pp.

DIFFERENCES IN ABLATION
OF THREE ADJACENT ALPINE GLACIERS,
INDIAN PEAKS REGION, FRONT RANGE, COLORADO

CHARLES COFER

Department of Geology
Stanford University
Stanford, California 94305

ABSTRACT

Ablation rates of three adjacent Colorado alpine glaciers over a 5-week period are compared with the average number of hours per day of direct sunlight to which more than 50% of each glacier's surface was exposed, and with average wind speed; the influence of glacier size on ablation is also considered. Direct sunlight was found to influence ablation, surface wind speed had a lesser influence, and glacier size had no apparent influence. A 24-hr continuous ablation record of one glacier is correlated with weather conditions recorded during the study period. The amount of global radiation (direct and diffuse short-wave radiation) shows moderate correlation with ablation during the period of measurement, while relative humidity had a lesser correlation. Temperature variations during this cloudy 24-hr period had no immediate correlation with the measured rate of ablation.

INTRODUCTION

Snow ablation of the Isabelle, Navajo, and Fair glaciers in the Front Range, Colorado, was studied during July and August, 1970. Previous studies of alpine glaciers have suggested that the primary factors of ablation are net radiation (absorbed short-wave, plus incoming long-wave, minus outgoing long-wave radiation) and convection (Paterson, 1969, p. 57). The present study seeks to determine the effect of these factors as they relate to differences among individual rates of ablation of adjacent alpine glaciers.

The three glaciers selected for study are located with in a 2-km² area in the Indian Peaks region (Figure 1), northwest of Boulder, Colorado. All three glaciers are influenced by approximately the same weather conditions (air temperature, relative humidity, percentage of cloudiness) and probably have a similar albedo. The Isabelle and Navajo glaciers occupy a compound cirque at the head of the South Saint Vrain Valley; both glaciers are presently facing northeast, though the Isabelle's cirque is oriented to the southeast. The Fair Glacier, one of the few Front Range glaciers on the west slope of the Continental Divide, is north-facing. The glaciers lie between 3,520 and 4,020 m a.s.l. The Institute of Arctic and Alpine Research's highest weather station (D-1, 3,747 m) is located 2.5 km to the east of Navajo Peak, on Niwot Ridge. Weather conditions (temperature, global radiation, and relative humidity) recorded at this station are used to examine the relation between hourly ablation on the Isabelle Glacier and immediate weather conditions. Though there is doubt as to whether this direct extrapolation of climatic data from D-1 to a site 2.5 km away is justified (D. Alford, pers. comm., 1972), it provides an approximation.

Arctic and Alpine Research, Vol. 4, No. 4, 1972, pp. 349-353.

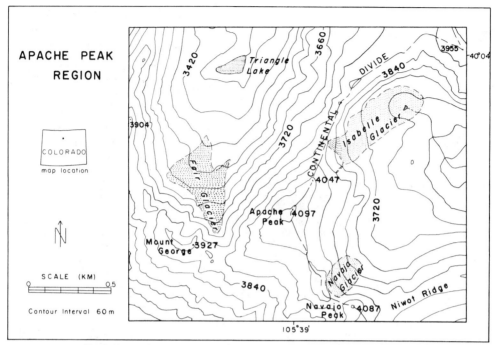

FIGURE 1. Topographic map of northern Indian Peaks region, Colorado. Adapted from U.S.G.S. Monarch Lake (7.5') Quadrangle.

ABLATION DIFFERENCES AMONG THE GLACIERS

Ablation stake networks of aluminum poles (3.66 m long, 5mm diameter) were established on each glacier in early July 1970. Weekly measurements of ablation were compiled, in terms of water equivalent, for a 5-week period (July 6 to August 10). A ratio between ablation rates of each glacier was then derived based on the ablation of the Isabelle Glacier, which was defined as unity (1.00). This ratio

of ablation rates stabilized at 1.04:1.00:0.83 (Navajo:Isabelle:Fair). Two physical factors varied among the glaciers: (1) the daily amount of insolation received by each glacier (a function of the direction of exposure), and (2) the average wind speed on each glacier (a factor in the transfer of sensible and latent heat at the glacier surface). This provides a partial explanation for the ratio of ablation

TABLE 1

Ratios between ablation, insolation, and size of Navajo, Isabelle, and Fair Glaciers

Factor	Navajo	Isabelle	Fair
Ablation, Ratio	1.04	1.00	0.83
Value (cm w.e. week^{-1})	23.9	23.0	19.1
Estimated Hours Direct Sunlight, Ratio	1.20	1.00	0.50
Value (hr day^{-1})	6	5	2.5
Estimated Surface Wind Speed, Ratio	1.05	1.00	0.95
Value (m sec^{-1})	1.6	1.5	1.4
Size (Surface area), Ratio	0.31	1.00	1.12
Value (m^2)	45,700	153,000	171,000

TABLE 2

Weekly ablation ratios

Period	Ratio[a]
July 6-July 13	1.39:1.00:0.97
July 13-July 20	1.16:1.00:0.75
July 20-July 27	1.05:1.00:0.85
July 27-Aug. 3	1.06:1.00:0.83
Aug. 3-Aug. -0	1.02:1.00:0.81

[a]Navajo:Isabelle:Fair

rates. Previous studies of temperate glaciers have shown insolation and wind convection to be strongly correlated with ablation (Paterson, 1969, pp. 56-62). The average number of hours per day during which more than 50% of each glacier's surface was exposed to direct sunlight, and the average wind speed were estimated for each glacier; a ratio of these values was computed for comparison with the previously derived ratio of ablation. The ratios obtained (Table 1) indicate that variation in the amount of direct sunlight received by each glacier compares favorably with ablation variation, while variation in estimated surface wind speed shows a weaker comparison. Differences in size, as expected, do not correlate with ablation variation among the three glaciers. The size ratios were calculated from data on surface area obtained from maps made of the glaciers in early August 1970 by the author.

The computed ratio of ablation varied over the 5-week period but tended to stabilize from mid-July to early August (Table 2). An average was taken of the stabilized values (July 20 to August 10), because these are probably more representative than those obtained earlier in the ablation season. This stabilization can perhaps be explained by noting that the overlying snow density was essentially the same on all the glaciers by July 20 (5.7 ± 0.5 g cm^{-3}), thus early instability of the ablation ratio could have been a function of unequal snowpack-consolidation rates on the three glaciers.

Table 1 suggests that differences in ablation among these glaciers are largely a function of differences in quantity of radiation received at the surface; the second part of this study seeks to determine how strongly ablation of an individual glacier is correlated with global radiation.

TWENTY-FOUR-HOUR ABLATION/WEATHER CORRELATION— ISABELLE GLACIER

Ablation on the Isabelle Glacier was measured hourly over a 24-hr period in mid-July 1970. The previously established stake network provided 34 data points on the 153,000-m^2 surface. Continuous ablation data is correlated with weather conditions recorded at D-1 (Figure 2). The 24-hr period was characterized by (1) extreme (100%) cloudiness with clouds enveloping the glacier, stillness, and unusual warmth from 1800 to 0400 MDT, (2) intermittent (50%) cloudiness from 0400 to 1000 MDT, (3) heavier (80%) cloudiness from 1000 to 1400 MDT, and (4) clearing (30% cloudiness) with freshening winds from 1400 to 1800 MDT. Most summer days in this region are characterized by clear mornings with cumulus cloud build-up during the afternoon. The 24-hr period is, therefore, not representative of the entire ablation season.

Figure 2 illustrates a striking comparison between relative humidity and ablation rate during a cloudy period. Water vapor in the air (relative humidity) both emits long-wave radiation and condenses on the glacier surface, adding latent heat to the calorie exchange at the glacier surface in both cases; this effects an increased rate of ablation (Wallén, 1948, pp. 28-76). Correlation between global radiation (measured by an actinograph) and ablation is positive ($r^2 = 0.29$), as is the lesser correlation between relative humidity and ablation ($r^2 = 0.13$). These graphs show the least correlation between temperature and ablation ($r^2 = -0.04$); significantly, temperature is the sole parameter of the "cumulative-degree-day index," the most widely used index of the surface energy flux that determines the stability of ice in all its forms (Gartska, 1964, pp. BF-34 = BF-35). However, the rate of melting of ice at 0°C cannot be expected to respond immediately to sharp fluctuations of air temperature over a 24-hr period because of the stabilizing effect of the near-surface calorie exchange between ice at 0°C, meltwater, and the surrounding air.

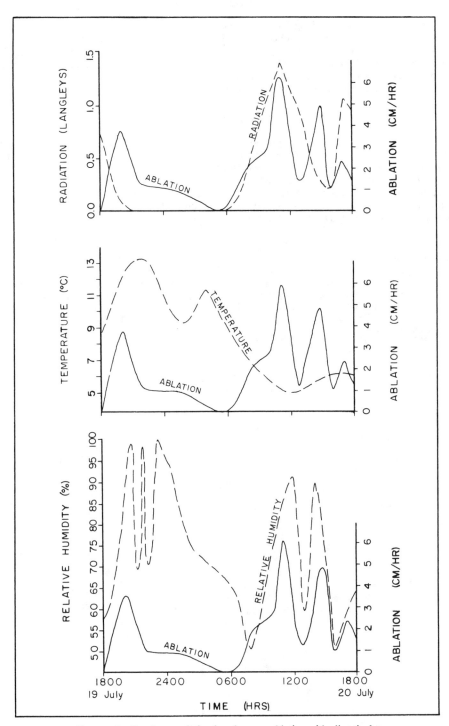

FIGURE 2. Graphs correlating hourly snow ablation with climatic data.

CONCLUSIONS

Ablation differences among the three glaciers studied are found to be produced by variations in the amount of direct sunlight received by each glacier. A continuous 24-hr ablation record of one glacier shows ablation to be only moderately correlated with measured global radiation ($r^2 = 0.29$). Differences in the amount of solar radiation received by each glacier may be reflected by differences in ablation rates among the three glaciers, but global radiation is not the only factor influencing ablation of an individual glacier.

ACKNOWLEDGMENTS

The basis for this study was developed at the Institute of Arctic and Alpine Research's Mountain Research Station during a Summer Science Training Program supported by the National Science Foundation, under the direction of Dr. J. D. Ives. Supervision during the study was provided by Dr. J. T. Andrews and Mr. D. Alford, and their help is gratefully acknowledged. Drs. J. C. Ingle and A. D. Howard critically reviewed a draft of this manuscript, but responsibility for its contents is my own. Assistance in the field was energetically supplied by Mr. R. Jackson.

REFERENCES

Gartska, W.
  1964 : Snow and snow survey. *In* Chow, V. T., (ed.), *Handbook of Applied Hydrology*. New York, McGraw-Hill Book Co., BF-1-BL-57.
Paterson, W. S. B.
  1969 : *The Physics of Glaciers*, Pergamon Press. Oxford, 250 pp.
Wallén, C. C.
  1948 : Glacial-meterological investigations on the Karsa Glacier in Swedish Lappland 1942-1948, *Geogr. Ann.*, 30: 28-76, 150-165.

AN ESTIMATE OF WATERSHED EFFICIENCY FOR A COLORADO ALPINE BASIN

Tom Carroll*

INTRODUCTION

The demand for water in semiarid areas has always exceeded the readily available supply. This problem becomes critical in areas of rapid population growth and expanding economy, characteristic of the eastern slope of the Rocky Mountains today. One approach to this problem is to manage the primary water-producing areas in a way that will enhance streamflow. The alpine zone is defined as that area above natural treeline; it has been estimated that as much as eleven percent of montane Colorado is in the alpine zone. However, little is known about the snow accumulation and stream discharge from alpine areas (Martinelli, 1975). This study is an attempt to determine the water budget and basin efficiency (output expressed as a percentage of input) of an alpine basin in central Colorado.

NATURE AND OBJECTIVES

The project has three objectives. The first is to establish a water budget for the Green Lakes Valley in the Colorado Front Range for the period of May to October, 1973. The second is an attempt to determine the efficiency (i.e., generated discharge expressed as a percentage of snowmelt input) of an alpine basin. Intuitively, it seems that the efficiency of an alpine basin would be higher than that of a forested basin largely because of the low evapotranspiration losses associated with alpine areas.

Presented at the Western Snow Conference, April 20-22, 1976, Calgary, Alberta

*Institute of Arctic and Alpine Research and
Department of Geography
University of Colorado
Boulder, Colorado 80309

The third objective is to define the significance to water yield of areas in the basin which are based on topographic factors.

With some additional observations, the realisation of these objectives would allow computation of a water budget for the alpine area. The study can, therefore, be approached in terms of a catchment water budget:

$$Q = P - Et - \Delta S \qquad\qquad (1)$$

where: Q = stream discharge;
      P = one or more precipitation terms;
    Et = sum of evaporation, sublimation and transpiration losses and gains;
  Δ S = sum of storage changes within the basin (in the snowpack, soil and ground water and lakes).

In evaluating equation (1), all terms must be stated in the same units, usually as depths of water (cm) or as volumes (m^3). In this study, it has not been possible to define a water budget for the basin with a short time resolution although some of the terms in equation (1), particularly Q, can easily be treated on a daily, or shorter, frequency.

Equation (1) is treated here in two parts. The first concerns the input of water to the stream system and involves both summer rainfall and storage changes within the basin that occur on snowmelt. The second comprises the basin outflow, either as stream discharge or through evapotranspiration.

FIELD SITE

The Green Lakes Valley (40° 3' N; 105° 37' W) is a glaciated valley in the Indian Peaks sector of the Front Range of central Colorado approximately twenty miles west of Boulder. The 2.08 km^2 basin runs east from the Continental Divide with an elevation of 4,087 m to the outlet of 3,554 m 2.4 km down valley. The basin has two small lakes which, together with areas of bogs, scrub willows, and standing water, constitute seven percent of the basin area. Tundra vegetation composes thirteen percent of the basin while eighty percent of the basin is bare rock surface of talus and bedrock. During 1973, the basin was instrumented with a hygrothermograph, a stage recorder, and a recording rain gage.

The long-term climate of the Green Lakes Valley can be estimated from the records of the D-1 station (3,750 m) located on Niwot Ridge immediately to the north of the valley. These records have been analysed by Barry (1973). They show mean temperatures of -13.2° C in January and 8.3° C in July with an annual mean of -3.8° C. The mean annual precipitation is 102.1 cm (based on only five years of record) with a slight maximum in winter and a minimum in the fall. An important characteristic of the D-1 site is its windiness (mean annual wind speed is

10.3 m sec^{-1}) which is important in drifting and sublimation of
the winter snowfall and concentrating the water stored as snow
in drift situations.

Data from the three Boulder Creek snow courses maintained
by the Soil Conservation Service indicate that on May 1, 1973,
the snow water equivalent of the snowpack was 159 percent greater
than the previous year and 132 percent greater than 1953-1967
average snow water equivalent for the same time (Washichek,
1973). The above normal snow accumulation will influence discharge values but not stratum or basin efficiencies.

BASIN STRATIFICATION

A snow course of 89 points was used to estimate snow water
equivalent and measure ablation. In setting out the course,
the basin was stratified by elevation, slope, aspect, and estimated snow depth (Table 1). Any one of the 89 points on the
snow course can be described by a four-element term which defines its characteristics.

SPRING PEAK SNOW WATER EQUIVALENT

Depth and density measurements were made on May 18, 1973,
with a Federal snow sampler at each of the 89 points of the
snow course to determine the snow water equivalent held on the
basin at the time of peak snow accumulation. A correction of
9.8 percent was made which compensated for the over-estimate of
the sampler (Work et al., 1965). At peak accumulation it was
determined that an average 67.6 cm w.e. of snow was distributed
over the basin. Table 1 also gives the mean snow water equivalent held on each of the thirteen stratifications and the number
of snow course points on each stratum. Through the relatively
small elevational range of density samples (372 m), density was
not found to vary with elevation. However, data from the 89
points on the Green Lakes snow course suggest that in the
alpine, snow water equivalent at peak accumulation increases
74.3 cm per 1000 m. Other workers have found similar results
in the Rocky Mountains (Caine, 1975; Meiman, 1968; Storr and
Golding, 1973).

ABLATION

Ablation measurements were taken at weekly intervals during
the nine weeks from June 16 to August 20, 1973, using the 89
snow course survey points as the sites of ablation stakes. An
estimate of the nine week snow water equivalent contributed from
each segment can be derived from the product of the ablation,
snow density measured during the ablation season, and proportion
of snow covered area of each segment. The ablation efficiency
of a segment is some measure of how expediently the snowpack
ablates from a given segment or stratum. The efficiency of a

TABLE 1
Basin Stratification and Snow Water Equivalent at Peak
Accumulation

Elevation	four elevational zones of roughly equal area	No. of Points	SWE (cm)
1	3554 to 3566 m	12	52.7
2	3566 to 3658 m	29	63.9
3	3658 to 3780 m	26	76.0
4	3780 to 4087 m	22	51.3
Slope	three slope angle classes		
steep	over 20°	45	64.9
medium	7.5° - 20°	24	78.6
flat	less than 7.5°	20	78.8
Aspect	four aspect classes		
north facing		24	48.7
south facing		26	73.7
east facing		19	105.6
flat (same as the flat area of the slope category)		20	78.8
(Since the basin runs west to east, west facing slopes are practically absent.)			
Depth	three depth classes (based on air photos)		
deep	deep drifted areas	34	121.2
medium	areas other than deep and light	33	68.2
light	blown clean areas throughout year	22	10.9
		basin mean =	67.6

stratum is derived by dividing the percent of a total melt from
each stratum by the percent of total area of each stratum. This
gives a basin mean efficiency of 1.00 with a minimum of 0.66
for north facing slopes and a maximum of 1.23 for south facing
slopes. Both the minimum and maximum exceed $\pm$1.64 standard
deviations from the mean. Table 2 gives the ablation efficiency
for each stratum. Efficiency is probably a function of ablation
controls and snow accumulation patterns which may in turn be
influenced by mesotopography and local wind patterns even though
radiation patterns and medium snow depths are relatively uniform.

SUMMER PRECIPITATION

Precipitation was measured with a shielded Belfort weigh bucket rain gage located at the lower end of the basin. The summer precipitation data was corrected in order to compensate for the systematic underestimate associated with rigidly shielded gages (Hamon, 1972; Larson and Peck, 1974). From May 18 to October 31, 1973, 32.5 cm of precipitation fell; 13.1 cm of this fell in the period June 19 to August 20 when the ablation measurements were taken.

DISCUSSION

The largest input to an alpine water budget is that of winter accumulation. In order to estimate the volume of input from the winter snowpack on a weekly basis, estimates of ablation, snow density, and snow cover are necessary. Ablation was measured at weekly intervals and snow density at monthly intervals because density is relatively invariable. Snow cover was estimated empirically from the generated discharge (U.S. Army, 1956, p. 277). The product of ablation, density, and snow cover at weekly intervals gives a rough estimate of the volume of input to the water budget during the interval. The estimate of areal snow cover probably introduces most of the error into the weekly estimates of volume input. However, the error is reduced when the volume of input is considered on a greater time scale.

The second input to the water budget is summer precipitation. Weekly estimates of input from precipitation may be in error since areal variation of basin precipitation will not be compensated for in the short term. However, errors associated with areal variation of precipitation are minimized over the season. Consequently, the error of the precipitation term in the seasonal water budget is acceptably low.

OUTPUT FROM THE SEASONAL WATER BUDGET

Stream Discharge

Stream stage was measured at a natural section (3,554 m) with a Leupold-Stevens float recorder. The section was rated with a Price current meter during the melt period. Error associated with the rating curve is less than five percent. The stage record begins approximately two days after flow began and a linear extrapolation backwards was used to estimate stream flow on these days.

Generated Discharge

Generated discharge is defined as the volume of stream flow at the gaging point produced by snowmelt. Other workers

TABLE 2
Stratum Efficiency

Main Category	Strata	% of nine week melt	% total area	Efficiency
Elevation	1	10.7	10.6	1.01
	2	23.1	23.0	1.00
	3	32.0	30.6	1.05
	4	34.2	36.5	0.94
Slope	Steep	70.8	69.6	1.02
	Medium	12.9	13.6	0.95
	Flat	16.3	16.8	0.97
Aspect	Flat	16.3	16.8	0.97
	North	21.5	32.4	0.66
	South	41.1	33.5	1.23
	East	21.1	17.3	1.22
Depth	Deep	16.1	15.0	1.07
	Medium	55.7	52.9	1.05
	Light	28.2	32.1	0.88

$\bar{X} = 1.00$

(Garstka et al., 1958; Leaf, 1969; U.S. Army, 1956) have estimated flow generated by each snowmelt day which is defined as the period of time from one trough in the hydrograph to the next one, normally about 24 hours (Leaf, 1971). However, this requires a more accurate estimate of the recession coefficient than is available for the Green Lakes Valley. The net flow generated from each snowmelt week (i.e., seven snowmelt days) was isolated on the discharge type hydrograph by means of the recession curve (Garstka et al., 1958; U.S. Army, 1956). Each week corresponds to the week in which ablation measurements were made throughout the basin (June 19 to August 20).

Generated runoff values (Q_{gen}) from the gaging station were computed from observed daily runoff volumes by equation (2):

$$Q_{gen} = Q_{obs} + Stg1 - Stg2 \qquad (2)$$

where: Q_{obs} = the observed runoff during the snowmelt week;

Stg1 = the initial volume of storage on the watershed at the beginning of the snowmelt week;

Stg2 = the terminal volume of storage on the watershed at the end of the snowmelt week.

Storage is used here as a groundwater or basin storage term and specifically excludes lake, stream, or snowpack storage. The volume of water in storage (Stg1 and Stg2) is a function of the discharge rate and is estimated as the integration of the area under the recession curve (Garstka et al., 1958). In this way, basin storage can be separated from snowpack storage and each can be considered separately.

Evapotranspiration

Evapotranspiration is the second output of the water budget (Hamon, 1966; Harris, 1972; Storr, 1973). This includes evaporation from rock, stream, lake, and soil surfaces as well as the volume of transpiration from the vegetation in the basin. Different plant types transpire at different rates while moisture evaporates at different rates from different surface types. Evaporation and transpiration are combined and an attempt is made to compute potential and actual evapotranspiration for the basin. Daily values of potential evapotranspiration have been estimated from mean daily temperature observations by the procedure of Hamon (1963):

$$E_p = C \ D^2 \ P_t \tag{3}$$

where: E_p = average potential evapotranspiration in cm per day;
D = possible hours of sunshine in units of 12 hours;
P_t = saturated water vapor density (absolute humidity) at the daily mean temperature in grams per cubic meter;
C = 2.17×10^{-3} chosen to give appropriate yearly values of potential evapotranspiration as indicated by observation reported in the literature.

Equation (3) allows an estimate of potential evapotranspiration for the basin but this is only useful in the parts of the basin where the water supply is unlimited. Consequently, the basin was divided into three sub-areas based on the vegetation: (1) areas where water is not limiting (e.g., lakes, areas of willow scrub and bogs), (2) areas of tundra vegetation, and (3) areas of bare rock (i.e., bedrock and talus). Actual evapotranspiration for the wet areas was assumed to be the same as potential evapotranspiration for those areas; actual evapotranspiration for areas of vegetation with medium water holding capacity was taken to be .23 times the potential. Recent work on Niwot Ridge (LeDrew, 1975), immediately north of the Green Lakes basin, indicates that actual evapotranspiration rates for a tundra vegetation can be computed from potential evapotranspiration by the use of equation (4):

$$E = \frac{.212 \ E_p}{1.0 - 1.275 \ E_p} \tag{4}$$

where: E = actual evapotranspiration in ly min^{-1};

E_p = potential evapotranspiration in ly min^{-1}.

For the bedrock and talus areas of the basin, evaporation rates are somewhat more difficult to calculate. Little work has been done in either measuring or calculating evapotranspiration from bare or lichen covered rock surfaces. Consequently, it was assumed that evaporation from areas of bare rock accounted for the amount of surface detention, taken to be 1 mm of water, after every summer rainstorm which is followed by at least six hours with no rain. Where the storm total is less than 1 mm, it is assumed to be totally evaporated. This estimate gives a runoff coefficient of approximately .85 for the bare rock areas. Runoff coefficients for streets and downtown business areas vary from .70 to .95 (Todd, 1970, p. 77).

The estimates used for evapotranspiration from areas of alpine tundra and alpine talus and bedrock may introduce error into total evapotranspiration term. It has been estimated that actual evapotranspiration rates from alpine tundra can vary from .83 to .27 mm per day (P.J. Webber, pers. comm., 1974). This is in good agreement with the estimate of actual evapotranspiration used in this study which was derived from potential evapotranspiration.

A second check on the evapotranspiration loss from the basin can be made from pan evaporation data. In 1969, data from four evaporation pans in the basin were collected. A high correlation between pan evaporation and actual evapotranspiration has been found (Hargreaves, 1958).

An estimate of the actual evapotranspiration for the basin based on the Hargreaves equation and the 1969 pan evaporation data is 3.2 cm and indicates that the values of actual evapotranspiration found in the 1973 study are reasonable.

In areas where water is not limiting (14.6 ha) the nine week estimate is 11.1 cm; in areas of tundra vegetation (26.6 ha) actual evapotranspiration is estimated at 2.6 cm; and in areas of bare rock (166.8 ha) the nine week estimate of actual evapotranspiration is 2.1 cm. The average nine week evapotranspiration distributed over 2.08 km^2 alpine basin is estimated at 2.8 cm while the total twenty-four week (May 17–October 29) evapotranspiration is estimated as 6.5 cm.

WATER BUDGET FOR THE GREEN LAKES VALLEY

The water budget of equation (1):

$$Q = P - E_t - \Delta S \tag{1}$$

can be redefined using the units considered already as:

$$Q_{gen} = S_n + P - E \tag{5}$$

where: Q_{gen} = generated discharge;
         S_n = snowmelt from winter accumulation;
          P = precipitation;
          E = basin wide evapotranspiration.

Generated discharge has previously been defined as simply discharge resulting from snowmelt. However, in using generated discharge to compute a water budget, precipitation and evapotranspiration must be considered. Consequently, generated discharge here includes the evaporation and precipitation term as well as the snowmelt term. The change of storage term of equation (1) is included in the Q_{gen} term of equation (5). When a large portion of the input to a water budget is derived from snowpack depletion, it is useful to evaluate the water budget in terms of equation (5).

The weekly estimates of snowmelt and precipitation were used as inputs to the water budget. Summer precipitation contributions are relatively straight forward and have been discussed. However, estimates of contributions from snowmelt are more difficult to quantify. From density and snowpack lowering measurements it is possible to estimate ablation over snow covered areas.

The major outflow from the water budget is that of generated discharge. Snowmelt and precipitation during a given period contributes to groundwater recharge and observed discharge, both of which constitute generated runoff.

Watershed efficiency (generated runoff expressed as a percentage of snowmelt and precipitation input) was computed also for the first five weeks (June 19-July 23), the first nine weeks (June 19-August 20), and for the entire season (May 17-October 29). Calculated efficiencies exceeded 90 percent in all cases (Table 3).

TABLE 3
Water Budget (cm)

Weeks	Q_{gen}	Snow-melt	P	E (wet)	E (medium)	E (unveg.)	Error	Efficiency (Percent)
	1	2	3	4	5	6		
1-5	63.50	59.46	8.54	.45	.13	1.04	-2.88	93.4
1-9	79.65	66.54	13.12	.78	.23	1.68	2.68	99.9
Year (May 18-Oct. 31)	94.53	67.63	32.48	1.54	.45	4.33	.73	94.4

Note: The evapotranspiration term is the estimate from each of the three areas distributed over the total basin.

       Error = 1 - (2 + 3 - 4 - 5 - 6)

$$\text{Efficiency} = \frac{1}{2 + 3} \times 100$$

Conclusion

A water budget of the basin was computed for three time intervals; two of the intervals represent a composite of field ablation measurements taken in order to use a snowmelt input term. The snowmelt input term for the seasonal interval was computed as the total snow water equivalent held on the basin at peak accumulation. Generated discharge was also computed for the same intervals. As seen in Table 3, more than two thirds of the seasonal stream flow volume was generated during the first five week period (June 19-July 23). Snowmelt produced virtually all of the runoff from this alpine basin.

In contrast, other studies have indicated a much lower efficiency for subalpine basins. For the period from 1943 to 1954 Fool Creek in the Fraser Experimental Forest in Colorado has a mean efficiency of 39 percent while Deadhorse Creek averaged 39 percent efficiency in 1969. Deadhorse Creek is divided into an upper and lower basin; during 1969 the average efficiency of the upper basin was 54 percent while the average efficiency of the lower basin was only 20 percent. The Fool Creek and Deadhorse stream gages are at 2926 m and 2880 m respectively.

It has been estimated that other alpine basins in Colorado have efficiencies also in excess of 90 percent (Leaf, 1975). The high efficiency of many alpine basins is apparently the result of: (1) a high snow cover at the time when seasonal snowmelt rates are near a maximum on all aspects, (2) a delayed and short snow cover depletion season, (3) relatively low recharge, and (4) evapotranspiration losses which are in part, compensated for by condensation on alpine snowfields during some months (Martinelli, 1975).

Partially as a result of the high watershed efficiencies found in alpine areas, it has been suggested that these areas might be used as to increase water supply to lower populated areas of the western United States. For the past twenty years, Martinelli (1975) has experimented with snowfences as a means of augmenting the alpine snowpack. Other techniques are available and include: (1) terrain modification; (2) intentional avalanching; and (3) artificially creating massive accumulations of ice from winter streamflow (Martinelli, 1975).

It may soon become feasible to utilize some of the above techniques to improve water yields from alpine zones largely because of the high watershed efficiencies which characterize areas above treeline in the Rocky Mountains.

ACKNOWLEDGMENTS

The project was made possible by research agreement No. 16-292-CA given by the Eisenhower Consortium for Western Environmental Forestry Research and administered through the Rocky Mountain Forest and Range Experimental Station, U.S.D.A., Fort Collins, Colorado. The principal investigator was Dr. Nel Caine of the Institute of Arctic and Alpine Research, University of Colorado, Boulder, Colorado. Drs. Nel Caine and Charles Leaf reviewed this manuscript and made helpful suggestions.

REFERENCES

Barry, R.G. 1973. A climatological transect on the east slope of the Front Range, Colorado. *Arctic and Alpine Research*, 5(2): 89-110.

Caine, N. 1975. An elevational control of peak snowpack variability. *Water Res. Bull.*, 11(3): 613-621.

Garstka, W.U., L.D. Love, B.C. Goodell, and F.A. Bertle. 1958. *Factors Affecting Snowmelt and Streamflow*. U.S. Government Printing Office, Washington, D.C. 189 pp.

Haeffner, A.D. and C.F. Leaf. 1973. *Areal Snow Cover Observations in the Central Rockies, Colorado*. U.S.D.A. Forest Service, General Technical Report RM-5. 15 pp.

Hamon, W.R. 1961. Estimating potential evapotranspiration. *Proc. Amer. Soc. Civil Engineers*, 87(HY3): 107-120.

_____. 1963. Estimating potential evapotranspiration. *Proc. Amer. Soc. Civil Engineers*, 128(1): 324-342.

_____. 1966. Evapotranspiration and water yield prediction. In: *Evapotranspiration and its Role in Water Resources Management*, 13: 8-9.

_____. 1972. Computing actual precipitation. *World Meteorological Organization Symposium on Distribution of Precipitation in Mountain Areas*, 1: 15-30.

Harris, S.A. 1972. Three modifications to produce more accurate measurements of snowfall and evapotranspiration. *Canadian Geogr.*, 16(3): 271-277.

Hargreaves, G.H. 1958. Closing discussion on irrigation requirements based on climatic data. *Proc. Amer. Soc. Civil Engrs., J. Irrigation and Drainage Div.*, 84(IRI): 7-8.

Larson, L.W. and E.L. Peck. 1974. Accuracy of precipitation measurements for hydrologic modeling. *Water Res. Res.*, 10(4): 857-864.

Leaf, C.F. 1969. Aerial photographs for operational streamflow forecasting in the Colorado Rockies. *Proc. West. Snow Conf.*, 37: 19-28.

_____. 1971. *Aerial Snow Cover and Disposition of Snowmelt Runoff in Central Colorado*. U.S.D.A. Forest Service, Research Paper RM-66. 19 pp.

_____. 1975. *Watershed Management in the Central and Southern Rocky Mountains*. U.S.D.A. Forest Service, Research Paper RM-142. 28 pp.

LeDrew, E. 1975. The energy balance of a mid-latitude alpine site during the growing season, 1973. *Arctic and Alpine Research*, 7(4): 301-314.

Martinelli, M., Jr. 1975. *Water-yield Improvement From Alpine Areas*. U.S.D.A. Forest Service, Research Paper RM-138. 16 pp.

Meiman, J.R. 1968. Snow accumulation related to elevation, aspect, and forest cover. *Proc. of Workshop Seminar in Snow Hydrology*. New Brunswick, Canada 35-46.

Storr, D. 1973. *Monthly and Annual Estimates of Evapotranspiration at Marmot Creek, Alberta, by the Energy Budget Method* (in review).

Storr, D. and D.L. Golding. 1973. A preliminary water balance evaluation of an intensive snow survey in a mountainous watershed. *Advanced Concepts and Techniques in the Study of Snow and Ice Resources*. Monterey, California, pp. 294-302.

Todd, D.K. (ed.). 1970. *The Water Encyclopedia*. Water Information Center, Port Washington, New York. 559 pp.

U.S. Army Corps of Engineers. 1956. *Snow Hydrology*. Portland, Oregon. 435 pp.

_____. 1961. *Runoff from Snowmelt*. Portland, Oregon. 59 pp.

Washichek, J.N. 1972. *Summary of Snow Survey Measurements for Colorado and New Mexico*. Soil Conservation Service, Denver, Colorado. 208 pp.

Work, R.A., H.J. Stockwell, T.G. Freeman, and R.T. Beaumont. 1965. *Accuracy of Field Snow Surveys*. C.R.R.E.L. Technical Report 163. 43 pp.

SNOW-FENCE EXPERIMENTS IN ALPINE AREAS

By M. MARTINELLI, Jr

(Rocky Mountain Forest and Range Experiment Station,* Forest Service, U.S. Department
of Agriculture, Fort Collins, Colorado 80521, U.S.A.)

ABSTRACT. Snow fences built up-wind of natural snowdrifts at four alpine sites in the Colorado Rocky
Mountains changed snow accumulation appreciably. The 3 m tall fences increased the amount of snow at
three sites but decreased it at the fourth. At two of the three sites where snow was increased, there was no
change in melt rate, so the additional snow prolonged the melt period 1–3 weeks. Fences most successfully
augmented natural snow accumulation at sites with level or gently sloping terrain down-wind from the
accumulation site. Between 15 and 30 m of fence was needed to produce an extra 1 000 m³ of water equivalent in the snowfields at the beginning of the melt season. Fences of the type described here, if properly
located, are a means of increasing summer stream flow from alpine areas.

RÉSUMÉ. *Experimentation de barrières à neige en zone alpine.* Des barrières à neige construites à l'amont de
congères naturelles dans quatre sites de montagne dans les Colorado Rocky Mountains ont modifié de
manière appréciable l'accumulation de la neige. Des barrières hautes de 3 m ont accru l'enneigement en
trois sites mais l'on diminué au quatrième. Sur deux des trois sites où l'enneigement avait augmenté, il n'y
avait pas de changement dans la vitesse de fusion. Les barrières se montrèrent les plus efficaces pour aug-
menter l'accumulation naturelle de la neige dans les endroits où il y avait un terrain horizontal ou à faible
pente sous le vent du lieu d'accumulation. Il fallait entre 20 et 30 m de barrières pour produire un supplé-
ment de 1 000 m³ d'équivalent en eau dans le manteau neigeux en début de saison de fusion. Les barrières
du type décrit ici, si elles sont convenablement placées, sont un moyen d'accroître les écoulements hydro-
logiques à partir des zones de montagne.

ZUSAMMENFASSUNG. *Versuche mit Schneezäunen im Gebirge.* Schneezäune, die im Luv der natürlichen
Schneedrift an vier alpinen Stellen in den Rocky Mountains von Colorado errichtet wurden, veränderten die
Schneeablagerung beträchtlich. Die 3 m hohen Zäune erhöhten die Schneemenge an drei Stellen, aber
verringerten sie an der vierten. An zwei der drei Stellen mit erhöhter Schneemenge änderte sich die Schmelz-
geschwindigkeit nicht, so dass der zusätzliche Schnee die Schmelzperiode um 1–3 Wochen verlängerte.
Zäune erhöhten die natürliche Schneeablagerung am wirkungsvollsten leeseits von Stellen im ebenen oder
leicht abfallenden Gelände. Für eine Zunahme von 1 000 m³ Wasserwert in den Schneefeldern am Beginn
der Schmelzperiode waren Zäune zwischen 15 m und 30 m Länge notwendig. Zäune der hier beschriebenen
Art sind, wenn sie richtig gesetzt werden, ein Mittel zur Erhöhung des sommerlichen Abflusses aus Gebirgs-
gebieten.

LAND managers have long been interested in improving water yields from mountainous areas,
especially in the semi-arid parts of middle latitudes. For the high-elevation, wind-swept
alpine areas where vegetation manipulation is not practical, snow fences or other artificial
wind barriers have been suggested to improve late summer stream flow (Martinelli, 1959,
1966). Fences properly located along the windward edge of deep natural snowfields create
additional snow deposition and thus increase the amount of snow available for summer
stream flow. 5 years' experience with such fences at several sites in the lee of a major ridge
and at one site on a windy ridge crest in the Front Range of central Colorado have been
reported (Martinelli, 1965). The lee sites showed mixed results, with fences giving good
additional accumulation at some places, but reducing natural accumulation at others. Best
results were obtained at Straight Creek Pass—the ridge-crest site.

This paper discusses how snow fences changed snow accumulation at Straight Creek Pass
and three other windy alpine sites selected to give a range of topographical conditions.

STUDY SITES

Deep natural snowfields at windy sites between elevations of 3 700 and 3 800 m (12 000
and 12 500 ft) in the Front Range of central Colorado were selected for study. At Straight
Creek Pass (Fig. 1) the snowfield is in a long trough immediately to the lee of a north–south

* Central headquarters maintained in cooperation with Colorado State University, Fort Collins, Colorado
80521, U.S.A.

ridge crest. The windward (west) approach is a smooth grassy up-slope with a gradient of about 15° for a distance of 120–150 m (400–500 ft). The down-wind area is also grass-covered and slopes gently upward from the eastern edge of the snowfield. A major stream flows to the south-west. There is an east–west ridge about 1.2 km (0.75 mile) north of the site. Only one isolated knob on this ridge exceeds the elevation of the study site. Winds during snowfall and snowdrifting are mostly westerly. Snow normally lasts until mid-August.

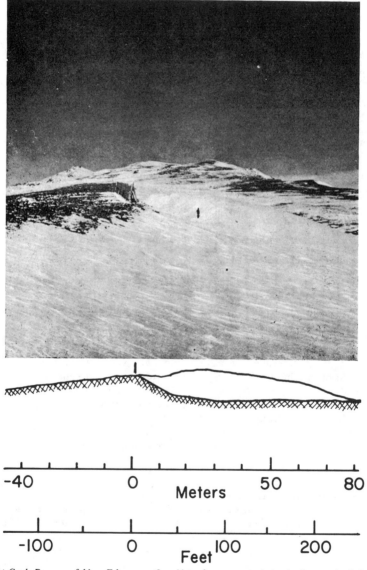

Fig 1. Straight Creek Pass snowfield, 3 February 1963. Natural snow accumulation in foreground of picture. Person is standing in a depression caused by wind blowing under the fence. The profile is a generalization of maximum snow accumulation behind the fence. (Vertical and horizontal scales are equal.) Wind flows from left to right.

The Mount Evans snowfield (Fig. 2) occupies the nearly flat floor of a solifluction terrace in the middle of a broad grass-covered valley that slopes gently (8–10°) downward to the east for almost 3.2 km (2 miles). Mountains to the north, west and south form a crescent of higher terrain. The peaks to the north and west are 150–300 m (500–1 000 ft) higher than the study site; those to the south-west are 600 m (2 000 ft) higher. Winds funnel through the gaps

Fig. 2. *Mount Evans snowfield, 1 August 1965, 1 d after a 15 cm (6 inches) snowfall. Two people on the snow give scale. The profile is a generalization of maximum snow accumulation behind the fence. (Vertical and horizontal scales are equal.) Wind flows from left to right.*

244

Fig. 3. Teller Mountain snowfield, 14 July 1966. Dirty snow in lower right edge of photograph is left over from summer of 1965. The profile is a generalization of maximum snow accumulation behind the fence. (Vertical and horizontal scales are equal.) Wind flows from left to right.

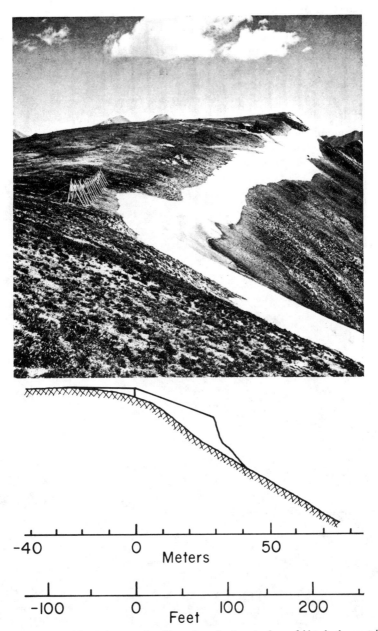

Fig. 4. *Glacier Mountain snowfield, 6 August 1965. The tendency for the natural snowfield to be drawn up-hill behind the fence is noticeable in this photograph. The profile is a generalization of maximum snow accumulation behind the fence. (Vertical and horizontal scales are equal.) Wind flows from left to right.*

between the peaks but they are mostly westerly down the valley. The long axis of the field is roughly north–south. Snowfall at this site is thought to be about half that at the other sites because of its location east of the Continental Divide. Snow normally persists in the deeper parts of the snowfield until early September.

At the Teller Mountain snowfield (Fig. 3), snow accumulates on a bench in the lee of a north-west–south-east break in the terrain. Beyond the bench the lee slope drops steeply to the valley below. Early in the season the snowfield extends all the way across the northern end of the bench, but only about two-thirds of the way across the southern end. The windward approach to this site is complex. North-west winds blow across a flat, grass-covered area 1.2 km (0.75 mile) long. South-west winds flow up a valley that is 0.5 km (0.3 mile) wide. It is not certain how westerly winds are channeled by the terrain. Snow usually persists all summer at this site.

Glacier Mountain snowfield (Fig. 4) forms along the moderately steep (25°) south-east side of this north-east–south-west orientated mountain. The snow accumulates on the side of

Fig. 5. *Snow fence of the type used in this study. Doubled end poles and stout back braces were needed at these windy sites. The guy wires are satisfactory if no snow accumulates on them. If they become buried, snow settlement exerts tremendous pressure on the fence.*

the mountain and not in a depression as it does at all the other sites. The study site is east of a gap or shallow saddle in the main ridge, which increases gently in elevation north-east and south-west of the study site. The mountain is rounded in cross-section, grass-covered and relatively smooth. North-westerly winds flow directly through the gap toward the study site. Down-wind of the snowfield the slope drops at a gradient of 25° for about 150 m (500 ft) then flattens out into a bench. Snow normally is gone from this field by the end of August.

METHODS

At each study site, a snow fence 60–100 m (180–330 ft) long was built along the windward edge of the natural snowfield. Fences were built by attaching two 1.2 m (4 ft) tiers of a commercially available mat made of narrow wood slats and wire to a stout framework of wooden poles and steel cables. The barriers had a density of 42% (58% open) and were 3–3.7 m (10–12 ft) tall including the gap between the fencing and the ground. The face of the barrier was tilted down-wind about 6–7° from the perpendicular to increase the efficiency of the back braces (Fig. 5).

During spring and summer, vertical angle and slope distance were measured at 7–14 d intervals along four parallel lines across the snowfield. Two of these profile lines, called test lines, were behind the fence and two, called control lines, were beyond the influence of the fence.

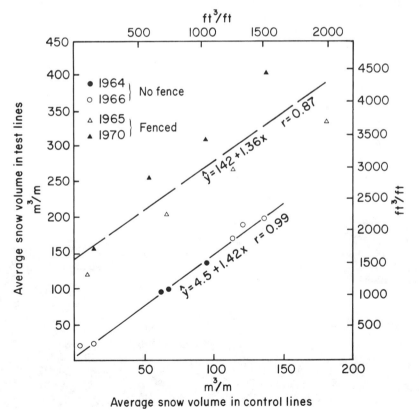

Fig. 6. Snow volume, average snow depth and length of snow-profile lines behind the fence (test lines) as a function of natural conditions (control lines) at Straight Creek Pass.

Cross-section areas of the snowdrifts were determined by planimetering scale drawings of the ground and snow profiles for estimates of snow volumes. Horizontal lengths of the snow profiles were measured directly from the drawings. Average snow depths were calculated by dividing cross-section areas by horizontal lengths.

Graphs and regressions were developed for snow volume, average snow depth, and length of profile lines for the test lines as a function of the control lines under natural and fenced conditions at each field. Differences in the amount of snow in the test lines for years with fences compared to years without fences were considered to be fence effects. This is justified because the fields tend to fill uniformly and because there was enough snow most years to saturate the control area. The analysis worked well for all but Teller Mountain, where a slight modification, described later, was used.

RESULTS

Best results were obtained at Straight Creek Pass. Here the fence increased total snow volume at the start of the melt season by 135 m³ of snow per lineal meter of fence (1 500 ft³/ft) or about 75–80% and average snow depth by 2 m (6.5 ft) (Fig. 6). Ablation rates were not affected so snow persisted about 3 weeks longer with the fence than without it (Fig. 7). Little effect could be noticed on length of the snow-profile lines until late July or early August, when the fenced lines remained 12–18 m (40–60 ft) longer than the unfenced due to slower recession of the deep drift behind the fence. The upward slope of the terrain beyond the eastern edge of the normal snowfield tended to shorten fence effect and prevent a significant increase in length of line behind the fence.

Fig. 7. Best fence results were obtained at Straight Creek Pass. On 9 August 1962, the additional 1.8–2.1 m (6–7 ft) of snow accumulated behind the fence is still obvious.

The smooth up-slope approach, together with the ridge-crest location of the fence and the 0.6 m (2 ft) gap beneath the fence, prevented a windward drift and allowed the fence to operate efficiently all winter. The absence of a windward drift not only gives best fence effect but it also eliminates the damage to a buried fence caused by snow settlement.

At maximum snow depth, a distance of 3.5–4.5 m (12–15 ft) behind the fence was blown clear of snow by air jetting under the fence. The snow then deepened rapidly into a distinct mound that had a steep lee face early in the winter, but usually filled to a gently rounded surface by spring. This was in sharp contrast to the normal streamlined filling of the terrain depression at this site (foreground of Figure 1).

At Mount Evans, the fence increased volume of snow 55–73 m³/m of fence (600–800 ft³/ft) (Fig. 8), average snow depth 0.6–0.8 m (2–2.5 ft), and length of profile lines 12–15 m (40–50 ft). The down-slope approach resulted in a windward drift that engulfed the fence in spite of a 1.2–1.4 m (4–4.5 ft) gap beneath the fence.

At maximum snow depth, most of the 3.7 m (12 ft) fence was buried and the entire area had a smooth rounded appearance. Damage to the fence from snow settlement was extensive each year. The gentle down-slope gradient east of the snowfield combined with the normal fence effect to give an increased volume that resulted from added length as well as depth.

At Teller Mountain, wind direction during snowdrifting proved to be different than expected. Field observations in the early summer of 1965 indicated that the drift from the ence fell more on the control lines adjacent to the fence than on the test lines behind the fence.

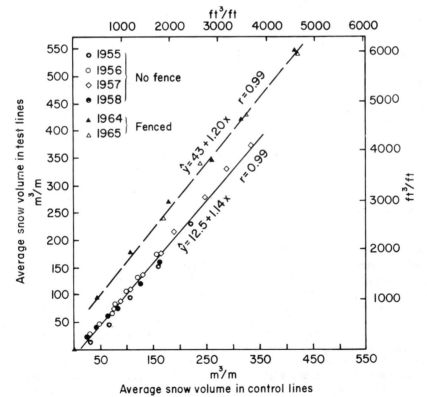

Fig. 8. *Snow volume, average snow depth and length of snow-profile lines behind the fence as a function of natural conditions at Mount Evans.*

250

Additional fence was built along the northern side of the field in an attempt to confine fence effect to the test lines. Erratic results indicated the additional fence did not completely correct the problem. It was therefore decided to use the control lines on Glacier Mountain to measure fence effect on all four profile lines at Teller Mountain. The Glacier Mountain control lines appeared to be free of fence effect, and the two sites were only 4.8 km (3 miles) apart and in similar terrain.

The long fence (1966 and 1967) at Teller Mountain increased early summer snow volumes and average snow depths 150 m³/m of fence (1 650 ft³/ft) and 1.7 m (6 ft), respectively (Fig. 9). This early season increase did not persist through the melt season, however, so that by late summer there was less snow with the fence up than under natural conditions. Why the depletion rate increased so sharply with the long fence is not known. It could be the short period of record or poor control.

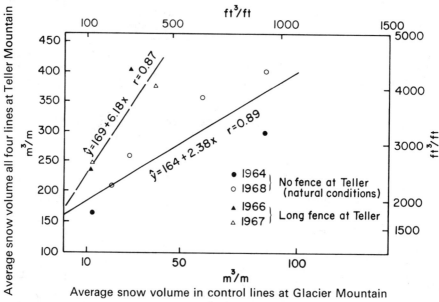

Fig. 9. *Snow volume, average snow depth and length of snow-profile lines in all four lines at Teller Mountain as functions of natural conditions at Glacier Mountain.*

The fence at Glacier Mountain reduced the volume of snow 56 m³/m of fence (600 ft³/ft) (Fig. 10), average snow depth 1.5 m (5 ft), and length of the profile lines about 9 m (30 ft). In the fenced part of the field, snow volume and average snow depths decreased more slowly and average length of profile more rapidly than under natural conditions (Fig. 10), possibly because the drift behind the fence was a little more in the shade of the ridge than before. These reduced rates, however, did not compensate for the large initial volume deficit, 85 m³/m (1 000 ft³/ft), so that at the end of the summer there was still almost 27 m³/m (300 ft³/ft) less snow behind the fence than under natural conditions.

The fence location at Glacier Mountain was something less than ideal for our purpose. The natural snowfield was about 35–40 m (110–130 ft) leeward of the ridge crest. The best fence site for keeping the fence free of a windward drift and maintaining high trapping efficiency all winter would have been the ridge crest. A fence here, however, would have thrown a drift well up-slope of the natural snowfield.

The location chosen was 5–8 m (15–25 ft) up-slope of the western edge of the snowfield and about 30 m (100 ft) to the lee of the ridge crest. It seemed necessary to take the risk of a windward drift burying the fence in order to get the fence effect to fall on the natural snowfield, as required by our primary objective of creating drifts deep enough to contribute to late summer stream flow. The first winter (1964–65) a windward drift did partially bury the fence, so the density of the lower tier of fencing was reduced to 20%. This helped a little but the lee drift still formed close to the fence and net snow accumulation was reduced from natural conditions.

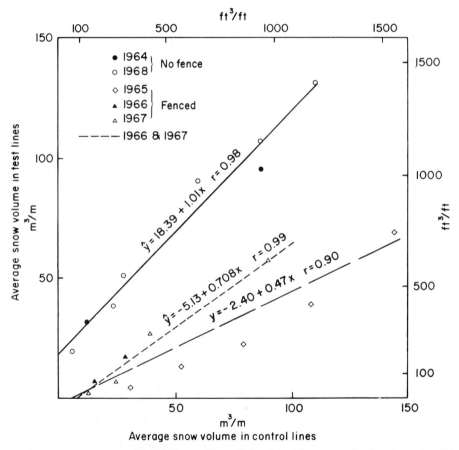

Fig. 10. Snow volume, average snow depth and length of the profile lines behind the fence as a function of natural conditions at Glacier Mountain.

CONCLUSIONS

At three of four alpine sites in the central Rocky Mountains, large snow fences appreciably increased snow accumulation on natural snowfields. At two of these sites, the increased accumulation persisted all summer and prolonged the melt season 1–3 weeks. Extra accumulation at the third successful site was accompanied by a more rapid melt rate so that early summer run-off was increased, but the melt season was not prolonged. The fence at the fourth site decreased the amount of snow normally present in the natural snowfield.

All successful fences were windward of snowfields that had level or gently sloping terrain beyond their down-wind edges. The unsuccessful fence was part-way down a lee slope that became steep just below the fence and remained steep for some distance beyond the snowfield. Schmidt (1970), in his discussion of wind-flow data taken at these sites, pointed out that fences above steep slopes encourage a reverse wind flow that can become strong enough to erode the natural snowdrift. This, together with the blocking of the gap below the fence by the windward snowdrift, is probably what happened at Glacier Mountain.

Net fence effect at Mount Evans was only half that at Straight Creek Pass. It is interesting to speculate what could be achieved at the Mount Evans site, if a barrier could be devised that would not become buried and would therefore remain effective all winter.

It is significant that, at both Straight Creek Pass and Mount Evans, the rate of depletion of snow volume and average snow depth was the same for fenced and natural conditions. This means the snow added by the fence will prolong the melt season and not just increase early summer run-off.

TABLE I. REGRESSIONS, EQUATIONS AND CORRELATION COEFFICIENTS (r) FOR SNOW VOLUME IN TEST LINES $(\hat{T})$ AS A FUNCTION OF SNOW VOLUME IN CONTROL LINES (x)

Snowfield	Natural		Fenced	
Straight Creek Pass	$\hat{T} = 4.5 + 1.42x$	$r = 0.99$	$\hat{T} = 142 + 1.36x$	$r = 0.87$
Mount Evans	$\hat{T} = 12.5 + 1.14x$	$r = 0.99$	$\hat{T} = 43 + 1.20x$	$r = 0.99$
Teller Mountain* (long fence)	$\hat{T} = 164 + 2.38x$	$r = 0.89$	$\hat{T} = 169 + 6.18x$	$r = 0.87$
Glacier Mountain	$\hat{T} = 18.4 + 1.01x$	$r = 0.98$	$\hat{T} = -5.1 + 0.71x$	$r = 0.99$

Conditions at the field

* Snow volume in the four lines at Teller Mountain was estimated from the volume in the two control lines at Glacier Mountain because the Teller Mountain control lines were not free of the fence effect.

Increases in snow volume (Table I) were greatest where the fence remained free of snow all winter. This was achieved at sites with a level or up-slope approach to the fence. Reducing the density of the lower half of one fence where a windward drift partly buried the fence helped but did not solve the problem. Damage to fences buried in their own drift was so extensive that another type of barrier should be considered for such places. At a good drift site like Mount Evans, it is possible that a rock or earth wall would induce a drift much like the one caused by the buried fence, and the more massive structure would not be damaged by snow settlement.

Based on an average snow density of 500 kg m⁻³ in these fields, the following amounts of snow fence were needed to produce an extra 1 000 m³ of water at the beginning of the melt season:

Straight Creek Pass	15 m	(60 ft of fence/acre-ft of water)
Mount Evans	31 m	(125 ft of fence/acre-ft of water)
Teller Mountain	27 m	(110 ft of fence/acre-ft of water)

These amounts compare favorably with the 50 m of the same type of fence needed per 1 000 m³ of water (200 ft of fence/acre-ft of water) for lower-elevation grasslands of eastern Wyoming (Tabler, 1970).

Land managers planning to use fences to modify the natural snowpack should select the sites with care. Fences should remain free of their own drifts to assure winter-long efficiency and to avoid the structural damage caused by settling snow. Sites should be chosen so the modification caused by the fence will contribute to the primary management goal, whether this be increasing spring run-off, decreasing snow depths in avalanche-prone areas, or supplementing late summer stream flow. Snow fences located with care and discretion can be a useful resource management tool, but the indiscriminate construction of fences along entire ridge crests or up-wind of a random assortment of natural snowfields will seldom achieve the desired results.

REFERENCES

Martinelli, M., *jr.* 1959. Alpine snowfields—their characteristics and management possibilities. *Union Géodésique et Géophysique Internationale. Association Internationale d'Hydrologie Scientifique, Colloque de Hannoveisch Münden, 8-14 Sept. 1959,* Tom. 1, p. 120-127.
Martinelli, M., *jr.* 1965. Accumulation of snow in alpine areas of central Colorado and means of influencing it. *Journal of Glaciology,* Vol. 5, No. 41, p. 625-36.
Martinelli, M., *jr.* 1966. Possibilities of snowpack management in alpine areas. (*In* Sopper, W. E., *and* Lull, H. W., *ed. Forest hydrology : proceedings of a National Science Foundation advanced science seminar held at the Pennsylvania State University . . . , Aug. 29–Sept. 10, 1965.* Oxford and New York, Pergamon Press, p. 225–31.)
Schmidt, R. A., *jr.* 1970. Locating snow fences in mountainous terrain. (*In* Snow removal and ice control research. Proceedings of an international symposium held April 8–10, 1970. [*U.S.*] *Highway Research Board. Special Report* 115, p. 220–25.)
Tabler, Ronald D. 1971. Design of a watershed snow fence system, and first-year snow accumulation. *Proceedings of the Western Snow Conference,* 39th annual meeting, 1971, p. 50–55.

PREDICTION OF SNOWDRIFT ACCUMULATION AT ALPINE SITES

(Summary of Doctoral Dissertation)

Neil H. Berg

INTRODUCTION

Field observations at alpine sites show the redistribution of fallen snow to the lee of meso-scale ridges which define traps for blowing snow. The results of this wind redistribution is especially striking in late spring and early summer when snow banks may survive only to the lee of alpine solifluction terraces. These snowdrifts provide a reservoir whose significance in the water balance of alpine watersheds remains incompletely known. They are also an important influence on vegetative growth in alpine areas. The relationships between topography and snow redistribution are incompletely understood, often in only a qualitative way. The research reported here was intended to provide a more rigorous, physical base to our knowledge of these relationships.

A COMPUTER SIMULATION

A set of hypotheses concerning the development of snow-drifts on natural terrain in alpine areas was developed and transformed into a computer simulation model. The model predicts the location and extent of drift accumulations on hetero-geneous terrain by specifying locations in the lower atmospheric boundary layer where topographic changes cause air flow expansion. The consequent reduction in wind velocity to less than that required to keep snow particles in eolian transport results in the accumulation of snow drifts.

Several zones of air flow are involved, including (1) a region upwind of the topographic disturbance in which the logarithmic law for vertical wind speed gradients applies, (2) an eddy zone immediately leeward of the topographic break, (3) an area of intense mixing which interfaces the eddy zone below and the logarithmic law profile region above, and (4) a region beyond the flow reattachment point where the boundary layer redevelops downwind (Figure 1).

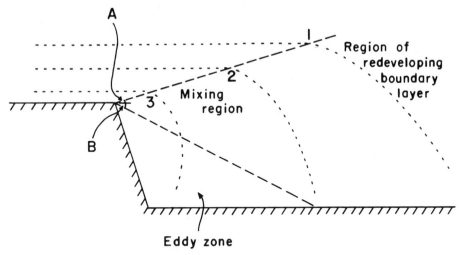

Undisturbed boundary layer flow

Figure 1. Schematic representation of snow particle movement
at a topographic step. Angle A defines the line
separating the region of undisturbed boundary layer
flow from the zone of intense turbulent mixing.
Angle B specifies the line separating the mixing
region from the zone of reverse eddy flow. Beyond
the eddy zone the boundary layer redevelops. Snow
grains moving at height 1 blow past the trap while
those at height 3 enter the eddy zone and add to the
drift accumulation.

Snow grain movement is described in the model prior to en-
trance to the mixing region in terms of the creep, saltation
and suspension modes of particle transport. On entry to the
mixing region, the grain trajectories are calculated and followed until eventual settlement in the drift or re-entrainment
beyond the trap (Figure 1).

In addition, the model:

1. apportions the mass of wind-blown being transported
    within the lower atmospheric boundary layer to dif-
    ferent vertical zones,
2. allocates the total transport between the suspension,
    saltation and creep modes of particle movement,
3. specifies the vertical and horizontal wind-speed gra-
    dients for air moving across a step-like boundary, and
4. tabulates the amount, density and spatial location of
    snow infilling the site.

Variations in grain characteristics are accommodated by allowing up to three size diameters and three shape factors to be considered sequentially at each blowing snow event. Thus, the effect of particle size and shape on the resulting deposit can be assessed. Time-sequencing is utilized so that the contribution of multiple blowing snow events at a single drift site can be analyzed. In essence, the model snowdrift deposition is a sedimentological process such that facies analysis in the geological sense could be undertaken.

The results of simulation experiments with the model converge with commonly observed characteristics of snowdrifts and show that:

1. there is relatively little deposition beyond the brink of the drifts;
2. grains of smaller diameter carry farther and are deposited farther downwind;
3. wind velocity is a major determinant in the amount and location of snow deposition in that:
   a. as wind speed increases grains go into suspension at the expense of saltation and creep and thus are more likely to blow past the trapping site,
   b. an increase in velocity also increases the horizontal component of the grain trajectory to similarly promote blowpast,
   c. deposition downwind from the brink of the drift is maximized at moderate wind speeds; at higher velocities blowpast predominates while at lower speeds there is insufficient energy to propel grains far leeward;
4. with wind speeds of less than twenty meters per second, all grains moving in saltation settle immediately to the lee of the brink of the drift;
5. the ground topography windward of the snow trap is an important control of the volume of drift accumulation. If the air flows downslope to the drift, its length will be reduced. A moderate upslope approach, on the other hand, lengthens the drift, increases its accumulation by reducing blowpast, and promotes cornice development,
6. the proportion of the total transport blowing past the trap remains constant and low, approximately ten percent of total transport, until approximately eighty percent of the trap is filled, after which blowpast increases sharply,
7. snow deposition is initiated only at sites where the divergence of the ground slope angle reaches nine degrees.

FIELD OBSERVATIONS

The correspondence between these model characteristics and experience suggests that the model performed reasonably well. Additional information on alpine snowdrift development can be gained from a "sensitivity" analysis and a comparison of field observations with model predictions.

The sensitivity analysis shows most of the parameters in the model to have a regular and predictable influence upon the outcome although the angle of divergence of the wedge of unmodified air flow emanating from the lip of the trap has an unduly large effect on the predicted snow surface. It seems that a maximum value must be assigned to this parameter to ensure that the drift accumulation does not extend toward infinity under some topographic conditions.

In a general way, drift infill on a Niwot Ridge site is adequately mimicked by the drift accumulation model. A cornice develops on all the drifts studied in the field but only for a short period during the early part of the accumulation season. In contrast, the model retains the cornice stage for much longer. Unfortunately, this comparison and test is of only limited value since the input parameters selected force the model to develop one drift over a field area which involves three drifts.

Several other conclusions derived from the field observations:

1. at some sites by mid-season a stable or equilibrium state of snow accumulation is reached; numerous deposition-erosion cycles occur whose net result is a constant level of accumulation. Such a steady-state is reached most readily at shallow sites and is maintained until spring when heavier snow, which tends not to drift, blankets the alpine (Figure 2).

2. although redistribution of fallen snow starts with the first snow fall, infill at lower elevations is postponed several weeks. Presumably the snow requirements of lee drifts associated with timberline vegetation must be fulfilled before accumulation at lower elevations commences (Figure 2).

3. infill is most rapid early in the season especially at shallow, exposed sites; at one location forty percent of the entire seasonal accumulation occurred in the first two weeks of drift accumulation (Figure 2).

4. snowdrifts at the same elevation fill in contemporaneously. Even where several traps are situated in line downwind, they all acquire snow simultaneously and it is not necessary for the upwind trap to be saturated before deposition farther downwind.

5. drift development is initiated when the angle of slope divergence exceeds approximately eight degrees measured over a five meter horizontal distance. There appears

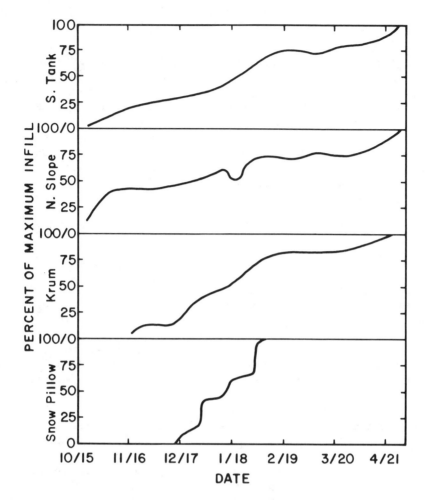

Figure 2. Snowdrift accumulation at four Niwot Ridge locations, 1974-1975. The top two graphs are based upon data from locations entirely in the alpine while the third location is at a slightly lower elevation immediately downwind of a large stand of krummholz. Note the delay in the onset of infill at the third site. The bottom graph portrays drift accumulation at a snow pillow at a still lower altitude in the upper montane forest.

to be no minimum height that a topographic irregularity must attain before deposition occurs: topographic discontinuities of only few centimeters height generate snowdrifts.
6. the snowdrifts studied on Niwot Ridge hold up to three-hundred cubic meters of water per linear meter perpendicular to the wind. This value is comparable to that measured on other alpine Rocky Mountain sites.

Part 4
Climatology

Overview
*Roger G. Barry**

Scientific interest in the climates of the Colorado mountains has a history spanning more than a century. Between 1874-88 and 1892-94 the Signal Service, and its successor the Weather Bureau, maintained an observatory on the summit of Pikes Peak (4300 m) which provided regular and detailed weather observations (U.S. Army, Chief Signal Officer, 1889; also, summary of results in Thompson and Dodd, 1958). Early workers used data from high-level stations to illustrate the altitudinal effect on temperatures and the significant occurrence of inversion conditions (temperatures increasing with height), especially in the elevated 'parks' (Henry, 1911-12). Most of the recent records at the higher elevations, however, have been of a climatological nature from unattended stations, or spanning only limited periods. Winter data are available from Berthoud Pass (3,450 m) since 1949, for example, with less regular records back to 1926 (Judson, 1977).

Four climatological stations established by J.W. Marr in 1952 along an altitudinal transect on the east slope of the Front Range up to 3,750 m, west of Boulder, have been operated by the Institute of Arctic and Alpine Research more or less continuously up to the present, providing invaluable year-round information. These last records (up to 1970) are analyzed in the first of the papers selected for inclusion in this chapter (Barry, 1973). By comparison with the data available for the conventional climatological elements, there is very little information on components of the energy budget at the surface. Indeed, studies by LeDrew (1973) and Greenland (1978) provide the only detailed information on solar radiation and surface energy budgets at high elevations in the Rocky Mountains.

*Institute of Arctic and Alpine Research
University of Colorado
Boulder, Colorado 80309

Two major branches of climatological research are represented by the papers included here -- synoptic climatology,
dealing with the control exerted by the large-scale circulation
on local climatic conditions (Barry, 1973; Hjermstad, 1970;
Greenland, 1978), and physical climatology, dealing with the
physical processes of heat and moisture exchanges at the ground-
air interface (Greenland, 1978; LeDrew, 1975; Ives, 1973). A
topic of early interest, which has received little subsequent
attention, is the possible therapeutic role of high altitude
climates (Williams, 1893). More specifically meteorological
problems concerning the effects of mountain barriers in setting
up lee wave motion, or in causing chinook conditions or downslope windstorms in their immediate lee, are also not considered
here. These subjects are fully treated in papers by Brinkmann
(1971, 1976) and Klemp and Lilly (1975). By contrast, much less
is known about wind conditions in the alpine regions of the
Colorado mountains.

Analysis of data from the transect of climatological stations on the east slope of the Front Range (Barry, 1973) demonstrates the importance of the regional atmospheric circulation
for local temperature and precipitation conditions. It also
serves to identify the sharp transition from an "upslope regime"
of precipitation, with a spring maximum, which occurs up to at
least 3,050 m, to a "west slope regime" at the Niwot Ridge site
at 3,750 m which is still 2 km east of the Divide. A larger
scale study of wintertime precipitation across the Continental
Divide by Hjermstad (1970) shows the effect of orography on the
west slope to be most pronounced between 2,100 m and 3,200 m
with totals approximately 50 percent larger at the base of the
east slope than at the same elevation on the west slope. Again,
rates of orographic increase are shown to depend strongly on
airflow direction although further work on total winter snowfall
indicates the major control exerted by topographic slope within
20 km of a particular site and by the number of upstream barriers
to precipitation-bearing airflows (Rhea and Grant, 1974). Some
of the implications of these analyses extend into the meteorological studies of winter cloud-seeding potential over the
Colorado mountains carried out at Colorado State University
(Mielke, Grant and Chappell, 1970) and the mapping of precipitation frequency by the National Weather Service (Miller et al.,
1973). Work of a complementary nature on summer rainstorms in
the San Juan mountains (Caine, 1976), suggests that their statistical properties, at least, resemble those at lower elevations. A seasonal trend is also apparent, with the shorter,
more intense storms tending to occur in mid-summer. Studies of
shower distribution indicate that, for southwestern Colorado,
when synoptic conditions are only marginally favorable, the few
showers that do occur are mainly in the mountains (Sullivan and
Seversen, 1966). However, in the area of the Continental Divide,
where valleys are of limited extent, there is less contrast
between mountain and valley locations. Radar studies indicate

that over the east slope of the Front Range, convective buildup
begins by mid-morning, with preferred locations near Estes Park,
Idaho Springs and southwest of Pueblo (Karr and Wooten, 1976).

Research on physical climatology has been concentrated
almost entirely on Niwot Ridge. Pioneer studies of high-altitude radiation conditions, microclimatology of the alpine
tundra environment, and their plant physiological implications
have been made by Gates and Janke (1966), and by Caldwell (1968).
However, their differing conclusions on altitudinal effects on
ultraviolet radiation are yet to be resolved and a thorough
study of the variation of solar and infrared radiation with
elevation remains to be performed, although the effect of weather
types on the altitudinal variation of solar radiation has recently
been investigated by Greenland (1978). A significant first step
in defining the energy budget regime of the alpine tundra in
summer is represented by the research of LeDrew (1975; LeDrew
and Weller, 1978), carried out in conjunction with the studies
of the International Biological Program, U.S. Tundra Biome. It
is of particular interest that, as a result of the strongly
advective regime, evaporation proceeds throughout the 24 hours,
dependent on soil moisture availability. Sublimation/evaporation
from alpine snow packs has been shown by several studies to be
generally negligible compared with melt (Martinelli, 1959),
although exceptions may occur in warm, dry, windy conditions.
Santeford (1972), however, concluded that sublimation of wind-
blown snow in early/mid winter, combined with in situ sublimation later in the season, led to the removal of 80 percent of
the winter snowfall from an alpine area above timberline (with
no redeposition of wind-blown snow in the forest). Almost
nothing is known about variations from year-to-year, or about
the energy regime in winter. In view of the demonstrated
occurrence of permafrost at favorable sites above 3,500 (Ives,
1973), the measurement of annual regimes of energy budget conditions over different alpine surfaces is an important task
awaiting attention. Another major gap in knowledge concerns
the variation of climatic conditions across timberline. Although this has been examined on the macroscale by Sharpe (1970)
using the moisture budget approach of C.W. Thornthwaite, it
remains for detailed microclimatic studies, like those of
Aulitzky (1961) in the Alps, to be carried out. It is in such
respects that our understanding of high mountain climatology is
still in its infancy.

REFERENCES

Aulitzky, H. 1961. Die Bodentemperaturverhältnisse an einer
    zentralalpinen Hanglage beiderseits der Waldgrenze. (I).
    Arch. Met. Geophys. Biokl., B10: 445-532.
Brinkmann, W.A.R. 1971. What is a Foehn? *Weather*, 26: 230-239.
    _____. 1974. Strong downslope winds at Boulder, Colorado.
    Monthly Weather Review, 102: 592-602.

262

Greenland, D. 1978. Spatial distribution of radiation on the Colorado Front Range. *Climatol. Bull.* (McGill University), 24: 1-14.

Henry, A.J. 1911-12. Variations of temperature at summit and base stations in the central Rocky Mountain region. *Bull. Mount. Weather Observ.*, 4: 103-114.

Ives, J.D. 1973. Permafrost and its relationship to other environmental parameters in a midlatitude, high-altitude setting, Front Range, Colorado Rocky Mountains. In: *Permafrost: North American Contribution (to the) Second International Conference. International Conference on Permafrost.* Washington, National Academy of Sciences, pp. 121-125.

Judson, A. 1977. Climatological data from the Berthoud Pass area of Colorado. *U.S. Department of Agriculture, Forest Service, General Tech. Rept. RM-42*, Fort Collins, Colorado. 94 pp.

Karr, T.W. and R.L. Wooten. 1976. Summer radar echo distribution around Limon, Colorado. *Monthly Weather Review*, 104: 728-734.

Klemp, J.B. and D.K. Lilly. 1975. The dynamics of wave-induced downslope winds. *Jour. Atmos. Sci.*, 32: 320-339.

LeDrew, E.F. and G. Weller. 1978. A comparison of the radiation and energy balance during the growing season for arctic and alpine tundra. *Arct. Alp. Res.*, 10: 665-678.

Martinelli, M., Jr. 1959. Some hydrologic aspects of alpine snowfields under summer conditions. *Jour. Geophys. Res.*, 64: 451-455.

Mielke, P.R., Jr., L.O. Grant, and C.F. Chappell. 1970. Elevation and spatial variation effects of wintertime orographic cloud seeding. *Jour. Appl. Meteorol.*, 9: 476-488.

Miller, J.F., R.H. Frederick, and R.J. Tracey. 1973. *Precipitation-frequency Atlas of the Western United States. Vol. III. Colorado.* National Weather Service, Office of Hydrology, Silver Spring, Maryland (NOAA-Atlas 2, Vol. III). 47 pp.

Rhea, J.O. and L.O. Grant. 1974. Topographic influences on snowfall patterns in mountainous terrain. In: *Advanced Concepts and Techniques in the Study of Snow and Ice Resources.* National Academy of Science, Washington, D.C., pp. 182-192.

Santeford, H.S., Jr. 1972. *Management of Windblown Alpine Snows.* Unpublished Ph.D. thesis, Colorado State University, Fort Collins, Colorado. 182 pp.

Sharpe, D.M. 1970. The effective climate in the dynamics of alpine timberline ecosystems in Colorado. *Publ. in Climatology* (Elmer, New Jersey), 23(1). 82 pp.

Sullivan, W.G. and J.O. Seversen. 1966. Areal shower distribution--mountain versus valley coverage. *Weather Bureau Central Region Tech. Mem. 3* (ESSA), Kansas City, Missouri. 3 pp. + figures.

Thompson, W.F. and A.V. Dodd. 1958. Environmental handbook for the Camp Hale and Pikes Peak areas, Colorado. Headquarters Quartermaster Research and Engineering Command, U.S. Army, *Tech. Rept. EP-79*, Natick, Massachusetts. 90 pp.

U.S. Army, Chief Signal Officer. 1889. Meteorological observations made on the summit of Pike's Peak, Colorado (latitude, 38°50'N., longitude, 105°2'W., height 14,134 feet). January 1874 to June 1888. *Annals, Astron. Observ., Harvard University*, XXII. 475 pp.

Williams, C.T. 1893. The high altitudes of Colorado and their climates. *Quart. Jour. Roy. Meterol. Soc.*, 19: 65-82.

A CLIMATOLOGICAL TRANSECT ON THE EAST SLOPE
OF THE FRONT RANGE, COLORADO

R. G. Barry

*Institute of Arctic and Alpine Research
and Department of Geography
University of Colorado
Boulder, Colorado 80302*

ABSTRACT

Climatological data collected from 1952 to 1970 at four ridge sites on the east slope of the Front Range, west of Boulder, Colorado, at elevations between 2,195 m and 3,750 m are analyzed using the TAXIR data retrieval system. Significant results of the climatography include the demonstration of a much greater mean annual precipitation at the two upper stations than previously reported. The mean total exceeds 100 cm at 3,750 m. Solar radiation totals show little or no change with elevation between 2,590 and 3,750 m for the annual average. Extremes of minimum air temperature for October 1969 at the two lower stations lay outside the theoretically expected 100-year return period for these stations. Daily precipitation and maximum and minimum temperatures are analyzed in terms of 700-mb circulation types in mid-season months, 1952 to 1970. Precipitation data are also examined with respect to 700-mb wind velocity over Denver. The paper concludes with some recommendations for further studies.

INTRODUCTION

Climatic records have been collected at four elevations between 2,195 and 3,750 m on the east slope of the Front Range, west of Boulder, Colorado, more or less continuously since October 1952. So far as is known, these form the most comprehensive series of mountain station records in the Rocky Mountains. The four principal stations were located on ridge sites in each of the major ecological belts by J.W.Marr, formerly of the Institute of Arctic and Alpine Research, University of Colorado. Marr's (1961) terminology is Lower Montane Forest, Upper Montane Forest, Sub-Alpine Forest, and Alpine Tundra, but Löve (1971) recommends that the term subalpine be restricted to the forest-tundra ecotone. The forest belts would then be submontane, middle montane, and up-per montane. For the period October 1952 to September 1953 observations were taken at four sites—north-facing slopes, valley floor, and ridge top—in each of the four ecological belts. An ecological survey of the east slope of the Front Range has been given by Marr (1961), together with a preliminary account of the results from the 16 stations operated in 1952 and 1953. The basic data have been tabulated through 1964 (Marr, 1967; Marr *et al.,* 1968a, 1968b) but not analyzed.

This paper presents a climatological analysis of the records for 1952 to 1970 in which the data were organized into magnetic tape data banks using the TAXIR information storage and retrieval system (Brill, 1971).

Arctic and Alpine Research, Vol. 5, No. 2, 1973, pp. 89-110.

DATA AND METHODS

The stations form a nearly east-west transect from just west of Boulder almost to the Continental Divide (Figure 1). The three lower stations—Ponderosa (A-1) at 2,195 m, Sugarloaf (B-1) at 2,591 m, and Como (C-1) at 3,048 m—are located in clearings in the montane forest while Niwot Ridge (D-1) at 3,750 m is on the alpine tundra. The sites of the two upper stations are illustrated in Figures 2 and 3. The stations were initially instrumented with thermohygrographs (regularly calibrated and checked with maximum and minimum thermometers and psychrometers), standard 8-inch precipitation gauges installed with the rim 1 m above ground, totalizing anemometers (at 2 m height at Niwot Ridge and ca. 0.7 m above the general level of tree crowns at the other three stations), and maximum and minimum soil thermometers at ca. 15 and 30 cm depth. Recording precipitation gauges were installed at Como in 1962 and during 1964 and 1965 at the other stations. The installation in the clearings was positioned so that the gauge rim subtended an angle of 45° to the tree crowns although the most effective angle is 30° according to Leaf (1962). Recording wind velocity systems, provided by the National Center for Atmospheric Research, Boulder, were operated from 1962 at the same elevation 3.5 km north of Sugarloaf, at Como and at Niwot Ridge. Solar radiation

data were obtained from bimetallic actinographs at Como for 1964 and 1965, at Sugarloaf in 1965, and at Niwot Ridge in 1965 and 1968 to 1970. Data post-1965 at Como are integrated chart records from an Eppley pyranometer. Generally, the stations were serviced at weekly intervals.

Three data banks have been constructed for daily data: (1) sixteen station bank for October 1952 to September 1953; (2) daily bank, part I for four stations for 1952 to 1964; and (3) daily bank, part II, for four stations for 1962 to 1970 (six in 1965). A "weekly" bank was also constructed for 1952 to 1964 incorporating observations made only at servicing visits (run-of-wind, total precipitation, soil temperatures, and snow depth).

In addition to the observational data, the banks included some simple parameters, such as mean and range of daily temperature and relative humidity, derived from the records in a data conversion program during the formation of the banks. Synoptic parameters chosen to characterize the daily atmospheric conditions over the area, on both a local and a large scale, were also incorporated. The local descriptors were 1200 GMT data from the Denver RAWINSONDE at 700 mb (temperature, relative humidity, and wind speed and direction) and height of the freezing level. The large-scale

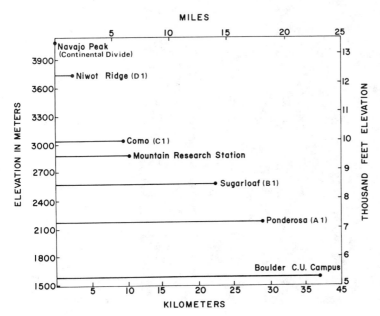

FIGURE 1. Elevation of the stations and proximity to the Continental Divide.

266

FIGURE 2. View westward along Niwot Ridge toward the Continental Divide. The Niwot Ridge station (3,750 m) and the IBP Tundra Biome alpine site are indicated. The peaks rise to over 4,000 m. The Green Lakes Valley is on the left.
(Photo J.D. Ives.)

FIGURE 3. Site of the Como station (3,050 m) in the upper montane forest. (Photo NCAR.)

synoptic situation was represented by a classification of the 700-mb height field and of the 700-mb height departure from the 1952 to 1970 mean for that month derived by the statistical method of Lund (1963). The similarity between pairs of daily maps was determined by the correlation coefficient for height data on a 31 point diamond grid over the sector 20 to 60°N, 95 to 125°W. The correlation threshold employed to determine the groups was $r \geqq 0.95$ for October to March and $r \geqq 0.922$ for April to September, in the case of the height patterns, and $r \geqq 0.7$ for the deviation patterns. In view of the size of the correlation matrix it was necessary to treat each month separately for the 18-year period, but the types distinguished for each month were then correlated among themselves in order to determine month-to-month continuity in the major patterns. Details of this analysis are given in Barry (1972).

The principal advantage of the TAXIR system is that it facilitates retrieval of any specified subsets of the data. This may be in tabulated form or on magnetic tape file suitable for use with a wide variety of statistical routines (see Brill, 1971, pp. 32-51, 49-50; Barry, 1972, Appendix 2).

CLIMATOGRAPHY

A primary purpose of the analysis was to provide a thorough documentation of the climatological characteristics of the area. This is essential as a background to studies in ecology, geomorphology, glaciology, and hydrology, being carried out by the Institute of Arctic and Alpine Research in the Front Range, as well as serving to identify climatological problems meriting further investigation.

Wind data are considered first since these have important implications for other climatic elements. Table 1 shows daily mean wind speeds based on 10-min averages at each hour (where there are at least 12 observations per day). Niwot Ridge experiences high mean speeds in the winter months although it is still much less windy than at the Mount Washington, New Hampshire, observatory (1,909 m), for example. The extreme gusts are certainly too low since the recorders had an upper limit of 100 m.p.h. (45 m sec⁻¹). The number of days with a peak gust $\geqq 45$ m sec⁻¹ at Niwot Ridge during the period January 1966 to April 1970 was 5.6% of days with records; observations were missing for 21% of the period. Nearly all of these extreme gusts occurred in October through February. The wind data at Como and Sugarloaf are more complete but the mean speeds at Como are probably unrepresentative also since the anemometer is close to tree-top height and the upwind distance to the edge of the clearing is only about 50 m.

Temperature data are summarized in Table 2. The mean annual air temperature of $-3.8°C$ at Niwot Ridge is almost identical with that at Nome, Alaska (64°N), although the summer on Niwot Ridge is somewhat cooler. The frost-free season, defined with respect to daily minimum temperatures (at 1.5 m) above 0°C, has a mean duration as follows:

Ponderosa	125 days	(maximum 160, minimum 92 in 17 years)
Sugarloaf	104 days	(maximum 156, minimum 64 in 17 years)
Como	59 days	(maximum 98, minimum 28 in 18 years)
Niwot Ridge	47 days	(maximum 74, minimum 26 in 18 years)

Winter conditions are particularly severe when the mean wind speed is taken into account.

The data in Table 2 illustrate the normal daytime lapse of temperature with elevation and the tendency for the topographic lapse rate to be affected by local conditions at night, especially in summer at the higher elevations. From June to September the mean minimum at Como is within 1.5°C of that at Niwot Ridge. This may be a result of nocturnal downslope drainage of cold air (Bergen, 1969) or it may reflect the influence of the clearing in which the Como station is located. As shown in Figure 4, the diurnal range of temperature in summer at Como is more like that at the two lower stations, both of which are sited in forest openings, than Niwot Ridge. Detailed wind measurements are required to explain the observed conditions at Como.

The diurnal temperature range (Figure 4) decreases markedly at the highest elevation where mixing of the surface layer with the free air is promoted by the high wind speeds. Differences of temperature between sites with different exposure also diminish with increasing elevation. For 1952 to 1953, the average differences between south-facing and valley sites, which generally show the maximum contrast, are given in Table 3. The steepness of the south slopes involved was only between 14 and 18%, however. Additional data relating to

TABLE 1

Mean wind speed and percentage frequency of peak daily gusts, 1965-1970

(a) Mean wind speed (for months with observations on at least 25 days)[a]

Station	Jan.	Feb.	Mar.	Apr.	May	June	July	Aug.	Sept.	Oct.	Nov.	Dec.	Year
Niwot Ridge	13.9(1)[b]	11.8(3)	12.1(4)	9.5(4)	8.9(3)	7.8(2)	5.8(2)	5.7(4)	7.9(4)	12.5(4)	13.4(3)	13.6(3)	10.3
Como	5.8(4)	3.1(5)	3.9(4)	3.3(4)	2.8(3)	2.2(2)	1.9(4)	2.0(4)	2.2(4)	3.6(4)	4.3(3)	4.4(4)	3.4
Sugarloaf	3.6(3)	2.7(4)	2.4(4)	2.1(4)	1.6(4)	1.4(4)	1.3(4)	1.3(4)	1.3(4)	2.0(4)	2.4(3)	2.8(3)	2.1

(b) Percentage frequency of daily peak gusts

Station	m sec⁻¹	Jan.	Feb.	Mar.	Apr.	May	June	July	Aug.	Sept.	Oct.	Nov.	Dec.	Year
Niwot Ridge (Jan. 1966-Apr. 1970)	≤ 8	0.6	0	0.8	0	0.8	0	0.8	0.8	0	0	0	0	0.8
	8-17	1.9	13.5	7.3	7.3	14.5	10.0	28.2	29.0	30.9	3.2	5.0	5.0	4.0
	17-32	21.3	31.2	37.9	49.3	50.0	58.9	29.8	56.4	50.1	50.8	36.7	33.0	33.0
	33-44	21.3	29.1	26.6	18.7	14.5	15.6	1.6	3.2	16.7	35.5	30.8	30.6	30.6
	≥ 45	6.5	14.1	1.6	3.5	3.2	0	0	0.8	0	4.8	13.3	11.3	11.3
Missing data		48.4	12.1	25.8	21.3	16.9	15.6	40.3	1.0	2.5	5.7	14.2	20.2	20.2
Total number of days		155	141	124	150	124	90	124	124	120	124	120	124	124
Como (Feb. 1966-May 1970)	≤ 8	0.8	15.6	14.2	10.7	20.2	34.2	46.0	37.9	32.5	12.9	10.0	9.7	9.7
	8-17	23.4	26.2	23.9	29.3	41.9	36.7	48.4	53.2	48.3	30.7	19.2	20.2	20.2
	17-32	57.2	51.8	40.6	39.3	20.2	14.2	2.4	4.0	15.8	47.6	49.2	47.6	47.6
	33-44	17.7	5.7	5.2	0.7	2.4	0.8	0	0	0	2.4	5.8	12.9	12.9
	≥ 45	0	0	0	0	0	0	0	0	0	0	0	0	0
Missing data		0.8	0.7	16.1	20.0	15.3	14.2	3.2	4.8	3.3	6.5	15.8	9.7	9.7
Total number of days		124	141	155	150	124	120	124	124	120	124	120	124	124
Sugarloaf (Gold Hill) (Feb. 1966-Dec. 1969)	≤ 8	20.4	31.9	32.3	42.6	51.6	55.8	76.7	75.1	70.0	37.9	25.0	23.4	23.4
	8-17	35.5	35.4	45.2	41.7	38.7	38.4	21.0	21.0	28.3	46.0	38.3	39.5	39.5
	17-32	38.7	31.0	18.6	13.4	5.6	3.3	2.4	1.6	1.7	12.9	15.8	21.0	21.0
	33-44	4.3	0.9	1.6	1.7	0	0	0	0	0	0	1.7	4.0	4.0
	≥ 45	1.1	0	0	0	0	0	0	0	0	0	0	0	0
Missing data		0	0.9	2.4	0.8	4.0	2.5	0	2.4	0	3.2	19.2	12.1	12.1
Total number of days		93	113	124	120	124	120	124	124	120	124	120	124	124

[a] Data are given in m sec⁻¹. Number of months are in parentheses.
[b] Confirmed by a mean of 13.9 for 3 years with $\geq$ 21 days/month.

steeper (and in the alpine more representative) slopes are needed.

Precipitation data for Niwot Ridge are virtually useless prior to October 17, 1964, when a large snow fence was erected around the recording gauge. The necessity for this at windy sites, in order to obtain anything approaching a realistic total, has been amply demonstrated

TABLE 2

Temperature data[a]

	Ponderosa (2,195 m)		Sugarloaf (2,591 m)		Como (3,048 m)		Niwot Ridge (3,750 m)	
(a) Mean daily maximum and minimum temperature, October 1952-September 1970[b]								
Jan.	4.6	−7.3	2.2	−9.2	−2.9	−11.8	−10.1	−16.2
Feb.	5.4	−6.9	3.0	−9.1	−2.2	−11.7	−10.3	−16.2
Mar.	6.5	−6.3	4.6	−8.3	−0.8	−11.3	−8.2	−15.2
Apr.	11.6	−1.5	9.0	−4.1	3.8	−6.8	−3.7	−11.1
May	17.5	4.1	14.9	1.7	9.6	−1.1	3.1	−4.6
June	22.8	8.8	20.2	6.4	15.1	1.9	8.6	0.5
July	27.8	12.7	24.8	10.5	19.0	5.0	12.5	4.4
Aug.	26.6	11.8	23.6	9.6	17.9	4.3	11.3	3.4
Sept.	21.5	7.3	18.9	5.2	14.2	0.9	7.3	−0.7
Oct.	16.2	2.6	14.2	0.6	9.2	−2.7	1.7	−5.4
Nov.	8.9	−3.2	6.4	−5.2	1.9	−7.9	−5.5	−11.6
Dec.	5.5	−5.9	2.8	−8.0	−1.8	−10.8	−9.1	−15.3
Year	14.6	1.4	12.1	−0.8	6.9	−4.4	−0.2	−7.3
(b) Temperature Extremes								
Jan.	17	−34	16	−36	12	−37	4	−37
Feb.	21	−27	16	−31	13	−32	5	−32
Mar.	27	−23	19	−26	12	−29	5	−30
Apr.	27	−17	25	−18	17	−22	11	−22
May	31	−11	29	−13	21	−16	14	−22
June	38	−3	34	−5	25	−7	19	−12
July	37	4	33	2	25	−2	18	−3
Aug.	37	2	33	−1	25	−7	18	−7
Sept.	34	−8	30	−9	25	−14	16	−14
Oct.	31	−18	26	−19	18	−18	11	−22
Nov.	21	−22	18	−23	13	−27	7	−29
Dec.	18	−24	17	−26	13	−27	4	−32

[a]Data are given in °C.

[b]Data are missing for Jan.-June 1956. Means were determined from the following number of years' data: Ponderosa —17, except July and Dec. (18); Sugarloaf —17, except April (16); July, Sept., Oct., and Dec. (18); Como —17, except Feb. and Mar. (16); July, Aug., Oct., and Dec. (18); Niwot Ridge —17, except Jan., Feb., Nov., Dec. (14); Mar. (15); July, Aug. (17).

by Larson (1971). The gauge rim is at 2 m so as to reduce the collection of drifting snow. The means from the recording gauges of 102 cm (40.2 inches) at Niwot Ridge and 77 cm (30.3 inches) at Como (Table 4) contrast markedly with 65.5 cm (25.8 inches) at both stations determined with unshielded standard 8-inch gauges for 1953 to 1964 (Marr *et al.*, 1968b). An average of 105 cm (41.4 inches) was recorded during 1907 to 1912 at Corona Pass (3,554 m) on the Continental Divide 19 km south of Niwot Ridge. The annual averages of Ponderosa and Sugarloaf are almost identical and this is confirmed by the record over the whole period (Table 4b). Hjermstad (1970) suggested that there is a minimum zone of winter precipitation on the eastern slopes of the Divide at about 2,600 m and there is some evidence for this in the data shown in Table 4.

The vertical distribution of precipitation varies markedly with season. The highest averages occur at 3,750 m from November through April and probably between 3,050 and 3,750 m from June through September. In May and October the distribution changes dramatically between different years. Very large falls on the lower slopes in May and October 1969 with 29.4 cm and 17.0 cm, respectively, at Ponderosa unduly bias the averages for 1965 to 1970, but using the 1952 to 1970 means for these months at Ponderosa and Sugarloaf the pattern of vertical distribution is still not clear cut.

The seasonal precipitation regime at the two lower stations is almost identical (Sugarloaf is not shown in Figure 5) with a pronounced maxmium in May and a minimum in mid-winter, whereas Niwot Ridge is more like stations west of the Divide in having a winter maximum and fall minimum. There is a similar regime to Niwot Ridge in the Green Lakes Valley immediately to the south although in individual years, such as 1969, it may not be apparent (N. Caine, pers. comm., 1972). The regime at Como resembles that at the two lower stations although the maximum and minimum are less pronounced.

The solar radiation data (Table 5) are available for only a short period at more than one station. Nevertheless, the observed variations with elevation are of considerable interest. The question of the altitudinal variation in global solar radiation has been considered from both a theoretical (Gates and Janke, 1966) and an observational standpoint (Sauberer and Dirmhirn, 1958). The actinograph data for 1965 (Table 5) indicate no increase with elevation on an annual basis, confirming Caldwell's (1968) view of the effect of cloud cover over the mountains on incident radiation. On a seasonal basis there is an increase from 2,600 to 3,050 m in December through May while in June through October there is some increase from 3,050 to 3,750 m. However, this latter feature was not observed in 1969. Independent cloud data are not available to examine these differences further and the sample sizes of the circulation types were too limited to use in this regard.

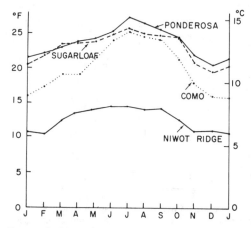

FIGURE 4. Mean daily range of temperature at the four stations.

TABLE 3

Average temperature differences between south-facing and valley sites, 1952 to 1953[a]

Approx. elevation (m)	December-February		June-August	
	Max.	Min.	Max.	Min.
2,195	3.5	3.9	5.1	7.6
2,590	1.4	2.1	1.3	5.3
3,050	2.6	1.3	4.0	1.7
3,750[b]	−1.4	−1.4	−1.0	−1.1

[a]Temperature data are given in °C.
[b]The valley site here was 180 m lower than the south-facing one. The negative sign indicates that the former was warmer.

TABLE 4

Mean precipitation

Station	Jan.	Feb.	Mar.	Apr.	May	June	July	Aug.	Sept.	Oct.	Nov.	Dec.	Year
(a) 1965-1970													
Ponderosa (2,195 m)	1.32(4)	2.49(5)	5.33(5)	5.08(5)	10.47(5)	7.29(5)	3.84(5)	4.78(5)	5.64(5)	5.99(4)	2.62(4)	3.05(4)	57.89
Sugarloaf (2,591 m)	1.35(5)	2.79(5)	4.75(5)	4.98(4)	9.63(5)	7.37(5)	4.88(5)	5.61(5)	5.77(5)	5.94(4)	2.39(5)	2.59(5)	57.79
Como (3,048 m)	4.83(6)	4.90(6)	7.09(6)	7.72(6)	9.55(6)	8.36(6)	8.15(6)	6.17(6)	5.61(5)	4.72(5)	5.44(4)	4.52(5)	77.06
Niwot Ridge (3,750 m)	13.77(5)	9.07(4)	10.54(4)	10.19(5)	6.78(4)	6.99(5)	8.03(4)	5.72(4)	7.16(4)	3.89(3)	11.20(4)	8.76(5)	102.08
(b) Oct. 1952-Sept. 1970													
Ponderosa (2,195 m)	2.18(16)	2.72(17)	5.26(17)	5.77(17)	9.22(17)	5.97(17)	5.03(17)	4.88(17)	4.50(17)	3.48(17)	3.23(17)	2.26(17)	54.48
Sugarloaf (2,591 m)	2.13(17)	3.23(17)	4.95(17)	5.64(16)	8.69(17)	5.44(17)	5.77(17)	5.89(17)	4.39(17)	3.58(17)	2.95(18)	2.44(18)	55.09

[a]Data are given in cm. Number of months with ≥ 25 days' record shown in parentheses.

TABLE 5

Mean daily radiation 1965 and ratios between stations[a]

Month	Means 1965			Ratios 1965			Ratio D-1/C-1		
	Sugarloaf B-1	Como C-1	Niwot D-1	C-1/B-1	D-1/B-1	D-1/C-1	1968	1969	1970
Jan.	157.7	186.5	180.0	1.18	1.14	0.96		0.96	1.05
Feb.	238.9	290.4	293.6	1.22	1.23	1.01		1.01	1.04
Mar.	303.5	378.9	343.9	1.25	1.13	0.91		1.15	1.14
Apr.	417.0	513.1	503.7	1.23	1.21	0.98		1.13	1.05
May	429.7	473.1	513.2	1.10	1.19	1.09		1.06	1.00
June	507.7	405.3	472.5	0.80	0.93	1.17		1.25	
July	489.0	387.7	482.6	0.77	0.98	1.24		0.89	
Aug.	514.8	402.9	451.0	0.78	0.87	1.12		0.95	
Sept.	355.7	307.0	347.0	0.86	0.98	1.13		0.99	
Oct.	341.7	311.9	325.5	0.91	0.95	1.04	0.93	0.83	
Nov.	222.3	202.7	181.3	0.91	0.82	0.89	0.96	0.94	
Dec.	161.7	167.7	169.0	1.04	1.05	1.01	0.86	1.02	
Year	345.0	335.6	355.3	0.97	1.03	1.06		1.01	

[a]Radiation is given in cal · cm^{-2} · day^{-1}. $n \geq 23$ days in each month.

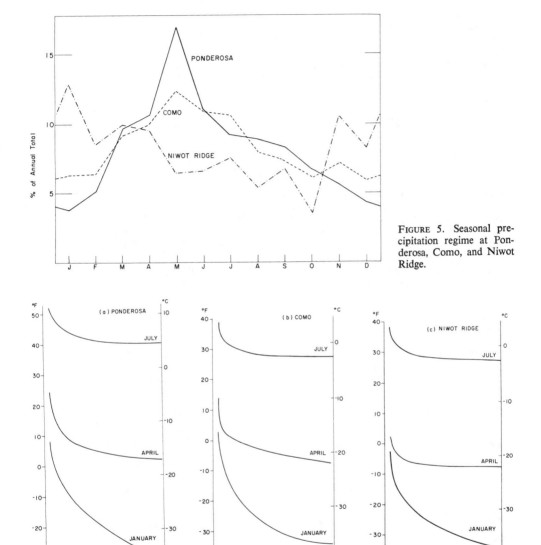

FIGURE 5. Seasonal precipitation regime at Ponderosa, Como, and Niwot Ridge.

FIGURE 6. Return periods of monthly minimum temperature for January, April, and July. (a) Ponderosa, (b) Como, and (c) Niwot Ridge. The return period is plotted for $(n + 1)/(n + 1 - m)$ where n = number of observations, m = rank of the observed value.

TEMPERATURE VARIABILITY AND TRENDS

The completeness of the temperature data permitted an examination of return periods and trends. Monthly minima for January, April, July, and October were analyzed with respect to return periods by Dr. E. S. Joseph (during an NSF Research Participation Program). Figure 6a-c shows that the 17- to 18-year records at Ponderosa, Como, and Niwot Ridge provide a reasonable characterization of the range of temperature conditions in January, April, and July. The curves for October are close to those for April at Como and Niwot Ridge. However, at the two lower stations the results for October 1969 lie just outside the 100-year recurrence interval (Figure 7). The synoptic events of that month, related to several spells of weather dominated by an upper cold low and heavy snowfalls on the lower eastern slopes, were evidently most effective below 3,000 m.

Although the series is a relatively short one, it is of considerable interest to examine the temperature record for any evidence of climatic fluctuations in view of Lloyd's (1970) claim of a downward trend. Figure 8 shows mean temperatures at Como for June to August (the main ablation season on the Front Range glaciers) extended with the latest data. There is a downward trend of 0.07°C year^{-1} which is significant at the 5% level by Student's t test. This trend is apparent in both maximum and minimum temperatures at the station, suggesting that it is unlikely to be the result of a site factor. However, similar analysis for Niwot Ridge reveals no statistically significant trend,

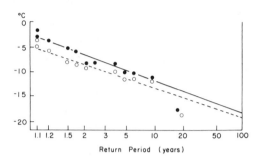

FIGURE 7. Return periods of monthly minimum temperature for October at Ponderosa and Sugarloaf.

although the sign of the regression coefficients is negative. Information supplied by Mr. Arthur Judson (pers. comm., 1973) indicates no trend in summer temperatures for 1962 to 1972 at Berthoud Pass (3,448 m) some 29 km from Niwot Ridge.

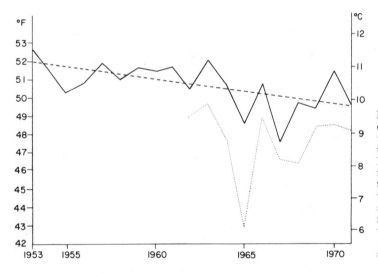

FIGURE 8. Trend of mean daily temperature for June to August at Como, 1953 to 1971, and Berthoud Pass, 1962 to 1971 (information supplied by Arthur Judson). Dashed line was determined by regression techniques. Five-year running means at Berthoud Pass for 1962 to 1972 and 1967 to 1971 are both 8.7°C.

SYNOPTIC CLIMATOLOGY

Analysis of the characteristics of the synoptic patterns has been carried out principally for daily temperature and precipitation data. The results obtained so far relate to the height patterns although a future examination of the deviation patterns is planned. Comparison of the discrimination of the 700-mb height pattern types with respect to temperature levels at Como, compared with that provided by nine classes of the 700-mb wind direction at Denver, shows that the former are considerably more effective in separating different temperature conditions, particularly in winter.

Mean maximum and minimum temperatures for days with the specified 700-mb circulation pattern types in mid-season months are given in Table 6 for three of the stations. The data are ranked with respect to maximum

TABLE 6

Mean maximum and minimum temperature and standard deviation for 700-mb circulation pattern types[a]

Circulation type	Days	Max.	Min.	Circulation type	Days	Max.	Min.
January 1953-1955, 1957-1970				April 1953-1955, 1957-1970			
Ponderosa				Ponderosa			
6	14	49.7(7.1)	26.5(7.5)	4	30	63.3(7.7)	35.0(6.3)
5	23	49.0(6.9)	26.2(7.5)	1	188	58.2(10.2)	32.8(8.3)
2	64	44.9(8.7)	23.9(8.7)	6	14	53.4(12.7)	28.9(5.5)
1	204	43.6(8.3)	22.9(9.4)	3	35	51.0(10.7)	29.8(6.2)
9	10	38.9(3.4)	18.4(6.7)	5	22	50.7(12.7)	26.0(8.9)
3	69	35.1(9.4)	11.3(12.0)	2	60	48.8(10.7)	25.4(8.5)
4	40	28.1(11.1)	4.6(11.7)	7	22	46.1(7.6)	26.9(5.2)
				8	13	44.7(13.1)	23.8(6.7)
8	8	52.0(4.1)	30.1(6.0)	9	10	37.3(9.3)	20.6(7.9)
13	7	22.6(4.2)	6.1(9.0)				
				14	3	73.7(6.7)	44.0(2.6)
Total	439			Total	397		
Mean (17-year)		40.2	18.8	Mean (17-year)		52.9	29.3
Como				Como			
6	14	40.1(5.1)	14.9(8.8)	4	30	47.7(6.9)	24.7(8.0)
5	23	36.8(7.7)	17.0(11.7)	1	188	43.1(8.1)	23.4(7.9)
2	64	31.4(7.9)	15.4(8.4)	6	14	39.3(8.6)	17.9(8.1)
1	203	27.8(8.4)	13.3(9.3)	3	35	38.2(8.2)	19.9(7.1)
9	10	24.9(3.3)	10.8(5.8)	5	22	37.7(10.3)	17.4(8.2)
3	69	21.2(7.8)	5.7(10.4)	2	60	34.9(8.6)	17.1(8.4)
4	34	19.2(7.9)	4.3(9.1)	8	13	33.2(8.3)	15.2(7.1)
				7	22	32.9(7.4)	15.6(5.4)
8	8	39.4(5.2)	21.1(8.8)	9	10	29.3(8.8)	12.8(7.4)
13	5	15.6(11.5)	−2.0(8.0)				
				14	3	57.0(2.6)	29.3(2.1)
Total	425			15	7	28.7(7.8)	16.7(5.6)
Mean (16-year)		26.9	10.9	12	7	30.7(4.7)	12.6(7.5)
				Total	411		
				Mean (17-year)		38.8	19.7
Niwot Ridge				Niwot Ridge			
6	14	26.0(4.8)	11.2(4.7)				
5	21	20.7(7.1)	9.0(7.7)	4	28	33.4(7.8)	18.2(7.1)
2	60	16.7(7.4)	6.7(8.3)	1	179	29.5(8.4)	15.6(7.4)
1	190	14.6(7.9)	4.0(8.8)	6	13	27.5(6.8)	14.5(5.6)
9	10	11.6(3.8)	0.3(8.2)	5	22	25.0(8.2)	11.0(7.9)
3	61	8.7(8.3)	−0.9(7.8)	3	34	24.3(8.5)	10.8(7.1)
4	33	7.4(6.8)	−1.9(7.8)	7	21	21.8(6.3)	6.7(5.9)
				2	60	21.2(8.6)	8.7(8.1)
8	8	23.3(4.8)	15.8(5.2)	9	10	19.4(4.3)	5.6(5.7)
13	5	1.8(14.9)	−11.8(6.4)	8	13	18.2(7.4)	7.7(6.6)
Total	402			14	3	43.0(2.6)	27.7(3.1)
Mean (14-year)		13.8	3.1	15	7	16.3(8.5)	6.6(6.8)
				Total	390		
				Mean (16-year)		25.5	12.1

Table 6 *continued*

Circulation type	Days	Max.	Min.	Circulation type	Days	Max.	Min.
		July 1953-1970				October 1952-1969	
		Ponderosa				Ponderosa	
8	10	*86.7*(4.3)	57.2(2.6)	9	12	*72.6*(3.8)	44.8(4.5)
4	13	85.7(5.5)	57.2(2.0)	5	16	70.6(7.3)	*45.7*(6.2)
2	77	84.9(5.9)	56.8(4.0)	6	15	68.5(10.7)	42.3(8.2)
11	11	84.5(2.3)	*57.3*(1.4)	2	86	68.0(8.8)	43.2(6.7)
5	12	83.8(6.5)	55.6(4.0)	7	13	66.6(10.0)	40.2(4.6)
1	200	83.3(7.6)	56.1(4.4)	1	139	63.6(9.6)	37.2(8.5)
6	12	80.6(8.4)	53.7(3.9)	4	32	63.0(9.0)	38.3(7.2)
3	55	79.2(6.8)	51.8(4.5)	8	14	61.5(6.9)	36.0(6.6)
7	12	79.1(7.4)	52.1(5.2)	3	49	58.3(11.0)	32.7(7.4)
				12	10	58.2(14.8)	38.1(7.2)
13	6	*71.3*(4.3)	*48.0*(3.0)	13	11	56.6(10.3)	27.5(6.6)
				11	15	54.9(10.2)	30.3(7.4)
Total	408			10	11	47.6(9.4)	23.8(7.7)
Mean (18-year)		82.0	54.9	14	5	*46.8*(6.0)	*23.2*(5.1)
		Como		Total	428		
				Mean (17-year)		61.2	36.7
8	10	68.2(4.8)	41.0(2.5)				
2	82	67.9(4.3)	42.8(4.8)			Como	
4	14	67.6(3.3)	41.6(4.0)				
11	11	67.6(2.7)	41.1(1.8)	9	12	*56.8*(3.7)	*33.9*(7.1)
1	210	67.2(5.3)	41.8(4.5)	5	16	56.2(4.4)	32.9(4.9)
5	13	66.8(4.3)	42.8(4.8)	7	13	54.4(5.7)	30.2(4.7)
3	57	65.3(4.5)	38.4(4.9)	6	15	54.2(9.2)	27.3(5.8)
6	14	64.6(5.9)	39.3(3.8)	2	87	53.4(6.9)	31.5(5.2)
7	12	64.6(4.2)	39.5(4.9)	12	10	50.1(9.6)	28.1(4.9)
				1	144	49.5(7.8)	28.3(7.3)
13	6	*60.2*(5.3)	*37.3*(3.1)	4	32	48.8(6.9)	27.5(5.2)
12	8	66.6(2.4)	*43.4*(4.4)	3	51	47.1(8.2)	24.2(6.0)
				8	14	46.3(5.9)	27.5(6.1)
Total	437			13	11	42.2(8.6)	21.2(4.8)
Mean (18-year)		66.2	41.0	11	15	39.3(12.0)	24.5(8.7)
				14	5	*30.4*(9.5)	*16.8*(10.1)
		Niwot Ridge		Total	425		
				Mean (18-year)		48.6	27.1
8	10	*56.5*(2.1)	*41.9*(1.9)				
11	10	56.0(2.1)	41.7(1.8)			Niwot Ridge	
4	14	55.9(3.3)	40.9(2.4)				
1	205	55.3(4.4)	41.3(3.3)	5	15	*42.5*(4.9)	28.8(4.0)
2	79	55.2(4.0)	41.4(2.9)	7	11	41.8(6.2)	28.4(4.9)
5	13	55.1(2.5)	40.2(3.4)	6	15	40.9(7.5)	28.4(6.4)
3	57	53.4(4.3)	37.9(4.6)	2	76	39.7(7.5)	27.0(6.2)
6	13	52.8(4.4)	38.2(2.9)	12	10	39.1(6.7)	22.4(8.7)
7	12	52.5(4.3)	38.1(4.0)	1	133	35.1(7.7)	22.7(7.3)
				3	46	34.4(7.8)	22.2(6.7)
13	5	*48.6*(2.4)	*34.0*(2.0)	4	32	33.3(7.5)	20.3(7.5)
				8	13	32.2(5.4)	16.9(6.4)
Total	418			10	10	27.4(5.7)	15.9(5.1)
Mean (17-year)		54.5	40.0	11	15	24.4(11.8)	12.6(9.2)
				14	5	*17.0*(8.7)	*6.2*(10.5)
				9	7	40.3(13.8)	*30.5*(2.4)
				Total	388		
				Mean (16-year)		35.1	22.3

[a]Types which occurred on at least 10 days are shown together with types for which the highest and lowest mean daily maximum and minimum temperatures (given in italics) were observed. Data are given in °F.

temperature since this is less subject to influence by local site factors. In January, warmer than average days at all stations are associated with Anticyclonic Westerly (type 6, Figure 9) and Northwesterly anticyclonic (type 5) patterns, while colder than average ones occur with Northwesterly cyclonic patterns (type 3 and type 4, Figure 10). In April, warmer than average days occur with Southwesterly pattern (type 4) and with Westerly Zonal flow (type 1) which is the most frequent pattern; colder than average conditions are associated with Northwesterly cyclonic patterns, particularly when there is a northeast-southwest tilted trough (type 9). The mean temperatures of the groups

show less spread in July. The warmest days occur with a major 700-mb level anticyclone over the southwest U.S. (type 8) and with Southwesterly flow components (types 2, 4 and 1) while the coldest conditions are on days with a Northwesterly flow (types 7 and 13). The warmest days in October occur with Southwesterly (type 5, Figure 11) and Westerly (type 9) flows and the coldest ones with Northwesterly flow (types 11 and 14) and with a weak ridge pattern (type 10).

Precipitation occurrences have been examined in relation to 700-mb wind speed and direction over Denver as well as to the 700-mb height patterns. In view of the limited sample

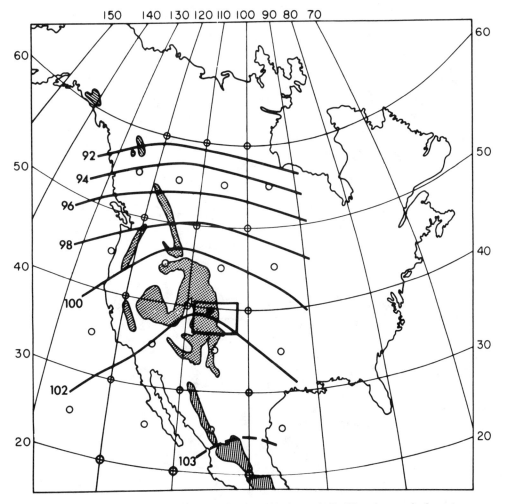

FIGURE 9. 700-mb heights (hundreds of feet) with Anticyclonic Westerly type in January.

sizes (relating to the 5-year period of daily data) only generalized results will be presented.

In January, when westerly flow predominates, the highest elevations receive the largest precipitation totals with lower elevations in the precipitation shadow. In all mid-season months except July the greatest totals occur at the highest elevation with northwesterly flow. In the summer when the 700-mb airflow direction is more variable, some precipitation occurs with southerly and easterly winds at all elevations, but less than with winds from southwest to northwest. In April, southerly winds at 700-mb give the most precipitation at the two lower stations while at Como northerly winds give

slightly more than southerly ones. Northwesterly and westerly winds are still associated with most precipitation at Niwot Ridge in April. In May northeasterly and easterly upslope winds give the highest precipitation at the two lower stations with a significant contribution at Como. The small sample size makes the results for October less clear-cut.

The precipitation characteristics of the 700-mb circulation types contributing most of the total for mid-season months are given in Tables 7-10.

There is clear evidence of increasing frequency and intensity of precipitation at higher altitudes with types 1 and 3 (Northwesterly)

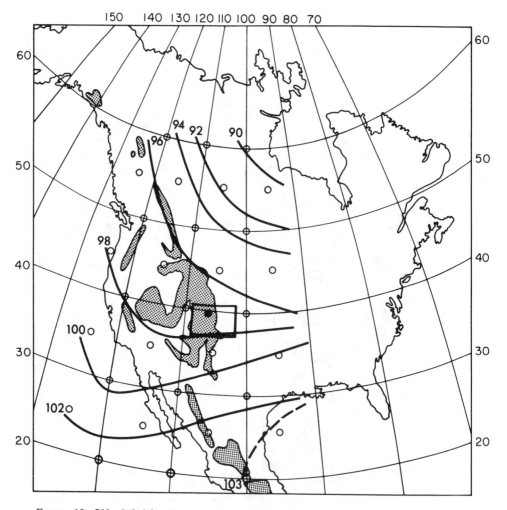

FIGURE 10. 700-mb heights (hundreds of feet) with Northwesterly cyclonic type in January.

and type 2 (Southwesterly) in January. The first two types account for 66% of the total at Como and Niwot Ridge, although the large number of dry days which also occur with these types demonstrates that additional synoptic and topographic criteria would be required if the synoptic situation were to be used as a predictor. At the two lower stations there are no dominant types or, at least, the type samples are too small for firm conclusions to be drawn.

In April, type 1 (Westerly) and type 9 (Trough, Northerly)· account for 21 to 23% and 26 to 29% of the 1966 to 1970 totals, respectively, at Ponderosa and Sugarloaf. The percentage is similar at Como and Niwot Ridge

for type 1, but that with type 9 decreases to 7% at Niwot Ridge. At the two higher stations types 3 (Southwesterly), 7 (Westerly cyclonic), and 15 (Northwesterly cyclonic) make important contributions to the total. These five types account for 64% of the total precipitation at Como and 52% at Niwot Ridge.

In July, type 1 (Westerly anticyclonic) contributes about 25% of the total at Sugarloaf and Niwot Ridge and just over 33% at Ponderosa and Como. The variability with altitude may be a result of the different years for which data were available. At Ponderosa no other single type is a major contributor to the total precipitation, whereas at Como and Niwot Ridge types

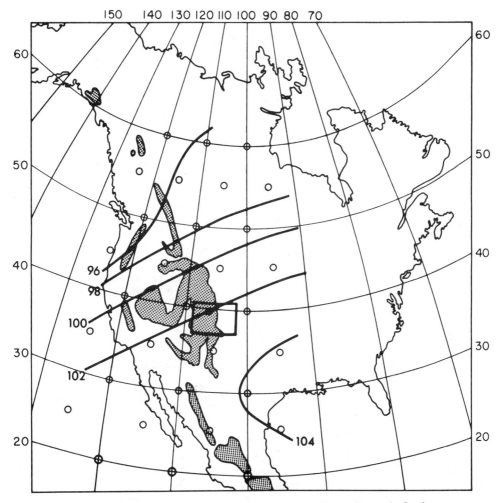

FIGURE 11. 700-mb heights (hundreds of feet) with Southwesterly type in October.

2 (Southwesterly anticyclonic) and 3 (North-westerly) jointly account for a further 25% of the total. Types 2 and 3 are also important at Sugarloaf. It is interesting that in this respect the latter is more like Como in this month, whereas in the other months Sugarloaf is more like Ponderosa. There are no clearly dominant types in October at any of the stations, apart from the "unclassified" days.

The considerable totals with unclassified days, especially in October, raises an important problem. Scrutiny of these cases shows that a few heavy falls account for much of the total in many instances. For example, 5.2 cm (2.05 inches) in 4 days at Niwot Ridge in January, 4.2 cm (1.65 inches) in 5 days at Ponderosa in October. Heavy precipitation on May 5 to 7, 1969, also occurred on days which were

TABLE 7

Precipitation for 700-mb circulation pattern types, January

Circulation type	Days with precip.	Total precip. (in)	Mean daily precip. (in)	Days without precip.	Missing days
Ponderosa (1966-1970)[a]					
1	6	0.21	0.05	46	6
2	1	0.08	0.08	27	4
3	3	0.72	0.24	10	0
12	3	0.75	0.25	1	0
Other types	2	0.05	0.03	21	1
Unclassified	4	0.47	0.12	11	5
Total	19	2.28	0.12	116	16
Sugarloaf (1966-1970)					
1	7	0.29	0.04	52	0
2	5	0.35	0.07	28	0
3	5	0.78	0.16	8	0
12	4	0.72	0.18	0	0
Other types	1	0.02	0.02	23	8
Unclassified	4	0.46	0.12	16	0
Total	26	2.62	0.10	127	8
Como (1965-1970)					
1	28	3.37	0.12	38	2
2	14	1.37	0.10	25	0
3	10	3.51	0.35	5	5
Other types	12	1.85	0.15	23	1
Unclassified	6	0.73	0.12	17	0
Total	70	10.83	0.15	108	8
Niwot Ridge (1965-1970)					
1	49	10.72	0.22	18	1
2	21	2.98	0.14	17	1
3	13	8.24	0.63	7	0
9	3	1.04	0.35	0	0
Other types	15	3.09	0.21	14	3
Unclassified	11	2.49	0.23	10	2
Total	112	28.56	0.26	66	7

[a]20 days of 1966 missing from Ponderosa.

unclassified. The synoptic maps for the un-classified dates with heavy precipitation show in many cases a typical cut-off cold low at 500 mb affecting Colorado. In other instances of heavy precipitation the low pressure area forms part of a deep trough extending from Hudson Bay. The heaviest falls on the east slope gen-erally occur with strong southerly to easterly flow components at 500 mb. For the maximum precipitation to occur at Ponderosa appears to

TABLE 8

Precipitation for 700-mb circulation pattern types, April

Circulation type	Days with precip.	Total precip. (in)	Mean daily precip. (in)	Days without precip.	Missing days
Ponderosa (1966-1970)					
1	10	2.11	0.21	36	0
2	3	0.39	0.13	10	0
3	4	0.58	0.15	8	0
9	6	2.84	0.47	0	0
Other types	9	1.23	0.13	12	0
Unclassified	11	2.83	0.26	16	0
Total	43	9.98	0.23	107	0
Sugarloaf (1966-1970)					
1	8	2.20	0.28	38	0
2	4	0.24	0.06	9	0
3	3	0.29	0.10	3	6
9	6	2.44	0.41	0	0
Other types	14	1.13	0.08	30	2
Unclassified	13	3.07	0.24	14	0
Total	48	9.44	0.20	94	8
Como (1965-1970)					
1	9	3.33	0.37	38	0
2	7	0.69	0.10	7	0
3	12	2.26	0.19	6	0
7	8	1.51	0.19	1	0
9	6	2.75	0.46	0	0
15	4	1.82	0.46	0	0
Other types	14	2.01	0.14	24	0
Unclassified	18	4.07	0.23	12	0
Total	78	18.44	0.24	89	0
Niwot Ridge (1965-1966, 1968-1970)					
1	23	4.27	0.19	27	0
2	8	1.58	0.20	6	0
3	9	1.79	0.20	2	0
7	4	1.07	0.25	2	1
9	6	1.42	0.24	0	0
15	3	1.72	0.57	1	0
Other types	16	2.94	0.88	16	0
Unclassified	20	4.88	0.24	5	1
Total	89	19.67	0.22	59	2

require frontal activity in the area of Colorado. For the maximum precipitation to occur at Niwot Ridge also requires this situation at the surface, but the upper low in these cases is to the west or northwest, rather than to the southwest, so that the upper flow, at least, has a westerly component.

In view of the significance of these situations, which are generally unclassified in the 700-mb height types, attention is being given to finding a means of identifying them as an additional group. Shortage of time and computer funds has so far prevented a similar analysis of the 700-mb deviation types in relation to precipitation.

CONCLUDING REMARKS

The climatological data collected at the stations operated by the Institute of Arctic and Alpine Research on the east slopes of the Colorado Front Range since 1952 have now been organized in the framework of a data retrieval system for permanent record and subjected to

TABLE 9

Precipitation for 700-mb circulation pattern types, July

Circulation type	Days with precip.	Total precip. (in)	Mean daily precip. (in)	Days without precip.	Missing days
Ponderosa (1966-1970)					
1	19	2.74	0.14	40	0
2	4	0.24	0.06	12	0
3	3	0.58	0.19	6	0
Other types	8	1.28	0.16	9	0
Unclassified	29	2.64	0.09	25	0
Total	63	7.48	0.12	92	0
Sugarloaf (1966-1970)					
1	15	2.37	0.16	44	0
2	10	1.25	0.13	11	0
3	6	1.17	0.20	5	0
Other types	12	2.34	0.12	13	0
Unclassified	14	2.44	0.11	15	0
Total	57	9.52	0.17	88	0
Como (1965-1970)					
1	36	6.66	0.19	40	3
2	10	2.48	0.25	16	0
3	11	2.24	0.10	5	0
Other types	10	1.79	0.18	18	1
Unclassified	19	5.50	0.29	15	2
Total	86	18.67	0.22	92	6
Niwot Ridge (1965-1966, 1968-1970)					
1	22	3.67	0.16	30	14
2	8	2.49	0.31	11	3
3	6	1.33	0.22	9	0
Other types	9	1.30	0.14	11	5
Unclassified	13	4.34	0.33	14	0
Total	58	13.08	0.23	75	22

analysis. The sparsity of observational records at high elevations, especially for stations which are not in valley locations, and the comparatively long series, gives this climatic transect along the east slopes particular significance. The major climatological findings are as follows:

(1) The solar radiation data show no evidence for any increase in annual totals with

TABLE 10

Precipitation for 700-mb circulation pattern types, October

Circulation type	Days with precip.	Total precip. (in)	Mean daily precip. (in)	Days without precip.	Missing days
Ponderosa (1966-1969)					
1	3	0.34	0.11	27	0
2	1	0.01	0.01	8	0
3	2	0.22	0.11	6	0
4	3	0.45	0.15	8	0
14	3	0.59	0.20	0	0
Other types	8	0.76	0.10	24	0
Unclassified	18	6.98	0.39	14	0
Total	38	9.45	0.25	87	0
Sugarloaf (1965-1969)					
1	5	1.27	0.25	35	2
2	2	0.33	0.17	9	1
3	2	0.24	0.12	10	1
4	1	0.01	0.01	12	0
14	2	0.50	0.25	1	0
Other types	6	0.87	0.14	28	3
Unclassified	14	6.45	0.40	20	0
Total	32	9.67	0.30	115	7
Como (1965-1969)					
1	5	0.88	0.18	27	0
2	3	0.28	0.09	9	0
3	2	0.36	0.18	11	0
4	4	0.79	0.20	8	1
14	3	0.86	0.29	0	0
Other types	10	1.27	0.13	26	2
Unclassified	11	4.02	0.37	20	3
Total	38	8.46	0.22	111	6
Niwot Ridge (1965-1969)					
1	7	0.97	0.14	35	0
2	3	0.37	0.12	8	0
3	3	0.29	0.10	10	0
4	3	0.81	0.27	8	2
14	3	1.29	0.43	0	0
Other types	7	0.70	0.10	19	12
Unclassified	8	1.97	0.25	16	10
Total	34	6.40	0.19	96	24

elevation. There is an increase in radiation with elevation during December-May but it is not clear whether this is the case above 3,050 m (10,000 ft). The available data were insufficient to examine the effect of different synoptic patterns although such a study is highly desirable.

(2) The daily precipitation records since 1965 have drastically revised the annual averages at the two upper stations. Annual precipitation increases with elevation to the highest station (3,550 m; 12,300 ft), where it is estimated to be 102 cm (40 inches). There is little or no difference between the annual totals at 2,200 and 2,600 m where about 56 cm (22 inches) is recorded. The 1965 to 1970 records at these two stations are essentially in line with those for 1952 to 1964. The vertical distribution of precipitation shows not only major seasonal contrasts, with a winter maximum at the highest elevation and a May maximum at the other stations, but it also varies markedly in the same month in different years. This is primarily in response to the occurrence of upslope events in spring and fall in association with upper cold lows or troughs. At the highest elevation most precipitation occurs with northwest flow (at 700 mb) in all mid-season months except July.

(3) The 700-mb synoptic classification and the other 700-mb descriptors have provided a useful basis for examining some of the synoptic climatological characteristics of the stations. The characteristics of the 700-mb deviation types in particular appear to warrant further analysis since it is in these patterns that upslope situations are most clearly represented.

Some of the recommendations which follow stem from experience gained in the analysis and attempted interpretation of the available data. Others are ideas stimulated by consideration of the general problems created by scale interactions in a mountain environment.

(1) The original chart records still contain much unused information. The analysis of precipitation gauge records by storm events would probably be of most value and to date this has not been carried out systematically due to shortage of manpower. Similarly, hourly temperature, humidity, and wind velocity data could be extracted from the chart records and some work along these lines is desirable, at least to assess how much information is being lost through the extraction of only daily maxima and minima and mean wind speed.

(2) The record lengths at the two upper stations provide an adequate characterization of temperature conditions but certainly not of precipitation. However, the downward trend in summer temperature at Como warrants continued study and other requirements necessitate continued measurements at Niwot Ridge. For example, the ongoing ground temperature and glaciological programs can be reliably linked in to the 18-year record if several years of concurrent data are collected. It may prove preferable in terms of logistics, with consequently more complete records, if the main high level station were maintained at the Saddle, 2 km farther east along Niwot Ridge, in conjunction with the IBP Tundra Biome alpine site, although greater windiness and blowing snow is a problem there. From climatological and ecological points of view the records at Ponderosa and Sugarloaf are still too short, but the generally smaller changes with altitude on the lower slopes allows consideration to be given to the discontinuation of one or other station.

(3) The major shortcoming of the measurement program up to now has been the inadequacy of data on the energy and moisture balances. The International Biological Programme at the Saddle is collecting such information for the alpine belt but consideration of the vertical and spatial variation is required for an adequate climatonomy of the mountains. Moreover, this approach is essential for a proper analysis of problems connected with snowmelt patterns, vegetation productivity, geomorphic and pedologic processes, and so on. The background climatic data now available provides only limited input to problems in these areas as it is more suited to purely climatological questions.

ACKNOWLEDGMENTS

This analysis was supported by the Atmospheric Sciences Section, National Science Foundation (GA-15528). The study was made possible only by the painstaking collection of data, since 1951, by many individuals associated with INSTAAR, notably J. M. Clark, A. W. Johnson, J. W. Marr, M. W. Paddock, and W. S. Osburn, Jr. Invaluable logistical support was maintained, often under severe weather conditions, by Ralph Greene. The measurement program, which was initiated and directed until 1967 by J. W. Marr, was variously supported by the U.S. Army Office of the Quartermaster General, U.S. Army Research Office and Natick Laboratories, U.S. Atomic Energy Commission, NASA, the National Science Foundation, the National Center for Atmospheric Research, and the University of Colorado. The author has been greatly assisted in the present analysis by R. C. Brill, Waltraud Brinkmann, J. M. Clark, G. F. Estabrook, J. Z. Little, Margaret Eccles, and Jill Williams. The encouragement of Jack D. Ives in supporting the observational program with Institute funds since 1967 and the office support of the Institute are much appreciated.

REFERENCES

Barry, R. G.
1972 : Climatic environment of the east slope of the Colorado Front Range. *Inst. Arct. Alp. Res. Occas. Pap.*, 3, Univ. of Colorado, Boulder. 206 pp.

Bergen, J. D.
1969 : Cold air drainage on a forested mountain slope. *J. Appl. Meteorol.*, 8: 884-895.

Brill, R. C.
1971 : The Taxir Primer. *Inst. Arct. Alp. Res. Occas. Pap.*, 1, Univ. of Colorado, Boulder. 72 pp.

Caldwell, M. M.
1968 : Solar ultraviolet radiation as an ecological factor for alpine plants. *Ecol. Monogr.*, 38: 243-268.

Gates, D. M. and Janke, R.
1966 : The energy environment of the alpine tundra. *Oecol. Plant.*, 1: 39-62.

Hjermstad, L. M.
1970 : The influence of meteorological parameters on the distribution of precipitation across central Colorado mountains. *Atmos. Sci. Pap.*, No. 163, Colo. State Univ., Fort Collins. 78 pp.

Larson, L. W.
1971 : Shielding precipitation gages from adverse wind effects with snow fences. *Water Resourc. Ser.*, No. 25, Univ. of Wyoming, Laramie. 161 pp.

Leaf, C. F.
1962 : Snow measurement in mountainous terrain. Unpub. M.S. Thesis, Colo. State Univ., Fort Collins. 93 pp.

Lloyd, D. T.
1970 : The Isabelle Glacier, Front Range, Colorado, during the 1968-1969 budget year. Unpub. M.A. Thesis, Univ. of Colorado, Boulder. 133 pp.

Löve, D.
1970 : Subarctic and Subalpine: where and what? *Arct. Alp. Res.*, 2: 63-72.

Lund, I. A.
1963 : Map-pattern classification by statistical methods. *J. Appl. Meteorol.*, 2: 56-65.

Marr, J. W.
1961 : Ecosystems of the east slope of the Front Range in Colorado. *Univ. of Colorado, Ser. Biol.*, No. 8. 124 pp.

1967 : Data on mountain environments I. Front Range, Colorado, sixteen sites, 1952-1953. *Univ. of Colorado, Ser. Biol.*, No. 27. 110 pp.

Marr, J. W., Johnson, A. W., Osburn, W. S., and Knorr, O. A.
1968a: Data on mountain environments II. Front Range, Colorado, four climax regions, 1953-1958. *Univ. of Colorado, Ser. Biol.*, No. 28. 170 pp.

Marr, J. W., Clark, J. M., Osburn, W. S., and Paddock, M. W.
1968b: Data on mountain environments III. Front Range, Colorado, four climax regions, 1959-1964. *Univ. of Colorado, Ser. Biol.*, No. 29. 181 pp.

Sauberer, F., and Dirmhirn, I.
1958 : Das Strahlungsklima. *In* Steinhauser, F., Eckel, O., and Lauscher, F. (eds.), *Klimatographie von Österreich*, 3(1), Springer, Vienna, 13-102.

ADDENDUM. The means of temperature for individual months given in Barry (1972, Table 3.1) have been redetermined to include certain extreme readings previously omitted from the daily bank because their exact date was uncertain. The changes are mostly minor but revised tables will be provided on request.

THE INFLUENCE OF METEOROLOGICAL PARAMETERS ON THE DISTRIBUTION OF PRECIPITATION ACROSS CENTRAL COLORADO MOUNTAINS

(Summary)

L. M. HJERMSTAD

This study has focused on obtaining a better understanding of mountain precipitation and the parameters that affect its spatial distribution. Precipitation distributions from 256 and 264 precipitation days, respectively, for a west-east[1] and a south-north[2] profile across the Continental Divide have been analyzed to (1) establish the mean distribution of precipitation with elevation, to (2) study the influence of the 500 mb wind direction, velocity, and temperature on precipitation distributions with elevation and to (3) identify the synoptic conditions producing variations in the distribution of precipitation across a north-south oriented mountain range. The results of this climatological study may be summarized as follows:

1. For an openly exposed mountain barrier, an average of 4.74 times more precipitation is observed near the crest at 3200 m msl than is observed at an average elevation of 1500 m msl on either side of the mountain. There is an average of 5.83 times more precipitation observed at the crest than at an average western slope base. All of the significant increase in west slope precipitation with respect to increased elevation occurs between 2100-3200 m (Avg. 62.5 cm per 1,000 m).

2. The ratio of the 1500 m precipitation amounts on the western slopes to the maximum amount recorded near the openly exposed ridge line increases from 1:3.0 to 1:11.3 as the 500 mb wind direction shifts from an orientation nearly parallel to the ridge to one perpendicular to it. The same ratio increases from

---

Published in full as:
Atmospheric Science Paper No. 163
Dept. of Atmospheric Science
Colorado State University
Fort Collins, Colorado

[1]Grand Junction-Vail Pass-Denver

[2]Saguache-Fremont Pass-Grand Lake

1:2.3 to 1:7.5 for a sheltered mountain pass which is oriented parallel to the main mountain range.

3. The ratio of the 1500 m precipitation amounts on the western slopes to the maximum amounts observed near the openly exposed ridge line increases from 1:4.5 to 1:10.3 when 500 mb winds increase in velocity from less than 7 ms^{-1} to greater than 25 ms^{-1}. The same ratio increases from 1:3.2 to 1:8.7 for the same respective wind velocities for the sheltered mountain ridge parallel to the main mountain range.

4. General decreases of about 55% in average precipitation amounts are noted at the 1500 m elevations as temperatures decrease from -20°C to -30°C. Smaller decreases of about 35% in the maximum precipitation amounts near the crest of the profile are noted for the same range of temperature decrease.

5. For an openly exposed ridge, the influence that orography has on the distribution of low to high elevation precipitation amounts and their resulting ratios reaches its maximum for 500 mb wind velocities greater than 25 ms^{-1} which are oriented perpendicular to the ridge line with 500 mb temperatures below -30°C. The orographic influence is minimized when 500 mb wind velocities are less than 15 ms^{-1} and oriented nearly parallel to the ridge line with 500 mb temperatures between -16°C and -20°C.

6. Greater amounts of precipitation are observed at the lowest elevation windward precipitation sites and on the western slopes relative to that observed on the ridge line when a 500 mb trough and associated surface cyclonic storm system are west of the mountain range. When the 500 mb trough and associated surface storm system are east of the Continental Divide, greater amounts of precipitation relative to the lowest elevation western slope precipitation sites are observed near or on the east side of the ridge line.

The results of this study present a detailed picture of the mountain precipitation patterns that are associated with variations in meteorological parameters and synoptic weather patterns. Knowledge of the variations in the precipitation patterns over a single mountain range can lead to a better understanding of the total precipitation picture over mountainous regions.

THE ENERGY BALANCE OF A MID-LATITUDE ALPINE SITE DURING THE GROWING SEASON, 1973

Ellsworth F. LeDrew

Institute of Arctic and Alpine Research
and Department of Geography
University of Colorado
Boulder, Colorado 80309

ABSTRACT

The surface energy balance of an alpine tundra in the Front Range of Colorado is determined for the summer season 1973. The problems of using conventional flux-profile relationships to estimate the turbulent fluxes over an alpine tundra are discussed. Because of the massive advection of cool dry air and heterogeneity of the surface, these one-dimensional models must be discarded. An empirical formula for evapotranspiration is derived for the Niwot Ridge site from lysimeter measurements of the vapor flux and vertical profiles of humidity and temperature.

The average partition of energy was as follows:

Net radiation
   298 cal $\cdot$ cm^{-2} $\cdot$ day^{-1} (100%)

Enthalpy flux
   148 cal $\cdot$ cm^{-2} $\cdot$ day^{-1} (49%)

Evapotranspiration
   113 cal $\cdot$ cm^{-2} $\cdot$ day^{-1} (39%)

Soil heat flux
   37 cal $\cdot$ cm^{-2} $\cdot$ day^{-1} (12%)

Bowen ratio 1.31

INTRODUCTION

Studies of the energy balance of an alpine tundra have been hampered by the difficulty of maintaining the required complex instrumentation in a remote environment. The only serious work in the North American Alpine (Terjung *et al.*, 1969) was based on 11 hours of observation under clear sky conditions. In connection with studies of the dynamics of the tundra ecosystem under the International Biological Programme, research has been carried out on the moisture and energy exchanges of a mid-latitude alpine tundra at 3,500 m on Niwot Ridge, Colorado. This paper summarizes the results for the sum- mer period from June 25 to August 24, 1973.

Since the turbulent fluxes of energy are seldom measured directly, limitations of the modeling of these fluxes in the Alpine are discussed and an empirical model validated for the site. When available, direct measures of the turbulent fluxes are used to examine some temporal characteristics of the surface energy balance. The seasonal course of the energy balance is estimated from these data, coupled with predictions of the empirical model, and compared with similar data for an arctic tundra site at Barrow, Alaska.

SITE LOCATION AND CHARACTERISTICS

The instrumentation for this study was located in the "Saddle" at 3,500 m on Niwot Ridge (40°03′23″N, 105°35′06″W) in the Front Range, Colorado. The site is approximately mid- point in elevation between the Como (3,048 m) and Niwot Ridge (3,750 m) climatological stations maintained by the Institute of Arctic and Alpine Research (INSTAAR) since 1952. A climatology of the Front Range based on data from these and two lower stations (Sugarloaf, 2,951 m, and Ponderosa, 2,195 m) has been presented by Barry (1973).

The surface cover in the instrument area consists of low perennial sedges and grasses broken by rock debris. The immediate vegetation is dominantly *Kobresia*. The local vegetation distribution is given in Figure 1.

Niwot Ridge is subject to the direct influence of the westerlies, modified only slightly by the Continental Divide (Figures 2 and 3). To minimize the effects of the massive advection of cold dry air, the instrumentation was located as far away from the leading edge of the ridge as possible (0.2 km) while maximizing the fetch over uniform terrain. Even with these two criteria optimized, there is considerable variation in slope and surface composition in the immediate area. Slope angles in the vicinity of the site range up to 10°.

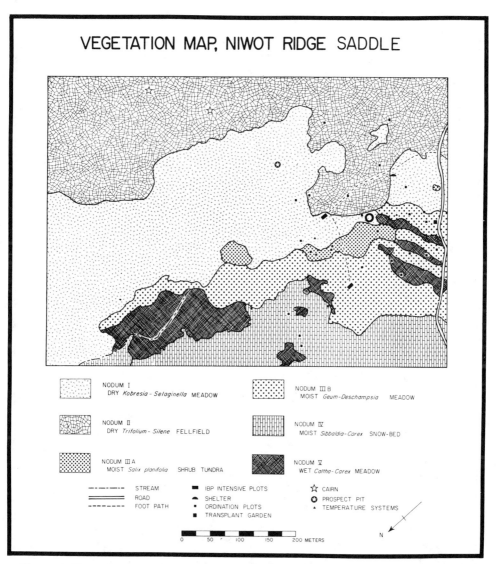

FIGURE 1. Vegetation map, Niwot Ridge, Saddle. The micrometeorological instrument array is denoted by open circle. (From Webber *et al.*, in prep.)

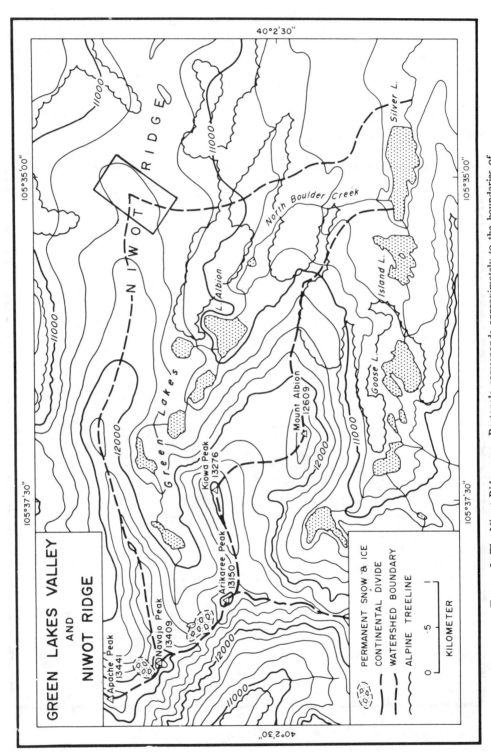

FIGURE 2. The Niwot Ridge area. Rectangle corresponds approximately to the boundaries of Figure 1. (Figure courtesy of D. Ebert May.)

INSTRUMENTATION

Net radiation was measured with a calibrated Funk-type net radiometer placed at 2 m and recorded continuously on strip chart. Soil heat flux at −2.5 cm was sensed with a calibrated soil heat flux disk and recorded hourly by means of a calibrated potentiometer. At 20-, 40-, 80-, and 160-cm air temperatures at 15-min intervals and 15-min wind passage were recorded simultaneously. Air temperatures were measured by calibrated thermistors housed in radiation shields. The wind sensors were a matched set of Thornthwaite sensitive anemometers. The wet-bulb depression at 20 and 80 cm was measured hourly with an aspirated psychrometer. During August, evapotranspiration was determined at 2-hr intervals with a weighing lysimeter described in LeDrew and Emerick (1974). Observations of all parameters were taken from 0800 to 1400 hours local (mountain) standard time. The observation routine was maintained for 24 hours one day per week (Thursday).

MODELING THE TURBULENT FLUXES OVER AN ALPINE TUNDRA

The net radiant energy (R_n) at a surface is dissipated by turbulent and conductive transport. These fluxes are related through the energy balance:

$$R_n + H + LE + G = 0 \qquad (1)$$

The symbols are defined in the Appendix. By convention, an energy gain at the surface is positive and an energy loss is negative.

This expression, as presented and defined. is valid only at the surface. When applied to the atmospheric boundary layer (e.g., between 20 and 160 cm height) changes of atmospheric storage must be included in equation (1) if there is vertical divergence or convergence of the turbulent or radiative fluxes. Divergence within a layer results in cooling of that atmospheric layer while convergence results in heating. Divergence or convergence of the turbulent terms occurs when there is a horizontal removal or addition of the transport property (enthalpy or water vapor) in the atmosphere immediately above the layer under consideration. This horizontal removal or addition of the property (advection) takes place only when there is a horizontal gradi-

FIGURE 3. The Saddle site (3,500 m), looking west to the Continental Divide. Wind is dominantly from slightly left of the 8-m mast (west wind). The 160 cm thermistor and anemometer array described in the text is immediately to the right of the 8-m mast. (Photo courtesy of J. Clark.)

ent of that property (Rao *et al.*, 1974). With the massive advection of cool dry air by westerly airflow at the Saddle, we can expect changes of atmospheric storage in the boundary layer to be significant.

The radiative and conductive components (R_n and G) of equation (1) were measured directly. Unfortunately lysimetric measurements of the vapor flux (E) were available for only part of the season. To examine the seasonal energy balance, the turbulent fluxes must be inferred from statistical flux-profile relationships validated against the lysimeter data.

For neutral stratification of the atmosphere (when an adiabatic temperature lapse exists), the vertical profiles of velocity and temperature are logarithmic (Sellers, 1965) and the Thornthwaite-Holzman flux-profile model used by Terjung *et al.* (1969) is valid. However, an examination of velocity and temperature profiles show that the logarithmic assumption is invalid at Niwot Ridge (Figure 4, Table 1). These data were recorded simultaneously at all levels under steady-state conditions; wind direction was predominantly from the west for these samples. The concave structure of the profiles is characteristic of diabatic conditions (cf. Deacon, 1969) when flux transport is by both thermal and mechanical turbulence. Models based on log-laws can lead to considerable errors under these conditions (Brooks *et al.*, 1965). To adjust the logarithmic flux-profile models for nonadiabatic conditions, a stability-dependent universal function, Φ (Obukhov, 1946; Monin and Obukhov, 1951; Lettau, 1949), must be applied to the log-law relationships for the flux of enthalpy (H):

$$\frac{\partial \phi}{\partial z} = \Phi_h \, H \, (\rho C p U^* k Z m)^{-1} \qquad (2)$$

and the vapor flux (E)

$$\frac{\partial q}{\partial z} = \Phi_w \, E \, (\rho U^* k Z m)^{-1} \qquad (3)$$

The symbols are defined in the Appendix. In this study, the friction velocity (U^*) is computed from 20 cm velocity and averaged roughness lengths (Table 2). Φ has been experimentally related to the gradient Richardson number (Ri) through:

$$\Phi = (a \pm bRi)^{\pm c} \qquad (4)$$

where a, b, and c are empirically derived constants. Given vertical gradients of velocity, temperature, and humidity, the fluxes of enthalpy and water vapor may be computed from equations (4) and (2) or (3) using constants in

equation (4) derived under well-controlled field conditions (e.g., Swinbank, 1964, 1968; Businger *et al.*, 1971; Morgan *et al.*, 1971).

For the constants in equation (4) to be universally applicable, similarity between the field sites must satisfy three criteria (Swinbank, 1964):

(1) The terrain must be uniform and surface homogeneous.
(2) Advection must be negligible.
(3) The fluxes must be constant with height.

This is essential since the characteristics of the turbulence, and therefore of the nature of the turbulent transport, are developed along the upwind fetch (cf. Bradley, 1968). The studies of Swinbank (1964, 1968), Businger *et al.* (1971), and Morgan *et al.* (1971) satisfied these constraints. If these criteria are not satisfied, the problem becomes two-dimensional in that horizontal as well as the vertical gradients of the atmospheric properties must be measured. The one-dimensional equations (2), (3), and (4) are not applicable under such situations. An evaluation of the advective problem has been made by Rao *et al.* (1974) using numerical techniques. The modification of the boundary layer structure of velocity by upwind surface heterogeneities has been investigated by Panofsky and Townsend (1963), Bradley (1968), and Taylor (1969). However, if the horizontal gradients are not measured and the similarity criteria cannot be applied successfully, wholly empirical models must be derived for each site.

At the Saddle site, the first significant surface obstruction to airflow is a 0.5-m rise 100 m upwind. Between this rise and the instrument site, the surface is flat and of homogeneous composition. Theoretical and experimental studies (Bradley, 1968) have suggested that the minimum height-fetch ratio, defined as the height of the boundary layer completely adjusted to the local terrain to the fetch of the unobstructed surface, is $1/150$. For this study, with 100 m of unobstructed upwind fetch, the observations at the 20- and 40-cm levels may be assumed to be completely adjusted to the terrain characteristics of the site. The similarity hypothesis as applied to criterion (1) is accepted for this site.

Using data for the vapor flux determined at 2-hr intervals by lysimeter, the enthalpy flux was calculated as a residual of equation (1) for neutral and diabatic conditions. Φ_h was computed from equation (2) using data at 20 and 40 cm and plotted against the absolute value of the gradient Richardson number in Figure 5. The relationship expected, if all criteria of the similarity hypothesis hold (Morgan *et al.*, 1971), is indicated for comparison. Included is the range of scatter for the Morgan data. The largest source of error in this analysis undoubtedly is in

the measurement of the soil heat flux (Stearns, 1969), which cannot be evaluated precisely. However, the instruments and data-reduction techniques used in this study are of comparable

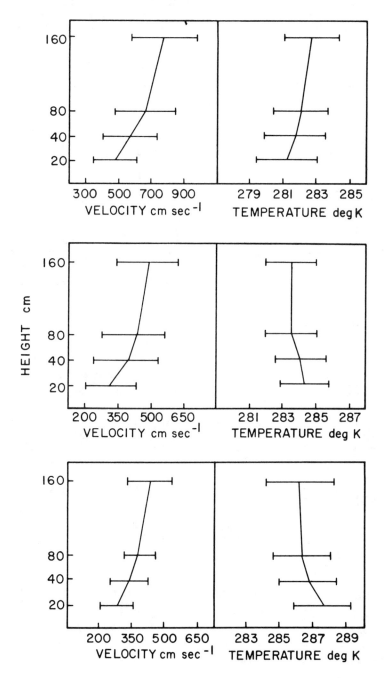

FIGURE 4. (a) Average velocity and temperature profiles for 0400 L.S.T. Horizontal bars indicate standard deviation. Statistics are in Table 1. (b) Average velocity and temperature profiles for 0800 L.S.T. (c) Average velocity and temperature profiles for 1200 L.S.T.

finesse to those described in the literature, and a comparison of scatter in the data points of Figure 5 is valid. As apparent from the wide scatter of Figure 5, the expected relationship (Morgan et al., 1971) would not be statistically significant for the data of this study. Also, a statistical re-evaluation of equation (4) is impossible for the Niwot Ridge site.

The poor association is probably a consequence of cold air advection. The resulting vertical flux divergence between 20 and 40 cm is associated with a change of the temperature gradient with height (McIlroy and Angus, 1964; Monteith, 1965). Measured profiles will not be representative of those at the surface where the energy balance, as defined in equation (1), is

TABLE 1

Averaged velocity and temperature profiles on Niwot Ridge for selected periods[a]

					Time	0400		
					Sample size	4		
					Richardson number	Mean	0.078	
						S.D.	0.150	
						Max	0.303	
						Min	0.002	

Height (cm)	Velocity (cm sec^{-1})				Temperature (°K)			
	Mean	S.D.	Max	Min	Mean	S.D.	Max	Min
160	778.2	405.0	1016.3	173.1	282.8	3.1	284.4	278.2
80	677.1	363.8	888.3	133.3	282.1	3.3	283.8	277.1
40	581.9	327.0	772.7	92.9	281.8	3.6	283.8	276.5
20	483.7	268.7	641.3	82.1	281.3	3.6	283.3	276.0

					Time	0800		
					Sample size	47		
					Richardson number	Mean	−0.018	
						S.D.	0.495	
						Max	2.298	
						Min	−1.707	

Height (cm)	Velocity (cm sec^{-1})				Temperature (°K)			
	Mean	S.D.	Max	Min	Mean	S.D.	Max	Min
160	483.4	297.1	1224.2	91.2	283.5	3.1	292.0	277.9
80	439.7	269.2	1078.7	84.0	283.5	3.1	291.8	277.8
40	393.9	292.6			284.1	3.1	292.4	278.2
20	314.5	199.1	810.1	72.0	284.3	3.1	292.4	278.5

					Time	1200		
					Sample size	117		
					Richardson number	Mean	−0.135	
						S.D.	0.777	
						Max	0.290	
						Min	−8.260	

Height (cm)	Velocity (cm sec^{-1})				Temperature (°K)			
	Mean	S.D.	Max	Min	Mean	S.D.	Max	Min
160	427.2	208.1	1762.0	106.5	286.2	4.0		277.4
80	390.4	185.3	1532.7	98.1	286.4	3.6	294.0	277.4
40	345.8	170.7	1298.4	61.5	286.8	3.6	294.5	277.8
20	295.5	155.4	849.0	75.6	287.7	3.7	295.5	278.0

[a]Data are based on observations taken at 15-minute intervals.

valid, leading to an underestimation of Φ_h for diabatic conditions. The existence of flux divergence also means that the fluxes are not independent with height; this independence is a requirement for the Monin-Obukhov one-dimensional analysis. Criteria (2) and (3) are not satisfied for this site.

An error estimate of the model predictions can be attempted. The enthalpy flux data computed from equation (2) using the empirical relation (equation 4) determined by Morgan *et al.* have been compared with those determined from the energy balance relation (equation 1) and lysimeter data for Niwot Ridge. The difference varies from −2400% to +2200% of the observed 2-hr flux. The mean difference for diabatic conditions was −23%. W. C. Swinbank (pers. comm., 1973) noted that even small-scale advection over a well-developed homogeneous terrain can alter the computed flux by 20%. Stewart and Thom (1973) found values of $LE + H$, using the flux-profile relationships of Dyer and Hicks (1970), that were smaller than the measured values over a forest canopy by a factor of 2.5 ± 0.5. They later suggested (Thom *et al.*, 1975) that the discrepancy may be due to an additional "diffusing" mechanism generated by turbulent wakes behind individual roughness elements (trees in their study) which may find a counterpart in the broken surface debris in some areas at the Niwot Ridge site; however, data are not available to investigate this possi-

bility. These examples emphasize the need for verification of the Monin-Obukhov and similar models at each study site.

In light of these difficulties, an empirical model for the water vapor flux for diabatic conditions has been derived for the Niwot Ridge site. Potential evapotranspiration (*PLE*) is com-

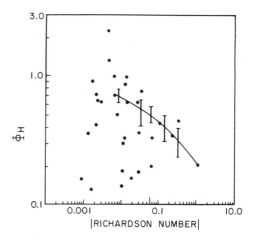

FIGURE 5. Analysis of the Monin-Obukhov relation for the enthalpy flux. The curve is the relationship suggested by Morgan *et al.* (1971, Fig. III-2). The limits of their data scatter is also indicated by vertical bars. The Richardson number is given as the absolute value.

TABLE 2

Roughness lengths for the Niwot Ridge site, 1973[a]

Period	Roughness length	Sample size	Standard error of the mean
June 21-30	0.757 cm	75	0.015
July 1-10	0.750 cm	22	0.042
July 11-20	1.024 cm	27	0.018
July 21-30	1.030 cm	34	0.024
July 31-Aug. 9	1.125 cm	69	0.055
Aug. 10-19	1.008 cm	71	0.019
Aug. 20-24	1.006 cm	13	0.039

[a]Values of the roughness lengths (z_o) were calculated for neutral condition ($-0.03 \leq Ri \leq 0.03$) from the formula of Sanders and Weber (1970):

$$\log z_o = \frac{U_{n+1}\log z_n - U_n \log z_{n+1}}{U_{n+1} - U_n}$$

puted as a fraction of available energy $(Rn\text{-}G)$ using the method of Priestley and Taylor (1972). The appropriate equation is

$$PLE = \alpha[s/(s + \gamma)]\ (Rn{-}G) \quad (5)$$

where

$$\alpha = \frac{L\Delta q}{[s/(s+\gamma)]\ (L\Delta q + Cp\Delta T)}, \quad (6)$$

s is the slope of the saturation specific humidity-temperature curve at the surface temperature, and γ is Cp/L. The formula is relatively insensitive to the errors in the measurement of the wet-bulb depression discussed by Fuchs and Tanner (1970). An error of $1°C$ in the wet-bulb depression at one level which results in a 15% change of Δq between 80 and 20 cm alters α by less than 1%.

Setting actual evapotranspiration equal to potential evapotranspiration as suggested by Rouse and Stewart (1972) for a lichen dominated site in the Hudson Bay lowlands allowed only 15% of the variance to be explained with an insignificant F-statistic. Their approach is

evidently not valid for all tundra environments, probably as a result of different plant resistance characteristics between the regions and a greater variability of moisture stress conditions on the Niwot Ridge site.

Setting LE/PLE as some function of LE yielded the predictive relation (Figure 6):

$$LE = 0.212\ PLE\ (1.0{-}1.275\ PLE)^{-1} \quad (7)$$

with a correlation coefficient of 0.86. The F-statistic of 65.2 is significant at the 99.95% level. The 95% confidence limits are drawn on Figure 7.

It should be emphasized that equation (7) is entirely empirical and little physical significance can be attached to it, except that the actual evapotranspiration is a slowly varying function of the potential evapotranspiration. It is valid only for the range of physiological resistance characteristics of the Niwot Ridge vegetation during the period of observations and for the profile structure as determined by the range of advection experienced at the site during the summer of 1973.

MOISTURE FLUXES BASED ON LYSIMETER MEASUREMENTS

Values of the Bowen ratio $(\beta = H/LE)$ for August 1973 range from -2.57 for the period 2000 to 2300 L.S.T. on August 9 to 5.45 on August 10 for the period 1200 to 1400 L.S.T. The negative value indicates opposing directions for the water vapor and enthalpy flux, with the vapor flux directed away from the surface and much smaller in magnitude than the enthalpy flux.

The diurnal trends of the vapor flux for three sample days are plotted in Figure 7. For each example, the vapor flux is away from the surface at all times; there is no recorded instance of dewfall, even during periods of negative net radiation. We can attribute this to the effects of dry air advection forcing a negative humidity gradient over a moist surface. Rao et al. (1974) have successfully modeled this feature for a transition from a dry to moist surface. McIlroy and Angus (1964) have noted similar negative vapor fluxes for a short-cropped turf in Australia during periods of negative net radiation when dry air advection was significant.

The general trend is for an early morning maximum of the vapor flux to change to a minimum around solar noon (probably related to

stomatal closure in response to the higher energy input during this period), with a secondary maximum in late afternoon. The examples show that the energy of evapotranspiration can exceed the net radiation while the latter is still positive during this late afternoon maximum. Monteith (1965) has noted a similar "oasis" effect for freely transpiring surfaces surrounded by drier areas.

The vapor flux varies seasonally with the moisture content of the soil. Three days prior to the August 9 example there was 5 mm of precipitation. At solar noon on August 9, the Bowen ratio was -0.28, indicating a regime of negligible moisture stress. No precipitation fell between this date and August 17 when the Bowen ratio at solar noon was 4.04. The vapor flux was comparatively small and there was a high moisture stress after this drying-out period. The period August 23-24 followed a rain of 13 mm on August 22 and a large proportion of the available energy was again used for evapotranspiration. These examples illustrate the significance of the aerial moisture supply in alpine water relations.

THE SEASONAL ENERGY BALANCE

Actual evapotranspiration was computed from equation (7) for hourly data during periods of

positive net radiation and collated as 5-day means for the summer season. The empirical

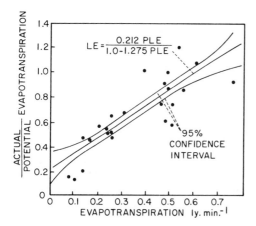

FIGURE 6. The predictive model for evapotranspiration based on lysimeter measurements during August 1973.

model was derived from data representing a wide range of moisture stress conditions and we can feel confident extrapolating it beyond the period of validation.

Since the model was not validated for nighttime conditions (periods of negative net radiation), daily totals of the vapor flux must be estimated. Analysis of 12 lysimeter measurements recorded during three nights in August suggested that the nighttime energy balance did not vary significantly. Evaporation rates averaged 1.01 × 10^{-5} mm min^{-1}. Table 3 and Figure 8 were constructed by assuming that the nighttime energy balance was constant through the entire season. This is justified in part by noting that the nighttime net radiation was nearly constant through the period of examination. Nighttime totals of evaporation determined in this manner were added to the daytime totals estimated from equation (7).

There is no discernible seasonal trend of evaporation that can be associated with the net radiation curve (Figure 8). The small temporal variations are probably more intimately related to the moisture regime (cf. discussion of Figure 7). The seasonal amplitude of the enthalpy flux curve, however, is greater and seems to correspond closely with the net radiation curve. The variation of the soil heat flux represents a balance between the available net radiation and the energy requirements of the turbulent fluxes. Note that there is a distinct mid-season minimum of net radiation during the period July 23 to 27. This is related to increased attenuation of insolation during this period of increased convective cloud development.

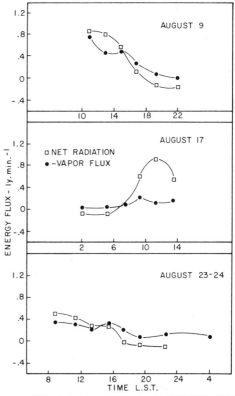

FIGURE 7. Examples of the vapor flux on Niwot Ridge as determined by lysimeter measurement.

For daytime diabatic conditions, 5-day averages of noon-hour Bowen ratios range from 3.80 to 11.39 (LeDrew, 1974) illustrating low evapotranspiration rates that are suggestive of a regime of high moisture stress during the day. However, immediately apparent from an examination of 24-hr average Bowen ratios (Table 3) is the fact that 24-hr evapotranspiration totals are much higher than the daytime data would suggest. Although there is significant moisture stress, evapotranspiration proceeds at all times (Figure 7) and 24-hr totals can be large (2.2 mm day^{-1}, August 6 to 10). The pattern of large daytime losses with smaller magnitudes of nighttime condensation which is common at low altitude agricultural sites is not evident in the Alpine.

The data for July have been summed and compared with similar data for the arctic tundra at Barrow, Alaska, from 1957 and 1958 (Mather and Thornthwaite, 1958) and 1971 (Weller and Holmgren, 1974) in Table 4. The

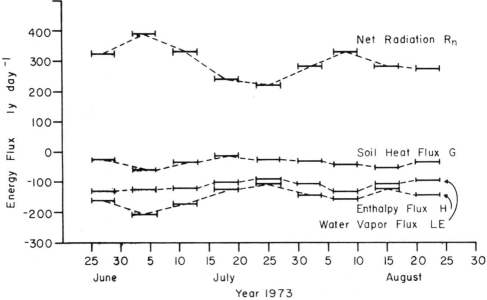

FIGURE 8. The seasonal energy balance. Data are 5-day averages, the period is denoted by the horizontal bars.

TABLE 3

Daily totals of the energy balance components for Niwot Ridge[a]

Period	R_n	H	LE	β	G
Day 176-179 (June 25-29)	323	−162	−131	1.23	−30
Day 183-187 (July 2-6)	391	−208	−124	1.70	−59
Day 190-194 (July 9-13)	331	−174	−121	1.46	−36[b]
Day 197-201 (July 16-20)	246	−126	−101	1.26	−19
Day 204-208 (July 23-27)	222	−90	−105	0.85	−27
Day 211-215 (July 30-Aug. 3)	282	−146	−108	1.35	−28
Day 218-222 (Aug. 6-10)	333	−159	−131	1.21	−43
Day 225-229 (Aug. 13-17)	281	−120	−108	1.10	−53
Day 232-236 (Aug. 20-24)	275	−144	−95	1.51	−36

[a]Data are averages for the periods given. Unit is ly day^{-1}. Symbols are defined in the Appendix.
[b]Estimate.

TABLE 4

Comparison of the July energy balance for Niwot Ridge, Colorado, and Barrow, Alaska[a]

	Niwot Ridge 1973		Barrow 1957, 1958		Barrow 1971 (July 15-18)	
R_n	298	(100)[b]	287	(100)	238	(100)
H	−148	(49)	−149	(52)	−77	(32)
LE	−113	(39)	−116	(40)	−157	(66)
G	−37	(12)	−22	(8)	−4	(2)
β	1.31		1.28		0.49	

[a]Unit is ly day^{-1}. Symbols are defined in the Appendix.
[b]Figures in parentheses are percent of net radiation.

magnitudes of the turbulent fluxes and the Bowen ratio for Niwot Ridge are almost identical to those for Barrow 1957 and 1958. The difference in net radiation (12 cal · cm^{-2} · day^{-1}) is almost entirely absorbed by the difference in soil heat flux (13 cal · cm^{-2} · day^{-1}). This suggests that the processes of turbulent transfer are equally efficient at both sites and the moisture stress is very similar for the two periods (1957 to 1958 and 1973). The discrepancy between the Niwot Ridge and 1971 Barrow data must be attributed to different regimes of moisture availability. The standing water which covered a large percentage of the Barrow tundra during 1971 (Weller and Holmgren, 1974) provided a continuous moisture source that was not available at Niwot Ridge.

DISCUSSION

There is a tendency among microclimatologists to consider data "contaminated" which do not correspond closely to the established norms. With the complexity and sophistication of instrumentation, it is easy to attribute small errors in fit to even smaller errors in observation. For example, a 10% error in the calculation of the vertical momentum flux between the surface and 16 m may be attributed to a 1% variation in wind speed along the fetch 100 m upwind (Swinbank, 1964), a variation well within instrumental accuracy. These errors are no doubt present in this investigation, but other problems peculiar to the Alpine are even more significant; the heterogeneity of the surface composition and the massive advection of cool dry air over an insolated and relatively moist surface. One-dimensional flux-profile models cannot be expected to be valid in such locations and must be replaced by two dimensional models, for which both vertical and horizontal gradients of the flux properties are required, or by empirical models that are valid only for the characteristics of that site. On account of the lack of necessary instrumentation, an empirical model was validated for this study on Niwot Ridge.

In the Alpine, each location is unique in a microclimatological sense. Variations in moisture availability, gradients of topography which give rise to moisture and insolation gradients, advection gradients, and gradients of vegetation type (cf. Figure 1) which are themselves nonlinear functions of these variables, all give rise to an infinite range of energy balance possibilities. The analysis presented in this study describes the energy relationships at one location on Niwot Ridge. It cannot be assumed to characterize those relationships for all alpine tundras in Colorado, or even in the vicinity of Niwot Ridge. It is, however, the first such seasonal study in the alpine tundra and has served to identify the problems and present a data base for future, more extensive, examinations of the microclimates of this type of environment.

Year to year variability has not yet been determined for this site. It is entirely possible that the results may be biased by the synoptic situations of the 1973 summer season. Several additional seasons of data are required to evaluate properly the energy balance of the Niwot Ridge site.

The seasonal energy balance for the 1973 summer was as follows:

Net radiation (R_n)
298 cal · cm^{-2} · day^{-1} (100%)
Enthalpy flux (H)
148 cal · cm^{-2} · day^{-1} (49%)
Evapotranspiration (LE)
113 cal · cm^{-2} · day^{-1} (39%)
Soil heat flux (G)
37 cal · cm^{-2} · day^{-1} (12%)
Bowen ratio (β) 1.31

These data compare favorably with those for an arctic tundra at Barrow, Alaska, for the 1957 and 1958 summer seasons.

The seasonal course of the enthalpy flux corresponds closely to that of the net radiation. The evapotranspiration responds to soil moisture availability more directly than to energy sources and the amplitude of the seasonal wave is much reduced from that of the enthalpy flux. A daytime moisture stress is evident; however, evapotranspiration proceeds at all times and 24-hr totals may be large. The pattern of daytime loss by evapotranspiration and nighttime gain by condensation common to low altitude agricultural sites is not evident in the Alpine. The soil heat flux is small, being a residual of the radiant energy supply and the energy demands of the turbulent terms (H and LE).

ACKNOWLEDGMENTS

This project was supported by the International Biological Programme, Tundra Biome (NSF Grant No. GV-29350 to J. D. Ives). Instrumentation and field logistics support was provided by the Institute of Arctic and Alpine Research. Provision of computer time by the National Center for Atmospheric Research, Computing Facility is also acknowledged. Financial support was also provided by the Council on Research and Creative Work, University of Colorado. I wish to thank R. G. Barry for his advice during the course of this work and constructive comments on the manuscript.

APPENDIX

Definition of Symbols

Cp specific heat of air, cal · g^{-1} · K^{-1}

E evapotranspiration, cm · cm^{-2} · min^{-1}

G soil heat flux, cal · cm^{-2} · min^{-1}

g acceleration of gravity, cm sec^{-2}

H enthalpy flux, cal · cm^{-2} · min^{-1}

k von Karman constant, $k \sim 0.4$

L heat of vaporization, cal cm^{-3}

Ri gradient Richardson number,

$$Ri = \frac{g}{T} \cdot \frac{\frac{\partial T}{\partial z}}{(\frac{\partial u}{\partial z})^2}$$

R_n net radiation, cal · cm^{-2} · min^{-1}

s slope of saturation specific humidity-temperature curve

T temperature, °K

U^* friction velocity, cm sec^{-1}

u wind velocity, cm sec^{-1}

z height above surface, cm

Zm geometric mean height between sensors, cm

z_o roughness length, cm

β Bowen ratio, $\beta = H/LE$

Φ_h Obukhov parameter for enthalpy flux

Φ_w Obukhov parameter for water vapor flux

ρ air density, g cm^{-3}

ϕ potential temperature, °K

γ Cp/L

301

REFERENCES

Barry, R. G., 1973: A climatological transect along the east slope of the Front Range, Colorado. *Arct. Alp. Res.*, 5: 89-110.

Bradley, E. F., 1968: A micrometeorological study of velocity profiles and surface drag in the region modified by a change in surface roughness. *Quart. J. Roy. Meteorol. Soc.*, 94: 361-379.

Brooks, F. A. and Pruitt, W. O., 1965: *Investigation of Energy, Momentum and Mass Transfer Near the Ground*. Dept. of Water Sciences and Engineering, University of California. 259 pp.

Businger, J. A., Wyngaard, J. C., Isumi, Y., and Bradley, E. F., 1971: Flux profile relationships in the atmospheric surface layer. *J. Atmos. Sci.*, 28: 181-189.

Deacon, E. L., 1969: Physical processes near the surface of the earth. *In* Flohn, H. (ed.), *General Climatology*, Vol. 2. Elsevier, N.Y., 39-104.

Dyer, A. J. and Hicks, B. B., 1970: Flux-gradient relationships in the constant flux layer. *Quart. J. Roy. Meteorol. Soc.*, 96: 715-721.

Fuchs, M. and Tanner, C. B., 1970: Error analysis of Bowen Ratios measured by differential psychrometry. *Agric. Meteorol.*, 7: 324-334.

LeDrew, E. F., 1974: The radiation and energy budget of an alpine tundra in Colorado during the growing season, 1974. Unpubl. M.A. Thesis, University of Colorado. 170 pp.

LeDrew, E. F. and Emerick, J. C., 1974: A mechanical balance-type lysimeter for use in remote environments. *Agric. Meteorol.*, 13: 253-258.

Lettau, H. H., 1949: Isotropic turbulence in the atmospheric surface layer. U.S. Air Force Cambridge Research Laboratories, *Geophys. Res. Pap.*, No. 1.

Mather, J. R. and Thornthwaite, C. W., 1956: Microclimatic investigations at Point Barrow, Alaska, 1956. Drexel Institute of Technology, Laboratory of Climatology, Vol. IX, No. 1. 51 pp.

————, 1958: Microclimatic investigations at Point Barrow, Alaska, 1957-1958. Drexel Institute of Technology, Laboratory of Climatology, Vol. XI, No. 2. 89 pp.

McIlroy, I. C. and Angus, D. E., 1964: Grass, water and soil evaporation at Aspendale. *Agric. Meteorol.*, 1: 201-224.

Montieth, J. L., 1965: Evaporation and environment. *Symp. Soc. Exp. Biol.*, 19: 205-234.

Monin, A. S. and Obukhov, A. M., 1954: Basic laws of turbulent mixing in the ground layer of the atmosphere. *Amer. Meteorol. Soc. Transl.* T-R174, AF 19.

Morgan, D. L., Pruitt, W. O., and Lourence, F. J., 1971: Analysis of energy, momentum and mass transfers above vegetative surfaces. *ECOM Tech. Rept.* 68-610-F, University of California, Davis, California. 120 pp.

Obukhov, A. M., 1946: Turbulence in an atmosphere with a non-uniform temperature. Transl. from Russian, *Bound. Layer Meteorol.* (1971), 2: 7-29.

Panofsky, H. A. and Townsend, A. A., 1963: Change of roughness and the wind profile. *Quart. J. Roy. Meteorol. Soc.*, 90: 147-155.

Priestley, C. H. B. and Taylor, R. D., 1972: On the assessment of surface heat flux and evaporation using large-scale parameters. *Mon. Weather Rev.*, 100: 81-92.

Rao, K. S., Wyngaard, J. C., and Coté, O. R., 1975: Local advection of momentum, heat, and moisture in micrometeorology. *Bound. Layer Meteorol.*, 7: 331-348.

Rouse, W. R. and Stewart, R. B., 1972: A simple model for determining evaporation from high latitude upland sites. *J. Appl. Meteorol.*, 11: 1063-1070.

Sanders, L. D. and Weber, A. H., 1970: Evaluation of roughness lengths at the NSSL-SKY meteorological tower. *ESSA Tech. Mem.* ERLTM-NSSL 47. 24 pp.

Sellers, W. D., 1965: *Physical Climatology*. University of Chicago Press, Chicago. 272 pp.

Stearns, C. R., 1969: Application of Lettau's theoretical model of thermal diffusion to soil profiles of temperature and heat flux. *J. Geophys. Res.*, 14(2): 532-541.

Stewart, J. B. and Thom, A. S., 1973: Energy budgets in pine forest. *Quart. J. Roy. Meteorol. Soc.*, 99: 154-170.

Swinbank, W. C., 1964: The exponential wind profile. *Quart. J. Roy. Meteorol. Soc.*, 90: 119-135.

————, 1968: A comparison between predictions of dimensional analysis for the constant-flux layer and observations in unstable conditions. *Quart. J. Roy. Meteorol. Soc.*, 94: 460-467.

Taylor, P. A., 1969: On wind and shear-stress profile above a change in surface roughness. *Quart. J. Roy. Meteorol. Soc.*, 95: 75-91.

Terjung, W. H., Kickert, R. N., Potter, G. L., and Swarts, S. W., 1969: Energy and moisture balance of an alpine tundra in mid-July. *Arct. Alp. Res.*, 1(4) 247-266.

Thom, A. S., Stewart, J. B., Oliver, H. R., and Gash, J.H.C., 1975: Comparison of aerodynamic and energy budget estimates of fluxes over a pine forest. *Quart. J. Roy. Meteorol. Soc.*, 101: 93-105.

Webber, P. J. and May, D. E. (In preparation), The structure and productivity of alpine tundra vegetation, Niwot Ridge, Colorado.

Weller, G. and Holmgren, B., 1974: The microclimates of the arctic tundra. *J. Appl. Meteorol.*, 13: 854-862.

SPATIAL DISTRIBUTION OF RADIATION IN

THE COLORADO FRONT RANGE

by

David Greenland*

Introduction

The increasing attention being given to solar energy as an alternate
energy source has also given rise to many studies concerning the potential
availability of solar energy. Most of these have pointed to the sparsity of
the global solar radiation observational network in North America. The paucity
of the network itself has stimulated a few investigations of the spatial
dimensions of an optimum sampling network and its correlate the predictability
of global solar radiation (from here on referred to as radiation) at a given
distance away from an observation station (Wilson and Petzold, 1972; Suckling
and Hay, 1976). The aim of the present paper is to extend this work in two
directions. First the extension will be into mountainous terrain and investigations will focus on the Colorado Front Range. Secondly the extension will
be in the temporal sense in which an examination of the relationships between
recorded values of radiation at two sites will be made with respect to different
seasons and aspects of the synoptic climatology of the Front Range.

The data used in this paper come from two separate investigations,
one made in 1965 by J.M. Clark and J.W. Marr (Clark and Marr, 1966) and one
undertaken in 1977 by D. Dickson as a student project. First the data will be
described then attention will be addressed to relationships between the data
themselves and then between the data and synoptic weather conditions.

---

* David Greenland is Associate Professor in the Department of Geography and
  Institute of Arctic and Alpine Research, University of Colorado, Boulder,
  Colorado.

Climatological Bulletin, 1978, No. 24, pp. 1-14.

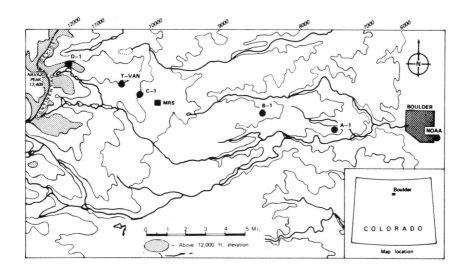

Fig. 1. Location of Observation Sites.

Location and Instrumentation

The Institute of Arctic and Alpine Research has maintained meteorological observing sites across the Colorado Front Range since 1952. The location of the four main sites A1, B1, C1 and D1 is shown on Figure 1 together with the sites of the supplementary T-Van, MRS (Mountain Research Station) and NOAA observing stations. Figure 2 shows the sites to cover an altitudinal range from 3749m at D1 to 1615m at NOAA. The transect runs eastwards from the continental divide, the closest station being D1 which is 2.6km from the divide and the furthest being the NOAA site at 37.0km from the divide. The horizontal distances and elevational differences between the stations used in this study are indicated in Table One. The area lies at approximately 40°N, 105°W.

The instruments used for recording radiation in the 1965 year were Robitzsch bimetallic actinographs operated at sites B1, C1 and D1. Clark and Marr (1966) have considered the accuracy of these recordings and have concluded that when instrumental and data reduction errors are taken into account daily totals of short wave radiation are given to an overall accuracy of ±15%. These authors describe in detail the care with which calibrations were carried out between the actinographs and between the actinographs and a 50 junction Eppley pyrheliometer (itself calibrated

304

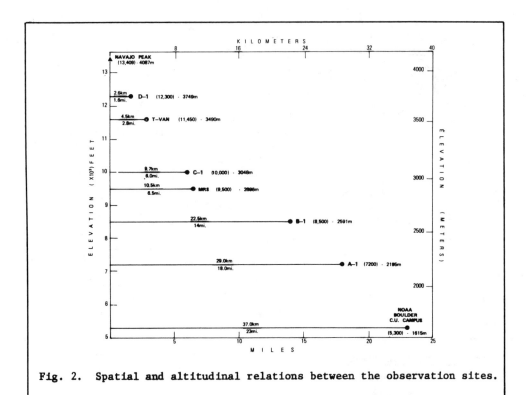

Fig. 2. Spatial and altitudinal relations between the observation sites.

TABLE ONE

Matrices of Distance and Elevation Differences between
Recording Sites Used in the Study

(a) Distance in Kilometres

	C1	D1	T-VAN
B1	12.8	19.9	
C1		7.1	
NOAA			32.5

(b) Elevation Differences in Metres

	C1	D1	T-VAN
B1	456	1158	
C1		702	
NOAA			1921

TABLE TWO

Mean Values of Radiation Receipt in $MJm^{-2}day^{-1}$ for
the Periods Involved in this Study.

Data Period	Mean Radiation Receipt B1	C1	D1	Boulder NOAA	T-VAN	Number of Cases
All Year 1965	14.6	14.0	14.4			365
Jan., Feb. 1965	8.5	10.1	9.7			59
Mar. - May 1965	15.9	18.1	19.1			92
June - Sept. 1965	19.8	16.0	17.2			122
Oct. - Dec. 1965	10.3	9.6	8.9			92
All data 1977				17.6	17.5	110
Jan. - Feb. 1977				8.3	8.5	25
Mar. - May 1977				19.0	19.2	66
June 1977				22.6	21.4	21

TABLE THREE

Variables Used in 1965 Data Analyses.

Variable	Abbreviation	Mean	Standard Deviation	Unit
Radiation at B1 (Sugarloaf)	R1	14.6	7.5	$MJm^{-2}day^{-1}$
Radiation at C1 (Como)	R2	14.0	7.1	$MJm^{-2}day^{-1}$
Radiation at D1 (Niwot Ridge)	R3	14.4	7.6	$MJm^{-2}day^{-1}$
Mean Temp at B1	TMEANC1	5.2	8.7	°C
Mean Temp at C1	TMEANC2	0.7	8.0	°C
Mean Temp at D1	TMEANC3	-4.1	8.4	°C
Relative Humidity at B1	RHMEAN1	63.1	19.2	%
Relative Humidity at C1	RHMEAN2	67.4	15.6	%
Relative Humidity at D1	RHMEAN3	70.3	26.4	%
Denver Freezing Level	FRELEV	2316.0	2194.1	metres
Denver 1200 GMT temp at 700mb	TEMP	1.5	8.2	°C
Denver 1200 GMT rel. hum. at 700mb	RH	45.1	22.2	%
Denver 1200 GMT wind direction at 700mb	WINDIR	25.0	8.5	degrees
Denver 1200 GMT wind velocity at 700mb	VEL	7.7	5.0	$msec^{-1}$

against ESSA pyrheliometers) operated at C1. An important point with regard
to operating efficiency is that radiation instruments on Niwot Ridge seldom
suffer from icing or condensation problems because of the dryness of snow,
and the general low humidities and high winds encountered in this area.
Another point is that all instrument sites are well exposed. No skyline
obstructions are significant such that errors due to them would be larger
than the errors already inherent in the cosine responses of the instruments.

The instruments used to collect the 1977 data were Eppley precision
pyranometers. Both instruments were interfaced with integrating equipment
and both had been previously indirectly calibrated together.

Certain other meteorological data were collected during 1965 at
the same time as the radiation data. Temperatures and relative humidities
were recorded at sites B1, C1 and D1. Mean daily temperatures and relative
humidities were computed from the daily maximum and minimum values of these
parameters. Data were also taken from the Denver radiosonde observations
made at 1200GMT daily. 700mb level observations of temperature, relative
humidity, wind direction and velocity were noted. 700mb is the approximate
level of the C1 and D1 sites and the Denver radiosonde station is approximately 80km from Niwot Ridge.

Aspects of the Synoptic Climatology of the Front Range

There are three major sources of moisture for the eastern slope
of the Front Range (James 1966) and the moisture bearing clouds obviously
affect insolation values recorded in this location. Moisture for winter
(Nov - Feb) precipitation is carried from the Pacific Coast. Spring
(March to May - June) precipitation is mainly derived from Gulf air, while
summer (June - July to September) precipitation results from local convective
activity.

Between November and February the largest precipitation and by
implication cloud amounts are found at the higher elevations (D1). It is
quite possible for this station to be covered by crest or foehn wall clouds
while the lower elevations remain free. An exception to this is when
inversions over the plains cause low level clouds leaving the upper elevations
cloud free. As a result, 1965 data can be interpreted to show that during
the months of November to February, D1 had more hours of daylight cloud
than either B1 or C1.

During the spring months (March to May or June) Gulf air frequently
moves up the eastern slope giving the heaviest precipitation to, and causing
cloud cover over, the lower and middle elevation stations. This effect does

TABLE FOUR

Correlation Coefficient Martix for 1965 Data (All Year). Coefficients greater than 0.5 are underlined.

	R1	R2	R3	TMEANC1	TMEANC2	TMEANC3	RHMEAN1	RHMEAN2	RHMEAN3	FRELEV	TEMP	RH	WINDIR
R2	.81555												
R3	.69265	.71660											
TMEANC1	.64302	.42860	.42808										
TMEANC2	.60179	.38573	.40870	.97936									
TMEANC3	.59520	.36248	.41409	.95309	.96721								
RHMEAN1	-.28418	-.30467	-.14120	-.37866	-.29894	-.22157							
RHMEAN2	-.20529	-.24794	-.13481	-.31026	-.29237	-.21473	.74078						
RHMEAN3	-.22359	-.23441	-.19540	-.24299	-.22361	-.26296	.41198	.46030					
FRELEV	.49850	.32940	.38448	.70839	.73009	.72727	-.08230	-.12169	-.11653				
TEMP	.49712	.26342	.27319	.93651	.94194	.92460	-.31605	-.26527	-.20379	.70580			
RH	-.22532	-.22829	-.03189	-.33632	-.26777	-.20836	.69303	.53335	.30479	-.13667	-.37443		
WINDIR	.03778	.08557	-.01348	-.09269	-.11118	-.16958	-.23493	-.20453	-.08841	-.13528	-.14068	-.12690	
VEL	-.16383	-.07186	-.19230	-.27320	-.25372	-.32490	.05086	.05494	.07347	-.20300	-.23986	-.00408	.28229

not usually penetrate above 3000m.

Spectacular cumulus and cumulonimbus clouds are typical of the summer months (June – July to September). Such clouds have the effect of decreasing daily totals of global solar radiations from their potential level. There is some evidence that such clouds tend to be located more over the mountainous rather than the plains areas (Reynolds 1977).

Precipitation and cloud conditions are therefore best explained on the seasonal basis discussed above. As a result the 1965 radiation data were analyzed, not only for the whole year, but also along the seasonal divisions examined here.

Procedure and Results

Before proceeding to the spatial analyses it is appropriate to address briefly the question of increased radiation receipt with altitude. Assuming a solar constant of $1352Wm^{-2}$, the altitudinal difference examined in this study between 1615m and 3749m under clear sky conditions would lead to a difference of incident energy of between $1103Wm^{-2}$ and $1186Wm^{-2}$ which amounts to 7.6% (Pope, 1977). The existence of cloud reduces this difference. Sutovik (1971) has shown that for Boulder the percentage hours of sun total available ranges from 40% in April to 60% in November. Clark and Marr (1966) use their 1965 radiation data to compute for D1 the percentage of daylight hours with cloud ranges from 41% in October to 84% in August. As a result only three sets of the mean radiation receipt data (Table Two) show a clear increase in radiation receipt with altitude. Thus for the purposes of this initial analysis it has been decided to ignore the altitudinal effect while at the same time acknowledging its existence.

The 1965 data were first analysed using simple and multiple regression techniques. Table Three shows the variables inserted into this analysis together with their abbreviations, units used, and annual means and standard deviations. As a matter of general interest Table Four shows the correlation coefficient matrix between all these variables for the complete year's data. This indicates radiation values and temperature values at the mountain sites to be correlated well between themselves and with the 700mb Denver temperature values. Relative humidity values at the mountain sites are also correlated well among themselves and with the 700mb relative humidity at Denver. This simply illustrates the expected cohesion among these meteorological variables which are observed within a rather small area, as the time scale and sample size becomes rather large.

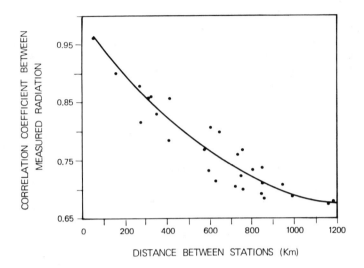

(a)   Distance and measured radiation

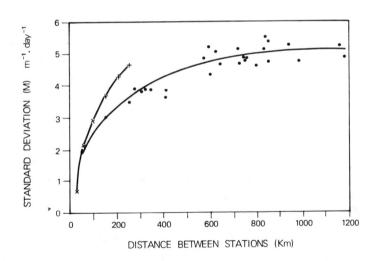

(b)   Distance and standard deviations

Fig. 3. Correlations between stations.

TABLE FIVE

Variables taken into multiple regression equations where
radiation at three sites is used as the dependent variable.
Variables are listed in the order in which they were taken
into the regressions equations.

Data Period	R1 best explained by variables:	R2 best explained by variables:	R3 best explained by variables:
All Year	R2, TMEANC1, R3	R1, R3, TMEANC3, RHMEAN1	R2, R1, RH, VEL
Jan., Feb.	R2, TMEANC3, RH, RHMEAN2	R1, RHMEAN2, R3, TMEANC2	R2, VEL, FRELEV, TMEANC3
March, April, May	R2, RHMEAN1	R1, R3	RHMEAN2, R2, RH, TMEANC1
June, July, Aug., Sept.	R2, TMEANC1	R1	R2, TMEANC3, TEMP
Oct., Nov., Dec.	R2, FRELEV	R1, R3	R2, FRELEV, RHMEAN3

The stepwise multiple regression technique was used to indicate by
which of the variables the radiation observations are best explained. This
is shown when the radiation at the three sites is taken in turn as being
the dependent variable (Table Five). Although all variables were taken into
account in this analysis only those which improve the value of the multiple
correlation coefficient by 0.01 when taken into the regression are included
in Table Five. The results given in Table Five show that with the aggregate
annual data and the seasonally stratified data, the radiation at one site
can be estimated from the radiation at the other mountain sites. Furthermore, in most cases values of temperature and relative humidity taken at the
same site or at nearby sites can also help improve predictions (more strictly
post-dictions) of radiation at that site. With one exception, only the
Niwot Ridge radiation is significantly explained by data from the free air
over Denver, and this effect is most marked in the winter months. The
multiple regression equations used in this analysis are not quoted because
they do not, in themselves, have much physical significance. Yet the lowest
multiple regression correlation coefficient among them is 0.684 significant
at the 99% level and clearly they could be usefully employed to fill in
missing data or to estimate radiation receipt at the stations on the Front
Range.

It is unlikely however that any one area would have as much data
as used in this analysis, so relationships between the radiation values

TABLE SIX

Simple Regression Relationships between the 1965 Radiation Values.
R1 = radiation at B1, R2 = radiation at C1
R3 = radiation at D1. Units = $MJm^{-2}day^{-1}$.

Data Period	Regression Equations	Correlation Coefficients	Cases
All Year	R1 = 0.87R2 + 2.41	0.82	365
	R1 = 0.69R3 + 4.73	0.69	365
	R2 = 0.66R3 + 4.43	0.72	365
Jan, Feb	R1 = 0.64R2 + 2.01	0.84	59
	R1 = 0.33R3 + 5.19	0.51	59
	R2 = 0.53R3 + 4.93	0.61	59
Mar, April, May	R1 = 0.59R2 + 5.20	0.74	92
	R1 = 0.75R3 + 1.44	0.61	92
	R2 = 0.97R3 - 0.48	0.63	92
June, July, Aug, Sept	R1 = 1.09R2 + 2.37	0.90	122
	R1 = 0.56R3 + 10.23	0.59	122
	R2 = 0.47R3 + 7.99	0.59	122
Oct, Nov, Dec	R1 = 0.97R2 + 0.78	0.90	92
	R1 = 0.64R3 + 4.55	0.78	92
	R2 = 0.62R3 + 4.22	0.81	92

TABLE SEVEN

Standard Deviation of Radiation Differences between pairs
of stations using the 1965 data. Units = $MJm^{-2}day^{-1}$.

Data Period	Station Pair	Mean	Standard Deviation	Cases
All Year	B1 - C1	0.6548	4.7337	365
	B1 - D1	-0.3881	5.9594	365
	C1 - D1	-1.0428	5.8393	
Jan - Feb	B1 - C1	-1.6780	2.3816	59
	B1 - D1	-1.2971	4.3488	59
	C1 - D1	0.3809	4.1337	59
Mar, April, May	B1 - C1	-2.1913	5.7435	92
	B1 - D1	-3.2586	5.5478	92
	C1 - D1	-1.0673	6.5877	92
June, July, Aug, Sept	B1 - C1	3.8296	3.3080	122
	B1 - D1	2.6281	7.0309	122
	C1 - D1	-1.2015	6.5577	122
Oct, Nov, Dec	B1 - C1	0.5249	1.7954	92
	B1 - D1	1.3840	3.1626	92
	C1 - D1	0.8591	2.9467	92

above are next examined. Table Six shows these relationships. As might be expected the highest correlations are between the stations nearest to each other. B1-C1, C1-D1 and B1-D1 is the order of highest correlation both for the year and when the data are stratified into seasons. In view of the synoptic climatology of the area this ordering of degree of correlation is reasonable. In winter the values of lower stations are best correlated because the higher station is suffering from frequent foehn cloud cover. In spring the lower stations' values are best correlated because they are both affected by the cloud of the upslope conditions. In summer they are best correlated because they are least affected by the cumulonimbus cloud which forms first over the higher elevations. Thus, the interesting situation arises where the order of the degree of correlation between the stations remains the same in different seasons but this occurs for different reasons which rest in the changing synoptic scale conditions.

Suckling and Hay (1976) have demonstrated that there is a fairly steady distance decay function between the correlation coefficient of radiation measured at pairs of stations and the distance between the stations. Their hand drawn curve is reproduced as Figure 3a superimposed on which are the relevant points for the Colorado Front Range 1965 all year data. It is apparent from this and from the correlation coefficients of the stratified data listed in Table Six that the Suckling and Hay relationship does not hold in the mountainous area being considered. The same is true when the standard deviations of radiation differences between station pairings are considered (Fig. 3b).

Figure 3b also includes the results of the study by Wilson and Petzold (1972) which indicates higher values of the standard deviation for a given distance than the Suckling and Hay study. The latter suggest that this could be due to 1) Wilson and Petzold's study being for summer only when high radiation values might give rise to higher standard deviations relative to those for an entire year and 2) the scale of weather systems influencing western Canada being larger than those influencing south eastern Canada, the location of Wilson and Petzold's study. Standard deviations of values of radiation at pairs of stations in the Front Range 1965 data (Table Eight) shows that higher standard deviations are found in the summer for two out of three pairs examined. This supports Suckling and Hay's first point. The second point is also substantiated by the Front Range analysis inasmuch as the synoptic weather conditions affecting the Front Range cloudiness actually manifest themselves as local mesoscale systems within the area being considered.

However, it is necessary to raise the qualification that much of western
Canada is mountainous terrain and the present study illustrates that neither
the correlation coefficient nor the standard deviation relationships with
distance hold in at least one example of mountainous terrain. Hay and
Suckling addressed this problem inconclusively in a paper given to the AAG
last year.

TABLE EIGHT

Statistics derived from the 1977 data relating
radiation receipt between the NOAA station at
Boulder and TVAN station on Niwot Ridge.

Data Period	Regression Equation	Correlation Coefficient	SD of Pair	Cases
All data	$R_{NOAA} = 0.97R_{TVAN} + 0.61$	0.86	4.17	110
Jan., Feb.	$R_{NOAA} = 0.87R_{TVAN} + 0.92$	0.85	1.89	25
Mar., April, May	$R_{NOAA} = 1.00R_{TVAN} - 0.23$	0.80	4.52	66
June	$R_{NOAA} = 0.77R_{TVAN} + 6.22$	0.79	4.70	21
Upslope Conditions	$R_{NOAA} = 0.90R_{TVAN} - 1.99$	0.83	3.78	16
Downslope Conditions	$R_{NOAA} = 0.87R_{TVAN} + 3.86$	0.91	3.36	16

Analyses of the daily T-Van and Boulder NOAA data for 110 days in
1977 were made along the same lines as above (Table Eight). However the
results from these analyses are not directly comparable to those of 1965
because of nonstationarity and the different amounts of data analyzed. Nevertheless, the results of Table Eight support in a general way the conclusions
already reached above. The only major difference is the low standard deviation of the difference in values between the paired stations for January and
February. The overall similarity lends support to the conclusions reached
in the previous discussion and lends credibility to the earlier less accurate
data.

As a minor extension to the 1977 analysis an examination of daily
synoptic charts was made in an attempt to determine days with upslope and
downslope wind conditions along the Front Range. Although this was rather
subjective, of all the 1977 data, 16 days in each category were selected

when it was likely that upslope and downslope conditions existed. Results of the regression analysis for these days are added to Table Eight and show that the relationships between the two stations are quite strong for these periods. The mean values of $MJm^{-2}day^{-1}$ for upslope conditions are NOAA (Boulder) 9.07 and TVAN 12.26 implying, as expected, more cloud cover at the lower site. The corresponding values for downslope conditions are NOAA (Boulder) 16.22 and TVAN 14.22 implying (again as expected) greater cloud cover at the upper site. Thus once more the 1965 data results are supported and the importance of synoptic conditions in the spatial relationships of radiation receipt along the Colorado Front Range is demonstrated.

Conclusions

The principal conclusions in this study are:

1) Daily radiation values and mean temperature values at the Front Range sites are well correlated between themselves and with the 700mb Denver temperature values.

2) Values of radiation at one mountain site can be estimated from values at nearby sites and the estimations can be improved by including data on temperature and humidity.

3) Across the Front Range the order of the degree of correlation between radiation values at the three stations remains the same throughout the year (1965) but the result is given by different synoptic conditions.

4) Neither the correlation coefficient nor the standard deviation variation with distance relationships of Suckling and Hay (1976) and Wilson and Petzold (1972) hold over the small distances examined in the Colorado Front Range.

Acknowledgement

Gratitude is expressed to Mr. J.M. Clark of INSTAAR, Mr. D. Dickson of Dept. of Geography, both University of Colorado, and Mr. E. Flowers of NOAA for assistance in the work described here. The work was partially supported by a grant from the University of Colorado Council on Research and Creative Work.

REFERENCES

Clark, J.M. and J.W. Marr, 1966: "Insolation and Other Environment Factors During 1965 in Three Ecological Regions in the Front Range, Colorado", Final Report on Contract DA49-092-AR046.

James, J.W., 1966: "Route 40 Mountain Environment Transect Colorado and Utah", Final Report on Contract DA 19-129-AMC-472( ). Project No. IKO 2400 IA 129. U.S. Army Natick Laboratories, Natick, Mass. Chapter VIII.

Pope, J.H., 1977: "Computations of Solar Insolation at Boulder, Colorado", NOAA Technical Memo, NESS 93, 13pp.

Reynolds, A.J., 1977: "A Study of the Occurrence of Mountain Thunderstorms in the Colorado Front Range", Unpublished Student Report.

Suckling, P.W., and J.E. Hay, 1976: "The Spatial Variability of Daily Values of Solar Radiation for British Columbia and Alberta, Canada", Climatological Bulletin, McGill University, Montreal, No. 20, pp. 1-7.

Sutovik, J.A., 1971: "Summary of Seeing Hours for Boulder Solar Observatory", Internal Memo, Space Environment Lab, ERL/NOAA, U.S. Dept. of Commerce, Boulder, Colorado, 5pp.

Wilson, R.G. and D.E. Petzold, 1972: "Daily Solar Radiation Differences between Stations in Southern Canada: a Preliminary Analysis", Climatological Bulletin, Dept. of Geography, McGill University, Montreal, No. 11, pp. 15-22.

PERMAFROST AND ITS RELATIONSHIP
TO OTHER ENVIRONMENTAL PARAMETERS
IN A MIDLATITUDE, HIGH-ALTITUDE SETTING,
FRONT RANGE, COLORADO ROCKY MOUNTAINS

JACK D. IVES

INTRODUCTION

Except for those relatively few areas where extensive ground temperature data exist (Sumgin, 1937; Black, 1954; Brown, 1960, 1966, 1968; Kudryavtsev (1959), maps showing permafrost distribution on a worldwide scale depend on broad extrapolations and an assumed relationship between mean annual air and mean annual ground temperatures. Use of the mean annual air (screen) temperature of -1.0 to -2.0°C to approximate the southern limit of permafrost, for instance (Brown, 1968), is justifiable for those extensive areas of the subarctic where little or no ground temperature data are available. This approach, however, may lead to inaccuracies in excess of 100 km when locating zonal boundaries.

The location and extent of permafrost in high mountain areas is even more uncertain. Since an increasing number of people are using the mountain areas of the earth for recreation, it would seem logical that there should be comparable growth in our knowledge of those areas. This study represents a systematic attempt to investigate the relationships between permafrost and other environmental parameters in a midlatitude, high-altitude setting.

THE NIWOT RIDGE STUDY SITE

The site chosen for a long-term permafrost research program is Niwot Ridge and adjacent areas in the Colorado Front Range,

Published in:
PERMAFROST: The North American Contribution
to the Second International Conference
ISBN 0-309-02115-4
National Academy of Sciences
Washington, D.C. (1973), pp. 121-125.

40°N. Treeline lies at about 3,400 m and the Continental Divide
follows the north-south crest of the range for 20 km. Individual
summits exceed 4,000 m from which slopes descend precipitously
into a series of cirques and U-shaped valleys. Glacial activity
during the late-Cenozoic glaciations has helped produce two contrasting sets of land-form assemblages--one typical of the glaciated, alpine mountains (*hochegebirge* (Troll, 1972)); the other
characterized by broad flowing contours, enclosing low hills and
ridges rising more than 300 m above treeline, and typical of a
periglacial landscape. Niwot Ridge is the longest of these
ridges. It is perpendicular to the Divide and 10 km in length,
and the westernmost 2 km forms a knife-edged arête (Figure 1).

Eight thermistor strings, set to depths between 160 and
418 cm with a 1-m vertical spacing, were installed along the
ridge in 1970 and 1971 through an altitude range of 300 m. Six
supplementary sets, emplanted to depths between 100 and 150 cm
with thermistors placed at 25, 50, 75, 100, and 150 cm were
added in 1972. Standard climatological observations have been

FIGURE 1. Low-level oblique air photo showing the middle section of Niwot Ridge with the forest-tundra ecotone in
the foreground and Institute of Arctic and Alpine Research's access road. The 3,750-m station is shown
by the letter s, and the site of the new 3,565-m station (x). Note the well-developed stone-banked lobes
and terraces (t) and goletz terraces (g).

taken at an alpine (3,750 m) and an upper montane forest site (3,000 m) since 1952 (Marr, 1961; Barry, 1972), and a new station for energy budget determination was established at 3,565 m in July 1972 as part of the United States Tundra Biome Program. A remote data platform, in association with analysis of the Earth Resources Technology Satellite (ERTS-1) performance, was added in October 1972 and is currently transmitting ground temperature and other data.

The available ground temperature data are still relatively sparse; more installations and a longer period of record are needed. However, sufficient data have been collected to approximate permafrost distribution and to draw some initial inferences concerning relationships between ground temperature, air temperature, precipitation and snowcover, vegetation, aspect, and short-wave radiation.

Climatic Characteristics of the Study Area

The basic climatic parameters for the 3,750-m station on Niwot Ridge, based on 19 years of record (1952-1970), are given in Table 1. Data from another station, maintained for 18 months at 3,500 m, gave a specific mean annual air temperature for October 1968-September 1969 of -0.8°C. At this site, wind-swept and snow-free in winter but with a copious water supply from a nearby snow-accumulation site, depths to permafrost measured in early autumn 1968 and 1969 were 190 and 183 cm, respectively (Fahey, 1971; Ives and Fahey, 1971). From the viewpoint of possible permafrost occurrence, the most significant environmental conditions on Niwot Ridge are relatively low mean annual air temperatures (about -1.0°C at 3,500 m and -4.0°C at 3,750 m) and very high westerly winds in winter that generally maintain a snow-free condition for all but lee slopes above treeline.

TABLE 1. Selected Climate Data[a] from Station 3,750 m, 1952-1970.

Annual air temperature	-3.9°C
July temperature	8.3
January temperature	-13.2
Monthly temperature range	21.5
Annual precipitation[b]	102.1 mm
Annual wind speed[b]	10.2 m s^{-1}
Wind speed for	
November	13.4
December	13.6
January	13.9
February	11.8
March[b]	12.1

[a]Values given are means.
[b]Values recorded from 1965 to 1970.

During spring (April-May) low-pressure systems moving north-ward from the Gulf of Mexico along the eastern flank of the Rocky Mountains bring up-slope storms that produce a precipitation maximum in the form of wet snow. As a result, snow cover usually reaches its greatest extent in April and May, or early June, i.e., at a time when the mid-winter period of most extensive heat loss is well past. The wet spring snowcover is important, however, in absorbing a large proportion of the available solar energy during the melting process and, because of the ensuing high al-bedo, in reflecting it back into the atmosphere. The critical nature of a wet snowcover in May and June is especially impor-tant, because it usually coincides with the first half of the annual period of high-angle sun and maximum short-wave radiation.

The summer (mid-June, July, August) is characterized by clear mornings and frequent afternoon thunderstorms typical of mountain systems in continental interiors. In relation to the onset of periods of low air temperature, the incidence of first snow in September, October, or November should also be critical in terms of marginal permafrost occurrence.

Ground Temperature Conditions, 1970-1971

The 1970-1971 maximum and minimum recorded temperatures at various depths from five selected sites are shown in Figure 2. At site (a) (3,750 m), the 381-cm-deep thermistor has remained below $0^{\circ}C$ through three summers, so that a depth to the perma-frost table of approximately 340 cm has been established. At sites (b) and (c), it was impracticable to install thermistors deep enough to substantiate a permafrost table. It is possible, however, to infer the probable presence of permafrost by ex-tending the maximum and minimum temperature curves until they intersect the $0^{\circ}C$ level. Such extrapolation is believed justi-fied, because at each site the temperature maxima continue to drop rapidly toward the $0^{\circ}C$ position with increasing depth to the lowest level of effective installation (418 cm and 382 cm, respectively) and because in each case the recorded maxima are only fractionally above the freezing point. Site (d) (3,485 m), on the other hand, is probably not underlain by permafrost, and at site (e) (3,490 m) the indication is no permafrost could exist. A thermistor string was installed to 5 m on the summit of Mt. Evans (4,300 m) on a horizontal surface, and the first readings (28 August 1970) showed the ground to be frozen below 320 cm. Unfortunately, soon after these readings were taken, the instal-lation was destroyed by tourists.

The five graphs in Figure 2 provide representative examples of the types of sites under investigation. From these data, from probing and digging, and from mining operations that en-counter frozen ground in late-August and September, it is pos-tulated that permafrost is widespread in the higher, wind-swept, and especially north-facing areas of the Colorado Rocky Moun-tains.

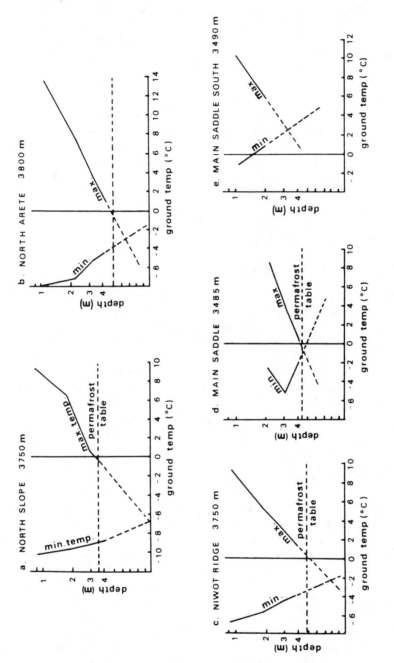

FIGURE 2. Maximum and minimum ground temperatures at various depths for 5 sites, 1970-1971, drawn on semilog paper. Permafrost either certainly or probably occurs under sites (a), (b), and (c), probably does not under site (d), and certainly does not under site (e).

Comparison of Conditions, 1970-1971 and 1971-1972

Figure 3 is an 18-month temperature record from four depths on a steep (40°) north-facing slope at 3,750 m. Comparison between the two melt seasons, subject to some data limitation, indicates that the rise in ground temperatures in the spring of 1972 may have been earlier and may have been more rapid than during the preceding year. Also, the warm phase of the cycle was about 12 days longer in 1972 and maxima were slightly higher. The overturn of temperatures in the early spring occurred nearly 6 weeks earlier in 1972 and the autumn reversal 2 weeks later.

Explanation of these differences between the two seasons at the one site can be related directly to weather conditions. February and March 1972 were comparatively warm and dry with a minimal snowcover, while April and May experienced one of the lightest wet spring snowfalls during the period of record (1952-1972). In addition, solar radiative flux, determined with an actinograph maintained at 3,750 m, was much higher for July 1972 than for July 1971. Conditions during August 1971 and 1972 were similar. Winter and spring periods for 1971 were much closer to normal.

The weekly observations through the middle of July 1971 caused speculation that no below-zero temperatures would be retained in the autumn. The sudden leveling off, beginning July 20, was related to a change in weather from warm and clear in the first part of the month to cloudy and very wet between July 19 and 28. This strong correlation between local weather and ground temperature trends was not repeated in 1972, yet temperatures at the 82- and 182-cm depths began to fall by the end of July, and the overall shape of the curves is very similar. The 1972 trends can be accounted for by reduced solar radiation, resulting from the progressive lowering of the sun's angle with increasing time from the summer solstice, accentuated by the northern exposure of this particular site. For comparative purposes, 1970-1971 and 1971-1972 temperature curves for a ridge crest site at 3,800 m are produced as Figure 4. The same general comparisons can be made, although the temperature decline from the summer maxima at two depths were delayed until late August, undoubtedly because of the longer exposure of the site to direct sunlight.

SUMMARY

The ground temperature data presented here, together with the large number of field observations of frozen ground in late summer and autumn, indicate that permafrost occurs extensively throughout the Colorado Rocky Mountains. It is much more widespread than hitherto believed, since few of the numerous reports by the pioneer miners of the last century penetrated the scientific literature despite Weiser's publication of 1875 and Baranov's (1959) speculation upon its existence in his world survey. Permafrost occurrence in Colorado, however, would seem marginal,

322

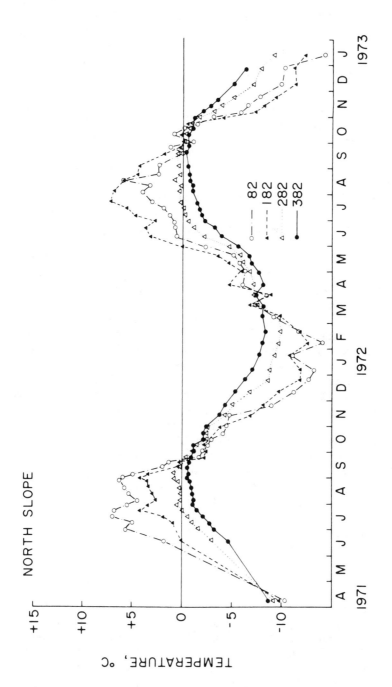

FIGURE 3.   Ground temperature record from April 1971 to January 1973 for a north-facing
site at 3,750 m. Following June 1971, thermistors at 82, 182, 282, and 382
cm were read weekly during the summer and approximately once every 2 weeks
during the winter. The 382-cm thermistor ceased to function in December 1972.

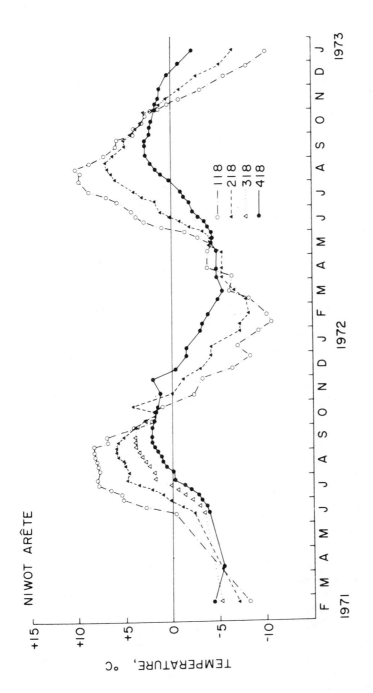

FIGURE 4. Ground temperature record for February 1971 to January 1973 from a ridge-crest site at 3,800 m for comparison with Figure 3. Thermistors were installed at 118, 218, 318, and 418 cm. The 318-cm thermistor ceased to function in October 1971.

although the numerous summits exceeding 4,000 m and extensive
areas of north-facing slopes should retain perennially negative
temperatures. One of the most important environmental parameters
in this high-altitude and relatively low-latitude region is incoming short-wave radiation and hence slope angle and aspect;
another is the interrelationships of wind, snow distribution,
and topography. The work already accomplished is only a beginning. A second stage will be a careful analysis of the relative
importance of the various secondary environmental parameters
affecting permafrost distribution, and this is currently under
way together with an energy balance study of a representative
alpine study site. It should then be feasible to make comparisons with and extrapolations to other high-mountain regions in
similar latitudes, since it is contended that the arctic and
subarctic experience is not fully comparable. For the present,
and despite the earlier implied criticism of the correlation
between mean annual air temperature and ground temperature, it
is worth reiterating that the lowest proven occurrences of
permafrost in the Front Range coincide with a mean annual air
temperature of approximately -1.0°C. The following conclusions
seem warranted:

1. At elevations of 3,500 m and above, i.e., immediately
above treeline, patches of permafrost should be expected under
wet sites that are largely blown free of snow during winter.
    Thickness of the active layer may be less than 2 m and
freezeback to the permafrost table may not be complete until
mid-February or early March. There will be no permafrost under
dry sites, south-facing slopes, and snow-accumulation sites.
South-facing slopes may experience very high temperatures in
late summer -11.9°C at 115 cm and 8.6°C at 215 cm.

2. Above about 3,750 m, permafrost will occur quite extensively under wet sites that are wind-swept in winter with an
active layer less than 2 m thick. Dry south-facing slopes, and
probably also wet south-facing slopes, and snow-accumulation
sites will be free of permafrost. Horizontal surfaces with
relatively little or no winter snowcover will probably be underlain by permafrost. North-facing slopes will be extensively
underlain by permafrost, and dry sites will show a depth of 3-4
m to the permafrost table.

3. The highest summits of the Front Range (4,000-4,400 m),
with an extrapolated mean annual air temperature of about -9°C
for 4,400 m, should be extensively underlain by permafrost of
considerable thickness.

4. The predominantly dry conditions and extensive areas of
bedrock outcrop severely limit the accumulation of significant
amounts of ground ice. Nevertheless, the possible presence of
permafrost is sufficient to indicate that any mountain development should take it carefully into account.

REFERENCES

Baranov, I.Y. 1959. Geographical distribution of seasonally frozen ground and permafrost. *In: Principles of Geocryology, Pt. 1, General Geocryology*. National Research Council of Canada, Ottawa. (Technical Translation 1121 by A. Nurklik), pp. 193-219.

Barry, R.G. 1972. Climatic environment of the east slope of the Colorado Front Range. *INSTAAR Occasional Paper*, No. 3, University of Colorado, Boulder, Colorado. 206 pp.

Black, R.F. 1954. Permafrost--a review. *Bull. Geol. Soc. Amer.*, 65: 839-856.

Brown, R.J.E. 1960. The distribution of permafrost and its relation to air temperatures in Canada and the U.S.S.R. *Arctic*, 13: 163-177.

_____. 1966. The relation between mean annual air and ground temperatures in the permafrost region of Canada. *In: Permafrost: Proceedings of an International Conference*. National Academy of Sciences, Washington, D.C., pp. 214-247.

_____. 1968. Permafrost map of Canada. *Can. Geogr. J.*, 2: 56-63.

Fahey, B.D. 1971. *A Quantitative Analysis of Freeze-thaw Cycles, Frost Heave Cycles and Frost Penetration in the Front Range of the Rocky Mountains, Boulder County, Colorado*. Ph.D. thesis, University of Colorado, Boulder, Colorado. 305 pp.

Ives, J.D. 1973. Permafrost. *In* Ives, J.D. and R.G. Barry (eds.), *Arctic and Alpine Environments*. Methuen, London.

Ives, J.D. and B.D. Fahey. 1971. Permafrost occurrence in the Front Range, Colorado Rocky Mountains, U.S.A. *J. Glaciology*, 10(58): 105-111.

Kudryavtsev, V.A. 1959. Temperature, thickness and discontinuity of permafrost. *In: Principles of Geocryology, Pt. 1: General Geocryology*. National Research Council of Canada, pp. 219-273. (Technical Translation 1187 by G. Belkov.)

Marr, J.W. 1961. Ecosystems of the east slope of the Front Range in Colorado. *Univ. Colo. Stud., Ser. Biol.*, No. 8. 134 pp.

Sumgin, M.I. 1937. *Perennially Frozen Soil Within the U.S.S.R.* 1st edition, Vladivostok, Moscow. 186 pp.

Troll, C. 1972. Geoecology and the world-wide differentiation of high-mountain ecosystems. *In* Troll, C. (ed.), *Geoecology of the High-mountain Regions of Eurasia. Erdwissenschaftliche Forschung*, Vol. 4. Franz Steiner Verlag, GMBH, Wiesbaden, pp. 1-16.

Weiser, S. 1875. Permanent ice in a mine in the Rocky Mountains. *Philos. Mag.*, 49: 322.

Part 5
Plant Ecology

Overview
Jack D. Ives and Patrick J. Webber*

There were many early contributions to Colorado botany. By 1908 a thorough bibliography listed over 500 entries (Allison, 1908), many of which concerned the mountains and the alpine. Many famous American botanists contributed to the early studies, for example, Frederic E. Clements, T.D.A. Cockerell, William S. Cooper, George Engelmann, Asa Gray, Edward L. Greene, R.F. Griggs, Theodor Holm, and P.A. Rydberg. Amongst these early contributions there were several attempts to lay foundations for long-term systematic research in plant ecology. One such attempt, which was made by Clements, is related in a delightful book by his wife (Edith S. Clements, 1960). She describes how Clements at the beginning of this century established an Alpine Laboratory on Pikes Peak. Ramaley (1908), as related in the Preface to this volume, also made a lasting impression and entitled a paper "Botanical opportunity in Colorado" and at almost the same time two papers from superb ecologists were published which concerned the alpine flora (Cockerell, 1906) and alpine vegetation (Cooper, 1908). Ramaley, Cockerell, and Cooper not only made fundamental studies but also through their contributions as teachers laid the foundations for the present plant ecology of the Front Range.

The latest attempt at long-term systematic study in the Front Range was initiated under the auspices of the United States International Biological Programme (IBP) in the early 1970s (Blair, 1977). A Tundra Biome Program concentrated on the alpine and facilitated the gathering of a significant number of scientists and graduate students representing many disciplines (Tieszen, 1978). Six selections in this chapter were derived from the alpine studies of the Tundra Biome.

Much of the early Colorado plant ecological work is summarized effectively in Gregg's (1963) monograph on the ants of

*Institute of Arctic and Alpine Research
University of Colorado
Boulder, Colorado 80309

Colorado. In particular Gregg indicates that the details of Merriam's (1890, 1891) life-zones for Colorado had been first worked out by Cary in 1911. Gregg goes on to discuss the views of several biologists concerning the value and implications of the life-zone concept. He quite correctly postulates (pp. 76-77) "that the life-zones were recognized on the basis of natural distribution patterns first, quite apart from any supposed temperature laws, and therefore (that they) have a biological reality independent of whether we know their causation."

It is to Marr (1961), however, that we must turn for the first major description and analysis of the Front Range east slope ecosystems. This monograph can perhaps be described as the fruit of Ramaley's inspiration; it emerged as the first phase of the development of INSTAAR. Marr recognized four major altitudinal vegetation belts beginning above the High Plains at the lower timberline. He named these: Lower Montane Forest; Upper Montane Forest; Subalpine Forest; Alpine Tundra. The Lower Montane is characterized by striking contrast in the density of vegetation on north- and south-facing slopes with a predominance of ponderosa pine. Douglas fir becomes co-dominant with ponderosa pine on the more moist north-facing slopes and has the potential to reduce the number of pines through natural processes to a few scattered individuals. Marr's Lower Montane Forest covers the altitudinal range of about 1,850 m (6,000 ft) to 2,380 m (7,700 ft) above sea level. The Upper Montane Forest, extending from about 2,450 m (8,000 ft) to 2,770 m (9,000 ft), is characterized by a predominance of Douglas fir in moderate sites of all aspects. Ponderosa pine is still abundant in the less mesic ridge-top and south-facing sites. Lodgepole pine and Aspen, with Limber pine, are important species which justify distinguishing this belt from the Lower Montane. Marr's third belt, the Subalpine Forest, extends from about 2,860 m (9,300 ft) to 3,400 m (11,000 ft). Here Engelmann spruce and Subalpine fir predominate with Aspen and Lodgepole pine conspicuous in the lower half and Limber pine extending with the spruce-fir association to timberline and species limit at 3,400 m (11,000 ft) and 3,520 m (11,400 ft) respectively.

Marr's work is also important because of his introduction of climate observing stations at representative sites within each of the four major ecosystems. This has ensured collection of many fundamental data upon which a great deal of subsequent work has depended (Barry, 1973). Similarly, the climatic station sites were used for locating a series of transplant gardens which in turn enabled completion of comparative studies on seed germinability and analysis of the growth and development of agronomic species as part of a mountain and circumpolar program (Amen and Bonde, 1964; Bonde, 1968; Bonde et al., 1973; Bonde and Foreman, 1973). Marr's work concentrated on the major ecosystems and while he delineated the three transitions, or ecotones, little detailed attention has been paid them, with the exception of the forest-tundra ecotone (Marr, 1977; Marr and Marr, 1973).

Certainly Marr's work is not without its critics, both with respect to delineation of vegetational belt boundaries and terminology. Gregg (1963, p. 85) objects to Marr's subalpine-upper montane boundary. He states that it is 200 to 300 m lower than it is usually placed by others (see Table 1): "A montane zone... of only 1000 feet seems much too narrow to me, and a subalpine zone of 1700 feet seems too broad. From observations, the reverse appears to fit more closely the actual conditions." D. Löve (1970) and Barry and Ives (1974) prefer the European altitudinal belt terminology and restrict the term subalpine to the forest-tundra ecotone. In this case the first altitudinal forest belt below the alpine tundra becomes the "Upper Montane Forest" and so on. Nevertheless, Marr's monograph with his subsequent papers (Marr, 1964a, 1964b, 1977) will remain a basic reference for many years to come. Peet (1978a and b) has recently made important contributions to Front Range forest ecology.

As mentioned previously, the forest-tundra ecotone has attracted special attention the world over (Wardle, 1974; Tranquillini, 1979). It has also been the object of scientific interest in the Front Range, although its full potential as a field research site has not nearly been fully realized. The first paper reproduced in this chapter is one of the more significant forest-tundra ecotone studies. By careful year-round observations on Engelmann spruce (Picea engelmannii Engel.) at its upper altitudinal limit, Wardle (1967) was able to demonstrate the importance of desiccation of windward needles as a timberline control and to bring timberline studies in the North American West more closely into line with extensive research characteristic of the Eastern Alps. The value of the Niwot Ridge site, in comparison to those in many other parts of the world, is that it is representative of the natural or near-natural timberlines of the Rocky Mountain region. This contrasts with other regions where timberline has been extensively lowered due to massive human impacts over several centuries. Other aspects of timberline research in the Front Range have been acknowledged although not adequately pursued. One aspect is fluctuation of the altitude of timberline through time. The palynological studies of Maher (1972) represent only a beginning, which have been supplemented in the San Juan Mountains by Andrews et al. (1975) and Petersen and Mehringer (1976) (see Ives, 1978; this chapter). Another important aspect is simple determination of the age of individual trees both within the uppermost forests and within the ecotone. Krebs has discovered Bristlecone pine (P. aristata Engel.) up to 1,750 years old on Mount Evans (Krebs, 1973) and Ives (1973) collated a number of scattered observations on the age of "ancient" Limber pines and Engelmann spruce below Niwot Ridge. Of comparable interest is the present-day dynamics of the ecotone (Marr, 1977) and the question of the age of individual krummholz forms that appear to be able to maintain themselves indefinitely by a combination of layering (vegetative reproduction), windward kill and leeward migration, so that Ives

(1973, 1978) has been tempted to hypothesize that the present forest-tundra ecotone and species limit along the Front Range is a relict of a warmer past climate, dating back possibly for more than 3,000 to 5,000 years. Because it may serve to spur additional timberline research, the short 1978 paper is reproduced as part of this chapter. Finally, the forest-tundra ecotone group of papers is rounded off with a study by Grant and Mitton (1977) that seeks to show genetic differentiation among growth forms of Engelmann spruce and Subalpine fir at treeline.

Several valuable studies on tundra research in the Front Range of an individual nature had been completed previous to IBP (Osburn, 1958; Holway and Ward, 1963; Marr, 1964a and b; Spomer and Salisbury, 1968, amongst others). These, together with the preeminent work of Billings, Bliss (for example, Bliss, 1956, 1966; Billings and Bliss, 1959; Billings and Mooney, 1968), and their collaborators, in many alpine and arctic regions, provided the critical platform of knowledge upon which the alpine components of the U.S. Tundra Biome were erected. Similarly, effective plant ecology will always depend heavily upon an adequate identification and classification of flora. In this respect, much of the Front Range endeavor would not have been so successful without the contribution of Harrington (1954) and especially that of W.A. Weber whose Flora of the Rocky Mountains (1976) and assiduous attention to the development and maintenance of the University of Colorado Herbarium represent achievements without compare. Also, the pioneering cytotaxonomical studies of Askell and Doris Löve (1966, 1971, 1974; D. Löve, 1970; Löve et al., 1971) have permitted major progress in development of our understanding of the evolution of the arctic-alpine flora. The papers by Webber (1974), Billings (1974a), and Löve and Löve (1974), together with the proceedings of a symposium on: The Evolution of Biotic Communities: The Alpine Biota, published as a group of four papers with an introduction by Löve and Löve (Arctic and Alpine Research, 1974) should help to place the Niwot Ridge papers, reprinted here, in proper perspective.

It must also be emphasized that the Niwot Ridge work was a relatively small component of the U.S. Tundra Biome endeavor. The main effort was focussed on an arctic coastal tundra ecosystem at Barrow, Alaska (Tieszen, 1978) itself linked to an international, circumpolar complex (Wielgolaski, 1975). Thus the alpine Tundra Biome component on Niwot Ridge was intended, amongst many other objectives, to throw light on the traditional arctic-alpine comparisons and contrasts. While much was gained from this, and the Caldwell et al. (1974) paper is included here to illustrate one aspect, it also serves to emphasize a certain questioning of Tundra Biome strategy -- how representative are the study sites? It is reasonable to maintain that the Niwot Ridge site is well representative of the Central Rocky Mountain alpine tundra, and Webber and May (1977), reproduced here, claim a much wider representativeness. The northern Alaska coastal tundra, however, may well be rather special and is not represent-

ative of the vast expanses of circumpolar arctic tundras in all
their varieties.

Prior to initiation of U.S. Tundra Biome research many fundamental questions had presented themselves and had been reasonably well defined. Thus, it was commonly understood that tundra
plant communities contrasted with the communities of most other
biomes (excepting grasslands and semi-deserts) in that belowground biomass greatly exceeded that aboveground -- was this an
adaptation to the "severe" environment with a short growing
season, moderate to low temperatures and, in the case of alpine
tundras, cold nights? Tundra life forms sensu Raunkaier (1934),
virtual absence of annuals, importance of tap roots of many of
the species that make up the fell field communities, and many
related characteristics, had been identified long since and yet
not adequately analyzed. Similarly, the close relationship
between snow and soil moisture distributions and plant community
patterns had been recognized several decades ago, but not fully
quantified. Thus resolution of these and other issues within
the context of a study of the structure and functioning of alpine tundra ecosystems in general became a major focus.

Even within the relatively small area of Niwot Ridge and
the Front Range, intensive and extensive study sites covered
only a minute proportion of the total area. Thus the desire-
ability of a vegetation map was emphasized early, and the paper
and map by Komárková and Webber (1978), reproduced here, is the
result, at least for Niwot Ridge itself. The careful mapping of
plant associations, using the Braun-Blanquet vegetation classification hierarchy on a scale of 1:10,000, not only allows determination of total above-timberline biomass by extrapolation from
the two major intensive and many extensive study sites, it can
be used in many other ways. Thus the zoologist, or animal ecologist, has an essential base for studies of the feeding ecology
of individual mammal and bird species (cf. May and Braun, 1972,
reproduced in Chapter 7). In addition a vegetation map readily
lends itself to derivation of soils maps, terrain sensitivity
and lichen-cover maps, and in the long-run should provide a
vital tool for mountain land-management, along the lines of the
soon to be published atlas on the Prudhoe Bay tundra (Walker et
al., in press). In addition, together with the topographical
map and micro- and macro-climatic data (Barry, 1973; LeDrew, 1975
and Chapter 5), it will provide a much more accurate and sophisticated base for future long-range ecological research and monitoring.

The abstract and introduction of Billings (1974) paper is
reproduced here to strengthen the relationship of Front Range
alpine ecology with that of tundra ecology at large. In this
paper Billings discusses two important long-range foci: (1) how
do alpine plants meet the challenges presented by cold, short
growing seasons at high elevations? and (2) from what sources
have alpine floras and vegetations been derived by migration and
evolution?

Flock's (1978) paper, produced here only in abstract, is
the first systematic attempt to analyze lichen-bryophyte patterns in the Front Range alpine. She reemphasizes the importance
of snow cover and soil moisture as the primary factors in controlling the distribution of vegetation above timberline. The
paper goes on to demonstrate the close interrelationships between
snow cover/soil moisture, on the one hand, and lichen-bryophyte
distribution, form, species composition, and biomass, on the
other.

The remaining three papers (Johnson and Caldwell, 1974;
Caldwell et al., 1974; Webber and May, 1977) are central alpine
products of the U.S. Tundra Biome, although by no means the
only members of the genre. They are also closely linked with
many other papers published in this volume and elsewhere. Realization that information on the relationship between photosynthesis and growth in individual leaves may lead to a better
understanding of how alpine plants cope with their harsh environment provided the incentive for the Johnson and Caldwell study.
They were able to show that leaf relative growth rates were
directly proportional to high or increasing photosynthetic
activity. This occurred primarily in the early part of the
growing season. A long middle stage was characterized by no
net change in leaf length with photosynthetic activity eventually
showing a steady decrease. A third, and final, stage showed
negative relative growth rates and a marked decline in CO_2 uptake, indicating senescence. It was also found that one to
several leaves on each plant studied operated at near maximal
photosynthetic capacity for prevailing conditions throughout
the growing season.

Caldwell et al. (1974) studied the relationships between
tundra canopy structure (in the form of foliage area indices)
and utilization of incoming solar radiation for both Niwot Ridge
alpine and Barrow arctic plant communities. They demonstrate
that the greater radiation intensities presented at higher solar
altitudes were well utilized by the denser alpine tundra communities. In the arctic the long day compensated to the extent that
lower radiation intensities presented at lower solar altitudes
are nearly equally well utilized in the much more sparsely stocked
arctic tundra communities. An increase in the amount of standing
dead led to reduced radiation receipts, but this reduced radiation, coupled with lower wind speeds, served to reduce water loss
by transpiration and thus diminish the effects of moisture stress.

Ehleringer and Miller (1975), not reproduced here, demonstrate that moisture stress can be high in the alpine tundra and
may limit primary production. The final paper to be included
here (Webber and May, 1977) also demonstrates the importance of
moisture stress in alpine plant communities, but somewhat incidentally to their arduous task of studying the magnitudes and
distribution of belowground plant structures. Despite the acquisition of a large data bank it was not possible to assess
the traditional concept that low aboveground to belowground

biomass ratios are an adaptation to a "severe" environment. It proved impossible to demonstrate correlations between such ratios and the environmental factors. They found that the magnitude of the ratio was more directly a function of species composition and growth form. Their determinations of aboveground primary production, ranging from 100 to 300 gm^{-2} yr^{-1} for different alpine plant communities represent about twice that for comparable arctic situations. This is probably the result of higher solar radiation receipts and higher growing season canopy and ground temperatures at 40°N. Moisture stress later in the growing season probably depresses primary production, and the approximately 50% higher production on San Juan Mountain sites (Webber et al., 1976) can be accounted for by heavier summer precipitation there compared to that received on the Front Range.

In addition to the formal, academic alpine ecological research referred to here, the Front Range has also been the site of potentially important initiatives to study applied aspects. In particular, the doctoral dissertation work of Beatrice Willard (1963) on Trail Ridge, Rocky Mountain National Park, led to a series of publications that took some first steps to quantify visitor impacts, especially hiker impacts, on alpine tundra, and to lay out permanent bench-mark study plots (Willard and Marr, 1970, 1971; Marr and Willard, 1970). Studies of the ecological impacts of winter cloud-seeding on the San Juan Mountain ecosystems (Steinhoff and Ives, 1976) is also worthy of mention in this context, particularly the plant ecology sections (Bock, 1976; Webber et al., 1976). Furthermore, the systematic mapping of vegetation, soils, surficial deposits, natural hazards, human impacts, land-management units, and so on, that will form the basis of the Indian Peaks Environmental Atlas (Ives et al., 1979), is an early movement toward a new stage of applied geoecological research. This type of work, with deliberate and strong linkages with the land manager, will likely play an increasing role in the future. Certainly, this is not to imply that traditional university research in the Front Range can be allowed to slow down; rather the reverse. Our present state-of-knowledge is such that we can only claim to have sharpened some of the basic questions and posed new ones. In this sense the foundations for long-term ecological research and monitoring have been laid. The creation of the Niwot Ridge Biosphere Reserve will now necessitate production of complete check lists, and precise mapping on a better topographical map scale than is presently available. It will also require a much fuller understanding of species and community interrelationships with both the indigenous and transient fauna, including man, and with the abiotic elements. The monumental treatise of Komárková (1979) has already carried the process many steps forward for the alpine and it will remain as a basic reference for the foreseeable future.

Preservation of the gene pool, as one of the objectives of the International Biosphere Reserve Network, through the Unesco Man and the Biosphere (MAB) Program, may seem somewhat esoteric.

But it is highly meaningful at the more prosaic level of determining how to manage mountain wilderness adjacent to a large
and rapidly growing population corridor on the adjacent High
Plains. Much more information on primary production, aboveground and belowground, for all Front Range communities, will
be needed, not only to facilitate development of a series of
sophisticated ecosystem models, but also, in relation to carrying
capacity determinations, for intelligent and justifiable management. The concept of ecosystem fragility, or rather, resiliency
(Webber and Ives, 1978) needs to be developed and further tested.
Thus there is an immediate need for the development of a synthesis of all available knowledge and for the construction of
long-range research team efforts crossing over into many disciplines of the life, earth, atmospheric, as well as the human
sciences. The most important and urgently needed future research endeavors, however, fall into four major categories: (1)
cycling of plant nutrients, including an impact assessment of
the recently reported acid precipitation over Niwot Ridge (Lewis
and Grant, 1980), (2) plant reproductive strategies, including
studies of life cycles, phenology, and reproductive success,
(3) development of plant communities, and (4) plant-animal interactions.

REFERENCES

Allison, E.M. 1908. Bibliography and history of Colorado
    Botany. *Univ. Colo. Stud.*, 6: 51-75.
Amen, A.D. and E.K. Bonde. 1964. Dormancy and germination in
    alpine *Carex* from the Colorado Front Range. *Ecology*, 45(4):
    881-884.
Andrews, J.T., P.E. Carrara, F.B. King, and R. Stuckenrath.
    1975. Holocene environmental changes in the alpine zone,
    northern San Juan Mountains, Colorado: evidence from bog
    stratigraphy and palynology. *Quaternary Research*, 5: 173-
    197.
Arctic and Alpine Research. 1974. The evolution of biotic
    communities: the alpine biota. Proceedings of a symposium
    edited by Askell and Doris Löve, 6(2): 105-142.
Barry, R.G. 1973. A climatological transect on the east slope
    of the Front Range, Colorado. *Arctic and Alpine Research*,
    5(2): 89-110.
Barry, R.G. and J.D. Ives. 1974. Introduction. *In* Ives, J.D.
    and R.G. Barry (eds.), *Arctic and Alpine Environments*.
    Methuen, London, pp. 1-13.
Billings, W.D. 1974a. Arctic and alpine vegetation: plant
    adaptations to cold summer climates. *In* Ives, J.D. and
    R.G. Barry (eds.), *Arctic and Alpine Environments*. Methuen,
    London, pp. 403-444.
_____. 1974b. Adaptations and origins of alpine plants.
    Arctic and Alpine Research, 6(2): 129-142.

Billings, W.D. and L.C. Bliss. 1959. An alpine snowbank environment and its effects on vegetation, plant development, and
productivity. *Ecology*, 40(3): 388-397.

Billings, W.D. and H.A. Mooney. 1968. The ecology of arctic
and alpine plants. *Biological Review*, 43: 481-529.

Blair, W.F. 1977. *Big Biology: the US/IBP*. US/IBP Synthesis
Series 7, Dowden, Hutchinson & Ross, Inc., Stroudsburg,
Pennsylvania. 261 pp.

Bliss, L.C. 1956. A comparison of plant development in microenvironments of arctic and alpine tundras. *Ecological
Monographs*, 26: 303-337.

_____. 1966. Plant productivity in the alpine microenviron-
ments on Mt. Washington, New Hampshire. *Ecological Monographs*, 36: 125-155.

Bock, J.H. 1976. The effects of increased snowpack on the
phenology and seed germinability of selected alpine species.
In Steinhoff, H.W. and J.D. Ives (eds.), *Ecological Impacts
of Snowpack Augmentation in the San Juan Mountains, Colorado*.
Final Report to Bureau of Reclamation, Colorado State University, Fort Collins, Colorado, pp. 265-280.

Bonde, E.K. 1968. Survival of seedlings of an alpine clover
(*Trifolium nanum* Torr.). *Ecology*, 49(6): 1193-1195.

Bonde, E.K. et al. 1973. Growth and development of three agro-
nomic species in pots ("phytometers"). *In* Bliss, L.C. and
F.E. Wielgolaski (eds.), *Primary Production and Production
Processes, Tundra Biome*. Proceedings on a conference,
Dublin, April 1973, Swedish IBP Committee, Wenner-Gren
Center, Stockholm, pp. 99-110.

Bonde, E.K. and M.F. Foreman. 1973. Growth and development of
arctic and alpine grasses in experimental gardens at various
altitudes in Colorado, USA. *In* Bliss, L.C. and F.E. Wielgolaski (eds.), *Primary Production and Production Processes,
Tundra Biome*. Proceedings on a conference, Dublin, April
1973, Swedish IBP Committee, Wenner-Gren Center, Stockholm,
pp. 87-98.

Caldwell, M.M., L.L. Tieszen, and M. Fareed. 1974. The canopy
structure of tundra plant communities at Barrow, Alaska,
and Niwot Ridge, Colorado. *Arctic and Alpine Research*,
6(2): 151-159.

Cary, M. 1911. *A Biological Survey of Colorado*. U.S. Dept. of
Agric., North American Fauna, No. 33. 256 pp.

Clements, E.S. 1960. *Adventures in Ecology*. Pageant Press,
New York, New York. 244 pp.

Cockerell, T.D.A. 1906. The alpine flora of Colorado. *Amer.
Naturalist*, 40: 861-873.

Cooper, W.S. 1908. Alpine vegetation in the vicinity of Long's
Peak. *Botanical Gazette*, 45: 319-337.

Ehleringer, J.R. and P.C. Miller. 1975. Water relations of
selected plant species in the alpine tundra, Colorado.
Ecology, 56(2): 370-380.

Flock, J.W. 1978. Lichen-bryophyte distribution along a snow-cover-soil moisture gradient, Niwot Ridge, Colorado. *Arctic and Alpine Research*, 10(1): 31-47.

Grant, M.C. and J.B. Mitton. 1977. Genetic differentiation among growth forms of Engelmann spruce and Subalpine fir at treeline. *Arctic and Alpine Research*, 9(3): 259-263.

Gregg, R.E. 1963. *The Ants of Colorado*. University of Colorado Press, Boulder, Colorado. 792 pp.

Harrington, H.D. 1954. *Manual of the Plants of Colorado*. Sage Books, Denver, Colorado. 666 pp.

Holway, J.G. and R.T. Ward. 1963. Snow and meltwater effects in an area of Colorado alpine. *American Midland Naturalist*, 69(1): 189-197.

Ives, J.D. 1973. Studies in the high altitude geoecology of the Colorado Front Range. *Arctic and Alpine Research*, 5(3), Pt. 2: A67-A75.

_____. 1978. Remarks on the stability of timberline. *In* Troll, C. and W. Lauer (eds.), *Geoecological Relationships Between the Southern Temperate Zone and the Tropical Mountains*. Franz Steiner Verlag, Wiesbaden, pp. 313-317, plus illustrations.

Ives, J.D., R. Baumgartner, S. Burns, V. Dow, K. Hansen, A. Ketchin, D. Luff, B. McCord, and M. Plam. 1979. The Indian Peaks Environmental Atlas, Colorado Front Range. *Second Conference on Scientific Research in National Parks*, San Francisco, November 1979 (in press).

Johnson, D.A. and M.M. Caldwell. 1974. Field measurements of photosynthesis and leaf growth rates of three alpine plant species. *Arctic and Alpine Research*, 6(3): 245-251.

Komárková, V. 1979. Alpine vegetation of the Indian Peaks area, Front Range, Colorado Rocky Mountains. *Flora et Vegetatio Mundi*, Bd VII, J. Cramer. 591 pp., plus illus. and maps.

Komárková, V. and P.J. Webber. 1978. An alpine vegetation map of Niwot Ridge, Colorado. *Arctic and Alpine Research*, 10(1): 1-29, with map.

Krebs, P.V. 1973. Dendrochronology of bristlecone pine (*Pinus aristata* Engel.) in Colorado. *Arctic and Alpine Research*, 5(2): 149-150.

LeDrew, E.F. 1975. The energy balance of a mid-latitude alpine site during the growing season, 1973. *Arctic and Alpine Research*, 7(4): 301-314.

Lewis, W.M., Jr. and M.C. Grant. 1980. Acid precipitation in the western United States. *Science*, 207: 176-177.

Löve, A. and D. Löve. 1966. Cytotaxonomy of the alpine vascular plants of Mount Washington. *University of Colorado Studies, Series in Biology*, 24: 1-74.

_____. 1967. Continental drift and the origin of the arctic-alpine flora. *Rev. Roam. Biol., Sér. Bot.*, 12: 163-169.

_____. 1971. Polyploidie et géobotanique. *Nat. Canada*, 98: 469-494.

_____. 1974. Origin and evolution of the arctic and alpine floras. *In* Ives, J.D. and R.G. Barry (eds.), *Arctic and Alpine Environments*. Methuen, London, pp. 572-603.

Love, A., D. Love and B.M. Kapoor. 1971. Cytotaxonomy of a century of Rocky Mountain orophytes. *Arctic and Alpine Research*, 3(2): 139-165.

Love, D. 1969. *Papaver* at high altitudes in the Rocky Mountains. *Brittonia*, 21: 1-10.

_____. 1970. Subarctic and Subalpine: where and what? *Arctic and Alpine Research*, 2(1): 63-72.

Maher, L.J., Jr. 1972. Absolute pollen diagram of Redrock Lake, Boulder County, Colorado. *Quaternary Research*, 2(4): 531-553.

Marr, J.W. 1961. Ecosystems of the east slope of the Front Range in Colorado. *University of Colorado Studies, Series in Biology*, 8: 1-134.

_____. 1964a. Utilization of the Front Range tundra, Colorado. *In: Grazing in Terrestrial and Marine Environments*, Blackwells, London, pp. 109-118.

_____. 1964b. The vegetation of the Boulder area. *In* Rodeck, H.G. (ed.), *Natural History of the Boulder Area*. University of Colorado Museum, Leaflet No. 13, pp. 34-42.

_____. 1977. The development and movement of tree islands near the upper limit of tree growth in the southern Rocky Mountains. *Ecology*, 58: 1159-1164.

Marr, J.W. and R.E. Marr. 1973. Environment and phenology in the forest-tundra ecotone, Front Range, Colorado. *Arctic and Alpine Research*, 5(3), Pt. 2: A65-A66.

Marr, J.W. and B.E. Willard. 1970. Persisting vegetation in an alpine region in the southern Rocky Mountains. *Biol. Conserv.*, 2(2): 97-104.

May, T.A. and C.E. Braun. 1972. Seasonal foods of adult white-tailed ptarmigan in Colorado. *Journal of Wildlife Management*, 36(4): 1180-1186.

Merriam, C.H. 1890. *Results of a Biological Survey of the San Francisco Mountain Region and the Desert of the Little Colorado, Arizona*. U.S. Department of Agriculture, North American Fauna, No. 3. 136 pp.

_____. 1891. *Results of a Biological Reconnaissance of South Central Idaho*. U.S. Department of Agriculture, North American Fauna, No. 5. 127 pp.

Osburn, W.S., Jr. 1958. *Ecology of Winter Snow-free Areas of the Alpine Tundra of Niwot Ridge, Boulder County, Colorado*. Ph.D. thesis, Univ. of Colorado, Boulder, Colorado. 76 pp.

Peet, R.K. 1978a. Forest vegetation of the Colorado Front Range: patterns of species diversity. *Vegetatio*, 37(2): 65-78.

_____. 1978b. Latitudinal variation in southern Rocky Mountain forests. *Journal of Biogeography*, 5: 275-289.

Petersen, K.L. and P.J. Mehringer. 1976. Postglacial timberline fluctuations, La Plata Mountains, southwestern Colorado. *Arctic and Alpine Research*, 8(3): 275-288.

Ramaley, F. 1908. The botanical opportunity in Colorado. *University of Colorado, Studies in Biology*, Boulder, Colorado, pp. 5-10.

Raunkaier, C. 1934. *The Life Forms of Plants and Statistical Plant Geography*. Clarendon Press, Oxford. 632 pp.

Spomer, C.G. and F.B. Salisbury. 1968. Ecophysiology of *Geum turbinatum* and implications concerning alpine environments. *Botanical Gazette*, 129(1): 33-49.

Steinhoff, H.W. and J.D. Ives (eds.). 1976. *Ecological Impacts of Snowpack Augmentation in the San Juan Mountains, Colorado*. Final Report to Bureau of Reclamation, Colorado State University, Ft. Collins, Colorado. 489 pp.

Tieszen, L.L. (ed.). 1978. *Vegetation and Production Ecology of an Alaskan Arctic Tundra*. Ecological Studies 29, Springer-Verlag, New York. 686 pp.

Tranquillini, W. 1979. *Physiological Ecology of the Alpine Timberline*. Ecological Studies 31. Springer-Verlag, New York. 137 pp.

Walker, D.A., K.E. Everett, P.J. Webber, and J. Brown. 1980. Geobotanical Atlas of the Prudhoe Bay region, Alaska. CRREL Report (in press).

Wardle, P. 1968. Engelmann spruce (*Picea engelmannii* Engel.) at its upper limits on the Front Range, Colorado. *Ecology*, 49(3): 483-495.

_____. 1974. Alpine timberlines. *In* Ives, J.D. and R.G. Barry (eds.), *Arctic and Alpine Environments*. Methuen, London, pp. 371-402.

Webber, P.J. 1974. Tundra primary productivity. *In* Ives, J.D. and R.G. Barry (eds.), *Arctic and Alpine Environments*. Methuen, London, pp. 445-473.

Webber, P.J., J.C. Emerick, D.E. May, and V. Komárková. 1976. The impact of increased snowfall on alpine vegetation. *In* Steinhoff, H.W. and J.D. Ives (eds.), *Ecological Impacts of Snowpack Augmentation in the San Juan Mountains, Colorado*. Final Report to Bureau of Reclamation, Colorado State University, Fort Collins, Colorado, pp. 201-264.

Webber, P.J. and J.D. Ives. 1978. Damage and recovery of tundra vegetation. *Environ. Conserv.*, 5(3): 171-182.

Webber, P.J. and D.E. May. 1977. The magnitude and distribution of belowground plant structures in the alpine tundra of Niwot Ridge, Colorado. *Arctic and Alpine Research*, 9(2): 157-174.

Weber, W.A. 1976. *Rocky Mountain Flora*. 5th Ed., Univ. of Colorado Press, Boulder, Colorado. 479 pp.

Wielgolaski, F.E. (ed.). 1975. *Fennoscandian Tundra Ecosystems Part I: Plants and Microorganisms*. Springer-Verlag, New York. 366 pp.

Willard, B.E. 1963. *Phytosociology of the Alpine Tundra of Trail Ridge, Rocky Mountain National Park, Colorado*. Ph.D. thesis, University of Colorado, Boulder, Colorado. 245 pp.

Willard, B.E. and J.W. Marr. 1970. Effects of human activities
on alpine tundra ecosystems in Rocky Mountain National
Park, Colorado. *Biol. Conserv.*, 2(4): 257-265.

_____. 1971. Recovery of alpine tundra under protection
after damage by human activities in the Rocky Mountains of
Colorado. *Biol. Conserv.*, 3(3): 181-190.

ENGELMANN SPRUCE (*PICEA ENGELMANNII* ENGEL.) AT ITS UPPER LIMITS ON THE FRONT RANGE, COLORADO

Peter Wardle*

Abstract. Engelmann spruce is the dominant tree at timberline in the Front Range at approximately 3,350 m elevation; it occurs as krummholz in the forest-tundra ecotone up to about 3,500 m, and occasional individuals are found in the tundra up to 3,730 m. Temperatures decrease with increasing altitude above timberline, whereas wind velocity increases, especially during winter. Winter snow is deeper and persists longer in the forest than in the krummholz above, its depth in the latter tending to remain constant once the lower portions of the plants are packed. Soil temperatures fluctuate widely beneath tundra vegetation in the neighborhood of krummholz plants, whereas under forest variations are small and there is a prolonged period in spring when they remain within $0.6^{\circ}C$ ($1^{\circ}F$) of freezing point.

Krummholz growth forms of spruce arise through death of needles and shoots exposed to the prevailing westerly winds. Even in summer young exposed needles tend to be somewhat chlorotic, and many show lesions. In winter windward needles dry out, become bleached, and are eventually shed. Certain needles, instead of becoming bleached during winter, turn brown and dry out in early spring. In krummholz, even within a single shoot, sharply contrasting differences develop in winter between leeward needles that show only small seasonal decreases in water content, and windward needles that dry out and die. Desiccation is usually confined to krummholz, mainly affecting small needles on stunted shoots and the distal needles of long, robust shoots, but in the winter of 1961-62, following a cold, wet September, it extended to leading shoots of saplings below timberline. Replenishment of water in needles during winter is probably from water stored in sapwood above the snow pack, since sapwood beneath the snow pack remains frozen in both forest and krummholz.

Late-lying snow delays the spring growth of seedlings below timberline, but they occur even where snow persists until late June. Above timberline, spruce seems to be less tolerant of late-lying snow.

It is concluded that though the position of timberline is correlated with summer temperatures, dry winter winds are the immediate, though probably not the ultimate, cause of the krummholz growth forms in the forest-tundra ecotone.

Ecology, Vol. 49, No. 3, 1968, pp. 483-495.

*Botany Division, Department of Scientific and Industrial Research, Christchurch, New Zealand

INTRODUCTION

Engelmann spruce (*Picea engelmannii* (Engel.)) and subalpine fir (*Abies lasiocarpa* Nutt.) are the most common trees in the upper part of the subalpine forests throughout the mountains of Colorado. Spruce is the dominant species and generally forms the timberline, the upper limit of symmetrically formed tall trees, at altitudes of 3,350–3,600 m. However, timberline seldom sets an abrupt limit to the upward distribution of this species, for wind-deformed spruce occurs well up into the alpine tundra as compact islands of krummholz that become smaller in area, lower in

FIG. 1. On the upper part of this slope, trees and krummholz are confined to spurs and ridges. Deep snow, prone to avalanche, accumulates in the hollows. The path of the avalanches is occupied by stunted, broken fir and spruce. Neversummer Range, Colorado.

stature, and more widely scattered with increasing altitude. Even below timberline, the continuity of the subalpine forest is broken by grassy meadows, parkland, and scrub. Trees and krummholz are usually more abundant and ascend higher on convex surfaces (ridges, spurs, knolls) than on concave surfaces (valleys, hollows; Fig. 1), though convex surfaces below timberline that are extremely exposed to wind can be occupied by tundra. Steep, high north-facing slopes and avalanche paths also often lack trees or krummholz. Particularly depressed timberlines and correspondingly broad belts of wind-deformed krummholz were noted on east-facing terrain at several points on the eastern side of the Continental Divide. There is also a tendency for trees to be reduced to krummholz on the floors of cirque-like valley heads, even though forest can ascend several hundred feet higher on the valley sides further downstream.

A healthy tree of Engelmann spruce below timberline is characteristically spire shaped, with main branches sweeping downwards from an erect central trunk. This growth form may be regarded as fundamental, and other growth forms as modifications imposed by severe habitat (Fig. 2). In closed forest, the lowest branches usually become suppressed and die, but on spruce trees growing

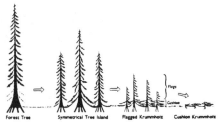

FIG. 2. Derivation of common growth forms of Engelmann spruce, increasingly deformed from left to right.

in open meadows they often persist and produce adventitious roots where they make contact with the ground. Once rooting occurs, such a branch is freed from domination by the original central stem and develops its own central axis. The proximal part of the branch ceases to grow and eventually dies. In this way, groups or islands of trees develop. Islands which have become hollow through death of the original central stem have been aptly called "timber atolls" by Griggs (1938) in his description of timberline on Sheep Mountain, Wyoming.

Above timberline, spruce is stunted and adventitious rooting of the lower branches is very pronounced. In sheltered localities (such as parts of the San Miguel Mountains and in some favored spots in the Front Range) krummholz islands can remain symmetrical, but their taller stems tend to die back in winter and, perhaps as a consequence, their stature decreases with increasing altitude. Far more commonly in Colorado, however, krummholz islands are deformed by the interaction of wind and snow. Exposure to prevailing westerly winds leads to desiccation and death of exposed shoots and needles during winter, giving krummholz a light brownish green color which contrasts with the dark green of the forest below. Foliage buried within the snow pack is protected from this kind of damage, but molds become damaging if burial is too prolonged. In the most severe sites towards the extreme upper limit of spruce, islands are reduced to cushions of contorted stems and needles, shorn off level with the surface of the winter snow pack. These are referred to as "cushion krummholz." In less severe sites, in the lower part of the ecotone, erect stems with branches only on their leeward sides rise above the cushions, to produce "flagged krummholz."

Daubenmire (1943) and Marr (1961) refer to many papers that mention aspects of the ecology of Engelmann spruce at timberline. However, there have been no detailed accounts of the environment throughout the year at timberline in North America, nor any concerning the physiological basis of krummholz growth forms, with the exception of a paper by Goldsmith and Smith (1926) dealing with seasonal changes in the chemistry of spruce needles at different altitudes. In Europe, on the other hand, Michaelis (1934) intensively studied the influence of the winter environment on *Picea excelsa* Link.

The chief aims of the present research were, therefore, (1) to measure the environmental factors at timberline and to relate them to the distribution, growth forms, and phenology of spruce; and (2) to investigate the processes involved in death of exposed needles and shoots. Most of the work was done on Niwot Ridge on the Front Range, about 4 miles east of the Continental Divide, at 105° 35′ W, 40° 03′ N. The data used in this paper were collected mainly from September 1962 to August 1963, with some measurements being continued into 1964. In another paper timberlines of Engelmann spruce are compared with timberlines of other species in North America and New Zealand, and further references that bear on the present study are presented (Wardle 1965).

The Environment on Niwot Ridge

Climatological stations fitted with standard instruments have been maintained on a series of broad, ridge-top sites in the Front Range since 1953 by the Institute of Arctic and Alpine Research (Marr 1961). Those relevant to the present studies are C–1 at 3,050 m in a forest clearing and D–1 at 3,750 m in open tundra. At the end of 1962 an intermediate station, C–7, was set up at 3,350 m, just below timberline on a flat area where fire destroyed forest of spruce and fir over 60 years ago. Records for 1963 and 1964 at station C–7 are summarized in Fig. 3, and Table 1 gives mean climatic values for 1963 at the three stations. These measurements were supplemented with observations and measurements of the local varia-

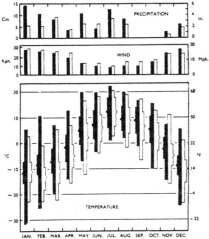

Fig. 3. Climatic records at station C–7, 3,350 m, Front Range, Colo. The solid and hollow histograms represent 1963 and 1964 records respectively. The points on the temperature histograms, from top to bottom, are: maximum for month; mean daily maximum; mean of daily maximum + minimum; mean daily minimum; minimum for month. Precipitation data incomplete for September and October.

Table 1. Mean climatic values at stations C-1 (3,050 m), C-7 (3,350 m), and D-1 (3,750 m), Front Range, Colorado—1963

Item	C–1	C–7	D–1
Temperature, mean of daily maximum and minimum (°C)	2	0.5	–2.5
Temperature, mean daily minimum (°C)	–4	–4	–6
Wind, mean velocity (kph)	13	18	29
Precipitation, total (mm)	767	>864	815

tion in snow depth, snow and soil temperatures, and soil moisture in the area near station C–7.

Air temperature

An altitudinal decline in temperatures is evident, but it by no means has a constant or consistent rate when data for the entire year are compared. Also, C–7 temperatures lie closer to those at C–1 than its altitudinal position would lead one to expect. Two circumstances seem to contribute to this. First, when the prevailing downslope wind blows there is not only a steepened temperature gradient (the föhn effect), but areas close to the Continental Divide, including D–1, are often enveloped in orographic cloud and rain or snow when the weather is clear at the other two stations. Secondly, minimum temperatures are often lower at C–1 than at C–7, indicating occurrence of inversions.

In connection with a study of the patchy distribution of spruce seedlings in meadows, nocturnal minimum temperatures were measured at 2.5 cm above the ground from June 27 to August 11, 1963. The lowest temperature, –5°C, occurred on July 28. Local differences of up to 3.5°C were measured, and while no firm conclusions could be drawn, there was notable coincidence between presence of seedlings and high minima, while low minima seemed to be characteristic of narrow openings in krummholz.

Wind

Average wind velocity increases with altitude, but as with temperature, velocities at C–7 are more similar to those at C–1 than at D–1. Most of this wind occurs as strong westerlies during winter, but even in near-calm weather, there are perceptible downslope and down-valley breezes, especially at high altitudes and at night. Fig. 3 demonstrates the close inverse relationship between wind velocity and mean temperature from month to month.

Precipitation

From October through March all precipitation falls as snow, and C–7 receives more than the other stations, doubtless because it is augmented by snow blown off the crest of Niwot Ridge. In the remaining months, when most precipitation is in the form of rain and soft hail, station C–7 usually receives an amount intermediate between those received at C–1 and D–1. In 1963 and 1964 July and August were the only months during which no snow fell.

Distribution of snow

Two kinds of snowfall are experienced at high altitudes in Colorado. Fine, "dry," very cold snow, usually brought in Pacific air masses, falls from October onwards, but mainly in the winter, and is rapidly re-distributed by wind. Heavy, "wet" snow, much less prone to drift, is usually brought in air masses from the Gulf of Mexico and falls mainly during March, April, and May, but in some years it can also come in an autumn storm.

The depth of the snow pack was measured at 27 sites near C–7, and data for five of these are shown in Fig. 4. In forest and meadow just below timberline, the snow pack builds up from December onwards, to reach a maximum depth of 60–300 cm in March. Its depth is more uniform under trees than in the open, and it persists longer, the last patches not disappearing until the beginning of July. Some stony, south-facing meadows below timberline gain their snow cover late and lose it early.

In flagged krummholz, the flags remain exposed throughout the winters in most years, but drifted snow builds up to completely pack the lower, or cushion, portions of the islands from late in December and maintains a constant depth until the beginning of May. Cushion krummholz is packed with snow from late in October, but the separate drifts captured by each island often lose their identity beneath larger, deeper drifts that build up in the later part of the winter. Despite this, cushion krummholz emerges early in the spring, most islands being completely free by the middle of May, but they are liable to temporary re-burial, even in June.

Much of the open tundra, especially on ridge crests and the upper parts of west-facing slopes, is blown free of snow all winter. In other places snow accumulates, especially towards the base of leeward slopes and in hollows, and many such drifts persist through all but the hottest summers.

Temperatures within the snow pack

Snow temperatures were first measured on March 17, 1963. Below timberline on this date, the lowest temperatures (down to −10.5°C in a small meadow) were in the top 12 inches of the profile; temperatures increased below this, to reach −1°C at the base of the snow pack at a depth of 114 cm. On exposed tundra, the temperature at the base of a snow pack 70 cm deep was only −4°C. As spring advanced, the snow pack warmed, and by May 4 had become nearly isothermal at 0°C, both above and below timberline.

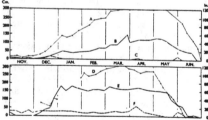

Fig. 4. Depth of snow at five sites, Front Range, Colo. All but D measured in winter 1963–64. A. In a small meadow below timberline. B. Under the forest canopy. C. On open tundra (*Kobresia* meadow). D. Same site as A, but winter 1962–63. E. At the leeward end of an island of flagged krummholz. F. At the leeward end of an island of cushion krummholz.

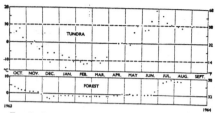

Fig. 5. Soil temperatures measured at 15 cm. Above: Tundra, blown free of snow all winter. Below: Under the forest canopy (B in Fig. 4).

Soil temperatures

Soil temperatures were measured at six sites with interchangeable thermistors at depths of 15 cm and 60 cm, using a bridge designed and built by Mr. Robert H. Swanson of the Rocky Mountain Forest and Range Experiment Station. Fig. 5 shows the fluctuations at 15 cm for two of the sites in 1963–64. Temperatures at 60 cm were similar to those at 15 cm, though their fluctuations were of smaller magnitude. Results for 1962–63 differ only in that they reflect the earlier arrival and earlier melting of the snow pack.

At most sites three periods are distinguishable: a winter period, when temperatures fall substantially below freezing point, and a spring transitional period when temperatures are held close to 0°C, through the influence of water percolating from melting snow banks. Thermistors under forest showed the smallest variations, through being insulated by trees and, in winter, by deep snow. Temperatures remained within 0.5°C of freezing point from late winter until the last snow disappeared from the site in June. The most extreme soil temperatures and the shortest transitional period were experienced near an island of cushion krummholz in tundra blown free of snow all winter. At the leeward end of an island of flagged krummholz, variations were slightly greater than under forest, but much smaller than in exposed tundra. On a stony, south-facing meadow below timberline, insolation kept summer soil temperatures high and, by continually melting snow, kept winter soil temperatures within 0.5°C of freezing point from November 29, 1963, to June 12, 1964.

Soil moisture and soil texture

Occasionally, gravimetric determinations of water content were made on soil samples screened through a 2-mm mesh, but values are only approximate since no special precautions were taken against water loss during screening. The following conclusions are tentatively drawn.

The highest values (up to 150% on a dry weight basis) are found in samples from humus-rich upper horizons, which occur widely under forest, but very patchily under other vegetation.

Many profiles consist of angular stones and boulders, with sandy interstitial material which has such poor water-holding capacity that there is little difference in moisture content between samples which are visibly moist and those which are dust-dry, most values ranging between 7% and 14%.

Material containing both humus and finer mineral components but few stones is characteristic of most forest profiles beneath the superficial humus, and also occurs to the leeward of islands of cushion krummholz. Moisture contents vary between 16% and 30%.

Lowest moisture contents prevail in autumn when melt-water is exhausted and summer thunderstorms have ceased. During November and December thawing of early snow leads to some replenishment, though sub-freezing soil temperatures seem to result in most of the water being held in a frozen crust in the top few inches of the profile. The greatest increase in soil water coincides with the melting of the snow pack from mid-April to mid-June when many areas are flooded for weeks at a time. On the other hand, areas where there is little accumulation of snow and no run-off from snow banks further upslope remain dry.

The vertical distribution of spruce roots is closely related to soil texture and may be conveniently described at this point. Seven pits, each 0.3 m (1 ft) square, were examined. Roots were sorted out from successive layers of soil, and the total length in each layer determined, partly by direct measurement and partly by estimation from weighing. The results for four pits, expressed as mean length of root per centimeter of depth in each layer of soil, are shown diagrammatically in Fig. 6. In the forest, roots are very abundant in the fine-textured humus-rich soil near the surface, decreasing sharply with depth. A pit beside a symmetrical tree island on a stony, south-facing slope and one beside a flagged krummholz island did not show the great concentration of roots near the surface, apparently because there is no upper horizon of fine soil. The three pits by a cushion krummholz reveal a remarkably asymmetrical distribution of roots, re-

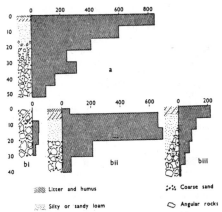

Fig. 6. Distribution of spruce roots, in four 1-ft-square pits. The vertical axes represent soil depth in centimeters, and the horizontal axes represent mean length (cm) of root per centimeter of depth in a column of 1 ft² (930 cm²) cross-sectional area.
a. At the edge of an opening in the forest, 1.8 m from the base of a 50-cm-diameter spruce.
bi. 20 cm beyond the windward edge of an island of cushion krummholz, and 64 cm from the nearest rooted part of a stem.

bii. Within the same island, 30 cm inside the leeward edge and 75 cm from the nearest rooted part of a stem.
biii. 53 cm beyond the leeward edge of the same island, and 175 cm from the nearest rooted part of a stem.

lated mainly to the accumulation of blown soil beneath and to the leeward of the plant—an accumulation which is, incidentally, the mirror image of that of drifted snow.

OBSERVATIONS ON ENGELMANN SPRUCE DURING THE GROWING SEASON
Growth of shoots

The opening of buds and the growth of new needles in spruce on Niwot Ridge were observed during the summer of 1963, and on selected shoots of seedlings and older plants the increase in distance between the base of a marked old needle and the tip of the most distal young needle was periodically recorded. This measurement includes components due to growth and flexure of young needles, but to have measured more accurately to the tip of the shoot itself would have risked damage to the bud. Since the exact date when growth began proved difficult to determine, the period of maximum increment was used for the more critical comparisons. In nearly every shoot more than 90% of the growth was completed within 1 month.

Seedlings.—On a warm, dry, stony, open area at 3,140 m new needles had emerged by June 11. By June 17 seedlings on similar sites at timberline (3,350 m) were at the same stage, and thereafter the flush spread to seedlings in other habitats. Table 2 shows the effect of late-lying snow on the

TABLE 2. Shoot growth of spruce seedlings in relation to melting of snow pack, as expressed by the number of shoots having their maximum growth increment in three successive time periods[a]

Date of snow clearance	June 24–July 2	July 2–July 9	July 9–July 16
Before April 20	2		
Before May 9	6		
May 9–22	3	6	
May 22–June 4		7	1
June 4–10		1	9

[a]The seedlings were 8–30 cm tall and growing at 3,350 m in a small meadow below timberline. Thirty-five shoots were measured on 26 seedlings.

growth of seedlings in a small meadow at 3,350 m, just below timberline. The relationship is not directly proportional, for a month's difference (May 9 to June 10) in the date of emergence of seedlings from the snow pack resulted in a difference in time of maximum growth of only about 15 days. Indeed, where snow had disappeared prior to May 9, differences in date of emergence were not reflected in growth, and at the other extreme, sites which were not clear of snow until about June 26 still supported spruce seedlings. However, they were absent from areas subjected to prolonged flooding by melt-water from snow drifts.

The few measurements among flagged krummholz indicated only that seedlings commence growth as early as at timberline. In areas occupied by cushion krummholz, spruce seedlings were too rare to yield phenological data.

Saplings.—The flushing time of three saplings in the meadow at 3,350 m was not related to the date of disappearance of snow around their bases. The six shoots measured grew over a longer period than those of seedlings and adult trees, with two very vigorous leading shoots growing from mid-June until the beginning of August.

Older plants.—On trees and krummholz near timberline, new needles began to emerge during the second half of June, and by the end of the month the flush had spread to the uppermost krummholz at 3,540 m. Buds developing into strobili swelled and opened earlier than vegetative buds. As with the saplings, late-lying snow had no discernible effect on the phenology of tall trees, and on one site trees which had snow around their butts until the first week of July still opened their buds at the normal time.

Growth of roots

The appearance of white, fleshy tips was taken as indicating the beginning of root growth in summer. The earliest excavations on June 24 and 26 showed new tips common under forest. Under krummholz, growing tips were hard to find on these dates, but they were common at 3,330 m on July 3.

Summer damage to young needles

Fully mature spruce needles withstand the lowest temperatures encountered in their natural environment, but new needles are quite liable to be frosted as they emerge from the bud. No such damage was noted in Colorado in 1963, but there was severe frosting in 1962, to judge from the black shrivelled remains of newly emerging shoots. It affected seedlings in meadows below timberline and the cushion foliage of krummholz, especially of plants at the highest altitudes, and almost certainly is attributable to a cold snap on July 15, when the minimum air temperature at Station C-1 (3,050 m) fell to −2°C.

Small, circular lesions occur abundantly on the dorsal surfaces of wind-exposed needles in the krummholz. Under the microscope, the mildest show as depressed areas on the needle surface, underlain by collapsed epidermal and hypodermal cells which, instead of the normal thick walls, have thin walls and brown coloration. The cuticle is left loose and wrinkled through the collapse of the underlying cells. More severe lesions in-volve mesophyll in the collapse, and the worst show as contorted, collapsed patches of tissue, including epidermis, hypodermis, and underlying mesophyll, usually with loose fragments of cuticle adhering to the surface. It is not known whether these degrees of severity lie on a time sequence.

Lesions were seen on November 21, 1962, but they certainly must have developed earlier, since in 1963 they were noted on July 16 on new needles which had flushed only 2 weeks before. The earliest appearance was in cushion krummholz, but by August the damage had spread down into flagged krummholz.

WINTER DEATH OF NEEDLES AND SHOOTS

In healthy trees on sheltered sites below timberline the needles remain green throughout the winter, despite repeated freezing and thawing, and persist many years; needles 17 years old were noted on one shoot. Needles are paler on the south side of isolated trees, and seedlings growing in strongly insolated places have pale needles except on their more shaded branches. However, no yellowing or death of needles resulting from strong winter sunshine on the south side of trees was noticed, though this phenomenon has frequently been observed in Europe (e.g. Holzer 1959).

Needles from forest trees can therefore be used as controls in studies of desiccation and death in foliage of krummholz, and to this end fluctuations in water content of needles were measured in 1962–63 on five trees surrounding the small meadow at 3,350 m. For this and similar measurements in krummholz, shoots were cut from the plants, placed in polythene bags, and as soon as possible (usually within 30 min) needles were clipped off at the junction with the petiole and placed in screw-cap vials. In most instances 20 needles comprised the sample in each vial. In the laboratory the vials and fresh needles were weighed, dried at 95°C, and re-weighed to provide the data for calculations of moisture content expressed as a percentage of dry weight. Needles flushed in 1962 and taken at 6 m above the ground gave the following values (each value being based on two samples from each of the five trees):

Date		Moisture content (% dry weight)
November	25	131
December	8	130
January	5	124
February	9	124
March	9	122
April	6	116
May	25	108
August	1	113

The fluctuations, though small, are regular and highly significant (B. A. Hayman, *personal communication*). Needles that flushed in 1963 had a moisture content of 213% on August 1, but that of needles which had flushed in 1961 had decreased to 111% when measured on April 6. Nearly identical seasonal variations in water content were measured at 1–2 m and 11–12 m above the ground.

Color change, desiccation, and abscission

Death of exposed needles in krummholz is usually accompanied by changes in color, though some needles, usually small ones, dry out and are shed while still green. External color changes were therefore followed by comparing needles with a chart of standard colors (Ridgway 1912), and changes in internal color and structure were examined in freehand sections. Most often needles undergo bleaching to pale yellow, which becomes noticeable once water contents fall below about 45%, and involves loss of chlorophyll, first from the outer mesophyll on the exposed side near the apex of the needles, and thence progressively downwards and inwards. At the same time the mesophyll shrinks and pulls in the stomatal grooves. Many needles show abrupt partition into a basal portion which is still turgid and green and a distal portion which has lost or is losing its chlorophyll and water; some even show a bleached band intervening between green zones.

Instead of bleaching, some dried-out needles develop a brown coloration that extends throughout the leaf tissues from epidermis to stele, appearing to pervade both cell wall and lumen, except in the epidermis and hypodermis, where only the lumen and inner parts of the thick walls are colored. Unlike the bleaching process, which takes place during the winter and ceases by the beginning of May, the browning was rarely observed before April. It shows first in windward needles of krummholz cushions (again, in contrast to bleaching, which is almost confined to flags) as they emerge from the ablating snow pack, and develops so rapidly as to suggest that the needles were already lethally damaged before they were buried. Later, during May, flag needles which had bleached and dried out only in their distal portions during the winter, dry out and turn brown in their hitherto green basal portions. Abrupt partition of needles into brown and green, or even into bleached, brown, and green parts, was again noted. Needles, which otherwise were bleached, sometimes developed the brown coloration in stomatal guard cells and in the stele.

Once a certain water content (probably about 20%) is reached at the base of a drying needle, it is shed. It seems that a well-defined abscission zone forms early in the life of a needle, and that its operation depends merely on stresses developed while drying, for when shoots were dried in the laboratory, either slowly or rapidly, the needles were shed in the same manner, even in the case of those which had flushed recently and were still soft (see also Sifton 1965).

Often, winter desiccation does not cease with the death of windward needles, but involves dying back of the shoot itself. It nearly always proceeds basipetally, whether from the tip of an individual needle, from the apex of a shoot, or from the top of a whole plant and, in addition, it proceeds from the most windward parts of the plant towards the leeward. Desiccation of shoots can be distinguished from other forms of damage through the absence of disruption to the tissue other than abscission of the needles. Even the leaf primordia remain undistorted, green but dry and lifeless, within the buds of shoots which have died back.

Incidence of desiccation in area and time

In collections for determination of water content in flagged krummholz, robust needles on the leeward sides of the plants, showing no apparent bleaching and desiccation, were sampled separately from those on the windward side. Leeward samples from flags showed seasonal changes which do not seem to differ from those found below timberline, while needles of cushions buried in the snow pack showed no real change in water content during the winter. On the windward sides of flags, on the other hand, though neither observation nor sampling revealed any abnormally dry needles as late as November 21, by December 26 there was extensive desiccation with water contents ranging down to 32%. Not only does the winter water content of needles contrast on the opposite sides of a flag, but even within a single shoot the leeward needles can remain green and turgid when the windward needles have dried out, as the following ranges and means show: leeward needles, 105–129, 116%; windward needles, 43–68, 55%. These figures are based on paired measurements made on February 3 on each of 10 shoots, using the method already described.

When desiccation of needles was first noticed on December 26, it appeared to be confined to the more exposed and stunted krummholz, but by March and April had extended down to timberline. In most winters there seems to be little desiccation below timberline, but during the winter of 1961–62 many leading shoots of young trees and saplings tall enough to be exposed above the snow pack were affected. It was most severe just below timberline and petered out at lower elevations (Table 3). That winter did not show any

TABLE 3. Incidence of desiccation in spruce in two forest areas as indicated by the percentage of plants with leading shoots which have died back—winter 1961–62

	Openings in forest (3,350 m elevation)		In cut-over forest (3,150 m elevation)	
Height (dm)a	Total plants examined	Percentage with die back	Total plants examined	Percentage with die back
9–21	28	11	25	4
24–31	13	62	24	0
34–46	13	69	17	6
49–61	11	55	18	17
64–76	7	71	9	22
79–91	4	100	8	0
94–107	3	100		
9–107	79	48	101	7

aHeights were measured to the nearest foot (3dm).

TABLE 4. Water content (percentage of dry weight) of spruce needles from selected depauperate shoots and normal shoots from krummholz flags

Date of sampling	Number of shoots	Range	Mean
Normal shoots			
November 17	32	121–145	134
December 22	10	114–133	125
February 3	10	117–137	126
Depauperate shoots			
November 17	7	140–170	152
December 22	10	109–182	130
February 3	3	43–56	51

unusual weather features, but September 1961 had been the wettest September in the 12-year Institute record (precipitation at station C–1 of 132 mm, cf. average for the month of 40 mm). Snow lay on the ground below timberline after two storms, and in most respects it was also the coldest September recorded.

Predisposition of needles to desiccation

Needles destined to dry out during winter already differ from other needles in several respects in the preceding summer and fall. First, they often bear lesions. Secondly, young needles develop differences in color before they have fully emerged from the protective bud scales in June. Newly emerging needles on the upper sides of horizontal or inclined shoots are often purplish, instead of pale green, on their dorsal surfaces, and this color extends into the mesophyll. Within 10–20 days of emergence the purplish tints have gone, but needles which showed it fail to develop the normal color, instead remaining pale, yellowish green. In cushion krummholz yellowishness of needles and the preceding purplish tints are most evident on the exposed, windward sides of the islands, whereas leeward foliage is normal healthy green. There is a similar contrast between windward and leeward needles on individual exposed shoots, and even within one needle the tip is paler than the more sheltered base. However, this chlorosis is possibly caused by exposure to excessive sunlight rather than by wind; for wind-training ensures that windward needles are always those on the upper sides of horizontal or inclined shoots, so that they are more strongly insolated.

Thirdly, branches which have suffered damage such as repeated death of shoots through winter desiccation tend to produce stunted shoots (4–12 cm) with small, crowded yellowish needles (needles, 4–11 mm; 50–72 needles/cm of shoot), instead of normal, robust shoots (7–27 cm) and needles (needles 12–16 mm; 29–44 needles/cm of shoot).

Water contents (dry weight basis) of the needles of selected depauperate shoots were compared with those of normal, robust shoots from krummholz flags (Table 4), using the method described earlier. The higher water contents among depauperate needles in the fall presumably reflects their lack of hardiness, for most succumb during the winter, few being available for sampling by February.

Finally, especially robust shoots—in particular the leading shoots of saplings and krummholz flags—also show more tendency to die back through winter desiccation than robust shoots of more limited growth. Leading shoots of saplings grow on later into the summer than most shoots, and paired measurements on seven plants on August 11 suggest that their later-formed needles have slightly higher water contents than those of shoots on the same plants which completed growth earlier in the summer (202% cf. 186%); this may be correlated with a lower degree of hardiness.

Water supply of stems and foliage during winter

During December, five excised branchlets were left to dry at 1 m above the ground in the forest clearing, and another five above the cushion of a flagged krummholz island. Each week a sample of 10 needles was removed from each shoot and the moisture content determined. At the krummholz site the mean value for the five shoots decreased from 133% to 126% during the first week, and from 83% to 65% during the 5th week. Corresponding values at the forest site were 127% and 127% (i.e., no change), and 111% to 89%. Spruce needles thus cannot completely prevent evaporation from their surfaces during winter, despite their xeromorphic structure. However, the rate of drying of the needles in this admittedly crude experiment was slow at first, suggesting that initial losses could be replenished from water in the supporting twigs. Likewise, the reduction in water content of most needles in situ during the winter is slight, indicating that they are supplied through the stems. Yet it is unlikely that any water can pass into the upper part of the plant from the roots, since thermistor readings (Fig. 7) and coring indicate that the sapwood of the part of the trunk within the snow pack remains frozen throughout the winter and does not rise above 0°C until the middle of May. On the other hand, stems above the snow pack thaw intermittently, at least after mid-March, and therefore possibly provide a reservoir of water for the needles. In trees below timberline and in the portions of krummholz stems that spend winter beneath the snow pack, visibly moist sapwood is usually 3–6 cm wide, whereas in flags it is usually less than 1 cm wide, indicating that the water reserves of the latter could be more readily exhausted during winter.

Water contents of many wood cores and several cross-sectional discs were determined to compare seasonal variations in krummholz and forest trees, but inconsistent results indicate that more refined methods should be used.

Damage by snow molds

Snow molds cause extensive damage to foliage of spruce. Especially obvious is *Herpotrichia*, which forms a black, smothering weft over lower foliage. Less obvious, but no less serious, is a mold which Dr J. M. Staley of the Rocky Mountain Forest and Range Experiment Station identified tentatively as a species of *Phoma*. Affected needles turn brown as they emerge from the snow pack and contain hyphae that penetrate the cells of the mesophyll. It occurs mainly on seedlings subjected to prolonged snow cover and on cushion foliage on the leeward sides of krummholz islands.

DISCUSSION

Factors governing distribution of spruce

Engelmann spruce very obviously decreases in abundance and stature between timberline and the highest outliers of cushion krummholz. Climatic measurements show that temperatures similarly decrease with increasing altitude and that wind velocity increases, and are therefore equivocal concerning two important theories bearing on the climatic reasons for timberline. The more generally accepted of these theories is that timberline is determined by summer growing conditions (Daubenmire 1954), and in keeping with this, Colorado timberlines are among the highest in the world, despite desiccating winds and low temperatures during winter. The mean July temperature measured at timberline on Niwot Ridge

(11.5°C at station C–7, 3,350 m) may be compared with Köppen's hypothesis that timberlines correspond with a mean temperature of 10°C during the warmest month of the year (discussed by Schröter 1926, p. 46–47).

On the other hand, Griggs (1938, p. 557) concluded that "it is wind rather than temperature that determines actual timberline" in the Rocky Mountains. While I cannot agree that the temperature factor is "entirely theoretical," there doubtless is a strong connection between distribution and growth forms of spruce and exposure to wind. Thus, absence of trees and krummholz on ridge crests is correlated with full exposure to the prevailing westerlies. Whether this is a direct effect of wind, however, is uncertain, for these sites are blown clear of snow so that not only is there a lack of protection for seedlings during winter, but an absence of melt-water to moisten the soil in spring; and the soils in turn are gen-

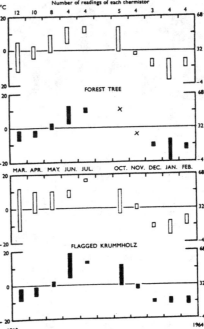

FIG. 7. Range of temperatures measured in sapwood over monthly periods, using thermistor probes inserted 3.8–4.8 cm from the surface of the bark. All readings between 0930 and 1800 hr. Temperatures in the lower portion of the stem that is buried in the snow pack during winter and in the upper portion that is exposed all winter are represented by solid and hollow bars respectively.

erally rocky and coarse-grained, and their water-holding capacity is low.

On sites where the prevailing westerly winds blow strongly downwards against the timberline, the latter is depressed and the belt of wind-deformed krummholz is correspondingly broad. Thus, timberline on Niwot Ridge generally lies at the relatively low altitude of 3,350 m, and on exposed lakeshores in a nearby valley krummholz descends to 3,110 m. On the other hand, forest can ascend to maximum altitudes where the westerlies blow upslope, so that each tree benefits from shelter provided by a tree down wind from it (Fig. 8).

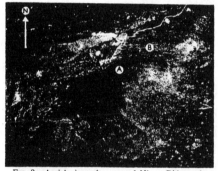

Fig. 8. Aerial view of a part of Niwot Ridge, where differences in exposure to westerly winds determine whether a site is occupied by forest (A) or krummholz (B). (From U.S. Geological Survey, Photo No. ECB-8-149).

Snow also has been postulated as a cause of timberlines (e.g., Shaw 1909). Late-lying snow delays the growth of seedlings in meadows below timberline on Niwot Ridge, but was not found to prevent their establishment except indirectly through flooding by melt-water. Krummholz above timberline loses its snow cover earlier than the forest below, possibly indicating that as the growing season becomes curtailed with increasing altitude, spruce becomes decreasingly tolerant of late-lying snow. The highest spruce recorded during the present study are islands of cushion krummholz at 3,730 m just below the crest of a ridge, on a steep slope with southeasterly aspect (Fig. 9). On sites such as this, plants receive the benefits of shelter from the prevailing wind, constant protection through the winter by snow which has drifted from the windward side of the slope, and very early emergence from the snow pack in the spring. Avalanches can prevent establishment of forest on the steeper mountains of Colorado, but not on the gentle topography of

Fig. 9. Cushion krummholz at 3,730 m on a southeasterly aspect near Loveland Pass, Colorado. May 26, 1963.

Niwot Ridge though movement in deep drifts here causes some crippling of young spruce.

Well-established principles of microclimatology (e.g. Geiger 1957), supported by results of the present environmental study, indicate that any one of several factors may underlie the preference for convex surfaces shown by spruce and other tree species. Convex surfaces are more favorable than concave ones in that insolation and drainage are better, snow is less likely to avalanche or persist late into summer, and nocturnal inversions of temperature are less likely to develop. Locally, these advantages can be offset by exposure to wind (aggravated by lack of protective snow in winter) and by shallower soils.

No obvious explanation can be advanced for the absence of forest, and its replacement by krummholz, in cirque-like valley heads. Nor does there seem to be any general explanation of open meadows below timberline, though some of those on Niwot Ridge occupy south-facing slopes that receive only a shallow snow pack during winter and have rocky, coarse-textured soils which are very dry during summer and fall.

Factors causing krummholz growth forms and winter desiccation

Even to a casual observer, the appearance of krummholz in the forest-tundra ecotone indicates severe winter conditions, and this is supported by the investigations described in this paper. The environmental studies confirm the prevalence of strong winds that blow mainly in winter, increase in velocity above timberline, and have a prevailing westerly direction that coincides with the direction of deformation of the krummholz. There is also a very close relationship between the pattern of snow accumulation and growth form. On the most severe sites, krummholz is reduced to low cushions surviving under the protection of the snow that they accumulate, while on less severe sites, islands of krummholz are differentiated into a lower cushion portion that spends the winter within the snow pack and taller flagged stems that are exposed above the snow.

Clausen (1965) suggests that growth forms at timberline differ genotypically, but in Colorado the correspondence between growth forms of spruce and environment is so close that in the field it is usually not possible to distinguish a genetic component in the phenotypic variation. However, several plants were seen which grew only as cushions, although neighboring plants produced flags or even developed into trees. Excavations of one of these showed that there was no layering, even of branches that were buried in the soil. The branchlets were short and spurry, like those in the crown of a mature tree, and bore cones in abundance; there were no vigorous leading shoots like those produced by saplings which originate from seed or layers. Possibly a genetic aberration has allowed these individuals to achieve a mature, fertile state, without passing through the normal, sterile, juvenile stage which enables plants to increase in height and spread through layering.

Wind-training of krummholz is effected through basipetal desiccation and death of exposed needles and shoots during the winter. On the lee sides of krummholz islands, as in forest, there are only slight, nonlethal decreases in water content during winter. Goldsmith and Smith (1926) also found that needles of Engelmann spruce below timberline showed seasonal fluctuations in water content, falling from a summer maximum at time of flush to a spring minimum which varied between 91% and 99% (converted to dry weight basis). Needles from krummholz gave a different pattern, in that a very low spring minimum (75%) was followed by a sharp rise to 128% in July, but this result appears to arise from failure to differentiate, while sampling, between needles showing a normal seasonal fluctuation, and those showing winter desiccation leading to death and abscission.

The water deficits that lead to death of foliage above timberline could arise in several ways. The increase in wind with increasing altitude may cause increased evaporation, though some experiments suggest that at high wind speeds there is little more transpiration than at low speeds (Satoo 1962). Alternatively, less water may be available to the foliage because of soil conditions. My data support the expectation that a fine-textured, humus-rich upper horizon holds much more water than the predominant rocky soils poor in organic matter, and also contains the greatest density of spruce roots (not that density of roots is necessarily an indication of absorptive activity). Such a horizon is generally lacking in krummholz areas

on Niwot Ridge except in restricted pockets, such as in the lee of islands of cushion krummholz.

Due to the insulating effect of canopy and snow in the forest, soil temperatures were above $-2°C$ during most of the winter suggesting that unfrozen water might be available, at least at depth. On sites supporting cushion krummholz, on the other hand, soil temperatures as low as $-14°C$ were recorded, and it is unlikely that unfrozen water was present in the rooting zone during winter. However, the temperature readings in sapwood suggest that trunks frozen within the snow pack present a barrier to passage of water to the foliage in both krummholz and forest during winter. Perhaps more relevant are the apparently small reserves of water in flagged stems. A possibility which was not tested is that snow clinging to leeward foliage after storms provides moisture which can be absorbed into the needles. In *Picea excelsa*, according to Michaelis (1934), winter deficits can be balanced by nocturnal uptake of atmospheric water vapor by needles.

In addition to high rates of water loss and low rates of replenishment as possible underlying causes of winter desiccation, there is the possibility of needles being already predisposed to dry out. Exposed needles show distinct chlorosis from the time that they emerge from the buds in the summer and are apt to develop lesions, needles which are small and crowded on their shoots are especially prone to winter desiccation, and likewise needles with water contents above average during fall tend to be killed. In other words, winter desiccation of needles is influenced by events in preceding seasons, perhaps as far back as the initial formation of the buds some 18 months before. The dying back of leading shoots below timberline after the exceptionally cold, wet September of 1961 leads one to suggest, in agreement with Michaelis (1934), that unfavorable conditions during the growing season lead to inadequate hardening of tissues. Probably spruce resembles many other tree species in that leading shoots show rapid, prolonged growth and are apt to be still succulent and frost-tender in their distal portions at the onset of winter.

Perhaps the most puzzling feature noted in this study is the contrast between the water contents of desiccated needles and other needles— even leeward needles on the same shoot—the latter exhibiting only normal, seasonal decreases in water content in the order of 20% (dry weight basis). One might expect all the needles of a flagged stem above the snow pack to lose water steadily during the winter; instead there appears to be a physiological mechanism ensuring that while the most exposed needles undergo rapid and irreversible drying, remaining needles maintain their turgor. It may be that once water becomes critically short in a stem, it is withdrawn from the most suceptible needles in an orderly vital process that also involves removal of chlorophyll.

Several authors (e.g., Rubner 1953, p. 81; Klikoff 1965) have stated that abrasion by wind-propelled particles of ice is an important factor in the origin of krummholz. When lesions on needles were first noticed during the present study, it was assumed that they also resulted from abrasion, but this is disproved by the intact condition of the cuticle over the lesions and the discovery that they are already present on young needles in July. Their cause remains unknown; possibly they reflect disturbances in cellular growth resulting from an environment at the extreme limit tolerated by spruce.

Though the elevation of timberline in Colorado can be broadly correlated with summer warmth, dry winter winds that kill exposed foliage and impose krummholz growth forms are effective in the forest-tundra ecotone. The detailed pattern of winter damage to foliage, together with the occurrence of symmetrically formed dwarfed trees with dead tops above timberline in sheltered localities indicates, however, that wind may not be the ultimate cause of winter desiccation and stunting.

ACKNOWLEDGMENTS

The work was carried out at the Institute of Arctic and Alpine Research, University of Colorado, and supported by a grant from the United States Forest Service. A Fulbright award enabled the author to travel from New Zealand. Grateful acknowledgment is made to the director (Dr. J. W. Marr) and staff at the institute, especially Miss M. A. Adams; the director of Botany Division, Department of Scientific and Industrial Research, New Zealand, for granting time to work on this paper; and D.S.I.R. staff, especially Dr. B. I. Hayman and Messrs. H. E. Connor, A. P. Underhill, C. J. Miles, S. L. Kircher, and K. R. West.

LITERATURE CITED

Clausen, J. 1965. Population studies of alpine and subalpine races of conifers and willows in the Californian High Sierra Nevada. Evolution 19: 56–58.

Daubenmire, R. 1943. Vegetational zonation in the Rocky Mountains. Bot. Rev. 9: 325–393.

——. 1954. Alpine timberlines in the Americas and their interpretation. Butler Univ. Bot. Stud. 11: 119–136.

Geiger, R. 1957. The climate near the ground. (Translation of 2nd German ed.) Harvard Univ. Press, Cambridge, Mass. 494 p.

Goldsmith, G. W., and J. H. C. Smith. 1926. Some physico-chemical properties of spruce sap and their seasonal and altitudinal variation. Colorado Coll. Pub. Gen. Ser. 137. 71 p.

Griggs, R. F. 1938. Timberlines in the northern Rocky Mountains. Ecology 19: 548–564.

Holzer, K. 1959. Winterliche Schäden an Zirben nahe der alpinen Baumgrenze. Centralbl. Ges. Forstwesen. 76: 232–244.

Klikoff, L. G. 1965. Microenvironmental influence on vegetational pattern near timberline in the central Sierra Nevada. Ecol. Monogr. 35: 187–211.

Marr, John W. 1961. Ecosystems of the east slope of the Front Range in Colorado. Univ. of Colorado Stud. Ser. Biol. 8. 134 p.

Michaelis, P. 1934. Ökologische Studien an der alpinen Baumgrenze. IV. Zur Kenntnis des winterlichen Wasserhaushaltes. V. Osmotischer Wert und Wassergehalt während des Winters in den verschiedenen Höhenlagen. Jahrb. Wiss. Bot. 80: 169–247, 337–362.

Ridgway, R. 1912. Color standards and color nomenclature. A. Hoen & Co. Press, Baltimore, Maryland. 44 p.

Rubner, K. 1953. Die pflanzengeographische Grundlagen des Waldbaues. Neumann Verlag, Radebeul und Berlin. 583 p.

Satoo, T. 1962. Wind, transpiration, and tree growth, p. 299–310. In T. T. Kozlowski [ed.] Tree growth. Ronald Press Co., New York.

Schröter, C. 1926. Das Pflanzenleben der Alpen. Albert Raustein Verlag, Zurich. 1288 p.

Shaw, C. H. 1909. The causes of timberline on mountains; the role of snow. Plant World 12: 169–181.

Sifton, H. B. 1965. On the abscission region in leaves of the blue spruce. Can. J. Bot. 43: 985–993.

Wardle, P. 1965. A comparison of alpine timberlines in New Zealand and North America. New Zealand J. Bot. 3: 113–135.

REMARKS ON THE STABILITY OF TIMBERLINE

Jack D. Ives

SUMMARY

The conventional approch to equating timberline with present-day climate is, at best, approximate and frought with danger since the life span of high-altitude trees will substantially exceed the period of secular climate change. The prospect of great age ($<$ 1,000 to 3,000 years) of ecotonal trees, surviving by the process of layering is introduced with specific examples from the Colorado Front Range. It is concluded that, since predominantly natural timberlines in Colorado must be considered as deriving, in part at least, from the Hypsithermal period of 3,500 to 5,000 BP, especial care must be taken when discussing timberlines in other parts of the world. They will be controlled by a composite not only of present and past climates, but also of extensive anthropogenic processes.

Biogeographers and ecologists have long sought to select environmental parameters to fit the position of timberline (polar timberline, or upper alpine timberline) and to show by inference a causal relationship between present-day climate and this dramatic vegatational limit. Köppen's, Nordenskjold's, and Thornthwaite's attempts are among the better known and have proven the most durable in textbook popularity.* References to the 10 °C isotherm for the warmest month are particularly frequent in discussions on the "causes" of timberline. TROLL (1973a and b) has adequately stressed the complexities of the relationship between timberline and environmental parameters. Perhaps an elaboration of one aspect of this problem may prove useful, particularly since palaeoecologists, working in mountain areas, rightly regard evidence of former timberline, higher or lower than that of the present, as especially strong indications of changing climatic conditions through time.

While the theme of this symposium has been a comparison of tropical and southern hemisphere timberlines, the information upon which the present discussion is based is derived largely from the Colorado Rocky Mountains. This can perhaps be justified partly because, as pointed out by WARDLE (1973, 1974), their timberlines are among the least influenced by anthropogenic processes of any in the world, and partly because ideas derived from study of this area may be applicable to world treelines in general.

The Front Range of Colorado extends north-south for a distance of some 120 km and rises to over 4000 m within 30 km of the High Plains. Since the strong prevailing westerly winds, accentuated in winter by fierce downslope storms, cross the range perpendicularly, a degree of timberline asymmetry between the west and east slopes might be expected. Late-Cenozoic glaciation was restricted to producing a series of cirques and glacial troughs,

---

* Different approaches have been used by HARE (1950), BRYSON (1966), BARRY (1967), BARRY and KREBS (1970); and HUSTICH (1966) has made an important contribution to our understanding of the arctic timberline and forest tundra ecotone in Northern Europe.

In Troll, C. and W. Lauer (eds.), *Geoecological Relations Between the Southern Temperate Zone and the Tropical Mountains*. Franz Steiner Verlag GMBH, Wiesbaden, pp. 313-317.

generally not more than 15 km in length, so that the landform assemblage is a combination of the hochgebirge forms (TROLL, 1972) close to the divide, with wide interfluve and plateau remnants displaying the gentle slopes of unglaciated mountains subject for long periods to cold climate (or periglacial) processes.

Timberline (defined as the upper limit of symmetrically formed tall trees) occurs at approximately 3,350 m on the east slope of the Front Range, with the forest-tundra eco-tone extending to about 3,500 m and individual cushion-krummholz forms occasionally reaching as high as 3,730 m (WARDLE, 1968). Four climatological stations, maintained continuously since 1951 through an altitudinal range of 2,200 m to 3,750 m (BARRY, 1973), indicate that the 10 °C July mean air isotherm lies within the forest-tundra ecotone, although there is still no adequate micro-climatic cross-section through the ecotone.

A single, quite simple theme will form the main focus of these remarks: discussion of the hypothesis that much of the forest-tundra ecotone is a relic of a warmer climate in the distant past; that it was established more than 3,500 years ago. *Photos 131–135 (Plates XXXIII/XXXIV)* provide a transect across the forest-tundra ecotone on the east slope of the Front Range.

Let us consider the question of the form and age of the individual tree species in the Front Range. Four species of conifer form the timberline and extend upwards as the forest components of the ecotone, although several deciduous shrubs and junipers are found in close association. They are, in decreasing order of numerical superiority, Engelmann spruce, *Picea engelmannii;* subalpine fir, *Abies lasiocarpa;* limber pine, *Pinus flexilis:* and bristlecone pine, *Pinus aristata.* The upper limit of fullgrown, symmetical, tall trees contains individual firs and pines that have been dated at 900 years (*pers. comm.* W.S. OSBURN, for *Pinus flexilis*), 700–800 years (*pers. comm.* Doris LÖVE, for *Abies lasiocarpa*), and 1650 years (KREBS, 1973, for *Pinus aristata*). Attempts to date individuals in the upper limits of the forest-tundra ecotone (cushion krummholz) by dendrochronology have not been particular-ly successful, yet at least suggest that firs and pines in the characteristic shrub form probably exceed 600 to 700 years in age.

As is well known, the trees of the forest-tundra ecotone rarely produce viable seeds, but maintain themselves by the process of layering. The severe westerly winds, at least on the east slope of the Front Range, largely restrict the layering process to the lee side, which in turn induces down-wind migration of the entire tree, since the west-facing side is progres-sively killed off. With progressive down-wind migration sections of the main stem die, weather, and become separated from the living tree. Examination of the upper forest-tundra ecotone has revealed the existence of snags, or remnants of stems, up to at least 5 m distan-ce from the living tree. An initial attempt, with the assistance of Dr. Val LAMARCHE of the Geochronology Laboratory, Tucson, Arizona, to date such a remnant through cross-corre-lation with the increment record of upright trees at lower elevations failed. Another ap-proach was to date the deadwood through 14_C assay. While this was still not completely satisfactory, it permitted, as a first approximation, the statement that the tree's rate of down-wind migration was of the order of 2.5 cm/yr (5 m in 200 years) (IVES, 1973). Measurement of shoot elongation on krummholz forms produced an annual growth figure average of 20–25 mm (MARR and MARR, 1973). Extrapolation through 200 years would indicate that the rough indication derived from the 14_C assay is reasonable (MARR, *pers. comm.*, 1972). From this it is also reasonable to assume that a krummholz tree 7 m long will have a minimum age of about 300 years. If we now consider the long-term migration, then the krummholz clone may well have persisted for more than 1,000 years.

Let us now turn to the question of regeneration of conifers near timberline. A large area of upper subalpine forest and forest-tundra ecotone on Niwot Ridge, east slope of the Front Range, was burned over in 1901. The upper two-thirds of the burned area shows no regeneration, with the exception of occasional seedlings surviving downwind from mature krummholz forms. Even below the former limit of tall trees, regeneration is extremely slow. The obvious question therefore arises: When was the forest-tundra ecotone established?

If survival of trees in the ecotone through the last 100 years or so has depended upon the species' ability to propagate through layering, it would seem unlikely that timberline and the ecotone would have been established during the last phase of the Neoglacial. Thus we must look at least as far back as the sub-hypsithermal, or in North Atlantic parlance, the Viking Period. So far no evidence has been found to support the contention that the Colorado Rocky Mountains experienced a significant warm period between 800 and 1 200 A.D. The few data available (MAHER, 1972; ANDREWS et al, 1973) indicate for the Front Range and San Juan Mountains that the most recent period of higher timberline occurred between 3,500 and 5,000 BP. The stratigraphic, macrofossil and radiocarbon data of ANDREWS et al (1973) for the San Juan Mountains, only 250 km distance from the Front Range, indicate that treeline was somewhat higher or equal to its present elevation from about 5,500 to 3,500 BP. Their inferences are based upon analysis of peat sections close to present timberline that were taken from valley-bottom, potentially wet sites, where even today krumm-

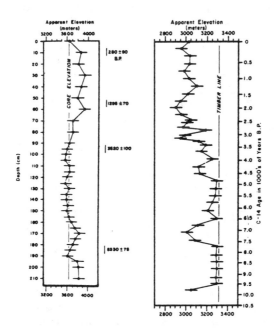

Fig. 1: Two profiles showing interpretations of treeline fluctuations through time based upon micro- and macro-fossil analysis of peat cores, together with radiocarbon dates. The left-hand diagram is from the San Juan Mountains; the right-hand diagram is from the Colorado Front Range. Collected by ANDREWS/ CARRARA and MAHER, respectively. Note that the two trends are essentially out of phase (see text).

holz forms exist 50–100 m higher on nearby relatively dry interfluves. The Front Range interpretations of MAHER (1972) would indicate treeline fluctuations synchronous with those interpreted for the San Juan Mountains but with an opposite sign. The two profiles are compared in *Figure 1*. MAHER's conclusions are based upon variations in spruce/pine pollen ratios with altitude and through time and may not be so reliable as the stratigraphic sections and macrofossils of trees. On the other hand, timberline variations in the two mountain areas may have occurred out of phase. Despite these uncertainties, the macrofossil evidence of ANDREWS *et al.* (1973) indicates a warmer climate and a higher timberline some 3,500 to 5,500 years ago. It also indicates that trees were growing on the floors of high cirques nearly 10,000 years ago, close after the end of the last major glacial stade (Pinedale).

In the Mt. Washington area of Nevada, LAMARCHE and MOONEY (1972) provided substantial evidence of timberline fluctuations and persistence of dead snags of bristlecone pine, *Pinus longaeva*, from the period 2,000 to 4,000 years ago. Their conclusion is that during this period timberline, as well as the ecotone altitude, was approximately 150 m higher than today. This would require a *wet* hypsithermal since *P. longaeva* at high altitude is dependent at least as much on moisture availability as upon temperature of the growing season. More recently BRADLEY (1974) has shown that within the period of instrumental record (1870–1970) climatic fluctuations across the southwestern United States most emphatically do not match fluctuations in eastern United States and Northwest Europe. Furthermore, KREBS (1972) concluded that individual mountain ranges, and even individual sites within 50 km distance in Colorado, have not shown synchrony in climatic change over the longer period of the life span of her bristlecone pines, such that her hopes of constructing a master chronology for the state could not be realized.

From the foregoing, it would seem that despite the paucity of palaeoecological data, two considerations must be recognized: (1) the difficulty of making long-distance palaeoclimatic correlations in southwestern United States, and perhaps in mountainous areas in general, and (2) the strong likelihood of the persistence of trees far beyond the timescale of secular climatic change.

In conclusion, it would seem that any attempt to relate natural timberlines in Colorado to climatic parameters of the twentieth century will have an air of unreality in face of the trees' ability to persist through perhaps several thousand years. If timberline and present climate are not in equilibrium in an area noted for the relatively slight impact of man, how much more will this apply to areas that have experienced massive anthropogenic impacts? Is it not appropriate, therefore, to regard timberlines and the forest-tundra ecotones above them, in part at least, as relics of a former warm climate, or climates? In the case of the arctic timberline of central Canada, NICHOLS (1976) has developed a similar thesis. To what extent would the main working hypothesis of this paper be applicable to tropical and southern hemisphere timberlines? In terms of making comparisons, would it not prove worth-while to attempt assessment of anthropogenic impacts as well as determination of the degree of causal incompatibility between timberlines and present climate? To what extent would systematic determination of altitudinal limits of seedlings and sexually propagating trees throw light on this problem? Systematic study of these and related problems could be profitably incorporated into the developing research program of the IGU Commission on Mountain Geoecology.

ACKNOWLEDGEMENTS

The writer is indebted to Dr. Harvey NICHOLS, Institute of Arctic and Alpine Research, for extensive discussions on the problems raised in this paper.

REFERENCES

ANDREWS, J.T., CARRARA, P.E., BARTOS, F., and STUCHENRATH, R. (1973): Holocene stratigraphy and geochronology of four bogs (3,700 m a.s.l.) San Juan Mountains, SW Colorado, and implications to the Neoglacial record. Geol. Soc. Amer., Abstracts with Programs, 5(6): 460—461.

BARRY, R.G. (1967): Seasonal location of the arctic front over North America. Geogr. Bull., Ottawa, Vol. 9(2): 79—95.

— (1973): A climatological transect along the east slope of the Front Range, Colorado. Arctic and Alpine Research, 5(2): 89—110.

BRADLEY, R.S. (1974): Secular changes of precipatation in the Rocky Mountains and adjacent western states. Ph.D. thesis, University of Colorado, 444 pp.

BRYSON, R.A. (1966): Air masses, streamlines, and the boreal forest. Geogr. Bull., Ottawa, Vol. 8(3): 228—269.

HARE, F.K. (1950): Climate and the zonal divisions of the boreal forest formations in Eastern Canada. Geogr. Rev., 40: 615—635.

HUSTICH, I. (1966): On the forest-tundra and the northern tree-lines. Ann. Univ. Turku., A, II, 36 (Rep. Kevo Subarctic Sta. 3), 7-47.

IVES, Jack D. (1973): Studies in high altitude geoecology of the Colorado Front Range: A review of the research program of the Institute of Arctic and Alpine Research, University of Colorado. Arctic and Alpine Research, 5(3, Pt. 2): A67—A75.

MARR, J.W., and MARR, R.E. (1973): Environment and phenology in the forest-tundra ecotone, Front Range, Colorado (Summary). Arctic and Alpine Research, 5(3, Pt. 2): A65—A66.

KREBS, J.S., and BARRY, R.G. (1970): The arctic front and the tundra-taiga boundary in Eurasia. Geogr. Rev., 60: 548—554.

KREBS, P.V. (1972): Dendrochronology and the distribution of the bristlecone pine (Pinus aristata Engelm.) in Colorado. Unpub. Ph. D. dissertation, University of Colorado, 211 pp.

KREBS, P.V. (1973): Dendrochronology of the bristlecone pine (Pinus aristata Engelm.) in Colorado, Arctic and Alpine Research, 5(2): 149—150.

MAHER, L.J., Jr. (1972): Absolute pollen diagram of Redrock Lake, Boulder County, Colorado. Quaternary Research, 2(4): 531—553.

LaMARCHE, V.C., and MOONEY, H.A. (1972): Recent climatic change and development of the bristlecone pine (P. longaeva Bailey) krummholz zone, Mt. Washington, Nevada. Arctic and Alpine Research, 4(1): 61—72.

NICHOLS, H. (1976): Historical aspects of the northern Canadian treeline. Arctic, 29(I): 38—47.

TROLL, C. (1972): Geoecology and the world-wide differentiation of high-mountain ecosystems, Geoecology of the High-Mountain Regions of Eurasia. Ed. Carl Troll, F. Steiner, Verlag GBMH, Wiesbaden, 1—16.

— (1973a): The upper timberlines in different climatic zones. Arctic and Alpine Research, 5(3, Pt. 2): A3—A18.

— (1973b): High mountain belts between the polar caps and the equator: Their definition and lower limit. Arctic and Alpine Research, 5(3, Pt. 2): A19—A27.

WARDLE, P. (1968): Englemann spruce (Picea engelmannii Engel.) at its upper limits on the Front Range, Colorado. Ecology, 49: 483—495.

Photo 131 "Wolf" trees at the upper limit of full-sized trees, Niwot Ridge. This photo also shows the beginnings of the subalpine meadows.   Photo: Ives

Photo 132 One hundred meters higher, flagging and other wind-deformed characteristics are apparent. This is approximately the middle zone of the forest-tundra ecotone.   Photo: Ives

Photo 133 Fifty meters higher the trees are significantly subdued in height, and in snow accumulation sites "skirts" are well developed, the result of kill by snow mould.

Photo: Ives

Photo 134 The extreme upper limit (3,500 m) of the forest-tundra ecotone on Niwot Ridge showing the greatest extent of wind-deformation. These "cushion-krumm-holz" forms are migrating down-wind (eastward) leaving behind remnants of dead stem that have been used in attempts to assess age of the individuals. Photo: Ives

358

Photo 135   The upper limits of the forest-tundra ecotone and the alpine belt on Niwot Ridge as seen from a low-flying aircraft. Note the pronounced east-west orientation of the tree-islands, due to wind training.   Photo: Ives

Photo 136 De-tail of wind-oriented krumm-holz and the upper limit of tree-species on the east slope of the Front Range, Colorado.

    Photo: Ives

GENETIC DIFFERENTIATION AMONG GROWTH FORMS OF ENGELMANN SPRUCE AND SUBALPINE FIR AT TREE LINE

MICHAEL C. GRANT AND JEFFRY B. MITTON

Department of Environmental, Population and Organismic Biology
and Institute of Arctic and Alpine Research
University of Colorado
Boulder, Colorado 80309

ABSTRACT

Starch gel electrophoresis was used to assay for genetic variation in Engelmann spruce (*Picea engelmannii*) and subalpine fir (*Abies lasiocarpa*) near tree line in the Rocky Mountains of Colorado. Substantial differentiation of peroxidase enzymes was detected along an elevational gradient in samples marked by different growth forms. The genetic differentiation observed runs counter to a commonly held view that extensive gene flow among these wind pollinated long-lived plants would maintain genetic homogeneity. The differentiation among peroxidase enzymes may be related to their fungicidal properties and the occurrence of snow molds in spruce and fir near the tree line.

INTRODUCTION

One of the most striking features of high elevation and high latitude areas is tree line — the ecotone marking the disappearance of certain tree species or their change into krummholz or elfinwood forms (Clausen, 1963). Three distinctly different morphological forms are often associated with the transition from typical forest to alpine or arctic tundra regions. At lower elevations and latitudes, coniferous trees generally exhibit the spire shape typified by one dominant stem with bifurcations being uncommon (Figure 1a). As tree line is approached, the trees begin to exhibit a shorter more branched appearance with abundant secondary branching below the still identifiable main stem. This main stem bears lateral branches only on the leeward side and thus earns the name flag tree (Figure 1b). Finally, at the distributional limits, the tree form is a low, prostrate shrub with no dominant erect stem. Lateral branch rooting or layering on the downwind side of the tree island is common in these krummholz or elfinwood forms (Figure 1c).

The nature of tree line and its causes has been the subject of several investigations (e.g., Daubenmire, 1954; Marr, 1961; Clausen, 1963, 1965; Wardle, 1965, 1968, 1971; Bliss, 1966; Billings and Mooney, 1968; Löve et al., 1970). Most of these studies have been autoecological, providing information on the relationships between individual metabolism and climatic variables such as temperature, wind, and available moisture. Clausen (1963, 1965) addressed the question of whether or not these distinct growth morphs which characterize many tree lines have a genetic basis. Tigerstedt (1973) also considered the question of genetic architecture near tree line, although from a slightly different point of view.

Clausen (1965) argues in favor of some genetic basis to the krummholz forms while Löve et al. (1970) argue in favor of a strictly

360

FIGURE 1. Examples of the three growth forms studied with a meter stick pictured for scale. Top left (a) is the spire form, top right (b) is the flag form, and the krummholz form is at the bottom (c).

environmental explanation for krummholz formation. Clausen's argument is based on the presence of dwarfed growth forms among spire-shaped trees. Löve *et al.* advance the view that various growth forms are the result of interaction between coumarin, its derivatives, and high elevational environmental parameters such as ultraviolet radiation. In the opinion of Löve *et al.*, no genetic component other than the general capability to form krummholz is involved. A second argument in favor of the absence of a genetic basis to these growth form variations is that gene flow via both pollen and seeds among forest trees in general can extend across distances substantially greater than the few hundred meters commonly separating these morphologically distinct subpopulations (Koski, 1970; Tiger-

stedt, 1973; Stern and Roche, 1974; Hamrick, 1976).

These three morphs, spire, flag, and krummholz, are clearly correlated with different microenvironments and thus are likely to be subject to substantially different selective regimes. In order to generate data relevant to the question of genetic differentiation of trees marked by different growth forms, we have used gel electrophoresis to assay genetic variation of enzymes from samples of individuals identified as spire, flag, and krummholz. In an attempt to test the generality of the degree of genetic differentiation associated with growth form, we have sampled two sympatric species of trees that exhibit similar patterns of variation in morphology.

MATERIALS AND METHODS

We collected needle samples from the two dominant tree species *Picea engelmannii* (Parry) Engelm. (Engelmann spruce) and *Abies lasiocarpa* (Hook) Nutt. (subalpine fir) from one transect along the southern slope of Niwot Ridge, Front Range, Colorado, immediately to the north of the University of Colorado's Mountain Research Station. This transect was along the same general region previously studied by Wardle (1968). We sampled 72 spire, 73 flag, and 56 krummholz of Engelmann spruce and 41 spire, 63 flag, and 54 krummholz of subalpine fir. Each sampling region was approximately 300 to 500 m apart. Care was taken to ensure that only separate individuals were sampled.

Fresh, green needles were ground with an aqueous solution of 1% polyvinylpolypyrrolidone and extracts were subjected to standard horizontal starch gel electrophoresis and stained for peroxidase by the method of Shaw

and Prasad (1970). Peroxidase enzymes from both species resolved satisfactorily in a discontinuous tris-citric acid buffer system (gel buffer pH 7.7, 18.16 g tris, 0.63 g monohydrate citric acid diluted to 1 liter; electrode buffer pH 7.5, 1.24 g sodium hydroxide, 18.54 g anhydrous boric acid diluted to 1 liter. Our studies have focused exclusively on peroxidase enzymes because that is the only enzyme system currently accessible technically at all times of the year from all individuals.

Interpretation of the gel phenotypes as representing segregating alleles is based on (1) presence of all expected genotypes, (2) the conformity of these genotypes to Hardy-Weinberg equilibrium, and (3) our experience with similar organisms and enzyme systems (e.g., Mitton *et al.*, 1977). Although we are confident that our interpretations are correct, confirming formal genetic analyses are being undertaken.

RESULTS AND DISCUSSION

The gene and genotype frequencies of the three polymorphic alleles in each species are listed in Table 1 according to growth form. There are clearly significant differences in gene frequencies among krummholz, flag, and spire growth forms for each species. The frequencies for each allele were tested for homogeneity by the χ^2 test (Workman and Niswander, 1970). The observed heterogeneity of allele frequencies is such that a consis-

tent linear trend is present for two alleles in each species. These results indicate dramatic differentiation in peroxidase traits correlated with spire, flag, and krummholz morphs. This study differs somewhat from many electrophoretic surveys in that we have found enzymic differentiation which corresponds to clear morphological differentiation. Most previous examples of microdifferentiation in plants have involved herbaceous forms of pre-

362

TABLE 1

Gene and genotypic frequencies for peroxidase polymorphisms in elevational transect of Engelmann spruce and subalpine fir

Species	Tree Morphology	Genotypes						N	Gene Frequencies ± S.D.		
		11	12	22	13	23	33		$f(1)$	$f(2)$	$f(3)$
Engelmann spruce											
	krummholz	35	17	3	0	1	0	56	.78 ± .04	.21 ± .04	.01 ± .01
	flag	18	34	11	4	6	0	73	.51 ± .04	.42 ± .04	.07 ± .02
	spire	12	26	28	0	5	1	72	.35 ± .04	.60 ± .04	.05 ± .02
χ^2 Test of homogeneity									$p < .001$	$p < .001$	$.05 < p < .10$
Subalpine fir											
	krummholz	2	7	17	4	11	0	41	.18 ± .04	.64 ± .05	.18 ± .04
	flag	1	8	36	1	16	1	63	.09 ± .02	.76 ± .04	.15 ± .03
	spire	2	7	40	1	4	0	54	.11 ± .03	.84 ± .03	.05 ± .02
χ^2 Test of homogeneity									$p > .10$	$p < .01$	$p < .05$

sumably short generation times (e.g., Antonovics, 1971; Antonovics *et al.*, 1971; Linhart, 1974). Engelmann spruce and subalpine fir represent the opposite ecological extreme by having long generation times, potentially long-range pollen and seed flow, and vegetative reproductive (in flag and krummholz) habits, all of which usually oppose the effects of disruptive selection between closely adjacent habitats. Considering these aspects of tree line ecology, this example of genetic microdifferentiation may well represent the extreme of situations where classical theory predicts no genetic differentiation. In particular, our data are consistent with recent trends in microevolutionary thinking which deemphasizes the role of gene flow in maintaining species cohesiveness via swamping effects (cf. Mayr, 1963; Ehrlich and Raven, 1969; Dickinson and Antonovics, 1973; Endler, 1973; Antonovics, 1976).

We are not yet in a position to demonstrate the adaptive significance of the polymorphic alleles studied here. However, Wardle (1968) considers snow molds (*Herpotrichia* and *Phoma* spp.) to be a significant feature of krummholz formation. He argues that an important balance exists between (1) protection from desiccation by snow cover and (2) the increased damage from molds when snow cover is prolonged. Peroxidases have been demonstrated to possess fungicidal properties (Lehrer, 1969) and the differences in allele frequencies reported here may, in part, reflect selection regimes associated with snow cover and resulting fungal infection.

In any case, the one tiny window through which we have viewed the genetic architecture of the six subpopulations indicates substantive differences in genetic make up. It seems most reasonable to infer that other genetic differences, in particular ones affecting growth form, are also present.

ACKNOWLEDGMENTS

We thank Michael Reynolds and Yan Linhart for assisting with field and laboratory work as well as for helpful criticism of the manuscript. We acknowledge partial support from NSF grants BMS 75-14050, DEB 76-02266, and SMI 76-04815, logistical support from the University of Colorado Mountain Research Station, and cooperation from the U.S. Forest Service.

REFERENCES

Antonovics, J., 1971: The effects of a heterogeneous environment on the genetics of populations. *Amer. Sci.*, 59: 593-599.

———, 1976: The nature of limits to selection. *Ann. Missouri Bot. Gard.*, 63: 224-247.

Antonovics, J., Bradshaw, A. P. and Turner, R. G., 1971: Heavy metal tolerance in plants. *Adv. Ecol. Res.*, 7: 1-85.

Billings, W. D. and Mooney, H. A., 1968: The ecology of arctic and alpine plants. *Biol. Rev.*, 43: 481-530.

Bliss, L. C., 1966: Plant productivity in alpine microenvironments on Mt. Washington, New Hampshire. *Ecol. Monogr.*, 36: 125-155.

Clausen, J., 1963: Tree lines and germplasm—a study in evolutionary limitations. *Proc. Nat. Acad. Sci.*, 50: 860-868.

———, 1965: Population studies of alpine and subalpine races of conifers and willows in the California High Sierra Nevada. *Evolution*, 19: 56-68.

Daubenmire, R., 1954: Alpine timberlines in the Americas and their interpretation. *Butler Univ. Bot. Stud.*, 11: 119-136.

Dickinson, H. and Antonovics, J., 1973: Theoretical considerations of sympatric divergence. *Amer. Natur.*, 107: 256-274.

Ehrlich, P. R. and Raven, P. H., 1969: Differentiation of populations. *Science*, 1965: 1228-1232.

Endler, J. A., 1973: Gene flow and population differentiation. *Science*, 179: 243-249.

Hamrick, J. L., 1976: Variation and selection in Western montane species II. Variation within and between populations of White Fir on an elevational transect. *Theor. Appl. Genet.*, 47: 27-34.

Koski, V., 1970: A study of pollen dispersal as a mechanism of gene flow in conifers. *Commun. Inst. For. Tenn.*, 70(8).

Lehrer, R. I., 1969: Antifungal effects of peroxidase system. *J. Bacteriol.*, 99: 361-365.

Linhart, Y. B., 1974: Intra-population differentiation in annual plants. I. *Veronica peregrina* L. raised under non-competitive conditions. *Evolution*, 28: 232-243.

Löve, D., McLellan, C., and Gamow, I., 1970: Coumarin and coumarin derivatives in various growth types of Engelmann spruce. *Svensk. Bot. Tidskr.*, 64: 284-296.

Marr, J. W., 1961: Ecosystems of the east slope of the Front Range in Colorado. *Univ. of Colorado Stud., Ser. Biol.*, No. 8. 134 pp.

Mayr, E., 1963: *Animal Species and Evolution.* Belknap Press, Cambridge, Mass. 797 pp.

Mitton, J. B., Linhart, Y. B., Hamrick, J. L., Beckman, J. S., 1977: Observations on the genetic structure and mating system of ponderosa pine in the Colorado Front Range. *Theor. Appl. Genet.* (in press).

Shaw, C. R. and Prasad, R., 1970: Starch gel electrophoresis of enzymes—a compilation of recipes. *Biochem. Genet.*, 4: 297-320.

Stern, K. and Roche, L., 1974: *Genetics of Forest Ecosystems.* Springer-Verlag, New York. 330 pp.

Tigerstedt, P. M. A., 1973: Studies on isozyme variation in marginal and central populations of *Picea abies. Hereditas*, 75: 47-60.

Wardle, P., 1965: A comparison of alpine timberlines in New Zealand and North America. *N.Z. J. Bot.*, 3: 113-135.

———, 1968: Engelmann spruce (*Picea engelmannii* Engel.) at its upper limits on the Front Range, Colorado. *Ecology*, 49: 483-495.

———, 1971: An explanation for Alpine timberline. *N.Z. J. Bot.*, 9: 371-402.

Workman, P. L. and Niswander, J. D., 1970: Population studies on Southwestern Indian tribes. II. Local genetic differentiation in the Papago. *Amer. J. Human Genet.*, 22: 24-49.

AN ALPINE VEGETATION MAP OF NIWOT RIDGE, COLORADO

Věra Komárková and P. J. Webber

Institute of Arctic and Alpine Research and
Department of Environmental, Population and Organismic Biology
University of Colorado
Boulder, Colorado 80309

ABSTRACT

Niwot Ridge represents an altitudinal, east-west oriented gradient on the east slope of the Front Range. A large scale (1:10,000) map of its alpine vegetation provides information on the extent and the spatial and environmental relationships of the mapped units of a Braun-Blanquet vegetation classification hierarchy. Patterns of moisture and snow, influenced to a high degree by wind and topography, appear to be the factors controlling vegetation distribution. Distance from the Continental Divide combined with altitude, rather than altitude alone, appears to be of importance for the distribution of most vegetation units. The average elevation of treeline on the ridge is 3406 m s.m. Treeline is lowered on the south slope by strong westerly winds; it is higher in valleys than on ridges, lowest positions occurring below snowpatches. The net aboveground vascular productivity of the mapped alpine area is estimated at 1.725 ton ha^{-1} yr^{-1}. The Braun-Blanquet system was found to be very suitable for mapping and analyzing vegetation at this large scale. Areas with vegetation composition of higher units of the Braun-Blanquet hierarchy (alliances in particular) that appear to represent average environmental conditions on the ridge are considerably larger than the areas of individual associations.

INTRODUCTION

Niwot Ridge is an interfluve almost 8 km long in the Indian Peaks area on the east slope of the Front Range in the Colorado Rocky Mountains (Figure 1). Niwot Ridge carries the largest extent of alpine vegetation in the Indian Peaks where much of the landscape above the treeline is covered by bedrock and scree. On its gentle, overall little-disturbed surface, the ridge supports a number of well-developed vegetation types. It is a relatively isolated ridge oriented east-west and can be regarded as an altitudinal gradient on an interfluve with more or less uniform topography. The ridge is, therefore, suitable for comparison of vegetation on north and south slopes. The altitudinal gradient shows the combined effects of altitude and distance from the Continental Divide.

Niwot Ridge is easily accessible from the University of Colorado Mountain Research Station, located on its south side and has been a center of considerable research activity. A study site of the Tundra Biome of the U.S. International Biological Programme, including intensive study plots and transplant gardens, was located on Niwot Ridge. Several vegeta-

FIGURE 1. Looking westward along Niwot Ridge toward the summit of Navajo Peak (4087 m s.m.). The ridge supports the largest continuous area of alpine vegetation in the Indian Peaks area. On the south side of the ridge are the Green Lakes and North Boulder Creek valley; on the north side is Lake Isabelle and South St. Vrain Creek valley. The Continental Divide follows the line connecting the highest peaks. (Photo by J. D. Ives.)

tion studies (Osburn, 1958; Marr, 1961; Webber, 1972; D. C. E. May, 1973; Webber and D. E. May, 1977) distinguish some vegetation types and noda, but no vegetation map of the entire site has been available. The present work is based on the Braun-Blanquet vegetation units described for the Indian Peaks area by Komárková (1976, 1978); the Niwot Ridge map is also included but not analyzed in this work. Braun-Blanquet vegetation units have been described in other areas of the southern Rocky Mountains by Cox (1933), Kiener (1939), and Willard (1963). The floristic-sociological, or Braun-Blanquet, approach to classification and interpretation of plant communities uses diagnostic species to organize communities into a hierarchical classification (Westhoff and Maarel, 1973). Long (1969) has pointed out that mapped vegetation represents an integration of the environment. The present map was made with the following objectives in mind:

(1) to determine spatial and cover relationships of the principal Braun-Blanquet hierarchy units;

(2) to relate the distribution of these units and of the treeline course to the meso-environment;

(3) to compare the results with existing maps which provide partial coverage of the ridge and to compare mapping techniques.

DESCRIPTION OF THE STUDY AREA

The study area is located in the southern part of the North American tundra (Figure 2) in an area of continental climate in the south- ern Rocky Mountains. Niwot Ridge, a continuation of the east ridge of Navajo Peak (4087 m s.m.), forms an interfluve between

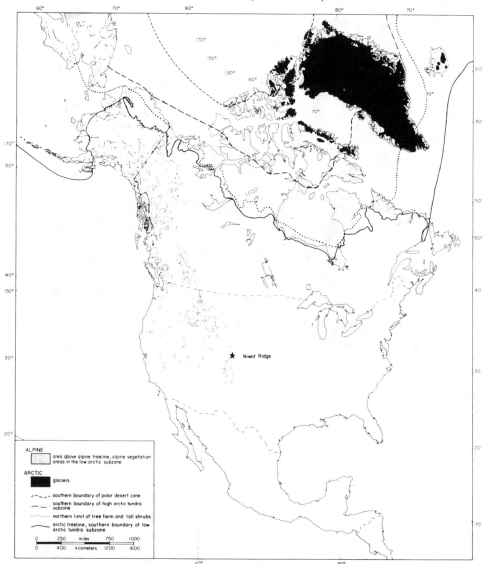

FIGURE 2. The distribution of North American tundra compiled from several sources. The map shows the distribution of alpine tundra and the northern treeline. Above the northern treeline the low arctic and high arctic subzones of the arctic tundra zone and the polar desert zone are shown. The location of Niwot Ridge is indicated by a star. (Major sources: Hermes, 1955; Hare, 1959; Rowe, 1959; Alexandrova, 1970; other sources: Lavrenko and Sochava, 1956; Hämet-Ahti, 1965; Ontario Dept. of Lands and Forests, 1969; Aleksandrova, 1971; Joint Federal-State Land Use Planning Commission for Alaska, 1973; Löve, Á., 1975, personal communication.)

the Lake Isabelle and Green Lakes valleys, rising gently westward, from about 3400 to 3750 m s.m. The ridge appears on U.S. Geological Survey Colorado 1:24,000 quadrangles, Ward and Monarch Lake. Altitudinally, the study area (6.99 km²) is limited by the alpine treeline (defined as the tree species limit at which the tree species cover at least 25% of the surface area) and by scree slopes which surround the western part of the ridge; thus, the study area consists of the alpine belt (Löve, 1970). Most of the alpine vegetation on the ridge belongs to the upper alpine belt; the lower alpine belt communities are found close to and in the area of the treeline (Komárková, 1976, 1978). Figure 3 shows that Niwot Ridge has a more extensive alpine vegetation than other parts of the Indian Peaks area. The width and the area of the subalpine (Löve, 1970) and subnival (Höller-

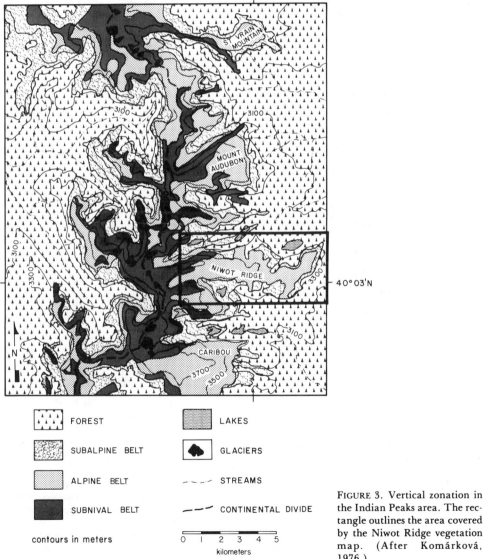

FIGURE 3. Vertical zonation in the Indian Peaks area. The rectangle outlines the area covered by the Niwot Ridge vegetation map. (After Komárková, 1976.)

368

mann, 1964) belt on the ridge are comparable to those on other interfluves on the east slope of the Front Range; the interfluves on the west slope are less extensive, which is probably the result of the action of the dominant westerly winds.

On a transect along Niwot Ridge precipitation increases with altitude, but annual average solar radiation totals show little or no change between 2590 and 3750 m s.m. The mean duration of the frost-free season (defined as the season with daily minimum temperatures, at 1.5 m, above 0°C) decreases with increasing altitude. The diurnal temperature range is lowest at the highest elevation; differences of temperature between sites with different exposure diminish and mean wind speed increases with increasing elevation (Barry, 1973). South-facing slopes are significantly warmer than north-facing slopes (Barry, 1972). The period from January through April is wet while a dry period occurs

in August through October (Figure 4). Permafrost occurs under north-facing slopes, areas blown free of snow in winter, and under wet sites (Ives and Fahey, 1971; Ives, 1973).

The geology of Niwot Ridge is documented by Gable and Madole (1976). The eastern part of the ridge is formed by cordierite- and magnetite-bearing sillimanite-biotite gneiss and by cordierite-bearing garnet-sillimanite-biotite gneiss; Silver Plume quartz monzonite also occurs. Solifluction deposits, characterized by hummocks, turf-bank lobes, and terraces, occur chiefly in the wet areas of the alpine tundra concentrated in the western part of the ridge. These deposits, together with a Pleistocene or Tertiary diamicton, cover most of the upper part of the ridge where the main rocks are quartz monzonite, monzonite, and syenite.

The Niwot Ridge surfaces may not have been glaciated during the Wisconsin time; the surface is deeply mantled in weathering

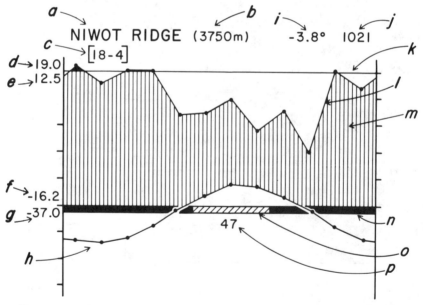

FIGURE 4. Climatic diagram for Niwot Ridge. After Walter and Lieth (1967) on the basis of data from Barry (1972, 1973) (Komárková, 1976). Abscissa: months (January-December), ordinate: one division = 10°C or 20 mm precipitation. a—station name, b—elevation in meters, c—duration of observation in years (the first figure indicates temperature, the second precipitation), d—highest recorded temperature in °C, e—mean daily maximum temperature of the warmest month, f—mean daily minimum temperature of the coldest month, g—lowest recorded temperature, h—curve of mean monthly temperature, i—mean annual temperature, j—mean annual precipitation in mm, k—line of 100 mm precipitation, l—curve of mean monthly precipitation, m—the relative humid season, n—months with mean daily minimum temperature below 0°C, o—months with absolute minimum below 0°C, p—mean duration of frost-free period in days (after Walter, 1973).

debris. Turf-bank terraces are mostly restricted to gentle south- and east-facing snow-accumulation slopes where snow provides a moisture supply; inactive sorted polygons occur at the western end of the ridge, while stone-bank terraces occur on relatively steep, south-southeast-facing slopes in lee situations (Benedict, 1970). The majority of these features appear to have developed in the upper western part of the ridge, and are probably associated with generally more moist conditions there. The orientation of turf-bank terraces and ponds is related to the dominant westerly winds. *Dryas*-banked terraces, found at the eastern end of the ridge, are oriented either parallel to or perpendicular to the local prevailing winter wind direction, whichever orientation most closely contours the slope (Benedict, 1970). Contemporary geomorphic activity in the Front Range appears to be very low (Caine, 1974).

Some Niwot Ridge soil profiles have been described by Osburn and Cline (in Soil Survey Staff, 1959) and Cline (in Soil Survey Staff, 1967). Komárková (1976, 1978) found mainly cryochrepts, cryorthents, cryofibrists, and cryaquents on interfluves in the Indian Peaks area. Mahaney (1970, 1974) and Mahaney and Fahey (1976) discuss Quaternary soil stratigraphy of the Front Range.

The treeline on Niwot Ridge is formed by *Picea engelmannii* Parry, *Abies lasiocarpa* (Hook.) Nutt., and *Pinus flexilis* James. Some aspects of the treeline in Colorado and on Niwot Ridge have been discussed by Wardle (1965, 1968, 1974), Löve *et al.* (1970), Lüllau (1974), Komárková (1976, 1978), Buckner (1977), Grant and Mitton (1977), and Ives (1977).

Weber (1965) emphasized the circumpolar and Asiatic relationships of the alpine flora in the southern Rocky Mountains, where the greatest concentration of circumpolar species at their southernmost limits is found. Komárková (1976, 1978) analyzed the alpine flora of the Indian Peaks area.

Osburn (1958) and Marr (1961) noted that wind and snow distribution, influencing the moisture supply, are major abiotic factors in determining the vegetation on Niwot Ridge. Webber (1972), D. C. E. May (1973), and Webber and D. E. May (1977) used ordination and nodal analysis to study the vegetation in the Saddle area. They found substrate moisture, snow cover, and substrate disturbance to be the major controlling environmental factors. Flock (1976, 1978) studied the influence of snow cover and soil moisture on bryophyte and lichen distribution on Niwot Ridge. D. C. E. May (1976) presented a map of the Saddle area based on the nodal analysis, and Keammerer (1976, unpublished; Figure 5) produced a vegetation map (1:80,000) of the ridge with the aid of color infrared aerial photographs. Komárková (1976, 1978) constructed the Braun-Blanquet vegetation unit hierarchy for the Indian Peaks area, including Niwot Ridge, and provided a description of its vegetation units. The vegetation on the ridge is somewhat disturbed by biotic factors; pocket gopher (*Thomomys talpoides fossor* Allen) activities are especially noticeable in the lower tundra regions on Niwot Ridge according to Osburn (1958), who also found areas where microtines grazed very heavily. Sheep grazing has occurred in the past.

METHODS

The vegetation units presented in Komárková (1976, 1978) served as a framework for the Niwot Ridge mapping units which represent the Braun-Blanquet syntaxa, mostly associations. Higher units were mapped both when the stands approximated an average species composition of a higher syntaxon and when the stands consisted of a mosaic of subordinated associations.

The standard Braun-Blanquet mapping method was used in the preparation of the map (e.g., Tüxen, 1963). The mapping was carried out in the field. In many cases it was necessary to generalize since only areas about

30 to 50 m in diameter could be represented cartographically at a scale of 1:10,000. The work on the map manuscript was considerably aided by the use of color aerial photographs. Black and white photographs, helpful in distinguishing small-scale vegetation units, were of little use in the unit differentiation at the detailed level employed in this study; Becking (1959) also made this observation. This is because black and white photographs reflect the percentage of vegetation cover rather than vegetation type in the low herbaceous vegetation of alpine tundra where rocks cover most of the nonvegetated surface;

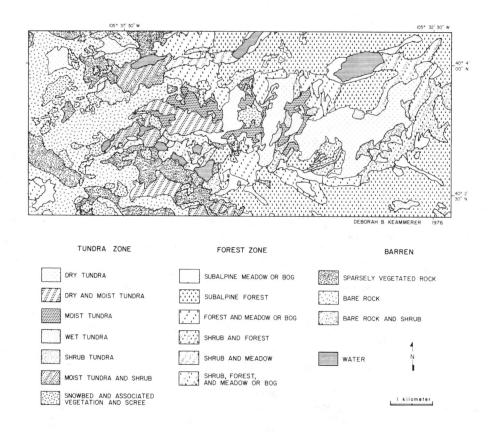

FIGURE 5. Niwot Ridge vegetation map produced by D. B. Keammerer in 1976. The initial photo interpretation for this map was done using NASA color infrared conventional aerial photography at a scale of
1:50,000 and a black and white copy of NASA color positive conventional aerial photography which was
enlarged to 1:17,000. The vegetation units were mapped primarily on the basis of color differences.
Almost all interpretation was done using the color infrared photography and the interpreted areas were
then transferred to a 1:24,000 U.S.G.S. topographic map and field checked. Figure 5 is approximately
1:80,000.

subtle color differences between various vegetation types are, on the other hand, quite apparent on a color photograph. Although
methods involving LANDSAT image analysis
(Hoffer and Staff, 1975) and color enhancing
of conventional black and white aerial photographs (Walker, 1977) were available, they
provided less information than the present
method (see also Morain, 1974).

The base map was redrawn from the U.S.
Geological Survey topographic maps
(1:24,000) and enlarged to 1:6,000 for the
production of the manuscript. The map was
contoured in meters by interpolation using
the U.S.G.S. base.

The manuscript copy for reproduction was

produced in three parts: black line and letter-
ing work; black vegetation unit boundaries;
and a full-color copy for the vegetation units.
The color copy was prepared using Pantone
color tint overlays (made by Letraset USA
Inc., Bergenfield, N. J. 07621) for four-color
separation. The map was reproduced by
photo-offset.

Colors for the vegetation units were selected
primarily to reflect the moisture regimes of
the habitats of the units. The sequence blue,
through green, to yellow and brown reflects
decreasing moisture. Red and purple were
used to indicate and emphasize vegetation in
areas of snow accumulation. These colors
proved more suitable for our large-scale map

of alpine vegetation than colors available in the international vegetation mapping system of Unesco (1973), although our colors do provide additional information about the environment of the mapping units.

Braun-Blanquet (1964) considers scales of 1:1,200, 1:5,000, or 1:20,000 suitable for representation of associations. Friedel (1956) found the scale of 1:5,000 large enough for mapping individual syntaxa. Our 1:10,000 scale was determined by the need for a field vegetation map of the widely used research area and by the production costs. For an accurate detailed vegetation map a larger scale would be necessary, perhaps 1:2,000, to accommodate the frequently small stands of associations in the alpine, which are limited by steep alpine environmental gradients.

The map area was divided into four sections: higher altitude–north slope, higher altitude–south slope, lower altitude–north slope, and lower altitude–south slope. When altitude alone was used as the basis for the altitudinal division, less vegetationally homogeneous map sections emerged than when the division was made on the basis of the distance from the Continental Divide which is located beyond the left map margin in the north-south direction. A north-south line through the Saddle area (3525 m s.m.) separates the higher western from the lower eastern section. Each map section was analyzed by planimetry (Tables 1 and 2). The area of each mapping unit in each section was cut out and weighed and percentage area of each calculated (the percentage weight is equivalent to percentage area). The mapping unit 22, coniferous krummholz and treeline, was omitted from this analysis because it does not constitute part of the alpine belt. The accuracy of the map (Switzer, 1971) was not computed. Because the map is based on field mapping, its accuracy is limited by the need to generalize to the smallest mappable area at the reproduction scale of 1:10,000.

The course of the treeline was analyzed by reading its elevation at 0.5-cm intervals on the map (50 m field distance). Resulting values, averaged for each section, were segregated into topographical categories (ridge, valley, snowpatch) and statistically treated. Since all differences in elevation between individual topographical categories and map sections were significant, the results of statistical significance tests are not presented (see Table 3).

MAP ANALYSIS

DESCRIPTION OF THE MAPPING UNITS
AND THEIR DISTRIBUTION

Short descriptions of each mapping unit follow. The Braun-Blanquet hierarchy system, which is outlined in the map legend, is presented in Komárková (1976, 1978) along with detailed descriptions of each syntaxon. The map and its planimetric analysis (Table 1) provided the basis for discussion of the spatial-environmental distribution of the mapped vegetation units.

Mapping unit 1: Association *Caricetum elynoidis* Willard 1963

The stands of this association, which belongs to the communities of well-drained habitats, are dominated by *Carex elynoides* Holm (Figure 6). It is one of the associations with the highest number of vascular species and a very poorly developed cryptogam layer. *Caricetum elynoidis* is close to *Trifolietum dasyphyllum* (mapping unit 3). Its habitats are usually warm, xeric, and snow covered in winter.

This mapping unit occurs only on the south slope at middle and higher altitudes. The total area of this unit is not extensive except for the south slope–higher altitude section.

Mapping unit 2: Alliance *Kobresio-Caricion rupestris* Komárková 1976 (except for *Dryadetum*)

This mapping unit includes communities of well-drained habitats, usually rich in lichens (Figure 7). It occurs predominantly on the ridge top in places where communities are either intermediate between the various associations of *Kobresio-Caricion rupestris* (except for *Dryadetum*) or constitute a mosaic of these communities which could not be mapped in detail. *Eritricho-Dryadetum octopetalae* was mapped separately (mapping units 5 and 7) because its distribution is distinctly limited.

This unit makes up the largest portion of the total map. High area percentages are found at lower altitudes, especially on the south slope, and very low area percentages occur in the higher altitude sections. Although this mapping unit contains stands with abundant *Kobresia myosuroides* (Vill.) Fiori & Paol. and small patches of drier stands of *Selaginello-Kobresietum*, its distribution contrasts with the distribution of *Selaginello-Kobresietum* (mapping unit 6) which is the only association of *Kobresio-Caricion rupestris* found in greater proportions at higher altitudes and on north slopes. The distribution of this mapping unit appears to be associated with xeric conditions at lower altitudes and on south-facing slopes.

Mapping unit 3: Association *Trifolietum dasyphyllum* Willard 1963

Communities of well-drained habitats in which *Trifolium dasyphyllum* T. & G. has a high cover, and which are related to *Caricetum elynoidis* (mapping unit 1) belong to this unit. These communities are rich in vascular species and poor in cryptogams and occur on well-stabilized subxeric sites which are usually snow covered in winter.

This unit has the largest area on the south slope at higher altitudes where the largest area of the related mapping unit 1, *Caricetum elynoidis,* is also found.

Mapping unit 4: Association *Sileno-Paronychietum* Willard 1963

This is a distinct fellfield association dominated by dicotyledonous cushion plants. It is found in extremely wind-exposed xeric habitats which are snow free in winter. Lichens predominate in the cryptogam layer and the number of vascular species is low (Figure 8).

FIGURE 6. *Caricetum elynoidis* (mapping unit 1). South slope of Niwot Ridge (3500 m s.m.).

Among the principal plants are *Paronychia pulvinata* A. Gray, *Trifolium nanum* Torr., *Lidia obtusiloba* (Rydb.) Löve & Löve, and *Silene acaulis* L. ssp. *subacaulescens* (F. N. Williams) C.L. Hitchc. & Maguire.

The occurrence of this association is limited to exposed ridge tops or summits oriented at right angles to the prevailing wind direction from the west.

FIGURE 7. Communities of the mapping unit 2, *Kobresio-Caricion rupestris* (except for *Dryadetum*). South slope of Niwot Ridge (3485 m s.m.).

TABLE 1

Areal extent and elevational and directional distribution of the map units [a]

Mapping unit	Higher altitude		Lower altitude		Altitude		Slope		Total map	Unit area (ha)
	North slope	South slope	North slope	South slope	Higher	Lower	North	South		
1. Association Caricetum elynoidis	0	17.02	0	0.80	7.62	0.40	0	6.34	3.05	21.31
2. Alliance Kobresio-Caricion rupestris (except for Dryadetum)	5.27	1.77	34.63	55.78	3.70	45.22	23.13	37.32	29.96	209.29
3. Association Trifolietum dasyphyllum	3.73	6.24	0.54	1.96	4.85	1.25	1.79	3.42	2.57	17.95
4. Association Sileno-Paronychietum	0.18	0	0.14	0.85	0.09	0.50	0.16	0.56	0.35	2.44
5. Association Eritricho-Dryadetum octopetalae	2.67	0	13.93	0.08	1.47	6.98	9.52	0.05	4.96	34.65
6. Association Selaginello-Kobresietum myosuroidis	21.67	19.47	19.19	16.63	20.68	17.90	20.15	17.60	18.92	132.12
7. Alliance Kobresio-Caricion rupestris and association Eritricho-Dryadetum octopetalae	0	0	16.04	0.46	0	8.22	9.75	0.30	5.20	36.32
8. Alliance Deschampsio-Trifolion parryi	32.07	27.45	2.69	2.95	30.00	2.82	14.18	11.32	12.81	89.48
9. Association Acomastylidetum rossii	4.38	6.46	5.64	3.93	5.31	4.78	5.15	4.79	4.98	34.79
10. Association Deschampsio-Trifolietum parryi	1.97	1.44	0.20	0.15	1.73	0.18	0.90	0.59	0.75	5.24
11. Association Stellario-Deschampsietum caespitosae	2.58	2.99	1.13	1.19	2.76	1.16	1.69	1.81	1.75	12.23
12. Association Vaccinietum scoparium-cespitosum	0.55	0	0.05	4.13	0.30	2.09	0.24	2.72	1.43	9.99
13. Association Solidagini-Danthonietum intermediae	0	0	0.32	0.77	0	0.55	0.20	0.51	0.35	2.44

TABLE 1 (cont.)

| | Map Section | | | | | | | | | |
| Mapping unit | Higher altitude | | Lower altitude | | Altitude | | Slope | | Total map | Unit area (ha) |
	North slope	South slope	North slope	South slope	Higher	Lower	North	South		
14. Order Sibbaldio-Caricetalia pyrenaicae	1.19	2.18	0.02	0.13	1.63	0.07	0.48	0.83	0.65	4.54
15. Association Toninio-Sibbaldietum	1.57	2.37	0.27	0.93	1.93	0.60	0.78	1.42	1.09	7.61
16. Association Caricetum pyrenaicae	1.01	0.65	0.17	0.43	0.85	0.30	0.50	0.50	0.50	3.49
17. Association Juncetum drummondii	0.88	0.47	0.17	1.50	0.70	0.84	0.45	1.15	0.79	5.52
18. Order Pedicularí-Caricetalia scopulorum	0	0.08	0.25	0.20	0.04	0.22	0.15	0.16	0.16	1.12
19. Association Caricetum scopulorum	2.49	2.69	2.98	1.52	2.58	2.24	2.78	1.92	2.37	16.56
20. Alliance Salicion`planifolio-villosae	5.89	3.84	1.63	5.30	4.97	3.47	3.30	4.80	4.02	28.08
21. Class Montio-Cardaminetea	0.27	0.25	0	0	0.26	0	0.11	0.09	0.10	0.70
23. Scree	11.64	4.65	0.09	0.32	8.51	0.20	4.61	1.80	3.25	22.70

[a] Mapping unit 22, Coniferous krummholz and treeline, has been omitted from this analysis.
Values in all but the last column are percentages of the mapped area; the last column gives area in ha.

Mapping unit 5: Association *Eritricho-Drya-detum octopetalae* Kiener 1939 corr. Komárková 1976

This association develops best on terraces formed by wind, frost action, and solifluction; its stands are dominated by *Dryas octopetala* L. ssp. *hookeriana* (Juz.) Hultén, in the cryptogam layer by lichens (Figure 9). It occurs in xeric, little-stabilized habitats, which have little snow cover in winter and where the soils have high percentage base saturation.

The stands of this mapping unit are concentrated on the north slope at lower altitudes close to the treeline, where also stands of the mapping unit 7, alliance *Kobresio-Caricion rupestris* and association *Eritricho-Dryadetum octopetalae,* have their highest area percentages. This distinct distribution, which is probably connected with edaphic conditions, is discussed in Komárková (1976, 1978) in more detail.

Mapping unit 6: Association *Selaginello-Kobresietum myosuroidis* Cox 1933 corr. Komárková 1976

Kobresia myosuroides dominates stands of this association and lichens predominate among cryptogams, especially in xeric habitats (Figure 10). More mesic stands are related to *Trifolio-Deschampsietalia.* The habitats are xeric to mesic, usually snow covered in winter and well stabilized. The best-developed stands are found in intermediate, mesic habitats.

FIGURE 8. *Sileno-Paronychietum* (mapping unit 4) on the south slope of Niwot Ridge (east of Martinelli's snowbank) in winter (3500 m s.m.).

This is the only association of well-drained habitats which has the highest percentage area at higher altitudes and on the north slope; this is probably related to higher habitat moisture in such situations. Stands of this association at higher altitudes occur on soli-

FIGURE 9. *Eritricho-Dryadetum octopetalae* (mapping unit 5). North slope of Niwot Ridge (3430 m s.m.).

FIGURE 10. *Selaginello-Kobresietum myosuroidis* (mapping unit 6). Niwot Ridge (3535 m s.m.).

fluction terraces. This mapping unit, with the second largest total area, shows a wide ecological amplitude.

Mapping unit 7: Alliance *Kobresio-Caricion rupestris* and association *Eritricho-Dryadetum octopetalae*

Stands of *Kobresio-Caricion rupestris* in which occurs *Dryas octopetala* ssp. *hookeriana* and mosaics of communities of this alliance and of *Eritricho-Dryadetum octopetalae* are included in this mapping unit. This unit was separated from the mapping unit 2, alliance *Kobresio-Caricion rupestris*, because the occurrence of *Dryas octopetala* ssp. *hookeriana* on Niwot Ridge is localized.

Like the mapping unit 5, association *Eritricho-Dryadetum octopetalae*, this mapping unit is practically limited to the north slope of the study area, where it occurs near the treeline. It includes stands combining mapping units 2 and 5 and, like these units, generally does not occur at higher altitudes.

Mapping unit 8: Alliance *Deschampsio-Trifolion parryi* Komárková 1976

Communities of snowpatches with prolonged snow cover which melts relatively early in the season are included here. These include mosaics of individual associations and intermediate stands. The principal habitats are earlier-melting snowpatches which are mesic and well stabilized.

This mapping unit shows the third highest area percentage for the total map; it covers the largest areas at higher altitudes of the north slope. All the individually mapped subordinated associations (mapping units 9 through 11) also have higher area percentages at higher altitudes and all, except for *Stellario-Deschampsietum caespitosae*, have higher area percentage on the north slope.

Mapping unit 9: Association *Acomastylidetum rossii* Willard 1963

Acomastylis rossii (R.Br.) Greene ssp. *turbinata* (Rydb.) W. A. Weber dominates the stands of this association; the cryptogam layer is poorly developed (Figure 11). *Acomastylidetum* is closely related to *Kobresio-Caricetalia rupestris*. Its habitats are mesic, more or less well stabilized, and with the shortest snow cover in *Deschampsio-Trifolion parryi*.

This association shows slightly higher area percentage at higher altitudes, but there is no obvious pattern in its distribution other than that it is related to depressions and snowpatches; it covers the largest areas in the middle part of the ridge.

Mapping unit 10: Association *Deschampsio-Trifolietum parryi* Komárková 1976

The communities of this mapping unit are dominated by *Trifolium parryi* A. Gray ssp. *parryi*. They occur in mesic to xeric snowpatch sites with early snowmelt, which are little to well stabilized. The snow cover lasts longer than in stands of *Acomastylidetum rossii*.

As with other associations of *Deschampsio-Trifolion parryi*, this mapping unit covers slightly larger area percentage on the north slope and at higher altitudes; it shows its smallest area percentage on the south slope at lower altitudes. The stands of this mapping unit are also associated with snowpatches.

Mapping unit 11: Association *Stellario-Deschampsietum caespitosae* Willard 1963 corr.

Komárková 1976

Deschampsia caespitosa (L.) Beauv. dominates the stands of this well-defined association; the cryptogam layer is poorly developed on account of the dense herb layer (Figure 12). Habitats are mesic, well stabilized, and belong to snowpatches which melt earlier in the season.

This mapping unit covers larger areas at higher altitudes but not on the north slope. Its stands are associated with snowpatches and depressions and they do not generally occur at lower altitudes.

Mapping unit 12: Association *Vaccinietum scoparium-cespitosum* Komárková 1976

The herb layer of the communities of this species-rich association is dominated by *Vaccinium scoparium* Leiberg and *V. cespitosum* Michx. A *Toninia* sp. is an important lichen in the cryptogam layer. This mapping unit and the related following mapping unit 13, association *Solidagini-Danthonietum intermediae*, belong to a different alliance of earlier-melting snowpatches, *Vaccinio-Danthonion intermediae*. The habitats of *Vaccinietum* are mesic to subxeric, more or less stabilized, and have substantial but earlier-melting snow cover.

This mapping unit is most widespread on the south slope at lower altitudes; it does not occur at higher altitudes. Like *Solidagini-Danthonietum*, *Vaccinietum* is most often found close to the treeline and close to snowpatches.

FIGURE 11. *Acomastylidetum rossii* (mapping unit 9). South slope of Niwot Ridge (3480 m s.m.).

Mapping unit 13: Association *Solidagini-Danthonietum intermediae* Komárková 1976

The stands of this mapping unit are domi-

FIGURE 12. *Stellario-Deschampsietum caespitosae* (mapping unit 11). Niwot Ridge (3650 m s.m.).

378

FIGURE 13. *Solidagini-Danthonietum intermediae* (mapping unit 13). Niwot Ridge (3470 m s.m.).

FIGURE 14. Order *Sibbaldio-Caricetalia pyrenaicae* (mapping unit 14). South slope of Niwot Ridge (3470 m s.m.).

nated by *Danthonia intermedia* Vasey. *Polytrichum piliferum* Hedw. can be an important cryptogam (Figure 13). This mapping unit is related to the preceding *Vaccinietum*, but occurs in more mesic habitats. The habitats are earlier-melting snowpatches, subxeric to mesic, and usually well stabilized.

The distribution of *Solidagini-Danthonietum* is very similar to the distribution of *Vaccinietum*; the largest area covered by this mapping unit occurs on the south slope at lower altitudes and it does not occur at higher altitudes. Its stands are usually associated with snowpatches.

Mapping unit 14: Order *Sibbaldio-Caricetalia pyrenaicae* Komárková 1976

This order includes the communities of later-melting snowpatches, both mosaics of stands of subordinated associations and, to a lesser degree than in other higher syntaxa, stands intermediate between them. Habitats are subxeric to subhygric, eroded to well-stabilized snowpatch centers with the latest-melting snow cover. Small stands of rare associations are mapped in this unit (Figure 14).

This mapping unit covers a relatively small area. It occurs, along with the three following subordinated associations, in snowpatch centers on east-oriented slopes; this is not reflected in the map analysis. Most of the later-melting snowpatch localities are found at middle altitudes. Communities of this mapping unit are most extensive on the south slope at higher altitudes.

Mapping unit 15: Association *Toninio-Sibbaldietum* Willard 1963

Sibbaldia procumbens L. dominates the stands of this association; *Polytrichum piliferum* can predominate in the cryptogam layer (Figure 15). *Toninio-Sibbaldietum* is related to the preceding order *Trifolio-Deschampsietalia* with which it sometimes forms intermediate stands. The habitats range from open, unstabilized, subxeric to stabilized, well vegetated, subhygric. The habitats always have later-melting snow cover.

The distribution of this mapping unit is similar to that of the preceding unit; it occurs

FIGURE 16. *Juncetum drummondii* (mapping unit 17). South slope of Niwot Ridge (3438 m s.m.).

FIGURE 15. *Toninio-Sibbaldietum* (mapping unit 15). South slope of Niwot Ridge, near Martinelli's snowbank (3560 m s.m.).

most extensively on the south slope at higher altitudes. It covers a larger area than any other association of *Sibbaldio-Caricetalia pyrenaicae* in later-melting snowpatches.

Mapping unit 16: Association *Caricetum pyrenaicae* Willard 1963

Stands included in this mapping unit are dominated by *Carex pyrenaica* Wahlenb.; the importance of cryptogams and bare soil varies. It is closely related to mapping unit 17, association *Juncetum drummondii*, with which it forms intermediate stands. The habitats of this association have the longest snow cover in *Sibbaldio-Caricion pyrenaicae*, are subxeric to mesic and little to well stabilized.

Also, this mapping unit covers larger areas in later-melting snowpatches at higher altitudes, but its areal extent on the north and south slopes is approximately the same. The distribution of *Juncetum drummondii* is somewhat different.

Mapping unit 17: Association *Juncetum drummondii* Willard 1963

Stands of this association are dominated by *Juncus drummondii* E. Meyer in Ledeb.; *Polytrichum piliferum* can be an important cryptogam (Figure 16). It has one of the highest vascular species numbers in *Sibbaldio-Caricion pyrenaicae*, and it is closely related to mapping unit 16, *Caricetum pyrenaicae*. The habitats are subxeric to mesic, little to more stabilized, and with shorter snow cover than the habitats of most other associations of *Sibbaldio-Caricion pyrenaicae*.

Juncetum drummondii has higher area percentages at lower altitudes and on the south slope. Its stands usually occur near the treeline, while stands of *Caricetum pyrenaicae* are best developed at higher altitudes.

Mapping unit 18: Order *Pediculari-Caricetalia scopulorum* Komárková 1976

All associations of marshes other than *Caricetum scopulorum*, which was mapped separately (mapping unit 19), are included here. Marshes usually do not form mosaics or intermediate stands as their development in the study area, except for *Caricetum scopulorum*, is limited. The habitats are mesic to hydric, little to well stabilized, and with early to moderately late snowmelt.

The communities of this order show considerably lower area percentages than do the communities of the separately mapped subordinated *Caricetum scopulorum*. They are most widespread at lower altitudes and on the north slope.

Mapping unit 19: Association *Caricetum scopulorum* Kiener 1939 em. Willard 1963

Carex scopulorum Holm var. *scopulorum* dominates the stands of this association; bryophytes can have high cover in some stands (Figure 17). *Caricetum scopulorum* has the highest number of vascular species in *Pediculari-Caricion scopulorum* and forms intermediate stands with *Deschampsio-Trifolion parryi* associations. The habitats are subhygric to subhydric, well stabilized, and with somewhat prolonged snow cover.

This mapping unit is most extensive on the north slope at lower altitudes, but there is not much difference between the south and north exposures at higher altitudes. Its stands occur in wet areas, especially below snowpatches and on solifluction terraces.

FIGURE 17. *Caricetum scopulorum* (mapping unit 19). North slope of Niwot Ridge near Lake Isabelle (3400 m s.m.).

Mapping unit 20: Alliance *Salicion planifolio-villosae* Komárková 1976

Willow shrub communities, which consist of stands dominated by *Salix planifolia* Pursh and *S. villosa* Hook. (= *S. glauca* auct.), and which are found above the alpine treeline, are included in this mapping unit (Figure 18). As tall herb communities are very poorly de-

FIGURE 18. Alliance *Salicion planifolio-villosae* (mapping unit 20) at the treeline on the south slope of Niwot Ridge (3450 m s.m.).

veloped in the study area, the mapping of *Salici-Trollietalia* was limited to willow stands. The habitats of *Salicion planifoliovillosae* are subxeric to subhygric, with varied lengths of snowmelt and are little to well stabilized. The composition of the understory varies mainly with the amount of moisture.

This mapping unit shows the highest area percentages on the north slope at higher altitudes and on the south slope at lower altitudes, which is perhaps associated with the largest scree slopes. Generally, its stands are found along the treeline and in krummholz islands, but they also occur on solifluction terraces at higher altitudes.

Mapping unit 21: Class *Montio-Cardaminetea* Br.-Bl. & Tx. 1943

The spring communities are very poorly developed in the study area and are, therefore, included in a higher syntaxon of the Braun-Blanquet hierarchy. *Primula parryi* A. Gray and *Saxifraga ondontoloma* Piper are the most important vascular plants in these stands and bryophytes usually have high cover. The habitats are subhydric to hydric, snow covered in winter and little to well stabilized.

This mapping unit is very rare on Niwot Ridge and mappable stands do not occur at lower altitudes which are on the whole more xeric. It is usually found near later-melting

snowpatches and its extent on the north and south slopes is similar.

Mapping unit 22: Coniferous krummholz and treeline

As mentioned earlier, the alpine treeline, which constitutes the lower boundary of the study area, is defined here as a tree species limit at which the tree species cover at least 25% of the surface area. Small tree and krummholz islands, surrounded by alpine communities, were mapped individually and not included in the treeline.

The cover values of the tree and krummholz islands were not included in the computation of the final percentages since they are not a part of the alpine belt (see Methods). They have the highest cover values on the south slope at lower altitudes and on the north slope at higher altitudes as does the mapping unit 20, alliance *Salicion planifoliovillosae.*

Mapping unit 23: Scree

This mapping unit includes surfaces with little or no vegetation, covered by scree of various origin. The upper limit of the study area is marked by scree. The highest area percentages for this mapping unit are found on both the north and south slopes at higher altitudes.

KEY TO MAPPING UNITS

These mapping units can be identified according to the following key. Similar keys were constructed by Brassard (1971) and Webber and Walker (1975). The present key is based on the species dominance, simple plant physiognomy and, occasionally, on the properties of the habitat.

1. a. Little or no vegetation cover . . . . Mapping unit 23
   b. At least 25% of vegetation cover 2
2. a. Tree species cover > 25% of surface . . . . Mapping unit 22
   Tree species cover ≤ 25% of surface 3
3. a. Shrubs present . . . . Mapping unit 20
   b. Shrubs absent 4
4. a. Lichens abundant 5
   b. Lichens rare 8
5. Class *Elyno-Seslerietea*, order *Kobresio-Caricetalia rupestris*
   a. *Carex elynoides* dominant . . . . Mapping unit 1
   b. *Carex elynoides* not dominant. 6
6. a. *Dryas octopetala* ssp. *hookeriana* dominant. . . . . Mapping unit 5
   b. *Dryas octopetala* ssp. *hookeriana* present but not dominant . . . . Mapping unit 7
   c. *Dryas octopetala* ssp. *hookeriana* absent 7

7. a. *Trifolium dasyphyllum* abundant .... Mapping unit 3
   b. Cushion dicotyledonous species abundant .... Mapping unit 4
   c. *Kobresia myosuroides* dominant .... Mapping unit 6
   d. None of the above .... Mapping unit 2
8. a. Communities of habitats with high moisture,
      bryophytes usually abundant 9
   b. Communities of snowpatch habitats, usually
      with low moisture, bryophytes rarely abundant 11
9. a. Marshes, water stagnant 10
   b. Springs, running water .... Mapping unit 21
10. Class *Scheuchzerio-Caricetea fuscae*
   a. *Carex scopulorum* var. *scopulorum* dominant .... Mapping unit 19
   b. Other species than *Carex scopulorum*
      var. *scopulorum* dominant .... Mapping unit 18
11. Class *Salicetea herbaceae*
   a. Vegetation cover usually closed, snowpatch margins 12
   b. Vegetation cover usually open, snowpatch centers 14
12. Order *Trifolio-Deschampsietalia*
   a. Communities dominated by *Vaccinium cespitosum*
      or *V. scoparium* .... Mapping unit 12
   b. *Danthonia intermedia* dominant .... Mapping unit 13
   c. Other species dominant .... Mapping unit 8 13
13. a. *Acomastylis rossii* ssp. *turbinata* dominant .... Mapping unit 9
   b. *Trifolium parryi* ssp. *parryi* dominant .... Mapping unit 10
   c. *Deschampsia caespitosa* dominant .... Mapping unit 11
14. Order *Sibbaldio-Caricetalia pyrenaicae*
   a. *Sibbaldia procumbens* dominant .... Mapping unit 15
   b. *Carex pyrenaica* dominant .... Mapping unit 16
   c. *Juncus drummondii* dominant .... Mapping unit 17
   d. Other species dominant .... Mapping unit 14

DISTRIBUTION OF HIGHER SYNTAXA AND ENVIRONMENTAL RELATIONSHIPS

Higher units of the Braun-Blanquet hierarchy also show clear differences in their cover in the different map sections (Table 2). Well-drained communities, *Kobresio-Caricetalia rupestris*, especially *Kobresio-Caricion rupestris*, have their largest extents at lower altitudes. Except for *Caricion foeneo-elynoidis*, the higher syntaxa of well-drained communities have similar area percentages for both south and north slopes; *Kobresio-Caricion rupestris*, which covers the largest area on the ridge of any alliance, shows somewhat higher values for the north slope. Snowpatches with *Salicetea herbaceae* show the next highest area percentage, especially the alliance of earlier-melting snowpatches, *Deschampsio-Trifolion parryi*, which has similar values for both north and south slopes. *Vaccinio-Danthonion intermediae* (also earlier-

melting snowpatches) is most widespread on the south slope at lower altitudes, while the communities belonging to later-melting snowpatches, *Sibbaldio-Caricetalia pyrenaicae*, show higher area percentages at higher altitudes. Marshes *Pediculari-Caricetalia scopulorum* do not show much difference in area among the various map sections. *Salici-Trollietalia*, tall herb and shrub communities, which are virtually limited to shrub communities in the study area, have their maximum extent on the north slope at higher altitudes and on the south slope at lower altitudes. Spring communities *Primulo-Cardaminetalia* are found only at higher altitudes.

It appears from the overall inspection of the map that both the distance from the Continental Divide and altitude, rather than altitude on its own, contribute to the control of the distribution of vegetation, of well-drained communities and earlier-melting snowpatches

TABLE 2

Areal extent and elevational and directional distribution of the higher Braun-Blanquet syntaxa[a]

Syntaxon	Map Section									
	Higher altitude		Lower altitude		Altitude		Slope		Total map	Unit area (ha)
	North slope	South slope	North slope	South slope	Higher	Lower	North	South		
Class *Elyno-Seslerietea*										
Order *Kobresio-Caricetalia rupestris*	33.52	44.50	84.47	76.56	38.41	80.47	64.50	65.59	65.01	454.08
Alliance *Caricion foeneo-elynoidis*	0	17.02	0	0.80	7.62	0.40	0	6.34	3.05	21.31
Alliance *Kobresio-Caricion rupestris*	33.52	27.48	84.47	75.76	30.79	80.07	64.50	59.28	61.96	432.77
Class *Salicetea herbaceae*	46.20	44.01	10.66	16.11	45.21	13.39	24.57	25.64	25.10	175.33
Order *Trifolio-Deschampsietalia*	41.55	38.34	10.03	13.12	40.10	11.58	22.36	21.74	22.07	154.17
Alliance *Deschampsio-Trifolion parryi*	41.00	38.34	9.66	8.22	39.80	8.94	21.92	18.51	20.29	141.74
Alliance *Vaccinio-Danthonion intermediae*	0.55	0	0.37	4.90	0.30	2.64	0.44	3.23	1.78	12.43
Order *Sibbaldio-Caricetalia pyrenaicae*	4.65	5.67	0.63	2.99	5.11	1.81	2.21	3.90	3.03	21.16
Class *Scheuchzerio-Caricetea fuscae*										
Order *Pediculari-Caricetalia scopulorum*	2.49	2.77	3.23	1.72	2.62	2.46	2.93	2.08	2.53	17.68
Class *Betulo-Adenostyletea*										
Order *Salici-Trollietalia*	5.89	3.84	1.63	5.30	4.97	3.47	3.30	4.80	4.02	28.08
Class *Montio-Cardaminetea*										
Order *Primulo-Cardaminetalia*	0.27	0.25	0	0	0.26	0	0.11	0.09	0.10	0.70

[a] Values in all but last column are percentages. The last column gives the area in ha.

in particular, along the combined (altitude and distance from the Continental Divide) environmental gradient on Niwot Ridge (see also Methods). The green (more mesophilous communities) and yellow-brown (more xerophilous communities) parts of the map are clearly separated this way rather than on the basis of altitude alone. This implies that the distance from the Continental Divide plays a role in the distribution of precipitation on Niwot Ridge; however, this factor cannot be separated from the available weather data (Barry, 1973) as direct evidence. The effects of wind and topography on the vegetation patterns can be illustrated best by the distribution of later-melting snowpatches (*Sibbaldio-Caricetalia pyrenaicae*). In general, the snowpatch occurrence seems to be little related to altitude and to be a function of the wind direction and topography, resulting in the redistribution of precipitation; later-melting snowpatches are found mainly on east-, southeast- and southwest-oriented slopes, in the lee of the dominant westerly winds. The distribution of several vegetation types, predominantly moisture-related communities, is associated with turf-bank terraces which occur mainly on the upper part of the ridge (Benedict, 1970).

Except for the two notable exceptions, *Caricetum elynoidis* and *Eritricho-Dryadetum,* the distribution of vegetation other than later-melting snowpatches appears to be in general related to the altitude—distance from the Continental Divide factor rather than to the slope orientation. This supports the contention that the distribution of moisture and snow, controlled by wind and topography, are the primary abiotic factors determining vegetation distribution on Niwot Ridge (Osburn, 1958; Marr, 1961; Webber, 1972; D. C. E. May, 1973; Komárková, 1976, 1978; Webber and D. E. May, 1977).

TREELINE

The average altitude for treeline on Niwot Ridge is 3406 m s.m. Along its course, the treeline appears to be little disturbed except for the effects of the approach jeep road and a burned area located on the south slope east of the road (Table 3). Predictably, treeline is higher by 45.8 m on the higher part of the ridge than in the lower part. The overall position of treeline on the south slope is lower than on the north slope by 18.8 m; this is also true for the lower altitudes (the difference there is 23.1 m). At higher altitudes the north slope shows lower treeline (by 28.9 m) than the south slope. Generally, the treeline should be higher where conditions are warmer and more continental (e.g., Ramaley, 1909; Brockmann-Jerosch, 1919; Lüdi, 1961). At higher altitudes treeline might be affected by the large monzonite scree on the north slope (which has and is probably lowering the treeline), or the slope orientation effect may be different from that at lower altitudes due to overall higher moisture; however, at lower altitudes the treeline should be higher on the south slope. The physiognomy of the treeline suggests that the factor causing its lower position on the south slope is the strong wind from the west; the wind-depressed treeline on the east slope of the Front Range was observed by Wardle (1965, 1968), Lüllau (1974), and Komárková (1976, 1978). Wind-formed krummholz forms can be much more often observed on the south slope than on the north slope (Figures 19, 20; see also Lüllau, 1974). A ribbon forest-krummholz pattern (Billings, 1969; Buckner, 1977) has developed on the north slope of the eastern end of the ridge.

The ridge, valley, and snowpatch values for the individual landforms for the total map show that the treeline is higher in valleys than on ridges by 26.6 m, which is probably connected with the protection of the treeline in the valleys from winds. That the treeline ascends higher on convex surfaces than on concave ones was observed in the Front Range by Wardle (1968); these results also agree well with the findings of Komárková (1976, 1978) for the cirque and ridge categories in the Indian Peaks area. On Niwot Ridge, snowpatches show the lowest treeline values of all landforms (41.9 m lower than the valleys). This is probably due to the prevention of tree development by a shortened growing season and in some cases due to associated high water tables. This pattern is evident in all map sections except for the north slope-higher altitude where the large scree slope affects the treeline position. The smallest differences between the three topographical categories occur on the south slope at lower altitudes (4.1 m), the largest on the north slope at higher altitudes (106.9 m).

TABLE 3
Evaluation of treeline position in various map sections

| | Higher altitude | | | | | |
| | North slope | | | South slope | | |
	Ridge	Valley	Snowpatch	Ridge	Valley	Snowpatch
Sample size	54	17	17	13	16	7
Mean m s.m.	3406.0	3512.9	3432.6	3466.5	3470.9	3421.4
Standard error of mean	6.7	7.7	7.7	6.3	6.3	10.3

| | Lower altitude | | | | | |
| | North slope | | | South slope | | |
	Ridge	Valley	Snowpatch	Ridge	Valley	Snowpatch
Sample size	83	42	34	76	29	69
Mean m s.m.	3412.3	3414.4	3377.9	3383.4	3384.5	3380.4
Standard error of mean	4.9	3.2	5.3	4.2	9.5	5.4

| | Higher altitude | | Lower altitude | |
	North slope	South slope	North slope	South slope
Sample size	87	36	159	174
Mean m s.m.	3430.8	3459.7	3405.5	3382.4
Standard error of mean	6.7	4.8	3.1	3.2

| | Altitude | | Slope | |
	Higher	Lower	North	South
Sample size	123	333	246	210
Mean m s.m.	3439.2	3393.4	3414.4	3395.6
Standard error of mean	5.4	2.4	3.4	3.65

| | Landform | | | |
	Ridge	Valley	Snowpatch	Total Map
Sample size	226	104	127	457
Mean m s.m.	3404.2	3430.8	3388.9	3406.0
Standard error of mean	3.1	5.6	3.9	2.4

DISCUSSION

The importance, purpose, and use of vegetation maps have been discussed by many authors (e.g., Tüxen, 1963; Küchler, 1967, 1973, 1974; Anderson, 1976; Webber *et al.*, 1976). The purpose of this map, besides providing a basic vegetation inventory, was to elucidate some vegetation-environment relationships in the study area. Comparable map analysis was, for example, carried out by Hesjedal (1975). The present map can also assist in the future management of the area, which is part of the Roosevelt National Forest. It can also serve as the ground truth for the production of smaller scale maps, based on remote-sensing imagery, of larger areas in the Front Range (e.g., Hoffer and Staff,

FIGURE 19. Krummholz on the south slope of Niwot Ridge.

FIGURE 20. Trees on the north slope of Niwot Ridge.

1975). Various uses of vegetation maps are enumerated by Küchler (1953). For instance, the present map could be of value to a zoologist; T. A. May (1975) mapped Niwot Ridge with respect to utilization by white-tailed ptarmigan. Secondary maps for special purposes such as, for example, terrain sensitivity and lichen cover (Webber and Walker, 1975; Everett *et al.*, 1978) also could be derived. Figure 21 shows a map of alpine soils on Niwot Ridge; it is partly based on the present 1:10,000 vegetation map. Correlation be-

tween soils and vegetation has been documented implicitly by many authors in the southern Rocky Mountains and also by Komárková (1976, 1978).

Despite the problems of comparing vegetation maps (Küchler, 1956), some comparisons can be made with other maps in the study area, based on different mapping units; comparisons with vegetation maps of other alpine areas can be made on the basis of the Braun-Blanquet classification. Fairly good agreement exists between the smaller scale

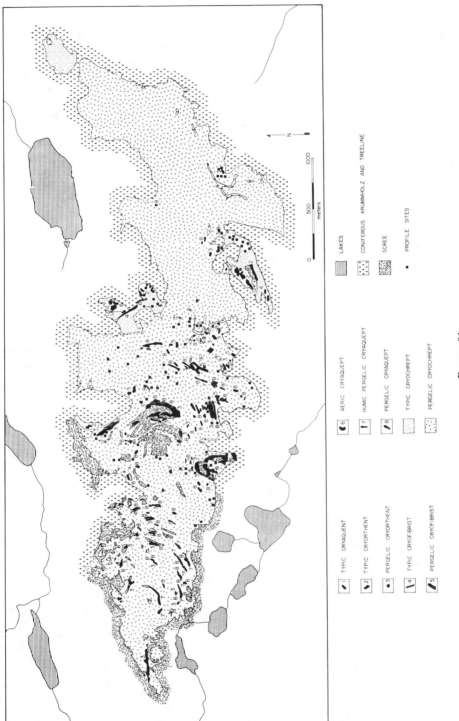

FIGURE 21.

(1:80,000) vegetation map of Keammerer (Figure 5) and the present map. Table 4 relates the noda distinguished by Webber (1972), D. C. E. May (1973), and Webber and D. E. May (1977), which were used as mapping units for the Saddle area on Niwot Ridge by D. C. E. May (1976), to the mapping units of the present map. D. C. E. May (1973) determined net aboveground vascular production for the noda; it is possible then to estimate approximate production values for the mapped Niwot Ridge alpine area. The net aboveground vascular productivity of the mapped alpine area is 1.725 ton

ha^{-1} yr^{-1} (172.5 g m^{-2} yr^{-1}); for herbaceous vegetation alone it is 1.665 ton ha^{-1} yr^{-1} (166.5 g m^{-2} yr^{-1}) and for woody vegetation (willow shrub) it is 0.060 ton ha^{-1} yr^{-1} (6.0 g m^{-2} yr^{-1}).

The Braun-Blanquet vegetation classification system was found very suitable for mapping and map analysis at this scale (1:10,000). Küchler (1967) pointed out that even though Braun-Blanquet considered his classification of vegetation not adapted to mapping except at very large scales, it has been demonstrated that it is feasible to employ this method also on maps of medium

TABLE 4

Correlation between the mapping units and noda of Webber (1972), D. C. E. May (1973), and Webber and D. E. May (1977).

Nodum	Mapping Unit
I. Moderately dry sedge meadow with a yearly snowfree period between 150 and 200 days, dominated by *Kobresia myosuroides, Selaginella densa,* and *Acomastylis rossii*	6 Association *Selaginello-Kobresietum myosuroidis*
II. Exposed dry fellfield with more than 200 snowfree days, dominated by *Trifolium dasyphyllum, Silene acaulis,* and *Carex rupestris*	3 Association *Trifolietum dasyphyllum* 4 Association *Sileno-Paronychietum*
III A. Moist shrub tundra, with a snowfree period of 100 to 150 days, dominated by *Salix planifolia*	20 Alliance *Salicion planifolio-villosae*
III B. Moist meadow with a snowfree period of 100 to 150 days, dominated by *Acomastylis rossii* and *Deschampsia caespitosa*	8 Alliance *Deschampsio-Trifolion parryi* 9 Association *Acomastylidetum rossii* 11 Association *Stellario-Deschampsietum caespitosae*
IV. Snowbank community with a snowfree period less than 75 days, dominated by *Sibbaldia procumbens* and *Carex pyrenaica*	14 Order *Sibbaldio-Caricetalia pyrenaicae* 15 Association *Toninio-Sibbaldietum* 16 Association *Caricetum pyrenaicae*
V. Wet meadow with a snowfree period approximately 100 days, dominated by *Caltha leptosepala* and *Carex scopulorum*	18 Order *Pediculari-Caricetalia scopulorum* 19 Association *Caricetum scopulorum*

FIGURE 21 (facing). Map of principal alpine soils on Niwot Ridge which was partly derived from the vegetation map. One hundred and five soil profiles were examined in the map area. In the areas with no profiles the soils were mapped according to their correlation with the vegetation and on the basis of field observations. The soil mapping units were named according to *Soil Taxonomy* (Soil Survey Staff, 1975); they are among the alpine soils recognized in the Indian Peaks area by Komárková (1976, 1978), who also presented profile descriptions representative for the Niwot Ridge soil mapping units and the properties of these profiles. The mean annual soil temperature at the station Niwot Ridge (3750 m s.m.) falls within the range of pergelic soils (mean annual soil temperature at 51 cm lower than 0°C) (Retzer, 1974, on the basis of data from Marr et al., 1968). The alpine soils descending below the usual treeline elevation were arbitrarily designated as typic since, in the absence of more detailed soil temperature measurements, it probably can be assumed that the mean annual temperature of these soils lies outside the range of pergelic soils (mean annual soil temperature at 51 cm lower than 0°C).

scale (1:100,000 to 1:1,000,000). There have been no problems in recognizing mapping unit boundaries; according to Friedel (1956), the gradient between phytocenoses is often much steeper than could be expected because they remain unchanged in a changing environment until a certain threshold value is passed (Küchler, 1973).

Areas of the higher syntaxa of the Braun-Blanquet hierarchy which consist of vegetation with an intermediate character and of vegetational mosaics are considerably larger than the areas of individual associations. This topic was discussed by Friedel (1956) and others. The intergradation of vegetation types usually involves associations of the same alliance, seldom orders or classes. In this sense, a multidimensional (but not spatial) continuum exists on Niwot Ridge among units of *Kobresio-Caricion rupestris* or *Deschampsio-Trifolion parryi*, reflecting moderate environmental gradients in the habitats of well-drained communities. Braun-Blanquet (1964) wrote that higher units (alliances, orders, classes) can be shown on small scale maps but that the vegetation corresponding to orders (excluding the vegetation corresponding to the subordinated syntaxa—alliances and associations) covers only very small areas. On the Niwot Ridge map the mapping units which encompass an order or class (*Montio-Cardaminetea,* *Sibbaldio-Caricetalia pyrenaicae* and *Pediculari-Caricetalia scopulorum*) have very small extent and include small stands of individual associations which have not been mapped separately. Alliances, on the other hand, cover the largest areas on the map and include stands intermediate between the subordinated associations. McVean and Ratcliffe (1962) in the Scottish Highlands and Oberdorfer (1968) in Germany observed that mixed vegetation may cover larger areas and be more important than the units they distinguished. Ellenberg (1963) pointed out that continuous transitions between various vegetation patches are more common than pure communities in the alpine belt, and that both at higher and lower altitudes the communities of extreme habitats are better characterized than those growing under average conditions. The latter often predominate in large areas.

ACKNOWLEDGMENTS

Map survey and drafting were supported by NSF grant GV-29350 (U.S. IBP Tundra Biome). NASA imagery was supplied by grant NGL 06-003-200. Map printing costs were supplied by a grant from Colorado University Scholarly Publication (CUSP) committee.

The base map was originally drawn by C. R. Grounds, York University, Toronto. Lois Perkins, Marilyn Joel, and Vicki Dow drafted the map; Vicki Dow prepared the color copy and drafted Figures 2, 3, 4, and 5. Kathleen Salzberg helped with the final editing of the map. Frederic Printing, Denver, Colorado, printed the map. We are indebted to Deborah B. Keammerer for the permission to use her map in Figure 5. Ken Bowman carried out the map analysis and calculations and drafted Figure 21. Dr. Jack D. Ives kindly supplied the color aerial photographs used in the study and Figure 1. Also, he made several useful suggestions during text preparations.

REFERENCES CITED

Alexandrova [Aleksandrova], V. D., 1970: The vegetation of the tundra zones in the USSR and data about its productivity. *In* Fuller, W. A. and Kevan, P. G. (eds.), *Productivity and Conservation in Northern Circumpolar Lands.* Int. Union Conserv. Natur., Morges, Switzerland, Publ. N.S. 16, 93-114.

Aleksandrova, V. D., 1971: Printsipy zonal'nogo deleniya rastitel'nosti Arktiki [The principles of zonal subdivision of arctic vegetation]. *Bot. Zh.,* 56: 3-21.

Anderson, J. H., 1976: Research needs in descriptive vegetation science in Alaska with special regard for land-use planning and management. *In* Evans, M. N. (ed.), *Proceedings of the Surface Protection Seminar, January 19-22, 1976, Anchorage, Alaska.* U.S. Department of the Interior, Bureau of Land Management, Alaska State Office, 214-231.

Barry, R. G., 1972: Climatic environment of the east slope of the Colorado Front Range. *Inst. Arct. Alp. Res., Univ. Colo., Occas. Pap.,* 3. 206 pp.

———, 1973: A climatological transect on the east slope of the Front Range, Colorado. *Arct. Alp. Res.,* 5: 89-110.

390

Becking, R. W., 1959: Forestry applications of aerial color photography. *Photogramm. Eng.*, 25: 559-565.

Benedict, J. B., 1970: Downslope soil movement in a Colorado alpine region: rates, processes, and climatic significance. *Arct. Alp. Res.*, 2: 165-226.

Billings, W. D., 1969: Vegetational pattern near alpine timberline as affected by fire-snowdrift interaction. *Vegetatio*, 19: 192-207.

Brassard, G. R., 1971: The mosses of northern Ellesmere Island, Arctic Canada. I. Ecology and phytogeography, with an analysis for the Queen Elizabeth Islands. *Bryologist*, 74: 233-311.

Braun-Blanquet, J., 1964: *Pflanzensoziologie, Grundzüge der Vegetationskunde*. 3 ed. Springer, Vienna and New York. 865 pp.

Brockmann-Jerosch, H., 1919: Baumgrenze und Klimacharakter. *Beitr. geobot. Landesaufn. Schweiz*, Zürich, 6. 255 pp.

Buckner, D. L., 1977: Ribbon forest development and maintenance in the central Rocky Mountains of Colorado. Ph.D. thesis, University of Colorado, Boulder, Colorado. 224 pp.

Caine, N., 1974: The geomorphic processes of the alpine environment. *In* Ives, J. D. and Barry, R. G. (eds.), *Arctic and Alpine Environments*. Methuen, London, 721-748.

Cox, C. F., 1933: Alpine plant succession on James Peak, Colorado. *Ecol. Monogr.*, 3: 299-372.

Ellenberg, H., 1963: *Vegetation Mitteleuropas mit den Alpen in kausaler, dynamischer und historischer Sicht. In* Walter, H. (ed.), *Einführung in die Phytologie*. Vol. IV, *Grundlagen der Vegetationsgliederung*. Pt. 2. Ulmer, Stuttgart. 943 pp.

Everett, K. R., Webber, P. J., Walker, D. A., Parkinson, R. J., and Brown, J., 1978: A geoecological mapping scheme for Alaskan coastal tundra. Unpublished manuscript to be presented at the Third International Conference on Permafrost, Edmonton, Alberta, July 10-13, 1978.

Flock, J. W., 1976: The influence of snow cover and soil moisture on bryophyte and lichen distribution, Niwot Ridge, Boulder County, Colorado. Ph.D. thesis, University of Colorado, Boulder. 168 pp.

———, 1978: Lichen-bryophyte distribution along a snow cover-soil moisture gradient, Niwot Ridge, Colorado. *Arct. Alp. Res.*, 10: 31-47.

Friedel, H., 1956: *Die alpine Vegetation des obersten Mölltales (Hohe Tauern)*. Wagner, Innsbruck. 153 pp.

Gable, D. J. and Madole, R. F., 1976: *Geologic Map of the Ward Quadrangle, Boulder County, Colorado*. U.S. Geological Survey. 1:24,000. Map 6Q-1277.

Grant, M. C. and Mitton, J. B., 1977. Genetic differentiation among growth forms of Engelmann spruce and subalpine fir at tree line. *Arct. Alp. Res.*, 9: 259-263.

Hämet-Ahti, L., 1965: Notes on the vegetation zones of Western Canada, with special reference to the forests of Wells Gray Park, British Columbia. *Ann. Bot. Fenn.*, 2: 274-300.

Hare, F. K., 1959: A photo-reconnaissance survey of Labrador-Ungava. *Geogr. Branch, Mines and Technical Surveys*, Ottawa, *Mem.* 6. 83 pp.

Hermes, K., 1955: Die Lage der oberen Waldgrenze in den Gebirgen der Erde und ihr Abstand zur Schneegrenze. *Kölner geogr. Abhandl.*, 5. 277 pp.

Hesjedal, O., 1975: Vegetation mapping at Hardangervidda. *In* Wielgolaski, F. E. (ed.), *Fennoscandian Tundra Ecosystems Part I: Plants and Microorganisms*. Springer, New York, 74-81.

Hoffer, R. M. and Staff, 1975: *An Interdisciplinary Analysis of Colorado Rocky Mountain Environments Using ADP Techniques*. Laboratory for Applications of Remote Sensing LARS/Purdue University, West Lafayette, Indiana, Res. Bull. 919 (LARS Info. Note 061575). 124 pp.

Höllermann, P., 1964: Rezente Verwitterung, Abtragung und Formenschatz in den Zentralalpen am Beispiel des oberen Suldentales (Ortlergruppe). *Z. Geomorph., N.F. Suppl.*, 4: 1-257.

Ives, J. D., 1973: Permafrost and its relationship to other environmental parameters in a midlatitude, high-altitude setting, Front Range, Colorado Rocky Mountains. *In: Permafrost, North American Contribution to the Second International Permafrost Conference, Yakutsk, USSR*, U.S. National Academy of Sciences, Washington, D. C., 121-125.

———, 1977: Remarks on the stability of timberline. *In: Erdwissenschaftliche Forschung*. Franz Steiner, Wiesbaden (in press).

Ives, J. D. and Fahey, B. D., 1971: Permafrost occurrence in the Front Range, Colorado Rocky Mountains, USA. *J. Glaciol.*, 10: 105-111.

Joint Federal-State Land Use Planning Commission for Alaska. 1973. Major ecosystems of Alaska [map].

Keammerer, D. B., 1976: Niwot Ridge vegetation map 1:24,000. Unpublished manuscript on file at Institute of Arctic and Alpine Research, University of Colorado, Boulder, Colorado 80309.

Kiener, W., 1939: Sociological studies of the alpine vegetation on Longs Peak. Ph.D. thesis,

University of Nebraska, Lincoln, Nebraska. 68 pp. *In: Univ. Nebr. Stud. N.S.*, 34, 1967. 75 pp.

Komárková, V., 1976: Alpine vegetation of the Indian Peaks area, Front Range, Colorado Rocky Mountains. Ph.D. thesis, University of Colorado, Boulder, Colorado. 655 pp.

——, 1978: *Alpine Vegetation of the Indian Peaks Area, Front Range, Colorado Rocky Mountains.* Tüxen, R. (ed.), *Flora et Vegetatio Mundi.* Cramer, Vaduz (in press).

Küchler, A. W., 1953: Some uses of vegetation maps. *Ecology*, 34: 629-636.

——, 1956: Classification and purpose in vegetation maps. *Geogr. Rev.*, 46: 155-167.

——, 1967: *Vegetation Mapping.* Ronald Press, New York. 472 pp.

——, 1973: Problems in classifying and mapping vegetation for ecological regionalization. *Ecology*, 54: 512-523.

——, 1974: A new vegetation map of Kansas. *Ecology*, 55: 586-604.

Lavrenko, E. M. and Sochava, V. B. (eds.), 1956: *Rastitel'nyi pokrov SSSR* [Vegetation cover of the USSR]. Akad. nauk SSSR, Moscow-Leningrad. 971 pp.

Long, G., 1969: Perspectives nouvelles de la cartographie biogéographique végétale intégrée. *Vegetatio*, 18: 44-63.

Löve, A., 1975: Personal communication. 5780 Chandler Court, San Jose, California 95123.

Löve, D., 1970: Subarctic and subalpine: where and what? *Arct. Alp. Res.*, 2: 63-73.

Löve, D., McLellan, C., and Gamow, I., 1970: Coumarin and coumarin derivates in various growth-types of Engelmann spruce. *Svensk bot. Tidskr.*, 64: 284-296.

Lüdi, W., 1961: Botanische Streifzüge durch die Rocky Mountains Nordamerikas. *Veröff. geobot. Inst. Rübel*, Zürich, 32: 217-236.

Lüllau, I., 1974: Studien und Beobachtungen zum Landschaftsgefüge in der östlichen Front Range, Colorado. Staatsarbeit in Geographie, Münster. 120 pp.

Mahaney, W. C., 1970: Soil genesis on deposits of Neoglacial and late Pleistocene age in the Indian Peaks of the Colorado Front Range. Ph.D. thesis, University of Colorado, Boulder. 246 pp.

——, 1974: Soil stratigraphy and genesis of Neoglacial deposits in the Arapaho and Henderson cirques, Central Colorado Front Range. *In* Mahaney, W. C. (ed.), *Quaternary Environments: Proceedings of a Symposium.* Geographical Monographs 5, York University Series in Geography, 197-240.

Mahaney, W. C. and Fahey, B. D., 1976: Quater-

nary soil stratigraphy of the Front Range, Colorado. *In* Mahaney, W. C. (ed.), *Quaternary Stratigraphy of North America.* Dowden, Hutchinson, Ross, Stroudsburg, Pennsylvania, 319-352.

Marr, J. W., 1961: Ecosystems of the east slope of the Front Range in Colorado. *Univ. Colo. Stud., Ser. Biol.*, 8. 134 pp.

Marr, J. W., Clark, J. M., Osburn, W. S., and Paddock, M. W., 1968: Data on mountain environments. III. Front Range, Colorado, four climax regions, 1959-64. *Univ. Colo. Stud., Ser. Biol.*, 29. 181 pp.

May, D. C. E., 1973: Models for predicting composition and production of alpine tundra vegetation from Niwot Ridge, Colorado. M.A. thesis, University of Colorado, Boulder, Colorado. 99 pp.

——, 1976: The response of alpine tundra vegetation in Colorado to environmental variation. Ph.D. thesis, University of Colorado, Boulder, Colorado. 164 pp.

May, T. A., 1975: Physiological ecology of white-tailed ptarmigan in Colorado. Ph.D. thesis, University of Colorado, Boulder, Colorado. 311 pp.

McVean, D. N. and Ratcliffe, D. A., 1962: *Plant Communities of the Scottish Highlands.* Monographs of Nature Conservancy 1, Her Majesty's Stationery Office, London. 445 pp.

Morain, S. A., 1974: Interpretation and mapping of natural vegetation. *In* Estes, J. E. and Senger, L. W. (eds.), *Remote Sensing.* Hamilton Publishing Company, Santa Barbara, California, 127-165.

Oberdorfer, E., 1968: Assoziation, Gebietsassoziation, Geographische Rasse. *In* Tüxen, R. (ed.), *Pflanzensoziologische Systematik, Bericht über das 8. internationale Symposion in Stolzenau/Weser 1964 der internationalen Vereinigung für Vegetationskunde.* Junk, The Hague, 124-131.

Ontario Department of Lands and Forests, Lands and Surveys Branch, 1969: *Vegetation Patterns of the Hudson Bay Lowlands North of the 52nd Parallel in the Province of Ontario.* (Originally described by Brokx, P. and modified by Bates, D. N. and Simkin, D.) Map 3269.

Osburn, W. S., Jr., 1958: Ecology of winter snow-free areas of the alpine tundra of Niwot Ridge, Boulder County, Colorado. Ph.D. thesis, University of Colorado, Boulder, Colorado. 77 pp.

Ramaley, F. 1909. The silva of Colorado. IV. Forest formations and forest trees. *Colo. Univ. Stud.*, 6: 249-281.

Retzer, J. L., 1974: Alpine soils. *In* Ives, J. D. and Barry, R. G. (eds.), *Arctic and Alpine Environ-*

392

ments. Methuen, London, 771-802.

Rowe, J. S., 1959: *Forest Regions of Canada.* Canada Department of Northern Affairs and National Resources. Forestry Branch. Bulletin 123. Ottawa. 71 pp.

Soil Survey Staff, 1959: *Lincoln Soil Survey Laboratory Report for Selected Soil Samples (1957) from Alpine Areas of Colorado.* U.S. Dept. of Agric., Soil Survey Laboratory, Soil Conserv. Service. Lincoln, Nebraska

—— , 1967: *Soil Survey Laboratory Data and Descriptions for Some Soils of Colorado. Soil Survey Investigations Rep.* No. 10. U.S. Dept. of Agric. and Colorado Agric. Exp. Station.

—— , 1975: *Soil Taxonomy: A Basic System of Soil Classification for Making and Interpreting Soil Surveys.* Soil Conserv. Service, U.S. Dept. of Agric. Handbook, 436. 754 pp.

Switzer, P., 1971: Mapping a geographically correlated environment. *In* Patil, G. P., Pielou, E. C., and Waters, W. E. (eds.), *Statistical Ecology.* Vol. 1. Penn. State Univ. Press, Univ. Park, Pennsylvania, 235-267.

Tüxen, R. (ed.), 1963: *Bericht über das internationale Symposion für Vegetationskartierung vom 23.-26. 3. 1959 in Stolzenau/Weser.* Cramer, Weinheim. 500 pp.

Unesco, 1973: *International Classification and Mapping of Vegetation.* Unipub, New York. 93 pp.

Walker, D. A., 1977: The analysis of the effectiveness of a television scanning densitometer for indicating geobotanical features in an ice-wedge polygon complex at Barrow, Alaska. M.A. thesis, University of Colorado, Boulder, Colorado. 129 pp.

Walter, H. 1973. *Vegetation of the Earth.* Springer, New York. 237 pp.

Walter, H. and Lieth, H., 1967: *Klimadiagramm-Weltatlas.* Gustav Fischer, Jena.

Wardle, P., 1965: Comparison of alpine timber lines in New Zealand and North America. *N. Z. J. Bot.,* 3: 113-135.

—— , 1968: Engelmann spruce (*Picea engelmannii* Engel.) at its upper limits on the Front Range, Colorado. *Ecology,* 49: 483-495.

—— , 1974: Alpine timberlines. *In* Ives, J. D. and Barry, R. G. (eds.), *Arctic and Alpine Environments.* Methuen, London, 371-402.

Webber, P. J., 1972: Comparative ordination and productivity of tundra vegetation. *In* Bowen, S. (ed.), *Proceedings 1972 U.S. Tundra Biome Symposium, Lake Wilderness Center, University of Washington, July 1972.* U.S. Tundra Biome, U.S. International Biological Program and U.S. Arctic Research Program, 55-60.

Webber, P. J. and May, D. E., 1977. The distribution and magnitude of belowground plant structures in the alpine tundra of Niwot Ridge, Colorado. *Arct. Alp. Res.,* 9: 155-166.

Webber, P. J. and Walker, D. A., 1975: Vegetation and landscape analysis at Prudhoe Bay, Alaska: A vegetation map of the Tundra Biome study site. *In* Brown, J. (ed.), *Ecological Investigations of the Tundra Biome in the Prudhoe Bay Region, Alaska.* Biological Papers of the University of Alaska, Spec. Rep. 2: 81-91.

Webber, P. J., Walker, D. A., and Komárková, V., 1976: Large scale mapping of Alaskan tundra vegetation. *In: Science in Alaska, Proceedings 27th Alaska Science Conference,* 1: 224-225.

Weber, W. A., 1965: Plant geography in the Southern Rocky Mountains. *In* Wright, H. E., Jr. and Frey, D. G. (eds.), *The Quaternary of the United States.* Princeton University Press, Princeton, N.J., 453-468.

Westhoff, V. and van der Maarel, E., 1973: The Braun-Blanquet approach. *In* Tüxen, R. (ed.), *Handbook of Vegetation Science.* Part 5, Whittaker, R. H. (ed.), *Ordination and Classification of Communities.* Junk, The Hague, 617-726.

Willard, B. E., 1963: Phytosociology of the alpine tundra of Trail Ridge, Rocky Mountain National Park, Colorado. Ph.D. thesis, University of Colorado, Boulder, Colorado. 245 pp.

ADAPTATIONS AND ORIGINS OF ALPINE PLANTS*

W. D. BILLINGS

*Department of Botany
Duke University
Durham, North Carolina 27706*

ABSTRACT

Alpine environments are characterized by short, cold, unpredictable growing seasons. Outside of the Arctic this growing season is characterized by cold nights as well. Alpine plant adaptations are much like those of the Arctic in morphological and physiological characteristics. However, they appear to acclimate metabolically to changes in temperature more easily than do arctic ecotypes. In fact, almost all representatives of arctic-alpine species are ecotypically different from their congeners in the Arctic. This is particularly true in reproduction and metabolism, the real heart of adaptation to cold alpine environments.

While there are relatively ancient alpine plant taxa, the accelerated rise of new mountain ranges in late Pliocene and Pleistocene times has led to new floristic aggregations in alpine vegetations by migration and adaptive radiation. Fluctuations in Pleistocene glaciations have alternately allowed migrations and blocked them. Interglacial refugia may be more important than glacial refugia in consolidating evolutionary changes in alpine taxa which evolve in response to decreasing temperatures, increasing light intensities, and in some cases to increasing drought stress.

INTRODUCTION

Except on equatorial mountains, vegetational mosaics of arctic and alpine areas show many resemblances to each other. Even the vegetation of polar deserts has its counterparts in arid high elevations such as the White Mountains of eastern California. In the Northern Hemisphere, there also is considerable overlap in the floras of arctic and alpine regions. At least 500 of the ca. 1,000 vascular plant species of the Arctic occur to some extent in alpine regions farther south. Alpine representatives of these arctic-alpine species are almost always ecotypically or ecoclinally different from their congeners in the Arctic. This is due partly to isolation and evolution during the glacial phases of the Pleistocene. These ecotypes also reflect rather marked differences in arctic and alpine environments. In fact, the uniqueness, isolation, and diversity of high mountain environments has resulted in the total alpine flora of the Northern Hemisphere being many times richer than the arctic flora. If the high elevation floras of the equatorial and Southern Hemisphere mountains are added to those of North America and Eurasia, the total alpine flora of the earth is very large as compared to that of the Arctic.

This paper is addressed to two questions:

(1) How do alpine plants meet the challenges presented by cold, short growing seasons at high elevations?
(2) From what sources have alpine floras and vegetations been derived by migrations and evolution?

The answers to the first question, while far from complete, are easier to obtain because the problems are subject to quantitative observation and experimentation in the field and in the laboratory. While there is much information

---

*Presented at "The Alpine Biota" symposium at the First International Congress of Systematic and Evolutionary Biology, Boulder, Colorado, August 7, 1973.

394

available to help answer the second question, it is far more difficult because of its complexity and the fact that most of the substantiation depends upon past events. Because of this situation and the almost total lack of fossils of alpine plants, the question of origin has been the subject of considerable speculation and hypothesis. Until recently, most of the evidence has come from cytotaxonomic studies.[1]

While answers to either question will vary somewhat from taxon to taxon and from one mountain range to another, it should be remembered that no individual or local population of a species lives and evolves in isolation from other organisms and the alpine environment. Answers must be reached in the context of whole alpine ecosystems whether the substantiating data are derived from field observations and experiments or from the laboratory.

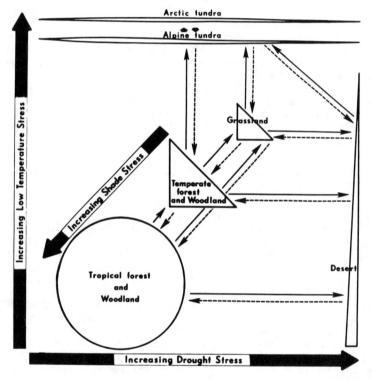

FIGURE 1. Diagrammatic representation of migratory and evolutionary pathways leading to the formation of alpine floras and vegetation. Solid lines indicate the direction of principal gene flow. Dashed lines indicate possible back flow. The large arrows denote increasing environmental stresses.

LICHEN-BRYOPHYTE DISTRIBUTION ALONG A SNOW-COVER-SOIL-MOISTURE GRADIENT, NIWOT RIDGE, COLORADO

JoAnn W. Flock

Department of Environmental, Population, and Organismic Biology
University of Colorado
Boulder, Colorado 80309

ABSTRACT

Although a number of snow-cover-soil-moisture plant distribution studies have been carried out in the Front Range of the Rocky Mountains of the United States, the emphasis of such studies has been on vascular plants, and lichens and bryophytes have received little attention. Bryophytes and lichens are seldom a conspicuous element of the plant community above timberline in the Front Range. They rarely form large masses but usually exist as small individual specimens hidden by the canopy of vascular plants or plant litter and are often overlooked or ignored.

A study was made of the percentage cover and abundance of 92 lichen taxa and 39 bryophyte taxa in 42 stands in a 1-km² area in the lower alpine zone of Niwot Ridge in the Colorado Front Range. The percentage of total area covered by individual species was seldom very high, but taken collectively the cover of lichens and bryophytes combined averaged 38%.

Species Index values for all individual lichen and bryophyte taxa in each of the 42 stands were calculated by comparing frequency and percentage cover of each lichen and bryophyte in a stand with the total lichen and bryophyte frequency and cover in the stand. The Species Index value for each lichen and bryophyte was then plotted against a gradient of snow cover and surface soil moisture. As a group, bryophytes appeared to have a wider range of distribution across the gradient but reached their highest Species Index values in the wet sites with deep, late-lying snow cover. Species Indices for individual lichens reached the highest values in moist sites with moderate snow cover, but a large number of lichen species with low Species Index values occurred in the low-snow-cover dry-soil portion of the gradient.

The largest number of lichen taxa (51%) was found on rock substrates while no bryophytes occurred on rock. Saxicolous lichens covered 0.7 of the available rock substrate in areas of little snow cover, 0.4 where snow cover was moderate, and none in areas of deep snow accumulation. Fifteen species of lichens were found on *Selaginella densa* detritus and their presence was restricted to the dry sites with little snow cover where *Selaginella densa* grew. The crustose growth form was the most common lichen growth form (accounting for 66% of all lichens). Acrocarpous mosses were most abundant in dry areas with light snow cover, while pleurocarpous mosses were most abundant in wet sites with deep snow cover. Few liverworts were found in the study area.

Arctic and Alpine Research, Vol. 10, No. 1, 1978, pp. 31-47.

FIELD MEASUREMENTS OF PHOTOSYNTHESIS AND LEAF GROWTH RATES OF THREE ALPINE PLANT SPECIES

Douglas A. Johnson and Martyn M. Caldwell

*Department of Range Science
and the Ecology Center
Utah State University
Logan, Utah 84322*

ABSTRACT

Leaf photosynthetic measurements using a portable $^{14}CO_2$ field system were carried out and leaf relative growth rates, R_l, were determined at different leaf positions of three alpine plant species throughout the growing season. Initially there was a period of high R_l associated with a period of high or increasing photosynthetic activity. Following this stage was a long period of no net change in length of the living leaf with photosynthetic activity eventually exhibiting a steady decrease. The final ontogenetic stage was a period of negative R_l denoting leaf senescence which was associated with a marked decline in leaf CO_2 uptake. Ontogenetic timing of these alpine species is geared with the surge and decline of individual leaf photosynthetic activity so that one to several leaves operating at near maximal photosynthetic capacity for existing conditions are always maintained during the growing season for each plant.

INTRODUCTION

Photosynthesis of individual leaves increases after leaf emergence, levels off before or after full leaf expansion, and declines with leaf senescence. This pattern has become apparent from field CO_2 uptake studies done for individual leaves of agricultural species (Beuerlein and Pendleton, 1971; Turner and Incoll, 1971). In alpine areas where the growing season is short and relatively severe, field photosynthesis measurements of whole plants have been carried out (e.g., Scott and Billings, 1964; Moser, 1973). Information on the relationship between photosynthesis and growth in individual leaves may lead to a better understanding of how alpine plants cope with their harsh environment. The present study with three major alpine tundra species investigated the field photosynthetic response of individual leaves at several leaf positions and correlated this response with the seasonal progressions of leaf growth rate during the alpine growing season.

METHODS

Leaf photosynthetic measurements were determined using a portable $^{14}CO_2$ field system. The field system and procedure have been described by Tieszen *et al.* (in press). The field system consists of a plexiglass leaf chamber which is temperature controlled by a Peltier thermoelectric stage. The procedure involves exposing an intact leaf to a $^{14}CO_2$ air mixture, immediately cooling the leaf sample in the field following exposure, subsequent drying of the exposed leaf sample, combusting this sample, and radioactivity counting using liquid scintillation techniques.

According to studies by Ludwig and Canvin (1971), net $^{14}CO_2$ uptake in a leaf is maximum at exposure periods less than 30 sec. This initial period approximates gross CO_2 influx. After 30 sec, net CO_2 uptake decreases as the exposure time in $^{14}CO_2$ is extended and after 10 min approaches normal net CO_2 exchange rates. This decrease in $^{14}CO_2$ uptake is associated with $^{14}CO_2$ evolution from the leaf. Thus, with exposure times of 1 min used in this study, CO_2 uptake measured was closer to gross CO_2 uptake than net photosynthesis.

All CO_2 uptake determinations were carried out under a constant chamber temperature of $10 \pm 0.5°C$ which is representative of the mean daytime growing season temperatures at the study area. Chamber temperatures were measured using a shielded copper-constantan fine wire thermocouple. Leaf temperatures were also monitored and were always within $\pm 1°$ C of chamber air temperature. Artificial irradiation was provided by a high intensity aircraft landing incandescent lamp (100 W) and was monitored with a Lambda Co. Model LI-190SR quantum sensor. A constant intensity of $2,700 \pm 200$ microeinsteins $\cdot$ m^{-2} $\cdot$ sec^{-1} in the 400 to 700 nm wavelength range was used for all determinations and is approximately equal to maximum midday solar radiation values. A period of 5 min was allowed for the leaf to attain a steady state gas exchange rate under these environmental conditions before $^{14}CO_2$ exposure. These temperature and radiation conditions were used consistently in this study in order to assess the combined influence of other factors such as leaf age and leaf position.

Leaf lengths and widths for *Deschampsia caespitosa* and *Kobresia myosuroides* were measured to the nearest 0.5 mm. This could lead to a ± 0.25 mm^2 error in area measurements and when compared to the smallest areas measured in these species would represent an accuracy of $\pm 5\%$. Area values for the highly dissected leaves of *Geum rossii* were estimated from regression relationships of leaf dry weight, leaf length and width, and leaf area which was determined by a modified optical planimeter (Caldwell and Moore, 1971) and have an accuracy of $\pm 8\%$. These basic relationships were determined at three times during the season.

For the leaf growth rate study, ten plants each of *Geum rossii* and *Kobresia myosuroides* in the *Kobresia* meadow site and ten plants each of *Deschampsia caespitosa* and *Geum rossii* in the *Deschampsia* meadow site were selected on June 15. These individual plants were observed and measured every 5 days for leaf emergence, leaf elongation, and senescence throughout the course of the growing season. Senescence was denoted as a recession of the green, apparently living tissue of the leaves. Leaf length was measured from the base of the plant to the most distal green portion of the outstretched leaf. Each leaf was individually measured and the same leaf was followed through emergence, expansion, and senescence.

From these individual leaf measurements, the mean leaf relative growth rate, R_l, was calculated by:

$$R_l = (\ln l_2 - \ln l_1)/(t_2 - t_1)$$
$$\text{length} \cdot \text{length}^{-1} \cdot \text{time}^{-1} \quad (1)$$

(Kvet *et al.*, 1971) where l_2 and l_1 are the lengths at times t_2 and t_1, respectively.

In both the leaf photosynthetic and R_l studies the same numerical identification of leaf position was used. The first green leaf present and thus the oldest living leaf on the plant was designated leaf No. 1, followed by the second green leaf to emerge as leaf No. 2 and so on.

STUDY AREA

The area of study was on Niwot Ridge (40° 04'N, 105°36'N) at an elevation of 3,476 m in the Front Range of the Colorado Rocky Mountains. The study sites were the U.S. International Biological Programme Tundra Biome intensive sites, one a *Kobresia* community and the other a *Deschampsia* meadow. The *Kobresia* site has a southwest aspect and 5° slope, while the *Deschampsia* site has a southeast aspect and a 4° slope.

Both sites are located on a gently sloping saddle and are characterized by low perennial grasses, sedges, and herbs. The *Kobresia* site is a well-developed mesic meadow, whereas the *Deschampsia* site is an area with heavy snow meltwater runoff. More detailed description of the study sites can be found in Fareed (1973). Plant nomenclature follows that of Weber (1967). The CO_2 uptake and leaf growth rate studies were initiated in June and continued through August 1972.

RESULTS AND DISCUSSION

Figures 1 and 2 illustrate the photosynthetic capacity and R_l of *Geum rossii, Deschampsia caespitosa,* and *Kobresia myosuroides* at different leaf positions throughout the growing sea-

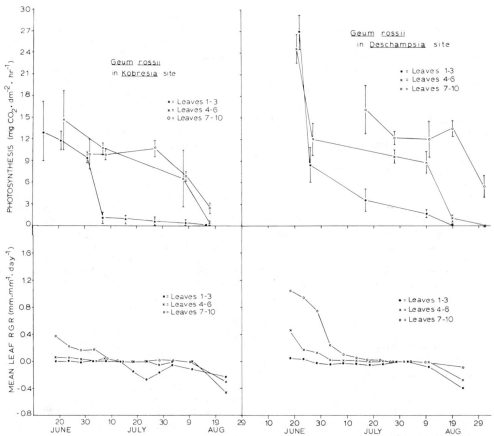

FIGURE 1. Leaf photosynthesis rates and R_l (RGL) of *Geum rossii* in the *Kobresia* site and the *Deschampsia* site. Each point on the photosynthesis figure is the mean of four to eight replicates with the vertical bars representing ± one standard error. Each point on the leaf R_l figure is the mean of ten plants with the standard errors ranging from 0.01 to 0.58. Negative R_l denotes leaf senescence.

son. In *Geum rossii* all leaves arose from the current year's growth. The first leaf in *Deschampsia caespitosa* and *Kobresia myosuroides* was one which typically had initiated growth in the prior season, but which had not attained complete exsertion and development. Thus, during the second season of growth, leaf elongation ensued.

In all species studied, the greatest R_l was exhibited by the upper leaves. In *Deschampsia caespitosa* and *Kobresia myosuroides* this period of rapid growth may have taken place the previous growing season and the leaves may have been completing exsertion in this subsequent growing season. Standard errors of the R_l means ranged from 0.01 to 0.94.

A similar ontogenetic pattern was exhibited

in all species studied. Initially there was a period of high R_l associated with a period of high or increasing photosynthetic activity. Following this stage was a long period of no net change in length of the living leaf with photosynthetic activity eventually exhibiting a steady decrease. The final leaf ontogenetic stage was a period of negative R_l denoting leaf senescence which was associated with a marked decline in leaf CO_2 uptake rate. All species studied exhibited a decrease in photosynthetic rate prior to negative R_l.

Snow meltoff was largely complete by May 22 in the *Kobresia* site. Therefore, there was an earlier opportunity for growth initiation as compared with the *Deschampsia* site where snow cover in this area remained until June 9 and

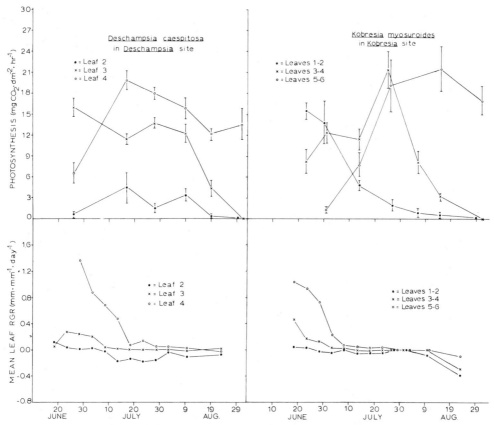

FIGURE 2. Leaf photosynthesis rates and R_l (RGL) of *Kobresia myosuroides* in the *Kobresia* site and the *Deschampsia caespitosa* in the *Deschampsia* site. Each point on the photosynthesis figure is the mean of four to eight replicates with the vertical bars representing ± one standard error. Each point on the leaf R_l figure is the mean of ten plants with the standard errors ranging from 0.01 to 0.94. Negative R_l denotes leaf senescence.

the first growth was noted near the middle of June (Diane Ebert May, unpublished data, 1972). Because of this early snowmelt in the *Kobresia* site substantial leaf growth had taken place before the first sampling period.

This difference between sites is particularly apparent when photosynthetic and leaf relative growth rates in leaf positions 7 through 10 of *Geum rossii* are compared. There were seldom more than 10 leaf positions on the *Geum* plants in 1972. Leaf positions 7 through 10 approached zero R_l near July 8 in the *Kobresia* site and July 18 in the *Deschampsia* site. In the *Kobresia* site, *Geum rossii* leaves in positions 7 through 10 declined earlier in their photosynthetic rates and exhibited less than 3 mg $CO_2 \cdot dm^{-2} \cdot hr^{-1}$ uptake by August 17. In the *Deschampsia* site comparable leaves ex-

hibited rates of more than 13 mg $CO_2 \cdot hr^{-1}$ on August 19. Even by August 31 these leaves had not declined to the low levels of CO_2 uptake exhibited by August 17 in the *Kobresia* site.

This earlier decline in leaf photosynthetic capacity and R_l of *Geum rossii* in the *Kobresia* site may be due to differences in plant age. The same ontogenetic sequence took place in *Geum rossii* in both the *Kobresia* and *Deschampsia* sites. However, due to the earlier snowmelt date in the *Kobresia* site, the ontogeny in the *Kobresia* site was initated earlier than in the *Deschampsia* site. Thus, as *Geum rossii* was completing its ontogenetic pattern in the *Kobresia* site, *Geum rossii* in the *Deschampsia* site was exhibiting a time lag of more than 10 days.

Differences in water stress may also account

400

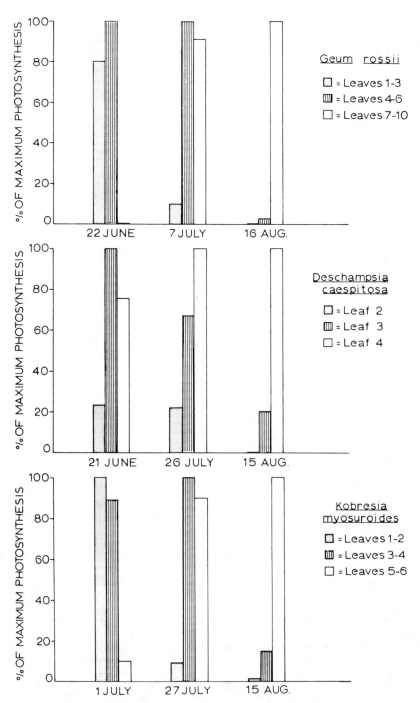

FIGURE 3. Relative photosynthetic contributions of *Deschampsia caespitosa*, *Geum rossii*, and *Kobresia myosuroides* at different leaf positions at three dates during the growing season. Each leaf position represents the mean of four to eight replicates.

for the earlier decline in the *Kobresia* site. Leaf water potentials for *Geum rossii* as measured by the Scholander pressure bomb technique (Waring and Cleary, 1967) were of the order of −18 bars by July 18 in the *Kobresia* site, whereas comparable leaf water potentials were not observed until July 29 in the *Deschampsia* site. Leaf water potential throughout the 1972 growing season ranged from −1 to < −30 bars in *Deschampsia caespitosa*, −1 to −20 bars in *Geum rossii*, and −7 to −29 bars in *Kobresia myosuroides*. Leaf photosynthetic capacities of *Geum rossii* and *Deschampsia caespitosa* have been shown to be significantly depressed with these decreases in leaf water potential for leaves of the same age (Johnson *et al.*, in press). In addition, the number of leaves operating at near maximal efficiencies at any specific time may also be reduced.

Leaves in the lower positions exhibited their highest photosynthetic capacity early in the season and generally showed a steady decline throughout the rest of the season. However, as photosynthetic activity in the older senescing leaves declined, new leaves were emerging to assume the function of the primary photosynthetic structures (Figure 3). Ontogenetic timing of these alpine species is geared with the surge and decline of individual leaf photosynthetic capacity so that one to several leaves operating at near maximal photosynthetic capacity for existing conditions are always maintained during the growing season of each plant. This generalized seasonal CO_2 uptake pattern has been shown for other species such as *Nicotiana sanderae* (Šesták and Čatský, 1962) and *Sorghum almum* and *Vigna luteola* (Ludlow and Wilson, 1971).

ACKNOWLEDGMENTS

This work was supported by the U.S. National Science Foundation grant number G.V. 29353X1 to M. Caldwell as part of the U.S. International Biological Programme Tundra Biome. We also gratefully acknowledge the assistance of Kathryn Johnson and the station support of the Institute of Arctic and Alpine Research, University of Colorado.

REFERENCES

Beuerlein, J. E. and Pendleton, J. W.
 1971 : Photosynthetic rates and light saturation curves of individual soybean leaves under field conditions. *Crop Sci.*, 11: 217-219.

Caldwell, M. M. and Moore, R. T.
 1971 : A portable small-stage photoelectric planimeter for leaf area measurements. *J. Range Manage.*, 24: 394-395.

Fareed, M.
 1973 : Canopy structure and phenology of alpine tundra vegetation. M.S. Thesis, Utah State University, Logan, Utah, 43 pp.

Johnson, D. A., Caldwell, M. M., and Tieszen, L. L.
 In press: Photosynthesis in relation to leaf water potential in three alpine plant species. *In* Wielgolaski, F. E. and Bliss, L. C. (eds.), *Proc. IBP Tundra Biome Primary Production Meeting, Dublin, Ireland, March 31-April 3, 1973.*

Kvĕt, J., Ondok, J. P., Nečas, J., and Jarvis, P. G.
 1971 : Methods of growth analysis. *In* Šesták, Z., Čatský, J., and Jarvis, P. G. (eds.), *Plant Photosynthetic Production Manual of Methods*. Junk, The Hague, 343-384.

Ludlow, M. M. and Wilson, G. L.
 1971 : Photosynthesis of tropical pasture plants. III. Leaf age. *Aust. J. Biol. Sci.*, 24: 1077-1088.

Ludwig. L. J. and Canvin, D. T.
 1971 : An open gas-exchange system for the simultaneous measurement of the CO_2 and $^{14}CO_2$ fluxes from leaves. *Can. J. Bot.*, 49: 1299-1313.

Moser, W.
 1973 : Licht, Temperatur und Photosynthese an der Station "Hoher Nebelkogel" (3184 m). *In* Ellenberg, H. (ed.), *Ökosystemforschung.* Springer-Verlag, Heidelberg, 203-223.

Scott D. and Billings W. D.
 1964 : Effects of environmental factors on standing crop and productivity of an alpine tundra. *Ecol. Monogr.*, 34: 243-270.

Šesták, Z. and Čatský, J.
 1962 : Intensity of photosynthesis and chlorophyll content as related to leaf age in *Nicotiana. Biol. Plant.*, 4: 131-140.

Straley, C. S. and Cooper, C. S.
 1972 : Effect of shading mature leaves of alfalfa and sainfoin plants on specific leaf weight of leaves formed in sunlight. *Crop Sci.*, 12: 703-704.

402

Tieszen, L. L., Johnson, D. A., and Caldwell, M. M.
   In press: A portable system for the measure-
      ment of photosynthesis using 14-
      carbon dioxide. *Photosynthetica.*
Turner, N. C. and Incoll, L. D.
   1971 : The vertical distribution of photosyn-
      thesis in crops of tobacco and sor-
      ghum. *J. Appl. Ecol.,* 8: 581-591.

Waring, R. H. and Cleary, B. D.
   1967 : Plant moisture stress: evaluation by
      pressure bomb. *Science,* 155: 1248-
      1254.
Weber, W. A.
   1967 : *Rocky Mountain Flora.* Univ. Colo-
      rado Press, Boulder, Colorado. 437
      pp.

THE CANOPY STRUCTURE OF TUNDRA PLANT COMMUNITIES AT BARROW, ALASKA, AND NIWOT RIDGE, COLORADO

Martyn M. Caldwell,* Larry L. Tieszen,† and Marcee Fareed*

ABSTRACT

The seasonal development of foliage area index (foliage area per unit ground surface, F) was compared by inclined point quadrat analysis for an arctic and two alpine tundra communities. An extensive series of other arctic and alpine communities were also compared at the peak of the vegetative season which occurred between July 25 and August 9 in 1971 in both the arctic and alpine areas. At this time, F values for living foliage of the arctic communities were all less than 1.0 while F ranged between 1 and 2.2 in the alpine sites. A simulation of radiation extinction in an arctic and an alpine community indicated that lower solar radiation intensities in the long arctic day were absorbed in the sparsely stocked canopy to about the same degree on a daily basis as the higher radiation intensities in the denser community of the alpine tundra. The significance of senescent foliage tissue displayed at the top of the alpine communities is also discussed.

INTRODUCTION

The tundra of arctic and alpine regions is remarkably similar in physiognomy and climate. The vegetative canopies in both regions reflect the harsh, windy, temperature-limited growing conditions. Under these conditions, aboveground primary productivity is generally reduced to less than 200 g m^{-2} year $^{-1}$ (Bliss, 1962). Even though the canopy is restricted to only 10 to 20 cm in height, recent simulations of an arctic tundra community (Miller and Tieszen, 1972) have shown a sensitivity of photosynthesis and primary production to changes in foliage area index and foliage inclination. We conducted a detailed investigation of the seasonal progression of the vertical canopy structure of arctic and alpine tundra communities in 1971 in order to compare these tundra systems. These studies were carried out concurrently on a grass-sedge community at Barrow, Alaska, and on a *Kobresia* and a hairgrass community on Niwot Ridge, Colorado.

METHODS

Inclined point quadrats were used to estimate the foliage area index (foliage area per unit ground surface area, F) of these vegetative canopies (Warren Wilson, 1960). A pin angle of 32.5° was selected as most suitable for these primarily erectophilic canopies (Warren Wilson, 1959). Foliage inclination was estimated by use of a protractor. At Barrow, Alaska (71°20'N, 156°46'W, 3 m elev.) an arctic tundra community dominated by *Eriophorum angustifolium* Honck., *Dupontia fischeri* R. Br., and *Carex aquatilis* Wahlenb. was studied. On Niwot Ridge in Colorado (40°04'N, 105°36'W, 3476 m elev.) two alpine communities were intensively sampled: (1) a *Kobresia* meadow community dominated by *Kobresia myosuroides* (Vill.) Fiori & Pool. with subdominants of *Geum rossii* (R. Br.) Greene and *Carex*

*Department of Range Science and The Ecology Center, Utah State University, Logan, Utah 84322.

†Biology Department, Augustana College, Sioux Falls, South Dakota 57102.

Arctic and Alpine Research, Vol. 6, No. 2, 1974, pp. 151-159.

rupestris All. and (2) a hairgrass meadow dominated by *Deschampsia caespitosa* (L.) Beauv., *Artemisia scopulorum* Gray and *Geum rossii*. These arctic and alpine sites were those used in the U.S. International Biological Programme Tundra Biome studies.

During 1971, each of these intensive sites were sampled approximately every 10 days between late June and late August. At each site 10 plots, each with 47 point quadrats, were used. In addition, during the peak of the vegetative seasons at both Barrow and on Niwot Ridge, foliage area indices were obtained from several other communities constituting an extensive series of sites. Foliage area indices were calculated at several height increments in the canopies. These were tallied separately for leaf, stem, and reproductive tissues but are reported here as total foliage. Living and dead tissues of each species were considered separately in these calculations.

RESULTS

LIVING FOLIAGE

Foliage area indices are presented in Figures 1, 3, and 5 for several height zones in the respective canopies. Complete tabular values of all data are available through the U.S. I.B.P. Tundra Biome data bank, University of Alaska, Fairbanks.

Maximum living aboveground biomass was attained at all three intensive sites in the period from July 25 to August 9 (F of 0.97 at Barrow, 2.2 for the Niwot *Kobresia* meadow, and 2.0 for the Niwot hairgrass site). At all three sites, maximum F values were apparent earlier in the season at the lower height zones in the canopies than at the higher zones. At all heights in the canopies, F values in both the intensive and extensive sites on Niwot Ridge were consistently greater than at Barrow.

All vegetation in the canopy at Barrow was below 15 cm (see Figures 1 and 2). The three dominant species contributed equally to the total F value and the maximum biomass occurred in the 2.5- to 5-cm height zone. Above 5 cm there was a steadily decreasing quantity of foliage area displayed with increasing height above ground.

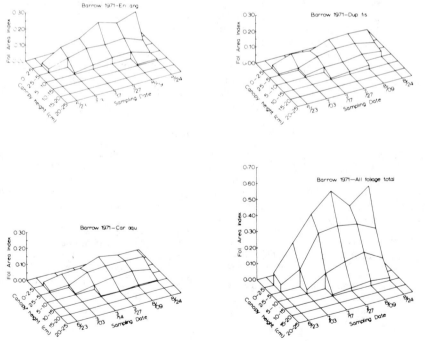

FIGURE 1. Foliage area indices for different height zones in the Barrow community during 1971.

Although foliage in the Barrow canopy was found at all angles of inclination, most of the foliage elements were inclined between 60 and 90° from the horizontal. *Carex aquatilis* and *Dupontia fischeri* possessed foliage predominantly in the 60 to 75° range of inclination angles. Less common species in the lower portion of the canopy had average inclination angles around 25°.

In the *Kobresia* meadow community on Niwot Ridge, most of the vegetation was below 10 cm in height (see Figures 3 and 4) although some foliage extended to 20 cm (primarily *Bistorta bistortoides* (Pursh) Small and *Ko-*

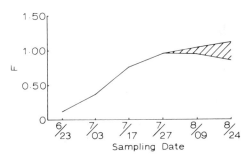

FIGURE 2. Total foliage area index for the Barrow community during 1971. That fraction represented by the hatched area is for foliage tissue which had undergone senescence during 1971. The remainder is living foliage tissues.

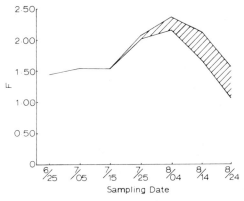

FIGURE 4. Total foliage area index for the Niwot Ridge *Kobresia* meadow community during 1971. That fraction represented by the hatched area is for foliage tissue which had undergone senescence during 1971. The remainder is living foliage tissue.

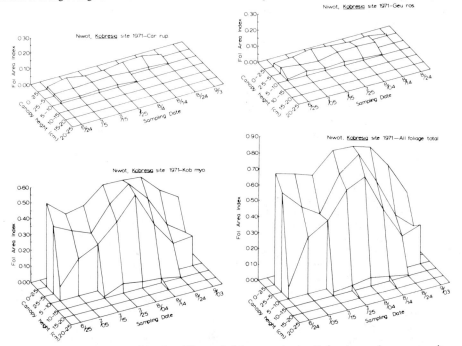

FIGURE 3. Foliage area indices for different height zones in the *Kobresia* meadow community on Niwot Ridge during 1971.

406

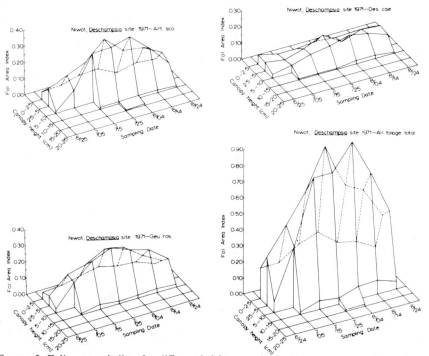

FIGURE 5. Foliage area indices for different height zones in the hairgrass community on Niwot Ridge during 1971.

bresia myosuroides). The contribution of the subdominant species, *Geum rossii* and *Carex rupestris* to the total F was very small.

Kobresia myosuroides had strongly erectophilic foliage on the lower portion of the plant with an average inclination angle of approximately 60° from the horizontal while most of the upper remaining foliage was in the orientation angle range of 80 to 90°. Foliage angles of *Carex rupestris* usually ranged between 70 to 90° from the horizontal. The other subdominant, *Geum rossii,* appeared to be the only other major species with reasonably horizontal foliage. Foliage inclination angles of the lowermost foliage elements ranged around 25° although some of the upper foliage approached 70°. Because of the overwhelming importance of *Kobresia* in the *Kobresia* meadow, this canopy should be characterized as highly erectophilic in nature.

The hairgrass meadow of Niwot Ridge did not reflect a single dominant species in terms of composition of living foliage material (see Figures 5 and 6). *Artemisia scopulorum* provided a somewhat greater contribution to the

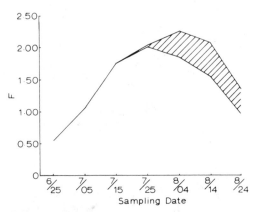

FIGURE 6. Total foliage area index for the Niwot Ridge hairgrass community during 1971. That fraction represented by the hatched area is for foliage tissue which had undergone senescence during 1971. The remainder is living foliage tissue.

total F; however, all three dominant species participated significantly in the above-ground biomass. Most of the vegetation in the hairgrass community was below 15 cm although some foliage elements did emerge to a height approaching 20 cm. The maximum amount of foliage was in the 5 to 10 cm height zone.

The hairgrass community was somewhat less erectophilic in nature than the *Kobresia* community. *Geum rossii* leaves ranged in inclination from 25° at the bottom of the plant to approximately 70° for the uppermost leaves. *Deschampsia caespitosa* leaves also ranged from 20° for the lowermost leaves on the plant to as high as 90° for the upper leaves. Most foliage was, however, between 45 and 60° from the horizontal. *Artemisia scopulorum* foliage ranged between 70 and 90°

SENESCENT FOLIAGE

Foliage tissue which was alive during the 1971 season and then died back later in the season is referred to as senescent foliage. Foliage area index values for senescent foliage are shown in Figures 2, 4, and 6. These values suggest differ-ences between the three intensively-studied communities. At Barrow, senescent F was about 25% of the quantity of the living F by the last sampling date of the season. Furthermore, at Barrow each of the dominant species contributed about equally to the total senescent F. In the hairgrass site on Niwot Ridge, senescent F was about 40% of the quantity of the living F at the last sampling date. A substantial portion of the total senescent F was *Geum rossii* foliage. In the *Kobresia* meadow, senescent F constituted a quantity approaching 45% of the living foliage F at this time. As with living foliage tissue, *Kobresia myosuroides* contributed most of the senescent tissue.

VARIABILITY IN CANOPY STRUCTURE

Mean live foliage area index values and variances for these means are given in Table 1. These indicate the magnitude of variation among the ten plots sampled in each community along with experimental errors.

DISCUSSION

Since experimental errors should be of a consistent magnitude at all sites throughout the season, the differences in variances among communities (Table 1) should indicate the comparative degree of structural homogeneity of these communities. For the total live foliage canopy, the Barrow community was consistently less variable than the two Niwot Ridge communities, while the greatest variability was evident in the hairgrass community. Changes in the relative magnitude of the variances for the same community or the same species within a community are quite apparent at different times of the season. This probably reflects differential growth and senescence rates of individual plants within the stand. This may also, however, result partially from changes in foliage element orientation caused by growth or exogenous factors such as wind and heavy precipitation.

When comparing the arctic and alpine tundra intensive sites it is readily apparent that foliage area index values were consistently higher at the Niwot Ridge intensive sites. Furthermore, in all but two of the ten extensive sites which were sampled at the peak of the growing season (August 4) on Niwot Ridge, total living F values exceeded 1.0 and ranged up to 2.1. The two extensive sites which possessed total F values less than 1.0 were cushion or fellfield plant communities where essentially all photosynthetic tissue was displayed in a single plane.

Both extensive and intensive sites at Barrow were never found to exceed F values of 1.0, except for a few minor community types in extremely wet sites.

Higher solar radiation intensities in alpine areas would seem to be better utilized by a more dense vegetative canopy when compared to arctic tundra communities. When the prevailing angles of incidence of the direct beam solar radiation are considered, this difference between arctic and alpine tundras is further amplified. In alpine areas, direct beam radiation is presented to the top of the canopy at greater solar altitudes than in the Arctic resulting in shorter optical path lengths through the alpine canopy. A comparison of radiation extinction in the Barrow and Niwot *Kobresia* communities is represented in Figures 7 and 8. This is depicted for clear (Figure 7) and overcast (Figure 8) days in late July (solar declination of 20°) when both communities were at peak vegetative development (F for Barrow $= 0.97$; F for *Kobresia* $= 2.2$, including senescent foliage). Global radiation for the appropriate solar altitudes was taken from measurements of the I.B.P. intensive site at Barrow using an Eppley pyranometer. Similar global radiation values from Niwot Ridge were supplied from Eppley pyranometer measurements of Caldwell (unpublished data) and Ehleringer and Moore (unpublished data). These measurements indicate

TABLE 1

Total mean live foliage area index values and variances of these means for two alpine communities and an arctic community in 1971

Community	June 25		July 5		July 15		July 25		Aug. 4		Aug. 14		Aug. 24	
	F	S^2	F	S^2	F	S^2	F	S^2	F	S^2	F	S^2	F	S^2
Kobresia Meadow														
Carex rupestris	0.04	9×10^{-4}	0.06	2.5×10^{-3}	0.05	1.6×10^{-3}	0.06	1.6×10^{-3}	0.05	2.5×10^{-3}	0.05	3.6×10^{-3}	0.02	9×10^{-4}
Geum rossii	0.08	6.4×10^{-3}	0.08	4.9×10^{-3}	0.09	4.9×10^{-3}	0.09	$4.9\times10^{-}$	0.07	8.1×10^{-3}	0.06	4.9×10^{-3}	0.01	4×10^{-4}
Kobresia myosuroides	1.04	0.0576	1.03	0.084	1.07	0.260	1.45	0.130	1.68	0.078	1.36	0.73	0.83	0.032
Total foliage	1.45	0.1225	1.54	0.504	1.57	0.250	2.03	0.240	2.16	0.109	1.73	0.102	1.09	0.058
Deschampsia community														
Artemisia scopulorum	0.16	8.1×10^{-3}	0.35	0.032	0.64	0.084	0.72	0.176	0.67	0.176	0.55	0.102	0.37	0.014
Deschampsia caespitosa	0.14	3.6×10^{-3}	0.13	0.022	0.19	0.04	0.27	0.022	0.28	0.058	0.26	0.022	0.17	0.01
Geum rossii	0.13	3.6×10^{-3}	0.39	0.026	0.59	0.022	0.60	0.090	0.55	0.102	0.46	0.062	0.25	0.048
Total foliage	0.55	2.5×10^{-3}	1.09	0.194	1.79	0.260	2.02	0.757	1.86	0.74	1.58	0.435	0.99	0.24

Community	June 23		July 3		July 17		July 27		Aug. 9		Aug. 24	
	F	S^2	F	S^2	F	S^2	F	S^2	F	S^2	F	S^2
Barrow community												
Carex aquatilis	0.03	5.6×10^{-4}	0.06	2.3×10^{-3}	0.14	9.3×10^{-3}	0.21	2.9×10^{-2}	0.20	2.7×10^{-2}	0.21	1.2×10^{-2}
Dupontia fischeri	0.02	4.3×10^{-4}	0.08	1.5×10^{-3}	0.13	7.3×10^{-3}	0.20	2.2×10^{-2}	0.23	3.7×10^{-2}	0.17	1.3×10^{-2}
Eriophorum angustifolium	0.04	1.1×10^{-3}	0.15	8.2×10^{-3}	0.22	3.2×10^{-2}	0.28	2.8×10^{-2}	0.29	1.9×10^{-2}	0.19	6.3×10^{-3}
Total foliage	0.12	1.7×10^{-3}	0.37	1.98×10^{-2}	0.77	4.4×10^{-2}	0.97	5.3×10^{-2}	0.96	8.0×10^{-2}	0.88	6.6×10^{-2}

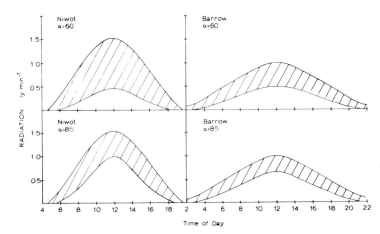

FIGURE 7. Simulated radiation extinction in the Barrow and Niwot Ridge *Kobresia* meadow communities for two foliage inclination angles (α = 60 and 85°) on clear days. In each graph the upper curve represents global radiation presented to the top of the canopy, the lower curve represents radiation penetrating to ground level, and the hatched area represents radiation extinction within the canopy.

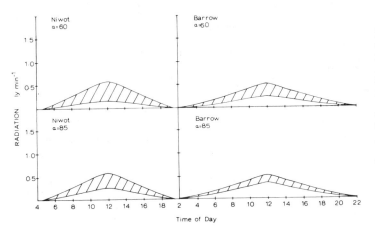

FIGURE 8. Simulated radiation extinction in the Barrow and Niwot Ridge *Kobresia* meadow communities for two foliage inclination angles (α = 60 and 85°) for overcast days. In each graph, the upper curve represents global radiation presented to the top of the canopy, the lower curve represents radiation penetrating to ground level, and the hatched area represents radiation extinction within the canopy.

that for clear days at both locations, direct beam solar radiation is generally about 85% of global radiation. This proportion has been used in these calculations. For the overcast conditions, all of the radiation is represented as diffuse.

Direct beam radiation extinction has been based on the classical modification of Beer-Lambert's law used recently by Miller and Tieszen (1972):

$$I_g/I_0 = e^{-KF} \qquad (1)$$

where I_g is direct beam radiation at ground level, I_0 is direct beam radiation at the top of the canopy, F is total foliage area index for the canopy, and K is an extinction coefficient based upon foliage inclination angle, α, and solar altitude, β (Miller and Tieszen 1972):

when $\alpha \leq \beta$

$$K = \cos \alpha \qquad (2a)$$

when $\alpha > \beta$

$$K = (\cos\alpha)/2 + (\sin\alpha)/\pi \, \tan\beta + [(\cos\alpha)/\pi] \, (2\theta = \sin2\theta) \qquad (2b)$$

where $\theta = \arctan(\cot\alpha \, \tan\beta)$.

For diffuse radiation, uniform sky brightness has been assumed and the hemisphere has been divided into nine angle classes from the horizon to the zenith. In this manner the proportion of radiation at all azimuth angles for each radial sky segment could be calculated according to:

$$PR_{\beta_1\beta_2} = \frac{\int_{\beta_1}^{\beta_2} 2\pi \ a \ \cos\beta \ \sin\beta \ d\beta}{\int_0^{\pi/2} 2\pi \ a \ \cos\beta \ \sin\beta \ d\beta} \qquad (3)$$

$$= \sin^2\beta_2 - \sin^2\beta_1$$

where $PR_{\beta_1\beta_2}$ is the proportion of radiation from a radial segment of the sky between angle β_1 and β_2 and a is an imaginary radius of the sky hemisphere (Stewart and Lemon, 1969).

In Figure 7 extinction of global radiation (depicted as 85% direct beam and 15% diffuse) is represented for foliage angles of 60 and 85° in the Barrow and Niwot *Kobresia* communities. These foliage angles were chosen as those angles which encompass most of the foliage in both tundra communities. In the absence of more refined foliage inclination data or community patterning, e.g., degree of clustered foliage element distribution, etc., more sophisticated models are not warranted in this comparison. Foliage is always assumed to be distributed randomly with respect to azimuth angle.

Considering that most of the daily photosynthetic carbon gain would occur during a 20-hr day at Barrow and in a 15-hr day on Niwot Ridge at this time of year, total daily irradiation values of 654 ly and 723 ly would be presented at the top of the canopy on clear days at Barrow and Niwot Ridge, respectively. At a foliage angle of 85°, the percentage of total daily radiation absorption by the two canopies would be nearly the same, 44% at Barrow and 51% at Niwot. At a foliage angle of 60°, radiation absorption would be about 22% greater at Niwot than at Barrow, i.e., 75% versus 58% of total daily radiation, respectively. For totally overcast conditions, a similar depiction of radiation penetration into arctic and alpine canopies is represented in Figure 8. For the same daylengths used for Figure 7, total daily irradiation values of 288 and 252 ly would be presented at the top of the canopy on overcast days at Barrow and Niwot Ridge, respectively. This irradiation would naturally vary somewhat with changes in cloud density. For the cases presented in Figure 8, at a foliage angle of 85°, 41% of the daily radiation would be absorbed in the Barrow canopy and 64% in the Niwot community. At 60° foliage inclination angle, these values would be 55 and 75%, respectively.

Although the Niwot canopy is more than twice as dense as the Barrow community, percentage daily radiation absorption in the Niwot community is usually no more than 20% greater than in the Barrow community at comparable foliage inclination angles for either clear or overcast days. Assuming a proportionality between radiation extinction in the canopy and radiation utilization in photosynthesis, it is apparent that radiation of greater intensities and presented at higher solar altitudes during clear days in the alpine area is well utilized by a denser tundra community, whereas lower radiation intensities presented at lower solar altitudes in the longer arctic day are nearly equally well utilized in a much more sparsely stocked tundra canopy. On overcast days these relationships also appear to apply although the radiation in this case is assumed to be totally diffuse and, therefore, there would be no differences in prevailing angles of incidence. This discussion is not meant, however, to imply that solar radiation is the single limiting factor for productivity and foliage development in these tundra communities.

The importance of standing dead material and senescent tissue from the current growing season should certainly not be overlooked. The significant quantity of dead foliage material displayed at the top of the canopy in the *Kobresia* meadow is of particular interest. Although this dead foliage would reduce radiation available for photosynthesis, reduced radiation intensities coupled with decreased wind speeds might also be expected to lessen water loss by transpiration from the live foliage beneath. The greatest quantity of senescent foliage displayed at the top of the canopy is in the *Kobresia* meadow (see Figures 2, 4, and 6). This community is also the driest of the three intensively studied sites, and the driest part of the year is in the mid- to late growing season when the quantity of this senescent foliage is at a maximum. The retention of this considerable quantity of senescent foliage attached to living foliage in the upper layer of this canopy as opposed to loss of this material to litter on the ground surface may serve to benefit the *Kobresia* community through reduced transpirational water loss.

ACKNOWLEDGMENTS

This work was financially supported by National Science Foundation grants GV-29343 and GB-25027 to Tieszen and GU-29353X1 to Caldwell and Tieszen. Kenneth Olsen, Roger

Hanson, Diane Hanson, Donald Hazlett, and Thomas Schoemaker provided field assistance in this study. Support provided by the Naval Arctic Research Laboratory, the Institute of Arctic and Alpine Research, University of Colorado, and the I.B.P. Tundra Biome Center, University of Alaska, is also gratefully acknowledged.

REFERENCES

Bliss, L. C.
1962 : Net primary production of tundra ecosystems. *In* Leith, H. (ed.) *Stoffproduktion der Pflanzendecke*. Gustav Fischer, Stuttgart, 35-45.

Miller, P. C. and Tieszen, L. L.
1972 : A preliminary model of processes affecting primary production in the arctic tundra. *Arct. Alp. Res.*, 4: 1-18.

Stewart, D. W. and Lemon, E. R.
1969 : The energy budget at the earth's surface: a simulation of net photosynthesis of field corn. Tech Rept. ECOM 2-68, I-6 (Available from Nat. Tech. Infor. Center, Springfield, Va.).

Warren Wilson, J.
1959 : Analysis of the distribution of foliage area in grassland. *In* Ivins, J. D. (ed.) *The Measurement of Grassland Productivity*. Academic Press, New York, 92-99.
1960 : Inclined point quadrats. *New Phytol.*, 59: 1-8.

THE MAGNITUDE AND DISTRIBUTION OF BELOWGROUND PLANT STRUCTURES IN THE ALPINE TUNDRA OF NIWOT RIDGE, COLORADO*

P. J. WEBBER AND DIANE EBERT MAY

*Institute of Arctic and Alpine Research and
Department of Environmental, Population and Organismic Biology
University of Colorado
Boulder, Colorado 80309*

ABSTRACT

The following generalized ranges of aboveground vascular productivity and of aboveground and belowground standing crop were measured: Aboveground productivity — 100 to 300 g m^{-2} yr^{-1}; aboveground biomass — 100 to 1500 g m^{-2}; aboveground total standing crop including litter — 500 to 3000 g m^{-2}; belowground biomass — 1000 to 5000 g m^{-2}; belowground standing crop of intact plant material — 2000 to 8000 g m^{-2}; and belowground standing crop of soil humus — 10 to 30 kg m^{-2}. Aboveground to belowground biomass ratios (A:B) varied from 1:3 to 1:25 and estimates of biomass turnover ranged from 1 to 5 yr for aboveground and from 16 to 26 yr for belowground.

No statistically significant correlations between the above variables and measured environmental variables were found. However, a combination of vegetation ordination and classification methods were used to look for general trends between plant and environmental variables. The principal controls of the species composition of the vegetation are, in order of importance, soil moisture, snow accumulation, and soil disturbance. Generally, productivity, rate of aboveground biomass turnover, rate of surface decay, belowground standing crop, and longevity of belowground biomass increased along the complex gradient of increasing soil moisture in the study area. The traditional concept of low A:B biomass ratios as an adaptation to a severe environment could not be assessed. A:B biomass ratios change from 1:14 in fellfield where there are some cushion plants to 1:25 in moist, graminoid-dominated tundra to 1:3 in shrub tundra. This sequence corresponds to a sequence of increasing aboveground productivity rather than a simple environmental gradient. Thus magnitude of A:B ratio is more directly a function of species composition and growth-form than the environment.

INTRODUCTION

Studies of the alpine tundra of Niwot Ridge carried out under the auspices of the United States Tundra Biome program of the International Biological Programme (IBP) have provided a very complete description of the vegetation. This description is based on detailed studies of the correlation of composition, structure, phenology, aboveground produc-

*A version of this paper was presented to the *Belowground Symposium: A Synthesis of Plant Associated Processes* held at Colorado State University, Fort Collins, September 5-7, 1973.

Arctic and Alpine Research, Vol. 9, No. 2, 1977, pp. 157-174.

tion, and decomposition with measured environmental variables (Webber, 1972; May, 1973; Webber and Ebert, 1973; May and Webber, 1975; May, 1976; Emerick, 1976; Flock, 1976; Komárková, 1976; Webber *et al.*, 1976; Komárková and Webber, 1977). Concurrently information was gathered on the variation of belowground plant material and it is this which is reported in this paper.

One of the most striking characteristics of the tundra ecosystem is the large proportion of vegetable matter which is belowground (Aleksandrova, 1958, 1970; Billings and Mooney, 1968; Bliss, 1970; Wielgolaski, 1972, 1975a). Grasslands and some deserts are the only major biome or vegetation types with this characteristic (Rodin and Bazilevich, 1967; Webber, 1974). This similarity between tundra, grassland, and desert ecosystems is a result of the similar structure in which trees are absent and the cryptophytic and hemicryptophytic life-forms of Raunkiaer (1934), comprised of many grass-like, ground-protected, or ground-hugging forms (Cain, 1950), are dominant. The concentration of plant matter near to or below ground is considered a strategy which takes advantage of the less fluctuating and more favorable microclimate than that aboveground (Bliss, 1962; Billings, 1974). Further strategies by the vegetation should take place belowground in tundra where the functions of absorption, storage, anchorage, and vegetative reproduction are critical (Daubenmire, 1941). These functions are critical because in the tundra the soils are often nutrient-poor (Dadykin, 1954; Bliss, 1963) and frequently unstable (Washburn, 1956), and sexual reproduction may be infrequent (Bliss, 1962; Billings, 1974). Spatial studies of the variation of belowground tundra material between plant communities and along environmental gradients have provided information on the nature of these strategies (Holm, 1927; Holch *et al.*, 1941; Scott and Billings, 1964; Bliss, 1966; Dennis and Johnson, 1970; Wielgolaski, 1975a). These studies often rely on a consideration of the ratio of aboveground to belowground (A:B) material. The A:B ratio may be seen as a measure of the allocation of primary production to aboveground or belowground structures. On the basis of certain assumptions concerning steady state, the A:B ratios may indicate longevity of various structures and overall productivity. Changes of the ratio

with respect to various gradients can be interpreted as adaptation to different environments. In a survey of the tundra literature on this topic, Wielgolaski (1975a) reported that the A:B derivative decreases along decreasing gradients of soil temperature, nutrients, aeration, and decomposition. The increase in the proportion of belowground material compared to that aboveground is considered to be an adaptation in which a higher belowground biomass would be compensatory through the means of increased efficiencies, for example, of storage or absorption. This phenomenon is demonstrated by several autecological studies which show a proportionally greater root development in severe environments (Holch *et al.*, 1941; Scott and Billings, 1964; Harper and Ogden, 1970; Bonde *et al.*, 1973). Scott and Billings (1964) found evidence that high wind speeds, dry soils, and low nutrient regimes in the Wyoming alpine would lead to a proportional increase of belowground biomass.

The definition of the position of the boundary between above- and belowground affects the size of the A:B derivative. In some tundra sites where lichens and especially mosses form a mat, which may even be expanding to bury the bases of the long-lived plants, the boundary definition is difficult (Dennis and Johnson, 1970; Tieszen, 1971; Wielgolaski, 1972). The inclusion of buried stem bases reduces the size of the ratio and further accentuates the subterranean characteristic of tundra. Standardization of methods is necessary to permit comparisons between localities and ecosystems. Boundary definition is not a problem on Niwot Ridge because the ground surface is usually mineral soil or at best a thin veneer of organic material and there is little aggradation of the soil surface. Another factor contributing to a reduction in the size of A:B is the completeness of the belowground harvest. Tundra vegetation not only has a large subterranean mass but may, in nonpermafrost areas, have deep penetration (Bliss and Cantlon, 1957; Bliss, 1966). Thus we should expect deep soil sampling to provide smaller ratios than shallow sampling.

In spite of the number of studies of the belowground phenomena in the tundra, these phenomena still remain poorly understood and there is a need for continued study (Bliss, 1971). The objective of this present study was to use some of the large body of existing data from the Niwot Ridge heritage to look at the spatial variation of tundra standing crops and biomass. This report is restricted to spatial rather than temporal variation of below-ground material and it is also confined to in-ferential hypotheses based on field observa-tions rather than hypotheses based on experi-mental manipulation. The data presented here are for the total vascular vegetation; they do not relate either to individual species or to cryptogamic plants.

DESCRIPTION OF THE STUDY AREA

Niwot Ridge is a wind-swept, tundra upland in the Colorado Front Range due west of Boulder. The main site for the IBP studies is called the Saddle (40°3′N, 105°36′W, ele-vation 3650 m s.m.). The bedrock of Niwot Ridge is igneous and metamorphic mainly of Precambrian age. During the late Pleisto-cene, glaciers occupied the valleys to the north and south of Niwot Ridge, but the ridge itself was not covered. A wide variety of peri-glacial features such as solifluction lobes, stone-banked terraces, and stone-nets occur (Benedict, 1970). Average length of the grow-ing season is 90 days. The July mean tempera-ture is 8.5°C with a mean July precipitation of 72.2 mm. The winters are cold with a January mean temperature of -13.2°C and mean January precipitation of 131.3 mm. The snow drifts extensively and while sheltered places may accumulate large amounts other places are kept virtually snowfree and exposed throughout the winter. Peak winds are stronger in January (49.9 km h⁻¹) than in July (20.9 km h⁻¹) (Barry, 1973).

Most soils are coarse textured, well drained, with thin organic-rich surface hori-zons, and often with a characteristic loess fraction in the upper horizons. Soils are pre-dominantly acid (pH 4.5 to 5.5) but occasion-ally mildly basic. Decomposition of plant matter proceeds at a moderate rate and is limited by available moisture. Surface decay proceeds slowest in fellfields and fastest in wet-to-moist sites. Permafrost is only sporadic on the ridge (Ives and Fahey, 1971) and is too deep to influence vegetation.

The ridge is bounded to the north, south, and east by a *Picea engelmannii–Abies lasio-carpa* forest. The forest-tundra transition is marked by krummholz forms at an elevation of from 3350 to 3500 m s.m. The flora of the ridge is comprised of some 200 vascular species, 100 bryophytes, and 50 lichens. The vegetation on the ridge is characterized by closed meadow on level ground with an abun-dance of herbs which gives way to disrupted mats where solifluction is prevalent. Some 40% of the ridge is covered with fellfield com-munities characterized by *Trifolium dasy-phyllum* and *Selaginella densa*; 20% is covered with meadows dominated by *Ko-bresia myosuroides* (Komárková and Webber, 1977). Both fellfields and *Kobresia* meadows are dry and have little winter snow cover. The remainder of the vegetation consists of moist and wet meadows, snowbeds, and shrub tundra.

Mosses and lichens are never abundant in any community type. Lichens are most abun-dant in dry sites where *Peltigera canina* and *Lecanora polytropa* are characteristic species. The predominance of fellfields and dry mead-ows is the result of the well-drained land-scapes and strong winds. Aboveground vascu-lar plant productivity on the ridge ranges from a few grams per square meter per year in stony fellfields to about 400 g m⁻² yr⁻¹ for shrub communities. A mean value for the en-tire ridge system above treeline has been esti-mated at 172.5 g m⁻² yr⁻¹ (Komárková and Webber, 1977).

Niwot Ridge is relatively undisturbed. Sheep grazing ceased in 1948 and was never extensive. Cows, goats, and horses occa-sionally cross the ridge. Vehicle traffic is re-stricted to an unpaved road. Scientists and a few hikers probably cause the largest impact on the ridge but it is insufficient to affect the majority of biological investigations. Never-theless disturbance and instability of sub-strates play a large role in the dynamics of this alpine tundra. The principal triggering agent for this disturbance is the pocket gopher (*Thomomys talpoides*) which lives beneath the vegetation and feeds on belowground plant organs (Osburn, 1958). The gopher is active year-round and brings to the surface large quantities of soil, which are subse-quently eroded by wind or runoff. This gopher-initiated erosion causes the meadows to erode which in turn increases the extent of the fellfield communities. Recovery of the fellfields is rare and may take many decades.

METHODS

The factors controlling the species composition of the vascular vegetation of the IBP site were assessed by constructing an indirect ordination (Bray and Curtis, 1957) of 30 permanently marked stands (May, 1973). The stands were chosen to represent the spectrum of vegetation occurring in the Saddle. Measurements for each stand of the soil moisture, soil water-holding capacity, soil nutrients, and number of snow-free days, and estimates of site instability based on burrowing activities of the pocket gopher and likelihood of wind erosion were correlated with the axes of the ordination. The factors having the highest correlation with each axis are considered the controlling factors of the principal complex environmental gradients operating in the Saddle.

The major vegetation units of the Saddle were identified by clustering the sampled stands on the basis of their species composition using the average linkage method of Sokal and Sneath (1963) (see Webber, 1971; May, 1973). The stand clusters or units are called noda and are given names based on their principal habit and physiognomy.

The ordination serves to study the response of vegetation to the principal controlling environmental gradients. This is done by plotting various vegetation responses, for example, standing crop or productivity, within the axes of the ordination. On the other hand, the identification of vegetation units allows for detailed studies or experiments at some key points within the vegetation continuum.

Net aboveground vascular productivity and above- and belowground standing crops were measured during the first week of August 1971, the period of peak aboveground vascular biomass. Standing crops were separated into biomass (live) and dead fractions. No attempt was made to estimate belowground productivity.

Aboveground sampling was achieved by clip-harvesting at the soil surface all 30 ordination plots. Each clip was separated into current year's growth, previous years' biomass, standing dead, and litter and prostrate dead. Details of the method are given in May (1973). The quantity of belowground plant matter was sampled in 1971 and 1973. In 1971 the 30 permanent plots were sampled from the clipped and cleared surface with a 7.6-cm diameter steel corer to the maximum possible depth. Two samples were taken from each plot. The depth of each sample varied; it always exceeded 10-cm, but seldom more than 30-cm because rocks and stones prevented deeper penetration. In 1973 a more complete sampling of belowground standing crop was made by coring at various depths into the wall of deep soil pits. Six soil pits, one in each major vegetation type, were excavated to bedrock or the water table. Two small $5 \times 5 \times 5$-cm monoliths were taken at each 5-cm interval throughout the soil profile. One monolith was taken for organic matter determination and the other for standing crop.

Belowground plant matter was extracted from the soil cores by washing over a No. 40 soil screen (0.42-mm mesh). An ultrasonic probe was used to dislodge small soil particles adhering to the belowground plant parts. All intact and distinct soil-free plant parts were separated into live and dead fractions. No attempt was made to separate roots from other belowground organs such as rhizomes, bulbs, and rootstocks. The distinction between live and dead roots was done on the basis of color after Dennis and Johnson (1970). White to tan was the distinguishing color of live roots, whereas dark brown to black colors indicated dead roots. Samples in which the outer sheath of the root was dark and the inner core was white or tan were classified as live material. Many small fine rootlets (less than 1-cm in length) were categorized as live roots because of their light color. This subjective separation of live from dead on the basis of color was considered acceptable.

All plant samples were dried at 105°C for 24-h before weighing. All standing crop fractions were expressed on a grams per square meter basis (g m^{-2}).

Organic matter or humus content of the soil profiles was determined by loss on ignition of an oven-dry sample. The weight loss was expressed on an area basis per 5-cm increment of the profile after bulk density and volume considerations.

RESULTS AND DISCUSSION

ORDINATION AND CLASSIFICATION

The ordination indicated that the principal controlling factors of the species composition of the vegetation of the Niwot Ridge Saddle are soil moisture, snow cover, and instability or disturbance. Six vegetation noda were identified in the Saddle. These major vegetation types are dry *Trifolium dasyphyllum* fellfield, dry *Kobresia myosuroides* meadow, moist *Salix planifolia* shrub tundra, moist *Deschampsia caespitosa* tundra, wet *Caltha leptosepala* meadow, and *Sibbaldia procumbens* snowbed. Figure 1 shows the distribution of the vegetation noda and the distribution of annual net aboveground (shoot) production, aboveground standing crop including litter, belowground biomass, and aboveground to belowground (A:B) biomass ratio within the ordination. The isolines in these figures are generalized and extreme high or low values are masked; however, the figures provide a ready visual description of the correlation between these vegetation responses and soil moisture, snow cover, and disturbance. Annual net shoot production is highest in sites which are moist, have moderate snow cover, and which have little or no disturbance; it is low in dry, snow-free sites, late snowbeds, and very wet sites. Along the individual gradients, production has an asymmetrical bell-shaped distribution, for example, productivity varies from around 150 g m^{-2} yr^{-1} in dry sites, to 300 g m^{-2} yr^{-1} in moist sites, and to around 100 g m^{-2} yr^{-1} in wet sites. Aboveground standing crop, which includes litter, reaches a maximum and may exceed 2000 g m^{-2} in moist, moderately snow-covered, stable sites which support willow shrub; wet sites have the smallest aboveground standing crops which are often less than 500 g m^{-2}. The aboveground standing crop pattern is a reflection of the rates of surface decay along the moisture gradient; dry sites have more litter and standing dead material than wet sites. Maximum belowground biomass coincides with maximum aboveground standing crop and may exceed 5000 g m^{-2}, but wet sites have a higher belowground biomass than drier sites in contrast to the aboveground standing crop; snowbeds have the smallest belowground biomass which may be less than 1000 g m^{-2}. A:B ratios range from greater than 1:10 to less than 1:20. Most snowbed and fellfield sites have values just greater than 1:10 and most dry meadow and moist tundra sites have values just less than 1:10. Although shrub tundra and wet meadow occupy similar positions in the ordination because they have moist to wet, stable soils with moderate snow cover there is a rapid change of the A:B ratio between them. Shrub tundra has consistently high ratios of greater than 1:10 while wet tundra has consistently low ratios of close to 1:20.

VERTICAL PROFILES

The belowground biomass values used in the construction of Figure 1 were obtained in 1971 from limited coring. The 1973 sampling using deep soil pits provides a more complete picture and higher total biomass and standing crop values (Figures 2 and 3 and Table 1). Figure 2 shows the limited aerial penetration and the extensive subterranean penetration of tundra vegetation; it also shows the concentration of the standing crop in the upper portions of the belowground profile. Commonly 50% of belowground standing crop occurs in the first 20 cm while 95% occurs within 50 cm of the surface. The profiles of soil humus, although showing a concentration of humus in the upper layers, are less truncated than the profiles of intact plant matter (Figure 2). This suggests a downward migration of humus from the upper to the lower region and that organic decomposition is slower at greater depth in the profile. Figure 2 also shows that the moist meadow has a taller stature and a larger belowground standing crop and humus fraction than the dry meadow. Figure 3 shows the vertical distribution of biomass for all six vegetation types. The striking generalization from this diagram is that the majority of living tundra plant matter occurs between 10 cm above and 10 cm below the tundra surface. In fact, greater than 80% of the biomass occurs in this -20-cm veneer with from 49 to 84% of the belowground biomass occurring in the first 10 cm of the soil. The predominant type of belowground structures change with depth. Fibrous roots of graminoids and fleshy rootstocks and stem bases are prevalent in the surface layers whereas tap roots and the roots of woody species penetrate to the bottom of the profiles.

The vertical distribution of biomass in each

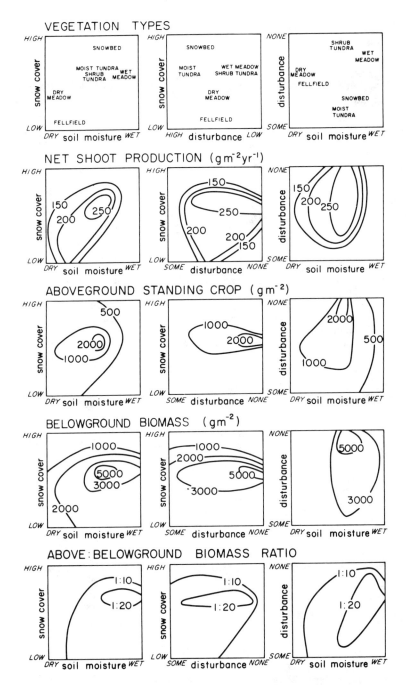

FIGURE 1. The distribution of six major vegetation types (noda), net shoot production, aboveground standing crop, belowground biomass, and above: belowground biomass ratios within an indirect ordination of vegetation (from Webber, 1972 and 1974). The factors correlating with the principal axes of the ordination are indicated. These data were gathered in 1971 at peak aboveground vascular plant biomass.

418

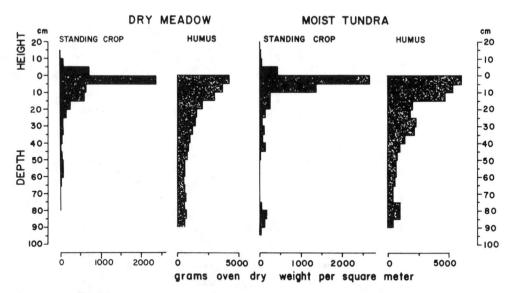

FIGURE 2. Vertical distribution above and below ground of standing crop and humus in the dry *Kobresia* meadow and the moist *Deschampsia* tundra at the period of peak aboveground biomass (August 1973). The aerial distributions were derived by proportion from the clip-harvest data using Leaf Area Index profiles which were measured using the inclined point-quadrat method (Warren Wilson, 1959).

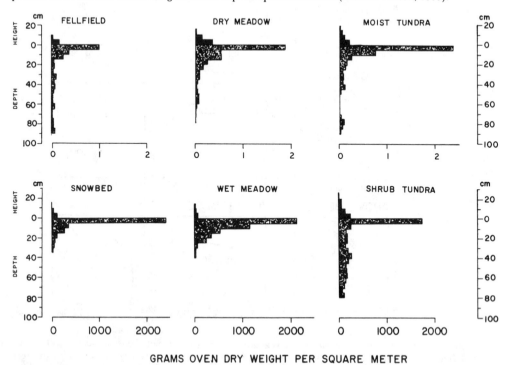

FIGURE 3. Vertical distribution above and below ground of biomass in the six vegetation noda at the period of peak aboveground biomass (August 1973).

TABLE 1

The relative cover of vascular plants with various belowground structures in the six vegetation noda of Niwot Ridge

Structures	Examples	Fellfield	Dry meadow	Snowbed	Moist tundra	Wet meadow	Shrub tundra	Mean
				Vegetation Noda				
Woody	*Salix planifolia*	0	0.1	0	0.1	3.7	28.6	5.4
Fibrous	*Kobresia myosuroides*	9.7	*73.8*[a]	*58.4*	36.2	47.2	18.3	40.6
Rhizomatous	*Carex scopulorum*	9.3	5.3	5.2	3.2	*28.6*	13.7	10.9
Rootstocked	*Acomastylis rossii*	17.8	10.8	*24.5*	*47.2*	15.2	19.1	22.4
Bulbous	*Lloydia serotina*	1.5	1.0	0	0.8	0	0.4	0.6
Tap rooted	*Silene acaulis*	*61.7*	9.0	11.9	12.5	5.3	19.9	20.1

[a]Values in italics serve to characterize each nodum.

TABLE 2

The relative cover of the major plant growth forms within each nodum of the Niwot Ridge vegetation

Growth form	Fellfield	Dry meadow	Snowbed	Moist tundra	Wet meadow	Shrub tundra	Mean
			Vegetation Noda				
Shrub	0	+	0	0	3	26	5
Forb	63	17	30	62	39	47	43
Graminoid	15	64	50	32	33	19	35
Bryophyte	6	5	19	5	24	7	11
Lichen	16	14	1	1	1	1	6

+ represents a relative cover of less than 0.5.

nodum is different (Figure 3). The belowground organs did not go as deep in snowbed and wet meadow as the other noda. The snowbed was situated on stony soil close to bedrock while the wet meadow had a high water table 30 cm from the surface. The snowbed and the wet meadow belowground profiles showed an extraordinary concentration of fibrous roots in the first 5 cm. Shrub tundra has the most different profile. It has the greatest aboveground stature and apart from a concentration of biomass in the top 5 cm it has a uniform distribution throughout the belowground profile. In spite of the coarse, stony substrate of fellfield, roots penetrated to the bottom of the soil pit (90 cm). Dry meadow and moist tundra have similar profiles with a well-developed layer of fibrous roots in the top 5 cm of the soil. Moist tundra has a taller plant canopy than the dry meadow.

No detailed separation of belowground structures into different categories was made. However, a surrogate of this was attempted by analyzing the vascular vegetation of each nodum in terms of the relative cover of the various species with particular belowground structures (Table 1). Each nodum has a distinct composition based on belowground structures. Fellfield has a predominance of species with tap roots; dry meadow and snowbed, fibrous roots; moist tundra, rootstocks; wet meadow, rhizomes; and shrub tundra, woody and tap roots. Snowbed has a higher proportion of species with fleshy rootstocks than dry meadow. The woody root form is restricted primarily to wet meadow and shrub tundra. Fibrous roots are abundant throughout all noda except fellfield. Rhizomes occur in all noda but are only abundant in wet meadow. Bulbous belowground organs which are typical of geophytes contribute little to the biomass in any nodum; they are most common in the fellfield. Taken as a whole the belowground material of the dry alpine tundra on Niwot Ridge is comprised mostly of fibrous roots, rootstocks and tap roots (Table 1). The fibrous roots originate primarily from graminoids and the rootstocks and tap roots from forbs (Table 2). Species with rhizomes are relatively unimportant in this predominantly dry tundra system.

TABLE 3
Some standing crop, productivity, and turnover estimates at or in the vicinity of the deep soil pits

	Noda (plot number)						
Variables	Fellfield (1)	Dry meadow (29)	Snowbed (16)	Moist meadow (30)	Wet meadow (9)	Shrub tundra (13)	Mean
1 Net top production[a] (g m⁻² yr⁻¹)	105	191	124	157	202	275	176
2 Aboveground biomass[a] (g m⁻²)	159	212	134	163	228	1285	364
3 Aboveground standing crop[a] (g m⁻²) (excluding litter)	503	703	271	409	542	1515	657
4 Aboveground standing crop[a] (g m⁻²) (including litter)	752	1204	685	639	876	2638	1132
5 Belowground biomass[b] (g m⁻²)	2267	3556	3245	4079	4485	4300	3655
6 Belowground standing crop[b] (g m⁻²)	2627	4536	3792	5396	6369	5150	4645
Above:belowground ratios							
7 Live (5 ÷ 2)	1:14	1:17	1:24	1:25	1:20	1:3	1:17
8 Live + dead (6 ÷ 3)	1:5	1:6	1:14	1:13	1:12	1:3	1:9
9 Live + dead + aboveground litter (6 ÷ 4)	1:3	1:4	1:6	1:8	1:7	1:2	1:5
Turnover rates (years)							
10 Aboveground biomass (2 ÷ 1)	1.5	1.1	1.1	1.0	1.1	4.7	1.8
11 Aboveground standing crop (excluding litter) (3 ÷ 1)	4.8	3.7	2.2	2.6	2.7	5.5	3.6
12 Aboveground standing crop (including litter) (4 ÷ 1)	7.2	6.3	5.5	4.1	4.3	9.6	6.2
13 Belowground biomass (5 ÷ 1)	21.6	18.6	26.2	26.0	22.2	15.6	21.7
14 Belowground standing crop (6 ÷ 1)	25.0	23.8	30.6	34.4	31.5	18.7	27.3

[a] 1971 peak-season clip
[b] 1973 soil pit cores

RATIOS OF ABOVEGROUND TO BELOWGROUND MATERIAL

The more complete and thus larger harvest of belowground material by the pit coring method than by the surface coring method produced ratios of above- to belowground biomass which are smaller than shown in Figure 1 (see Table 3). Thus the dry meadow A:B biomass ratio changes from around 1:10 (Figure 1) to 1:17 (Table 3) and A:B for the snowbed nodum changes from around 1:10 to 1:24. Harvesting to even greater depths would further reduce the A:B ratios but because of the concentration in the upper horizons any reduction will only be small. Further discrepancies exist between Figure 1 and Table 3 because Table 3 is based on one representative plot per nodum whereas Figure 1 is a generalization from several plots.

Table 3 provides a variety of ratios of various aboveground and belowground materials, and estimates of turnover rates of these various materials. The latter are based on the assumptions that the Niwot vegetation is in a steady state, that the production year of 1971 was representative, and that belowground production equals that aboveground (Johnson and Kelley, 1970; Wielgolaski, 1975a).

The ratios formed from the quantities of aerial and subterranean materials progressively get larger as the nonliving fractions are included. This increase in ratio may be explained by the slower rate of decay to be found aboveground in all noda (Webber *et al.*, 1976). Consistent with this is the general decrease of these ratios (excluding fellfield and shrub tundra because of their perennial aboveground structures) along the gradient of increasing rates of surface decay, that is from dry meadow and snowbed to moist wet meadow (Table 3).

The rate of turnover of aboveground biomass in meadow and snowbed tundra is essentially unity which indicates the annual nature of their aboveground biomass. In fellfield where several species, especially cushion plants, have longer-lived perennial structures the aboveground turnover rate for biomass is 1.5 yr and in shrub tundra with long-lived aerial stems the rate is 4.7 yr. Turnover rates for belowground biomass are much slower than those for aboveground biomass indicating the perennial nature of the belowground system. Belowground biomass turnover times of almost 26 yr are estimated for snowbed and moist tundra with an average value for all noda of 21.7 yr. Shrub tundra has the fastest belowground biomass turnover rate of 15.6 yr. The turnover rate for standing crops of all aboveground material including litter varies from 4.1 to 9.6 yr with average value for all noda of 6.2 yr. It is fastest in moist and wet meadows and slowest in fellfields and shrub tundra. The turnover rate for belowground standing crops of intact plant material varies from 18.7 (shrub tundra) to 34.4 (moist meadow) with a nodal mean of 27.3.

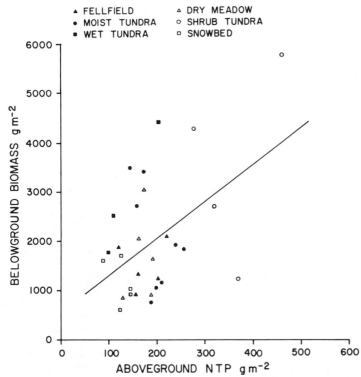

FIGURE 4. Belowground biomass plotted as a function of aboveground net shoot production (NTP). The data are from the 1971 extensive sampling.

When the total standing crop of soil humus, which ranges from around 10 kg m^{-2} in late snowbeds and fellfields to 30 kg m^{-2} in wet meadows and shrub tundra, and all other material of vascular plant origin are considered the turnover time ranges from 100 to 300 yr. However, the equilibrium time is very much longer and will be discussed in another paper by us in which we will elaborate upon the decomposition studies reported in Webber et al. (1976).

INTERRELATIONS BETWEEN THE STANDING CROP FRACTIONS AND ENVIRONMENTAL VARIABLES

No statistically significant correlations were found between the measured plant and abiotic substrate variables (that is, site and soil temperature, soil nutrients, soil moisture, surface and soil decomposition rates, snow cover, and soil stability). The variations about most mean values are large due to both sampling error and large point to point variation. The lack of statistically significant correlations between the variables prevents the construction of strong hypotheses concerning the environmental controls affecting the magnitude and distribution of the belowground structures on Niwot Ridge. Nevertheless, several quantitative and reasonably consistent trends were interpreted from the ordination results (Figure 1) and the detailed analysis of a few representative plots from each nodum (Table 3). The most striking trends are along the complex moisture gradient where productivity, rate of aboveground turnover, rate of surface decay, belowground standing crop, proportion of below- to aboveground material (B:A), and longevity of belowground biomass all increase as soil moisture increases. This generalization is weakened by the effects of some snowbed and shrub tundra stands which occur on moist-to-wet sites. These snowbeds may have low productivity and surface decay rates and yet some have relatively high belowground biomass values. Shrub tundra has a large, perennial aboveground biomass and is the most productive vegetation nodum. It is this complexity which further reduces the chances of significant biotic/abiotic correlations.

The distinct and somewhat similar patterns of aboveground production, aboveground biomass, belowground biomass, and the A:B

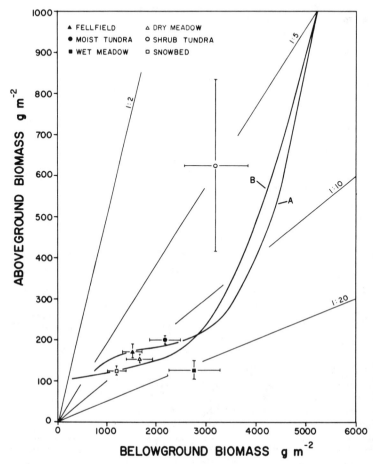

FIGURE 5. The aboveground vascular biomass for the six vegetation noda plotted as a function of belowground vascular biomass. Nodal means are plotted as a point with one standard error on either side of the mean as a bar. The straight lines represent above- to belowground biomass ratios of 2, 5, 10, and 20. The curved regression lines A and B are not based on the nodal averages but on the values for all 30 plots. Line A is a regression line of the form $Y = a + bx + cx^2$. Line B is a line of the same form which was forced through the point of zero biomass (i.e., where $a = 0$). The data are from the 1971 extensive sampling.

derivative within the ordination (Figure 1) suggest the presence of significant interrelationships. However, when these measures are studied in pairs through the use of graphs and regressions no unequivocal relationships can be seen (Figures 4 and 5). Nevertheless, we have tried to look for trends in the data which might at least serve as hypotheses for subsequent testing. In Figure 4 there is only the slightest positive correlation ($r = 0.1$) between aboveground production and belowground biomass in the herbaceous stands. When the stands of shrub tundra are included the correlation improves ($r = 0.5$), but it is barely significant. The regression equation for this relationship has a slope of 0.74 which suggests a belowground biomass turnover rate of 7.4 years. This is, however, a minimal estimate because the belowground data are from incomplete, shallow coring. In Figure 5 the

nodal means and the standard errors of aboveground biomass are plotted against those of belowground biomass. The four dry to moist, primarily herbaceous noda (fellfield, dry meadow, moist tundra, and snowbed) range around the A:B line of 1:10, the wet meadow close to 1:20, and the shrub tundra close to 1:5. A curvilinear regression of all 30 stands based on a second order polynomial equation provide lines A and B. Line A was forced through zero biomass while line B was not. These lines can be interpreted in terms of the A:B derivative by considering their position relative to the straight lines representing various A:B values. As aboveground and belowground biomass increase A:B first decreases from 1:5 through 1:10 to 1:15 and then increases through 1:10 to 1:5. The curves are skewed toward the higher biomasses of the shrub tundra. This skewed distribution of A:B with respect to increasing above- and belowground biomass would be absent if data from the shrub tundra were excluded. Then, the only trend that would be apparent for herbaceous tundra alone would be one in which A:B decreases as belowground biomass increases. This is primarily because the amount of herbaceous aboveground biomass varies very little along the various gradients and is relatively constant (100 to 250 g m^{-2}) while the amount of herbaceous belowground biomass varies much more (500 to 3500 g m^{-2}). However, we do consider it legitimate to keep the stands of shrub tundra in the regression because they are part of the natural continuum responding to the continuum of gradients. We also consider it legitimate to include woody stems containing dead sclerenchymatous cells in the biomass fraction. Wood which is covered by live cambium, phloem and bark does have some living ray cells (Zelawsky, 1962) and storage tissue and its live tissues are an important sink for photosynthetic materials (Dennis and Johnson, 1970).

COMPARISON WITH OTHER STUDIES

The vegetation types described on this small site have a close affinity with the plant communities recognized in other central and southern Rocky Mountain studies (Marr, 1961; Willard, 1963; Scott and Billings, 1964; Eddleman, 1967; Smith, 1969; Webber et al., 1976; and Komárková, 1976). These studies have also ranked soil moisture, snow accumulation, and soil disturbance or instability high on their lists of environmental controls of vegetation composition, structure, and productivity. The rate of primary production and size of standing crops estimated in this study are comparable to other studies from this Rocky Mountain region (Mooney and Billings, 1960; Paulsen, 1960; Scott and Billings, 1964). The broad physiognomic patterns and controls of the Niwot site are also reported from other North American alpine sites (e.g., Bliss, 1966, 1969) and other northern hemisphere sites (e.g., Dahl, 1956; Kjelvik and Kärenlampi, 1975; Wielgolaski, 1975b). In fact, the similarities go further and a case can be made to consider the site representative of tundra in general (Bliss, 1956, 1969; Webber, 1974) in spite of the contrasting climates and geomorphology. Certainly the productivity and standing crop patterns described here for

Niwot Ridge are similar to those reported for arctic regions (see Alexandrova, 1970).

Daubenmire (1941), Retzer (1956), and Scott and Billings (1964), have commented on the concentration of belowground material in the upper 25 cm. This is a characteristic in common with all tundra systems. However, the causes of this distribution may not be the same. In wet arctic tundra where impenetrable permafrost is often only 25 cm beneath the surface there is a clear mechanical cause (Dennis and Johnson, 1970). There is also a mechanical cause which prevents deep root penetration in wet meadow and some snowbed sites on Niwot Ridge where there is a high water table and bedrock is near the surface. In fact, these profiles (Figure 3) are very similar to those for wet arctic tundra (see Dennis and Johnson, 1970, or Dennis, 1977). In better drained sites in the arctic where the active layer is considerably deeper and on Niwot Ridge where permafrost has no influence on vegetation patterns, different causes must be in effect. No doubt temperature and nutrient availability from decomposition are more favorable to growth in the upper layers of the profile; however, root growth and uptake of minerals by tundra plants are remarkably efficient at low temperatures (Billings et al., 1977b; Chapin, 1977). A more proximate cause of this belowground pattern is probably the belowground root distributions of the hemicryptophytes and cryptophytes which comprise the majority of the vegetation.

The fact that broad belowground patterns of grassland which is comprised of the same predominant life-forms are the same as tundra (Dahlman and Kucera, 1965; Dennis and Johnson, 1970; Sims and Singh, 1971) supports the previous idea. Thus these standing crop patterns are not unique to tundra and this suggests that, while these growth-forms are successful in the tundra, the ultimate basis of tundra adaptations goes beyond basic plant form to the metabolic and physiologic characteristics.

Daubenmire (1941) examined the subterranean structural characteristics of Wyoming alpine plants. Although his survey did not examine monocotyledons and woody plants which comprise about half of the vascular plant standing crop, he concluded that no striking uniform adaptations were apparent. Adaptation may well be at a more subtle level than that of gross morphology. Billings et al.

(1977) have shown that certain tundra graminoids, while they have the same aboveground form, have very different rooting depths and longevity. On Niwot Ridge the various belowground structures show distinct patterns with respect to the various nodal environments (Table 1). For example, tap roots are prevalent on dry sites while rhizomes are prevalent on wet meadows. The same patterns are seen in the arctic tundra (Dennis and Johnson, 1970). Raup (1969) found that fibrous and tap roots were predominant over rhizomatous forms in the dry, rather barren vegetation of Northeast Greenland. The observation that rhizomes are relatively unimportant in dry, alpine tundra is at odds with Holch *et al.* (1941) who found that rhizomes were the commonest type of belowground system in the Colorado alpine. However, this discrepancy seems to lie in the definition of rhizome, for example, *Acomastylis rossii* in Table 1 is classified as having a rootstock while Holch *et al.* (1941) described it as rhizomatous. If rootstocks and rhizomes were combined as rhizomes in Table 1 they would be quite numerous and would rank only below fibrous roots in importance. Together they gain in importance in the wetter, colder noda. Although it may only be of incidental interest the alpine ecotype of *Oxyria digyna* has no rhizomes while its arctic ecotype does (Mooney and Billings, 1961).

The values for the amount of belowground standing crop found on Niwot Ridge are higher than those for some tundra sites (Mooney and Billings, 1960; Scott and Billings, 1964; Dennis and Johnson, 1970) but similar to others. For example, Bliss (1966) reports a value of 3634 g m^{-2} for the New England alpine and Alexandrova (1970) reports a value of 6226 g m^{-2} for Typical Arctic Tundra in the USSR. The present values also exceed those for grassland (Dahlman and Kucera, 1965; Sims and Singh, 1971).

A:B ratios vary considerably for tundra vegetation. Bliss and Mark (1974) have reported standing crop ratios of 1:0.5 and 1:0.8 for New Zealand cushion plant and herb fields. Dennis and Johnson (1970) reported A:B biomass ratios from 1:30 to 1:45. The mean value of 1:17 (Table 3) for the Niwot tundra is towards the lower end of the range of values reported by Wielgolaski (1975a) in his review. On the whole the Niwot biomass ratios compare very favorably with those for

Norwegian alpine tundra (Wielgolaski, 1972). The high values of 1:3 for shrub tundra are compatible with other values for shrub tundra (see Wielgolaski, 1975a). The ratio is increased when live and dead matter are combined; this has also been observed by Dennis and Johnson (1970) and Wielgolaski (1975a).

There are only a few estimates of turnover in the tundra literature. For wet Alaskan arctic tundra, turnover of aboveground standing crop material (including litter), seems to take between 4 and 5 yr (Dennis and Johnson, 1970; Johnson and Kelly, 1970). For a drier cushion and herb field communities in the New Zealand alpine where there is a larger aboveground standing crop turnover rates of between 8 and 15 yr have been estimated (Bliss and Mark, 1974). Niwot Ridge with a mean nodal value of 6 yr seems to be between these examples. The turnover rates of aboveground standing crop increase along the moisture gradient which is consistent with the observations on surface decay rates (Webber *et al.*, 1976). Dahlman and Kucera (1965) and Sims and Singh (1971) have estimated that belowground biomass in several prairie types turns over about every 4 yr. Beschel and Webb (1964) have shown that the main root of *Salix arctica* frequently lives longer than 50 yr. Dennis' (1968) estimates of belowground biomass turnover ranged from 10 to 20 yr in the wet Alaskan tundra. The Niwot Ridge belowground biomass turnover rates are similar to the latter although somewhat higher (15 to 26 yr — Table 3). These observations support the concept that the belowground tundra system is longer lived than that of grassland (Bliss, 1970).

The values of 10 to 30 kg m^{-2} for total soil organic matter on Niwot Ridge compares with 16.5 kg m^{-2} for Missouri Prairie (Dahlman and Kucera, 1965) and 22 to 45 kg m^{-2} for Barrow tundra (MacLean, 1974). Clearly large equilibrium times of several centuries are involved in these systems and large amounts of matter and energy are tied up in belowground organic matter. Very few of the several correlations and implied causal relationships between standing crop fractions and abiotic factors which are reported in the literature (see p. 158 and principally Scott and Billings (1964) and Wielgolaski (1975a)) were found in this study. For example, the A:B ratio did not increase with decreasing soil moisture or nutrients (cf. Billings and Scott, 1964), or decrease with decreasing temperature and decay rates (cf. Wielgolaski, 1975a). The only trend consistent with some reports is the decrease of A:B biomass ratio along the complex moisture gradient (Alexandrova, 1970; Wielgolaski, 1972).

Bliss (1966) has stressed that for tundra the errors of sampling and the large natural variation combine to weaken correlations. Scott and Billings (1964) and Smith (1969) also find that correlations between vegetation productivity and standing crops and environmental variables are low because in their view the total plant mass is the sum of the production of individual species reacting more or less independently to many environmental factors. Therefore it is not surprising that such correlations are low for A:B ratios because they are the combination of two partly independent production sums. However, a satisfactory resolution of the problem should not be entirely unattainable because tundra production is primarily the sum of only a few species and many of the factors controlling production affect all species similarly. Also, May (1973) was able to predict, albeit only at low levels of confidence, stand productivity of the Niwot tundra from environmental variables. We hope that better sampling methods may in the future provide more reliable insights into the controls of production and standing crop at the vegetation level.

The most frequent argument to be found in the literature on the cause of low A:B ratios of tundra is as follows. The A:B ratios of tundra are lower than the ratios given by Bray (1963) for herbaceous temperate vegetation, thus, the proportionate increase in belowground biomass may be a response to the more severe tundra environment (Scott and Billings, 1964: 264; Dennis and Johnson, 1970: 265; Bliss, 1970: 79; Wielgolaski, 1975a: 4). The

argument grew more emphatic with each successive use. There may be merit in the argument, but the explanation that the even smaller A:B ratios to be seen in the Niwot tundra when compared to the Barrow tundra is an expression of even more severe environment seems to be carrying the idea close to and even beyond its limits (Webber, 1974: 465). The within-site variation of A:B ratios seen here does not show a decrease with any gradient of increasing severity such as decreasing nutrients, temperature, or dessication. In fact, the decrease of A:B, excluding shrub tundra stands, follows the gradient of increasing productivity which could itself be regarded as an integrated measure of site favorability. Just as the concentration of biomass in the upper soil layers seems to be more directly a function of plant growth-form than it is of the environment, the magnitude of the A:B ratio seems to be more directly controlled by plant growth-form, which itself is a product of the environment. When cushion plants and shrubs are present A:B increases (Table 3 and Alexandrova, 1970; Bliss and Mark, 1974) and when belowground storage organs such as rootstocks and rhizomes become prevalent the A:B ratio decreases (Table 1 and Dennis and Johnson, 1970). Wielgolaski (1975a: 304) also pointed out that the A:B ratio is influenced by species composition in addition to environmental constraints. Clearly, more research into the nature of the A:B ratio is necessary. We suspect its value has been over-rated. One line of research to resolve the value of the A:B ratio is to continue the work started by Scott and Billings (1964), Bliss and Mark (1974), and Bell (1975) in which the A:B ratio of individual species were followed along the various field gradients. These results could then be compared with the ratios for the complete vegetation.

SUMMARY AND CONCLUSIONS

(1) The objective of this study was to examine the distribution of belowground biomass and standing crop along the various environmental gradients of the U.S. IBP Tundra Biome alpine site on Niwot Ridge, Colorado, with a view to determining their controls.

(2) An indirect ordination of 30 stands of vegetation was constructed to determine the principal environmental controls on the

species composition of vegetation at the site. They were, in order of importance, soil moisture, snow accumulation, and soil stability.

(3) Six major vegetation types or noda were identified within the continuum of the site. They were dry, *Trifolium* fellfield, dry *Kobresia* meadow, moist *Salix* shrub tundra, moist *Deschampsia* tundra, wet *Caltha* meadow, and *Sibbaldia* snowbed.

(4) Belowground biomass and standing

crops and aboveground vascular productivity were determined by soil coring and clip harvesting of the 30 ordination plots at the period of peak season aboveground vascular biomass. Each aboveground sample was separated into current year's growth, previous years' biomass, standing dead and litter and prostrate dead. Belowground biomass and standing crops were separated by washing. All results were expressed on an oven dry basis.

(5) Aboveground productivity varied from 100 to 300 g m^{-2} yr^{-1}; aboveground standing crops of biomass and standing dead reached values of 2000 g m^{-2}, and with the addition of litter reached 3000 g m^{-2}. Belowground biomass values ranged from 1000 to 5000 g m^{-2}, and belowground standing crops of intact material ranged from 1000 to 8000 g m^{-2}.

(6) The various productivity and standing-crop fractions were plotted within the framework of the ordination to determine how they varied along the principal complex environmental gradients. Aboveground productivity is highest on moist sites with moderate snow cover and little disturbance, and it is low on dry, winter snow-free sites, in late snowbeds, and very wet sites. Maximum aboveground standing crop coincides with the distribution of highest aboveground productivity (shrub tundra) but it is also high on dry sites where the decay of litter and standing dead material is slow; it is lowest on wet sites. Belowground biomass is highest beneath shrub tundra but it is also high beneath other wet sites; it is lowest beneath dry sites.

(7) In order to obtain a more detailed picture of the belowground distribution of vascular plant material a deep soil pit was dug in a representative stand of each nodum. This provided vertical profile distributions of biomass, standing crop, and soil humus.

(8) The vertical profiles showed that 49 to 84% of the belowground biomass occurs in the top 10 cm of the soil. Estimates of the belowground standing crop of soil humus provided values of 10 kg m^{-2} for dry sites and late snowbeds and up to 30 kg m^{-2} in moist and wet sites.

(9) The species comprising each nodum have a distinct suite of belowground plant organs. For example, fellfield has the most tap rooted plants and dry meadow has the most fibrous rooted plants. On the whole Niwot Ridge tundra has a predominance of fibrous rooted vegetation which is indicative of its overall dry character. However, along the moisture gradient which is also the gradient of increasing belowground biomass, the proportion of plants with rootstocks and rhizomes increased.

(10) Aboveground to belowground (A:B) ratios of biomass ranged from 1:3 to 1:25. When dead standing crop fractions were considered along with biomass, A:B ratios increased indicating slower decay rates aboveground than belowground. Ratios were highest in shrub tundra and lowest in moist tundra.

(11) Ratios of aboveground productivity to various standing crop and biomass fractions were used to indicate various turnover rates. Aboveground living structures in herbaceous tundra are essentially annual with turnover rates of 1 yr while in fellfield and in shrub tundra aboveground biomass turnover rates of 1.5 and 4.7 yr were estimated. Belowground structures have long average lives of about 20 yr; they seem to live longest in cold moist sites and least in shrub tundra.

(12) No statistically significant correlations could be found between measured site variables and the various productivity and standing crop fractions. Sampling errors and natural variation of both sets of variables seem to be responsible for this lack of correlation. However, one reasonably consistent set of trends emerged from the study. It is that along the complex moisture gradient productivity, rate of aboveground turnover, rate of surface decay, belowground standing crop, and longevity of belowground biomass all increase; the A:B biomass ratio tends to decrease along this gradient.

(13) The low A:B biomass ratios found in tundra are often considered as an adaptation to a severe environment; the significance of this could not be assessed because of the lack of correlations with the environmental factors. The magnitude of the A:B ratio seems to be more directly controlled by species and growth-form composition of the vegetation than the environment.

(14) A comparison of these results with the available tundra literature shows Niwot Ridge to be representative not only of the central Rocky Mountain alpine tundra but tundra in general. The values of productivity, standing crop, and derived variables such as A:B ratios and turnover rates are within the published

ranges.

(15) Methodological studies are required with a view to reducing sampling errors and to examine better the relationships between productivity, standing crops, and their controls. Only then can reliable generalizations about the nature of tundra vegetation be forthcoming.

ACKNOWLEDGMENTS

This study was supported by grant number GV 29350 from the National Science Foundation. We would like to thank the many field assistants who helped gather and process the data. In particular we should single out Sue Vetter Clark, Clare Priest, and Kim Sutherland for their unflagging efforts with the soil core washing and plant sorting. Ms. Kathleen Salzberg graciously assisted with the manuscript preparation. We wish to thank Dr. Frans Wielgolaski of the University of Oslo for his stimulation while we were developing the data. Finally we wish to thank Dr. John K. Marshall of the Commonwealth Scientific and Industrial Research Organization, Australia, who organized the symposium where these data were first presented; it was he who provided the idea for this report.

REFERENCES

Alexandrova, V. D., 1958: An attempt to measure the overground and underground productivity of plant communities in the arctic tundra. *Bot. Zh.*, 43: 1748-1762.

———, 1970: The vegetation of the tundra zones in the USSR and data about its productivity. *In* Fuller, W. A. and Kevan, P. G. (eds.), *Productivity and Conservation in Northern Circumpolar Lands*, Internat. Union Conserv. Natur., Morges, Switzerland, Publ. N.S., 16: 93-114.

Barry, R. G., 1973: A climatological transect on the east slope of the Front Range, Colorado. *Arct. Alp. Res.*, 5: 89-110.

Bell, K. L., 1975: Root adaptations to a polar semi-desert. *In* Bliss, L. C. (ed.), *Plant and Surface Responses to Environmental Conditions in the Western High Arctic.* Canada Dep. Indian and North. Affairs, Publ. QS-8056-000-EE-A1: 21-72.

Benedict, J. B., 1970: Downslope soil movement in a Colorado alpine region: rates, processes, and climatic significance. *Arct. Alp. Res.*, 2: 165-226.

Beschel, R. E. and Webb, D., 1964: Growth ring studies on arctic willows. *In* Müller, F. (ed.), *Axel Heiberg Island, Preliminary Report.* McGill University, Montreal, 189-198.

Billings, W. D., 1974: Arctic and alpine vegetation, plant adaptations to cold summer climates. *In* Ives, J. D. and Barry, R. G. (eds.), *Arctic and Alpine Environments.* Methuen, London, 403-443.

Billings, W. D. and Mooney, H. A., 1968: The ecology of arctic and alpine plants. *Biol. Rev.*, 43: 481-529.

Billings, W. D., Peterson, K. M., and Shaver, G. R., 1977: Growth, turnover and respiration of roots and tillers of tundra graminoids. *In* Tieszen, L. L. (ed.), *The Ecology of Primary Producer Organisms in the Alaskan Arctic Tundra.* Springer-Verlag, New York (in press).

Billings, W. D., Peterson, K. M., Shaver, G. R., and Trent, A. W., 1977: Root growth, respiration, and carbon dioxide evolution in an arctic tundra soil. *Arct. Alp. Res.*, 9(2): 127-135.

Bliss, L. C., 1956: A comparison of plant development in arctic and alpine tundras. *Ecol. Monogr.*, 26: 303-337.

———, 1962: Adaptations of arctic and alpine plants to environmental conditions. *Arctic*, 15: 117-144.

———, 1963: Alpine plant communities of the Presidential Range, New Hampshire. *Ecology*, 44: 678-697.

———, 1966: Plant productivity in alpine microenvironments on Mt. Washington, New Hampshire. *Ecol. Monogr.*, 36: 125-155.

———, 1969: Alpine community pattern in relation to environmental parameters. *In* Greenidge, K. N. H. (ed.), *Essays in Plant Geography and Ecology.* Nova Scotia Museum, Halifax, Canada, 167-184.

———, 1970: Primary production within arctic tundra ecosystems. *In* Fuller, W. A. and Kevan, P. G. (eds.), *Productivity and Conservation in Northern Circumpolar Lands*, Internat. Union Conserv. Natur., Morges, Switzerland, Publ. N.S., 16: 77-85.

———, 1971: Arctic and alpine plant life cycles. *Ann. Rev. Ecol. Syst.*, 2: 405-438.

Bliss, L. C. and Cantlon, J. E., 1957: Succession on river alluvium in northern Alaska. *Amer. Midl. Nat.*, 58: 452-469.

Bliss, L. C. and Mark, A. F., 1974: High-alpine environments and primary production on the Rock and Pillar Range, Central Otago, New

Zealand. *N. Z. J. Bot.*, 12: 445-483.

Bonde, E. K., Foreman, M. F., Babb, T. A., Kjelvik, S., McKendrick, J. D., Mitchell, W. W., and Wooding, F. J., 1973: *In* Bliss, L. C. and Wielgolaski, F. E. (eds.), *Primary Production and Production Processes, Tundra Biome.* International Tundra Biome Steering Committee, University of Alberta, Edmonton, Alberta, Canada, 99-110.

Bray, J. R., 1963: Root production and the estimation of net productivity. *Can. J. Bot.*, 41: 65-72.

Bray, J. R. and Curtis, J. T., 1957: An ordination of the upland forest communities of southern Wisconsin. *Ecol. Monogr.*, 27: 325-349.

Cain, S. A., 1950: Life forms and phytoclimate. *Bot. Rev.*, 16: 1-32.

Chapin, F. S., III, 1977: Temperature compensation in phosphate absorption occurring over diverse time scales. *Arct. Alp. Res.*, 9(2): 137-146.

Dadykin, V. P., 1954: Peculiarities of plant behavior in cold soils. *Vopr. Bot.*, 2: 455-472 (in Russian); 473-489 (in French).

Dahl, E., 1956: Rondane Mountain vegetation in South Norway and its relation to the environment. *Norske Vid.-Akak. Oslo I. Mat.-Nat. Kl. 3.* 374 pp.

Dahlman, R. C. and Kucera, C. L., 1965: Root productivity and turnover in native prairie. *Ecology*, 46: 84-86.

Daubenmire, R. F., 1941: Some ecological features of the subterranean organs of alpine plants. *Ecology*, 22: 370-378.

Dennis, J. G., 1968: *Growth of Tundra Vegetation in Relation to Arctic Micro-environments at Barrow, Alaska.* Ph.D. dissertation, Duke University. 289 pp.

―――― 1977: Distribution patterns of belowground standing crop in arctic tundra at Barrow, Alaska. *Arct. Alp. Res.*, 9(2): 111-125.

Dennis, J. G. and Johnson, P. L., 1970: Shoot and rhizome root standing crops of tundra vegetation at Barrow, Alaska. *Arct. Alp. Res.*, 2: 253-266.

Eddleman, L/E., 1967: A study of phyto-edaphic relationships in alpine tundra of northern Colorado. Ph.D. thesis, Colorado State University, Fort Collins. 148 pp.

Emerick, J., 1976: Effects of artificially increased winter snow cover on plant canopy architecture and primary production in selected areas of Colorado alpine tundra. Ph.D. thesis, University of Colorado, Boulder. 193 pp.

Flock, J. W., 1976: The influence of snow cover and soil moisture on bryophyte and lichen distribution, Niwot Ridge, Boulder County, Colorado. Ph.D. thesis, University of Colorado,

Boulder. 168 pp.

Harper, J. L. and Ogden, J., 1970: The reproductive strategy of higher plants I. The concept of strategy with special reference to *Senecio vulgaris* L. *J. Ecol.*, 58: 681-698.

Holch, A. E., Hertel, E. W., Oakes, W. O., and Whitwell, H. H., 1941: Root habits of certain plants of the foothill and alpine belts of Rocky Mountain National Park. *Ecol. Monogr.*, 11: 327-345.

Holm, T. H., 1927: The vegetation of the alpine region of the Rocky Mountains in Colorado. *Nat. Acad. Sci. Mem.*, 19: 1-45.

Ives, J. D. and Fahey, B. D., 1971: Permafrost occurrence in the Front Range, Colorado Rocky Mountains, USA. *J. Glaciol.*, 10: 105-111.

Johnson, P. L. and Kelley, J. J., Jr., 1970: Dynamics of carbon dioxide and productivity in an arctic biosphere. *Ecology*, 5(1): 73-80.

Kjelvik, S. and Kärenlampi, L., 1975: Plant biomass and primary production of Fennoscandian Subarctic and Subalpine Forests of Alpine Willow and Heath Ecosystems. *In* Wielgolaski, F. E. (ed.), *Fennoscandian Tundra Ecosystems Part I: Plants and Microorganisms.* Springer-Verlag, New York, 111-120.

Komárková, Vera, 1976: Alpine vegetation of the Indian Peaks Area, Front Range Colorado Rocky Mountains. Ph.D. thesis, University of Colorado, Boulder. 655 pp.

Komárková, V. and Webber, P. J., 1977: An alpine vegetation map of Niwot Ridge, Colorado. *Arct. Alp. Res.*, 9(4): in press.

MacLean, S. F., 1974: Production, decomposition, and the activity of soil invertebrates in tundra ecosystems: a hypothesis. *In* Holding, A. J., Heal, O. W., MacLean, S. F., and Flanagan, P. W. (eds.), *Soil Organisms and Decomposition in Tundra. Proceedings of a Working Group Meeting in Fairbanks, Alaska, August, 1973.* Tundra Biome Steering Committee, Stockholm, Sweden, 197-206.

Marr, J. W., 1961: Ecosystems of the east slope of the Front Range in Colorado. *Univ. Colo. Stud., Ser. Biol.*, 8. 134 pp.

May, D. E., 1973: Models for predicting primary production in alpine tundra ecosystems. M.A. thesis, University of Colorado, Boulder. 99 pp.

――――, 1976: The response of alpine tundra vegetation in Colorado to environmental variation. Ph.D. thesis, University of Colorado, Boulder. 164 pp.

May, D. E. and Webber, P. J., 1975: Summary of soil and plant canopy temperatures for the major vegetation types from Niwot Ridge, Colorado, for the period July 1972-October 1974. *U.S. Tundra Biome Data Rep. 75-80.* 129 pp.

Mooney, H. A. and Billings, W. D., 1960: The annual carbohydrate cycle of alpine plants as related to growth. *Amer. J. Bot.*, 47: 594-598.

Mooney, H. A. and Billings, W. D., 1961: Comparative physiological ecology of arctic and alpine population of *Oxyria digyna. Ecol. Monogr.*, 31: 1-29.

Osburn, W. S., Jr., 1958: Ecology of winter snow-free areas of the alpine tundra of Niwot Ridge, Boulder County, Colorado. Ph.D. thesis, University of Colorado, Boulder, Colorado. 77 pp.

Paulsen, H. A., Jr., 1960: Plant cover and forage use of alpine sheep ranges in the central Rocky Mountains. *Iowa State J. Sci.*, 34: 731-748.

Raunkiaer, C., 1934: *The Life Forms of Plants and Statistical Plant Geography.* Clarendon, Oxford. 632 pp.

Raup, H. M., 1969: The relation of the vascular flora to some factors of site in the Mesters Vig district of Northeast Greenland. *Medd. Grønland,* 176(5): 1-80.

Rodin, L. E. and Bazilevich, N. I., 1967: *Production and Mineral Cycling in Terrestrial Vegetation.* Oliver and Boyd, Edinburgh. 288 pp.

Retzer, J. L., 1956: Alpine soils of the Rocky Mountains. *J. Soil Sci.*, 7: 22-32.

Scott, D. and Billings, W. D., 1964: Effects of environmental factors on standing crop and productivity of an alpine tundra. *Ecol. Monogr.*, 34: 243-270.

Sims, P. L. and Singh, J. S., 1971: Herbage dynamics and net primary production in certain ungrazed grasslands in North America. *In* French, N. E. (ed.), *Preliminary Analysis of Structure and Function in Grasslands.* Colorado State Univ., Range Sci. Dep., Sci. Ser., 10: 59-124.

Smith, D. R., 1969: Vegetation, soils and their relationships at timberline in the Medicine Bow Mountains, Wyoming. *Sci. Monogr.*, 17, Agricultural Experiment Station, University of Wyoming, Laramie. 14 pp.

Sokal, R. R. and Sneath, P. H. A., 1963: *Principles of Numerical Taxonomy.* Freeman, San Francisco. 359 pp.

Tieszen, L. L., 1971: *Tundra Biome Plant Specialists Meeting, April 8–10, 1971, Kananaskis Research Station, University of Alberta, Calgary, Alberta, Canada.* US/IBP Tundra Biome, Analysis of Ecosystems Program. 14 pp.

Warren Wilson, J., 1959: Analysis of the distribution of the foliage area in grassland. *In* Ivins, J. D. (ed.), *The Measurement of Grassland Productivity.* Butterworth, London, 51-61.

Washburn, A. L., 1956: Classification of patterned ground and review of suggested origins. *Geol. Soc. Amer. Bull.*, 64: 823-866.

Webber, P. J., 1971: Gradient analysis of the vegetation around the Lewis Valley North-Central Baffin Island, Northwest Territories, Canada. Ph.D. thesis, Queen's University, Kingston, Canada. 366 pp.

——, 1972: Comparative ordination and productivity of tundra vegetation. *In* Bowen, S. (ed.), *Proceedings of the 1972 Tundra Symposium, Lake Wilderness Center, University of Washington.* U.S. Tundra Biome, U.S. International Biological Program and U.S. Arctic Research Program, 55-60.

——, 1974: Tundra primary productivity. *In* Ives, J. D. and Barry, R. G. (eds.), *Arctic and Alpine Environments.* Methuen, London, 445-473.

Webber, P. J. and Ebert, D. C., 1973: Ordination and production of tundra vegetation from Niwot Ridge, Colorado, and Point Barrow, Alaska. *U.S. Tundra Biome Data Rep.*, 73-22. 72 pp.

Webber, P. J., Emerick, J. C., May, D. C. E., and Komárková, V., 1976: The impact of increased snowfall on alpine vegetation. *In* Steinhoff, H. W. and Ives, J. D. (eds.), *Ecological Impacts of Snowpack Augmentation in the San Juan Mountains, Colorado.* Final Report of the San Juan Ecology Project. Colorado State University, CSU-FNR-7052-1, 201-264.

Wielgolaski, F. E., 1972: Vegetation types and plant biomass in tundra. *Arct. Alp. Res.*, 4: 291-306.

——, 1975a: Productivity of Tundra Ecosystems. *In: Proceedings of a Symposium on Productivity of World Ecosystems.* National Academy of Sciences, Washington, D.C., 1-12.

——, 1975b: Primary productivity of alpine meadow communities. *In* Wielgolaski, F. E. (ed.), *Fennoscandian Tundra Ecosystems Part I: Plants and Microorganisms.* Springer-Verlag, New York, 121-128.

Willard, B. E., 1963: Phytosociology of the alpine tundra of Trail Ridge, Rocky Mountain National Park, Colorado. Ph.D. thesis, University of Colorado, Boulder. 245 pp.

Zelawsky, W., 1962: Traumatogen respiration of living wood elements. *Acta. Soc. Bot. Pol.*, 31: 313-335.

Part 6
Animal Ecology

Overview
*Terry A. May**

Past emphasis and intensity of field studies of animals (both invertebrates and vertebrates) found at high altitudes in the Colorado Front Range and the quantity of the resulting information have been varied. As a result, current knowledge of individual species is uneven, at best. This is the case even though the Front Range is a highly attractive and biologically interesting area for study. Reasons for apparent gaps in knowledge are many: perhaps the most important is the absence of an animal ecologist in the past and present development of INSTAAR. Additional reasons include the vagaries of history and the logistical difficulties associated with conducting field studies at widely separated and undisturbed mountainous sites. As a result, there are great research needs and opportunities for future studies of animals in high altitude areas with both basic and applied objectives. Topics for consideration are limited only by individual imagination.

Papers reprinted in this chapter are not intended to give a complete portrayal of the available literature dealing with the ecology of animals of the Front Range. Rather, papers were selected to cover representative topics of inquiry which are biologically important and which should stimulate thought and discussion. All the studies selected have been conducted in the alpine in contrast to the high-altitude subalpine. This was done to emphasize the uniqueness of the extensive alpine tundra in Colorado and to stimulate a proportionately greater research effort in the alpine.

Of the papers included here, only Neldner and Pennak (1955) is concerned with aquatic systems. The fauna considered in their paper likely play minor roles in the functioning of tundra ecosystems, but much more importantly, the paper stresses that

*School of Forest Resources
University of Maine

little is known about the ecology of high altitude ponds and
lakes. It is unfortunate that relatively little new information
has been published since this paper was written over 20 years
ago. This paper is also noteworthy because of its detailed description of the abiotic environment of the tundra pool studied
and the conditions to which aquatic organisms are subjected
throughout the year.

Of the remaining six papers reprinted here, two (Alexander,
1951; Schmoller, 1971a) deal with invertebrates (Arthropods),
two (Campbell, 1970a; Spencer, 1971) deal with amphibians, one
(Stoecker, 1976) deals with mammals, and one (May and Braun,
1972) deals with birds. This breakdown should not be construed
as an indication of the relative understanding of these four
general categories of animals. Certainly, the arthropods (insects and their allies) include the greatest number of species
and individuals as well as being the faunal category with representatives occurring most uniformly over the alpine in all habitats. Arthropods play major roles in the functioning of tundra
ecosystems and are probably the least well known of the commonly
occurring faunal groups in the alpine.

It is particularly fitting that the papers by Alexander
(1951) and one of his students (Schmoller, 1971a) should be reprinted here. Dr. Gordon Alexander, a long-time professor at
the University of Colorado before his untimely death in 1973, is
directly and indirectly responsible for much that is known about
the ecology of arthropods in the Colorado alpine. In his paper,
he discusses the relative importance and ecological adaptations
of grasshoppers in tundra; however, he did not quantify the
impact of these herbivorous insects on tundra plants. This
seems to be an area of research that is of great relevance. In
addition, Alexander stresses the importance of air currents in
transporting grasshoppers from lower altitudes to the alpine,
but again this was not quantified. Anyone traversing tundra
snowfields in late spring and summer can readily verify Alexander's observation as many species of both winged and flightless
arthropods from lower altitudes are deposited on the snow surface
by strong upslope winds. Because these species are not adapted
to tundra environments, they are vulnerable to predation by
insectivorous birds and may be a major food source. Arthropod
fallout on ice and snow has been studied elsewhere (e.g., Edwards, 1972), but the resulting impact on tundra birds has not
been evaluated.

Dr. Ronald Schmoller has produced a series of significant
papers (1970, 1971a, 1971b) concerning Arthropoda as a result
of his doctoral research in Boulder, but only one of these (1971a)
is reprinted. This paper emphasizes that alpine tundra has a
significant nocturnal arthropod fauna while arctic tundra, presumably because of the high-latitude, long day, does not. This
is a good example of the ecological implications of differences
in photoperiods between mid- and high-latitude tundra sites.
More general studies considering ecological, physiological, and

behavioral differences, which are related to photoperiod, should
be conducted in all the faunal groups. Schmoller (1971a) also
stresses the potential ecological importance of arthropods as
predators on herbivorous diurnal arthropods. The reader is also
referred to a related paper by Tolbert *et al*. (1977) that resulted from the arthropod research program initiated on Niwot
Ridge by Schmoller in conjunction with the International Biological Program, U.S. Tundra Biome.

In comparison to the arthropods, the amphibians include the
fewest number of species and individuals as well as being the
faunal category with the most restricted distribution in the
alpine for obvious ecological reasons. The short papers by Campbell (1970a) and Spencer (1971) are reprinted to stress that at
least two species of amphibians are known to occur above timberline as a result of highly specialized adaptations which are
only partially known for boreal toads (*Bufo boreas boreas*)
(Campbell, 1970b, 1970c) and which should be known in detail for
both species.

Marr (1964) presented an overview of the Front Range tundra
with emphasis on grazing by free-living and domesticated animals.
This paper is important and should be read by everyone but was
not reprinted here because it includes material discussed in
more detail in Chapter 6. In his 1964 paper, Marr describes
and evaluates the utilization of tundra by mammals but largely
ignores tundra birds. This is understandable, because mammals
likely have the greatest and birds the least impact on tundra
ecosystems of all the commonly occurring faunal groups. Specifically, Marr (1964) suggested that the pocket gopher (*Thomomys
talpoides*) is probably the most influential tundra animal. This
idea is supported by recent studies of the dynamics of tundra
plant communities by Webber and May (1977); however, the actual
pattern and magnitude of the impact of pocket gophers on tundra
plant communities is only partially known. The most complete
study of this was by Stoecker (1976) which is reprinted here.

A number of other species of mammals ranging in size from
shrews (*Sorex* spp.) to elk (*Cervus canadensis*) and bighorn
sheep (*Ovis canadensis*) are common on the tundra during parts or
all of the year. These species are able to exploit tundra habitats as a result of many and varied strategies. The paper by
Johnson and Maxwell (1966) is emphasized because it illustrates
one of these strategies although it is not reproduced here.
This paper discusses the energy dynamics of pikas (*Ochotona
princeps*), a small rabbit-like animal characteristic of tundra
boulder fields on a year-round basis.

Even though tundra birds likely play minor roles in the
functioning of Colorado alpine ecosystems, they are readily
observable from spring through fall and are therefore of considerable aesthetic interest. As a result of the ease of observing tundra birds, previous studies have emphasized the
general ecology of species so that the natural histories of the
most commonly observed species breeding in the alpine (water

pipit (*Anthus spinoletta*), rosy finches (*Leucosticte* spp.), horned lark (*Eremophila alpestris*), and white crowned sparrow (*Zonotrichia leucophrys*)) are generally well known (e.g., Johnson, 1965; Verbeek, 1967, 1970; Morton *et al.*, 1972). However, these studies were conducted outside Colorado so that much comparative work remains to be done in the Colorado alpine.

West and Norton (1975) stressed the importance of the strategic distinction between permanent residents and summer visitors in tundra birds. All of the previously mentioned species are summer visitors while the only year-round resident in the Colorado alpine is the white-tailed ptarmigan (*Lagopus leucurus*). This species is well adapted to cold-dominated environments and has been the subject of a long-term, cooperative research effort in Colorado by Dr. Clait E. Braun, a wildlife researcher for the Colorado Division of Wildlife, and his colleagues. May and Braun (1972) is reprinted here as an example of the papers (Braun, 1971; Braun and Rogers, 1971; Braun and Schmidt, 1971; Braun *et al.*, 1976; Hoffman and Braun, 1975, 1977; May and Braun, 1973) produced from this project and because it summarizes the seasonal patterns of habitat selection and quantifies the foods eaten by Colorado ptarmigan.

Unfortunately, careful reading of the papers reprinted in this chapter provides little insight into future research needs and priorities. This is not surprising, but a major objective of this chapter is to stimulate interest and thought concerning the direction of future research in the animals of the Colorado alpine. Therefore, I offer the following statements which reflect my training, personal biases, and knowledge of the existing literature rather than a synthesis of published observations. At the risk of being overly simplistic, I maintain that:

1. Terrestrial systems are better known than aquatic systems;
2. The magnitude of environmental variability is better known than its predictability and significance to populations of animals;
3. Life histories of animals are better known than their roles and functions;
4. Dynamics of single species are better known than interactions between species;
5. Habitat selection by animals is more often defined in terms of the perception of the investigator rather than in terms of the perception of the organism;
6. The response of animals to vegetation patterns is better known than the influence animals have in creating and maintaining vegetation patterns; and
7. Densities of animals are better known than patterns of dispersion and their causes.

It is my hope that the reader will critically evaluate the reprinted papers as well as my introduction and that they will

serve as an impetus for new research efforts which will ultimately lead to a more complete and balanced understanding of
the ecology of animals in the Colorado Front Range tundra.

REFERENCES

Alexander, G. 1951. The occurrence of Orthoptera at high al-
    titudes, with special reference to Colorado Acrididae.
    Ecology, 32(1): 104-112.
Braun, C.E. 1971. Habitat requirements of Colorado white-
    tailed ptarmigan. *Proc. Western Assoc. State Game and
    Fish Commissioners*, 51: 284-292.
Braun, C.E. and G.E. Rogers. 1971. The white-tailed ptarmigan
    in Colorado. *Colorado Division of Game, Fish, and Parks*,
    Tech. Publ. 27: 1-80.
Braun, C.E. and R.K. Schmidt, Jr. 1971. Effects of snow and
    wind on wintering populations of white-tailed ptarmigan in
    Colorado. *In* Haugen, A.O. (ed.), *Snow and Ice Symposium*.
    Iowa Coop. Wildlife Res. Unit, Iowa State University, Ames,
    pp. 238-250.
Braun, C.E., R.W. Hoffman, and G.E. Rogers. 1976. Wintering
    areas and winter ecology of white-tailed ptarmigan in
    Colorado. *Colorado Division of Wildlife Special Report*,
    38: 1-38.
Campbell, J.B. 1970a. New elevational records for the boreal
    toad (*Bufo boreas boreas*). *Arctic and Alpine Research*,
    2(2): 157-159.
_____. 1970b. Hibernacula of a population of *Bufo boreas
    boreas* in the Colorado Front Range. *Herpetologica*, 26(2):
    278-282.
_____. 1970c. Food habits of the boreal toad, *Bufo boreas
    boreas*, in the Colorado Front Range. *J. Herpetology*, 4
    (1-2): 83-85.
Edwards, J.S. 1972. Arthropod fallout on Alaskan snow. *Arctic
    and Alpine Research*, 4(2): 167-176.
Hoffman, R.W. and C.E. Braun. 1975. Migration of a wintering
    population of white-tailed ptarmigan in Colorado. *J.
    Wildlife Management*, 39(3): 485-490.
Hoffman, R.W. and C.E. Braun. 1977. Characteristics of a
    wintering population of white-tailed ptarmigan in Colorado.
    Wilson Bulletin, 89(1): 107-115.
Johnson, D.R. and M. Maxwell. 1966. Energy dynamics of Colo-
    rado pikas. *Ecology*, 47(6): 1059-1061.
Johnson, R.E. 1965. Reproductive activities of rosy finches,
    with special reference to Montana. *Auk*, 82(2): 190-205.
Marr, J.W. 1961. Ecosystems of the east slope of the Front
    Range in Colorado. *Univ. Colo. Series in Biology*, 8: 1-134.
_____. 1964. Utilization of the Front Range tundra, Colorado.
    In Grazing in terrestrial and marine environments. *Black-
    well Scientific Publications*, pp. 109-118.

May, T.A. and C.E. Braun. 1972. Seasonal foods of adult white-tailed ptarmigan in Colorado. *J. Wildlife Management*, 36(4): 1180-1186.

May, T.A. and C.E. Braun. 1973. Gizzard stones from adult white-tailed ptarmigan (*Lagopus leucurus*) in Colorado. *Arctic and Alpine Research*, 5(1): 49-57.

Morton, M.L., J.L. Horstmann, and J.M. Osborn. 1972. Reproductive cycle and nesting success of the mountain white-crowned sparrow (*Zonotrichia leucophrys*) in the central Sierra Nevada. *Condor*, 74(2): 152-163.

Neldner, K.H. and R.W. Pennak. 1955. Seasonal fauna variations in a Colorado alpine pond. *American Midland Naturalist*, 53(2): 419-430.

Schmoller, R. 1970. Life histories of alpine tundra Arachnida in Colorado. *American Midland Naturalist*, 83(1): 119-133.

_____. 1971a. Nocturnal arthropods in the alpine tundra of Colorado. *Arctic and Alpine Research*, 3(4): 345-352.

_____. 1971b. Habitats and zoogeography of alpine tundra Arachnida and Carabidae (Coleoptera) in Colorado. *Southwestern Naturalist*, 15(3): 319-329.

Spencer, A.W. 1971. Boreal chorus frogs (*Pseudacris triseriata*) breeding in the alpine in southwestern Colorado. *Arctic and Alpine Research*, 3(4): 353.

Stoecker, R. 1976. Pocket gopher distribution in relation to snow in the alpine tundra. *In* Steinhoff, H.W. and J.D. Ives (eds.), *Ecological Impacts of Snowpack Augmentation in the San Juan Mountains, Colorado*. Final Report, San Juan Ecology Project, Colorado State University Publ., Fort Collins, pp. 281-287.

Tolbert, W.W., V.R. Tolbert, and R.E. Ambrose. 1977. Distribution, abundance, and biomass of Colorado alpine arthropods. *Arctic and Alpine Research*, 9(3): 221-234.

Verbeek, N.A.M. 1967. Breeding biology and ecology of the horned lark in alpine tundra. *Wilson Bulletin*, 79(2): 208-218.

_____. 1970. Breeding ecology of the water pipit. *Auk*, 87(3): 425-451.

Webber, P.J. and D.E. May. 1977. The magnitude and distribution of below ground plant structures in the alpine tundra of Niwot Ridge, Colorado. *Arctic and Alpine Research*, 9(2): 157-174.

West, G.C. and D.W. Norton. 1975. Metabolic adaptations of tundra birds. *In* Fernberg, F.J. (ed.), *Physiological Adaptation to the Environment*. Intext Educational Publ., New York, pp. 301-329.

Seasonal Faunal Variations in a Colorado Alpine Pond[1]

Kenneth H. Neldner and Robert W. Pennak
University of Colorado, Boulder

The peculiar and highly variable physical conditions prevailing in the alpine tundra make it one of the most rigorous of all types of environments. This is true for aquatic as well as terrestrial communities. The fauna of an alpine tundra pond, for example, must be adapted to a very short period of activity when the water is ice-free and to a long period of suspended activity in the frozen bottom of the pond during the winter. It must also be adapted to rapid and extensive daily temperature changes produced by alternating periods of cloudiness, high insolation, cold nights, frequent cold showers, and strong winds.

Although the seasonal hydrobiology of alpine lakes is poorly known, it is further true that even less is known about the hydrobiology of small alpine tundra ponds. The American literature on the ecology of high altitude ponds is exceptionally scanty, most of this information being limited to casual or occasional observations. The European literature is much more extensive, but it is unfortunate that the great majority of such studies are based upon single visits to particular ponds. A few investigations are based upon two, three, or rarely more visits. As a consequence, such publications are necessarily limited to short general discussions, brief descriptions of pond habitats, and lists of species collected during the one or several visits. Typical papers are those of Brink and Wingstrand (1949), Pesta (1933, 1935, 1943), Pichler (1939a, 1939b), Stirnimann (1926), Thomasson (1951, 1952), and Turnowsky (1946).

It therefore follows that our concept of the seasonal appearance, development, and disappearance of animal populations in tundra ponds is exceedingly sketchy, and it is the purpose of the present paper to give a seasonal characterization of a typical Colorado alpine tundra pond based on observations and collections distributed throughout the open season. Emphasis is placed on the seasonal abundance of the major aquatic organisms, exclusive of most of the microscopic forms. The collections were quantitative whenever possible. A few physical and chemical determinations were also made. The study extended from June 29 to October 29, 1950, and this period represents the entire open season of the pond in that year. The data were gathered on 15 trips at seven to 12-day intervals.

The writers are grateful to the National Park Service for permission to make these field collections in Rocky Mountain National Park.

Description of Trail Ridge Pond.—Trail Ridge Pond (hitherto unnamed) is located in Larimer County, Colorado, in the northwestern part of Rocky Mountain National Park at 40° 26′ north latitude and 105° 45′ west longi-

[1] Contribution No. 21, Limnology Laboratory, Department of Biology, University of Colorado.

tude. It may be seen nearly 700 feet below and southwest of Trail Ridge Road from a point about one-quarter mile northwest of the Iceberg Lake parking area (fig. 1). The pond is situated at an elevation of 3507 meters (11,500 feet), approximately at timberline near the head of Forest Canyon. This is well above the 3200 meters suggested by Pennak (1941) as the lower limit of the alpine limnological zone in northern Colorado.

The shape is roughly rectangular with a maximum length of 70 meters and width ranging from 28 to 37 meters (fig. 2). Maximum depth is one meter. Two small marshy sedgegrown islands lie near the southeast corner. The pond basin is saucer-shaped and is not to be confused with the staircase or thrust ponds characterized by Ives (1941).

Geologically, the rock bound basin was formed from rock plucking by a glacierette during late Wisconsin times. The organic fraction of the accumulated bottom deposits can perhaps be best described as a gyttja and förnasapropel combination (Lindeman, 1941). Much of the organic material is coprogenic, but there is also a quantity of macroscopic plant detritus derived from the peripheral sedge growths or blown in from the valley below by frequent strong updrafts. A small amount of sand and bits of angular and flaked siliceous gravel are intermingled with the organic material.

Much of the pond water is derived from surface drainage from the steep talus and tundra slopes to the north and east of the basin. Melting snows contribute much water through the middle or end of July, but thereafter showers and seepage are the chief sources. A broad sluggish outlet is present at the west end. In years when the months of August, September, and October are exceptionally dry, the maximum depth of the pond may fall to only 0.7 or 0.8 meters, but it is essentially a permanent body of water. The summer of 1950 was normal, and the pond maintained its maximum depth of about one meter throughout the period of field work.

Fig. 1.—Trail Ridge Pond as seen from Trail Ridge Road,
Rocky Mountain National Park, in midsummer.

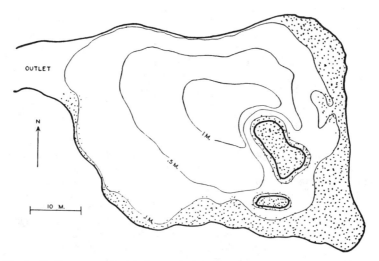

Fig. 2.—Outline map of Trail Ridge Pond. Only the 0.1, 0.5, and 1.0 meter contours are shown. Sedgy area indicated by dots. Note the two small sedgy "islands."

Materials and methods.—The steep and rocky climb between Trail Ridge Pond and Trail Ridge Road made it imperative that lightweight and compact sampling equipment be used. All sampling and measurements were done regularly between 10 a.m. and 3 p.m.

For bottom samples, a small flat-bottomed scoop (12 x 12 x 2.8 cm) was constructed of heavy sheet metal. The total area of bottom sampled with each such scoopful was one-seventieth of a square meter. Five samples were taken on each visit. They were sifted through a number 20 standard sieve, so that essentially all of the macroscopic bottom organisms could be recovered and transferred to vials of alcohol. The entire bottom of the pond was not representatively sampled. Even with hip boots it was impossible to get near the center of the pond because of the thick soft bottom deposits. The north edge of the pond was rocky and no bottom samples could be taken near shore. On the other hand, the five bottom samples taken on each visit were from a variety of depths and at scattered points so that the comoposite is believed to be a fair and representative qualitative and quantitative picture of the bottom fauna population.

Water samples for zooplankton counts were taken with a one-liter flask tied to a long pole, so that the flask was filled at a distance up to eight feet from the water's edge. Ten one-liter samples of water taken at random were considered to be a representative gross sample. The water was filtered through number 25 bolting silk, which is sufficiently fine to retain almost all zooplankters. The organisms were placed in vials of alcohol.

Qualitative collecting was also done along the shoreline and among the vegetation in order to get a more complete picture of the taxonomic groups involved in the economy of the pond.

Temperatures were taken regularly with a laboratory thermometer at a depth of 10 cm in water ranging from 30 to 80 cm deep. It was customary to take readings in several such places and derive an average.

CHEMICAL CONDITIONS

Several routine chemical determinations were made on the pond water, and in keeping with certain European studies, were found to be quite variable. Dissolved salts ranged from 21.5 to 48.1 mg per liter, and total organic matter 17.5 to 38.4 mg per liter. Bound carbon dioxide determinations were unusually high; they varied from 14.8 to 34.0 mg per liter. Most northern Colorado lakes and ponds of the alpine zone contain less than 10.0 mg per liter of bound carbon dioxide, and perhaps this is one factor that partially explains ·the unusually rich animal community occurring in the pond (at least *rich* as compared with other types of alpine ponds). Hydrogen ion determinations ranged from pH 6.5 to 7.3.

TEMPERATURE CONDITIONS

A preliminary visit to the pond was made on June 19, but the basin was completely obscured by snow and ice and there was no open water.

By June 29 the water temperature was 4.3°C, and the ice had disappeared from about half of the surface. Much of the bottom of the pond, however, was still covered with thick masses of ice. Trail Ridge Pond freezes solidly during the long winter, and the ice mass extends below the water-mud interface and well into the bottom deposits. The sudden spring melt of the pond ice first occurs at the surface and mid-depths, and the bottom layers apparently are insulated sufficiently so that melting is slower. It is possible for a layer of ice to remain on and in the bottom because it has intermingled aquatic plant roots and sufficient sand and gravel particles mixed in with it to give it weight and anchor it until the superimposed warm water thaws it out. Such bottom ice a common phenomenon in swift streams but is seldom reported from standing water.

By July 7 the water temperature at some distance from the edge of the pond had risen to 8.8°C, but snow and ice still remained along the north shore. By July 14 only a small amount of slush ice persisted on the north shore, and the average water temperature was 12.8°C.

Temperatures rose to a maximum of 16.1°C on July 29 and thereafter decreased slowly and irregularly. The first heavy snow fell on September 12, but the first ice appeared on the visit of October 12 when there was one-half inch along the east shoreline. The open water temperature was 5.5°C on this date. Slightly more ice was present on October 19 when the water temperature averaged 4.4°C. By October 29 the pond was frozen over except for a small area in the center; the ice was sufficiently thick to support a person's weight. The water temperature was 3.9°C. A few days later the Park roads were snowed in and closed to traffic until the following spring.

Thus in 1950 Trail Ridge Pond had an open season of about 120 days when the pond was either completely free of ice or only partially frozen over. In most years the season is considerably shorter. In 1951, for example, the pond was still completely covered with ice and snow on July 15, and in most years it freezes over before October 15. Ninety or 100 days of open water is therefore probably more typical.

Because of the alternating cold nights and high insolation during daylight hours, wide daily temperature variations are to be expected in Trail Ridge Pond. Pesta (1933) found daily variations of 7 to 20°C in alpine ponds, and Pichler (1939a, 1939b) found daily variations of 6.5 to 30°C. At the periphery of Trail Ridge Pond where the water was less than 10 cm deep, temporary mid-day temperatures in sunny weather sometimes were 5, 10, or even 20°C above those taken in deeper water.

Vegetation

Most tundra ponds have no true aquatic vegetation, perhaps because they usually dry up completely during much of the summer. Trail Ridge Pond, however, being permanent, supports a good emergent growth of the sedge, *Carex aquatilis*, along the east, south, and west shores. In a few places the sedge zone attains a width of 5 to 10 meters (fig. 3). The north shore has a rocky bottom unsuited to the establishment of rooted aquatics.

Carex undoubtedly provides additional ecological niches for the pond, for it was among these growths that the largest variety of metazoans, especially insects, was found.

Bottom Fauna

The quantitative bottom samples contained only three groups of numerically dominant organisms: seed clams (*Pisidium*), tendipedid larve (mostly *Tendipes*, *Calopsectra*, and *Procladius*), and small tubificid oligochaetes.

As shown in fig. 4, the tendipedid larvae were most abundant in the superficial bottom deposits early in the year, even before the surface ice had disap-

Fig. 3.—Trail Ridge Pond, looking west along the south shore.

peared. On June 29 an average population of 28 larvae per square meter was found. The water temperature was then only 4.3°C, and there was still a considerable amount of surface and bottom ice. The population increased enormously to 1512 per square meter by July 7 (water temperature 8.8°C), and 1904 on July 14 (water temperature 12.8°C). Thereafter the population dropped rapidly as the tendipedids pupated and quickly emerged as adults. On July 21 there were 1230 per square meter and on July 29 only 560. After August 16 the population varied irregularly and never exceeded 196 per square meter. Undoubtedly much of the irregularity of the curve in fig. 4 is produced by sampling errors. Thus Trail Ridge Pond had a simple unimodal annual curve for its tendipedid population. This is the usual situation in most temperate and subarctic lakes and ponds. It is quite possible, however, that one or more of the species represented had a two-year life cycle. Undoubtedly the larvae live at temperatures close to 0°C below the lower limit of ice in the frozen bottom during the long winter. With the rapid thawing of the water and bottom deposits in June and early July they migrate upward to the surface of the mud, where the great majority pupate and emerge as adults within two or three weeks. Although a few large larvae were found in the autumn just before the freeze, the great majority were undoubtedly in the egg stage or first larval instar, both of which will pass through the meshes of a number 20 sieve and escape detection. The second and third larval instars of many individuals were presumably attained during the winter and very early spring, even though temperatures were only 0 to 4°C. Thus it is difficult to avoid the conclusion that their threshold temperature for feeding and growth is exceptionally low. The occurrence of an abundance of active tendipedids on the bottom of most large cold lakes supports this familiar contention.

The *Pisidium* population curve (fig. 4) was strikingly similar to that for the tendipedid larvae, with a spring population burst which dropped off rapidly and remained at a low level from August through October. No *Pisidium* were collected on June 29 when there was still much ice on the pond, but by July 7 sufficient numbers had migrated to the surface layers from deeper parts of the mud to give an average population of 1162 per square meter. The maximum population, 1470 per square meter, was found on July 14. During the month following this peak the seed clams had a high mortality rate, and between August 16 and October 29 the residual population varied from 126 to 420 per square meter. Nothing is known about the reproductive habits of *Pisidium* in Trail Ridge Pond. A wide range of size was always found, but no one particular time was ever noted when there was a predominance of immature forms. It should be emphasized, however, that very young seed clams will pass through the meshes of a number 20 sieve and may thus have gone unnoticed. On the basis of our present knowledge of *Pisidium* biology, it is difficult to explain the occurrence of maximum numbers of large and mature individuals immediately after the ice melts in early summer. It is usually assumed that *Pisidium* is not active and does not ingest food while it hibernates below the mud surface during the cold months, but perhaps this assumption should be supported by actual observations. On the other hand, there certainly was not sufficient time between October 29 and the complete freeze of the pond a short time later to allow any appreciable growth in the late autumn.

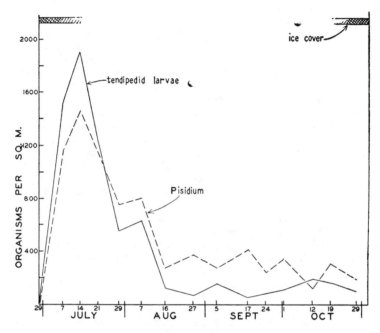

Fig. 4.—Seasonal population curves for tendipedid larvae and *Pisidium* in the bottom deposits of Trail Ridge Pond in 1950.

In keeping with the results obtained by many other investigators, it was found that the numbers of tubificid oligochaetes varied irregularly from place to place on the bottom and showed no distinct seasonal population trends. On several visits to the pond none were found in the five samples collected, and on October 1 a maximum of 168 individuals per square meter was collected. Oligochaetes apparently became active early in the season since 42 per square meter were found on July 7. Tubificids are notoriously difficult to sample quantitatively since many of them crawl through the meshes of the sieve and since they fragment very easily. Consequently the above figures are of little significance.

ZOOPLANKTON

The zooplankton population was exceedingly low, much lower in fact than those populations reported from the most barren of lakes. Copepod nauplii were the most abundant forms. On July 29 there was a peak of 121 individuals per liter, and on September 17 there were 9 per liter. On all other sampling dates there were negligible numbers of nauplii, or they were absent from the samples.

Small numbers of copepodid stages and adult copepods were found only occasionally, and it is obvious that there was a very high mortality of nauplii. The highest population of copepodids and adults occurred on September 17 when 0.9 individual per liter was taken. *Paracyclops fimbriatus* (Fischer) was the only plankton species found, but a few specimens of *Canthocamptus* sp., a bottom dweller, were also collected.

Daphnia pulex was the only cladoceran taken; a total of only 11 individuals was collected on the 15 sampling dates.

Several *Pedalia fennica* and *Brachionus* sp. were the only rotifers taken in the plankton samples. Population densities were always less than one individual per liter.

PHYTOPLANKTON

Casual observations were made on the phytoplankton. Like the zooplankton, the population was qualitatively and quantitatively scanty, much more scanty than the phytoplankton of a typical large oligotrophic lake. Several species of diatoms, filamentous blue-greens, and *Cosmarium* were noted. Late in the season a *Spirogyra* bloom covered part of the bottom of the pond. Otherwise no special algal pulses were observed.

LITTORAL AND MISCELLANEOUS ORGANISMS

The following discussion includes organisms collected in random sweeps of a metal sieve among the submerged parts of sedges and along the shoreline. Few of these organisms ever appeared in the quantitative bottom samples or plankton samples. Since they were not homogeneously distributed, no quantitative estimates could be derived.

Beginning on July 21, peculiar greenish balls (superficially similar to *Nostoc* balls) were observed on the bottom and attached to the sedges below the water surface. These were found to be colonies of an unknown ciliate protozoan containing symbiotic (?) algal cells. Along with them in the colony were numerous diatoms and desmids, the entire colony being held together by a threadlike and gelatinous matrix. By July 29 the colonies nearly covered the submerged sedge growth as well as other objects along the shore. Thereafter they decreased in abundance but did not disappear until the end of the season. Presumably these colonies served as browse for many macrometazoans.

The fairy shrimp *Branchinecta shantzi* Mackin (formerly *B. coloradensis* Packard) was certainly the most abundant and most obvious macrometazoan in the pond. With the exception of a Texas report, this species is restricted to western high altitude lakes and ponds. It was abundant throughout most of the season, and although no definite quantitative estimates of the *B. shantzi* population could be made, the general population trends could be easily followed by inspection on the 15 visits to the pond. Overwintering undoubtedly occurs in the highly resistant winter egg stage, as is usual among phyllopods. On July 7 (the second visit to the pond) many phyllopod nauplii were present in the plankton. Two weeks later the first sexually mature adults appeared swimming about among the sedges near shore, and on July 29 the adult population reached a dense maximum. Thereafter the population declined and reached a minimum on September 5. This was followed by a second population increase which reached its maximum on September 24. On October 29, the last collecting date, a few stragglers still remained. Thus, Trail Ridge Pond appeared to have had two distinct generations of phyllopods in 1950. The two population peaks, one in late July and the other in late September, were of about equal density.

Phyllopods are most characteristic of vernal ponds which are dry during much of the year and in which a single population maximum per year is attained. Little appears to be known about their seasonal population variations in permanent bodies of water.

Branchinecta shantzi was clearly the most characteristic macrometazoan in Trail Ridge Pond. In their studies on mountain waters of Swedish Lapland, Brink and Wingstrand (1949) were impressed with a comparable situation, and they distinguished *"Lepidurus* pools," which are shallow mountain ponds characterized by an abundant notostracan phyllopod population. In their physical, chemical, and biological characteristics, *Lepidurus* pools are strikingly similar to Trail Ridge Pond.

Limnephilus larvae (Trichoptera) were associated with the submerged portions of the sedge plants, especially on July 29 and August 7. Thereafter the population fell off gradually until only scattered living individuals could be collected at the end of October. Their cases were constructed of variable amounts of sand, fine gravel, bits of vegetation, and *Pisidium* shells. It was a considerable surprise to find that living *Pisidium* also were used in the construction of *Limnephilus* cases. No other reported instance of the use of living seed clams has come to the attention of the present writers. In addition to *Limnephilus,* a single specimen of *Phryganea* was found.

Dytiscid beetles were nearly always found along the shore but were never abundant. Adult *Agabus* were collected on nearly all visits to the pond, but *Ilybius* were collected only in July and August. Larvae were found early and late in the season, but there was a rather long mid-season when none could be found. It can therefore be concluded that these beetles have a single generation per year with the larvae (and possibly eggs) overwintering in the bottom deposits.

Aquatic Hemiptera were taken occasionally in the shallows, especially *Arctocorisa sutilis, Sigara alternata,* and one species of *Notonecta.* A few water striders were observed as early as July 7 but were not collected.

Hydracarina were most abundant during August and September. Representatives of *Eylais, Lebertia,* and *Limnesia* were found.

Small numbers of certain Diptera larvae were taken along the shoreline that did not occur in the quantitative bottom samples. These included *Prionocera* (Tipulidae), *Stratiomyia* (Stratiomyidae), *Aedes* (Culicidae), and a case-building *Metriocnemus* (Tendipedidae).

The only vertebrates found at the pond were two mature mountain toads (*Bufo boreas boreas*). They were swimming about slowly in the slush ice on July 29 and July 14. On the latter date a large mass of toad eggs was found. Small tadpoles 15 to 20 mm long were later collected on August 16 but not seen subsequently.

Discussion

The counterpart of Trail Ridge Pond does not appear to have been characterized in American hydrobiological literature. Blake (1945), however, briefly described "moraine ponds" in the Medicine Bow Mountains of Wyoming at an altitude of 10,200 feet. Such ponds have a longer ice-free season than Trail Ridge Pond and are surrounded by forests. They are also warmer and have a richer macrometazoan fauna, including several species of dragonfly and damselfly nymphs, whirligig beetles, a variety of other beetles, leeches, and the swamp cricket frog.

McClure (1943) described several tundra ponds and small lakes at Churchill on Hudson Bay. In certain respects some of these resemble Trail Ridge Pond. They contained essentially all of the major taxonomic groups occurring in the latter except for seed clams. In addition, most of them contained snails, leeches, turbellarians, hydras, odonate nymphs, and ostracods. Numerically, however, the Churchill ponds were enormously richer in both numbers of individuals and in numbers of species. One pond, for example, contained up to 80,000 metazoans per cubic foot of water at the height of the season. Judging from McClure's meager temperature data, the Churchill tundra ponds attain higher summer maximum temperatures and have an open season about 30 to 50 days longer than that for Trail Ridge Pond.

Numerous European workers have described "Almtümpeln" which in many ways are similar to the Trail Ridge Pond type. They seldom contain phyllopods, however, but have a richer phytoplankton, cladoceran, and rotifer population.

Several important major taxonomic groups were not collected from Trail Ridge Pond. These include ostracods, amphipods, mayfly nymphs, odonate nymphs, and snails. All of these are common in ponds at elevations below 10,000 feet, and it is not clear whether low summer temperatures, the complete winter freeze, or some other ecological factors are of prime importance as limiting factors.

Some species are able to maintain themselves from year to year in the pond because of their ability to burrow deeply into the bottom deposits below the ice line. Examples are tendipedids, *Pisidium*, tubificid oligochaetes, and perhaps beetle larvae. In accordance with the investigations of Lindeman (1942) and others, however, it is quite probable that a large percentage of these organisms die during the long period of winter anaerobiosis. Most other groups overwinter in the resistant egg stage which withstands freezing in the superficial layers of the bottom deposits.

In general, most of the taxonomic groups in the pond were represented by exceptionally small numbers of individuals, and populations were much more scanty than those found in ponds and small lakes at lower elevations. The zooplankton, for example, was almost negligible, and with the exception of Trichoptera and *Branchinecta*, the miscellaneous organisms collected along the shallow margins were never abundant. Seldom could more than ten specimens of any one species be taken from five meters of marginal area.

Nevertheless, the dominant elements of the Trail Ridge Pond community are obvious. They are tendipedids, *Pisidium*, and *Branchinecta*. Judging from repeated observations on many plains and mountain ponds in Colorado, a *Branchinecta* population possibly does not make its appearance every summer in Trail Ridge Pond. More typically it may be absent for a year or two and then reappear for one, two, three, or more consecutive years. This irregular and intermittent annual occurrence of vernal and permanent pond phyllopods has been considered at length in Ohio by Dexter (1943) and Dexter and Kuehnle (1948, 1951).

Permanent ponds such as Trail Ridge Pond are common above timberline in northern Colorado. They occur invariably where they receive melting snow water and rain seepage water from adjacent slopes. They range from 0.25 to 2.0 m in maximum depth, and their maximum dimensions range from about 5 to 100 m. Judging from casual observations made on many of them, the tendipedid—*Pisidium*—*Branchinecta* association is usually present.

A wide variety of temporary ponds and pools is also characteristic of the tundra, but these bodies of water are almost barren of macrometazoans and are not comparable with the permanent Trail Ridge Pond type.

Summary

Trail Ridge Pond is a permanent body of water about 30 x 70 m and 1 m deep at an elevation of 11,500 feet in northern Colorado.

The plankton and bottom fauna were sampled quantitatively during the entire open season at intervals of 7 to 12 days from June 29 to October 29, 1950. Qualitative studies were also made on the macrometazoans living in the shoreline areas and *Carex* growths.

The pond freezes solidly during the winter, and the 1950 maximum summer temperature was 16.1°C on July 29. Dissolved salts ranged from 21.5 to 48.1 mg per liter. Hydrogen ion concentration determinations ranged from pH 6.5 to 7.3.

Zooplankton and phytoplankton populations were much more scanty than those in large barren oligotrophic lakes. Entomostraca and rotifers each averaged less than one individual per liter of pond water.

Tendipedid larvae and *Pisidium* (seed clams) attained their maximum abundance in the superficial layers of bottom mud just as the last of the ice was disappearing from the pond on July 14. The former reached 1904 individuals per square meter and the latter 1470. On June 29 only small numbers of tendipedids and no *Pisidium* were found, and it is concluded that there was a mass migration out of the deeper strata of the bottom deposits during the ensuing two weeks. Following July 14 the population tapered off to a level of 100 to 400 per square meter during September and October.

Tubificid oligochaete populations varied irregularly from 0 to 168 individuals per square meter.

The phyllopod *Branchinecta shantzi* was the most characteristic macrometazoan in the pond. It had a bimodal population curve, with distinct peaks on July 29 and September 24.

Small numbers of the following were present near the shoreline: *Limnephilus* larvae (Trichoptera); *Agabus* and *Ilybius* (Coleoptera: Dytiscidae); *Arctocorisa*, *Sigara*, and *Notonecta* (Hemiptera); Hydracarina; *Prionocera*, *Stratiomyia*, *Aedes*, and *Metriocnemus* larvae (Diptera).

The dominant and characteristic organisms of Trail Ridge Pond are the tendipedid-*Pisidium*-*Branchinecta* community.

In general, the pond has an impoverished fauna, both qualitatively and quantitatively, and it is believed that the very short open season and the complete winter freeze of the water mass are important contributing factors.

Trail Ridge Pond is compared with other subarctic and mountain tundra ponds in both North America and Europe.

REFERENCES

BLAKE, I. H. 1945—An ecological reconnaissance in the Medicine Bow Mountains. Ecol. Monogr. 15:207-242.

BRINK, P. AND K. G. WINGSTRAND 1949—The mountain fauna of the Virihaure area in Swedish Lapland. Kungl. Fysiogr. Sällsk. Handl. N. F. 60:1-60.

DEXTER, R. W. 1943—A second survey of the anostracan phyllopods in Northeastern Ohio. Amer. Midl. Nat. 30:336-340.

——— AND C. H. KUEHNLE 1948—Fairy shrimp populations of northeastern Ohio in the seasons of 1945 and 1946. Ohio J. Sci. 48:15-26.

——— AND ——— 1951—Further studies on the fairy shrimp populations of northeastern Ohio. Ibid. 51:73-86.

IVES, R. L. 1941—Tundra ponds. J. Geomorph. 4:285-296.

LINDEMANN, R. L. 1941—The developmental history of Cedar Creek Bog, Minn. Amer. Midl. Nat. 25:101-112.

——— 1942—Experimental simulation of winter anaerobiosis in a senescent lake. Ecology 23:1-13.

McCLURE, H. E. 1943—Aspection in the biotic communities of the Churchill area, Manitoba. Ecol. Monogr. 13:1-36.

PENNAK, R. W. 1941—An introduction to the limnology of northern Colorado. Univ. Colo. Studies, Ser. D. 1:203-220.

PESTA, O. 1933—Beiträge zur Kenntnis der limnologischen Beschaffenheit ostalpiner Tumpelgewässer. Arch. Hydrobiol. 25:68-80.

——— 1935—Kleingewässerstudien in den Ostalpen. Ibid. 29:296-345.

——— 1943—Limnologische Untersuchungen an einem Hochgebirgstümpel der Ostmark. Ibid. 40:444-458.

PICHLER, W. 1939a—Der Alpentümpel als Lebensstätte. Eine ökologische Studie. Bioklimatische Beibl. 6:85-89.

——— 1939b—Ergebnisse einer Limnologischen Sammelreferat in den Ostalpen (Steiermark). Arch. Hydrobiol. 35:107-160.

STIRNIMANN, F. 1926—Faunistisch-biologische Studien an den Seen und Tümpeln des Grimselüberganges. Int. Rev. 16:233-271.

THOMASSON, K. 1951, 1952—Beiträge zur Kenntnis des Planktons einiger Seen im nordschwedischen Hochgebirge. Schweiz. Zeitschr. Hydrol. 13:336-351, 14:257-288.

TURNOWSKY, F. 1946—Die Seen der Schobergruppe in den Hohen Tauern. Carinthia II 8 (Sonderheft):7-78.

THE OCCURRENCE OF ORTHOPTERA AT HIGH ALTITUDES, WITH SPECIAL REFERENCE TO COLORADO ACRIDIDAE

Gordon Alexander*

Among the most abundant animals at high altitudes are the grasshoppers. In the alpine zone of the Colorado Rockies these apparently exceed all other kinds of insects -- in numbers of individuals if not in numbers of species. The statement that insects of complete metamorphosis predominate at high altitudes, whereas the "warmth-loving" Orthoptera are less well adapted to the cold of such regions (Hesse, 1924; Erhard, 1931), seems to be based on observations of conspicuous rather than abundant forms. The butterflies and beetles of high altitudes are per-haps better known than are the Orthoptera, as suggested by the summary of Holdhaus (1929), and the butterflies are certainly more conspicuous. Furthermore, more species of Coleoptera and Lepidoptera than of Orthoptera undoubtedly do occur at high al-titudes, but the same relationship holds at low altitudes. On the other hand, if we consider numbers of individuals, disre-garding numbers of species, we may safely say that grasshoppers are often the predominant insects at high altitudes, just as stated by Prenant (1933). They are certainly among the most significant ecological units of the alpine zone.

There seems to be no a priori reason for the statement that insects with complete metamorphosis are poorly adapted to the cold of high altitudes. The statement is not supported by the known facts of distribution. In the Alps, Collembola occur at higher altitudes than any other insects (Erhard, 1931). Hemip-tera as well as Orthoptera occur in considerable numbers in al-pine regions. Some primitive insects are actually dependent upon cold for survival. *Grylloblatta*, for example, cannot long survive at temperatures above approximately 60° F. (Walker, 1937), and its optimum temperature seems to be close to 39° F.

Published in:
Ecology, 1951, 32(1): 104-112

*University of Colorado
Boulder, Colorado

(Mills and Pepper, 1937). One of the Acrididae, an unnamed species from Mount Everest, appears to hold the high altitude record for an established insect species. Major Hingston (1925), who made observations on natural history while a member of the 1924 Everest Expedition, found early nymphs of a grasshopper at 18,000 feet above sea level, the limit of vegetation. Uvarov (1925) was unable to name these and stated that they were representatives of an undescribed species. In the same paper, Uvarov described a new genus of wingless grasshoppers, *Dysanema*. Appropriately enough, he named the two new species in this genus *irvinei* and *malloryi* after A.C. Irvine and G. Mallory, the two members of the Expedition who lost their lives in the final assault on the summit. The two species of grasshoppers occurred at altitudes of 15,000 and 16,000 feet on Mount Everest. Where vegetation occurs at such altitudes in any part of the world we may reasonably expect to find Orthoptera. Altitude, as such, is not a barrier.

Orthoptera have been recorded from alpine regions all over the world. Good general summaries of their occurrence have been given by Scudder (1898), Chopard (1928), and Uvarov (1928). In addition, some discussion of their occurrence has been combined with the excellent general accounts of alpine animal ecology by Hesse (1924) and Erhard (1931).

Most of the records of high altitude occurrence are, of course, scattered through taxonomic accounts of collections made in mountainous regions. Unfortunately, the importance of complete data -- even with reference to altitude alone -- was not recognized by early collectors, localities being designated by such vague expressions as Tibet, Colombia, or Rocky Mountains. The information on high altitude Orthoptera is naturally more complete from the mountains of Europe and North America than elsewhere. We were particularly fortunate in the United States in that the first great student of Orthoptera in this country, Samuel H. Scudder, was an ardent mountain climber. Limited collections, however, and individual variations led to an early multiplicity of names that seems more complex than in the taxonomy of lowland species. Mountain climbing is strenuous, too, and the accumulation of representative collections from scattered alpine areas is a long-time process.

TYPES OF ORTHOPTERA REPRESENTED

Not all groups of Orthoptera are well represented at high altitudes. Some, however, appear to be particularly well adapted to the cold conditions of the alpine zone. The Grylloblattidae, for example, are associated in general with cold, damp situations. They have been found in the mountains of western Canada and northwestern United States, among rocks at the edge of snow-fields, in areas covered with snow much of the year. Some of the Tetrigidae, likewise, are tolerant of cold, damp situations, and occur in the alpine zone.

Species which are quite active at night, as are many Gryllidae and Tettigoniidae, are absent from alpine regions. Nor are they likely to occur even as accidental visitors, because wind movements in mountains are usually downwind at night. Crickets appear to be absent from high altitudes, at least in the Holarctic Region. The diurnal Tettigoniidae, however, are represented by several high altitude species, in the Old World as well as in the New. In this country we have several species thoroughly adapted to alpine conditions. *Anabrus simplex* Haldeman, the Mormon "cricket," completes its life cycle in Colorado at altitudes up to 13,000 feet above sea level (at least as far north as Mount Evans). *Acrodectes philopagus* Rehn and Hebard, another decticine, was described from specimens collected near and at the summit of Mount Whitney (California), 14,500 feet, the highest mountain in the United States (Rehn and Hebard, 1920). One of the cave-crickets, *Ceuthophilus alpinus* Scudder, was collected above timber line on Mount Lincoln, in Colorado (Scudder, 1898). All of the forms just mentioned are flightless; wings, if present, are much abbreviated.

The majority of the alpine Orthoptera, some of which have wings of normal length, are members of the family Acrididae. Undoubtedly, hundreds of species in this family will eventually be known from the alpine regions of the world, where they occur as well-adapted resident insects. The activity of the American species with which I am familiar, at air temperatures below 50° F., is convincing evidence of efficient physiological adaptation to cold temperatures. The high altitude species are obviously better adapted to cold than are those of low altitudes, even when closely related taxonomically.

ECOLOGICAL CATEGORIES OF HIGH ALTITUDE SPECIES

When a flightless insect as large as the average decticine (or even a small grasshopper, for that matter) is found regularly at a given altitude we may consider this reliable evidence that it is able to complete its life cycle at that altitude. On the other hand, among the numerous species of fully-winged grasshoppers recorded from alpine regions we must distinguish carefully between those that are native to the altitudes in question and those that are accidental or casual in occurrence. Since grasshoppers are primarily diurnal in activity, and since diurnal air movements in mountainous regions are predominantly upward, we find that a large number of species at high altitudes are accidental. A combination of flight ability, which need not be great, and favorable wind currents is undoubtedly responsible for the arrival of such accidental visitors. The possibilities of passive dispersal of this sort have been summarized by Holdhaus (1929). In commenting upon the same phenomenon, Chopard (1938) has pointed out that this high degree of vagility is not necessarily accompanied by a high per cent of establishment in new areas. In other words, we are apparently dealing with species

that annually repeat on a large scale their invasions of the alpine region, but which, lacking the necessary preadaptation, have not yet become established there. Several of the species attributed to the alpine zone in Colorado, in particular *Melanoplus mexicanus mexicanus* and *Melanoplus occidentalis*, are apparently in this category. It is important, therefore, to know something of the life histories of long-winged species that occur at high altitudes. Without this information it is not possible to determine whether a species is present as a resident or merely as an accidental visitor.

In the ecological classification suggested by Hesse (1924), three types of alpine animals are recognized, eualpine, tychoalpine, and xenoalpine. Belonging to the first category are those that are exclusively alpine; to the second belong those that extend into the alpine zone from below and are able to complete their life cycles in the higher zone; in the third group are those that invade the alpine zone but are unable to establish themselves there.

This classification was devised for the fauna of the Alps, a mountain mass isolated from northern regions by intervening lowlands. It is not appropriate in the Rocky Mountains, however, for in the Rockies the populations of alpine species in southern latitudes are in more or less continuous geographic contact with populations of the same or closely related species at lower altitudes to the north. There are no eualpine species in the meaning of Hesse's term; a species which appears to be eualpine in the southern part of its range may not be alpine at all farther north. All our characteristic alpine species would be considered tychoalpine according to Hesse's classification. This, however, implies that they are related to species of the adjacent lowlands, whereas their affinities are with low altitude species which occur farther north. Xenoalpine or accidental species do occur in numbers, however, and these undoubtedly occur in mountains of all regions.

A satisfactory ecological classification of the alpine fauna of the Rocky Mountains appears to require only two categories. We must distinguish between species which can complete their life cycles in the alpine zone but cannot become established at that altitude. The former are characteristic of the zone; they are here designated "resident alpines." The numerous species which invade the alpine region from below but cannot become established are the "accidental alpines."

HIGH ALTITUDE GRASSHOPPERS IN COLORADO

Since the summer of 1931 I have been interested in the altitudinal distribution of Colorado grasshoppers. Collections at altitudes from the plains (5,000 feet) to over 13,000 feet above sea level have been made in northern Colorado throughout this period. These collections were chiefly in the Boulder region, but occasional trips have been made into the mountains of

other parts of the state. Personal observations were supplemented
during the season of 1949 by extensive collections made by H.A.
Fehlmann, graduate student at the University of Colorado, in the
alpine zone of the Culebra, Sangre de Cristo, and Mosquito Ranges.
Published records have been used to supplement personal observations and those of Mr. Fehlmann. In spite of the apparent
extensive coverage, however, there are still large areas of alpine country in Colorado where grasshoppers have not been collected.

The present report is limited to a discussion of grasshoppers
(Acrididae) of the alpine zone. This is the mountain zone which
occurs above timber line. Timber line in Colorado is at an altitude of about 11,000 feet in the northern part of the state,
at about 12,000 feet in the Culebra Range and other mountains of
southern Colorado. The Acrididae referred to are all listed in
the last section of this paper, preceding the Summary.

A geographic study of the distribution of species waits
upon additional collections and taxonomic reexamination of some
of the high altitude groups. Large series covering the entire
range of each species should be collected. Meanwhile, the recognition of the ecological category to which each species thus far
collected belongs may prove of value.

The method of recognizing a winged species as a resident
alpine is relatively simple if local life history studies are
available. If a species is collected above timber line in the
adult condition, and the flightless nymphs of the same species
are found in the same locality, it is considered characteristic
of the alpine zone. If, on the other hand, an adult grasshopper
is collected above timber line without juveniles of the same
species we must ask its source. If one knows from observations
at lower altitudes that it is just appearing as an adult some
five thousand feet lower down the assumption is clear that it
has been transported upward. If we follow this species through
the season at different altitudes we are able to determine its
maximum range of altitude as a resident. If it occurs anywhere
above that range it is accidental.

The special case of *Melanoplus mexicanus mexicanus* is highly
informative, particularly since it has been referred to as an
alpine form on the basis of adult specimens alone (Hebard, 1935,
1936). The species is highly vagile, and has repeatedly been
taken in numbers above timber line. One striking observation
illustrates the real nature of this occurrence. On July 18,
1948, I found numerous adults of this species frozen in the
surface of a snow bank at about 12,200 feet altitude on the
east side of Mount Audubon (Colorado). These grasshoppers had
fallen on the snow not many hours or days before, because the
snow bank had not yet receded to its size in the preceding
autumn. The alpine species in the adjacent area were still
juveniles, not having reached the adult condition, while *M. m.
mexicanus* was already a common adult on the plains seventeen
miles due east and seven thousand feet lower down. The adults

in the snow bank had undoubtedly flown or been carried on rising
air currents to the high altitude.

A more complete demonstration is afforded by the record of
collections during 1949, as these collections were made to determine the time of development at different altitudes. Early
juveniles of *M. m. mexicanus* were collected on the plains and
as high as 7,600 feet by the last of May, and these were adult
by the first of July. Juveniles were taken as early as the
third week in June at 8,500 feet, but the first adults did not
mature at that altitude until about the first week of August.
The highest elevation at which juveniles were collected was
9,800 feet. Juveniles appeared there as early as the first of
August, but the first adults associated with last instar nymphs
were not collected until after the first of September. As late
as October 1, juveniles and adults were both still present at
9,800 feet, but cold weather had already set in at that altitude. Meanwhile, on September 8, an adult female of this species was collected by H.A. Fehlmann at an altitude of 12,300
feet on Mount Evans. This grasshopper may have come all the
way from the plains; in any case it must have originated from
an altitude at least 2,500 feet lower than that at which it
was collected.

Other high altitude records of this species in Colorado
give additional evidence that *M. m. mexicanus* is not typical of
the alpine zone. On July 13, 1936, an adult male and three
adult females were collected above timber line, at 11,400 feet,
on Niwot Ridge (near Science Lodge, University of Colorado mountain laboratory). On July 20, the same year, three males and
eight females, all adults, were collected above timber line on
Mount Audubon, one of the females being collected on the cold
rocks of the windblown summit, at 13,300 feet above sea level.
H.A. Fehlmann collected adults during August 1949, from alpine
areas above 12,000 feet on Trinchera Peak (Culebra Range), Greenhorn Mountain, West Spanish Peak, Sierra Blanca, Pike's Peak,
and in the Mosquito Range west of Alma, Colorado. On Greenhorn
Mountain, which is quite close to the plains southwest of Pueblo,
thirteen adults were taken above 12,000 feet on August 3 and
twenty-six on August 25. No juveniles were collected in any of
these alpine areas, nor have I found any records of juveniles
taken above timber line in this region. Furthermore, we do know
that *M. m. mexicanus* is capable of flying or being carried many
miles (Munro and Sangstad, 1938). The evidence seems clear that
it is an accidental alpine.

The evidence with reference to *Melanoplus occidentalis* is
not so clear. It has been found above timber line on numerous
occasions, and was listed by Hebard (1929, 1935, 1936) as an alpine species in Colorado and New Mexico. On July 13, 1936, I
collected eight males and two females, all adult, above timber
line on Niwot Ridge. A single adult male was collected by
Robert J. Niedrach on August 10, 1933 at 13,600 feet on Mount
Evans. I have no records, however, of juveniles above timber

line, nor have I seen such records in the literature. Furthermore, the species is highly vagile (La Rivers, 1948). The evidence available thus far points, therefore, to recognition of this species as a purely accidental alpine grasshopper, which is not established above timber line.

Other species occasionally listed as alpine in distribution include *Melanoplus bivittatus* and *Melanoplus femur-rubrum*. The former completes its life cycle up to about 9,500 feet, but juveniles are scarce at that altitude. *M. femur-rubrum* apparently does not occur much above 8,000 feet in the juvenile condition. Both these species are collected not infrequently above timber line, where they are of course accidental.

Arphia conspersa, since of boreal affinities, is a species that we might expect to find established in the alpine zone. Adults are found above timber line (Hebard, 1929), but in the Boulder region I have not collected juveniles above approximately 9,800 feet. In favorable spots this species may be able to complete its life cycle above timber line, but at present I am inclined to consider its occurrence at such altitudes accidental.

Another one of the Oedipodinae listed by Hebard (1929) as alpine in Colorado is *Camnula pellucida*, but Hebard failed to list any alpine collecting localities. I have not collected this species above timber line but have taken both juveniles and adults from 6,000 to 10,000 feet. In favorable areas this species may be able to complete its life cycle above timber line. It should not at present be considered alpine, however.

One other macropterous species of uncertain status, *Chorthippus longicornis*, may upon further collecting prove to be a resident alpine. Adults have been taken above timber line, but this species is so highly restricted in habitat that a special search will have to be made at the right time and place before we can be sure that it does complete its life cycle above timber line. It does complete its life cycle in wet patches of sedges up to about 10,500 feet in the Boulder region, and my son and I have collected juveniles and adults on Hoosier Pass (11,500 feet), just at timber line.

One of the interesting aspects of the occurrence of accidental species above timber line is the observation that at certain times, apparently during quite warm weather, abnormally large numbers of these may be taken in a single day. I have previously referred twice to collections made July 13, 1936 on Niwot Ridge, near Science Lodge. Niwot Ridge, which at its eastern end extends only a few hundred feet above timber line, carries the tundra farther east than at any other place in northern Colorado. It is an alpine ridge extending in an east-west direction, its eastern end less than fourteen miles from the plains. On the day mentioned there occurred the most extensive invasion of the alpine tundra by lowland species of which I have record. The collection above timber line on that date included adults of the following species: *Aulocara elliotti* (4 males, 11 females); *Acropedellus clavatus* (1 male); *Amphitornus coloradus*

(1 male, 1 female); *Metator pardalinus* (2 males, 1 female); *Melanoplus bivittatus* (8 males, 2 females); *M. mexicanus mexicanus* (1 male, 3 females); *M. dodgei dodgei* (5 males, 2 females); *M. occidentalis* (8 males, 2 females); *M. packardii* (2 males, 3 females); *Hesperotettix viridis viridis* (1 female). Two of these species were typical alpines, *Aeropedellus clavatus* and *Melanoplus dodgei dodgei*. Eight juveniles of the former and seven of the latter were collected. On the other hand, no juvenile specimens of any of the other eight species were collected. They were all accidentals.

Among the observations made during the summer of 1949 by H.A. Fehlmann, at least one such unusual collection was noted. One or two accidental species were collected at almost every alpine collecting locality, but the most striking collection was made on Sierra Blanca, at 12,800 to 13,000 feet, on August 24, 1949. On that date adults of the following accidentally occurring species were collected: *Dissosteira carolina* (2 males, 2 females); *Melanoplus femur-rubrum* (5 males, 6 females); *M. mexicanus mexicanus* (1 male); *M. packardii* (1 male). Juveniles as well as adults of three resident alpine species were collected. These were *Aeropedellus clavatus*, *Melanoplus dodgei bohemani*, and *M. borealis monticola*. What weather conditions are associated with these invasions of high altitudes by lowland species we do not know, but the invasions are necessarily associated with rising air currents.

Among the grasshoppers with fully developed wings at least three species in the front range of the Colorado Rockies are resident alpines. These are: *Melanoplus alpinus*, of the northern Colorado mountains; *M. borealis monticola*, of the mountains of southern Colorado; and *Xanthippus corallipes altivolus*, with a wider north-south range than either of the other two species. The last of these forms has somewhat reduced wings, those of the female occasionally being too short to support sustained flight, but both species of *Melanoplus* have moderately long wings. I have collected many juveniles of *M. alpinus* and *X. c. altivolus* in the alpine zone in the mountains west of Boulder, Colorado. With H.A. Fehlmann I collected juveniles of *M. b. monticola* in the Culebra Range in July 1949, and during August of the same season he collected both juveniles and adults of this species on Greenhorn Mountain, on Sierra Blanca, in the northern Sangre de Cristo Mountains, and as far north as Pike's Peak. These three species are the only fully winged grasshoppers normally present in the alpine zone along the eastern range of the Rockies in Colorado.

A fourth macropterous form, *Melanoplus bruneri*, appears in the alpine zone of mountains in the central part of the state. This was recorded from an "alpine environment" near Gothic by Hebard (1929), two adult males and a juvenile female having been collected by Mary J. Brown. Under the name *Melanoplus excelsus* it was recorded from above timber line on Mount Lincoln by Scudder (1898).

Melanoplus borealis stupefactus is a brachypterous subspecies of *M. borealis* that occurs in the alpine zone of New Mexico and in the mountains west of the San Luis Valley and as far north as Gothic (Hebard, 1935). I find no definite record of its occurrence above timber line in Colorado, but there is a questionable record mentioned by Scudder (1898) under the name *Podisma stupefacta*.

The majority of the resident alpine species in Colorado are short-winged. *Aeropedellus clavatus*, of wide latitudinal range, appears to have the widest altitudinal range of any alpine species, completing its life cycle in the Boulder region at all altitudes from 5,500 to 13,500 feet. The short-winged *Melanoplus dodgei* complex, for which I use the nomenclature of Hebard's Colorado paper (1929), is represented by the small alpine subspecies in northern Colorado (*M. d. dodgei*) and a larger subspecies (*M. d. bohemani*) above timber line in the southern mountains of the state. Hebard, in a later paper (1935), recognized *bohemani* as a distinct species. I have retained the earlier name, however, as it indicates what appears to me to be a close relationship with *M. d. dodgei*.

Melanoplus oregonensis marshallii is another brachypterous form, its tegmina and wings being shorter even than those of *M. dodgei*. It occurs in alpine communities in the Mosquito Range and as far north as Loveland Pass. It occurs north of Loveland Pass below timber line. *Melanoplus kennicotti nubicola*, which has been recorded from a few alpine areas in the central part of the state, is unquestionably alpine, but its geographic distribution is not yet well understood.

I have collected juvenile and adult *Melanoplus fasciatus* a short distance above timber line in the Boulder region, and, for that reason, have listed the species as a resident alpine. However, it is possible that it should be considered accidental on the tundra in spite of the fact that it is relatively short-winged. It is ecologically associated with the forested portions of the mountains, and is able to complete its life cycle up to and within the dwarf forest at timber line. Even juveniles, at least in the later instars, could hop the short distance from the forest to the tundra areas where they have been collected.

In any particular alpine area of the front range the community of resident alpine grasshoppers appears to include not more than three species at the same time. *Xanthippus corallipes altivolus* is the only species that over-winters in the juvenile condition above timber line, and, consequently, it is the only species that becomes adult before mid-summer. In the latitude of Boulder, adults mature at 11,000 feet as early as the last week of June. By the middle of July, *Aeropedellus clavatus* and *Melanoplus dodgei* are adult. Both of the macropterous melanopli, *M. alpinus* and *M. borealis*, become adult toward the end of the season, about the middle of August, but while *A. clavatus* and *M. dodgei* are still present. Adults of Xanthippus have disappeared by that time, though juveniles hatch as early as the last

of August from eggs laid the same season. Since the two macropterous melanopli do not occur in the same locality, the usual
combination of species is: *A. clavatus*, *M. dodgei*, and either
M. alpinus (in the north) or *M. borealis* (in the south). Neither
of the last two species is necessarily present, however. If
Melanoplus oregonensis marshallii is present, *M. dodgei* appears
to be absent. Thus we have as the typical alpine grasshopper
population the wide-spread *A. clavatus*, a short-winged species
of *Melanoplus*, and a long-winged species of *Melanoplus*, all of
these following an early season form, the over-wintering *Xanthippus corallipes altivolus*.

COLORADO ACRIDIDAE COLLECTED IN THE ALPINE ZONE

The following is a list of all species of Acrididae known
from above timber line in Colorado. Most of these have been
collected by the writer. Some were collected by H.A. Fehlmann
in his 1949 expedition. If the only records available are his,
the names are followed by the initials H.A.F. in parentheses.
Some names are based on published records only. The sources for
these are indicated by reference to the literature list, likewise in parentheses following the names. Those Acrididae that
are resident alpine species, completing their life cycles above
timber line, are indicated by an asterisk preceding the name.
Species not so marked are considered of accidental occurrence.

Acridinae:
    *_Aeropedellus clavatus_ (Thomas)
    Ageneotettix deorum (Scudder)
    Amphitornus coloradus (Thomas)
    Aulocara elliotti (Thomas)
    Chorthippus longicornis (Latreille) (May be a resident
       alpine species)
Oedipodinae:
    Arphia conspersa Scudder (Hebard, 1929)
    Circotettix rabula altior Rehn
    Dissosteira carolina (Linnaeus) (H.A.F. collection)
    Metator pardalinus (Saussure)
    Spharagemon collare (Scudder)
    Trachyrhachis kiowa (Thomas)
    *_Xanthippus corallipes altivolus_ (Scudder)
Cyrtacanthacrinae:
    Hesperotettix viridis viridis (Thomas)
    *_Melanoplus alpinus_ Scudder
    M. bivittatus (Say)
    *_M. borealis stupefactus_ (Scudder) (Scudder, 1898; question-
       able)
    *_M. bruneri_ Scudder
    *_M. dodgei dodgei_ (Thomas)
    *_M. dodgei bohemani_ (Stal)
    *_M. fasciatus_ (F. Walker) (May be accidental)

M. femur-rubrum (DeGeer) (H.A.F. collection)
*M. kennicotti nubicola (Scudder) (Scudder, 1898, as *Podisma nubicola*)
M. mexicanus mexicanus (Saussure)
*M. mexicanus spretus (Walsh) (Extinct; juveniles reported by Scudder, 1898)
M. occidentalis (Thomas)
*M. oregonensis marshallii (Thomas)
M. packardii Scudder

It should be noted that of the total number of twenty-eight species and subspecies collected above timber line in Colorado only eleven (approximately 39%) may be considered characteristically alpine in distribution, and one of these (*Melanoplus mexicanus spretus*) is now extinct.

SUMMARY

1. Orthoptera of several families occur at high altitudes. The Acrididae are represented by the largest number of species. In numbers of individuals they are among the most numerous insects at high altitudes. Their abundance leads one to question the statement that insects with complete metamorphosis are better adapted to alpine climatic conditions than are those with incomplete metamorphosis.

2. High altitude Orthoptera of the Rocky Mountains of Colorado are of two ecological groups, resident alpines and accidental alpines. The former can complete their life cycles above timber line. Accidental alpines occur in the alpine zone only as adults, flying or being borne to the alpine areas on air currents. The majority of species of Acrididae recorded from alpine areas of Colorado are accidentals. Only eleven (approximately 39%) of the twenty-eight recorded species and subspecies are resident alpines.

3. *Melanoplus mexicanus mexicanus*, *M. occidentalis*, and several other species previously recorded as alpine grasshoppers are not resident species but accidental visitors. The resident alpine species of Colorado are: *Aeropedellus clavatus*, *Xanthippus corallipes altivolus*, *Melanoplus alpinus*, *M. borealis monticola*, *M. bruneri*, *M. dodgei dodgei*, *M. dodgei bohemani*, *M. fasciatus* (may be accidental), *M. kennicotti nubicola*, *M. mexicanus spretus* (now extinct), *M. oregonensis marshallii*. None of these is confined, except locally, to the alpine zone.

4. In any given alpine area along the eastern ridge of the Colorado Rockies the grasshopper population may include an early summer species which over-winters as a juvenile (*Xanthippus corallipes altivolus*), *Aeropedellus clavatus* and a short-winged *Melanoplus* in mid-summer, and a long-winged *Melanoplus* in late summer. Apparently two species of brachypterous melanopli or two species of macropterous melanopli do not occur at the same time and place.

REFERENCES

Chopard, L. 1928. La faune des Orthopteres des montagnes des
Etats-Unis et ses rapports avec la faune paléarctique.
Mem. Soc. Biogéographie, 2: 142-149.

_____. 1938. *La biologie des Orthopteres*. Paul Lechevalier,
Paris.

Erhard, H. 1931. Die Tierwelt der Alpen. *In* Brockhaus, F.U.
(Leipzig), *Alpines Handbuch*, pp. 107-204.

Hebard, M. 1929. The Orthoptera of Colorado. *Proc. Acad. Nat.
Sci. Phila.*, 81: 303-425.

_____. 1935. Orthoptera of the upper Rio Grande valley and
the adjacent mountains in northern New Mexico. *Proc. Acad.
Nat. Sci. Phila.*, 87: 45-82.

_____. 1936. Notes on North American Orthoptera of the
Arctic-Alpine Zone. *Ent. News*, 47: 13-15.

Hesse, R. 1924. *Tiergeographie auf ökologischer Grundlage*.
Gustav Fischer, Jena.

Hingston, R.W.G. 1925. Animal life at high altitudes. *Geogr.
Jour.*, 65: 186-198. (Reprinted in *Ann. Rept. Smithson.
Inst.*, 1925: 337-347.)

Holdhaus, K. 1929. Die geographische Verbreitung der Insekten.
In Schröder, C. (ed.), *Handbuch der Entomologie*. Gustav
Fischer, Jena, 2: 592-1057.

LaRivers, I. 1948. A synopsis of Nevada Orthoptera. *Amer.
Midl. Nat.*, 39: 652-720.

Mills, H.B. and J.H. Pepper. 1937. Observations on *Grylloblatta campodeiformis* Walker. *Ann. Ent. Soc. Amer.*, 30:
269-274.

Prenant, M. 1933. *Géographie des animaux*. A. Colin, Paris.

Rehn, J.A.G. and M. Hebard. 1920. Descriptions of new genera
and species of North American Decticinae (Orthoptera; Tettigoniidae). *Trans. Amer. Ent. Soc.*, 46: 225-265.

Scudder, S.H. 1898. The alpine Orthoptera of North America.
Appalachia, 8: 299-319.

Uvarov, B.P. 1925. Grasshoppers (Orthoptera, Acrididae) from
the Mount Everest. *Ann. Mag. Nat. Hist.* (Ser. 9), 16:
165-173.

_____. 1928. Orthoptera of the mountains of Palaearctic
region. *Mem. Soc. Biogéographie*, 2: 135-141.

Walker, E.M. 1937. *Grylloblatta*, a living fossil. *Trans. Roy.
Soc. Canada*, Sect. V, Ser. 3, 31: 1-10.

NOCTURNAL ARTHROPODS IN THE ALPINE TUNDRA OF COLORADO

Ronald Schmoller

*Department of Zoology and Entomology
and Graduate Program in Ecology
The University of Tennessee
Knoxville, Tennessee 37916*

ABSTRACT

Certain groups of insects, myriapods, and arachnids were collected by pitfall trap at 3,600 to 4,270 m elevation in the Colorado alpine tundra. The Cicadellidae (leafhoppers) adults, Acrididae (grasshoppers), Scarabaeidae (scarab beetles), Erythraeidae (erythraeid mites), Lycosidae (wolf spiders), and Thomisidae (crab spiders) appear to be mainly diurnal taxa. Most Carabidae (ground beetles) and Micryphantidae (dwarf spiders), and all Diplopoda (millipedes) appear to be mainly nocturnal taxa. Data for other taxa does not in- dicate significant day or night concentration in activity. There are indications that the nocturnal arthropod fauna extends to 4,270 m. The nocturnal arthropod fauna of the alpine tundra is shown to be of considerable size, contrary to earlier opinions. The cold night conditions (ca. 1 to 5°C) do not halt all arthropod activities. The arctic tundra is shown to lack most of the alpine tundra nocturnal taxa, probably due to lack of night conditions during the summer.

INTRODUCTION

Diel (24-hour) behavioral periodicities among arthropods include diurnal, nocturnal, and crepuscular species behavior. Williams (1962) found that phalangids in Britain are almost entirely nocturnal or crepuscular. Breymeyer (1966) found that most carabid beetles are nocturnal, while most crab spiders (Thomisidae) and jumping spiders (Salticidae) are diurnal. Although no intensive nocturnal studies have previously been done in the alpine tundra (i.e., that region above the tree line) high altitude biologists have generally been of the opinion that nocturnal arthropods are a negligible component of the alpine tundra biome. This study was done in order to document better the extent of arthropod nocturnality in the alpine tundra.

METHODS AND MATERIALS

Field work was done in the Colorado Front Range during July and August in 1967 and 1970. The 1967 study areas were on Trail Ridge in Rocky Mountain National Park at 3,600 m elevation and on Mt. Evans at 3,700 m; the 1970 study areas were on Mt. Evans at 3,800 m and 4,270 m. The habitats studied in 1967 included sedge turf, marsh, cushion vegetation, and shrubby sites (Schmoller, 1971). The 1970 areas were mainly *Geum* forb types.

Glass pitfall jars, 53 mm inside diameter and 55 mm deep, were used to sample the arthropods in 1967. Plastic cups, 63 mm inside diameter and 60 mm deep, were used in 1970. The traps were placed in the ground with their lips flush with the surface, 1 m apart in line patterns. About 10 mm of ethylene glycol was added to each pitfall as a preservative. A little detergent was used to reduce the surface tension. The traps were left unshielded.

Pitfall traps do not provide definite information about activity levels (e.g., diurnal vs. nocturnal) of the animals collected. Population densities, behavioral avoidance, weather, and the nature of the vegetation and soil surrounding the traps all influence the number of specimens collected. Despite their limitations, I believe that good data as to which arthropod taxa are diurnal and which are nocturnal can be obtained by means of pitfall traps. Weather interacting with arthropod activity levels is probably the only major variable of this study. The warmer day conditions might be expected to result in more arthropod activity by day, but as can be seen from my data below most taxa were collected in much greater numbers at night, indicating a high level of nocturnal activity.

Quantitative sampling was attempted in 1970 with a gasoline powered vacuum insect net (D-Vac) without success. Most arthropods in this extremely windy habitat are apparently well adapted to resist the push or pull of any strong wind.

Pitfall samples were taken on four nights in 1967. Twenty-seven jars were used on Mt. Evans during the nights of July 18-19 and July 31-August 1, and 24 jars were used on Trail Ridge on the nights of July 20-21 and August 3-4. The same jar-sites were used on both nights in each study area and to take 2-week arthropod samples in the periods immediately preceding and following each nocturnal sample. These 2-week day-plus-night samples were compared with the night samples.

The 1967 night sampling procedure was as follows. Every evening the pitfall jars were emptied of their 2-week day and night catches. Preservative was added and lids were screwed onto each jar. The lids were removed after dark and were not replaced until shortly before sunrise on the next day. Later that morning, when it was light enough to see, the arthopods were collected from the jars. The jars were then left in continuous day-night operation for 2 weeks after each nocturnal sampling.

The 1970 sampling procedure was somewhat different. Fifty-six cups were used to take separate day and night collections so that each night collection was preceded by a single day's collection. Collections were made on the days and ensuing nights of July 27, 28, and 29, and August 7, 8, and 9.

Only the ground cursorial predatory arthropods were collected in 1967. In 1970 all the arthropods taken in the pitfalls were collected except for the true flies (Diptera) and springtails (Collembola). For both years only data on the numerically dominant taxa were developed.

In 1967, night air temperatures were taken with a thermistor held 15 cm above the ground at about 8:15 p.m. and 4:20 a.m. (MST) on each night. In 1970 day and night air temperatures were taken with a recording thermometer (Pacific Transducer Corp. Model 615) and a maximum-minimum thermometer. The 1970 thermometers were placed beneath a large overhanging boulder in a shaded position.

TABLE 1

Expected (E) and observed (O) nocturnal catches of some important arthropods during four nights in 1967

Arthropods	E	O
Coleoptera (Carabidae)	24.9	45
Amara alpina Paykull	5.5	9
Amara quenseli Schonherr	9.7	19
Carabus taedatus Fabricius	7.1	10
Pterostichus lecontellus Csiki	0.5	4
Phalangida	8.0	26
Homolophus biceps (Thorell)	8.0	26
Acarina	12.2	2
Erythraeus sp.	12.2	2
Araneida	16.3	3
Gnaphosidae	2.7	2
Lycosidae (mainly *Pardosa* spp.)	11.2	0
Thomisidae	1.8	1

RESULTS

The pitfall collection data for the four nights in 1967 are given in Figure 1 and Table 1. On all four nights a total of 76 ground cursorial predatory arthropods were taken. In Figure 1 and Table 1 the number of specimens expected (E) is based on the hypothetical assumption that arthropod activity (as roughly indicated by pitfall trappings) is of an even intensity during a 24-hr diel cycle. In order to obtain E, the number of specimens taken in the 2-week sampling period, both preceding and following each nocturnal sample, was summed and the number of specimens expected on that night was determined. For example, during the 14-day sampling interval preceding the 8.5-hr night sample of July 20-21 and during the 14-day sampling interval following that night, a combined total of 1,349 ground cursorial predatory arthropods were collected from the 24 pitfall jars. Since 8.5 hr is 0.0126 of 28 days, then $0.0126 \times 1,349$ specimens = 17.0 specimens. If arthropod activity is of equal intensity during an average 24-hr diel cycle, E for the night of July 20-21 is 17; actually, 25 specimens (O or observed) were taken that night. During all four nights 60.3 individuals were expected while 76 were actually collected.

Every night except August 3-4 more arthropods of the combined groups counted were taken (O) than expected (E) (Figure 1). A substantial nocturnal arthropod fauna does, therefore, exist. On August 3-4 less than half as many specimens were taken as were expected. This small catch may have been due to the colder weather on that night, the only night of the four cold enough to frost the vegetation. Temperatures recorded on the other three nights were about 3°C warmer than the 4 and 1°C readings recorded at 8:15 p.m. and 4:20 a.m. on August 3-4. The three warmer night temperature minima (4:20 a.m. readings) are the same temperatures reported by Marr et al. (1968) as the mean July and August minima for a weather station op-

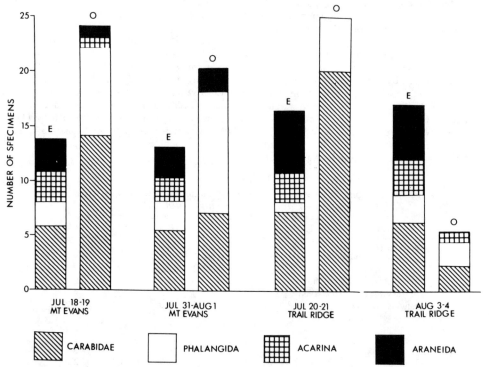

FIGURE 1. 1967 night pitfall samples. E is number of specimens expected (see text for explanation); O is number of specimens observed (i.e., actually collected). There were 27 jars used on Mt. Evans and 24 jars on Trail Ridge.

erating at nearby Niwot Ridge (3,700 m) during the period 1953 to 1964. The mean July and August temperature minima for 1967 was 4°C on Niwot Ridge (Schmoller, 1968).

Figure 1 and Table 1 indicate that the Acarina (mite) and Araneida (spider) faunas are apparently largely diurnal, while the Phalangida (harvestmen) and Carabidae (ground beetles) are apparently largely nocturnal. In fact, since the period of night trapping is approximately one third of the 24-hr diel cycle and since more than three times as many phalangids were collected than were expected, it is clear that night catches of phalangids could account for all the phalangids taken during the 24-hr cycles.

Collection data for the 6 days and nights studied in 1970 are given in Figure 2 and

Table 2. The data in Table 2 agree fairly well with the data of Table 1. A total of 1,799 arthropods were collected by day and 363 by night in 1970. The following arthropod groups were taken in markedly greater numbers during the day than at night: Cicadellidae (leafhoppers) adults, Acrididae (grasshoppers), Scarabaeidae (scarab beetles), Erythraeidae (erythraeid mites), Lycosidae (wolf spiders), and Thomisidae (crab spiders). The following taxa were taken in greater numbers during the night than by day: most Carabidae (ground beetles), and Micryphantidae (dwarf spiders), and all Diplopoda (millipedes).

Figure 3 shows the relationship between day and night temperatures and the number of arthropods collected in 1970. No direct relationship between temperatures and catch size

TABLE 2

Day and night pitfall catches at 3,760 m on Mt. Evans, 1970

	6 days	6 nights (× 1.39)[a]
Insects		
Cicadellidae (>95% 1 species)	1,252	105.7
Adults	1,188	45.9
Juveniles	64	59.8
Lygaeidae (2 spp.	19	2.8
Acrididae (>95% 1 species)	253	5.6
Aeropedellus clavatus (Thomas)	243	5.6
Formicidae (1 sp.)	66	36.1
Carabidae (6 spp.)	30	180.7
Amara alpina Paykull	11	12.5
Pterostichus surgens LeConte	5	4.2
Nebria gyllenhali Schonherr	5	77.8
Amara quenseli Schonherr	4	29.2
Carabus taedatus Fabricius	2	52.8
Scarabaeidae (1 sp.)	45	2.8
Cantharidae (1 sp.)	10	2.8
Myriapods		
Diplopoda (1 sp.)	2	13.9
Chilopoda (1 sp.?)	2	4.2
Arachnids		
Phalangida (2 spp.)	17	86.2
Homolophus biceps (Thorell)	17	80.6
Erythraeidae (1 sp.)	108	23.6
Araneae Subtotal	103	52.8
Lycosidae (4 spp.)	64	0.0
Thomisidae (5 spp.)	18	2.8
Gnaphosidae (3 spp.)	5	12.5
Micryphantidae (several spp.)	16	37.5

[a]Multiplication by 1.39 is done to give a catch time in hours equal to the day collection time.

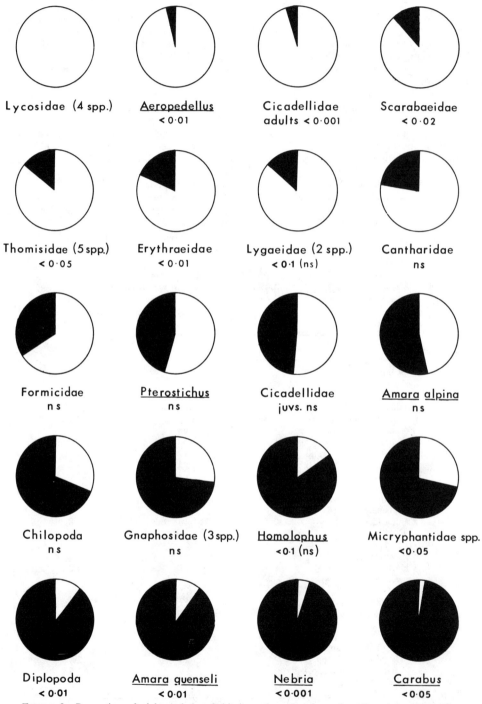

Lycosidae (4 spp.)

Aeropedellus
< 0·01

Cicadellidae
adults < 0·001

Scarabaeidae
< 0·02

Thomisidae (5 spp.)
< 0·05

Erythraeidae
< 0·01

Lygaeidae (2 spp.)
< 0·1 (ns)

Cantharidae
ns

Formicidae
ns

Pterostichus
ns

Cicadellidae
juvs. ns

Amara alpina
ns

Chilopoda
ns

Gnaphosidae (3 spp.)
ns

Homolophus
<0·1 (ns)

Micryphantidae spp.
<0·05

Diplopoda
< 0·01

Amara quenseli
< 0·01

Nebria
<0·001

Carabus
<0·05

FIGURE 2. Proportion of night and day (white) catches of arthropods collected in 1970. Significance of the day-night division of catches is indicated below each figure (t—test; ns = not significant).

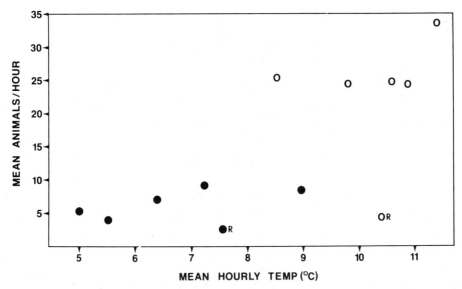

FIGURE 3. Relationship between mean hourly temperatures of each of the 6 days (open circles) and 6 nights (solid circles) of 1970 on Mt. Evans (3,800 m) and the mean number of animals taken per hour. Circles with letter "R" represent rainy or wet conditions.

is evident. Day catches for the total faunal segment studied are larger than the night catches. Maximum and minimum daily air temperatures on the six dates ranged from 11 to 15°C (6-day mean 14°C) and 3 to 5°C (6-night mean 5°C) compared with means of 12 and 4°C given by Marr et al. (1968) for a nearby similar tundra site during July and August in the period 1953 to 1964. Low catches, indicated by R in Figure 2, were associated with a heavy rainfall during the day (August 7) which left many pitfall cups nearly filled with water by evening. The tundra stayed wet all night long on August 7-8.

Nocturnal studies were also attempted at the very high altitude of 4,270 m on Mt. Evans in 1970, but were discontinued after one night's catch due to snow. On the night of July 25-26, 24 cups were emplaced for 8 hr. The air temperature that night was 5°C at 8:30 (MST) and 2°C at 4:00 a.m. Despite these cold conditions, nine arthropods including three *Homolophus* (a phalangid), three Carabidae, two Thomisidae, and one lycosid were taken. These 24 traps were left in operation after July 26 and allowed to collect arthropods until August 9 when they were sampled. During these 14 days and 14 nights 158 arthropods (Carabidae, Phalangida, Lycosidae, Thomisidae, Gnaphosidae, Micryphantidae, Nabidae, Lygaeidae,

and Curculionidae) were trapped. If the night of July 25-26 was a typical one, the expected (E) or hypothesized number of arthropods taken on that night would be four (i.e., 8 hr is 0.025 of 13.42 days and 0.025 of 158 arthropods is 3.95 specimens). It appears that nocturnal arthropods occur even at 4,270 m.

Nocturnal arthropod flying activity was observed on the night of July 25-26, 1970. Thousands of large noctuid moths, locally called "millers," were seen at 4,270 m on Mt. Evans flying upslope, possibly towards the well-lit restaurant located on the summit a hundred meters in elevation above. About five could be seen on the average instant in the beam of my flashlight at 9:00 p.m. (MST). Some even hit my face and body with heavy impact. At 4:15 a.m. on the next morning some moths were still flying uphill at 4,270 m although the air temperature was 2°C and the wind 4.5 m sec[-1] (10 mph). I have seen no nocturnal flying insects in the Colorado alpine tundra except for these large moths, although I did not search carefully. The only other possible components of the nocturnal arthropod fauna of the alpine tundra are subsurface and plant-surface inhabiting taxa. I have made no observations in these last two habitats.

I made field notes on the activities of arthropods by day and at night. Of the groups listed in Table 2, I have rarely seen carabid beetles or phalangids in the open on the tundra during the daytime. Occasionally a carabid or phalangid was seen walking about, mainly in the early morning. Other carabids and phalangids were often found beneath rocks in the daytime. Night observations (by flashlight) were frequently made of carabids and phalangids moving over the ground. Cicadellidae, Acrididae, Formicidae, Erythraeidae, Lycosidae, and Thomisidae were frequently observed moving about during the daytime, but almost never at night. Cicadellids and acridids were often seen at night, but they were immobile and moved slowly, if at all, when touched. On the night of July 26, 1966, I searched in vain for active lycosid spiders. Temperatures near the ground were 7 to 9°C. I finally found one sluggish lycosid under a rock.

DISCUSSION AND CONCLUSION

Up until the present time a nocturnal alpine tundra arthropod fauna had almost been discounted. Thus Alexander (1950), in reference to Colorado, said "nocturnal insects are practically non-existent at high altitudes." Mani (1968) stated that nocturnal species of arthropods are sometimes found at tree line, but with increasing elevation are completely replaced by diurnal forms. Mani (1962) gives activity figures for alpine tundra Diptera, Lepidoptera, and Hymenoptera, indicating complete cessation of surface activities for these groups during the night hours.

Two reports concerning nocturnal alpine tundra arthropods do exist. Swan (1961), working at 5,250 m in the Himalaya, noted that cursorial spiders go out to feed just after the sun has set behind the peaks and eat flying insects that are seeking shelter at that time. According to his graph the spider activity gradually subsided to zero just before complete darkness occurred. At this time the air temperature was about 4°C. Greenslade (1968) reports that the two species of carabid beetles which occur in the relatively low elevation (980 m) alpine tundra or montane habitat of Scotland are nocturnal.

Perhaps the main reason why the nocturnal alpine tundra arthropod fauna has been overlooked is due to the misconception that nights in the tundra are too cold for arthropod activities. There is evidence to the contrary. Mellanby (1940) working at 69°N in the Finnish arctic tundra experimented in the laboratory with the chill-coma temperature (i.e., that temperature at which and below which insects are immobilized by cold) of several insects. Mellanby found that an ant species, a beetle, and two mosquito species could crawl at temperatures ranging from 1 to 4°C if previously acclimatized to 7 to 12°C for 24 hr, or 3 to 5.5°C if previously acclimatized to 20 to 30°C. One of the mosquito species could probably fly at and above ca. 10°C. Bertram (1935) did a similar study in the arctic tundra at Scoresby Sound in eastern Greenland (70°N). Bertram found chill-coma temperatures of −4.5 to 10°C for 49 species of insects and spiders. The Greenland species came into complete activity at temperatures of −2 to 11°C. Bertram compared his results with similar data obtained by another scientist in Finland (67°N) working with sand dune insects in the taiga biome. The sand dune fauna had chill-coma and "complete activity" temperatures averaging about 8 or 10°C higher than the Greenland species. Besides the laboratory data given above, field observation indicates that certain chironomid midges in the high Canadian Arctic (82°N) can fly even at 3°C (Downes, 1965).

Thus it would appear that the alpine tundra does have a significant and distinct nocturnal arthropod fauna, the night environment not being cold enough to limit activities. According to Marr et al. (1968) the mean minimum air temperature for a weather station located in the Front Range alpine tundra of Colorado at 3,700 m was 1, 4, 3, and 1°C for the four summer months (June to September) in the period 1953 to 1964.

The arctic tundra, in contrast to the alpine tundra, lacks definite day and night periods. Thus, a significant or distinct nocturnal arthropod fauna could not exist. Along with this lack of nocturnal niche space comes a parallel poverty in the arctic tundra arthropod fauna. None of the predominantly nocturnal taxa of the Colorado alpine tundra (Carabidae, Diplopoda, Phalangida, or Gnaphosidae), except the Micryphantidae, occur as anything but rarities in the arctic tundra (Downes, 1962; Leech, 1966). Adult carabids are less than 8% as numerous at Point Barrow, Alaska, as their soil-inhabiting larvae (Brown and West, 1970). Downes (1965) suggests that arctic insects are often opportunistic in their feeding, flying, swarming, etc. behavior; tight rhythms fail to control or synchronize many activities.

The alpine tundra habitat, in contrast to the arctic tundra, is surprisingly rich in species of nocturnal taxa. I recorded 20 species of Carabidae, 3 species of Phalangida, and 14 species of Gnaphosidae from tree line and above in Colorado (Schmoller, 1971). Mani (1962) notes that Carabidae dominate the Himalayan alpine tundra beetle fauna, the carabids comprising 20 to 25% of the total Himalayan alpine insect fauna.

Many ecologically important activities are probably carried out by the night fauna. Most of the species are probably either predatory or scavenging. A considerable amount of predation upon the then torpid largely herbivorous diurnal fauna may occur at night.

In conclusion, it would appear that the nocturnal ecology of the alpine tundra is a more important facet than ecologists previously suspected. It should also be noted that there is no ecological counterpart of this fauna in the arctic tundra.

ACKNOWLEDGMENTS

I would like to thank Dr. Gordon Alexander and Dr. Lawrence Swan for encouraging me to do research in high altitude biology. The Kathy Lichty Memorial Fund (Department of Biology, University of Colorado) provided financial support in 1967, while the 1970 work was supported by Sigma Xi and faculty research money from the University of Tennessee and the Zoology Department, University of Tennessee. Denver University High Altitude Laboratory on Mt. Evans kindly provided living accomodations in 1970. The following individuals identified arthropods for me: Dr. G. E. Ball (Carabidae), Dr D. C. Lowrie (Lycosidae), Dr. C. J. Goodnight (Phalangida), Dr. W. J. Gertsch (Araneida), Dr. H. W Levi (Araneida), Dr. Beatrice Vogel (Lycosidae), Dr. R. X. Schick (Thomisidae), and Mr. Wilton Ivie (Araneida)

REFERENCES

Alexander, G.
1950 : The natural history of high altitudes. *The Biologist,* 33: 91-97.

Bertram, G. C. L.
1935 : The low temperature limit of activity of arctic insects. *J. Anim. Ecol.,* 4: 35-42.

Breymeyer, A.
1966 : Relations between wandering spiders and other epigeic predatory Arthropoda. *Ekol. Polska,* (A) 14: 27-71.

Brown, J. and West, G. C.
1970 : Tundra biome research in Alaska. The structure and function of cold-dominated ecosystems. U.S. Int. Biol. Prog. Tundra Biome Rep., 70-1. 148 pp.

Downes, J. A.
1962 : What is an arctic insect? *Ann. Rev. Entomol.,* 10: 257-274.
1965 : Adaptations of insects in the Arctic. *Ann. Rev. Entomol.,* 10: 257-274.

Greenslade, P. J. M.
1968 : Habitat and altitude distribution of Carabidae (Coleoptera) in Argyll, Scotland. *Trans. Roy. Entomol. Soc. London,* 120 (2): 39-54.

Leech, R. E.
1966 : The spiders (Araneida) of Hazen camp, 81°49'N, 71°18'W. *Quest. Entomol.,* 2: 153-212.

Mani, M. S.
1962 : *Introduction to High Altitude Entomology.* Methuen, London. 302 pp.
1968 : *Ecology and Biogeography of High Altitude Insects.* Junk, The Hague. 527 pp.

Marr, J. W., Clark, J. M., Osburn, W. S., and Paddock, M. W.
1968 : Data on mountain environments. III Front Range, Colorado, four climax regions 1953-1964. *Univ. Colo. Studies,* Ser. Biol., 28. 181 pp.

Mellanby, K.
1940 : The activity of certain arctic insects at low temperatures. *J. Anim. Ecol.,* 9: 296-301.

Schmoller, R. R.
1968 : Ecology of alpine tundra Arachnida and Carabidae (Coleoptera) in Colorado. Ph.D. Thesis, Univ. of Colorado. 81 pp.
1971 : Habitats and zoogeography of alpine tundra Arachnida and Carabidae (Coleoptera) in Colorado. *Southwestern Natur.,* 15: 319-329.

Swan, L. W.
1961 : The ecology of the high Himalayas. *Sci. Amer.,* 205 (4): 68-78.

Williams, G.
1962 : Seasonal and diurnal activity of harvestmen (Phalangida) and spiders (Araneida) in contrasted habitats. *J. Anim. Ecol.,* 31: 23-42.

NEW ELEVATIONAL RECORDS FOR THE BOREAL TOAD
(*BUFO BOREAS BOREAS*)

James B. Campbell

Institute of Arctic and Alpine Research
University of Colorado
Boulder, Colorado 80302

ABSTRACT

In July 1969 a large female boreal toad was found at timberline (3,557 m, 11,560 ft) in the Rocky Mountain National Park, Larimer County, Colorado. A total of 46 boreal toads have been found at different localities in the Colorado Front Range, all above 3,385 m (11,000 ft) elevation, and all within 200 m of timberline. These new records extend the known elevational range of the species upward more than 250 m. A brief description of the habitat of the two highest known localities is given.

The boreal toad (*Bufo boreas boreas*) is known to occur from sea level to timberline within its wide geographical range of mountainous regions of northwestern North America, from New Mexico to Alaska (Stebbins, 1954). Maximum known elevations for the boreal toad throughout its range are given in Table 1. Within the Colorado Front Range the boreal toad occupies a wide variety of habitats, with the largest populations occuring between 2,615 m (8,500 ft) and 3,385 m (11,000 ft).

On July 26, 1969, while investigating a small lake (30 m in diameter) at 3,557 m (11,560 ft) on the Fall River Road, Rocky Mountain National Park, Larimer County, Colorado, I found a single large female boreal toad (weight, 71 gms; snout-vent length, 98 mm). The toad was found at the margin of the lake on a moist substrate in an area of emergent sedges. The ground near the lake was quite boggy, with many small streamlets coursing through the surrounding vegetation.

Salix-Picea krummholz was the dominant vegetation near the lake. The krummholz showed obvious evidence of wind-trimming. The understory vegetation was dominated by mosses and sedges growing on the spongy substrate. No *Bufo* eggs or larvae were seen.

On July 25, 1968, a single large female boreal toad (snout-vent length, 90 mm) was found at King Lake, Boulder County, Colorado, elevation 3,508 m (11,400 ft). This individual was on a small island at the north end of the lake. The island was located within 20 m of the nearest *Picea* krummholz. The shore of lake consisted of semisubmerged talus and patterned ground. The dominant surrounding vegetation included sedges, mosses, and *Sedum*. King Lake occupies a cirque lying 62 m (200 ft) directly below the Continental Divide. No *Bufo* eggs or larvae were seen at this locality.

With the exception of a population of 29 boreal toads inhabiting an extensive bog at Albion, Boulder County, Colorado, elevation 3,385 m (11,000 ft), all of the boreal toads found above 3,385 m in the Colorado Front Range have been female. Reproduction is apparently unsuccessful

TABLE 1

Maximum elevational records for Bufo boreas boreas

Locality	Elevation		Source
Union Co., Oregon	1,077 m	3,500 ft	Ferguson, 1954a
Forbidden Plateau, Vancouver Island, British Columbia	1,415	4,600	Hardy, 1955
Big Lake, Linn Co., Oregon	1,429	4,645	Graf *et al.*, 1939
Mission Mountains, Montana	2,009	6,530	Brunson and Demaree, 1951
Wassowa Co., Oregon	615-2,154	2,000-7,000	Ferguson, 1952
Deschutes Co., Oregon	1,846-2,154	6,000-7,000	Dunlop, 1959
Crater Lake National Park, Oregon	2,154	7,000	Farner and Kezer, 1954
Washington	2,462	8,000	Schonberger, 1945
Oregon	2,462	8,000	Ferguson, 1954b
Elk Mountains, Colorado	3,077	10,000	Blair, 1951
Gothic Region, Colorado	3,077	"about 10,000"	Burger and Bragg, 1946
Near Alma, Colorado	3,077	"above 10,000"	Ellis and Henderson, 1915
Isabelle Glacier Trail, Boulder Co., Colorado	3,292	10,700	This study
Poudre Lake, Larimer Co., Colorado	3,308	10,750	Karlstrom, 1962
Jenny Lake, Boulder Co., Colorado	3,359	10,917	This study
Lake Albion, Boulder Co., Colorado	3,385	11,000	This study
Between Pumphouse and Corona Lakes, Grand Co., Colorado	3,462	11,250	This study
Rollins Pass, Grand Co., Colorado	3,462	11,250	This study
King Lake, Boulder Co., Colorado	3,508	11,400	This study
Fall River Road, Rocky Mountain National Park, Larimer Co., Colorado	3,557	11,560	This study

above 3,385 m. Above this elevation, eggs and larvae do not seem to survive the winter. This suggests that reproduction in the populations at about 3,385 m may be successful only every few years, and is never successful at elevations much above 3,385 m.

Apparently the individuals at the highest elevations are derived from populations in the lower valleys. Mark-recapture studies have shown that transient or wandering toads are a common feature of Front Range populations. These individuals, which do not establish a home range, presumably pioneer new habitats and thus serve to extend the local range of the population, assuming favorable conditions for colonization of the unoccupied habitat. The fact that only isolated adults are found at the highest elevations suggests that the pioneer occupation of vacant habitats is usually unsuccessful.

ACKNOWLEDGMENTS

I wish to thank David Vleck and Mercedes Russell, NSF Student Science Training Program (Pre-College) participants, for field assistance. Hobart Smith kindly commented on portions of the paper. This study was supported by NSF Science Faculty Fellowships G8027 and G0030.

REFERENCES

Brunson, R. B. and Demaree, H. A.
  1951 : The herpetology of the Mission Mountains, Montana. *Copeia,* 1951(4): 316-308.
Blair, A. P.
  1951 : Note on the herpetology of the Elk Mountains, Colorado. *Copeia,* 1951 (3): 239-240.

Burger, W. L. and Bragg, A. N.
  1946 : Notes on *Bufo boreas* (B. and G.) from the Gothic region of Colorado. *Proc. Oklahoma Acad. Sci.,* 27: 61-65.
Dunlop, D. G.
  1959 : Notes on the amphibians and reptiles of Deschutes County, Oregon. *Herpetologica,* 15: 173-177.

470

Ellis, M. M. and Henderson, J.
  1915 : Amphibia and reptilia of Colorado. *Univ. Colorado Studies II* (part 2): 253-263.

Farner, D. S. and Kezer, J.
  1954 : Notes on the amphibians and reptiles of Crater Lake National Park. *Amer. Midland Nat.* 50(2): 448-462.

Ferguson, D. F.
  1952 : The distribution of amphibians and reptiles of Wassowa County, Oregon. *Herpetologica,* 8(3): 67-68.
  1954a: An annotated list of the amphibians and reptiles of Union County, Oregon. *Herpetologica,* 10(3): 149-152.
  1954b: An interesting factor influencing *Bufo boreas* reproduction at high elevations. *Herpetologica,* 10(3): 199.

Graf, W., Jewett, S. G., Jr., and Gordon, K. L.
  1939 : Records of amphibians and reptiles from Oregon. *Copeia,* 1939(2): 101-104.

Hardy, G. A.
  1955 : The natural history of the Forbidden Plateau, Vancouver Island, British Columbia. *Rep. Prov. Mus. Victoria, B.C.,* 1954: B24-64.

Karlstrom, E. L.
  1962 : The toad genus *Bufo* in the Sierra Nevada of California. *Univ. California Publ. Zool.* 62: 1-104.

Schonberger, C. F.
  1945 : Food of some amphibians and reptiles of Oregon and Washington. *Copeia,* 1945(2): 120-121.

Stebbins, R. C.
  1954 : *Amphibians and reptiles of western North America.* McGraw-Hill Book Co., Inc., New York. 536 pp.

BOREAL CHORUS FROGS (*PSEUDACRIS TRISERIATA*) BREEDING IN THE ALPINE IN SOUTHWESTERN COLORADO

ALBERT W. SPENCER

Department of Biology
Fort Lewis College
Durango, Colorado 81301

ABSTRACT

Boreal chorus frogs, *Pseudacris triseriata borealis* (Weid), breed at and above timberline in the San Miguel and San Juan Mountains of southwestern Colorado. The location of two breeding sites at 3,670 m and 3,597 m are described. Males were observed calling at 3,720 m. These are the highest recorded breeding amphibians in North America.

I have found the chorus frog, *Pseudacris triseriata borealis* (Weid), breeding at and above the tree line in the San Miguel and San Juan Mountains of southwestern Colorado at elevations of 3,597 m (11,800 feet) and 3,670 m (12,040 feet). This is fully 300 m higher than the upper limit suggested by Maslin (1959) and Smith *et al.* (1965). To my knowledge, this is the only instance of frogs breeding in the alpine in the United States The precise locations of the breeding ponds are at the base of the southeast ridge of Mt. Wilson, San Miguel Mountains, Dolores County, at 3,597 m (approximately 37°49′15″N, 107°59′29″W; Mt. Wilson 7.5′ quad., U.S.G.S., 1963) and in Dog Rincon, a tributary of West Weminuche Creek, San Juan Mountains, Hinsdale County, at 3,670 m (approximately 37°37′30″N, 107°18′30″W; Weminuche Pass 7.5′ quad., U.S.G.S., 1964).

The Mt. Wilson pond is a spring-fed *Eleocharis* bog about 20 × 30 m in extent. The water is not more than 8 cm deep. The pond lies over a very soft muck more than 80 cm in depth. Tadpoles observed on July 12, 1970, appeared to be just recently hatched. Four males caught here ranged from 29 to 31 mm in length from snout to tip of urostyle. Each one had some uncommon peculiarities of pattern. They were calling very sporadically. The pond lies at the extreme upper edge of the forest on the edge of a willow and sedge bog. Only a few, very scattered clumps of krummholz lie above the pond.

The pond in Dog Rincon is one of several sedge-bordered bogs in the basin. Its dimensions are approximately 35 × 40 m, about two-thirds of which is open; its depth is at least 40 cm. Several males were calling vigorously here on July 22, 1970. The pond lies about 130 m above the upper limit of the forest. It is surrounded by dense willow bog. Krummholz averaging less than 1 m in height extends to about 3,720 m (12,200 feet) elevation in the basin. I also caught two lone males calling above 3,720 m but could find no signs of successful breeding. One of these sites was a pond higher in Dog Rincon; the other was a bog about 3 km distant on the Continental Divide between Grouse Rincon and the Squaw Creek Basin. I hope collectors will refrain from taking frogs from these and other high ponds. Observations in northern Colorado indicate that populations in marginal habitats often consist of a very few long-lived individuals. Yearly recruitment is very low. Removal of a half dozen individuals from these areas may seriously impair the chances for the survival of the population.

REFERENCES

Maslin, T. P.
  1959 : An annotated check list of the amphibians and reptiles of Colorado. *Univ. Colorado Studies,* Ser. Biol., No. 6: 1-98.
Smith, H. M., Maslin, T. P., and Brown, R. L.
  1965 : Summary of the distribution of herpetofauna of Colorado. *Univ. Colorado Studies,* Ser. Biol., No. 15: 1-52.

POCKET GOPHER DISTRIBUTION IN RELATION
TO SNOW IN THE ALPINE TUNDRA

ROBERT STOECKER

ABSTRACT

Winter distributions of pocket gophers (Thomomys
talpoides) were mapped in the Trout, Williams Fork,
and Eldorado lakes basins in the alpine tundra area
of the San Juan Mountains of Colorado. Higher densities were found in the Trout and Williams Fork
lakes areas than in the Eldorado Lake area. Winter
home ranges of gophers, estimated by measuring areas
of isolated soil cores, averaged 56.2 m^2 (600 ft^2).
The amounts of soil gophers brought to the surface
during the season of snow cover were 937 kg/ha on a
tundra snowdrift site and 561 kg/ha on a willow
clearing snowdrift site. During the snow free season,
amounts of soil transported were 329 kg/ha on a
tundra site and 765 kg/ha on a subalpine meadow site.
It was estimated that 43.5 percent of the ground
surface was covered by fresh soil after snow melt.
The percentages of vegetation known to have been
destroyed by gopher digging activities on two
alpine tundra sites were 14.7 percent and 24.4
percent. Photographic documentation of plant
recolonization and soil erosion on gopher mounds
was carried out over a two year period. Species
lists of mammals, birds, and invertebrates in the
alpine tundra were compiled.

INTRODUCTION

Snowpack augmentation may affect animal populations
directly through lower temperatures, increased snow
load, and increased soil moisture, and indirectly
through second order effects on the vegetation and
substrate components of the ecosystem. In the latter
case, studies of alpine animal ecology provide a link
between plant ecologic and geomorphic studies.

The principal objective of this project was to
monitor alpine animal populations in relation to
the snowpack. Densities of animal populations living
in the alpine zone could conceivably be increased or
decreased by greater accumulations of snow. If
residual snowpack during the summer months appreciably
reduced the spatial extent of plant communities,
less food and cover would be available to all
organisms comprising the consumer portion of the
food web. This overall reduction in resources
could significantly reduce populations of both
resident and migratory species. However, populations
limited by winter mortality due to low temperatures
rather than lack of food might benefit from the
insulating effects of a heavier or more extensive
blanket of snow. In this case, invertebrates over-
wintering as eggs or larvae, hibernating mammals,
or mammals that remain active all year might show
increases in population levels due to increased snow.
The increase could be great in especially favorable
situations.

Originally, the project design included population
studies of mammals, invertebrates, and birds.
These groups were censused during the summer of 1971
(Appendices A, B, and C).

However, after the 1971 field season, the
scope of the investigation narrowed to in-
depth studies of one mammal species, the pocket
gopher (Thomomys talpoides). The importance of
this species stems from its singular influence on
the alpine ecosystem. In wind-swept tundra areas,
pocket gophers are less numerous than in lower subalpine meadows; nevertheless, during their excavation
activities they bring large quantities of soil to
the tundra surface where it is then subjected to
erosion by wind and water. Unquestionably gophers
modify the vegetation by burying it; by providing a
seedbed for colonizing species; and by grazing. The
extent to which they affect the tundra system through
soil aeration, soil erosion, and patterned-ground
formation is not nearly so obvious.

From what is known of pocket gophers in other
mountainous areas (Ingles 1949, Ellison 1946) and
from the studies conducted in the San Juan alpine
area, snow is thought to be one of the important
controls of local population sizes. With this in
mind, emphasis was directed toward estimating the
winter distribution of pocket gophers from soil cores
deposited under the previous season's snow cover.
From these data and from snowdrift distributions
evident on air photographs, the relationship of
snow distribution to local pocket gopher movements
and to overwinter survival may be better understood.

Of equal importance to these studies are measurements
of the effects of pocket gophers on the plants and
soil. Such data indicate the significance of
pocket gophers in the alpine to plant community
composition and to soil erosion.

This project was terminated in 1973 when it was
realized that a much higher level of funding would
be required to reach the stated objectives, and
continuation at the original level of funding would
not yeild significantly better results. Pocket
gopher studies conducted during the two year period
concentrated on two problems: 1) estimation
of population distribution, and 2) effects of
gophers on soil erosion and vegetation cover. Both
were approached through observation and measurement
of soil cores deposited on the ground surface by
gophers.

LOCATION AND DESCRIPTION OF STUDY PLOTS

The study plots used in the Williams Fork Lake area
were not the same plots that were used by the plant
ecology and geomorphology teams. Four distinct
habitat-types were chosen and two study plots defined
in each. The following is a brief description of
these areas:

In Steinhoff, Harold W. and Jack D. Ives (Eds.) 1976. Ecological Impacts of Snowpack Augmentation in the
San Juan Mountains, Colorado.   Final Report, San Juan Ecology Project, Colorado State University Publ.,
Fort Collins.

(a) Snow free area. Plots A and B: Both study plots occur on alpine tundra. Plot B was located on a knoll immediately above Williams Fork Lakes. Plot A was positioned on the saddle (Continental Divide) north of the lakes. Plot A is contiguous with the tundra site studied by the plant ecology and geomorphology teams (Site W4). Snow is swept from these plots virtually all winter. Vegetation is mainly short sedges, grasses, and herbaceous plants adapted to withstanding the high winds and desiccation characteristic of alpine tundra areas.

(b) Moderate snow area. Plots C and D: Plot C was positioned on a willow slope immediately west of Williams Fork Lakes. Part of this same willow slope was studied by the plant ecology and geomorphology teams (Site W3). Plot D was positioned approximately 400 meters to the northeast of plot C. Plot C has a steep east-facing slope. The willows are from 1 to 3 meters tall, dense, and difficult to walk through. Snow is held by the willows during winter to depths of from 0.5 to 2.5 meters. Plot D is in a depression and is covered by an extensive snowdrift in winter. The willows here are much less dense than on plot C and become green several weeks later in the spring because of a longer lasting snow cover.

(c) Deep snow area. Plots E and F were positioned in a grass-forb meadow. The meadow has a gradual south-facing slope, good drainage, and a deep soil development. Its vegetation was composed of many sedges approximately 0.2 to 1 meter tall in early August, with some willow along drainages, and a few scattered trees. Snow depth in April varied from 1 to 3 meters.

(d) Shallow snow area. Plots G and H: Two study plots were positioned on the slope immediately west of Williams Fork Lakes, approximately 100 meters south of plot C. The slope is composed mainly of Geum rossii, which forms a low but very dense herbaceous ground cover. Snow is typically swept from the convex portions of this slope during winter. This site was also studied by the plant ecology and geomorphology teams (Site W2).

METHODS AND RESULTS

Gopher Distribution and Movement

During the study period, analysis of soil core data provided estimates of winter population distribution, home range size, and movement.

-Distribution

The two habitats for which data were collected in 1971 were alpine tundra and grass-forb meadow. Amounts of soil excavated differed appreciably between these two locations. The amount of soil brought to the surface by gophers during the summer in various habitat types depends on 1) population density of gophers, as well as on 2) type and depth of the soil. Gopher densities in these two habitats were not estimated quantitatively but the grass-forb

meadow appears to support more gophers than does the tundra. The higher population density is associated with weaker surface soil materials (14.6 kg cm^{-2} resistance to penetration as against 18.8 kg cm^{-2}).

Figure 1 shows the cumulative amounts of soil collected and weighed for the two habitats. It

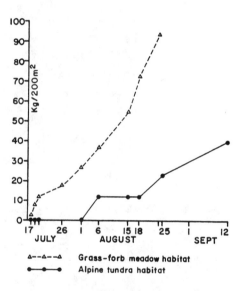

Figure 1. Cumulative amounts of soil removed by pocket gophers during summer in an alpine tundra habitat and a grass-forb meadow, Williams Fork Lakes.

indicates an increase in digging activity as the summer progressed toward fall. Little soil was excavated prior to mid-July as judged by field observations. In July, August, and September, 329 kg/ha were brought to the surface in the tundra habitat, and 765 kg/ha were brought to the surface in the meadow habitat. These weights are probably underestimated by the amount of soil scattered by rain and wind between collections.

It was not possible to collect soil as it was brought to the surface by gophers during the winter. However, in late spring and summer, areas where gophers were active during the winter are easily recognized by the conspicuous soil cores that remain on the soil surface after the snow melts (Figures 2 and 3). Two sites were chosen in 1971 that showed heavy winter use as judged by the abundance of soil cores. According to core measurements, 937 kg/ha were removed by gophers from the tundra snowdrift site and 461 kg/ha from the willow-clearing snowdrift site (Plot D) during the winter and spring.

Air photographs of the Trout, Williams Fork and Eldorado lakes areas were used as field maps for plotting winter pocket gopher distributions

474

Figure 2.   Surface channel dug by a pocket gopher in winter.

Figure 3.   Winter soil cores.

(Figures 4 and 5). These maps were carried in the field during June and July 1972 and locations of winter cores were marked on a 45 m square grid drawn over the air photograph. According to this work there are fewer pocket gophers in the Eldorado Lake area than in Trout and Williams Fork lakes areas. This is probably due to generally more shallow and rocky soils and to the higher, more alpine elevation of the Eldorado Lake basin.

-Winter Home Ranges

An estimate of the area inhabited by pocket gophers during the snow season was obtained by examining clusters of soil cores over wide areas in various plant communities. Where the gophers were not extremely abundant, clusters of soil cores occurred as recognizable units assumed to be the work of a single individual. Sixteen such clusters in the Trout and Williams Fork lakes area and ten in the Eldorado Lake area were located. For each case, the location, total length of all cores, and the approximate length and width of the core clusters were

recorded. In the lower subalpine meadows, the density of cores was so high as to form continuous networks over wide areas, making recognition of individual activity impossible.

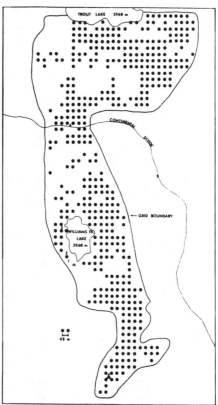

Figure 4.   Winter distributions of pocket gophers in the Trout and Williams Fork lakes areas.

Winter home range estimates are based on the assumption that an identifiable cluster of cores represents the work of a single gopher. This suggests that the home range of a pocket gopher in the alpine of San Juan Mountains is approximately 56 m^2 (608.7 sq. ft.). Howard and Childs (1959) estimated the home ranges of female pocket gophers (T. bottae) in California to be 119.6 m^2 (1,300 sq. ft.). Male home ranges were estimated to be 248.4 m^2 (2,700 sq. ft.). These results derive from work done on a different species of gopher in a habitat which is virtually devoid of snow. The estimates from the San Juan Mountains suggest that the presence of snow cover may severely restrict home range size.

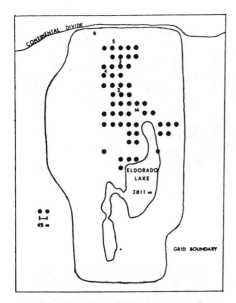

Figure 5. Winter distribution of pocket gophers in the Eldorado Lake area.

-Movement Patterns in Relation to Snowdrifts

In the Trout and Williams Fork lakes area, 18 snow-drifts were located during June 1972, as sites where pocket gophers were thought to have over-wintered. Observations were made of these sites throughout the summer. Photographs were taken of each site periodically; melt date, vegetation, and substrate conditions were also recorded. Pocket gopher cores were eventually found at every site as the snowdrifts receded throughout the spring and early summer. Subsequent digging activity was then recorded during the field season to discern any relationship between pocket gopher occurrence and such local conditions as local inundation, frozen ground, soil depth, or soil texture.

Diagramatic representation of the data is given in Figure 6. There is some indication that gophers move seasonally against a moisture gradient, as indicated by the arrows within the circles repre-senting the snowbanks in Figure 6. However, this interpretation is subject to question since movement patterns are not obvious in every case. Data in Figures 6b, 6i, 6e, and 6h are examples which argue strongly for the moisture gradient hypothesis here suggested. The obscure or nonexistent patterns in Figures 6a and 6c may be caused by complex topo-graphic and substrate features of these sites which make delineation of the moisture gradient difficult. Figure 6f tends to support the hypothesis but data are limited; Figures 6d, 6g, and 6j are inconclusive.

Erosional Effect of Pocket Gophers in the Alpine

The effects of the gopher on soil erosion and vege-tation cover were estimated from measurements of

amounts of soil removed, and area of ground surface denuded by gopher activity. In addition, photographic documentation of plant succession and erosion on selected pocket gopher mounds monitored these pro-cesses during the study period.

-Soil Removal

In 1971, soil cores resulting from winter and summer activities at the Williams Fork Lakes area were collected, dated, and weighed; similar samples from both Williams Fork and Eldorado lakes were analyzed in order to determine class-size of component materials. In 1972, two subalpine meadow locations were chosen for measurement of the amount of soil brought to the surface by gophers during the winter. The meadow locations seemed to represent the optimal pocket gopher habitat at the higher elevations of the San Juan Mountains. The volumes and weights of the cores allowed conversion of percent-cover to mass of soil per area.

Core analysis indicates that during the period July-September, 329 kg/ha were brought to the surface on a tundra site and, 765 kg/ha brought to the surface on a meadow site. The mean value for weights of soil transported during the winter on two other meadow sites was 362 kg/ha.

-Patterned Ground Mosaic in the Tundra

The percentage of soil surface known to have been exposed by the digging activities of pocket gophers was estimated on two tundra sites in the Williams Fork Lake area in 1972 (Plots A & B).

On a site located on the Continental Divide, ele-vation 3661 m (12,011 ft.) (Plot A), 14.7 percent of the soil surface was denuded by gopher activity; a slightly lower site, elevation 3646 m (11,962 ft.) (Plot B), had 24.4 percent of its surface area un-covered by pocket gophers. These estimates under-estimate effect of gophers since bare areas of un-known origin were not recorded.

-Erosion and Plant Succession on Pocket Gopher Mounds

Eleven separate gopher mounds were located in the Williams Fork Lakes area in August, 1971 and permanently marked with numbered stakes. These sites were photographed at regular intervals in August, 1971 and during the summer of 1972. In addition, a number of older mounds showing various erosional and plant successional features were photographed.

The photographs show that mounds on windswept tundra sites lose much fine material through time and that coarse material is exposed (Figures 7, 8, 9). Deflation rates appear to vary with local topography: Mounds in small depressions eroded more slowly than mounds on relatively flat or slightly convex slopes. On the lower subalpine meadow sites, erosion was considerably less than that on any of the tundra sites (Figures 10, 11, 12). Plant succession (recolonization) has proceeded more slowly in the subalpine meadows than was anticipated.

DISCUSSION

Gophers in the alpine and subalpine areas of the San Juan Mountains occur over a very wide range of habitat-types, from moist meadows with deep soil and lush vegetation, to wind-swept, dry fell fields with shallow soils and sparse plant cover. Optimal

476

Figure 7. Fresh pocket gopher mound. Tundra.

Figure 10. Fresh pocket gopher mound. Meadow.

Figure 8. After 10 days.

Figure 11. After 10 days.

Figure 9. After 35 days.

Figure 12. After 35 days.

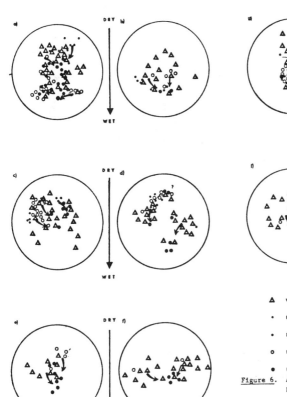

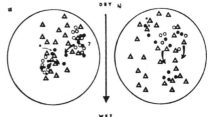

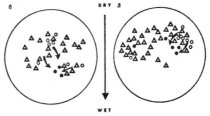

△ Winter sign (cores)

• Late June sign (mounds)

• Early July sign ("   )

○ Early August sign ("   )

● Late August sign ("   )

Figure 6. A diagramatic representation of seasonal pocket gopher activity in snowdrift sites.

habitats are grass-forb meadows although significant numbers of gophers occur in the alpine tundra. Talus slopes and bogs are almost the only major habitat types in the Williams Fork Lakes area where other mammals are present and gophers are absent. Within each of the habitats mentioned, differences in local features (microhabitats) occur which influence the suitability of the site for gopher habitation. The tundra is of particular interest in this regard. Depressions typically collect snow in winter and maintain permanent snowdrifts continuously through the winter season. Small knolls or convex slopes on the other hand are typically swept free of snow by the wind. This situation often causes abrupt differences in the microhabitats.

Snowdrifts are often favorable sites for gophers during winter. During this season, gophers will tunnel through the snow above the soil surface and build nests and food caches within the snow (Warren 1937). They use the snow tunnels to pack full of soil removed by their excavations. Hence, the soil cores are left conspicuously on the soil surface in the summer. Occasionally gophers burrow at the soil-snow surface interface, making well developed channels, which may subsequently be eroded by runoff (Figure 2). In summer gophers seem to prefer areas other than snow-drift sites.

The seasonal movements of gophers are related to changes in the local water table (Ingles 1949), soil temperature, and plant cover, all of which are influenced by local snowpack. Snow cover is important to gophers not only as an insulating blanket, but also as an avenue for dispersal across such barriers to summer movement as streams and exposed bedrock (Ingles 1949). But spring melt-off and consequent saturation of the soil can quickly cause favorable winter sites to become uninhabitable. How successful the gophers are in avoiding drowning, freezing and in finding food during the time snow is melting are difficult questions to answer because gophers bring up little soil at this time of year to indicate their abundance and location. Movements during the late summer and fall are more apparent, since gophers are actively digging at this time.

CONCLUSIONS

Pocket gophers alter their environment by transporting large quantities of soil to the ground surface during their tunneling activities. These activities in turn lead to second order effects on vegetation and soil erosion. Although there is some suggestion that gophers move seasonally against the moisture gradient, and that the presence of snow cover may restrict winter home range size, this two year study does not demonstrate any clear effect of snow on gopher distribution or activity. Nevertheless, the importance of these populations as agents of environmental change in the alpine tundra renders them suitable subjects for further monitoring studies.

LITERATURE CITED

Ellison, L. 1946. The pocket gopher in relation to soil erosion on Mountain Range. Ecology 27: 101.

Howard, W. E. and Childs, H. E. 1959. Ecology of pocket gophers with emphasis on Thomomys bottae mewa. Hilgardia 29: 277-358.

Ingles, L. G. 1949. Ground water and snow as factors affecting the seasonal distribution of pocket gophers, Thomomys monticola. J. Mamm. 30: 343-350.

Warren, E. R. 1937. Notes on pocket gophers. J. Mamm. 18: 473-477.

SEASONAL FOODS OF ADULT WHITE-TAILED PTARMIGAN IN COLORADO[1]

TERRY A. MAY, Department of Wildlife Biology, Colorado State University, Fort Collins[2]

CLAIT E. BRAUN, Wildlife Research Center, Colorado Division of Game, Fish and Parks, Fort Collins

Abstract: Crop contents of 286 adult white-tailed ptarmigan (*Lagopus leucurus*) collected between June 1966 and June 1971 in alpine and subalpine areas of Colorado were analyzed to describe seasonal trends in food selection. Except in summer, willow (*Salix* spp.) was the most abundant food. In winter, willow buds and twigs were eaten most often, with mountain dryad (*Dryas octopetala*) and alder (*Alnus tenuifolia*) being of secondary importance. In spring, ptarmigan utilized green leaves and flowers of mountain dryad, cinquefoil (*Potentilla diversifolia*), buttercup (*Ranunculus* spp.), and snowball saxifrage (*Saxifraga rhomboidea*), with leaves and buds of willows still being taken most often. Major foods during summer included the seeds and leaves of alpine bistort (*Polygonum viviparum*), sedges (*Carex* spp.), clovers (*Trifolium* spp.), willows, American bistort (*Polygonum bistortoides*), mouse-ear (*Cerastium* spp.), snowball saxifrage, alpine avens (*Geum rossii*), and mustards (Cruciferae). Early in the fall, willow leaves, buds, and twigs were again utilized most often, with alpine bistort, clovers, blueberries (*Vaccinium* spp.), and mouse-ear eaten before they became unavailable because of increasing snow depths.

The white-tailed ptarmigan, a small alpine grouse, occupies suitable habitats above tree line from north-central New Mexico north into Montana, Washington, and through the mountains of western Canada into southern Alaska. This little-studied bird is the only species of *Lagopus* confined to North America.

Intensive studies of foods utilized by white-tailed ptarmigan are lacking. Weeden (1967) presented the most complete analysis of foods taken by this species, although

[1] A partial contribution of Colorado Federal Aid in Wildlife Restoration Project W–37–R.

[2] Present address: Institute of Arctic and Alpine Research, The University of Colorado, Boulder.

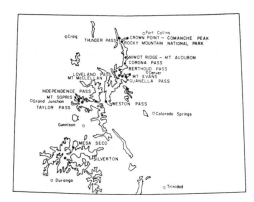

Fig. 1. Locations of collection sites in relation to distribution of white-tailed ptarmigan in Colorado.

Table 1. Contents[a] of 58 crops from adult white-tailed ptarmigan (14 males and 44 females) in winter.

CROP CONTENTS	PERCENT OF TOTAL DRY WEIGHT		
	Females	Males	Total
Willow	90 (44)[b]	84 (14)	89 (58)
Mountain dryad	3 (6)	15 (3)	6 (9)
Grit	4 (21)	—	3 (26)
Alder	3 (2)	—	2 (2)
Total	100	99	100

[a] Contents comprising more than 1 percent of aggregate weight are included.
[b] Sample size.

several workers (Judd 1905, Bailey 1927, Taylor and Shaw 1927, Bailey 1928, Beer 1948, Johnstone 1949) reported on the contents of a few crops taken at various localities. Field observations of white-tailed ptarmigan feeding were recorded by Chapman (1902), Taylor (1920), Pickwell (1941), Evans and Fisher (1958), and Choate (1960, 1963). Quick (1947) analyzed limited samples of winter droppings of ptarmigan in Colorado. The present paper describes the seasonal trends in food selection by adult white-tailed ptarmigan in Colorado.

R. A. Ryder and D. Hein, Department of Wildlife Biology, Colorado State University, provided helpful suggestions throughout the study. E. O. Nuzum, H. M. Small, D. M. Floyd, and S. D. Harness assisted with the separation of crop contents. We thank the Department of Wildlife Biology, Colorado State University; the Colorado Division of Game, Fish and Parks; and the Institute of Arctic and Alpine Research, the University of Colorado, for providing equipment and laboratory space to complete this work. Appreciation is extended to the National Park Service and Rocky Mountain National Park for permitting study within Rocky Mountain National Park.

A considerable portion of the data presented in this paper is included in a M.S. Thesis at Colorado State University (May 1970).

METHODS

Ptarmigan were located (Braun and Rogers 1971:7) and either captured (Zwickel and Bendell 1967) and sacrificed by suffocation or collected with a shotgun. Crops from ptarmigan shot by hunters were collected at check stations. Sexes of birds were identified using techniques described by Braun and Rogers (1967) and by examining gonads. After September 30, juvenile and adult collections were combined and arbitrarily considered to be adults. At that time, juveniles were approximately 10 weeks old and had replaced juvenal primaries one through eight; primary number eight was longer than 100 mm.

All crops had membranes and contents intact and were preserved by freezing. Contents were separated according to species, dried at approximately 80–90 C until a uniform weight was obtained, and weighed to the nearest 0.01 gram. Weights less than 0.05 gram were recorded as trace amounts. Identification of crop contents was from pressed specimens of Colorado alpine and subalpine plant species. Plant names used were generally according to Harrington (1954).

Samples were grouped into seasonal periods with foods being ranked and quantitatively described using frequency of occurrence and percentage of aggregate weight (Martin et al. 1946).

RESULTS AND DISCUSSION

Two hundred eighty-six crops were obtained from 16 locations in Colorado (Fig. 1) from June 1966 through June 1971. Samples were combined into one of four seasons: winter (October 20–April 30), spring (May 1–June 30), summer (July 1–August 31), and fall (September 1–October 19). Included in each season are 58, 26, 37, and 165 crops, respectively. Season boundaries were chosen primarily through observations of ptarmigan and climatic change.

Winter

During the winter, ptarmigan were found only in areas where willow was a dominant or codominant. Accumulated snow depths varied considerably; however, at all times, willow was available. In winter, ptarmigan ate willow almost entirely (89 percent of aggregate weight), and willow was also present in all crops in winter (Table 1).

Sexes segregated from late November to late March, with most males wintering in krummholz areas (11,000–12,000 feet elevation) that were alternately dominated by Engelmann spruce (*Picea engelmannii*) or willows (Braun and Schmidt 1971:242). Most females wintered in lower areas (8,500–11,800 feet elevation) where willows were dominant. Foods of secondary importance varied between males and females (Table 1). Although sample sizes

are small, the variance between males and females was probably the result of varying availability of vegetation in winter sites. Mountain dryad was available in greater amounts on high, windswept slopes near wintering males, and alder was most common in low protected areas near wintering females.

Weeden (1967) reported that white-tailed ptarmigan in Colorado ate mostly willow buds and twigs in winter, and that alder catkins were important in the winter diets of white-tailed ptarmigan in Alaska, with willow and birch (*Betula* spp.) being taken in lesser amounts. Differences in winter diets of white-tailed ptarmigan in Alaska and Colorado are probably related to a higher proportion of alder in northern areas and to competition for fairly restricted food supplies among the three species of *Lagopus* in Alaska (Weeden 1967).

Coniferous species such as subalpine fir (*Abies lasiocarpa*), Engelmann spruce, and lodgepole pine (*Pinus contorta*) are abundantly available to ptarmigan in winter areas in Colorado. Quick (1947) reported that subalpine fir needles comprised up to 10 percent by weight of winter droppings in Colorado. Data from our study do not substantiate Quick's finding even though ptarmigan were collected in areas examined by him.

Spring

In late winter (early April), numbers of ptarmigan in winter areas decrease, with most major winter sites used being essentially devoid of ptarmigan after April 20 (Braun and Schmidt 1971:243). Males initiate territorial behavior in mid- or late April and defend territories until late June or early July (Schmidt 1969:54). Females arrive on territories in early to mid-May. Pairing is complete by late May. Even though winter snow cover is prevalent in

Table 2. Contents[a] of 26 crops from adult white-tailed ptarmigan (16 males and 10 females) in spring.

CROP CONTENTS	PERCENT OF TOTAL DRY WEIGHT		
	Females	Males	Total
Willow	85 (10)[b]	85 (15)	85 (25)
Grit	3 (5)	4 (4)	3 (9)
Mountain dryad	1 (2)	5 (4)	3 (6)
Cinquefoil	4 (7)	—	3 (11)
Buttercup	4 (1)	—	2 (1)
Unidentified	—	2 (9)	1 (13)
Snowball saxifrage	1 (3)	1 (2)	1 (5)
Total	98	97	98

[a] Contents comprising more than 1 percent of aggregate weight are included.
[b] Sample size.

Table 3. Contents[a] of 37 crops from adult white-tailed ptarmigan (24 males and 13 females) in summer.

CROP CONTENTS	PERCENT OF TOTAL DRY WEIGHT		
	Females	Males	Total
Alpine bistort	54 (9)[b]	2 (11)	26 (20)
Sedges	9 (4)	18 (8)	14 (12)
Clovers	4 (4)	13 (9)	9 (13)
Willow	9 (7)	4 (9)	6 (16)
Grit	3 (9)	9 (12)	6 (21)
American bistort	6 (4)	6 (10)	6 (14)
Mouse-ear	—	11 (6)	6 (7)
Snowball saxifrage	4 (7)	7 (8)	5 (15)
Alpine avens	4 (5)	6 (6)	5 (11)
Mustards	—	9 (12)	5 (19)
Cinquefoil	3 (2)	3 (7)	3 (9)
Rock jasmine (*Androsace septentrionalis*)	—	3 (7)	2 (13)
Fendler's sandwort (*Arenaria fendleri*)	—	3 (2)	1 (2)
Unidentified	—	2 (15)	—
Alp lily (*Lloydia serotina*)	—	1 (3)	—
Sage (*Artemisia* spp.)	—	2 (1)	—
Grasses (Graminae)	2 (1)	—	—
Lousewort (*Pedicularis* spp.)	—	1 (1)	—
Alum-root (*Heuchera parvifolia*)	—	1 (1)	—
Alpine sorrel (*Oxyria digyna*)	1 (1)	—	—
Total	99	101	94

[a] Contents comprising more than 1 percent of aggregate weight are included.
[b] Sample size.

early spring, all territories include areas that are free of snow by mid-May and that are adjacent to areas where willow is abundant. As tundra vegetation becomes green and snowfields decrease in size, territories are enlarged and most activities then occur on higher areas away from willow bushes (Schmidt 1969:64).

During spring, ptarmigan continued to select for willow buds and twig tips, with new green leaves of willow also being taken as plant growth was initiated. The various components of willow occurred in 96 percent of the crops in spring and comprised 85 percent of the total foods taken (Table 2). Other important foods taken at this time were the green leaves and flowers of mountain dryad, cinquefoil, buttercup, and snowball saxifrage. Weeden's (1967) data indicated that leaves and flowers of willows and mountain dryad were eaten in greatest quantities during the spring. There were no apparent differences between males and females in foods eaten in spring.

Summer

In July, males and females without broods move upslope to high, rocky, and, frequently, windswept ridges. These sites, characterized by abundant rocky cover and short vegetation, are frequently near late-lying snowfields or wet areas. Vegetation types used most often at this time are *Trifolium* Cushion Fellfields, *Carex* Rock Meadows, and *Carex–Geum* Rock Meadows (Braun 1971).

After hatching their clutches, females typically remain within several hundred meters of their nests for up to 1 week. They then move uphill to areas below where males and females without broods congregate, and hens with broods occupy sites intermediate between the *Carex*,

Carex–Geum Rock Meadows, and the Kobresia–Carex–Geum and Kobresia–Carex Alpine Meadows (Braun 1971). By late August, females with broods occupy sites similar to those used by males and females without broods.

Diets in summer were composed of a variety of foods of nearly equal importance (Table 3), with leaves and seeds of alpine bistort, sedges, clovers, willows, American bistort, mouse-ear, snowball saxifrage, alpine avens, and mustards comprising 82 percent of the total. This information agrees with Weeden's (1967) data, which indicated that leaves of willow and buttercups, fruits of bistorts, and seeds of sedges and grasses were eaten during the summer. Summer was the only season when willow was not eaten most often. Samples from females with and without broods were limited; however, gross examination of crop contents indicated that all hens were eating the same types of foods. There were definite differences in the diets of males and females (Table 3). Bulbils of alpine bistort comprised 54 percent of the food from crops of females and only 2 percent of the food from crops of males. Female ptarmigan ate a variety of items of secondary importance that included sedges (9 percent), willows (9 percent), American bistort (6 percent), clovers (4 percent), snowball saxifrage (4 percent), and alpine avens (4 percent). Males utilized a greater number of plant species as food with sedges (18 percent), clovers (13 percent), mouse-ear (11 percent), mustards (9 percent), snowball saxifrage (7 percent), American bistort (6 percent), and alpine avens (6 percent) eaten in greatest amounts.

Females fed selectively on alpine bistort bulbils in summer even though they occupied sites dominated by clovers, sedges, and alpine avens. Males, however, ate seeds and leaves of plants, such as sedges and clovers, in the approximate proportions in which they were available.

In late summer, ptarmigan move to areas where phenology of the vegetation is delayed. This typically results in uphill movements into or near areas of snow accumulation. At Crown Point, because of altitudinal differences and drying effects of grazing by domestic sheep on alpine vegetation, movements are horizontal and downhill into rocky and wet krummholz areas. At Independence Pass, ptarmigan are found near snow fences that increase local snow accumulation and delay melting. These distributional patterns are related to the availability of green vegetation. Thus, during summer, ptarmigan select particular species of plants that may provide a particular quality of food.

Fall

In early September, ptarmigan remain in areas they occupied during late summer. Downhill movements coincide with the first severe snowstorms, with some birds returning to summer areas as the weather moderates. Sites favored in late fall are near areas of late-lying snow accumulations. These sites are characterized by plants such as sage (Artemisia norvegica), dwarf willow (Salix nivalis), Parry's clover (Trifolium parryi), alpine avens, sibbaldia (Sibbaldia procumbens), buttercup, sedges, and tufted hairgrass (Deschampsia caespitosa), as Braun (1971) reported.

Willows were again eaten in greatest amounts and comprised 43 percent of the aggregate weight (Table 4). Dwarf willow was the principal species of Salix eaten during the fall, with leaves and seeds of alpine bistort, clovers, mouse-ear, and fruits of blueberries eaten regularly before ptarmigan moved to winter areas. Diets of males and females were similar during the fall period.

Table 4. Contents[a] of 165 crops from adult white-tailed ptarmigan (104 males and 61 females) in fall.

CROP CONTENTS	PERCENT OF TOTAL DRY WEIGHT		
	Females	Males	Total
Willow	30 (40)[b]	49 (77)	43 (117)
Alpine bistort	16 (20)	22 (47)	20 (67)
Clovers	7 (32)	3 (38)	5 (70)
Blueberries	1 (5)	5 (6)	4 (11)
Mouse-ear	3 (18)	4 (45)	4 (63)
Sedges	4 (25)	3 (31)	3 (56)
Mustards	5 (26)	2 (35)	3 (61)
Alpine sorrel	2 (12)	3 (13)	3 (25)
Alpine sandwort (*Arenaria obtusiloba*)	3 (27)	2 (41)	2 (68)
Mountain dryad	3 (6)	1 (10)	2 (16)
Grasses	7 (35)	2 (36)	3 (71)
American bistort	4 (5)	—	2 (16)
Grit	3 (31)	1 (33)	2 (64)
Pussy-toes (*Antennaria rosea*)	3 (5)	—	1 (8)
Sibbaldia	3 (12)	—	1 (18)
Cinquefoil	1 (7)	—	—
Snowball saxifrage	1 (18)	—	—
Total	96	97	98

[a] Contents comprising more than 1 percent of aggregate weight are included.
[b] Sample size.

Weeden (1967) found that the green leaves of willow and fruits of low-growing plants such as whitlow-wort (*Draba* spp.) and bistorts were most important in crops of white-tailed ptarmigan collected early in September. He also found that berries were absent from crops of white-tailed ptarmigan in Colorado during fall, a finding that our study confirmed. One exception to the lack of utilization of berries was found in our study at Crown Point where ptarmigan remained in subalpine areas and ate seeds of sedges and fruits of blueberries most often.

Movements of ptarmigan to winter areas were gradual and were greatly influenced by climatic conditions; however, by late October, birds were seldom observed away from winter areas (Braun and Schmidt 1971:242).

CONCLUSIONS

Data collected during this study indicate that white-tailed ptarmigan in Colorado depend heavily on various species of willow for food from October to June. Willow comprises the bulk of the foods taken during the winter and is a major food item during all seasons. We have unpublished data on weights of 2,198 birds that suggest ptarmigan in Colorado rarely, if ever, undergo food shortages because weight changes are correlated with behavioral traits and not with changes in availability of food. Thus, food is probably not a limiting factor for populations of white-tailed ptarmigan in Colorado during any season. Exceptions may occur in localized areas due to habitat degradation by natural and artificial agents. Such occurrences were not detected during 1966–71. Future studies of feeding regimes of white-tailed ptarmigan should compare the nutrient availability in foods utilized in areas supporting significantly different numbers of birds. Additional studies of food habits of white-tailed ptarmigan would be profitable only in areas where vegetative composition is markedly different from that in Colorado, where behavior patterns are different, and where competition with other browsing gallinaceous birds occurs.

LITERATURE CITED

BAILEY, A. M. 1927. Notes on the birds of southeastern Alaska. Auk 44(2):184–205.

BAILEY, FLORENCE M. 1928. Birds of New Mexico. New Mexico Department of Game and Fish, Santa Fe. 807pp.

BEER, J. 1948. Notes on the food habits of some western grouse. Murrelet 29(2):18–20.

BRAUN, C. E. 1971. Habitat requirements of Colorado white-tailed ptarmigan. Proc. Western Assoc. State Game and Fish Commissioners 51:284–292.

———, AND G. E. ROGERS. 1967. Determination of age and sex of the southern white-tailed ptarmigan. Colorado Div. Game, Fish and Parks Game Information Leaflet 54. 3pp.

484

——, AND ——. 1971. The white-tailed ptarmigan in Colorado. Colorado Div. Game, Fish and Parks Tech. Publ. 27. 80pp.

——, AND R. K. SCHMIDT, JR. 1971. Effects of snow and wind on wintering populations of white-tailed ptarmigan in Colorado. 238–250pp. *In* A. O. Haugen [Editor], Snow and ice symposium. 280pp.

CHAPMAN, F. M. 1902. List of birds collected in Alaska by the Andrew J. Stone Expedition of 1901. Am. Museum Nat. Hist. Bull. 16(art. 19):231–247.

CHOATE, T. S. 1960. Observations on the reproductive activities of white-tailed ptarmigan (*Lagopus leucurus*) in Glacier Park, Montana. M.A. Thesis. Montana State Univ. 113pp.

——. 1963. Habitat and population dynamics of white-tailed ptarmigan in Montana. J. Wildl. Mgmt. 27(4):684–699.

EVANS, F., AND R. FISHER. 1958. Observations of white-tailed ptarmigan. *In* T. S. Choate. 1963. Ecology and population dynamics of white-tailed ptarmigan (*Lagopus leucurus*) in Glacier National Park, Montana. Ph.D. Thesis. Montana State Univ. 250pp.

HARRINGTON, H. D. 1954. Manual of the plants of Colorado. Sage Books, Denver. 666pp.

JOHNSTONE, W. B. 1949. An annotated list of the birds of the East Kootenay British Columbia. British Columbia Provincial Museum Occasional Papers 7. 87pp.

JUDD, S. D. 1905. The grouse and wild turkeys of the United States, and their economic value. U. S. Dept. Agr., Biol. Survey Bull. 24. 55pp.

MARTIN, A. C., R. H. GENSCH, AND C. P. BROWN. 1946. Alternative methods in upland gamebird food analysis. J. Wildl. Mgmt. 10(1): 8–12.

MAY, T. A. 1970. Seasonal foods of white-tailed ptarmigan in Colorado. M.S. Thesis. Colorado State Univ. 55pp.

PICKWELL, G. 1941. Above Mount Rainier's timberline. Audubon Mag. 43(4):337–345.

QUICK, H. F. 1947. Winter food of white-tailed ptarmigan in Colorado. Condor 49(6):233–235.

SCHMIDT, R. K., JR. 1969. Behavior of white-tailed ptarmigan in Colorado. M.S. Thesis. Colorado State Univ. 174pp.

TAYLOR, W. P. 1920. A new ptarmigan from Mount Rainier. Condor 22(4):146–152.

——, AND W. T. SHAW. 1927. Mammals and birds of Mount Rainier National Park. United States Department of the Interior, National Park Service, Washington, D. C. 249pp.

WEEDEN, R. B. 1967. Seasonal and geographic variation in the foods of adult white-tailed ptarmigan. Condor 69(3):303–309.

ZWICKEL, F. C., AND J. F. BENDELL. 1967. A snare for capturing blue grouse. J. Wildl. Mgmt. 31(1):202–204.